Hazardous Waste Regulation Handbook
A Practical Guide to RCRA and Superfund

Revised Edition

Sue M. Briggum
Greer S. Goldman
Daniel H. Squire
David B. Weinberg

EXECUTIVE ENTERPRISES
PUBLICATIONS CO., INC.
New York, New York

This publication is designed to provide accurate and
authoritative information regarding its subject matter.
It is sold with the understanding that the publisher is
not engaged in rendering legal, accounting, or other professional service. If legal advice or other expert
assistance is required, the services of a competent professional person should be sought. -- <u>From a Declaration
of Principles jointly adopted by a Committee of the
American Bar Association and a Committee of Publishers.</u>

ISBN 0-88057-401-1
Library of Congress Catalog Card No. 85-080589

Second Printing

Printed in the United States of America

PREFACE

In the three years since we published the first
Hazardous Waste Regulation Handbook, there have been many
significant developments in hazardous waste regulation. The
obligations imposed by the two principal federal statutes,
the Resource Conservation and Recovery Act ("RCRA") and the
Comprehensive Environmental Response, Compensation, and
Liability Act of 1980 ("CERCLA" or "Superfund") have been
greatly expanded. These changes result, in large part, from
major legislative amendments to RCRA and important regulatory amendments to both the RCRA and Superfund programs.
Moreover, as public awareness of the problems of hazardous
waste management has increased, litigation in this area has
mushroomed.

These developments have heightened corporate
environmental managers' concerns about their obligations for
waste management. Although there will continue to be
further, important changes in this area over the next few
years, the federal programs have now matured to the point
where we can discern the broad parameters of what will be
required of the regulated community with respect to hazardous waste management.

This book, like its predecessor, is written primarily for corporate environmental managers and their counsel to help them comply with the requirements of RCRA and

Superfund. While its focus thus is on statutory obligations and federal regulations, it also addresses related state programs and briefly describes non-statutory "common law" concepts of liability that relate to waste management activities.

Our objective, as before, has been to provide a practical, usable handbook. Rather than simply reprinting statutory or regulatory provisions, we have identified and described the principal obligations imposed by RCRA and Superfund, included compliance checklists, and directed the reader to the regulatory provisions, interpretations, or decisions that deal with specific concerns.

The organization of the materials reflects our objective. Part 1 provides a very broad overview of the two programs. Part 2 describes substances and waste practices subject to regulation under RCRA and Superfund. Because polychlorinated biphenyls ("PCBs"), regulated primarily under the Toxic Substances Control Act (and also under Superfund), are of such concern to environmental managers, Part 2 includes a discussion of the rules affecting their use, storage and disposal. Parts 3-7 explain the responsibilities of each participant in the waste management process -- generators, transporters, and treaters, storers, and disposers -- and discusses the relationships between the RCRA and Superfund requirements that affect each of them.

Part 8 discusses enforcement under RCRA and Superfund as well as related, non-statutory "common law" theories of liability for waste management activities being applied by the courts. Included also is a short review of liability insurance issues.

Following the text are a series of appendices designed to provide guidance on areas of particular concern and to explain more fully key regulatory provisions and obligations. Appendices A through G contain excerpts from some of the key RCRA regulations referenced in the text and the list of Superfund hazardous substances (and their reportable quantities). Appendices H through J present more detailed discussions of material in the text. Finally, Appendices K through O summarize in schematic and outline form major RCRA and Superfund requirements, including checklists of compliance obligations for hazardous waste generators, transporters, and owners and operators of waste management sites, and a chart listing the deadlines for regulatory action imposed by the 1984 RCRA Amendments.

We have not included in this volume copies of the statutes involved, nor have we reproduced all the current regulations promulgated thereunder. Unfortunately, these materials are too lengthy to be included in their entirety. Furthermore, while all references and citations presented in this book are current as of May 30, 1985, the regulations are

constantly changing, and persons facing compliance obligations will need to be sure that the regulations they consult
are complete and up-to-date. The federal government publishes these regulations annually in Title 40 of the <u>Code of</u>
<u>Federal Regulations</u>, available from the Superintendent of
Documents, U.S. Government Printing Office, Washington, D.C.
20402. Between annual updates, which are compiled in July
but generally not publicly available until November, changes
and modifications are published in the daily <u>Federal</u>
<u>Register</u>; indices of the <u>Federal Register</u> notices are
published monthly.

Finally, development of this volume has benefited
substantially from the assistance and guidance of our
colleagues at Wald, Harkrader and Ross. We particularly
wish to acknowledge the contributions of Stanley M.
Spracker, Susan D. Sawtelle, Donna B. Grossman, Daniel
Aibel, and our senior legal assistant Julie P. Hamre.
Without their valuable assistance, this volume would not
have been possible.

Sue M. Briggum
Greer S. Goldman
Daniel H. Squire
David B. Weinberg

May 30, 1985

TABLE OF CONTENTS

     Lead-Acid Batteries
     Being Reclaimed 59
4. Land Disposal Restrictions .. 60

CHAPTER V: SUPERFUND HAZARDOUS
               SUBSTANCES 64

A. Hazardous Substance Defined 64

    1. Substances Designated in
        Environmental Statutes 64
    2. Additional Designated
        Substances 66
    3. Hazardous Constituents 66
    4. Petroleum and Natural Gas
        Exclusion 67

B. Pollutants or Contaminants 67

C. Spill Reporting 68

CHAPTER VI: PCB REGULATION 74

A. Regulation of PCBs Under TSCA 75

    1. Regulated PCBs 75
    2. Marking Requirements 77
    3. Storage of PCBs 77
    4. Use, Servicing, and Inspection
        of Electrical Equipment
        Containing PCBs 78
        (a) Transformers 78
        (b) Capacitors 79
        (c) Other Equipment 80
    5. Disposal of PCBs 80
    6. PCB Spill Reporting and
        Cleanup 83

B. Superfund and Other Statutory
    Obligations Pertaining to PCBs ... 84

    1. Superfund Requirements 84
    2. Other Statutory
        Requirements 85

PART 1: OVERVIEW

This introductory section provides a broad overview of the RCRA and Superfund programs. It includes a description of their beginnings as well as recent and pending changes in their statutory schemes. Included also is a discussion of where to find specific statutory regulatory requirements. The differing role of the states under the two programs is explored. Part 1 concludes with a discussion of the basic principles underlying the RCRA and Superfund programs.

CHAPTER I

INTRODUCTION TO RCRA AND SUPERFUND

This handbook is intended to provide a usable and
concise summary of the federal and federally-authorized
state programs that regulate industrial hazardous waste
handling operations. Hazardous waste management obligations
arise principally under two federal statutes administered by
the United States Environmental Protection Agency ("EPA")
and their parallel state programs: the Resource Conservation and Recovery Act, commonly known as "RCRA," and the
Comprehensive Environmental Response, Compensation and
Liability Act ("CERCLA"), commonly known as "Superfund."
This chapter briefly discusses the relationship between
these programs.

A. RCRA

The Resource Conservation and Recovery Act was
enacted in 1976 as an amendment to the Solid Waste Disposal
Act, and amended in 1978, 1980, and 1984. It is codified in
Title 42 of the United States Code, beginning at Section
6901. Subtitle C of the statute establishes the framework
for a comprehensive, "cradle-to-grave" scheme of regulating
hazardous waste management. It imposes specific obligations
on waste generators, on those who transport waste, and on
those who treat, store, or dispose of waste. As of 1984,

a new Subtitle I authorizes a separate, comprehensive program for the management of underground storage tanks.

B. Superfund

Superfund (also commonly called "CERCLA") was enacted in 1980. It also is codified in Title 42 of the United States Code, beginning at Section 9601. Superfund established a $1.6 billion fund (the "Superfund" or "Fund") to begin to clean up hazardous substance spills and disposal problems, principally at abandoned hazardous waste sites that are not addressed by RCRA. Superfund identifies the persons who are responsible for hazardous substance cleanup, and who therefore may be ordered to undertake cleanup activities or to reimburse the Fund for government cleanup expenditures. Superfund also imposes certain spill release reporting requirements.

C. RCRA and Superfund Compared

Both RCRA and Superfund were enacted in a flurry of activity during the closing days of congressional sessions, after several years of consideration by the Congress. The result is that relatively little legislative history is available on the final language of the statutes. Thus, both statutes contain significant ambiguities which have generated a number of controversies between EPA, regulated industries, and environmental groups. Many of these ambi-

guities are addressed in this book.

The major differences between RCRA and Superfund
are the role of regulations in implementing each statute and
the time periods on which each statute focuses its primary
attention. First, like most environmental regulatory statutes, RCRA is largely not self-implementing. That is,
rather than directly telling regulated companies what they
must do, Congress instead directed EPA to promulgate regulations that would, in turn, control company activities. The
primary exceptions are certain obligations created by the
1984 Amendments to RCRA, which do not require implementing
regulations. Superfund, on the other hand, is principally a
program that establishes liabilities and obligations, and
does not require promulgation of regulations for implementation.

Second, RCRA focuses its attention on current and
future activities, while Superfund is principally retrospec-
tive. Generally speaking, RCRA requirements began to attach
to operations in 1980 and, with few exceptions, do not address
waste handling activities before that year. The exceptions,
most of which were added by the 1984 Amendments to RCRA, are
limited generally to situations in which prior activities
have current effects at operating facilities. Superfund, on
the other hand, focuses principally on liability for

historic waste management activities. Its current and future impacts are limited to obligations for spill response and establishing liability for possible future waste management failings.

D. Where to Find Specific Requirements

Because RCRA is largely not self-implementing, a company seeking to determine its RCRA obligations must look to the implementing regulations issued by EPA (and authorized states). EPA's RCRA regulations are set forth in Title 40 of the Code of Federal Regulations, Parts 260-271 (technical and permitting requirements) and Part 124 (administrative and hearing procedures). (Specific portions thus are often cited as 40 C.F.R. § ___.) Amendments and revisions are published in the daily Federal Register, and are collected annually in republished editions of the C.F.R. Regulatory amendments that are under consideration are listed in EPA's Regulatory Agenda, published semi-annually in April and October of each year, in the Federal Register.

In contrast, a company seeking to determine its Superfund obligations generally must turn to the statute itself, which is published at 42 U.S.C. §§ 9601 et seq., and to the increasing numbers of judicial decisions interpreting the meaning of the statute. One important exception to this rule is the National Contingency Plan, which, as the blueprint for government cleanup under Superfund, sets forth standards for cleanup activities and describes the relationship between various federal and state agencies responsible for Superfund implementation. It has been published in the Code of Federal Regulations at 40 C.F.R. Part 300. A second important exception is the release reporting regulations setting forth the requirements for reporting hazardous substance releases into the environment, which are published at 40 C.F.R. Part 302. These reporting requirements were published in the Federal Register on April 5, 1985, and until codified in the C.F.R. can be found at 50 Fed. Reg. 13474. They are included here as Appendix F.

Schematic outlines of the major requirements under both RCRA and Superfund appear at Appendices M and N.

E. The 1984 RCRA Amendments and Pending
    Superfund Legislation

As with all new programs, the RCRA and Superfund regulatory systems are still evolving. Although their parameters have been largely defined, changes in a number of the requirements inevitably will be made.

The principal source of pending changes in the RCRA program is the legislation enacted in November 1984, reauthorizing and revising the statute. The Hazardous and Solid Waste Amendments of 1984, Pub. L. No. 98-616 (hereinafter referred to as the "1984 RCRA Amendments") require EPA to promulgate new regulations governing numerous aspects of hazardous waste management during the next few years. The major provisions and the statutory deadlines for EPA rule-makings are noted in the text, and the deadlines are summarized in Appendix O. Noted also are the effective dates of some new requirements that take effect whether or not EPA issues regulations. In April 1985, EPA Administrator Lee Thomas signed a final rule (the "codification rule") to amend the hazardous waste regulations to reflect the statutory provisions with immediate or short-term effects on the regulated community. (As of May 30, 1985, these regulations had not yet been published in the Federal Register.) It will be important for environmental managers to monitor closely EPA's implementation of these RCRA amendments to assure that their companies are aware of new or different hazardous waste management obligations and their effect on company activities.

Changes in the Superfund program also are likely to result if, as expected, Congress amends and reauthorizes the Superfund legislation for a second five-year period when it expires in September 1985. Congress is expected to increase the size of the Fund substantially, through the imposition of new corporate taxes, and also to streamline and clarify the cleanup and liability provisions.

CHAPTER II

THE FEDERAL/STATE RELATIONSHIP UNDER RCRA AND SUPERFUND

A. States' Role Under RCRA

The RCRA regulatory program, like the Clean Water Act's National Pollutant Discharge Elimination System program and the State Implementation Plan program under the Clean Air Act, envisions substantial federal delegation of implementation and enforcement responsibilities to the states. The general concept is one of "federal standards, state implementation."

Unlike the Water and Air acts, however, RCRA provides for a two-stage delegation to the states. Unfortunately, the statute's relatively straightforward delegation process has been complicated by delays in the promulgation of the underlying federal regulations and by the fact that several states continue to impose independent regulatory schemes pending completion of EPA's program. As of May 1985, several stages and phases of delegation exist. These are discussed in the following paragraphs.

1. Authorization of State Programs

The statutory scheme envisions "interim authorization" and "final authorization" of state programs. "Interim authorization" is to be granted by EPA to states that have implemented programs that are "substantially equivalent" to the federal program. "Final authorization" is to be granted to states that have programs that are "equivalent" to and "consistent" with the federal program, and have "adequate" enforcement authority.

Within this statutory framework, states have some flexibility in developing their programs, provided their programs are substantially equivalent to the federal program during "interim authorization," and are no less stringent than the federal program during "final authorization." Moreover, one of the 1980 amendments to RCRA explicitly provides that a state may have requirements that are "more stringent" than those imposed by the federal regulations.

As delegation to the states has proceeded, the idea of "more stringent" yet "equivalent" and "consistent" state programs has been among the most difficult conceptual matters with which the Agency has had to deal, and the ultimate dimensions of state authority have not yet become clear. For example, it is theoretically debatable whether state programs that have operating requirements for facilities disposing of extremely hazardous wastes are merely stricter than, or inconsistent with, the federal program. In practice, however, it appears that EPA has tended to err on the side of giving states broad flexibility to have "more stringent" programs.

2. Interim Authorization: Phases I and II

EPA has divided "interim authorization" into two phases, and the latter phase into three components, A, B, and C.

Phase I allows the states to administer a hazardous waste program in lieu of, and corresponding to, those elements of the federal program first adopted in May 1980: restrictions covering identification and listing of hazardous wastes, regulation of generators and transporters, and "interim status" standards for existing hazardous waste treatment, storage, and disposal facilities. In states with only Phase I authority, EPA retains authority to manage the federal RCRA permitting program, while the state simultaneously may operate its own program. Thus, in such jurisdictions, regulated facilities may have to comply with both federal and state requirements.

Phase II allows states to establish a permit program for hazardous waste treatment, storage, and disposal facilities in lieu of, and corresponding to, the federal hazardous waste program for these types of facilities. Within Phase II, Component A provides for permitting storage and treatment in tanks and containers. Component B covers permitting for incinerators, and Component C covers permitting for land disposal facilities -- i.e., landfills, disposal surface impoundments, and land treatment facilities.

States may no longer apply for interim authorization. The deadline for all applications was January 26, 1983. All interim authorizations will expire on January 31, 1986, by which time a state must have final authorization, or management of its RCRA program will revert to EPA. As of May 1985, 45 states and jurisdictions had interim authorization for Phase I and 25 states for Phase II, as shown on the charts at pp. 12-13.

3.   Final Authorization

Once the basic elements of the federal program were in place, EPA announced that states could apply for final authorization, to become effective beginning January 26, 1983. After a state is granted final authorization, regulated companies within that state generally may, with the exception noted below, look only to the state hazardous waste regulations. As of May 30, 1985, 27 states had final authorization, as shown in the chart at p. 14.

4.   Authorization to Administer the 1984
     RCRA Amendments

All new requirements imposed by the 1984 RCRA Amendments take effect simultaneously in all states. EPA will administer each requirement until a state receives interim or final authorization to administer that requirement. (1984 RCRA Amendments § 228, amending RCRA § 3006.) Pending interim or final authorization, EPA and a state may agree to cooperate in administering any new requirement. (1984 RCRA Amendments § 227, amending RCRA § 3006.)

STATES GRANTED INTERIM AUTHORIZATION FOR PHASE I
(As of May 30, 1985)

	State	Date Authorized	FR Page Number
1.	Arkansas	18 November 1980	76144
2.	Utah	12 December 1980	81757
3.	North Dakota	12 December 1980	81758*
4.	North Carolina	18 December 1980	83229
5.	Louisiana	19 December 1980	83498
6.	Texas	24 December 1980	85016
7.	Mississippi	7 January 1981	1727
8.	Oklahoma	14 January 1981	3207
9.	Vermont	15 January 1981	3517
10.	Iowa	30 January 1981	9948
11.	Georgia	3 February 1981	10487
12.	Alabama	25 February 1981	14008
13.	Delaware	25 February 1981	14009
14.	Massachusetts	25 February 1981	14010
15.	South Carolina	25 February 1981	14012
16.	Montana	26 February 1981	14123†
		17 February 1982	6831
17.	Maine	18 March 1981	17194
18.	Kentucky	1 April 1981	19819
19.	Pennsylvania	26 May 1981	28161
20.	Rhode Island	29 May 1981	28850
21.	California	4 June 1981	29938
22.	Maryland	8 July 1981	35259
23.	Oregon	16 July 1981	36844
24.	Tennessee	16 July 1981	36846
25.	Kansas	21 September 1981	46576
26.	New Hampshire	3 November 1981	54544
27.	Virginia	3 November 1981	54545
28.	Wisconsin	15 January 1982	2314
29.	Connecticut	21 April 1982	17055
30.	Nebraska	14 May 1982	20773
31.	Illinois	17 May 1982	21043
32.	Florida	19 May 1982	19698††
33.	Arizona	18 August 1982	35967
34.	Indiana	18 August 1982	35970
35.	Puerto Rico	14 October 1982	45880
36.	New Jersey	2 February 1983	4661
37.	Guam	16 May 1983	21953
38.	Ohio	15 July 1983	32345
39.	Nevada	19 July 1983	32778
40.	Washington	2 August 1983	34954
41.	New Mexico	30 September 1983	44783
42.	Missouri	8 November 1983	51298
43.	D.C.	22 November 1983	52720
44.	New York	27 December 1983	56952
45.	West Virginia	28 March 1984	11836

*   North Dakota received partial Phase I Interim Authorization on
      December 12, 1980.

†   Montana was granted partial Phase I Interim Authorization
      on February 26, 1981. Complete Phase I Interim Authorization
      was granted on February 17, 1982.

††   Appeared in FR on May 7.

STATES GRANTED INTERIM AUTHORIZATION FOR PHASE II

(As of May 30, 1985)

	State (Component)*	Date Authorized	FR Page Number
1.	Texas (A & B)------------23	March 1982------------------12347	
	(C)-----------------1	September 1983-------------39623	
2.	North Carolina (A & B)----26	March 1982------------------12366	
3.	Arkansas (A & B)----------19	April 1982------------------16625	
4.	Georgia (A & B)-----------21	May 1982-------------------22096	
5.	Mississippi (A & B)-------31	August 1982----------------38323	
	(C)-----------26	April 1983-----------------18814	
6.	South Carolina (A & B)-----3	November 1982--------------49842	
7.	Oklahoma (A & B)----------13	December 1982--------------55680	
	(C)-------------24	June 1983------------------28989	
8.	California (A)------------11	January 1983----------------1197**	
9.	Kentucky (A & B)----------28	January 1983----------------3983	
10.	New Hampshire (A & B)-----31	March 1983------------------13430	
11.	Connecticut (A, B & C)----29	June 1983------------------29864	
12.	Nevada (A & B)------------19	July 1983------------------32778	
13.	Washington (A & B)---------2	August 1983----------------34954	
14.	Virginia (A & B)----------17	August 1983----------------37215	
15.	Maine (A, B & C)----------26	September 1983-------------43679	
16.	New Mexico (A & B)--------30	September 1983-------------44783	
17.	D.C. (A & B)--------------22	November 1983--------------52720	
18.	Maryland (A)--------------23	November 1983--------------52915	
19.	Florida (A & B)-----------29	December 1983--------------57342	
	(C)---------------24	February 1984-------------- 6900	
20.	Louisiana (A, B & C)------24	January 1984-------------- 2893	
21.	Vermont (A, B & C)--------24	January 1984-------------- 2894	
22.	West Virginia (A & B)-----28	March 1984------------------11836	
23.	New Jersey (A & B)---------6	April 1984------------------13697	
24.	Rhode Island (A) ---------15	May 1984-------------------20496†	
25.	Massachusetts (A, B & C)---3	August 1984---------------29377††	

* Note: Component A = authority to permit storage and treatment in tanks and containers

Component B = authority to permit incinerators

Component C = authority to permit land disposal facilities

** State is not authorized to control storage/treatment in
surface impoundments.

† Appeared in FR on April 29.
†† Appeared in FR on July 20.

STATES GRANTED FINAL AUTHORIZATION

(As of May 30, 1985)

	State	Date Authorized	FR Date	FR Page Number
1.	Delaware----------14	December 1983------------------55570*		
2.	Mississippi------- 2	June 1984--------13	June--------24377	
3.	Montana-----------25	July 1984--------11	July--------28245	
4.	Georgia-----------21	August 1984-------7	August------31417	
5.	North Dakota------19	October 1984------5	October-----39328	
6.	Utah -------------24	October 1984-----10	October-----39683	
7.	Colorado----------2	November 1984----19	October-----41036	
8.	South Dakota-------2	November 1984----19	October-----41038	
9.	Virginia----------18	December 1984-----4	December----47391	
10.	Texas-------------26	December 1984----12	December----48300	
11.	North Carolina----31	December 1984----14	December----48694	
12.	New Hampshire------3	January 1985-----18	December----49092	
13.	Oklahoma----------10	January 1985-----27	December----50362	
14.	Vermont-----------21	January 1985------7	January--------775	
15.	Arkansas----------25	January 1985-----11	January------1513	
16.	New Mexico--------25	January 1985-----11	January------1515	
17.	Kentucky----------31	January 1985-----17	January------2550	
18.	Tennessee----------5	February 1985----22	January------2820	
19.	Massachusetts------7	February 1985----24	January------3344	
20.	Nebraska-----------7	February 1985----24	January------3345	
21.	Louisiana----------7	February 1985----24	January------3348	
22.	Maryland----------11	February 1985----25	January------3511	
23.	Minnesota---------11	February 1985----28	January------3756	
24.	Florida-----------12	February 1985----29	January------3908	
25.	Kansas------------31	January 1986**--24	January------3343	
26.	D.C.--------------22	March 1985-------8	March--------9427	
27.	New Jersey--------21	February 985------7	February-----5260	

*   Reauthorized June 22, 1984; appeared in FR June 8, p. 23837.

**   Extension authorized.

B. States' Role Under Superfund

Superfund does not establish as complex a regulatory scheme as the one developed under RCRA. Instead, the
statute primarily establishes: (1) principles governing
liability for waste management practices, (2) a mechanism
for govermental funding of cleanup efforts when private parties have not undertaken, or cannot be forced to undertake,
cleanups, and (3) requirements for reporting releases of
hazardous substances into the environment.

The principal burden of implementing Superfund
rests with the federal government. For example, the federal
government was responsible for revision of the National
Contingency Plan (which originally was developed to deal
with spills into navigable waters under Section 311 of the
Clean Water Act, 33 U.S.C. § 1321) to cover Superfund
responses to spills and other releases onto land as well.
While Congress directed that this activity be completed by
June 1981, the final National Contingency Plan ("NCP") was
not published until July 1982. In addition, EPA has
published additional proposed revisions to the NCP that provide greater direction to federal cleanup response. 50 Fed.
Reg. 5862 (Feb. 12, 1985) (reprinted in Appendix E.)

The federal government also has principal responsibility for expending monies from the Superfund -- a
multi-million dollar account established by a tax on the

chemical and petroleum industry and contributions from the federal treasury -- and for seeking reimbursement of those funds from potentially liable parties. The job of responding to hazardous substance spills and other releases also falls initially on the federal government, through its National Response Center.

Nonetheless, the states play an important Superfund role. For example, pursuant to the National Contingency Plan, states may take principal responsibility for undertaking hazardous waste site cleanup activities by entering into a contract or cooperative agreement with the federal govern-ment. See 40 C.F.R. §§ 300.24, 300.62. Furthermore, regardless of whether it undertakes such a management role, each state must assure payment of ten percent of the funding for Superfund "remedial" (permanent cleanup) actions within its jurisdiction -- before more than $1 million of federal money may be spent at any site in that state. (CERCLA § 104(c)(1). In cases where disposal activities were con-ducted on land owned by a political subdivision of the state (e.g., a municipality), this contribution requirement increases to 50 percent. States also must assure future maintenance of short-term removal or more permanent remedial actions, and must assure the availability of a hazardous waste disposal facility to receive hazardous wastes as they are removed from a dump site. (CERCLA § 104(c)(3).)

One unresolved question under Superfund is the extent to which states may adopt their own "little Superfund" taxation schemes. Although there is little doubt that states have authority to adopt liability principles paralleling the federal program, it is unclear whether states are precluded by federal law from having their own parallel taxation programs.

The federal Superfund statute provides that "except as provided [in CERCLA], no person may be required to contribute to any fund, the purpose of which is to pay compensation for claims for any costs of response or damages or claims which may be compensated under this subchapter," except for taxes needed to finance the purchase of response equipment or preparations. (CERCLA § 114(c). Several lawsuits have been brought challenging state Superfund taxes on the basis that the federal provision preempts such state laws. As of May 1985, the most definitive ruling on this issue has come from the Supreme Court of New Jersey, which decided in September 1984 in a case entitled <u>Exxon Corp. v. Hunt</u> that Superfund does not preempt New Jersey's "little Superfund" so long as money from both funds is not used to clean up the same site. 97 N.J. 526, 481 A.2d 271 (1984). This case has been appealed to the U.S. Supreme Court. 53 U.S.L.W. 3509 (filed Dec. 17, 1984) (No. 84-978).

CHAPTER III

BASIC PRINCIPLES OF RCRA AND SUPERFUND

This chapter discusses the basic principles that underlie the complex RCRA and Superfund programs. The chapters that follow describe the specific requirements based on these principles.

A.   Solid Waste Includes Liquids and Gases

RCRA's statutory definition of "solid waste" includes liquids and "contained gases." Since "hazardous wastes" are a subcategory of "solid wastes," many liquids are regulated as hazardous waste under RCRA. This principle is particularly significant with regard to wastewater, since it means that many treatment systems built to comply with the National Pollutant Discharge Elimination System permit obligations are also RCRA-regulated hazardous waste treatment facilities.

B.   RCRA Imposes Major Responsibilities on
     Waste Generators

Perhaps the most fundamental practical change wrought by the RCRA regulatory scheme is the imposition of major responsibility for hazardous waste management on waste generators. For example, under the RCRA scheme, it is the waste generator's responsibility to determine whether a waste is hazardous. (See p. 88.)

Responsibility for initiation of a manifest "tracking" system also falls on generators. Basically, this system provides that each participant in the waste management cycle -- generator; transporter; treatment, storage, or disposal facility owner or operator -- sign a manifest and retain one copy of it for three years after a waste shipment. The responsibility for providing sufficient manifest copies, and reporting to governmental authorities if the manifest system is not complied with or the waste is "lost," is placed on waste generators. Furthermore, waste generators are obliged to identify the treatment, storage, or disposal facilities to which their wastes will be taken.

C. The RCRA Permit System Applies Only to Treatment, Storage, and Disposal Facilities

While the RCRA program imposes broad obligations on all participants in the hazardous waste management cycle, it requires permits only for hazardous waste treatment, storage, or disposal facilities ("TSDFs"), also called hazardous waste management ("HWM") facilities. Permits may be issued for an entire facility or on a unit-by-unit basis. Waste generators and waste transporters do not need a RCRA permit unless they also own or operate a TSDF, or they retain wastes for more than 90 days (in which case they are considered to be operating a storage facility). They may, however, need to register with the Department of

Transportation ("DOT") and/or obtain state or local permits or approvals.

With certain exceptions, all TSDFs need RCRA permits before construction and operation. A significant exception is granted to facilties in existence on November 19, 1980, or on the effective date of statutory or regulatory changes making the facility subject to RCRA. If such facilities comply with certain paperwork requirements (i.e., filing a notice and Part A of the permit application), they are grandfathered under a concept called "interim status." (This is not to be confused with "interim authorization," described at pp. 8-11, which applies to state delegation, not to permitting of privately-owned facilities.) The general rules for obtaining interim status are discussed in Chapter XI. Interim status facilities are treated as having a permit to operate until such time as EPA or an authorized state requests the filing of a RCRA Part B permit application under a time schedule adopted in the 1984 RCRA Amendments. If a facility fails to file its application by the prescribed deadline, it will lose its interim status.

Certain specified types of facilities may operate under simplified "permits by rule." If they file relatively brief notices and abide by certain operational requirements, they are treated as having a permit. Among the types of facilities currently covered by permits by rule are

wastewater treatment units and underground injection wells.
See 40 C.F.R. § 270.60.

EPA is considering permitting certain classes of facilities, e.g., containers and mobile treatment units, by issuing a single set of permit conditions in a class rulemaking; site-specific conditions would then be decided for each facility in a separate rulemaking. The purpose of this approach is to expedite the permitting process. It is expected that EPA will allow class permits only for facilities managing minimally hazardous wastes.

Finally, some facilities are specifically exempted from RCRA permitting requirements. These facilities are listed at 40 C.F.R. § 264.1, and are described at pp. 168-69.

D.   Superfund Imposes Liability for Past Activities

The most significant element of Superfund is its attempt to codify the principle that companies are now liable for damages resulting from waste management practices many years ago, regardless of whether any problems were foreseeable, the company acted in good faith, or state-of-the-art waste management practices were used at the time materials were disposed of. Thus, Section 107 of the statute provides that, subject only to very limited defenses, current and former site owners and operators, transporters, and some generators are responsible for cleanup costs and damages to natural resources (but not personal injury damages) resulting from hazardous substance spills and other releases. In more precise terms, the statute holds the following responsible parties liable for cleanup costs and damages to natural resources:

(1) the owner and operator of a vessel or facility;

(2) any person who at the time of disposal of a hazardous substance owned or operated the facility at which the substance was disposed;

(3) any person who arranged for disposal or treatment of hazardous waste, or arranged with a transporter for transportation for disposal or treatment by any other party at a facility owned or operated by any other party (this category generally includes the waste generator); and

(4) any person who accepted any hazardous substance for transport to disposal or treatment facilities selected by such person, from which there is a release, or a threatened release.

The defenses to liability are limited to acts of God, acts of war, and acts or omissions of a third party. The "third party defense" is further limited to apply only in situations where the third party involved is not now and has not been an employee or agent of the defendant or one whose act or omission occurred in connection with a contractual relationship with the defendant, and where the defendant can establish that he exercised due care with respect to the hazardous substance and took precautions against all foreseeable acts and omissions. CERCLA's liability provisions, therefore, are extraordinarily broad, and were intended to be so. The scope of these provisions is now being tested in the courts, which thus far have interpreted them very broadly -- in some cases, even more so than the literal statutory language would support -- to impose liability.

Parties that fall within any of the four categories of responsible parties under Section 107 may be held liable for the federal government's or state's full cost of cleaning up the site as well as damages to restore, rehabilitate or compensate for lost natural resources. Although the statute itself is silent on the subject, several courts have held that a responsible party may be held jointly and severally liable for the entire amount of costs and damages, regardless of that party's percentage contribution to the environmental situation at the site. The courts also have found a right of contribution (to apportion liability) against other responsible parties, but the party seeking to recover bears the risk of not prevailing.

Instead of responding to a site and seeking to recover its costs under Section 107, the federal government may exercise its authority under Section 106 of the statute to issue an administrative order requiring responsible parties to clean up the site if it poses "an imminent and substantial endangerment to the public health or welfare or the environment." The issuance of an order has an immediate and substantial impact in a Superfund action by shifting the cleanup burden from the government to one or more private parties. Failure to comply with the order carries a risk of substantial penalties. As an alternative to issuing an order, the federal government may seek injunctive relief from the courts to compel private cleanup.

PART 2:   REGULATED SUBSTANCES AND PRACTICES

The threshold issue in determining whether a company has RCRA or Superfund concerns, or indeed any environmental concerns, is to determine whether the company manages substances and engages in practices that are subject to regulation under the statute in question. This Part discusses this issue. Chapter IV discusses the materials and waste practices subject to hazardous waste regulation. Chapter V describes the broad category of hazardous substances covered by Superfund. Chapter VI discusses a specific substance, polychlorinated biphenyls ("PCBs"), which is of great concern to environmental managers. The use, storage, and disposal of PCBs is regulated under the Toxic Substances Control Act, as well as under Superfund. PCBs are not currently a RCRA hazardous waste. EPA or the Congress may at some time in the future list PCBs as a RCRA hazardous waste, in which case EPA will have to meld the TSCA and RCRA regulatory schemes.

CHAPTER IV

RCRA-REGULATED "HAZARDOUS WASTE"

This chapter describes in detail what materials and
practices are regulated under the RCRA hazardous waste
program as implemented by EPA.

A.   The Scope of RCRA Regulation

The key concept underlying the federal RCRA hazardous waste system is, not surprisingly, EPA's definition of
"hazardous waste." Only if a material is within that definition is it subject to hazardous waste regulation as implemented by EPA.

This is not to say that other wastes are unregulated. For example, although EPA has excluded some materials that otherwise would be considered hazardous from its
regulated category of hazardous waste, not all states have
adopted the same exclusions. Thus, state hazardous waste
regulations may apply to materials that are not deemed
hazardous under the federal program. Moreover, state solid
waste management programs developed under Subtitle D of RCRA
govern the land disposal of a much larger universe of
"nonhazardous" solid wastes. Also, a substance identified
by Congress as warranting special attention, polychlorinated
biphenyls ("PCBs"), is not currently a RCRA hazardous waste
(although it soon may be), but it is regulated under

the Toxic Substances Control Act (as well as Superfund), as explained in Chapter VI.

Nor is RCRA regulation exclusive. Indeed, substances that are RCRA hazardous wastes may be subject to additional regulation under other federal and state statutes. Superfund, most importantly, attaches responsibility to the management of "hazardous substances" -- a broad category that includes not only RCRA "hazardous waste," but also virtually all substances considered hazardous under the other major federal environmental statutes, as described in Chapter V. And the transportation of "hazardous materials" -- a broad category including hazardous waste -- is governed by the Hazardous Materials Transportation Act, discussed at p. 113 below.

Environmental managers must keep in mind these other potentially applicable statutes when analyzing their companies' waste management responsibilities.

B. The Definition of Hazardous Waste

Hazardous waste is a subset of solid waste. Thus, unless a material is a "solid waste," hazardous waste regulation will not attach. If a material is solid waste, it is deemed hazardous and subject to regulation if it is either (1) listed in the regulations or (2) exhibits certain characteristics identified in the regulations, and it is not specifically excluded from regulation. A schematic outline of the definition of hazardous waste appears in Appendix L. Only materials that meet this definition are subject to RCRA hazardous waste regulation.

The following sections explain how these criteria are applied by EPA, as well as the special restrictions and requirements that apply to certain regulated wastes and waste practices. Although authorized state RCRA programs may differ somewhat from the federal program, for example, by including more listed wastes, they must follow the federal approach for determining what solid wastes are hazardous, as described in this chapter.

C. Determining If a Material Is a Waste --
    the Definition of "Solid Waste"

Defining the term "solid waste" has been among the most difficult problems that has arisen for EPA in implementing RCRA. One man's waste may be another man's source material. This is most obvious in the context of "waste" solvents that have positive heat recovery value and often are burned as fuels. In May 1980, EPA defined solid waste in 40 C.F.R. § 261.2 as materials that are discarded or are being accumulated for discarding, or that are "sometimes" discarded. However, the meaning of the phrase "sometimes discarded" proved problematic, and on January 4, 1985, EPA issued a revised definition. (50 Fed. Reg. 614.)

The revised definition removes some of the uncertainty arising from the original definition of solid waste by eliminating the concept that a material may be a waste if it is "sometimes discarded." Instead, the revised definition delineates specific waste management practices, notably certain recycling and reuse activities, that are regulated. In fact, the primary focus of the revised definition is on those recycling and reuse activities that are made subject to RCRA hazardous waste regulation. The following discussion describes the revised definition, focusing on the recycled and reused materials that are subject to hazardous waste regulation. (The revised definition is included as Appendix A.) The reader should note that the following discussion applies only to wastes that also are hazardous for the purposes of the regulations implementing Subtitle C of RCRA, and does not apply to materials (such as ordinary non-hazardous scrap, paper, textiles, or rubber) that are not otherwise hazardous wastes and that are recycled. (50 Fed. Reg. at 663, amending 40 C.F.R. § 261.1.)

1.   Materials Subject to Regulation

Under the revised definition, a solid waste is "any discarded material" falling into any one of the following three categories. (50 Fed. Reg. at 664, amending 40 C.F.R. § 261.2(a)(1).)

(a) Abandoned Materials

Material is deemed abandoned and therefore subject
to regulation if it is: (1) disposed of; (2) burned or
incinerated; or (3) accumulated, stored or treated prior to
(1) and (2). This includes burning of materials in industrial and utility boilers or industrial furnaces for recovery
of usable energy, although (as of May 1985) EPA has temporarily exempted these units from regulation pending
further study.

If a material meets this criterion, it is a solid
waste. Next the evaluator must determine if it is hazardous, as explained at pp. 37-50. If it is, it is subject to
the RCRA hazardous waste program unless it is specifically
excluded by regulation, as explained at pp. 50-51.

(b) Inherently Waste-Like Materials

Material is deemed "inherently waste-like" and
therefore subject to regulation, whether or not it is
recycled or reprocessed, if EPA determines that it: (1) is
ordinarily disposed of, burned or incinerated, or (2) contains toxic constituents listed in Appendix VIII of 40
C.F.R. Part 261 (discussed at pp. 41-42 below and reprinted
as Appendix C to this Handbook) not ordinarily found in raw
materials or products for which the materials substitute;
and (3) may pose a substantial hazard to human health and
the environment. (50 Fed. Reg. at 664, amending 40 C.F.R.
§ 261.2(d).) An example is dioxin.

If a material is listed by EPA as inherently waste-like, it is a solid waste. Next the evaluator must determine if it is hazardous, as explained at pp. 37-50. If it is, it is subject to the RCRA hazardous waste program unless it is specifically excluded by regulation, as explained at pp. 49-50.

(c) Secondary Materials When Recycled in Specific Ways

The third category of solid wastes is composed of secondary materials, as defined by EPA, when recycled in specific ways. Secondary materials include: (1) spent materials (which are materials that have been used and as a result of contamination can no longer serve their original purpose without reprocessing); (2) pollution control sludges; (3) by-products (which are materials that are not the primary products of a production process and are not solely or separately produced); (4) discarded commercial chemical products listed in 40 C.F.R. § 261.33; and (5) scrap metals (which are bits and pieces of metal parts or metal pieces that may be combined with bolts or soldering). These secondary materials are subject to regulation when they are recycled as follows: (1) used in a manner constituting disposal; (2) burned for energy recovery, used to produce a fuel, or contained in fuel; (3) reclaimed; or (4) accumulated speculatively, as explained below. (50 Fed. Reg. at 664, amending 40 C.F.R § 261.2(c).)

(i) Secondary materials used in a manner constituting disposal

In EPA's view, the direct use of secondary materials on the land (such as dust suppressants, fertilizers and fill material) is virtually equivalent to unsupervised land disposal and is regulated as a "use constituting disposal." EPA also asserts jurisdiction under this provision over all secondary materials contained in products that are applied to the land. However, EPA has temporarily exempted hazardous waste-derived commercial products (like waste-derived cement) from hazardous waste management if the secondary material has undergone a chemical reaction in the course of manufacturing the product so as to become inseparable by physical means. This exemption allows the Agency the opportunity to develop a proposal for more limited regulation of what it concedes are beneficial recycling activities. (50 Fed. Reg. at 628.)

(ii) Secondary materials burned for energy recovery, used to produce a fuel, or contained in fuels

The revised definition makes all burning of secondary materials subject to hazardous waste regulation. However, not all combustion units are currently regulated. Incinerators are regulated. As noted above, boilers and industrial furnaces are temporarily excluded from regulation, although EPA intends to regulate these units in the future. Burning in these units is exempt, however, only if it is legitimate, as opposed to "sham," burning. This distinction is explained at 48 Fed. Reg. 11157 (March 16, 1983), and summarized at 50 Fed. Reg. 630.

To qualify a boiler as temporarily exempt from regulation, it must (i) have provisions for heat recovery, (ii) have a combustion chamber and heat sections that are of integral design, (iii) maintain, while in operation, a thermal energy recovery efficiency of at least 60 percent, and (iv) export and utilize at least 75 percent of the recovered energy, calculated on an annual basis. (50 Fed. Reg. at 661, amending 40 C.F.R. § 260.10.) The Agency may grant a variance from these criteria on a case-by-case basis and classify a unit as a boiler. Procedures to obtain such a variance are described in 40 C.F.R. § 260.33 (as added at 50 Fed. Reg. 662).

Industrial furnaces that are temporarily exempt are certain enumerated combustion units that are used as integral components of manufacturers' processes to recover materials or energy, not to destroy waste. While EPA has limited the current exclusion from regulation to those industrial furnaces listed in the regulation, the regulation includes criteria to add other combustion units to this list. (50 Fed. Reg. at 661, amending 40 C.F.R. § 260.10.)

(iii) Secondary materials being reclaimed

Reclamation constitutes either the processing of waste materials to recover usable products or the regeneration of waste materials by removing contaminants or impurities.

Most, but not all, secondary materials are deemed solid wastes when reclaimed. The exceptions to this rule are listed commercial chemical products, listed by-products and sludges exhibiting a characteristic of hazardous waste. (See pp. 37-51 for a discussion of listed waste materials and waste materials identified by hazardous characteristics.) Secondary materials that have been reclaimed but must be reclaimed further before the materials are completely recovered are subject to regulation as wastes until the reclamation process is completed unless granted a variance by the Regional Administrator. (50 Fed. Reg. at 662, adding 40 C.F.R. § 260.30(c); see also 50 Fed. Reg. at 655.)

(iv) Secondary materials accumulated
     speculatively

EPA has concluded that over-accumulation and speculative accumulation of secondary materials for recycling may pose environmental risks. Thus, the revised definition presumes that secondary materials are solid wastes if they accumulate before recycling unless the person accumulating the materials demonstrates that: (1) the materials have known recycling potential and can feasibly be recycled; and

(2) during a one-year calendar period, the amount of material recycled, or transferred to a different site for recycling, is at least 75 percent of the amount accumulated at the beginning of the year. Failure to make this demonstration subjects these materials to the standards for storage of recyclable materials in 40 C.F.R. § 261.6(c).

The Agency may grant a variance from operation of this provision to persons unable to recycle sufficient amounts of secondary materials in one year based upon a showing by the recycler that a reasonable likelihood exists that he can comply with this turnover provision with an extension of an additional year. If the recycler fails to recycle 75 percent of the materials on hand in the following year, he may petition for a new variance. (50 C.F.R. at 661-62, adding 40 C.F.R. §§ 260.30, 260.31.)

The following chart from EPA's preamble to the revised definition of solid waste summarizes the foregoing discussion of what secondary materials are defined as hazardous wastes when recycled in specified ways.

TABLE 1. Matrix of Which Types of Secondary Materials Will be Defined as Solid and Hazardous Wastes When Recycled and Which Types of Recycling Activities Constitute Waste Management.

	Use constituting disposal	Burning for energy recovery, or use to produce a fuel	Reclamation	Speculative accumulation
Spent materials (both listed and nonlisted/characteristic).	Yes	Yes	Yes	Yes.
Sludges (listed)	Yes	Yes	Yes	Yes.
Sludges (nonlisted/characteristic)	Yes	Yes	No	Yes.
By-products (listed)	Yes	Yes	Yes	Yes.
By-products (nonlisted/characteristic)	Yes	Yes	No	Yes.
Commercial chemical products listed in 40 CFR § 261.33 that are not ordinarily applied to the land or burned as fuels.	Yes	Yes	No	No.
Scrap metal	Yes	Yes	Yes	Yes.

Yes—Defined as a solid waste
No—Not defined as a solid waste.

2. <u>Recycled Materials That Are Not Solid Wastes</u>

The following recycled materials are deemed <u>not</u> to be solid wastes and therefore are not subject to regulation as hazardous wastes: (a) materials used or reused as ingredients in an industrial process to make a product; (b) materials used or reused as effective substitutes for commercial products; and (c) materials returned to the original process from which they were generated, without first being reclaimed. These concepts are explained below.

(a) Materials Used or Reused as Ingredients in an Industrial Process to Make a Product

EPA believes that these secondary materials function as raw materials in normal manufacturing operations and, accordingly, should not be regulated. For example, zinc-containing sludges used as ingredients in fertilizer manufacturing and chemical industry still bottoms used as feedstocks in the manufacturing process fall in this category. (50 Fed. Reg. at 619.)

(b) Materials Used or Reused as Effective Substitutes for Commercial Products

EPA has exempted these materials from regulation because they function as products in normal commercial applications. For example, spent pickle liquor used as a phosphorous precipitant and sludge conditioner in wastewater treatment falls in this category. (50 Fed. Reg. at 619.)

(c) Materials Returned to the Original
    Process From Which They Are Generated,
    Without First Being Reclaimed

This exemption applies to "closed-loop" recycling operations -- an ongoing production process using secondary materials. To qualify, secondary materials must be returned to a primary production process, e.g., one that uses raw materials as the majority of its feedstock, and must be returned as feedstock to the original production process and recycled as part of that process. Thus, a spent degreasing solvent returned to degreasing operations would not be excluded under this provision because it merely cleans equipment and is not involved in actual production. (50 Fed. Reg. at 639.)

A material that meets any of the foregoing criteria is a solid waste. Next the evaluator must determine if it is hazardous, as explained below. If it is, it is subject to the RCRA hazardous waste program unless it is specifically excluded by regulation, as explained at pp. 50-51.

D. Determining If a Solid Waste Is Hazardous

As noted above, a solid waste is deemed hazardous and thus subject to regulation under Subtitle C of RCRA either because it is listed or because it exhibits certain characteristics. (See Appendix L for a schematic outline of the definition of hazardous waste.)

1.   Listed Hazardous Wastes

There are three lists of hazardous wastes in EPA's regulations. If a waste appears on one of these lists, it must be handled as a hazardous waste unless it is specifically excluded from regulation, as described at pp. 50-51.

(a) Wastes from Non-Specific Sources

The first category of listed hazardous wastes consists of wastes that are considered hazardous regardless of their source. This list appears at 40 C.F.R. § 261.31, and is reprinted as of May 1985 in Appendix B. This category, sometimes called "generics," includes common solvents, certain wastewater treatment sludges and plating baths, and other metal treatment wastes. Any person who generates or manages one of these listed materials must handle it as a hazardous waste. Since its first printing in May 1980, this list has been expanded several times by EPA.

(b)   Wastes from Specific Sources

The second category of wastes are those that are considered hazardous when generated from specific sources. This list appears at 40 C.F.R. § 261.32, and is reprinted as of May 1985 in Appendix B. Wastes generated by various specific industries -- the wood preservation industry, the inorganic pigment industry, the organic chemical industry, and so forth -- are listed here. Since its first printing in May 1980, this list also has been expanded several times by EPA. Only persons included within the listed industry who generate these wastes must treat them as "hazardous wastes." As a practical matter, most of the wastes listed here are generated only by the industries for which they are listed. However, there are exceptions to this rule. For example, "API separator sludge" is a listed waste for the petroleum refining category, yet other industries may generate this waste from their oil-water separators. However, it is not a listed waste for any other industry.

In some cases, companies may have difficulty determining whether they fall within the industrial category set forth by EPA. EPA has explained the meaning of these categories in its "background documents." These documents, which explain the categorization and reasons for listing certain waste as hazardous, are available at EPA headquarters in Washington, in the various EPA offices, and from some consultants and attorneys who practice regularly in this area.

(c) Discarded Commercial Chemical Products

The third category of listed hazardous wastes consists of the discarded commercial chemical products. A list of these wastes is set forth at 40 C.F.R. § 261.33, and reproduced as of May 1985 in Appendix B. This list has been among the most confusing elements of the RCRA program, for several reasons. First, this category includes two subcategories, as to which slightly different requirements apply. One group (listed in Section 261.33(e) in Appendix B) includes acute hazardous wastes; the second group (listed in Section 261.33(f) in Appendix B) includes toxic wastes.

Second, many of these materials are in common use, and companies have not understood when RCRA regulation attaches to their handling. The key to whether these commercial chemical product materials are considered "hazardous waste" is whether they have been discarded, which, under the regulations, includes burning or land application in lieu of their original intended use. Thus, these products -- which include many pesticides and such commonly used industrial products as trichloroethylene and naphthalene -- are not regulated as hazardous waste when they are in stock or being used in industrial products or processes. However, they are considered hazardous waste when discarded, or intended to be discarded, as follows:

(1) in a commercial pure grade, in any technical grade, or in a formulation for which the listed chemical is the sole active ingredient;

(2) in any off-specification formulation if the material, had it met specifications, would have been a listed acute or toxic waste;

(3) as residues or inner liners of containers holding any commercially pure grade, technical grade, or

formulation in which the chemical is the sole active ingredient, unless the container is empty, as defined by 40 C.F.R. § 261.7(b)(3);

(4) as a residue or as contaminated soil, water, or other debris from a spill of a commercial pure grade, technical grade, or formulation for which the listed chemical is the sole active ingredient or off-specification version of such ingredient.

These listed materials are considered hazardous wastes only when discarded in one of these forms, not when they are constituents of process streams that are then discarded. Thus, a process waste that contains a material listed in 40 C.F.R. § 261.33 is not automatically hazardous, although it may be considered hazardous if it fails one of the tests described below or is mixed with other wastes. (See pp. 45-50.) The reader should note, however, that EPA is considering listing process waste streams that contain discarded commercial chemical products.

The third element of confusion arises because the list of discarded commercial products is often confused with another list, known as Appendix VIII, published by EPA in the regulations along with the listed hazardous wastes and reproduced in this text as Appendix C. This appendix includes numerous chemicals and, initially, was believed by some persons to be an additional list of wastes automatically considered to be hazardous. However, this is not the case. Instead, Appendix VIII serves other purposes: (a) it lists constituents the presence of which in a waste may lead EPA in the future to list that waste as hazardous; (b) it provides the basis for measuring adverse effect on groundwater by treatment, storage, and disposal facilities ("TSDFs") and for monitoring incinerators (see pp. 177 and 210-12); and (c) under the 1984 RCRA Amendments, releases of Appendix VIII constituents may have to be cleaned up by facilities as a condition to receiving a TSDF permit, and health assessments, when required, may have to consider potential public exposure to Appendix VIII constituents. Nevertheless, the fact that a waste stream contains one of these Appendix VIII wastes does not make it a listed hazardous waste until EPA specifically lists it.

(d)   Future Listings

The 1984 RCRA Amendments specify a number of wastes unlisted at the time of enactment of the Amendments in November 1984 that Congress wanted EPA to consider listing in the future. (1984 RCRA Amendments § 222, adding RCRA § 3001(e).) EPA was directed to determine by May 8, 1985, whether to list wastes containing chlorinated dioxins or chlorinated dibenzofurans (and EPA preempted this deadline by listing these substances on January 14, 1985, 50 Fed. Reg. 1978). By November 8, 1985, EPA must decide whether to list wastes containing halogenated dioxins and halogenated dibenzofurans. Rulemaking proceedings to list these latter two categories of wastes are pending as of May 1985. By February 8, 1986, EPA must decide whether or not to list as hazardous the following additional wastes:

chlorinated aliphatics   refining wastes
dioxin   chlorinated aromatics
dimethyl hydrazine   dyes and pigments
toluene diisocyanate   inorganic chemical
carbamates   industry wastes
bromacil   lithium batteries
linuron   coke byproducts
organo-bromines   paint production wastes
solvents   coal slurry pipeline
                                effluents

(In fact, EPA has already taken action and proposed listing some of these substances.)

The Amendments also direct EPA to list or identify those wastes that are hazardous solely because of the presence of certain types of constituents (such as carcinogens, mutagens, or teratogens) at levels that endanger human health. (1984 RCRA Amendments § 222, amending RCRA § 3001(b)(1).)

Furthermore, from time to time, the Agency adds to the lists of listed wastes. Wastes under consideration for listing are noted in EPA's semi-annual Regulatory Agenda, printed in the Federal Register every April and October.

(e) Delisting Procedure

The regulations provide that a company may demonstrate to the regulators that its waste materials, even though they would generally be considered listed hazardous wastes, need not be handled as otherwise required by these regulations.

The procedures for delisting are set forth in 40 C.F.R. 260.22, and explained in an EPA guidance manual entitled Petitions to Delist Hazardous Waste: A Guidance Manual (April 1985). The procedures are relatively straight-forward in that they require submission of certain data to EPA and analysis of the data by the Agency. Until 1984, the Agency granted many delisting petitions. However, the 1984 RCRA Amendments limit the Agency's discretion to grant such petitions by requiring EPA to consider additional factors (including additional constituents) beyond those for which a waste originally was listed in determining whether a waste is nonhazardous and may be delisted. (1984 RCRA Amendments § 222, adding RCRA § 3001(f).) For a waste to be delisted, EPA must conclude that it does not exhibit any of the characteristics of hazardousness or any toxicants at hazardous levels.

In a notice published on February 26, 1985, the Agency proposed a complex model for evaluating the hazard potential of a waste. See 50 Fed. Reg. 7882. If this model is adopted, it will complicate considerably the delisting process, notwithstanding that the 1984 RCRA Amendments require the Agency, to the extent practicable, to take final action on delisting petitions within two years of receipt.

2.   Characteristic Hazardous Wastes

Identification of "characteristic" hazardous wastes
is far more complex than recognizing "listed" wastes. There
are four criteria currently in the regulations for determining if a material that is not listed is nonetheless
hazardous. The criteria are ignitability, corrosivity,
reactivity, and toxicity. If a waste exhibits any of these
characteristics, or any additional characteristics EPA may
add in the future, it must be handled as a hazardous waste
unless it is specifically excluded from regulation, as
described at pp. 50-51 below.

(a) Ignitable Waste

Ignitability is determined in accordance with 40
C.F.R. § 261.21. Basically, liquids are ignitable if they
have a flash point of less than 60 degrees centigrade, using
standard ASTM tests. Nonliquids are ignitable if they are
capable, under standard temperature and pressure, of spon-
taneously causing fire through friction, absorption of
moisture, or spontaneous chemical changes and, when ignited,
burn so vigorously and persistently as to create a hazard.

(b) Corrosive Waste

Corrosivity is defined in 40 C.F.R. § 261.22.
Aqueous materials are considered corrosives if they have a
pH less than or equal to two, or greater than or equal to
12.5, as determined by specified test methods. Liquids also

are considered corrosive if they corrode steel at a rate of greater than 6.35 millimeters per year at a test temperature of 55 degrees centigrade, as determined under specified standard tests. Materials that do not contain a liquid portion that would, for example, settle out during storage cannot be considered corrosive under these tests, and thus are not regulated under this category.

(c) Reactive Waste

Reactivity is defined in 40 C.F.R. § 261.23. In general terms, a solid waste is considered a reactive hazardous waste if: (i) it normally is unstable and readily undergoes violent change with detonation; (ii) it reacts violently with water; (iii) it forms potentially explosive mixtures with water; (iv) when mixed with water, it generates toxic gas vapors or fumes in a quantity sufficient to present a danger to human health or the environment; (v) it is a cyanide or sulfur-bearing waste that when exposed to extremely high or low pH conditions can generate toxic gases, vapors, or fumes; (vi) it is capable of detonation or exposure reaction; or (vii) it is classified as a forbidden explosive or class A or class B explosive under Department of Transportation regulations.

(d) Toxic Waste

The RCRA definition of toxicity is set forth at 40 C.F.R. § 261.24. Unlike the other three criteria, the test of toxicity is not based on traditional industry testing procedures. Instead, a procedure was invented by EPA for the purposes of the RCRA rules. Currently, the test is the "extraction procedure" (or "EP") toxicity test, which in general terms requires that a sample of material be separated into solid and liquid phases and that an extract be produced from the solid phase. The extract is then analyzed and its constituents compared to a list of contaminents drawn from the Safe Drinking Water Act's list of National Interim Primary Drinking Water Regulation contaminants. If the concentrations of any of these materials in the extract exceed 100 times the Safe Drinking Water Act level, the material is considered an "EP toxic" hazardous waste.

The 1984 RCRA Amendments require EPA to examine the deficiencies of the EP toxicity characteristics as a predictor of the leaching potential of wastes. By March 8, 1987, EPA must make changes in the test to ensure that it accurately predicts the leaching potential of wastes that pose an environmental danger when mismanaged. By November 8, 1986, EPA also must promulgate regulations identifying additional characteristics of hazardous waste, including measures or indicators of toxicity. (1984 RCRA Amendments § 222, adding RCRA §§ 3001(g), (h).) As this edition goes to print, EPA is considering a replacement toxicity test, known as the "toxicity characteristic leaching procedure" (or "TCLP") which would amend the EP to include analysis of the organic content of wastes and to increase the concentration of inorganics extracted from a waste sample. EPA also is considering replacing the 100 times drinking water standard for judging whether waste leachate is hazardous with new, probably stricter standards. The result of these changes is likely to be that wastes formerly considered nonhazardous may be deemed hazardous wastes.

3. The Mixture Rule

In addition to listing and identifying by characteristics waste materials that are hazardous, the regulations also set forth a rule to determine when a mixture of nonhazardous waste materials and hazardous waste materials must be considered hazardous. The general rule is simple: mixtures of listed hazardous wastes with other waste materials are considered hazardous wastes until otherwise proven not to be, while combinations of characteristic hazardous wastes mixed with other solid waste materials are considered to be nonhazardous unless the resulting product meets a hazardousness criterion. (40 C.F.R. § 261.3(a)(2)(iv).)

Unfortunately, strict application of this rule leads to some absurd situations. For example, even minute quantities of listed solvents in wastewater could require that the entire quantity of wastewater be handled as a "hazardous waste." To clarify the situation, EPA in

November 1981 revised the regulation to exclude from the
mixture rule the following classifications of mixtures found
in wastewater discharged into surface water or into a
publicly-owned treatment works sewer system:

(1) the spent solvents carbon tetrachloride,
tetrachloroethylene, and trichloroethylene if the maximum solvent discharged weekly does not exceed one part
per million ("ppm") of the wastewater flow;

(2) the spent solvents methylene chloride,
1,1,1-trichloroethane, chlorobenzene, o-dichlorobenzene, cresols, cresylic acid, nitrobenzene, toulene,
methyl ethyl ketone, carbon disulfide, isobutanol, pyridine, and spent chlorofluorocabon solvents, if the maximum solvent discharged weekly does not exceed 25 ppm
of the wastewater flow;

(3) heat exchanger bundle cleaning sludge
from the petroleum refining industry;

(4) discarded commercial chemical products or
chemical intermediates arising from de minimis losses
during manufacturing (including spills, minor leaks,
sample purgings, relief device discharges, discharges
from personal safety equipment, and rinsate from
empty containers); and

(5) toxic wastes from laboratory operations if the
annualized average flow of laboratory wastewater does
not exceed one percent of the total wastewater flow.

To summarize, if a material is solid waste, and if it is also hazardous, it is subject to RCRA hazardous waste regulation unless it is specifically excluded, as described below.

E.   Excluded Materials

Based both on statutory directives and administrative decisions to create a workable hazardous waste management system that focuses on "problem" materials, EPA's rules exclude certain materials from regulation as hazardous wastes. These exclusions are set forth in 40 C.F.R. § 261.4, and include:

(1)   domestic sewage;

(2)   any mixture of domestic sewage and other waste that passes through a sewer system to a publicly-owned treatment works for treatment;

(3)   industrial wastewater discharges that are point source discharges subject to National Pollutant Discharge Elimination System regulation;

(4)   irrigation return flows;

(5)   source, special nuclear, or by-products material as defined by the Atomic Energy Act;

(6)   materials subjected to in-situ mining techniques that are not removed from the ground as part of the extraction process;

(7) pulping liquor that is reclaimed and reused in a pulping process unless it is accumulated speculatively;

(8) spent sulfuric acid used as a feedstock to produce virgin sulfuric acid unless it is accumulated speculatively;

(9) household wastes;

(10) agricultural wastes and manures that are used as fertilizers;

(11) mining overburden returned to the mine site;

(12) fly ash waste, bottom ash waste, slag waste, and flue gas emission control waste generated primarily from the combustion of coal or other fossil fuels;

(13) drilling fluids, produced waters, and other wastes associated with the exploration, development, or production of crude oil, natural gas, or geothermal energy;

(14) waste that would be considered toxic because of chromium that is exclusively or nearly exclusively trivalent chromium and will not create hexavalent chromium;

(15) solid waste from the extraction, beneficiation, and processing of ores and minerals (including coal), excluding phosphate rock and overburden from the mining of uranium ore;

(16)   cement kiln dust wastes;

(17)   solid waste that consists of discarded wood or wood products that would fail the test for toxicity only because it is an arsenic-treated wood; and

(18)   wastes that are generated in a product or raw materials storage tank, vehicle or vessel, pipeline, or manufacturing process unit that has been closed or from which waste is not removed.

F.   Residues in Empty Containers

Hazardous waste residues in "empty containers," as defined in the regulations, are not subject to hazardous waste regulation. 40 C.F.R. § 261.7(b) defines an "empty container" in terms of the type of waste that was in it. Containers that have held hazardous wastes other than compressed gases and the acutely hazardous materials listed in 40 C.F.R. § 261.33(c) are considered "empty" when all wastes have been removed that can be removed by common emptying practices, and the "empty" container contains no more than either (1) 2.5 cm (one inch) of residue, or (2) three percent of the weight of its total capacity, if it is 110 gallons or less in size, or 0.3 percent of the weight of its total capacity, if it is larger. Compressed gas containers are "empty" when opened to atmospheric pressure. For acutely hazardous wastes (as defined at 40 C.F.R. § 261.33(e)), an empty container is one that has been triple rinsed with an appropriate solvent or cleaned using another method to achieve equivalent removal, or has the inner liner removed.

G. Restrictions and Requirements Applicable to Certain Regulated Wastes and Waste Practices

   1. Differences in Handling Requirements for Listed and Characteristic Wastes

There are a number of differences in the way listed and characteristic hazardous wastes must be handled. The major differences are summarized in this section and explained in greater detail in the discussions of the various RCRA substantive requirements throughout the Handbook.

First, there are differences with respect to the effect of treating wastes. A listed hazardous waste remains a hazardous waste even if subsequently treated to reduce its toxicity. (40 C.F.R. § 261.3(c).) A characteristic waste, in contrast, may be treated to eliminate its hazardous characteristic, and the end result will be considered nonhazardous material. (40 C.F.R. § 261.3(d).)

Second, as discussed earlier in this chapter, there are differences with respect to the effects of mixing wastes. Materials contaminated by listed wastes must be treated as hazardous wastes. Thus, if a listed hazardous waste is mixed with solid waste, the entire mixture becomes a hazardous waste. (40 C.F.R. § 261.3(b)(2), discussed at pp.

48-49 above.) However, a mixture of a characteristic waste and a solid waste is hazardous only if the mixture also tests as hazardous. (40 C.F.R. § 261.3(b)(3).)

Third, there is a difference with respect to the applicability of the exemption for wastes generated in small quantities, in that listed _acutely_ hazardous waste is subject to a much lower threshold. (40 C.F.R. § 261.5(c), discussed at pp. 94-97 below.) Also, a container or the inner liner of a container that held a listed _acutely_ hazardous waste is considered hazardous waste itself until triple rinsed or the inner liner is removed. (40 C.F.R. § 261.33(d), discussed at p. 52 above.)

Fourth, recycled listed and characteristic wastes are treated somewhat differently under the revised definition of solid waste. The differences are discussed at p. 34, and summarized in a chart from EPA's Preamble to the revised definition, which appears at p. 35 above.

Finally, listed and characteristic wastes are subject to varied Superfund spill reporting requirements. Specifically, the quantities of spilled listed hazardous wastes and toxic wastes that must be reported under Superfund are identified at 40 C.F.R. § 302.4 (published at 50 Fed. Reg. 13475 and reprinted in Appendix F). Ignitable, corrosive, and reactive wastes are subject to the general 100 pound reportable quantity rule. (See discussion at pp. 68-73.)

2. Special Requirements for Wastes
   Generated in Small Quantities

Hazardous wastes generated in small quantities at any individual site are not subject to full RCRA hazardous waste regulation. See pp. 94-97 for a discussion of the special requirements applicable to small quantity generators.

3. Management Standards for Recycled Materials

For the future, EPA has promised a separate regulatory regime tailored to recycled materials. For the time being, however, the rules that were issued in conjunction with the revised definition of solid waste, 50 Fed. Reg. 614 (Jan. 4, 1985), generally impose on managers of recycled material current management standards for hazardous waste generators and transporters and current facility standards and permitting requirements for storage facilities. (These obligations are discussed in subsequent chapters of this Handbook.) This eliminates, for all practical purposes, any distinction between hazardous waste management and recycle/reuse activities, except that the rules do not regulate the actual recycling process.

The specific standards that apply are set forth in 40 C.F.R. § 261.6 and 40 C.F.R. Part 266 (published at 50 Fed. Reg. 665, 666-68). Limited exemptions have been granted for the following recycled materials: (a) industrial ethyl alcohol that is reclaimed; (b) used batteries returned to a battery manufacturer for regeneration;

(c) used oil exhibiting one or more of the characteristics of hazardous waste; and (d) scrap metal. (50 Fed. Reg. at 665, amending 40 C.F.R. § 261.6(a)(3).)

Part 266 currently contains management standards for five categories of recycled materials, as described below.

(a) Management Standards for Recycled Materials Used in a Manner Constituting Disposal

Subpart C of Part 266 makes generators and transporters of materials used in a manner constituting disposal, i.e., applied to land, subject to the standards for hazardous waste generators and transporters, discussed in Chapters VII and IX. Facilities that store and use these materials are made subject to the standards generally applicable to land disposal facilities, discussed in Parts 5 and 6. However, commercial fertilizers that contain recycled materials and waste-derived products that have undergone a chemical reaction during manufacturing are temporarily exempt from regulation as of May 1985. (50 Fed. Reg. at 666, adding 40 C.F.R. Part 266, Subpart C.)

(b) Management Standards for Hazardous Waste Burned for Energy Recovery

Subpart D of Part 266 currently imposes management standards on generators, transporters, and storers of hazardous waste fuels containing listed hazardous wastes and sludges. Pursuant to the 1984 RCRA Amendments, EPA will eventually expand these rules to apply to all hazardous waste fuels.

Specifically, Subpart D currently makes generators
and transporters of hazardous waste fuel composed of listed
hazardous wastes and sludges who send the fuel directly to
processors and burners subject to full regulation under the
hazardous waste system, 40 C.F.R. Parts 262 and 263, respectively, as described in Chapters VII and IX. Generators,
processors and burners of these same waste fuels who store
the fuels are subject to full regulation as hazardous waste
storage facilities under 40 C.F.R. Parts 264 and 265,
described in Parts 5 and 6. Persons who distribute but do
not process or blend these hazardous waste fuels are temporarily excluded from regulation as of May 1985.

Furthermore, as required by the 1984 RCRA
Amendments, any person who produces, distributes or markets
any hazardous waste fuel (with very limited exceptions) must
include a warning label that the fuel contains hazardous
wastes and list them. (1984 RCRA Amendments § 204, adding
RCRA § 3004(r), to be codified in the regulations at 40
C.F.R. § 266.34(d).) EPA is considering replacing the
labeling requirement with a manifesting requirement. (50
Fed. Reg. 1704 (Jan. 11, 1985).)

Finally, the 1984 RCRA Amendments establish substantial new requirements with respect to fuels containing
hazardous waste (listed and characteristic) and fuels containing used oil, applicable to all persons who produce,

use, distribute, or market the fuels. These new requirements include various notice and manifesting requirements to be effective no later than February 1986, and substantive standards for facilities that burn such fuels, to be promulgated by EPA no later than November 1986. EPA is authorized to exempt facilities burning such fuels if; (1) they burn de minimis quantities of hazardous waste at the same facility that generates the waste; (2) the waste is burned to recover useful energy; and (3) the waste is burned in a device determined by EPA to have sufficient destruction and removal efficiency to protect human health and the environment. (1984 RCRA Amendments § 204, amending RCRA §§ 3004, 3010.)

EPA has proposed rules that will implement some of these requirements. See 50 Fed. Reg. 1684 (Jan. 11, 1985). Under the proposed rules, generators, marketers, and burners of fuels containing hazardous waste or contaminated used oil must file a notification with EPA, use manifests for hazardous waste fuels, and keep certain records. Existing storage standards for hazardous waste under RCRA (see Parts 5 and 6) would be expanded to cover storage of processed or blended hazardous waste fuels. The proposed rules also prohibit the burning of hazardous waste fuels in nonindustrial boilers.

To implement further the 1984 RCRA Amendments, EPA plans to propose substantive controls on waste burning in industrial and utility boilers and furnaces, and to propose listing used oil as a hazardous waste by late 1985.

(c) <u>Management Standards for Recycled Used Oil</u>

Subpart E of Part 266 is reserved for used oil. EPA proposed regulations dealing with the burning of contaminated used oil, as discussed above, on January 11, 1985. (50 Fed. Reg. 1684.)

(d) Management Standards for Recyclable
Materials Utilized for Precious Metal
Recovery

Subpart F of Part 266 governs the reclamation of precious metals, e.g., gold, silver, platinum, and palladium. Owners and operators of such reclamation facilities are excluded from all regulations but the following: (1) notification requirements; (2) manifest requirements; and (3) requirements precluding over-accumulation of these materials and supporting recordkeeping. However, EPA explicitly reserves the right to impose full Subtitle C regulation on individual precious metal reclamation operations based on criteria set forth in the regulations. (50 Fed. Reg. at 662, adding 40 C.F.R. § 260.40.)

(e) Management Standards for Lead-Acid
Batteries Being Reclaimed

Subpart G of Part 266 regulates spent lead-acid batteries being reclaimed only when stored prior to reclamation at battery cracking or smelting operations. Spent batteries are not regulated, however, when handled by retailers, wholesalers, local service stations, intermediate collection centers, or during transportation. (50 Fed. Reg. at 667, adding 40 C.F.R. Part 266, Subpart G.)

4.   Land Disposal Restrictions

The 1984 RCRA Amendments establish a new national policy that is likely to affect dramatically the way in which all hazardous wastes are managed in the future. The legislation states that reliance on land disposal of hazardous wastes should be minimized or eliminated, and that land disposal, particularly in landfills or surface impoundments, should be the least favored method for managing such wastes. (1984 RCRA Amendments § 101, amending RCRA § 1002.) In establishing this policy, Congress intends that land disposal should be used only as a last resort, and should be replaced in most cases by advanced treatment, recycling, incineration, and other hazardous waste control technologies.

To implement this policy, the land disposal of specified categories of hazardous wastes is prohibited unless EPA determines that the prohibition of any particular method of land disposal of any particular type of waste is unnecessary to protect human health and the environment. (1984 RCRA Amendments § 201, amending RCRA § 3004.) The Amendments impose an immediate ban on disposal of bulk liquids in salt dome or salt bed formations, or in mines or caves. They also forbid the use of contaminated waste or used oil or other material for dust suppression or road treatment. Effective May 8, 1985, placement of bulk liquid hazardous wastes in landfills is prohibited. Beginning November 8, 1985, the disposal of nonhazardous liquids in landfills is prohibited, unless such disposal presents no risk of drinking water contamination and no safe alternative is reasonably available. The Amendments direct EPA to promulgate final regulations by February 8, 1986, to minimize the disposal of containerized liquid hazardous waste in landfills, and to minimize the presence of free liquids in these wastes. Until then, EPA regulations banning landfill disposal of these wastes unless certain conditions are met remain in effect.

Land disposal of certain spent solvents and wastes containing dioxins is banned effective November 8, 1986. Effective July 8, 1987, a group of hazardous wastes known as the "California list" (because they are banned from disposal in that state) is banned from land disposal. This list includes liquid wastes and sludges containing set concentrations of specified heavy metals or arsenic, highly acidic liquids, liquids containing 50 or more ppm of PCBs, and halogenated organic compounds. Underground injection of these wastes, dioxins, and solvents is prohibited effective August 8, 1988.

EPA is empowered to grant an exception to any of these bans on land disposal where the facility owner or operator demonstrates "to a reasonable degree of certainty" that there will be no migration of hazardous constituents from the disposal unit or injection zone for so long as the wastes remain hazardous. (1984 RCRA Amendments § 201, amending RCRA § 3004(d).)

The Amendments also require EPA to publish by November 8, 1986, a schedule for reviewing all other listed and identified hazardous wastes. EPA must then determine whether land disposal of those wastes should be prohibited. In accordance with deadlines prescribed in the legislation, EPA must promulgate regulations prohibiting those methods of land disposal for each waste that are not protective of human health and the environment. EPA must have reviewed all wastes for land disposal prohibition by May 8, 1990. After that time, a complete ban on land disposal of all hazardous wastes for which EPA has not promulgated regulations takes effect.

Moreover, once a hazardous waste becomes subject to EPA's land disposal prohibition, that waste may be stored only for the purpose of accumulating quantities necessary for proper treatment, recovery, or disposal.

Two types of limited variances from these land disposal prohibition will be available. First, EPA may postpone a land disposal prohibition for up to two years, if adequate alternative treatment, recovery, or disposal capacity for any particular waste is unavailable. Second, individual handlers may apply for a one-year variance, which EPA may grant if the applicant shows that there is a binding contract to construct or provide alternative capacity, which cannot be made available by the effective date due to circumstances beyond the applicant's control. Even where variances are granted, however, the waste may be disposed of only at facilities that meet new minimum technological requirements for landfills and surface impoundments (see pp. 139-40, 196-98).

CHAPTER V

SUPERFUND HAZARDOUS SUBSTANCES

        This chapter describes the substances covered by
Superfund's cleanup, liability and reporting provisions.

A.   Hazardous Substance Defined

        Almost all of the major provisions of Superfund are
tied to the definition of "hazardous substance" under
Section 101(14) of CERCLA. EPA has authority to respond to
the release or substantial threat of release of any
"hazardous substance" into the environment. (CERCLA
§ 104(a)(1).) Parties responsible for the release of a
"hazardous substance" -- including the generator of the
hazardous substance, the transporter, and the owner and
operator of the facility from which the release originates
-- may be held liable for cleanup. (CERCLA § 107(a).) In
addition, the person in charge of a vessel or facility immediately must report the release of a reportable quantity of
a "hazardous substance" into the environment. (CERCLA
§ 103(a).)

    1.   Substances Designated in Environmental Statutes

        Hazardous substances under Superfund include all
RCRA hazardous wastes, but include many additional substances
as well. This broader concept of a hazardous substance
under Superfund is defined with reference to all of the

major existing federal environmental statutes, and includes
any substance designated or regulated under any of the
following statutory provisions: (1) any hazardous substance
designated under Section 311 of the Clean Water Act; (2) any
toxic pollutant listed under Section 307 of the Clean Water
Act; (3) any hazardous waste under Section 3001 of RCRA, but
not including any waste the regulation of which under RCRA
has been suspended by Congress; (4) any hazardous air pollutant under Section 112 of the Clean Air Act; or (5) any
imminently hazardous chemical substance or mixture under
Section 7 of the Toxic Substances Control Act.

Close to 700 elements, compounds, and waste streams
are hazardous substances under Superfund by virtue of their
regulation under one or more of these other environmental
statutes. Approximately 300 of these substances are designated under Section 311 of the Clean Water Act and are
listed at 40 C.F.R. Part 116. The 65 toxic pollutants regulated under Section 307 of the Clear Water Act are listed at
40 C.F.R. § 401.15. Seven chemicals are designated under
Section 112 of the Clean Air Act and are listed at 40 C.F.R.
Part 61. All RCRA hazardous wastes, including those listed
under 40 C.F.R. Part 261 and those exhibiting any of the
four RCRA hazardous characteristics (see pp. 37-48) are
Superfund hazardous substances as well. There are currently

no chemical substances designated under Section 7 of the Toxic Substances Control Act.

All Superfund hazardous substances are listed alphabetically in Table 302.4 following 40 C.F.R. § 302.4, published at 50 Fed. Reg. 13475 and reprinted in Appendix F hereto.

2.   Additional Designated Substances

EPA also has authority to designate additional hazardous substances under Superfund through rulemaking. (CERCLA §§ 101(14), 102.) As of May 1985, however, EPA indefinitely deferred rulemaking on designating additional hazardous substances.

3.   Hazardous Constituents

EPA has taken the position, and the courts that had reached the issue as of May 1985 agreed, that a material may be a hazardous substance even if the material itself is not listed under one of the environmental provisions described above. For example, a waste that is nonhazardous under RCRA is still a Superfund hazardous substance if it contains constituents listed under Section 307 or 311 of the Clean Water Act or Section 112 of the Clean Air Act. In an April 1985 decision, the D.C. Circuit Court of Appeals held that even wastes suspended from regulation as hazardous under RCRA -- and therefore exempt from regulation as RCRA hazardous wastes under Superfund as well -- nevertheless are Superfund hazardous substances if they contain hazardous constituents listed under one of the listed statutes other than RCRA. <u>Eagle-Picher Industries, Inc. v. EPA</u>, No. 83-2259 (D.C. Cir. April 16, 1985).

    4.   <u>Petroleum and Natural Gas Exclusion</u>

Superfund expressly excludes from the definition of hazardous substance petroleum and natural gas, natural gas liquids, liquefied natural gas, and synthetic gas usable for fuel. The effect of the petroleum exclusion is that releases of oil into water are covered by federal law (under the Clean Water Act), but oil spills onto land are not. In particular, owners of oil facilities, and generators and transporters of oil disposed at an off-site facility, are not subject to the reporting or liability provisions of Superfund.

B.   <u>Pollutants or Contaminants</u>

Although most of Superfund's major provisions are tied to the definition of hazardous substance, EPA also has authority to expend Superfund monies in response to the release or substantial threat of release of any "pollutant or contaminant which may present an imminent and substantial danger to the public health or welfare." The term "pollutant or contaminant" is defined broadly to include any element, substance, compound, or mixture that may cause

disease in any organism in the environment. (CERCLA §
104(a).)

EPA therefore has broad residual authority to
respond to the release of virtually any substance, whether
or not it meets the statutory definition of hazardous
substance, if a potential imminent and substantial danger
can be demonstrated. The practical impact of this response
authority is limited by Section 107 of the statute, however,
which limits liability for response costs to those expended
in response to a hazardous substance. Section 106 of the
statute, which provides EPA with authority to compel private
cleanup, likewise is limited to hazardous substances.

C.   Spill Reporting

Superfund is for the most part a liability statute
which imposes cleanup responsibility on parties whose past
disposal practices contributed to existing waste sites. In
addition, however, Superfund imposes a few current regulatory obligations on owners and operators, generators, and
transporters of hazardous substances. Chief among these is
the release reporting requirement, which is contained in
Section 103(a) and which EPA has implemented through new
regulations. (40 C.F.R. Part 302, published at 50 Fed. Reg.
13474 (April 4, 1985) and reprinted as Appendix F.)

Under Superfund, a person in charge of a facility
or vessel must report any spill or other release of a

"reportable quantity" ("RQ") of a hazardous substance as soon as he has knowledge of the release. (CERCLA § 103(a).) If such a release has occurred, the person in charge of the facility immediately must notify the National Response Center (telephone: (800) 424-8802, or from Washington, D.C. (202) 426-2675). The regulations establish a 24-hour period within which a reportable quantity of a hazardous substance must be released for the release to be reportable, as is the rule for reporting spills under Section 311 of the Clean Water Act. (50 Fed. Reg. 13513, adding 40 C.F.R. § 302.6(a).) EPA has indicated its intention, for notification purposes, to treat the entire contiguous plant and grounds as one "facility," and to aggregate all concurrent releases of the same substance from a facility to determine if an RQ has been exceeded. (50 Fed. Reg. 13459.) Failure to report is punishable by a $10,000 fine and/or a year's imprisonment. (CERCLA § 103(b).)

The statute established an RQ for all hazardous substances at one pound, except where a higher RQ had been established under Section 311 of the Clean Water Act. (CERCLA § 102(b).) Under the new regulations, however, the RQs of approximately one-half of all CERCLA hazardous substances have been raised or lowered based on five primary criteria (aquatic toxicity, mammalian toxicity, ignitability, reactivity, and chronic toxicity) and the susceptibility of the substance to degradation (biodegradation, hydrolysis, and photolysis). The current RQs for all CERCLA hazardous substances, which range from 1 to 5000 pounds, are listed as "Final RQs" in Table 302.4 of the regulations, 50 Fed. Reg. 13475 (Appendix F). EPA also has proposed in a separate rulemaking to adjust the RQs of 105 additional CERCLA hazardous substances. (50 Fed. Reg. 13514.) EPA has deferred rulemaking on the RQs of potential carcinogens, PCBs, and other hazardous substances pending further evaluation. (50 Fed. Reg. 13470.)

For all listed hazardous substances, including all listed RCRA hazardous wastes, the regulations establish individual RQs based on the criteria listed above. For all unlisted RCRA hazardous wastes exhibiting the characteristic of ignitability, corrosivity, or reactivity, the regulations establish the reportable quantity of 100 pounds. For unlisted RCRA wastes exhibiting the characteristic of EP toxicity, the reportable quantity is the RQ listed in Table 302.4 for the particular contaminant on which the characteristic of EP toxicity for that particular waste is based. If a RCRA waste exhibits EP toxicity based on more than one contaminant, or exhibits EP toxicity and one or more other RCRA hazardous characteristics, the RQ for the waste is the lowest of the applicable reportable quantities. (50 Fed. Reg. 13513, adding 40 C.F.R. § 302.5.)

Under the same mixture rule that is applied under Section 311 of the Clean Water Act, releases of mixtures and solutions under Superfund are subject to the release reporting requirement only where a component hazardous substance of the mixture or solution is released in its reportable quantity. (50 Fed. Reg. 13512, adding 40 C.F.R. § 302.6(b).) Conversely, releases of several component hazardous substances of a mixture in amounts less than their respective reportable quantities need not be reported; in other words, RQs are not added to determine a reportable release.

For listed or unlisted RCRA hazardous wastes, the applicable RQ is normally applied to the entire waste. If, however, the concentrations of each hazardous component of a RCRA waste is known, the applicable RQ may be ignored in favor of reliance on the RQs of the particular hazardous components -- applied to the quantity of each individual component under the mixture rule. For example, if a spent halogenated solvent, identified as a listed waste from a non-specific source in 40 C.F.R. § 261.31 as "FOO2" (whose reportable quantity is one pound), has as its sole hazardous constituent chlorobenzene (whose reportable quantity is 100 pounds), the applicable RQ is 100 pounds; and if the con- centration of chlorobenzene in the waste is 50 percent, only a release of 200 pounds or more of the waste need be reported. In addition, if the person in charge knows that an RQ of a particular hazardous component of a RCRA waste has been released before the RQ of the entire waste has been exceeded, the release must be reported. (50 Fed. Reg. 13463.)

As applied to an unlisted RCRA hazardous waste exhibiting the ignitability, corrosivity, or reactivity characteristic, the release reporting rules currently require reporting only if the substance is a RCRA waste prior to its release. However, EPA also has proposed to subject substances to the reporting requirements even if they become wastes only by virtue of their release. (50 Fed. Reg. 13514.)

EPA has decided not to establish RQs for the many broad generic classes of organic and metallic compounds (e.g., "zinc and compounds") designated as toxic pollutants under Section 307 of the Clean Water Act. Therefore, the notification requirements apply only to those specific compounds for which RQs are listed in Table 302.4, rather than to the generic classes of compounds. (50 Fed. Reg. 13461.) In addition, EPA does not require notification of releases of twelve solid metals (antimony, arsenic, beryllium, cadmium, chromium, copper, lead, nickel, selenium, silver, thallium, and zinc) listed under Section 307 if the mean diameter of the particles released is larger than 100 micro-meters (0.004 inches). (50 Fed. Reg. 13513, adding 40 C.F.R. § 302.6.)

Exempt from the Superfund release reporting requirements are "federally permitted releases" under other federal environmental statutes and releases that have been exempted pursuant to reporting requirements under RCRA. In addition, continuous releases that already have been reported for a sufficient period of time need not be reported again. (CERCLA § 103(f)(1)-(2).) EPA previously indicated its intent to issue special rules on continuous releases, but as of May 1985 had deferred rulemaking indef-initely.

In order to avoid duplicative reporting, EPA has clarified its intention to allow one call to the National Response Center to satisfy similar reporting obligations to the NRC under Superfund, the Clean Water Act, RCRA, Hazardous Materials Transportation Act, and Section 8(e) of the Toxic Substances Control Act. (50 Fed. Reg. 13464.)

For further discussion of Superfund and other spill reporting requirements, see Appendix I.

CHAPTER VI

PCB REGULATION

Polychlorinated biphenyls ("PCBs") have been widely
used since the 1930s in electrical equipment and other
machinery as electric and cooling fluids, and continue to be
so used. They have not been commercially manufactured in
this country since the mid-1970s, although they are still
made in Europe.

Currently, PCBs are neither listed nor characteristic hazardous wastes under RCRA, although EPA is studying
whether it should list them as a hazardous waste. The only
application of the RCRA program to PCBs is that they are
among the RCRA 40 C.F.R. Part 261 Appendix VIII constituents
for which groundwater monitoring, cleanup, and health
assessments may be required for some treatment, storage, and
disposal facilities. (See pp. 177-78.) In addition, the
1984 RCRA Amendments impose certain restrictions on the
disposal of PCBs, as discussed below at pp. 81-82.

Instead, PCBs are subject to their own complex
regulatory scheme under section 6(e) of the Toxic Substances
Control Act ("TSCA"), 15 U.S.C. § 2605(e). These regula-
tions are set forth in 40 C.F.R. Part 761, as modified by 49
Fed. Reg. 28189 (July 10, 1984) and 49 Fed. Reg. 44638
(Nov. 8, 1984). PCBs also are regulated to some degree

under Superfund as hazardous substances, and under other statutes. This chapter describes both the TSCA and other statutory requirements regarding PCBs.

A. Regulation of PCBs Under TSCA

Generally, the manufacture, processing, and sale of any concentration of PCBs are now, with limited exceptions, prohibited unless a special exemption is obtained from EPA. The use of PCBs continues to be allowed in some cases, if the equipment is "totally enclosed" (essentially if it does not leak) or if EPA has specifically authorized the use. Equipment that meets one of these criteria is still subject to specific requirements relating to marking, storage, servicing, and disposal.

1. Regulated PCBs

Until July 1984, regulated PCBs were only those in concentrations of 50 parts per million ("ppm") or greater. PCBs in concentrations less than 50 ppm were not regulated, except that waste oil containing any PCBs could not be used for dust control or road oiling or as a herbicide.

As the result of judicially-ordered rulemaking completed in July 1984, EPA eliminated the general 50 ppm cutoff. Now, the use and manufacture of PCBs at any concentration is prohibited unless it is specifically allowed by the rules. For example, the rules allow the "inadvertent generation" of very low levels of PCBs incidental to various manufacturing processes and the use of certain "recycled" PCBs and PCBs below 50 ppm in hydraulic and heat transfer systems and in natural gas pipeline compressors. Some of the PCB rules, however, such as the disposal rules, still apply only to PCBs above 50 ppm. (49 Fed. Reg. 28189, amending 40 C.F.R. § 761.1.)

The regulations distinguish between various types of equipment and various concentrations of PCBs. For example, any equipment that contains 50 ppm PCBs or greater is classified as PCB Equipment. Within this broad category, electrical equipment containing 50 ppm or greater PCBs but less than 500 ppm PCBs is classified as PCB-Contaminated Electrical Equipment. All mineral oil-filled electrical equipment except circuit breakers, reclosers, and cable must be assumed to be PCB-Contaminated Electrical Equipment unless its concentration is known.

The rules also create different classes of trans- formers and capacitors. Transformers that contain 50 ppm PCBs or greater but less than 500 ppm PCBs are classified as PCB-Contaminated Electrical Equipment. However, transfor- mers that contain 500 ppm PCBs or greater are classified specifically as PCB Transformers. Capacitors also are bro- ken into two classes: Small Capacitors (those containing less than three pounds PCBs) and Large Capacitors (those

containing three or more pounds PCBs). (40 C.F.R. § 761.3.)
The regulatory requirements applicable to these classes
differ, as explained below.

2.   Marking Requirements

PCB Transformers and Large PCB Capacitors must be
marked with a special EPA-approved label identifying the
equipment as containing PCBs. Containers holding either
PCBs or equipment containing PCBs, PCB storage-for-disposal
areas, and certain PCB transport vehicles also must be
marked. No marking requirements are applicable to PCB-
Contaminated Electrical Equipment. (40 C.F.R. § 761.40.)

3.   Storage of PCBs

All PCBs that are stored for disposal, including
any electrical equipment containing PCBs and any PCB fluid
that is stored to service PCB Equipment, must be stored in a
special storage facility. These are often referred to as
"Annex III" storage facilities, named after the portion of
EPA's regulations in which they were originally described.
Such a facility must have a roof, walls, impervious floor,
continuous curbing, and must not be located in a 100-year
floodplain. The storage facilities must be inspected
monthly.

In some circumstances, PCBs also may be stored temporarily in an area that does not comply with Annex III
requirements. Non-leaking PCB Articles and Equipment,

leaking PCB Articles and Equipment if placed in a container with sufficient sorbent material, and containers containing either PCB Equipment or non-liquid PCBs (e.g., soil) may be stored for up to 30 days in non-compliance areas. (A PCB Article is any manufactured article, other than a PCB Container, that contains PCBs and whose surfaces have been in direct contact with PCBs). In addition, non-leaking Large PCB Capacitors and PCB-Contaminated Electrical Equipment may be stored adjacent to an Annex III facility, provided that they are inspected weekly and that the facility contains space equal to 10 percent of the volume of equipment stored outside of the facility. (40 C.F.R. § 761.65, as amended at 49 Fed. Reg. 28191.)

4. Use, Servicing, and Inspection of Electrical Equipment Containing PCBs

(a) Transformers

Currently, most transformers containing PCBs may continue to be used for the remaining useful life of the equipment. The one exception is PCB Transformers that pose a risk of exposure of PCBs to food or feed; these transformers must be phased out by October 1, 1985. (An exposure risk is posed if there is a potential pathway from the equipment to the food or feed. "Potential" is deemed to include foreseeable events such as a leak.) In addition, until these transformers are phased out, they must be inspected for leaks weekly. All other PCB Transformers must

- 78 -

be inspected quarterly unless they have secondary containment or contain under 60,000 ppm (6 percent) PCBs, in which case only annual inspection is required. No inspection requirements apply to transformers that contain less that 500 ppm PCBs. (40 C.F.R. § 761.30(a).)

In October 1984, EPA proposed to add further restrictions on the use of PCB Transformers to address the Agency's concern over by-products produced from building fires involving this equipment. (See 49 Fed. Reg. 39966 (Oct. 11, 1984).) A final rule, or a decision that no further rules are needed, is due in July 1985.

The servicing of transformers containing PCBs also is restricted. EPA considers servicing to be a type of use, so that unless the servicing of a particular type of equipment is authorized, the equipment may not be serviced. Servicing is subject to specific limitations, with the more stringent requirements applying to PCB Transformers. (40 C.F.R. § 761.30.) For example, no servicing can be performed on PCB Transformers if it requires the removal and reworking of internal components such as the transformer coil.

(b) Capacitors

Large PCB Capacitors located in restricted areas (either a restricted-access electrical substation or a contained and restricted-access indoor installation) can continue to be used for the remaining useful life of the equipment. Other Large PCB Capacitors that are not located in restricted areas, including those posing an exposure risk to food or feed, must be phased out by October 1, 1988. All Small Capacitors may continue to be used for their remaining lives. No inspection requirements apply to capacitors. (40 C.F.R. § 761.30(1).)

(c) Other Equipment

Most electromagnets containing PCBs may be used for their remaining useful lives. Those that contain 500 ppm PCBs or greater and pose an exposure risk to food or feed, however, may not be used after October 1, 1985. Until that date, they must be inspected weekly for leaks.

PCB-Contaminated Electrical Equipment may continue to be used indefinitely, subject to certain servicing restrictions. (40 C.F.R. § 761.30.)

The use of PCBs in heat transfer and hydraulic systems and in natural gas pipeline compressors was authorized in July 1984 for the remaining life of the equipment, subject to a requirement that the concentration not exceed 50 ppm and to certain other restrictions. (49 Fed. Reg. 28190, amending 40 C.F.R. §§ 761.30(d), (e).)

5. Disposal of PCBs

There are three basic types of facilities approved by the regulations for the disposal of PCBs in concentrations

of 50 ppm or greater. No restrictions apply to disposal of
PCBs in lesser concentrations.

The three types of approved facilities are: (1)
EPA-approved incinerators; (2) high-efficiency boilers that
meet EPA criteria and for which notice of intent to burn
PCBs has been sent to EPA; and (3) EPA-approved chemical
waste landfills. (40 C.F.R. § 761.60.) The rules provide
which type of facility may be used, according to the type of
equipment involved and the medium in which the PCBs are present. In addition, when incineration is required, application can be made to EPA for approval of the use of an
alternative method of disposal. EPA may grant such approval
if the alternate method provides destruction equivalent to
an approved incinerator or high-efficiency boiler and if the
alternative will not pose an unreasonable risk of injury to
health or the environment. (40 C.F.R. § 761.60(e).)

Liquid PCBs with concentrations of 500 ppm or
greater must be disposed of in an approved incinerator.
Liquids containing less than 500 ppm (but at least 50 ppm)
must be disposed of either in an approved incinerator, a
high-efficiency boiler or, currently, an approved landfill,
provided the liquid is not an ignitible waste (i.e., flash
point greater than 60 degrees centigrade). Under the 1984
RCRA Amendments, however, landfilling of liquid PCBs at 50
ppm or greater is prohibited after July 1987, or earlier if

EPA so directs. (1984 RCRA Amendments § 201(a), adding RCRA § 3004(d)(2)(D).) To determine the proper disposal method, batch testing of PCB liquids stored in bulk is permitted, subject to certain restrictions. (40 C.F.R. § 761.60(g).)

PCB Transformers must be disposed of in an approved incinerator or in a chemical waste landfill if the transformer has been drained of all fluid and flushed with solvent.

Large PCB Capacitors must be incinerated in an approved facility, except that capacitors containing greater than 50 but less than 500 ppm PCBs currently may be disposed of in an approved landfill. (40 C.F.R. §§ 761.60(b)(2)(iii), 761.60(b)(4).) However, the 1984 RCRA Amendments appear to eliminate this exception, so that after July 1987, or earlier if EPA so directs, Large PCB Capacitors containing from 50 to 499 ppm no longer will be permitted to be landfilled. Small PCB Capacitors may be disposed of as municipal solid waste, except that those owned by a former PCB Equipment manufacturer must be disposed of in an approved incinerator. (40 C.F.R. § 761.60(b)(2)(ii), (iv).)

The disposal of PCB-Contaminated Electrical Equipment (except capacitors) is not subject to any of the PCB disposal rules if it has been drained of all free-flowing liquid.

Finally, spill material (e.g., soil, rags, other debris) must be disposed of in an approved incinerator or landfill.

6.   PCB Spill Reporting and Cleanup

The PCB regulations contain no specific reporting requirements relating to spills of PCBs. PCB spills are subject only to the general requirement in TSCA § 8(e), which requires the reporting of any incident that poses a "substantial risk" to human health or the environment, and to the Superfund and Clean Water Act reporting requirements, discussed below and in Appendix F.

Under the PCB rules, any spill technically is deemed to be illegal, because EPA has defined disposal to include "spills, leaks, and other uncontrolled discharges" but has not authorized such occurrences as permissible disposal methods. (40 C.F.R. §§ 761.3, 761.60(d).) As a policy matter, though, EPA has stated it will not take any enforcement action for "improper disposal" if "adequate" cleanup measures are begun within 48 hours of discovery. (See 47 Fed. Reg. 37342, 37354 (Aug. 25, 1982).) Thus, EPA has chosen to address spills in the context of enforcement actions for inadequate, and therefore improper, disposal.

The level to which one must clean and the particular procedures one must follow are currently being debated. EPA considered, but rejected in 1982, establishing a requirement to clean to background levels in certain desig-nated "sensitive" areas. In the absense of a uniform policy, the various EPA Regional Offices have used differing cleanup standards, ranging from 50 ppm (the rationale being that disposal of PCBs is unregulated below that level) to background or non-detectable levels. As this Handbook goes to press, the Agency is in the process of developing a uni-form approach that would address cleanup levels and proce-dures nationwide.

B. Superfund and Other Statutory Obligations Pertaining to PCBs

1. Superfund Requirements

PCBs are deemed to be a "hazardous substance" under CERCLA § 101(14). Therefore, their presence can be, and has been, the rationale for inclusion of a site on EPA's National Priorities List for remedial action. (See p. 101.)

In addition, a spill of 10 pounds or more of PCBs (the "reportable quantity" for PCBs) from a vessel or facil-ity must be reported to the National Response Center (telephone: (800) 424-8802) by any person in charge of such vessel or facility. (CERCLA § 103(a).) The owner or opera-tor of such a facility also must notify potentially injured parties by publication in local newspapers serving the affected area. (CERCLA § 111(g).)

2. Other Statutory Requirements

EPA has listed PCBs under Section 311 of the Clean Water Act as a hazardous substance. Accordingly, as under Superfund, if there is a discharge of PCBs over the reportable quantity (10 pounds) from a vessel or facility, the person in charge must notify the National Response Center. (Clean Water Act § 311(b)(5).) In addition, the federal government may seek to force cleanup of such a spill or undertake cleanup itself and then seek to recover its costs. (Clean Water Act §§ 311(c), (e), (f).)

The transportation of PCBs in an amount above the reportable quantity is subject to the requirements of the Hazardous Materials Transportation Act, 49 U.S.C. §§ 1801 et seq., and the Department of Transportation's implementing regulations, as an "Other Regulated Material-E." Specifically, PCBs are subject to the shipping paper provisions of 49 C.F.R. Part 172, Subpart C, the marking requirements of 49 C.F.R. Part 172, Subpart D, and the packaging requirements of 49 C.F.R. Part 173, Subparts A and B and section 173.510.

PART 3: GENERATORS' OBLIGATIONS

As noted in Chapter III, RCRA and Superfund impose
major obligations on generators of hazardous waste. Indeed,
perhaps the most fundamental practical impact of RCRA is the
imposition of major responsibility for hazardous waste management on waste generators. Superfund in some circumstances
obligates generators to clean up abandoned waste sites and
to pay the cost of cleanup for and damages to natural
resources resulting from spills and other releases of hazardous substances. Chapters VII and VIII address these responsibilities.

CHAPTER VII

GENERATORS' RCRA OBLIGATIONS

One of the most important impacts of RCRA regulation is to impose on waste generators the obligation to determine whether their wastes are hazardous, to decide where their hazardous wastes will be disposed of or otherwise managed, and to assure that their hazardous wastes reach that designated location. All the requirements imposed on generators flow from this basic concept.

Federal regulations applying to waste generators are set forth at 40 C.F.R. Part 262. With the exception of generators who produce only small quantities of waste, all hazardous waste generators are required to:

(1) determine whether their wastes are hazardous;

(2) obtain an EPA identification number;

(3) initiate a manifest document that will follow the waste from "cradle to grave";

(4) properly package, label, and mark the waste;

(5) maintain records of waste shipments; and

(6) report to EPA if a copy of the completed manifest is not received from the designated facility within 45 days of the date the waste was accepted by the initial transporter.

Special requirements apply to generators of hazardous waste in small quantities, i.e. less than 1,000 kilograms of waste per month. They are described in the last section of this chapter.

We review each of the generators' requirements as administered by EPA. Although state requirements apply in authorized states in lieu of the federal rules, most states are adopting the federal program with minimal changes. (See pp. 8-14.) To be apprised of these changes and any additional requirements, generators should consult state and local requirements.

A. Waste Characterization

The previous chapter describes the method for determining whether a material is a hazardous waste. It is the generator's responsibility to make that determination. However, it is not necessary to test the waste in every case. That is, EPA's regulations allow a judgment as to the hazardousness of a waste to be based on the generator's "knowledge of the hazard characteristic of the waste in light of the materials or the processes used." Nonetheless, the ultimate burden of hazardousness identification falls on the generator. (40 C.F.R. § 262.11.)

B. Identification Number

If a waste generator determines that his wastes are hazardous, he must obtain an identification number from EPA. This is a relatively straightforward procedure, requiring EPA Form 8700-12. Identification numbers are assigned by Regional Administrators of EPA. A generator may offer his hazardous waste only to transporters or treatment, storage, or disposal facilities ("TSDFs") with EPA identification numbers. (40 C.F.R. § 262.12.)

C. Manifests

Manifest documents are the key to the "paper trail" established by RCRA. On March 20, 1984, EPA and the United States Department of Transportation ("DOT") published a Uniform Hazardous Waste Manifest to be used for all regulated shipments of hazardous waste. (49 Fed. Reg. 10490, reprinted here as Appendix G.) The information on the manifest includes the manifest number; information identifying the generator and all transporters; a description of the waste in accordance with DOT regulations; and the quantity of waste. Although states may use their own manifest forms, the information required must be basically the same as the information required on the federal form. (40 C.F.R. § 271.6(d).) State forms may include space for additional, state-required information.

A manifest must be used whenever hazardous waste is shipped off its site of generation. Basically, off-site shipment means shipment on or along a public highway. It does not matter whether the shipment is by vehicle owned by the generator, or to a site owned by the generator. If the shipment is off-site, a manifest must be used. (40 C.F.R. § 262.20.) EPA has been considering allowing an "alternate manifest" for shipments between a generator's own facilities, but has not published a formal proposal.

If the state to which the generator is shipping waste (the consignment state) requires its own manifest form, the generator must use that manifest. If the consignment state does not supply a form, the generator must use the form of the state in which he is located, if that state requires its own form. If neither state requires a form, the generator may obtain a manifest from any source. (40 C.F.R. § 262.21.) Special rules apply for water and rail transport. (40 C.F.R. § 262.23(c)-(d).)

The generator is responsible for designating on the manifest the treatment, storage, or disposal facility to which his waste is to be taken, and he may designate an alternate facility for delivery in the event that the designated facility is not available. If the waste cannot be delivered to either facility, the generator must instruct the transporter where to take the waste. (40 C.F.R.

§ 262.20.) The generator must sign a manifest certification assuring compliance with DOT labeling and packaging requirements; obtain the handwritten signature of the transporter; and give the transporter enough copies of the manifest so that every participant along the line can retain one and a copy can be returned to the generator. (40 C.F.R. § 262.22.) After September 1, 1985, generators must certify on the manifest form that they have a program in place to reduce the volume and toxicity of their waste as much as economically practicable. (1984 RCRA Amendments § 224, amending RCRA § 3002, to be codified in the regulations at 40 C.F.R. § 262.41(a).)

If the generator does not receive a copy of the manifest signed by the owner or operator of the designated facility within 35 days after the waste was accepted by the initial transporter, the generator must determine whether the waste was received at the designated facility. If this signed manifest has not been received within 45 days of the initial shipment, the generator must report this fact to the EPA Regional Administrator by filing an Exception Report containing a copy of the manifest and a letter explaining his efforts to trace the waste. This obligation applies even if the generator has received an explanation of the situation that he deems satisfactory. (40 C.F.R. § 262.42.)

D. Packaging and Labeling Requirements

The generator is responsible for packaging, labeling, marking, and placarding hazardous waste shipments according to DOT regulations. (40 C.F.R. Part 262, Subpart C;
49 C.F.R. Parts 172, 173, 178, 179; 50 Fed. Reg. 11048
(March 19, 1985).)

E. Accumulation Time

A generator may accumulate hazardous waste on site
for 90 days without a TSDF permit or without having interim
status, provided some regulatory requirements are met during
those 90 days. The generator must (1) store the material in
(a) good containers that are compatible with the waste they
contain and are inspected weekly, or (b) tanks that hold the
waste safely and are inspected daily for operational defects
and weekly for construction flaws (see Part 265, Subparts I
and J); (2) mark the first day of accumulation on the outside of each container; (3) label the container or tank
"Hazardous Waste"; (4) ship the waste to a permitted or
interim status facility within 90 days of the beginning of
accumulation; and (5) comply with several management standards, including personnel training, facility preparedness
and prevention, and contingency and emergency procedures.
(40 C.F.R. § 262.34.)

Very small amounts of waste are exempt from the 90-day accumulation rule. Hazardous waste may be collected in a number of so-called "satellite accumulation" areas throughout a generator's facility in 55-gallon drums (or, for 40 C.F.R. § 261.33(e) acutely hazardous waste, one-quart containers). Until these drums or containers are taken from their point of generation and placed in a central accumulation area, or the amount of waste at a particular point of generation exceeds one drum or one quart, respectively, the generator need not comply with the 90-day rule. The waste containers in satellite areas must be closed and in good condition, compatible with their contents, and marked with their contents or the words "Hazardous Waste." (49 Fed. Reg. 49568 (Dec. 20, 1984), to be codified at 40 C.F.R. § 262.34.)

Note that a small quantity generator (described below at pp. 94-97) is not subject to the 90-day accumulation rule.

F. Recordkeeping and Reporting

The generator is required to keep copies of all signed manifests for three years, and copies of Exception Reports for a similar period. In addition, all test results, waste analyses, and other data upon which a hazardous waste determination is made also must be kept for three years. (40 C.F.R. § 262.40.)

Hazardous waste generators must submit biennial reports to EPA. The reports are to include information on the types and amounts of hazardous waste generated, the disposition of those wastes, and efforts undertaken to reduce the volume and toxicity of wastes. Reports are due on March 1 of each even numbered year with respect to activities during the previous year. (40 C.F.R. § 262.41; 1984 RCRA Amendments § 224, adding RCRA § 3002(b).)

G. <u>International Shipments</u>

Special requirements apply to persons who export hazardous wastes to a foreign country or import hazardous wastes into the United States. These requirements are set forth in 40 C.F.R. § 262.50, and generally require notification to EPA, receipt of confirmation of waste delivery, and exception reporting. The 1984 RCRA Amendments establish further requirements for exports (scheduled to take effect no later than November 1986), including a requirement that the receiving country consent to the shipment. (1984 RCRA Amendments § 245, adding RCRA § 3017.)

H. <u>Special Requirements for Small Quantity Generators</u>

Under EPA regulations, generators of small quantities of hazardous waste at individual sites are not subject to full RCRA regulation. (40 C.F.R. § 261.5.) Prior to the 1984 RCRA Amendments, the general rule was that any waste generated in quantities of less than 1,000 kilograms per month was covered by this exclusion. Some regulatory requirements did apply, however. Most notably, the generator had to determine if his wastes were hazardous and had to send his wastes to be recycled or managed at a landfill or other facility regulated under some state or federal program. For acutely hazardous commercial chemical products listed in 40 C.F.R. § 261.33(e) and for contaminated soils resulting from the spill of these materials, levels lower than 1,000 kilograms per month apply. These limits are (1) one kilogram for the materials listed in 40 C.F.R. § 261.33(e) and off-specification variations, and (2) 100 kilograms of residues and contaminated soils resulting from the spill of these materials.

As a result of the 1984 RCRA Amendments, the requirements applicable to small quantity generators will be substantially increased. The Amendments require EPA to promulgate a number of new requirements for small quantity generators who generate between 100 and 1,000 kilograms of hazardous waste (other than acutely hazardous waste) per month. (The limited requirements for small quantities of acutely hazardous waste may remain the same.) By March 31, 1986, EPA must promulgate regulations for these generators, although the regulations may vary from those applicable to large quantity generators. For example, a small quantity generator may store wastes on-site for up to 180 days without a permit. If the generator must transport waste more than 200 miles for disposal, he may store up to 6000 kilograms on-site for up to 270 days without a permit. (1984 RCRA Amendments § 221, adding RCRA § 3001(d).)

EPA already has drafted regulatory amendments to implement these provisions (to be codified in the regulations at 40 C.F.R. § 261.5). The new rule creates three classes of small quantity generators for regulatory purposes:

(1) those generating between 100 kilograms and 1,000 kilograms of non-acutely hazardous waste per calendar month;

(2) those generating up to 100 kilograms of non-acutely hazardous waste per month; and

(3) those generating acutely hazardous waste in very small quantities, i.e., one kilogram of the commercial chemical products listed in 40 C.F.R. § 261.33(e) or 100 kilograms of spill residues and contaminated soils.

The requirements for the second and third categories will remain unaffected by the new regulations. However, beginning August 5, 1985, generators in the second category who ship wastes off site must use an abbreviated version of EPA's Uniform Hazardous Waste Manifest forms to track the wastes they ship. The form must contain the following information:

(1)   the name and address of the generator;

(2)   the U.S. Department of Transportation description of waste including the proper shipping name,
hazard class, and identification number;

(3)   the number and type of containers;

(4)   the quantity of waste being transported; and

(5)   the name and address of the designated facility.

Moreover, generators in this category may ship their wastes
only to interim states or permitted hazardous waste facilities, state-regulated facilities, or to recycling facilities.

As a result of these changes in the regulatory
program, it is estimated that approximately 75,000 more
businesses will be subject to RCRA regulation than had been
the case under the prior regulations.

CHAPTER VIII

GENERATORS' SUPERFUND OBLIGATIONS

A hazardous waste generator may be responsible under Superfund for the costs of cleaning up spills and other releases from waste disposal sites he used at any time in the past, and for reporting current spills and other releases from his own facility. This chapter briefly describes these obligations.

A. Responsibility for Cleanup

1. Liability Principle

The Superfund legislation states that anyone who arranges for "disposal" or "treatment" of hazardous substances at another person's facility is responsible as a waste generator for the hazard eventually posed by his disposal practices. (CERCLA § 107(a)(3).) If there is a release, or a substantial threat of a release, of a "hazardous substance" (see pages 64-68) from a facility into the environment, any and all generators who used the site may be held responsible for its cleanup.

The courts that have reached the issue have interpreted generator liability extremely broadly to impose liability on parties that do not easily fit within the definition of persons that "arranged for disposal or treatment." For example, two courts have held that a generator's sale of its waste does not in and of itself relieve the company of liability for disposal. New York v. General Electric Co., 592 F. Supp. 291 (N.D.N.Y. 1984); United States v. A & F Materials, Inc., 582 F. Supp. 842 (S.D. Ill. 1984). Other courts have applied a very flexible "causation" requirement to hold generators liable if they disposed of hazardous substances at a site and the site is leaking, without regard to whether the generators' wastes are the source of the problem. United States v. Wade, 577 F. Supp. 1326 (E.D. Pa. 1983); United States v. South Carolina Recycling & Disposal, Inc., 14 Envtl. L. Rep. 20272 (D.S.C. Feb. 23, 1984) (No. 80-1274-6).

Although the statute itself does not explicitly establish a standard of liability, several courts have applied a strict liability standard, or liability without regard to fault. E.g., United States v. Northeastern Pharmaceutical & Chemical Co., 579 F. Supp. 823 (W.D. Mo. 1984); United States v. Chem-Dyne Corp., 572 F. Supp. 802 (S.D. Ohio 1983). The statute allows a defense to liability only for releases caused solely by an act of God, act of war, or act or omission of a third party with whom the defendant has no contractual relationship. (CERCLA § 107(b)(1)-(3).)

An important exception to generator liability is that generators are not liable for "federally permitted" releases that occur in compliance with a permit issued under RCRA, the Clean Water Act, the Ocean Dumping Act, the Underground Injection Control Program, the Clean Air Act, or the Atomic Energy Act of 1954. Liability in connection with such releases, if any, is pursuant to other federal or state law. (CERCLA §§ 101(10), 107(j).)

2. Cleanup Activities

If there is a release or substantial threat of a release of a hazardous substance (or of a pollutant or contaminant posing an imminent and substantial danger) into water, land surface or subsurface strata, or ambient air, EPA has authority to assure that (a) the release is addressed by temporary "removal" cleanup activity, including removing released hazardous substances, monitoring, limiting access, or temporarily evacuating the area; and (b) remedial action is taken to eliminate the hazard more permanently by activities such as dredging, excavation, onsite treatment, incineration, and repair or replacement of leaking containers. (CERCLA § 104(a)(1).)

Removal actions must end within six months or when $1,000,000 is spent, unless there is a continuing emergency at the site. Remedial action must be cost-effective and cannot begin until EPA and the state agree on state participation in the cleanup and contribution toward its cost. The state must agree to pay 10% or 50% of the remedial action, depending on who owns the site (10% for privately owned sites, 50% for sites owned by the state or a municipality). In addition, EPA may take remedial action only at sites it has listed on the National Priorities List ("NPL") after notice to the public and an opportunity for comment. As of June 1985, EPA had listed 540 priority sites on the NPL (40 C.F.R. Part 300, App. B, as amended by 49 Fed. Reg. 37082 (Sept. 21, 1984) and 50 Fed. Reg. 6322 (Feb. 14, 1985)), and had proposed to include an additional 244 sites (49 Fed. Reg. 40320 (Oct. 15, 1984)). The Agency is required to update the NPL at least once annually, and has indicated that the list likely will be expanded to include approximately 2000 sites.

Any response activity undertaken by EPA, the state, or any other party must be consistent with the National Contingency Plan ("NCP"). (CERCLA § 105; 40 C.F.R. Part 300.) The NCP is principally important in describing governmental roles and procedures for evaluating remedial options. See 40 C.F.R. § 300.68. Typically, EPA (with the assistance of outside contractors) undertakes an extensive "remedial investigation" ("RI") to determine the nature and extent of the problem based on the particular physical characteristics at the site and the disposal practices utilized. EPA then performs a detailed "feasibility study" ("FS") to compare remedial options, and publishes a "record

of decision" justifying its selection of a remedial option.
The "RI/FS" process can easily take several months or more
than one year, and may involve the expenditure of $1 million
or more.

The Plan currently establishes a flexible cleanup
standard to resolve the central "how clean is clean" issue
which defines the extent and cost of the remedy chosen to
clean up the site. (40 C.F.R. § 300.68(j).) However, EPA
has proposed revisions to the NCP that would limit its
discretion and require cleanup in accordance with "applicable or relevant" standards for environmental quality
established under other federal environmental laws. The
effect of these revisions would be potentially to increase
the level of cleanup and remedial costs substantially.
EPA's proposed revisions to the National Contingency Plan,
50 Fed. Reg. 5862 (Feb. 12, 1985), are reprinted as Appendix E.

Instead of undertaking cleanup at a site, EPA may
issue an administrative order or seek an injunction against
responsible parties compelling private cleanup action, if an
actual or threatened release of hazardous substances poses
an imminent and substantial endangerment to public health or
welfare or the environment. (CERCLA § 106(a).) Where EPA
proceeds by issuance of an order, the courts have been
reluctant to review the merits of the order prior to EPA's

initiation of a judicial enforcement action. E.g., Lone Pine Steering Committee v. EPA, 600 F. Supp. 1487 (D.N.J. 1985). However, at least one court has held that if EPA provides no administrative hearing on the order, the penalties attaching to noncompliance (see p. 104) are unconstitutional. Aminoil, Inc. v. EPA, 21 Env't Rep. Cas. (BNA) 1817 (C.D. Cal. Sept. 28, 1984) (No. CV84-5853 Kn(Px)).

    3.   Costs

        When EPA designates a site for Superfund cleanup, it sends a "notice letter" to all known parties who may be responsible for the site. If none of them voluntarily begins the cleanup, EPA may take action to clear the site. No matter who undertakes the cleanup, each and every generator may be held strictly liable for all costs incurred by the federal or state government or by others who clean up the site, so long as the costs are expended in accordance with the NCP. (CERCLA § 107(a)(3).) Indeed, although the statute is silent, the courts consistently have held that each generator may be held jointly and severally liable for the entire cost of cleaning up the site at which his wastes were disposed, even if he contributed only a small portion of the wastes found at the site. E.g., United States v. A & F Materials, Inc., 578 F. Supp. 1249 (S.D. Ill. 1984); United States v. Chem-Dyne Corp., 572 F. Supp. 802 (S.D. Ohio 1983). The courts also have found a right of contribution against other liable parties, but the party found liable in the first instance for the government's costs proceeds at his own risk. E.g., United States v. A & F Materials, Inc., supra.

The generator's liability is limited in most cases to the cost of response action (which may exceed $10-20 million if there is groundwater contamination) plus up to $50 million for any damages to natural resources (including, for example, land, fish, wildlife, groundwater). (CERCLA § 107(c).) The Department of Interior has responsibility for issuing regulations for assessing damages from injury to or destruction of natural resources. (CERCLA § 301(c).) Although the Department has requested preliminary comments on the appropriate methodology for assessing damages, proposed regulations are not expected until the end of 1985.

Failure to comply with a Superfund administrative order to clean up a site also may result in substantial penalties. (CERCLA §§ 106(b), 107(c)(3).) A party that fails "without sufficient cause" to comply with an administrative order may be liable for punitive damages in an amount up to three times the government's subsequent cleanup costs. Failure to comply with an order also subjects the offender to penalties up to $5,000 per day. Superfund's enforcement provisions are discussed in Chapter XX.

B. Reporting Requirements

   1.   Spill Reports

        Generators in charge of a facility must report to
the National Response Center any spill or other release of a
reportable quantity of a hazardous substance as soon as they
have knowledge of the release. (CERCLA § 103.) This
release reporting requirement was discussed more fully at
pages 68-73.

        EPA also requires notice in a local newspaper to
persons who might be injured by a large-scale release
(although there are no specific penalties for failure to
provide such notice). (CERCLA § 111(g).)

   2.   Facility Reports

        Those generators who transported RCRA hazardous
wastes (as opposed to the broader category of Superfund
hazardous substances) to treatment, storage, or disposal
facilities of their choice were obligated to report the
existence of the facilities to EPA by June 9, 1981.
Permitted facilities and facilities with interim status
under RCRA did not have to be reported. (CERCLA § 103(c).)
The notification form requested information on the facility's location, waste contents, and suspected releases.
According to EPA, approximately 10,000 abandoned hazardous
waste sites were reported.

Persons who were unaware of this reporting requirement in 1981 and who wish to review its specific elements
should consult the interpretive notice that appeared at 46
Fed. Reg. 22144 (April 15, 1981).

PART 4: TRANSPORTERS' OBLIGATIONS

As the foregoing chapters imply, the burden of
RCRA regulation does not fall as heavily on hazardous waste
transporters as it does on generators and owners and operators of facilities. Basically, RCRA regulations obligate
the transporter to deliver hazardous waste as directed by
its manifest and to comply with reporting and recordkeeping
requirements. On the other hand, Superfund obligates hazardous waste transporters as well as generators to clean up
abandoned waste sites and to report spills. In addition,
the Hazardous Materials Transportation Act and the Clean
Water Act, among other statutes, impose further obligations
on hazardous waste transporters. Chapters IX and X address
these responsibilities.

CHAPTER IX

TRANSPORTERS' RCRA OBLIGATIONS

All persons transporting hazardous wastes off the site of their generation must comply with the requirements in 40 C.F.R. Part 263, developed jointly by EPA and the Department of Transportation ("DOT"). Both generator-owned and independent transporters must comply. Waste transporters are required to:

(1) obtain an EPA identification number;

(2) comply with the manifest signature requirements;

(3) deliver the waste in accordance with directions on the manifest;

(4) maintain records of the waste shipment; and

(5) properly respond to any spills during transportation.

In this chapter, we review each of these requirements as administered by EPA. Although state requirements apply in authorized states in lieu of the federal rules, most states are adopting the federal program with minimal changes. (See pp. 8-14.) To be apprised of these changes and any additional requirements, transporters should consult state and local requirements.

A. Identification Number

Chapter VII described the generator's obligation to obtain an EPA identification number by filing EPA Form 8700-12. A transporter may not transport hazardous waste unless he has received an EPA identification number. (40 C.F.R. § 263.11.)

B. Manifests

As a general rule, a transporter may not accept a hazardous waste shipment unless it is accompanied by a manifest signed by the generator. (40 C.F.R. § 263.20.) Shipments from small quantity generators are exempted from the rule, provided certain conditions are met. (40 C.F.R. § 261.5.)

The regulations require the transporter to sign and date the manifest, to acknowledge receipt of the waste and to return the signed copy to the generator before leaving the site. In addition, the transporter must assure that the manifest accompanies the waste until delivery to another transporter or to the designated waste treatment, storage, or disposal facility ("TSDF"). When he releases custody of the waste shipment, the transporter must have the recipient sign and date the manifest. The transporter then retains one copy of the manifest for his records, and gives the remaining copies to the next person along the delivery chain. (40 C.F.R. §§ 263.20, 263.21.)

Water and rail transporters may use shipping papers rather than manifests for rail transportation and water transportation of bulk shipments. The regulations require signatures by the initial transporters and the owners or operators of the designated TSDF, but do not require signatures from rail and water intermediate carriers. (40 C.F.R. § 263.20.)

C. Recordkeeping

Transporters must retain copies of signed manifests (and shipping papers, in the case of water and rail transporters) for at least three years. (40 C.F.R. § 263.22.)

D. Spill Reporting

If hazardous waste is spilled during transportation, the transporter must take immediate action to protect human health and the environment (for example, notify local authorities and dike the area to prevent run-off from the spill). He then must perform any cleanup activities required by federal, state, or local officials. (40 C.F.R. §§ 263.30, 263.31.) Additional spill reporting requirements arise under other statutes. (See pp. 68-73.)

E. Obligations for Waste Generation and Storage

Transporters who bring waste into the United States from abroad or who mix wastes of differing DOT shipping descriptions in one container also must comply with the

waste generator requirements discussed at in Chapter VII.
Transporters who store wastes prior to transport for more
than 10 days may subject themselves to the permitting requirements for storage facilities, as discussed in Parts 5
and 6.

CHAPTER X

TRANSPORTERS' SUPERFUND AND OTHER OBLIGATIONS

A hazardous waste transporter's obligations under
Superfund are similar to those imposed on hazardous waste
generators. This chapter briefly describes the transporter's cleanup and reporting duties as well as other obligations imposed for spills.

A. Responsibility for Cleanup

The liability of hazardous waste transporters
has been considerably expanded by Superfund. Like hazardous waste generators, transporters may be responsible for
the costs of cleaning up spills and other releases or
threatened releases of hazardous substances. (CERCLA §
107(a)(4).) The transporter shares the generator's liabilities, described at pp. 98-104, and generally all transporters who used a disposal site can expect to be joined in
any Superfund litigation pertaining to that site.

B. Reporting Requirements

1. Spill Reports

Transporters must comply with the Superfund
reporting requirements for spills and other releases
applicable to hazardous waste generators, discussed at
pp. 68-73. If a reportable quantity of hazardous waste is

released during transport, notification must be provided to the National Response Center (telephone: (800) 424-8802) and the local population in cases of potential injury. (CERCLA §§ 103, 111(g).)

    2. <u>Facility Reports</u>

Anyone who accepted hazardous waste for transport and selected its disposal site was subject to the CERCLA § 103(c) requirement to report the selected site to EPA by June 1981. (See p. 105.)

C. Hazardous Materials Transportation Act
    and Other Obligations

Transporters of hazardous materials and wastes also are subject to spill reporting requirements under the Hazardous Materials Transportation Act, 49 U.S.C. § 1801 <u>et seq</u>. A land or water common carrier or civil aircraft carrier must report to DOT any unintentional release of hazardous materials (materials listed in 49 C.F.R. § 172.101) or hazardous wastes (wastes subject to RCRA manifest requirements). Reports must be sent on DOT Form F 5800.1 within 15 days of discovery of the spill. (49 C.F.R. § 171.16(a).) If hazardous waste has been spilled, its RCRA manifest must be attached to the report. Certain spills involving consumer commodities, batteries, and small amounts of paint products need not be reported. (49 C.F.R. § 171.16(c).)

Immediate telephone notification (telephone: (800) 424-8802), as well as written notification, is required for a spill that results in death, injury, or property damage exceeding $50,000, or that involves radioactive materials or etiologic agents. (49 C.F.R. § 171.15(a).)

Finally, although this overview is not intended to be exhaustive, it should be noted that several other statutes apply to spills of hazardous substances during transport. Spills of oil or hazardous substances into water are subject to spill prevention, reporting, and cleanup requirements under Section 311 of the Clean Water Act. Regulations implementing these requirements appear at 40 C.F.R. Parts 110-117. Serious spills occurring during air transport must be reported to the Federal Aviation Administration Civil Aviation Security Office. (49 C.F.R. § 175.45(a).) Leaking containers of etiologic agents must be reported to the Center for Disease Control of the U.S. Public Health Service. (42 C.F.R. § 72.3(e).) For spill reporting requirements generally, see Appendix I.

Part 5: RCRA INTERIM STATUS FACILITIES -- OBLIGATIONS OF FACILITY OWNERS AND OPERATORS

Existing facilities that treat, store, or dispose of hazardous waste may qualify to operate under "interim status," without a permit, if they were in existence on November 19, 1980 (the date of enactment of the 1980 Amendments to RCRA) and they have complied with certain paperwork requirements. During interim status, they may operate only if in compliance with specified standards, known as the interim status standards, set forth in 40 C.F.R. Part 265, or analagous provisions of authorized state programs. In general, interim status standards are less restrictive than the standards for permitted facilities. Interim status terminates for all facilities unless a Part B RCRA permit application is submitted according to a spec- ified schedule.

This part describes EPA's procedures for obtaining interim status and the standards with which interim status facilities must comply, including both the general status standards applicable to all facilities and additional requirements for specific types of facilities.

CHAPTER XI

RCRA INTERIM STATUS PROCEDURES

This chapter describes EPA's procedures for
obtaining and operating under interim status, i.e., without
a permit. Although state requirements apply in authorized
state in lieu of the federal rules, most states are adopting
the federal program with minimal changes. (See pp. 8-14.)
To be apprised of those changes and additional requirements,
a facility owner or operator should consult state and local
requirements.

A.   Obtaining Interim Status

        Facilities that were in existence on November 19,
1980 (the date of enactment of the 1980 RCRA Amendments)
qualified for interim status if their owners or operators
filed with EPA a notice of hazardous waste activities by
August 18, 1980 and Part A of the RCRA permit application
by November 19, 1980. In addition, facilities in existence
on the effective date of RCRA statutory or regulatory amendments that for the first time make the facility subject to
RCRA regulation may apply for interim status by submitting
a Part A permit application within six months of publication
of such amendments or thirty days after they first become
subject to RCRA standards, whichever first occurs. (1984

RCRA Amendments § 213, amending RCRA § 3005, to be codified in the regulations at 40 C.F.R. §§ 270.10 and 270.70.)

For example, if an existing facility handles a waste that is newly added to the list of RCRA hazardous wastes, it may qualify for interim status if it files a Part A application within six months after the waste is designated as hazardous. If a facility that was handling a solid waste determines subsequently that the waste exhibits hazardous characteristics, it may qualify by filing a Part A application within 30 days of that determination. A formerly exempt facility also may qualify if a Part A application is filed (1) within six months of the time EPA first subjects the facility to regulation, or (2) within 30 days after a facility that was exempt from regulation loses its exempt status (e.g., when a facility that was an exempt small generator begins storing large quantities).

For a facility to have been considered "in existence" on November 19, 1980 or at the time of a statutory or regulatory amendment, it is not necessary that the facility actually have treated, stored, or disposed of hazardous waste on the critical date. A facility qualifies if, by that date, (1) the owner or operator has obtained all necessary pre-construction approvals or permits and (2) either continuous physical on-site construction has begun or construction contracts have been signed that cannot be changed without substantial loss. (40 C.F.R. § 270.2.)

Forms for the notice, if required, and Part A applications are available from EPA. (A more detailed description of the Part A application is found in Chapter XIV on RCRA permits.) The Part A application is identical for both permit and interim status applications.

B. Facilities That Fail to Qualify

Existing facilities that operate without interim status (or a permit) are subject to civil and criminal penalties, as discussed in Chapter XIX. However, EPA may excuse a late filing in some cases and allow an existing facility to operate without a permit under a compliance order or interim status compliance letter. (See 40 C.F.R. § 270.10(e).) Furthermore, EPA believes it has the discretionary power to apply Part 265 interim status standards to existing facilities regardless of whether they have filed for interim status or had their interim status terminated. (See 48 Fed. Reg. 52718, 52719 (November 22, 1983); 49 Fed. Reg. 46094 (November 21, 1984).)

C. Withdrawal from Interim Status

If a facility owner or operator determines that the facility for which he previously has filed notice and a Part A application is not, in fact, subject to the hazardous waste management regulations, he may file a request to withdraw from interim status. The request must be signed and certified by an authorized person in accordance with 40 C.F.R. § 270.11.

D. Modifications During Interim Status

   1. Part A Revisions

      If, during interim status, a facility plans to change its operations so that its Part A application would no longer be accurate, the owner or operator must submit a revised Part A application and, in most situations, obtain prior EPA approval. (40 C.F.R. § 270.72.)

      EPA approval is not required when a facility changes its operations to handle a new hazardous waste not previously identified in its Part A application. In those circumstances, the owner and operator only must submit a revised Part A application prior to making such changes. (40 C.F.R. § 270.72(a).) However, if the owner or operator wants to increase the design capacity of his processes, a revised Part A application must be submitted prior to such a change, and EPA approval must be obtained. Furthermore, approval is allowed in this circumstance only if there is a lack of available treatment, storage, or disposal capacity at other hazardous waste management facilities. (40 C.F.R. § 270.72(b).)

If the owner or operator wants to change his processes for treatment, storage, or disposal of a hazardous waste handled at the facility, he must submit a revised Part A application prior to such change and obtain EPA approval. Again, the circumstances in which approval may be granted are limited: it may be granted only if the change is necessary to prevent an emergency situation or to comply with federal or local laws. (40 C.F.R. § 270.72(c).) EPA will not approve changes to a hazardous waste facility during the interim status period that amount to reconstruction of the facility. (40 C.F.R. § 270.72(e).)

Finally, if ownership or operational control of a facility changes during the interim status period, the new owner or operator must apply for interim status by filing a revised Part A permit application no later than 90 days prior to the scheduled change. The old owner is responsible for assuring regulatory compliance until he has been notified by EPA that the transfer is approved. (40 C.F.R. § 270.72(d).)

2.   Additional Land Disposal Units, Replacement
      Units, and Lateral Expansions

The 1984 RCRA Amendments established stringent requirements for new units, replacement units, and lateral expansions to existing units that continue to receive waste at interim status land disposal facilities after May 8, 1985 (RCRA Amendments § 243, adding RCRA § 3015.) Beginning

in May, all such units must meet the new minimum technological requirements that the Amendments mandate for permitted facilities. These requirements are discussed in
Chapters XV and XVI. The owner or operator of a new,
replacement, or laterally expanded unit at an interim
status land disposal facility must notify EPA (or the
authorized state) 60 days prior to receiving waste at the
new unit. A Part B application for the facility must then
be filed within six months.

E.   End of Interim Status

Prior to the 1984 RCRA Amendments, a facility's
interim status ended in most cases when EPA or an authorized
state requested the filing of Part B of the permit application, and a permit either was issued or denied. Alternatively, interim status could be terminated for failure to
provide a complete Part B application upon request. (40
C.F.R. § 270.73.) Until Part B was requested, the facility
could operate under interim status.

The termination of interim status has been hastened
for all facilities by the 1984 RCRA Amendments. While EPA
and the authorized states continue to call in Part B applications, the Amendments have established an outer limit by
which interim status must terminate for all facilities
unless a Part B application is submitted according to a
schedule specified in the Amendments. Land disposal

facilities lose interim status on November 8, 1985, unless a Part B application is submitted by that date and the owner or operator certifies that the facility is in compliance with groundwater monitoring and financial responsibility requirements. Incinerators lose interim status on November 8, 1989, unless a Part B application is submitted by November 8, 1986. All other facilities lose interim status on November 8, 1992, unless a Part B is submitted by November 8, 1988. (1984 RCRA Amendments § 213, amending RCRA § 3005, to be codified in the regulations at 40 C.F.R. § 270.73.) The legislation also establishes a timetable by which EPA must render a final decision on these permit applications.

	Land Disposal Facilities	Incinerators	All Other Facilities
Date to complete application by submitting Part B	11/8/85	11/8/86	11/8/88
Date interim status will be lost if Part B is not filed	11/8/85	11/8/89	11/8/92
Date EPA must render decision	11/8/88	11/8/89	11/8/92

CHAPTER XII

GENERAL INTERIM STATUS STANDARDS

The interim status standards, set forth in 40 C.F.R. Part 265, include administrative and basic operating requirements applicable to all facilities, as well as specific standards applicable to particular types of facilities. In general, the standards are relatively straightforward and unambiguous, and compliance typically has not required substantial capital expenditures during the interim status period, although the 1984 RCRA Amendments may require retrofitting of many interim status surface improvements.

Interim status standards apply only to facilities qualifying for interim status. Certain types of facilities are specifically excluded from interim status obligations:

(1) licensed municipal and industrial solid waste facilities that treat, store, or dispose of hazardous waste from small quantity generators (Section 302 of the 1984 RCRA Amendments, which added RCRA § 4010, requires groundwater monitoring, siting, and corrective action obligations for such facilities by March 1988);

(2) facilities engaged in a limited range of reuse activities (see discussion at pp. 28-37);

(3) generators accumulating waste on-site in compliance with the 90-day accumulation rule (see pp. 92-93);

(4)   farmers disposing of pesticides according to labeling instructions;

(5)   permitted underground injection wells;

(6)   totally enclosed treatment facilities, in which hazardous waste is treated in a totally enclosed process directly connected to the industrial production process;

(7)   elementary neutralization units (tanks, containers, transport vehicles, or vessels containing corrosive wastes);

(8)   publicly-owned treatment works;

(9)   wastewater treatment tanks regulated under the Clean Water Act;

(10)   facilities responding to spills;

(11)   transfer facilities holding a transporters' manifested hazardous waste for no more than 10 days;

(12)   facilities adding absorbent material to hazardous waste in a container; and

(13)   ocean disposal facilities with permits issued under the Marine Mammal Protection, Research, and Sanctuaries Act.

(40 C.F.R. § 265.1(c).)   Furthermore, as discussed above, state standards apply to facilities operating in states with authorized RCRA programs, although most states have adopted the federal program with minimal changes.   (See pp. 8-14.)

The following discussion briefly summarizes the substantive standards applicable to interim status treatment, storage, and disposal facilities.

A. General Facility Standards

1. Identification Number

Every facility must have an EPA identification number. (40 C.F.R. § 265.11.)

2. Notification

The owner or operator of an active facility or a closed disposal facility subject to post-closure requirements (see pp. 133-34) must notify any new purchaser of the facility of the requirements of Parts 265 and 270. EPA must be notified four weeks in advance of the first receipt of wastes from a foreign source. (40 C.F.R. § 265.12.)

3. Waste Analysis

Before hazardous waste is treated, stored, or disposed of, the owner or operator must obtain a detailed chemical and physical analysis of a representative sample of the waste. This analysis must be updated when the facility manager has reason to believe the waste-generating process has changed or, for off-site facilities, when the waste does not meet the manifest's description. (40 C.F.R. § 265.13.) The procedures for this sampling must be described in a written waste analysis plan kept at the facility. Additional requirements tailored to specific types of facilities also may apply. (See, e.g., 40 C.F.R. § 265.193.)

4. Security

The owner or operator must prevent inadvertent and, to the extent possible, deliberate entry of people or livestock into the active portion of his facility, unless their contact with the waste will not cause injury to themselves or to facility integrity. In order to secure the site, the facility may need to have 24-hour surveillance, barriers surrounding the active portion of the waste management area, controls to entry, and signs barring unauthorized entry. (40 C.F.R. § 265.14.)

5. Inspections

The owner or operator must inspect his facility for malfunctions and deterioration, operator errors, and discharges, according to a written inspection plan retained at the facility. If any deterioration or malfunction is discovered, it must be remedied. A record of all inspections must be retained for at least three years. (40 C.F.R. § 265.15.) Additional requirements tailored to specific types of facilities also may apply.

6. Personnel Training

Facility personnel must complete a program of training in RCRA procedures and emergency response. A written description of the training program, its attendees, and instructors must be kept at the facility. (40 C.F.R. § 265.16.) (EPA has published a helpful background document on training, and it is available from EPA and many law firms regularly practicing in this field.)

     7.   Requirements for Ignitable, Reactive, or Incompatible Wastes

The owner or operator must take precautions to prevent accidental ignition or reaction of ignitable or reactive wastes, and to prevent adverse reactions caused by mixing incompatible wastes. (40 C.F.R. § 265.17.) Additional requirements tailored to specific types of facilities also may apply. (See, e.g., 40 C.F.R. §§ 265.176, 265.177.)

B.   Preparedness for and Prevention of Spills and Other Emergencies

All interim status facilities must have equipment adequate to deal with unexpected fires, explosions, or any unplanned sudden or non-sudden spill or other release of hazardous wastes. Required equipment includes internal communications or alarm systems; telephones, radios or other means of summoning emergency personnel; fire extinguishers or other fire control devices; and water or foam-producing equipment. Proper aisle space must be maintained for emergency equipment.

Emergency response procedures must be detailed in a contingency plan kept at the waste facility and submitted to state and local authorities. A Clean Water Act Spill

Prevention, Control, and Countermeasures ("SPCC") Plan may be used as the basis for the RCRA contingency plan. The RCRA plan must describe the personnel in charge of emergency response, emergency equipment, and evacuation procedures. (40 C.F.R. Part 265, Subparts C and D.)

C. Manifest System, Recordkeeping, and Reporting

    1. Manifests

        When a facility receives a shipment of hazardous waste accompanied by a manifest, the owner or operator must sign and date the manifest, note any significant discrepancies between the manifest and the waste received, give the transporter a copy of the signed manifest, send another copy of the manifest to the generator within 30 days, and retain his own copy for at least three years from the date of delivery. (40 C.F.R. § 265.71.) If the owner or operator cannot resolve significant discrepancies between the waste received and its manifest description (i.e., greater than 10 percent variations in bulk weight, variations in piece count, or obvious differences in waste type), he must report the discrepancy to EPA within 15 days of receiving the waste. (40 C.F.R. § 265.72.) If a facility receives any hazardous waste that is not accompanied by a manifest, the shipment must be reported to the Regional Administrator within 15 days. Although wastes from small quantity generators (see pp. 94-97 above) need not be accompanied by a manifest,

EPA recommends that the generator provide certification that the shipment is a lawful small generator waste shipment. (40 C.F.R. § 265.76.)

2. Recordkeeping

All records required to be kept by RCRA regulations (including the facility operating record of waste receipts, waste placement in the facility, and waste analyses; contingency plan reports; inspection logs; and monitoring data) must be available at all reasonable times for inspection by EPA representatives. (40 C.F.R. § 265.74.)

3. Biennial Report

The regulations currently require a report in March of each even-numbered year of the following: the EPA identification number of every generator from whom waste was received (or the name and address of foreign generators); a description and the quantity of each hazardous waste shipment received; the method of treatment, storage, or disposal used by the facility; groundwater monitoring data; and an estimate of closure costs. (40 C.F.R. § 265.75.)

D. Groundwater Monitoring and Response Requirements

1. General Requirements

Owners and operators of hazardous waste surface impoundments, landfills, and land treatment facilities must conduct interim status groundwater monitoring. The facility's groundwater monitoring program must be designed to determine the facility's impact on groundwater quality in the uppermost aquifer underlying the facility, whether or not the aquifer is an underground drinking water source. This groundwater monitoring must continue through the active life of the facility and through the 30-year post-closure care period. (See pp. 132-34.) At least one monitoring well must be placed upgradient of the facility to determine the background groundwater quality, and at least three wells downgradient to determine the impact of the facility. (40 C.F.R. Part 265, Subpart F.)

2. Waivers

If the facility owner or operator can demonstrate in writing a low potential for hazardous waste migration from the facility via the uppermost aquifer to water supply wells or to surface water, he can qualify for a self-implementing waiver of some or all of the monitoring requirements. (40 C.F.R. §§ 265.90(c), 265.301(c).) In addition, surface impoundments used solely to neutralize corrosive wastes are not subject to the groundwater monitoring requirements if the owner or operator can assure that there is no potential for migration of hazardous wastes from the impoundment. (40 C.F.R. § 265.90(e).) Finally, if a facility knows that hazardous waste migration is occurring, it may request EPA approval of an alternative groundwater monitoring program. (40 C.F.R. § 265.90(a).)

3. Monitoring Obligations

The interim status groundwater monitoring requirements became effective on November 19, 1981, and obligated each interim status facility in existence at that time to keep a groundwater monitoring and analysis plan at the facility. Each facility had to monitor groundwater at least quarterly through November 1982 (or for one year after becoming subject to RCRA interim status requirements) to establish background quality for pH, specific conductance, total organic carbon, and total halogen (groundwater contamination indicators); and for chloride, iron, manganese, phenols, sodium, and sulfate (groundwater quality parameters). In addition, the facility had to monitor the aquifer quarterly for one year to determine its suitability as a drinking water supply. After the initial one-year period, all wells must be sampled at least semi-annually for the four groundwater contamination indicators, and at least annually for the six groundwater quality parameters. (40 C.F.R. § 265.92.)

Should monitoring detect any statistically significant deterioration from background levels in the groundwater quality parameters, the facility must notify EPA within one week and, within 15 days, identify those parameters that exceeded background levels. The facility must submit a plan for assessing groundwater quality certified by

a qualified geologist or geotechnical engineer. If the
owner or operator determines that no hazardous waste has
entered the groundwater, he may reinstate the semi-annual
monitoring program for groundwater contamination indicators.
If hazardous constituents have entered the groundwater, he
must assess groundwater quality on a quarterly basis until
final closure of the facility. (40 C.F.R. § 265.93.) No
cleanup or other remedial action is required as part of the
interim status monitoring program, although EPA may order
corrective action at an interim status facility if
"necessary to protect human health or the environment."
(1984 RCRA Amendments § 233, adding RCRA § 3008(h).) All
groundwater data must be retained for the active life of the
site and, for disposal facilities, throughout the 30-year
post-closure care period. (40 C.F.R. § 265.94.)

E. Closure and Post-Closure Requirements

        The interim status regulations include general
closure and post-closure requirements for all interim
status facilities (40 C.F.R. Part 265, Subpart G) and
additional requirements for specific types of facilities.

        Closure is the period after wastes are no longer
accepted, during which the facility completes treatment,
storage, and disposal operations, applies a final cover to
or caps disposal units (if necessary), and disposes of or
decontaminates equipment. Post-closure is the period after

closure, during which owners or operators of disposal facilities must conduct certain monitoring and maintenance activities. All interim status facilities must have a written closure plan, post-closure plan (if wastes will remain at the site after closure), and cost estimates for closure and, if applicable, post-closure. The plans must be submitted to EPA at least 180 days before the facility expects to commence closure. (40 C.F.R. §§ 265.112, 265.117, 265.118.) This notification period may be shortened for some facilities. (See 50 Fed. Reg. 11090 (Mar. 19, 1985), proposing amendment to 40 C.F.R. § 265.112.)

1. Closure

Within 90 days of receiving the final volume of waste at a facility, all hazardous wastes must either be treated, removed from the site, or disposed of onsite according to the closure plan. The entire closure period may not exceed six months unless a longer period is authorized by EPA. (40 C.F.R. § 265.113.) When closure is completed, all facility equipment and structures must be disposed of or decontaminated, and closure must be certified by a registered professional. (40 C.F.R. §§ 265.114, 265.115.)

2. Post-Closure

The post-closure period extends 30 years after closure. During the post-closure period, all land disposal facilities must continue groundwater monitoring, maintenance of the cap or final cover and other containment structures, and maintenance of the facility's monitoring equipment. (40 C.F.R. § 265.117.) Access to the property will be restricted if necessary. In the land disposal regulations published in July 1982, EPA announced that all disposal facilities that accepted wastes after January 26, 1983, including those that closed during interim status, would be subject to the 40 C.F.R. Part 264 post-closure requirements (described at pp. 187-89). (47 Fed. Reg. 32274, 32336 (July 26, 1982).) Thus, an interim status facility may be required to go through full-scale permit review even if it is closed before a Part B application was requested by EPA (see pp. 121-22), if it accepted wastes after January 26, 1983. (See 40 C.F.R. § 270.1(c).)

3. Notice to Local Land Authorities

The fact that land has been used as a hazardous waste disposal site must be reported to local land authorities and must be recorded in the deed to the property. (40 C.F.R. §§ 265.119, 265.120.)

F. Financial Requirements

1. Financial Responsibility

All interim status facilities must have written estimates of the cost of closure, and disposal facilities also must estimate the cost of post-closure activities.

- 134 -

Moreover, owners or operators of these facilities must demonstrate the ability to satisfy closure and post-closure expenses by one of several means: (a) satisfying a financial test assuring that the owner's or operator's assets are sufficient to guarantee anticipated expenditures; (b) obtaining a corporate guarantee by the parent of the waste facility; (c) establishing a closure trust fund; (d) obtaining a financial guarantee bond; (e) obtaining a performance bond; (f) obtaining a letter of credit; (g) purchasing closure insurance; or (h) combining trust funds, surety bonds, letter of credit, and insurance. (40 C.F.R. §§ 265.140-.145.) These requirements, which parallel permitted facility requirements, are outlined in further detail at pp. 188-95.

2. Liability Coverage

All interim status facilities must obtain liability insurance coverage. All facilities must have coverage for sudden accidental occurrences in the amount of $1 million per occurrence and $2 million annual aggregate. Surface impoundments, landfills, and land treatment facilities must have coverage for non-sudden accidental occurrences in the amount of $3 million per occurrence and $6 million annual aggregate. (40 C.F.R. § 265.147.) The insurance requirement may be satisfied by having liability insurance, passing a financial test, or combining the two. These requirements, which parallel permitted facility requirements, are outlined in further detail at pp. 195-96.

CHAPTER XIII

ADDITIONAL REQUIREMENTS FOR SPECIFIC INTERIM
STATUS FACILITIES

In addition to the foregoing general requirements, other interim status standards apply only to specified facilities and types of equipment.

A. Containers

1. Applicability

The RCRA regulations define containers as any portable devices used to treat, store, dispose of, transport, or otherwise handle material. (40 C.F.R. § 260.10.)

2. Operating Requirements

Containers of hazardous wastes must be replaced if not in good condition, and the container material must be compatible with the wastes stored. Containers must be closed during storage, handled carefully to avoid leaks, and inspected weekly for deterioration. (40 C.F.R. §§ 265.171-.174.) The current regulations require that containers holding ignitable or reactive wastes be located at least 50 feet from the facility's property line (40 C.F.R. § 265.176), but EPA has proposed to amend this requirement to account for the effect of protective walls or construction techniques (see 49 Fed. Reg. 23290, 23299 (June 5, 1984)).

3. Closure

During closure, hazardous wastes and hazardous waste residues must be removed from a container storage facility or from that part of the facility being closed. By removing such wastes or residues, the owner or operator of the facility becomes a generator of hazardous wastes and must manage them according to 40 C.F.R. Part 262. See Chapter VII for those requirements.

B. Tanks

1. Applicability

A RCRA-regulated tank is defined as a stationary device constructed primarily of non-earthen materials (e.g., wood, concrete, steel, or plastic) designed to hold hazardous waste. (40 C.F.R. § 260.10.) RCRA standards have not yet been promulgated for underground tanks holding hazardous waste that cannot be entered for inspection, but these regulations are mandated by Section 207 of the 1984 RCRA Amendments (adding RCRA Section 3004(w)) and are expected in the fall of 1985. Standards for underground tanks holding non-RCRA hazardous materials will be developed under the new "LUST" program, described in Chapter XVIII.

2. Operating Requirements

Hazardous waste placed in tanks must be compatible with tank materials and capacity. A waste analysis is required when a substantially different hazardous waste is treated or stored, or a substantially different treatment process is used in the tank. (40 C.F.R. §§ 265.192, 265.193, 265.199.) Overflow must be avoided by means of two feet of freeboard or a containment structure. A continuously fed tank must be equipped with discharge control equipment (e.g., waste feed cutoff system or by-pass system). (40 C.F.R. § 269.192.)

Tank discharge control systems, monitoring equipment, and waste levels must be inspected daily, and tank construction materials and containment structures weekly. Any deterioration or malfunction must be remedied. (40 C.F.R. § 265.194.)

3. Closure

All hazardous waste and hazardous waste residues must be removed from tanks, discharge control equipment, and confinement structures at closure. (40 C.F.R. § 265.197.)

C. Surface Impoundments

1. Applicability

The RCRA regulations consider any natural topographic depression, man-made excavation, or impoundment composed primarily of earthen dikes (e.g., holding, storage, settling, or aeration pits, ponds, and lagoons) to be a surface impoundment. (40 C.F.R. § 260.10.)

2.   Operating Requirements

Impoundment overtopping must be prevented, and at
least two feet of freeboard must be maintained at an
impoundment. All dikes must have a protective cover to preserve their structural integrity. A waste analysis is
required when a substantially different hazardous waste is
contained or treatment process is used in an impoundment.
(40 C.F.R. §§ 265.222-.225.)

Weekly inspections are required to detect leaks and
deterioration, and the freeboard level must be inspected
daily. (40 C.F.R. § 265.226.)

3.   Retrofitting Required by 1988

(a) New Technological Requirements

The 1984 RCRA Amendments require many interim
status surface impoundments to retrofit by November 8, 1988
to meet the new minimum technological requirements applicable to permitted surface impoundments. The requirements,
which are discussed in Chapter XVI, include a double liner,
a leachate collection system, and groundwater monitoring.
If a facility does not meet the deadline, it may no longer
receive, store, or treat hazardous waste. (1984 RCRA
Amendments § 215, adding RCRA § 3005(i).)

Surface impoundments that become subject to RCRA
hazardous waste regulations due to newly promulgated or

newly defined characteristics of hazardous waste have four
years to comply with the minimum technological requirements.

(b) Exemptions

Certain types of surface impoundments are exempt
from the retrofitting requirements. First, an impoundment
is exempt if it meets each of three criteria: (1) it has at
least one non-leaking liner; (2) it is located more than
one-quarter mile from an underground source of drinking
water; and (3) it complies with the groundwater monitoring
requirements applicable to permitted surface impoundments.
For purposes of this exemption, a liner may be designed,
constructed, and operated to prevent hazardous waste either
from passing into the liner or from migrating beyond the
liner at any time during the facility's active life. The
effect of this definition is to allow use of either a
synthetic or a clay liner.

Second, wastewater treatment impoundments that meet
certain prescribed standards are exempt. Such impoundments
must be part of a facility conducting aggressive biological
treatment of wastewater subject to a permit under Section
402 of the Clean Water Act, or contain water that has been
so treated. These facilities must comply with the groundwater monitoring requirements applicable to permitted surface impoundments. In addition, the facility must be in
compliance with applicable effluent guidelines under the

Clean Water Act. If no such guidelines are applicable, the facility must be in compliance with a permit issued under Section 402 of the Clean Water Act, and be achieving a "significant degradation" of toxic pollutants and hazardous constituents in the untreated waste stream.

Finally, an interim status surface impoundment may be exempt from the minimum technological requirements, or the requirements may be modified for it, if the owner or operator demonstrates to EPA (or the authorized state) that the impoundment is located, designed, or operated so as to assure that there will be no migration of any hazardous constituent into ground or surface water at any future time. This standard, derived from EPA regulations, has caused confusion in the past, and it is difficult to envision what kind of demonstration can pass muster under the "at any future time" standard. In any event, EPA (or the state) must give notice and an opportunity for public comment before granting an exemption based on this standard.

The owner or operator of a surface impoundment that potentially is eligible for any of these exemptions must apply to EPA (or the authorized state) by November 8, 1986. The application must contain all pertinent evidence, including a Part B application, groundwater monitoring data, and certification by a registered professional engineer that the impoundment meets the applicable criteria for an exception.

EPA (or the state) must render a decision within one year. If a surface impoundment other than a wastewater treatment impoundment is determined to be exempt but at some future time no longer satisfies the criteria for the exemption due to a change in condition (such as the development of a leak in a liner), it must comply with the minimum technological requirements no later than two years after the change is discovered. Wastewater treatment impoundments have three years in which to comply.

The deadline to apply for an exemption for facilities that first become subject to RCRA due to newly promulgated listings or hazardous characteristics is two years after they first become subject to RCRA.

(c) Good Faith Compliance

When an interim status surface impoundment installs a liner and a leak detection system in good faith compliance with EPA's regulations and guidance documents, EPA may not require any different liners or leak detection systems as a condition of the first permit issued to the facility. EPA may, however, require installation of a new liner if there is reason to believe that any existing liner is leaking.

4. Closure and Post-Closure

At closure, the owner or operator may remove the hazardous wastes and residues, the liner (to the extent it is hazardous), and underlying and surrounding soil contaminated with hazardous waste. If he does so, the decontaminated facility no longer is subject to any further closure and post-closure requirements, although any hazardous wastes removed from the site must be treated as hazardous waste generated by the facility. The facility thus must comply with 40 C.F.R. Part 262 (see Chapter VII for those requirements). (40 C.F.R. § 265.228.)

If the owner or operator fails or decides not to remove all hazardous impoundment materials or fails to demonstrate that the materials left in place at the impoundment are nonhazardous, he must comply with the closure and post-closure care requirements for a landfill (described at p. 147). (40 C.F.R. § 265.228.)

D. Waste Piles

1. Applicability

Waste piles that are temporary accumulations must be managed in accordance with 40 C.F.R. Part 265, Subpart L. Waste permanently disposed of in a pile must be managed as a landfill under Subpart N. (40 C.F.R. § 265.250.)

2. Operating Requirements

The waste pile owner or operator must monitor each new placement of waste to assure that it is compatible with existing wastes. (40 C.F.R. §§ 265.252, 265.256, 265.257.) Waste piles subject to wind dispersal must be covered or otherwise managed to control dispersal. (40 C.F.R. § 265.251.)

If leachate or run-off from a waste pile is hazardous, run-on and run-off from the pile must be controlled by means of an impermeable base, an overflow prevention system, a run-off management system, and means to prevent precipitation and run-on from contacting the waste. No free liquids may be placed in the pile. (40 C.F.R. § 265.253.)

3. Closure and Post-Closure

A waste pile must be closed by removing or decontaminating all waste residue and all contaminated containment system components (e.g., liners), subsoils, and equipment. If any contaminated material remains after all reasonable efforts to remove or decontaminate the material fail, the pile must be closed as a landfill. (40 C.F.R. § 265.258.)

E. Land Treatment Units

1. Applicability

Facilities at which hazardous waste is applied onto or incorporated into the soil surface are known as land treatment facilities. (40 C.F.R. § 260.10.)

2. Operating Requirements

Hazardous waste may not be placed in or on a land treatment facility unless it can be made less hazardous or nonhazardous by the biological degradation or chemical reactions occurring in or on the soil. (40 C.F.R. § 265.272.) Waste must be analyzed before treatment, and a record of the

dates and rates of waste application must be maintained.
(40 C.F.R. §§ 265.273, 265.279.) Adverse reactions by
incompatible wastes must be avoided. (40 C.F.R. § 265.282.)
Run-on, run-off, and wind dispersal must be controlled. (40
(40 C.F.R. § 265.272.)

3. Food-Chain Crops

Food-chain crops may be grown in a land treatment
unit only if the owner or operator can demonstrate that
arsenic, lead, mercury, EP toxic constituents, and constituents for which a waste has been listed under RCRA will not
transfer from the waste into the food crop. (40 C.F.R.
§ 265.276.)

4. Unsaturated Zone Monitoring

In addition to groundwater monitoring, land treatment facilities must install unsaturated zone monitoring to
detect the vertical migration of hazardous waste under the
active portion of the facility and to provide information on
the background concentrations of hazardous waste in similar
but untreated soils nearby. The unsaturated zone must be
monitored to trace the concentrations of fast-moving, highly
soluble constituents by means of soil pore liquid monitoring
and slower-moving constituents such as heavy metals by means
of soil core monitoring. (40 C.F.R. § 265.278.)

5. Closure and Post-Closure

Land treatment facilities must consider removing contaminated soils, placing a final cover, and monitoring groundwater at closure in order to assure that releases from the facility are controlled. Run-on, run-off, and wind dispersal controls must be maintained, and unsaturated zone monitoring must continue. (40 C.F.R. § 265.280.)

F. Landfills

1. Applicability

The term "landfill" is used as a catch-all for facilities at which waste is placed on or in the land and which are not land treatment units, surface impoundments, or injection wells. (40 C.F.R. § 260.10.)

2. Operating Requirements

The contents of each landfill cell must be recorded in the facility's operating record. (40 C.F.R. § 265.309.) The owners and operators of landfills also must divert surface water run-on, collect precipitation run-off, treat any liquid wastes or semi-solid wastes so that they do not contain free liquids, control wind dispersal, and crush or shred most waste containers (other than small containers in lab packs) so that they cannot later collapse and cause subsidence and cracking of the cover. (40 C.F.R. §§ 265.302, 265.314-.316.)

3.   Closure and Post-Closure

A final cover is required for closure of a landfill, and the facility's closure plan must show how air,
groundwater, and surface water contamination will be
avoided. Site access must be controlled. (40 C.F.R.
§ 265.310.)

G.   Incinerators

1.   Applicability

Incinerators are enclosed controlled flame combustion devices other than boilers (which are designed for
energy recovery) or industrial furnaces (which are energy or
materials recovery devices that are integral components of
manufacturing processes). (50 Fed. Reg. at 661, amending
40 C.F.R. § 260.10.) Incinerators used to burn hazardous
waste are subject to RCRA regulation. (40 C.F.R.
§ 265.340.)

2.   Operating Requirements

Incinerator owners or operators must analyze any
new hazardous waste to determine its potential pollutants.
(40 C.F.R. § 265.341.) Incinerators must achieve normal
steady-state conditions before hazardous wastes are introduced. (40 C.F.R. § 265.345.)

3.   Monitoring and Inspections

Combustion and emission control instruments must be
monitored every 15 minutes, and operational corrections made

when necessary. All incinerator equipment must be inspected daily for leaks, spills, fugitive emissions, and equipment malfunction. (40 C.F.R. § 265.347.)

4. Closure

At closure all hazardous waste and residues must be removed from the incinerator. (40 C.F.R. § 265.351.)

H. Thermal Treatment Units

1. Applicability

Thermal treatment units elevate temperatures to change the chemical, physical, or biological character or composition of hazardous waste. This process can take the form of incineration, molten salt, pyrolysis, calcination, wet air oxidation, or microwave discharge. (40 C.F.R. § 260.10.)

2. Operating Requirements

Thermal treatment facilities (other than those employing a non-continuous, or "batch," treatment process) must achieve normal steady-state conditions using fuel before hazardous wastes are introduced. (40 C.F.R. § 265.373.) Any new hazardous waste to be treated in the unit must be analyzed to determine its potential pollutants. (40 C.F.R. § 265.375.) Only explosives may be treated by open burning. (40 C.F.R. § 265.382.)

Combustion and emission control equipment must be monitored at least every 15 minutes and operational corrections made when necessary. Stack plume emissions must be observed visually at least once every hour for normal appearance of color and opacity. The complete incinerator or thermal treatment facility and associated equipment must be inspected at least daily. (40 C.F.R. § 265.377.)

3. Closure

At closure, all hazardous waste and residues must be removed from the thermal treatment facility. (40 C.F.R. § 265.381.)

I. Chemical, Physical, and Biological Treatment Units

1. Applicability

Facilities treating hazardous wastes in other than tanks, surface impoundments, and land treatment units come under the catch-all category of chemical, physical, and biological treatment units. (40 C.F.R. § 265.400.)

2. Operating Requirements

Treatment and storage units must be operated to fully contain their wastes, and new wastes must be analyzed before being placed in the units if these wastes are substantially different from previous wastes or if a different process is being used. (40 C.F.R. § 265.402.)

3.   Closure

All hazardous wastes and treatment process residues must be removed from treatment processes or equipment, discharge control equipment, and discharge confinement structures at closure. Residues from hazardous waste treatment processes must be considered hazardous wastes unless the owner or operator can demonstrate otherwise. (40 C.F.R. § 265.404.)

J.   Special Regulations Pertaining to Underground Injection

Underground injection of fluid wastes through a bored, drilled, or driven well or through a dug well with greater depth than surface dimension is subject to regulation under both RCRA and the Safe Drinking Water Act. (See 40 C.F.R. § 265.1.) EPA applies the RCRA interim status standards to underground injection only if the facility lacks an Underground Injection Control permit issued under the Safe Drinking Water Act by a state with an approved UIC program.

The 1984 RCRA Amendments have limited the wells able to receive UIC interim status. The amendments prohibit underground injection of any hazardous waste into or above a formation that contains an underground source of drinking water within one-quarter mile of the injection well. This prohibition took effect May 8, 1984. (1984 RCRA Amendments § 405, adding RCRA § 7010(a).)

The amendments provide one important exception to this prohibition. Underground injection wells are permitted within one-quarter mile of a drinking water source if this injection is part of a Superfund response action or a RCRA cleanup program. The contaminated groundwater handled pursuant to this exception must be treated before injection, however, to substantially reduce the concentration of hazardous constituents.

PART 6: RCRA PERMITTED FACILITIES -- OBLIGATIONS OF FACILITY OWNERS AND OPERATORS

Chapters XIV-XVI outline the procedural and substantive permit requirements imposed on all new and existing treatment, storage, and disposal facilities, except facilities explicitly excluded from regulation under 40 C.F.R. § 264.1 and facilities operating in a state with an authorized RCRA permitting program. Although state rules apply in authorized states in lieu of the federal standards, most states are adopting the federal program with minimal changes.

As with interim status standards, the federal regulations contain both a series of administrative and basic operating standards applicable to all regulated facilities, and a series of additional requirements tailored to specific types of facilities and equipment. While a few of these permit requirements mirror the comparable interim status standards discussed in Part 5, most of them are more stringent than their interim status counterparts.

The requirements, as described in this Part, reflect the significant changes in the regulations brought about by the issuance of regulations covering land disposal of hazardous waste on July 26, 1982. With that rulemaking, EPA to a large extent completed its "cradle-to-grave" scheme for regulating waste management. Under this scheme, facilities temporarily holding waste prior to treatment, disposal, or storage elsewhere are considered storage facilities. Disposal facilities, in contrast, are considered permanent depositories of hazardous wastes. The regulatory approach to both types of facilities focuses upon containment of wastes during the facilities' active life and minimization of adverse environmental impacts after they are closed.

CHAPTER XIV

RCRA PERMIT PROCEDURES

This chapter describes the procedural requirements that must be met to obtain a RCRA permit. These appear at 40 C.F.R. Part 270 (permit application requirements) and Part 124 (procedures for decisionmaking). The substantive federal standards with which facilities must comply are discussed in the following two chapters. Although state substantive and procedural requirements apply in authorized states in lieu of the federal rules, most states are adopting the federal program with minimal changes. (See pp. 8-14.) To be apprised of these changes and any additional requirements, a facility owner or operator should consult state and local requirements.

A. When a Permit Must Be Obtained

The general rule is that every new hazardous waste management facility must obtain a RCRA permit before construction and operation. (40 C.F.R. § 270.10(f)(1).) An important exception is for PCB incinerators constructed and approved under the Toxic Substances Control Act for which RCRA permits may be sought to treat RCRA regulated hazardous waste. (1984 RCRA Amendments § 211, amending RCRA § 3005, to be codified in the regulations at 40 C.F.R. § 270.10(f)(3).)

Excepted also are facilities subject to permits by rule and exempt facilities, discussed at pp. 165 and 168-69.

With these exceptions, all new facilities must submit a complete two-part (i.e., Part A and Part B) permit application at least 180 days before beginning physical construction. (40 C.F.R. § 270.10(f).) In addition, all existing facilities that have filed Part A applications and are operating under interim status must complete their applications by filing Part B applications according to the prescribed schedule discussed at pp. 121-22 above. Reapplications must be submitted at least 180 days before expiration of a facility's expiring permit. (40 C.F.R. §§ 270.10(h).)

Permits may be issued for a term not to exceed ten years, although permits for land disposal facilities must be reviewed after five years. (40 C.F.R. § 270.50; 1984 RCRA Amendments § 212, amending RCRA § 3005(c), to be codified in the regulations at 40 C.F.R. § 270.50(d).) All hazardous waste management facilities must have permits throughout their active lives, and land disposal facilities also must have permits covering applicable post-closure activities and any compliance activities to correct groundwater contamination, as discussed in Chapter XVI below.

B. Application Requirements

1. General Requirements and Signatories

As noted above, RCRA permit applications consist of two parts. Part A contains general information on the facility, and Part B contains detailed information on the nature and scope of activities at the facility. When a facility is owned by one entity and operated by another, it is the operator's duty to obtain a permit, although the owner must sign the permit application. (40 C.F.R. § 270.10.)

Applications must be signed by both the owner and operator of the facility. For corporate applicants, 40 C.F.R. § 270.11 allows signature by either (a) a responsible corporate officer in charge of a principal business function or any other person who performs similar corporate functions, or (b) the manager of a major manufacturing, production or operating facility if the appropriate authority has been delegated. For federal permits, EPA must review the application for completeness within 30 days and notify the applicant if more information is required.

2. Part A Information

Part A must include a description of the activities requiring a RCRA permit, a list of the quantities of hazardous wastes to be handled, the exact location of the facility, information on the owner and operator, a scale drawing of the facility, a topographical map of the immediate neighborhood, a listing of all relevant environmental federal and state permits, and other specified information. (40 C.F.R § 270.13.) Forms for Part A are available from EPA and authorized state agencies.

3.   Part B Information

No forms are provided for Part B. Rather, Part B consists of detailed information reflecting the substantive, technical standards in 40 C.F.R. Part 264 (discussed in the following two chapters). For example, the Part B application must include chemical and physical analyses of the hazardous waste to be handled at the facility, operating plans, security and inspection procedures, contingency plans, employee training programs, closure and post-closure plans and costs, insurance coverage, and detailed geographical, geological, and hydrological studies. (40 C.F.R. § 270.14.) Additional, specific Part B information is required for each of the various types of facilities, i.e., containers, tanks, surface impoundments, waste piles, incinerators, land treatment units, and landfills. (40 C.F.R. §§ 270.15-.21.) For the protection of groundwater, detailed hydrogeologic and monitoring information is required for surface impoundments, waste piles, land treatment units and landfills. (40 C.F.R. § 270.14(c).)

Finally, the 1984 RCRA Amendments require exposure assessments for landfills and surface impoundments. (RCRA Amendments § 247, adding RCRA § 3019, to be codified in the

regulations at 40 C.F.R. 270.10(j).) Beginning August 8,
1985, all Part B applications for these facilities must
include information reasonably ascertainable to the owner or
operator on the potential for the public to be exposed to
hazardous substances through releases related to the unit.
Owners and operators who previously submitted Part B applications must provide the requested information by August 8,
1985.

If the Part B application is not sufficiently
detailed, EPA will issue a notice of deficiency and allow an
opportunity to cure the defects.

To speed the permitting process for certain, minimally hazardous classes of facilities, EPA has proposed
class permits for above-ground storage tanks and containers,
including an application form on which to provide all Part B
information. EPA is planning to expand the use of class
permits in the future. (See 49 Fed. Reg. 29524 (July 20,
1984).)

C. Permit Processing

    1. Consolidation of Permit Processing

        Whenever a facility needs a permit or permits under
both RCRA and another of EPA's permitting programs, these
permit proceedings may be consolidated. The final permits
then may be issued together, with simultaneous expiration

dates. It is important to note, however, that this consolidation is procedural only; separate, individual permits
will be issued under each program. (40 C.F.R § 124.4.)

2.   Draft Permits

After EPA (or an authorized state agency) reviews
a complete permit application, the agency makes a tentative
decision whether to grant or deny the permit. If that decision is affirmative, a draft permit is prepared incorporating all the permit conditions applicable to that
facility. If the decision is negative, a notice of intent
to deny is issued and processed under the same procedures as
a draft permit. (40 C.F.R. § 124.6(b).) In addition, a
"fact sheet" giving key information is prepared for major
hazardous waste management facilities; for all others, a
statement of basis for the draft permit is prepared. For
major facilities, a nonbinding project decision schedule
also is prepared. (40 C.F.R. §§ 124.7, 124.8.)

3.   Public Notice and Hearings

EPA and authorized states are required by statute
to notify the public and local authorities of all permit
applications, and to allow for public comment. (40 C.F.R
§ 124.10.) A public hearing must be held for RCRA permits
if any interested party requests one. Public hearings are
legislative in nature; that is, any person may testify or

submit written material, but no cross-examination of witnesses is allowed.   (40 C.F.R. § 124.12.)

In limited circumstances, a non-adversary panel ("NAP") hearing before a panel of EPA experts may be held in lieu of a public hearing. For example, the Regional Administrator may, in his discretion, order a NAP hearing for initial RCRA permits for existing hazardous waste management facilities. A permit applicant also may request a NAP hearing during the public comment period on the ground that there are genuine issues as to material facts that are determinative of major permit conditions. If the Regional Administrator denies this request, a brief statement must be sent to the applicant explaining the reasons for the denial. (40 C.F.R. § 124.12.) According to EPA, NAP hearings will be provided when there is a tentative decision to deny a permit for an existing facility or a disagreement on major permit conditions for an existing facility. (See 49 Fed. Reg. 17717 (April 24, 1984).) NAP hearings also may be provided if a RCRA permit application is consolidated with an NPDES application for the same facility, or whenever the Regional Administrator determines, in his discretion, that the more formalized NAP procedures should be used in lieu of a public hearing. (40 C.F.R. § 124.111.)

A formal, full-scale evidentiary hearing is authorized in the federal regulations in only two circumstances:

(1) when an existing RCRA permit is terminated (including termination of interim status for failure to provide information); and (2) when a RCRA permit is closely linked with the conditions of an NPDES permit as to which an evidentiary hearing has been granted. (40 C.F.R. § 124.71.)

4. Permit Conditions

All RCRA permits are subject to general conditions specified in the regulations, including the duty to comply with permit conditions, the duty to provide information, and obligations to provide monitoring reports, unmanifested waste reports, and biennial reports. (40 C.F.R §§ 270.30-.33.) Beginning September 1, 1985, these conditions will include the obligation to retain operating records, which must include the permittee's certification regarding efforts taken to minimize the amount and toxicity of wastes at the facility. (1984 RCRA Amendments § 224, amending RCRA § 3005, to be codified in the regulations at 40 C.F.R. § 270.30(j)(2).) Finally, the 1984 RCRA Amendments grant EPA and authorized state agencies broad authority to add additional permit conditions beyond those specified in the regulations, where they determine additional conditions are necessary to protect human health and the environment. (1984 RCRA Amendments § 212, amending RCRA § 3005, to be codified in the regulations at 40 C.F.R § 270.32(b)(2).)

5. Permit Issuance and Appeal

After the close of the public comment period, including any hearing, a final permit decision is issued and becomes effective 30 days thereafter unless an administrative appeal is filed, or a later date is specified, or no comments requested a change in the draft permit, in which case it becomes effective immediately. (40 C.F.R. § 124.15.) As noted above, there is a maximum ten-year term on all RCRA permits. (40 C.F.R. § 270.50.)

6. Review of Land Disposal Permits

As required by the 1984 RCRA Amendments, permits for land disposal facilities must be reviewed by EPA or the authorized state agency every five years. (1984 RCRA Amendments § 212, amending RCRA § 3005(c), to be codified in the regulations at 40 C.F.R. § 270.50(d).)

D. Changes to Permits

RCRA permits may be modified, revoked and reissued, or terminated for cause, at the request of any interested person or on the permitting agency's own initiative.

1. Major Modifications or Revocation and Reissuance

Major modifications to a RCRA permit or revocation and reissuance of a RCRA permit may be ordered only for cause as specified in 40 C.F.R. § 270.41. If EPA or the authorized state agency agrees with a proposed modification, it prepares a draft permit incorporating the changes. When a permit is modified, only the changed conditions are reopened. If a permit is revoked and reissued, the action is processed as an original permit application. If, after the public comment period, the permitting agency decides to incorporate the changes, it may either issue a modified permit or revoke the original permit and issue a new one. A RCRA permit may be modified for the following reasons:

(1) material and substantial alterations to the regulated facility or activity;

(2) new information;

(3) an amendment to the applicable standards or regulations, provided that the modification is requested within 90 days;

(4) good cause for modifying a compliance schedule;

(5) required modifications of a closure plan;

(6) specified changes in closure requirements;

(7) specified changes in financial responsibility requirements;

(8) corrective action has been unsuccessful;

(9) specified changes in groundwater monitoring;

(10) conditions applicable to new units at a facility;

(11) incomplete treatment at land treatment units;

(12) cause for termination (discussed below); and

(13) a proposed transfer of the permit.

The suitability of a RCRA facility's location will not be considered during modification or revocation and reissurance proceedings unless new information or standards indicate that a threat to human health or the environment exists which was unknown at the time of permit issuance.

2. Minor Modifications

Minor modifications of a permit with the permittee's consent may be made at the permitting agency's discretion without following the procedures of 40 C.F.R. Part 124. Minor modifications include limited extensions in compliance schedules, changes in closure date estimates, and changes in the facility's contingency and treatment plans. In addition, certain specified changes to land treatment permits have been designated minor modifications. (40 C.F.R. § 270.42.) EPA has proposed expanding the list of minor modifications. (See 49 Fed. Reg. 9850 (March 15, 1984).)

3. Transfer of Permits

RCRA permits may not be transferred unless the permit has been modified or revoked and reissued to identify the new owner and incorporate any necessary new conditions. (40 C.F.R. § 270.40.)

E. Termination of Permits

Grounds for termination include: (1) noncompliance; (2) failure to disclose fully, or misrepresentation of, relevant facts; and (3) a determination that the permitted activity endangers human health or the environment. (40 C.F.R § 270.43.) If the permitting agency decides to terminate a RCRA permit, it issues a notice of intent, and the permittee is entitled to a full-scale evidentiary hearing before an administrative law judge. An appeal of an EPA decision may be taken to the Administrator of EPA, and ultimately to the courts. See 40 C.F.R. Part 124, Subpart E.

F. Special Forms of Permits

    1. Permits by Rule

        The regulations specifically authorize permits by rule, provided some conditions are met, for: (1) ocean disposal barges or vessels having permits issued under EPA's ocean dumping regulations; (2) injection wells having underground injection permits; and (3) publicly owned treatment works having NPDES permits. No application need be filed. (40 C.F.R. § 270.60.)

    2. Emergency Permits

        In the event the permitting authority finds an imminent and substantial endangerment to human health or the environment, a temporary emergency permit may be issued to a non-permitted facility to allow treatment, storage, or disposal of hazardous waste or to a permitted facility to allow treatment, storage or disposal of hazardous waste not covered by an effective permit. The emergency permit, which may be oral or written, may be terminated at any time. (40 C.F.R § 270.61.)

3. Hazardous Waste Incinerator Permits

The regulations authorize special permits to conduct a trial burn to determine the operational readiness of hazardous waste incinerators following completion of physical construction. Detailed conditions apply. (40 C.F.R. § 270.62.)

4. Permits for Land Treatment Demonstrations

To allow a land treatment unit to demonstrate compliance with treatment requirements in 40 C.F.R § 264.272, the regulations authorize treatment demonstration permits. Permits may be issued for only the field test or laboratory analyses, or they may also cover the design, construction, operation, and maintenance of the land treatment unit. (40 C.F.R. § 270.63.)

5. Interim Permits for UIC Wells

In a state where there is no approved underground injection control program, two year federal permits are authorized for Class I wells (situated beneath the lowermost formation containing, within one-quarter mile of the well bore, an underground source of drinking water). (See 40 C.F.R. § 270.64.)

6. Research, Development, and Demonstration Permits

The 1984 RCRA Amendments encourage development of hazardous waste treatment technologies by authorizing EPA to issue special research, development, and demonstration permits for innovative and experimental treatment technologies or processes. (1984 RCRA Amendments § 214, amending RCRA § 3005, to be codified in the regulations at 40 C.F.R. § 270.65.) For a discussion of the requirements applicable to these special permits, see p. 213.

CHAPTER XV

GENERAL PERMIT STANDARDS

This chapter describes EPA's general substantive
standards for facilities that have obtained a RCRA permit.
It includes a discussion of the facility operating and financial responsibility standards, which are similar to interim
status standards, and it also describes the obligations with
respect to monitoring, facility design, and corrective
action, which are much more stringent than the obligations
imposed on interim status facilities.

A. Facilities Subject to RCRA Permit Requirements

With limited exceptions, all new hazardous waste
treatment, storage, and disposal facilities must obtain RCRA
permits and comply with the substantive permitting standards.
In addition, as discussed above at pp. 120-21, new units,
replacement units, and lateral expansions to existing units
at interim land disposal status facilities that continued to
receive waste after November 8, 1984, are subject to the
minimum technological requirements imposed on new disposal
facilities (i.e., a double liner for landfills and surface
impoundments, a single liner for waste piles, and a leachate
collection system at all three types of units).

However, some treatment, storage, and disposal units
are specifically excluded from permit obligations:

(1) licensed municipal and industrial solid waste facilities that treat, store, or dispose of hazardous waste from small quantity generators (Section 302 of the 1984 RCRA Amendments, which added RCRA § 4010, requires groundwater monitoring, siting, and corrective action obligations for such facilities by March 1988);

(2) facilities engaged in a limited range of reuse activities (see discussion at pp. 28-37);

(3) farmers disposing of pesticides according to labeling instructions;

(4) totally enclosed treatment facilities, in which hazardous waste is treated in a totally enclosed process directly connected to the industrial production process;

(5) elementary neutralization units (tanks, containers, transport vehicles, or vessels containing corrosive wastes);

(6) wastewater treatment tanks regulated under the Clean Water Act;

(7) facilities responding to spills;

(8) transfer facilities holding a transporter's manifested hazardous waste for no more than 10 days;

(9) facilities adding absorbent material to hazardous waste in a container; and

(10) generators accumulating waste on-site in compliance with the 90-day accumulation rule (see pp. 92-93).

(40 C.F.R. § 264.1.) Furthermore, the federal permitting standards do not apply to facilities operating in states with authorized RCRA programs. Although state rules apply in authorized states, most states have adopted the federal program with minimal changes.

The federal permitting standards are based on a two-part strategy to protect human health and the environment. First, the regulations mandate protection of soil, ground-water, and surface water by minimizing liquids in and around hazardous waste facilities. The regulations employ performance standards for facility design and operation (Part 264, Subparts K-N) and groundwater monitoring and response standards (Part 264, Subpart F) to limit the amount of liquid that may be placed into a waste facility, may run on or off a waste facility, or may leach out of a facility during its active life and after. Second, the effectiveness of a facility's design and operating standards is policed by a groundwater monitoring program that mandates corrective action if the strategy fails and contaminants in sufficient concentrations are released into the environment.

B. General Facility Standards

1. Identification Number

Every facility must have an EPA identification number. (40 C.F.R. § 264.11.)

2. Notification

The owner or operator of a facility receiving hazardous waste from an off-site source must inform the waste generator that the facility has obtained appropriate permits. EPA must be notified four weeks in advance of receipt of wastes from foreign sources. Before facility ownership is transferred, the new owner or operator must be notified of the requirements of Parts 264 and 270. (40 C.F.R. § 264.12.)

3. Waste Analysis

Before hazardous waste is treated, stored, or disposed of, the owner or operator must obtain a detailed chemical and physical analysis of a representative sample of the waste. This analysis must be updated when the facility manager has reason to believe the waste-generating process has changed or, for off-site facilities, when the waste does not meet the manifest's description. (40 C.F.R. § 264.13.) The procedures for this sampling must be described in a written waste analysis plan kept at the facility. Additional requirements tailored to specific types of facilities also may apply. (See, e.g., 40 C.F.R. § 264.341.)

4. Security

The owner or operator must prevent inadvertent and, to the extent possible, deliberate entry of people or livestock into the active portion of his facility, unless

their contact with the waste will not cause injury to themselves or to facility integrity. In order to secure the
site, the facility may need to have 24-hour surveillance,
barriers surrounding the active portion of the waste management area, controls to entry, and signs barring unauthorized
entry. (40 C.F.R. § 264.14.)

    5.   Inspections

The owner or operator must inspect his facility for
malfunctions and deterioration, operator errors, and
discharges, according to a written inspection plan retained
at the facility. If any deterioration or malfunction is
discovered, it must be remedied. A record of all inspections must be retained for at least three years. (40 C.F.R.
§ 264.15.) Additional requirements tailored to specific
types of facilities also may apply, as described below.

    6.   Personnel Training

Facility personnel must complete a program of
training in RCRA procedures and emergency response. A written description of the training program, its attendees, and
instructors must be kept at the facility. (40 C.F.R.
§ 264.16.) (EPA has published a helpful background document
on training, and it is available from EPA and many law firms
regularly practicing in this field.)

7. Requirements for Ignitable, Reactive, or
    Incompatible Wastes

The owner or operator must take precautions to prevent accidental ignition or reaction of ignitable or reactive wastes, and to prevent adverse reactions caused by mixing incompatible wastes. (40 C.F.R. § 264.17.) Additional requirements tailored to specific types of facilities also may apply. (See, e.g., 40 C.F.R. §§ 264.176, 264.177.)

8. Location Standards

Facilities located in areas of seismic activity must not place new treatment, storage, or disposal units within 200 feet of a fault, and facilities located within a 100-year floodplain must prevent washout of hazardous waste in amounts and concentrations that would adversely affect the environment. (40 C.F.R. § 264.18.)

C. Preparedness For and Prevention of Spills and
    Other Emergencies

All permitted facilities must have equipment adequate to deal with unexpected fires, explosions, or any unplanned sudden or non-sudden spill or other release of hazardous wastes. Required equipment includes internal communications or alarm systems; telephones, radios or other means of summoning emergency personnel; fire extinguishers or other fire control devices; and water or foam-producing equipment. Proper aisle space must be maintained for emergency equipment.

Emergency response procedures must be detailed in a contingency plan kept at the waste facility and submitted to state and local authorities. A Clean Water Act Spill Prevention, Control, and Countermeasures ("SPCC") Plan may be used as the basis for the RCRA contingency plan. The RCRA plan must describe the personnel in charge of emergency response, emergency equipment, and evacuation procedures. (40 C.F.R. Part 264, Subparts C and D.)

D. Manifest System, Recordkeeping, and Reporting

    1. Manifests

        When a facility receives a shipment of hazardous waste accompanied by a manifest, the owner or operator must sign and date the manifest, note any significant discrepancies between the manifest and the waste received, give the transporter a copy of the signed manifest, send another copy of the manifest to the generator within 30 days, and retain his own copy for at least three years from the date of delivery. (40 C.F.R. § 264.71.) If the owner or operator cannot resolve significant discrepancies between the waste received and its manifest description (i.e., greater than 10 percent variations in bulk weight, variations in piece count, or obvious differences in waste type), he must report the discrepancy to EPA within 15 days of receiving the waste. (40 C.F.R. § 264.72.)

If a facility receives any hazardous waste that is not accompanied by a manifest, the shipment must be reported to the Regional Administrator within 15 days. Although wastes from small quantity generators (see pp. 94-97 above) need not be accompanied by a manifest, EPA recommends that the generator provide certification that the shipment is a lawful small generator waste shipment. (40 C.F.R. § 264.76.)

2. Recordkeeping

All records required to be kept by RCRA regulations (including the facility operating records of waste receipts, waste placement in the facility, and waste analyses; contingency plan reports; inspection logs; and monitoring data) must be available at all reasonable times for inspection by EPA representatives. (40 C.F.R. §§ 264.73, 264.74.)

3. Biennial Report

The regulations currently require the facility owner or operator to submit a report in March of every even-numbered year detailing facility activities during the previous calendar year. (40 C.F.R. § 265.75.)

4. Certification

The 1984 RCRA Amendments require owners and operators of facilities permitted after September 1, 1985, that both generate and treat, store, or dispose of wastes to certify that a program is in place to reduce the volume and toxicity of the hazardous waste generated. (1984 RCRA

Amendments § 224, adding RCRA § 3002(g), to be codified in the regulations at 40 C.F.R. § 264.73.) The owner or operator also must certify that his method of treatment, storage, or disposal is the practicable method currently available to minimize threats to human health and the environment.

E. Groundwater Monitoring and Response Requirements

With few exceptions, all treatment, storage, and disposal facilities must comply with the 40 C.F.R. Part 264, Subpart F groundwater monitoring requirements. Before passage of the 1984 RCRA Amendments, a number of facilities (for example, double-lined surface impoundments, waste piles, and landfills located above the seasonal high water table) could obtain exemptions from RCRA groundwater monitoring requirements. (See 40 C.F.R. §§ 264.222, 264.252, 264.302.) The 1984 Amendments now mandate groundwater monitoring for nearly all new permitted surface impoundments, waste piles, land treatment units, and landfills. (1984 RCRA Amendments § 203, amending RCRA § 3004.) The 1984 Amendments allow EPA to continue exempting from groundwater monitoring requirements only (a) certain land treatment units in the post-closure period, (b) units with no potential for migration of liquid from the unit into the uppermost aquifer through the post-closure period, and (c) indoor waste piles. (1984 RCRA Amendments § 203, adding RCRA § 3004(p), to be codified in the regulations at 40 C.F.R. § 264.90(b).)

The only additional exemption from groundwater monitoring authorized by the 1984 Amendments is an engineered structure that meets the following critria: (1) does not receive or contain liquid waste or waste containing free liquids; (2) is designed and operated to exclude liquid from precipitation as run-off; and (3) uses multiple leak detection systems within the outer layer of containment that operate continuously through the end of the post-closure care period. (1984 RCRA Amendments § 203, amending RCRA § 3004, to be codified in the regulations at 40 C.F.R. § 264.90(b).) EPA may exempt such a structure from groundwater monitoring because these design and operating features give a reasonable certainty that hazardous constituents will not migrate beyond the outer layer of containment through the closure period.

For all other permitted facilities, a three-stage groundwater monitoring and response program is obligatory. Under this program, monitoring and response obligations range from the relatively simple "detection" monitoring to the more intensive "compliance" monitoring and eventually corrective action if a hazardous waste facility causes groundwater contamination.

1.   Groundwater Monitoring Program Requirements

The goal of the Part 264 groundwater monitoring and response program is avoidance or, if that fails, remediation of groundwater contamination. Contamination is identified in this program as violation of the "groundwater protection standard," which occurs when (a) the hazardous constituents listed in 40 C.F.R Part 261 Appendix VIII (reprinted in Appendix C) occur in concentrations significantly above the concentrations found in local groundwater upgradient to and unaffected by the hazardous waste facility, or (b) special maximum concentrations limits ("MCLs") based on the National Interim Primary Drinking Water Standards ("NIPDWS"), which appear in Table I of 40 C.F.R § 264.94(a) (reprinted in Appendix D) are exceeded. Variations from the ground-water protection standard, or alternative concentration levels ("ACLs") for specific hazardous constituents that exceed background levels, may be allowed for individual facilities, but an ACL will be granted only after the facility makes a detailed demonstration that the ACL will result in no substantial present or potential hazard to human health or the environment. (40 C.F.R. § 294.94(b).)

(a) <u>Establishing a Monitoring Program</u>

A facility's compliance with the groundwater protection standard must be monitored at a "compliance point," defined as the "vertical surface located at the hydraulically downgradient limit of the waste management area that extends down into the uppermost aquifer underlying the regulated units." (40 C.F.R. § 264.95(a).) The waste management area

is the site on which waste will be placed during the active
life of the regulated unit, and will be specified in the
facility permit. (40 C.F.R. § 264.95(b).) Where there is
more than one regulated unit at the facility, the waste
management area encompasses all regulated units.

A facility must ensure compliance with the groundwater protection standard for a "compliance period" which
begins to run upon detection of hazardous constituents in
the groundwater. Ordinarily, this period is equal to the
number of years a facility has been in active operation,
including any waste management activity occurring prior
to permitting and the closure period. (40 C.F.R.
§§ 264.96(a)(b).)

Most of the technical requirements for an individual facility's monitoring program are developed during the
permitting process, but there are some general performance
standards that apply to all groundwater monitoring systems.
First, the system must consist of a sufficient number of
wells, installed at appropriate locations and depths, to
yield groundwater samples indicating the quality of groundwater. (40 C.F.R. § 264.97(a).) Several construction
guidelines should be followed when establishing this system.
Well casings must maintain the integrity of the monitoring
well bore hole, and must be screened or perforated and
packed with gravel or sand, where necessary, to enable

collection of groundwater samples. In addition, the annular space above the sample depth must be sealed to prevent inadvertent contamination of samples and the groundwater. (40 C.F.R. § 264.97(c).)

The groundwater monitoring system, once constructed, must be operated in a manner that employs consistent sampling and analytical procedures. (40 C.F.R. §§ 264.97(d), (e); 47 Fed. Reg. at 32352.) An EPA publication, Test Methods for Evaluating Solid Waste ("SW-846") is to be used in establishing acceptable analytical methods and procedures for groundwater sampling and analysis. (See 49 Fed. Reg. 38786 (Oct. 1, 1984).)

(b) Detection Monitoring Program

Once a facility's groundwater monitoring system is installed, the facility must begin what is termed "detection monitoring" to determine if hazardous leachate from a waste management unit has entered the groundwater. (40 C.F.R. § 264.98.) In order to detect when a facility has begun affecting groundwater, the owner or operator must monitor for the release into groundwater of "indicator parameters," or the constituents most likely to migrate from the waste in his facility. These indicator parameters will be specified in the facility's permit, and are selected on the basis of:

(1) the types, quantities, and concentrations of hazardous constituents in wastes managed at the facility;

(2)   the quality of the leachate as it passes through soil beneath the facility;

(3)   the detectability of the potential monitoring parameters; and

(4)   the nature of background groundwater.

In order to identify when the presence of indicator parameters at certain concentrations show the facility is leaking into groundwater, the facility must be able to distinguish between background water quality and groundwater affected by hazardous leachate. In order to do this, the facility must establish background concentrations for each indicator parameter by sampling upgradient wells quarterly for at least one year. (40 C.F.R. § 264.97(g)(4).) Thereafter sampling should be done at least semi-annually. (40 C.F.R. § 264.98(c).) This background will then be compared with groundwater quality downgradient from and affected by the active portion of the waste facility in order to determine whether the hazardous waste facility is leaking.

Leakage is assumed by EPA if a statistically significant increase in concentration of hazardous constituents in downgradient leachate is identified. (40 C.F.R. §§ 264.98(g), (h).) The regulations rely on a standard statistical comparison using Cochran's Approximation to the Behrens-Fisher Student's t-test to identify a statistically significant increase. If such an increase in concentration

of hazardous constituents is detected, EPA presumes that the
hazardous waste unit is leaking, and the facility owner must
notify the Regional Administrator in writing within seven
days. (40 C.F.R. § 264.98(h)(1).)

A more intensive monitoring program must then be
implemented. To identify the range of hazardous constituents that may have entered the groundwater, all monitoring
wells must be sampled immediately for all constituents identified in Appendix VIII of Part 261 (reprinted in Appendix
D). (40 C.F.R. § 264.98(h)(2).) Once this sampling has
been completed, background values for each Appendix VIII
constituent present in the groundwater must be established.
(40 C.F.R. § 264.98(h)(3).) The facility owner or operator
then has 90 days to apply for a permit modification to
implement the compliance monitoring program, described below,
which is triggered by detection of a suspected leak from the
facility. The only way in which to avoid such a permit
modification is to submit a report to the Regional
Administrator within 90 days, demonstrating that the perceived increase in concentration of hazardous constituents
or parameters was caused by a source other than the disposal
unit or was the result of error in sampling, analysis, or
evaluation. (40 C.F.R. § 264.98(i).) To be prudent, this
report probably should be accompanied by a permit modification application, because if the report fails to demonstrate

error or that the contamination is from another source and no such application has been filed, the facility would be found in violation of its permit.

(c) Compliance Monitoring Program

The second phase of the groundwater protection strategy, "compliance monitoring," is triggered when the owner or operator of a facility detects a statistically significant increase in contaminants in downgradient ground-water. Sampling for all Appendix VIII constituents reasonably expected to derive from the facility must occur at least quarterly, and groundwater flow rate and direction also should be determined once a year. In addition, groundwater must be analyzed for all Appendix VIII constituents at least annually to determine whether additional hazardous constit-uents have entered the groundwater. (40 C.F.R. §§ 264.99(d)-(f).)

If compliance monitoring for all Appendix VIII constituents confirms that hazardous constituents are migrating from the unit, the owner or operator must notify the Regional Administrator within seven days. He also must prepare an application for a permit modification to establish a corrective action program designed to remediate the effect of the release of hazardous constituents from the facility. (40 C.F.R. § 264.99(i).) As with the detection monitoring program, the owner or operator may file a report along with, or in lieu of, a permit modification application, which explains why the statistically significant increase was caused by a source other than the disposal unit or that the increase was the result of error in sampling, analysis, or evaluation. (40 C.F.R. § 264.99(j).)

(d) Corrective Action Program

The goal of a corrective action program is to bring the regulated unit into compliance with its groundwater protection standard by removing hazardous constituents from groundwater or treating them in place. EPA believes that the precise measures that must be taken to accomplish this are highly dependent on site-specific factors, and therefore has avoided imposing rigid guidelines which might have the effect of stifling innovation in this area. (47 Fed. Reg. 32310.) As a result, the goal of corrective action is expressed as a performance standard requiring action to prevent "hazardous constituents from exceeding their respective concentration limits at the compliance point . . . ."
(40 C.F.R. § 264.100(b).)

Corrective action must begin within a reasonable period of time after the groundwater protection standard has been exceeded, and extend as long as necessary to achieve the groundwater protection standard. Furthermore, if corrective action is still needed at the end of the compliance period, the owner or operator must continue the remedial measures until the groundwater protection standard is not exceeded for a period of three years. (40 C.F.R. § 264.100 (f).)

The owner or operator must report semi-annually in writing to the Regional Administrator on the effectivensss of the program. (40 C.F.R. § 264.100(g).) If a corrective action program fails to comply with the groundwater protection standard, the facility owner must submit an application for a permit modification to make appropriate changes to the program. (40 C.F.R. § 264.100(h).)

2. Additional Corrective Action Obligations Imposed at the Time of Initial Permitting

Until enactment of the 1984 RCRA Amendments, there was nothing to prohibit EPA from granting a final permit to a facility that was causing groundwater contamination from an inactive unit. Only the groundwater monitoring and response obligations described above, which are applicable to active hazardous waste management units, would trigger corrective action obligations at a facility. To close this loophole, the 1984 RCRA Amendments stipulate that all permits issued after November 8, 1984, require corrective action for all releases of hazardous waste or hazardous constituents from any solid waste (not merely hazardous waste) management unit at a RCRA facility. This requirement applies regardless of when the waste was placed in the unit. If corrective action cannot be completed prior to issuance of a permit, the permit must contain a compliance schedule for corrective action and assurances of financial responsibility for completing such action. (1984 RCRA Amendments, § 206, adding RCRA Section 3004(u), to be codified in the regulations at 40 C.F.R. § 264.101.)

Moreover, the 1984 Amendments direct EPA to require corrective action beyond the boundary of a facility where such action is necessary to protect human health and the environment. This requirement may be waived only if the owner or operator of the facility demonstrates to EPA's satisfaction that, despite his best efforts, he has been unable to obtain the necessary permission from owners of adjacent property. (1984 RCRA Amendments § 207, adding RCRA § 3004(v).)

These new corrective action obligations have dramatically broadened the scope of RCRA. In addition to the obligations imposed on permitted facilities, the 1984 RCRA Amendments also authorize EPA to issue a corrective action order or to commence a civil suit whenever there has been a release of hazardous waste from an interim status facility. (1984 RCRA Amendments § 233, adding RCRA § 3008(g).) (See discussion at pp. 233-34.) Armed with this authority to compel cleanup, EPA has announced that it plans use its RCRA corrective action provisions, rather than Superfund, to achieve cleanup of releases from facilities subject to RCRA regulation. (See 50 Fed. Reg. 14116 (April 10, 1985).)

Indeed, the Agency has proposed to defer listing RCRA-regulated sites on the Superfund National Priorities List until it is determined that cleanup measures ordered under RCRA are unlikely to succeed. The new provisions are likely to have the effect of turning RCRA into a "little Superfund" by expanding EPA's ability to compel cleanup of RCRA-regulated facilities without resort to Superfund.

3. Closure and Post-Closure Requirements

The Part 264 regulations include general closure and post-closure requirements for all permitted facilities (40 C.F.R. Part 264, Subpart G) and additional requirements for specific types of facilities.

Closure is the period after wastes are no longer accepted, during which the facility completes treatment, storage, and disposal operations, applies final cover to or caps disposal units (if necessary), and disposes of or decontaminates equipment. Post-closure is the period after closure during which owners or operators of disposal facilities must conduct certain monitoring and maintenance activities. All permitted facilities must have a written closure plan, post-closure plan (if wastes will remain at the site after closure), and cost estimates for closure and, if applicable, post-closure. The plans must be submitted to EPA at least 180 days before the facility expects to commence closure. (40 C.F.R. §§ 264.112, 264.117.) This notification period may be shortened for some facilities. (See 50 Fed. Reg. 11068, 11090 (March 19, 1985).)

(a) Closure

Within 90 days of receiving the final volume of waste at a facility, all hazardous wastes must either be treated, removed from the site, or disposed of onsite according to the closure plan. The entire closure period may not exceed six months unless a longer period is authorized by EPA. (40 C.F.R. § 264.113.) When closure is completed, all facility equipment and structures must be disposed of or decontaminated, and closure must be certified by a registered professional engineer. (40 C.F.R. §§ 264.114-.115.)

(b) Post-Closure

The post-closure period extends 30 years after closure. During the post-closure period, facilities must continue groundwater monitoring, maintenance of the cap or final cover and other containment structures, and maintenance of the facility's monitoring equipment. (40 C.F.R. § 264.117.) Access to the property will be restricted if necessary. In the land disposal regulations published in July 1982, EPA announced that all disposal facilities that accepted wastes after January 26, 1983, including those that closed during interim status, would be subject to the 40

C.F.R. Part 264 post-closure requirements (described below). (47 Fed. Reg. 32274, 32336 (July 26, 1982).)

(c) Post-Closure Permits

Any facility that closed after January 26, 1983, must obtain a post-closure permit. (See 40 C.F.R. § 270.1(c).) Like other facilities that obtain a permit after November 8, 1984, facilities with post-closure per-mits may be required to schedule corrective action at the facility if necessary to clean up all releases of hazardous waste or constituents from any solid waste management unit at the facility. (1984 RCRA Amendment § 206, adding RCRA § 3004(u).)

(d) Notice to Local Land Authorities

The fact that land has been used as a hazardous waste disposal facility must be reported to a local land authority and EPA's Regional Administrator (or his state equivalent) and must be recorded in the deed to the prop-erty. (40 C.F.R. §§ 264.119, 264.120.)

4. Financial Responsibility

All treatment, storage, and disposal facilities must have written estimates of closure costs, and disposal facilities must also have written estimates of post-closure costs. Moreover, these facilities must demonstrate their ability to bear these costs.

(a) Cost Estimates

The required closure and post-closure cost estimates must be prepared based on the closure and post-closure plans for the facility, with all applicable closure costs included. The estimates must be based on the assumption that closure occurs at the point in the life of the facility when closure would be most expensive. (40 C.F.R. § 264.142(a), 264.144.)

The closure cost estimate must be revised whenever a change is made in the closure plan that would increase closure costs. (40 C.F.R. § 264.142(c).) The closure and post-closure cost estimates also must be revised for inflation yearly by multiplying the latest cost estimate by an inflation factor based on the annual Implicit Price Deflator for the Gross National Product, published by the Commerce Department. (40 C.F.R. §§ 264.142(b), 264.144(b).)

The owner or operator must retain a copy of the latest closure and post-closure estimates at the facility. (40 C.F.R. §§ 264.142(d), 264.144(d).)

(b) Financial Assurance

The owner or operator of each facility must demonstrate, by means of one of seven accepted methods, financial assurance for the closure of the facility. (40 C.F.R. § 264.143.) Similar requirements are imposed for post-closure financial responsibility when applicable. (40 C.F.R. § 264.145.)

(i) Closure Trust Fund

The owner or operator may establish a closure trust fund. The trust agreement must follow the exact wording of the form in 40 C.F.R. § 264.151, and must be signed and notarized. Schedule A, fixing the total amount of the current closure and/or post-closure cost estimate, must be updated within 60 days after a change in the current closure cost. Payments must be made annually over the term of the initial RCRA permit or the remaining life of the facility, whichever is shorter. This period is termed the "pay-in period." Payments must be equal to the current closure cost estimate, minus the current value of the trust fund, divided by the number of years left in the pay-in period. 40 C.F.R. § 264.143(a) contains more detailed requirements to cover contingencies which could arise.

(ii) Surety bond guaranteeing closure trust fund

A surety bond to guarantee eventual payment into a closure trust fund may be submitted to the Regional Administrator to satisfy the financial assurance require- ment. The wording of the surety bond must be identical to the form in 40 C.F.R. § 264.151, and the issuing company must be listed as an acceptable surety on federal bonds by the Treasury Department (in Circular 570). The owner or operator must also establish a standby trust fund. The trust fund can be either unfunded, to be funded by the bond proceeds at closure, or can be funded by payments by the owner or operator to the surety prior to closure (or following an order by EPA or a court). The bond must be

adjusted to reflect adjustments in closure cost estimates.
If the bond is cancelled, the owner or operator must offer
alternative financial assurances within 90 days. (40 C.F.R.
§ 264.143(b).

> ### (iii) Surety bond guaranteeing performance of closure

This is similar to the surety bond described above,
except that the surety does not become liable until the
owner or operator fails to perform in accordance with the
closure plan and other RCRA permit requirements. (40 C.F.R.
§ 264.143(c).)

> ### (iv) Irrevocable Letter of Credit

An owner or operator may submit an irrevocable
letter of credit sufficient to cover the entire amount of
the current closure cost estimate. This letter must follow
the exact wording of the form in 40 C.F.R. § 264.151. A
standby trust arrangement must be established similar to the
surety bond standby trust funds. (40 C.F.R. § 264.143(d).)

> ### (v) Closure insurance

The owner or operator may satisfy financial
assurance requirements with a closure insurance policy with
a face amount at least equal to current closure costs and
subject to adjustment as the estimate increases. This
policy must pay out funds whenever final closure occurs, to
such party or parties as the Regional Administrator directs.
If the Regional Administrator determines that closure costs

will exceed the value of the policy, payments on claims may be withheld pending determination of the owner or operator's financial responsibility. The insurer must agree not to cancel the insurance for any reason except non-payment of the premium after notice has been served on both the Regional Administrator and the owner or operator. The insurance cannot be cancelled in the event that the facility is abandoned, the RCRA permit is denied or terminated, closure is ordered by court order, or the owner or operator is named in bankruptcy proceedings. (40 C.F.R. 264.143(e).)

(vi) <u>Financial Test or Corporate Guarantee</u>

The owner or operator can establish financial assurance by providing evidence of financial stability under the guidelines in this section. (40 C.F.R. § 263.143(b).) There are three alternative methods of satisfying this requirement.

Under the first alternative, the owner or operator must satisfy two of the following three ratios: a ratio of total liabilities to net worth less than 2.0; a ratio of the sum of net income plus depreciation, depletion, and amortization to total liabilities greater than 0.1; and a ratio of current assets to current liabilities greater than 1.5. The owner or operator also must have net working capital and tangible net worth each at least six times the sum of current closure and post-closure estimates; tangible net worth over $10 million; and assets in the United States amounting to either 90 percent of total assets or at least six times current closure and post-closure cost estimates.

Under the second alternative, all of above requirements except for the required ratios must be demonstrated. Instead, the owner or operator must have a current rating for the most recent bond issuance of AAA, AA, A, or BBB under the Standard and Poor's ratings or, Aaa, Aa, A, or Baa under Moody's ratings.

A third financial test is a "corporate guarantee" from the parent corporation of the owner or operator. This parent corporation must fulfill the requirements of one of the above two alternatives.

For any alternative, required evidence must be submitted yearly in the form of (1) a letter from the Chief Financial Officer, (ii) a copy of the independent auditor's report on the company's latest annual financial report, and (iii) a special report from a CPA certifying the information in the chief financial officer's letter. The Regional Administrator has the power to require additional reports, or to disallow qualification on the basis of the auditor or CPA reports.

(vii) Combination of financial responsibility requirements

An owner or operator may combine any of the above mechanisms, as long as the combination meets the financial requirements of ensuring the availability of full closure costs at the necessary times. (40 C.F.R. § 264.143(a)).

A new mechanism also may be used to cover several facilities, as long as the total amount of funds available is equal to the aggregate current closure costs of the various facilities. (40 C.F.R. § 264.143(h).)

    5.   Liability Coverage

    (a) Applicability

All active treatment, storage and disposal facilities must have liability coverage for sudden accidental occurrences of at least $1 million per incident and $2 million as an annual aggregate, exclusive of legal costs. In addition, landfills, surface impoundments, and land treatment facilities must have and maintain non-sudden accident liability coverage of at least $3 million per incident and $6 million as an annual aggregate, exclusive of legal costs. (40 C.F.R. § 264.147.)

These requirements became effective at different times depending on the size of the owner or operator. Owners or operators with total revenues, from all lines of business, in excess of $10 million were subject to the requirement as of January 16, 1983. Those with between $5 million and $10 million in revenues were subject to the requirement as of January 16, 1984, and all others as of January 16, 1985.

(b) <u>Demonstration of Coverage</u>

Coverage may be shown either by an insurance policy worded according to a form in 40 C.F.R. § 264.151(i) and issued by a licensed insurance broker, or by the owner or operator passing a financial test identical to the financial test described earlier (pp. 193-94). (40 C.F.R. § 264.147 (f).) However, no corporate parent guarantees are permitted. An owner or operator may also combine these methods.

(c) <u>Variances or Adjustments</u>

An owner or operator may petition the Regional Administrator for a downward adjustment of liability coverage requirements, as part of a permit modification request. The request must demonstrate that the current requirements are not consistent with the degree and duration of the risk involved in the facility.

The Regional Administrator may also require more liability coverage than otherwise required, where it is deemed necessary to protect human health and the environment. Such adjustment is to be based on an assessment of the degree and duration of the risk associated with the facility. (40 C.F.R. § 264.147(c).)

6. <u>Leak Detection System</u>

The 1984 RCRA Amendments require that new landfill units, surface impoundment units, waste piles, underground tanks, and land units for hazardous waste storage, treatment, or disposal utilize approved leak detection systems. (1984 RCRA Amendments § 202, amending RCRA § 3004.) EPA must promulgate standards for such systems by May 8, 1987. The requirements will apply to all units on which construction begins after that date. The standards must provide for a system capable of detecting leaks of hazardous constituents at the earliest practicable time.

7. Liner and Leachate Collection Requirements

The 1984 RCRA Amendments require that all new landfills and surface impoundments, as well as replacement units and lateral expansions of existing units, have two or more liners and a leachate collection system between the liners. (1984 RCRA Amendments § 202, amending RCRA § 3004.) Landfills must also have a leachate collection system above the liners. These requirements apply to all facilities submitting Part B permit applications after November 8, 1984. Existing permitted facilities are exempt.

EPA must issue regulations or guidance documents implementing these requirements by November 8, 1986. The standards that apply until that guidance is developed are described at pp. 202-03 below.

EPA may waive the double liner and leachate collection system requirements if the owner or operator of a facility successfully demonstrates that alternative design and operating practices, together with location characteristics, will provide equivalent protection from migration of any hazardous constituents into ground or surface waters. EPA also may waive the double liner requirement for a monofill containing only hazardous wastes from foundry furnace emission controls or metal casting molding sand, if certain conditions are met.

CHAPTER XVI

ADDITIONAL REQUIREMENTS FOR
SPECIFIC PERMITTED FACILITIES

In addition to the foregoing general requirements, other substantive standards apply to specific permitted facilities and types of equipment.

A. Containers

    1. Applicability

The RCRA regulations define containers as any portable devices used to treat, store, dispose of, transport, or otherwise handle material. (40 C.F.R. § 260.10).

    2. Operating Requirements

Containers of hazardous wastes must be replaced if not in good condition, and the container material must be compatible with the wastes stored. Containers must be closed during storage, handled carefully to avoid leaks, and inspected weekly for deterioration. (40 C.F.R. §§ 264.171-.174, 264.177.) The current regulations require that containers holding ignitable or reactive wastes be located at least 50 feet from the facility's property line (40 C.F.R. § 264.176), but EPA has proposed to amend this requirement to account for the effect of protective walls or construction techniques. (49 Fed. Reg. 23290 (June 5, 1984).)

3. Closure

During closure, hazardous wastes and hazardous
waste residues must be removed from a container storage
facility or from that part of the facility being closed.
By removing such wastes or residues, the owner or operator
of the facility becomes a generator of hazardous wastes and
must manage them according to 40 C.F.R. Part 262. See
Chapter VII for those requirements.

B. Tanks

1. Applicability

A RCRA-regulated tank is defined as a stationary
device constructed primarily of non-earthen materials (e.g.,
wood, concrete, steel, or plastic) designed to hold hazardous waste. (40 C.F.R. § 260.10.) RCRA standards have not
yet been promulgated for underground tanks holding hazardous
waste that cannot be entered for inspection, but these regulations are mandated by Section 207 of the 1984 RCRA Amendments (amending RCRA § 3004(w)) and are expected in the fall
of 1985. Standards for underground tanks holding non-RCRA
hazardous materials will be developed under the new "LUST"
program, described in Chapter XVIII.

2. Operating Requirements

Hazardous waste placed in tanks must be compatible
with tank materials and capacity. (40 C.F.R. §§ 264.192,
264.199.) Overflow must be avoided by means of sufficient

freeboard or a containment structure, and a continuously fed tank must be equipped with discharge control equipment (e.g., waste feed cutoff system or by-pass system). (40 C.F.R. § 264.192.)

Tank discharge control systems, monitoring equipment, and waste levels must be inspected daily, and tank construction materials and containment structures weekly. The tank must be entered for inspection at intervals justified by its contents and expected corrosion. Any deterioration or malfunction must be remedied. (40 C.F.R. § 264.194.)

3. Closure

All hazardous waste and hazardous waste residues must be removed from tanks, discharge control equipment, and confinement structures at closure. (40 C.F.R. § 264.197.)

C. Surface Impoundments

1. Applicability

The RCRA regulations consider any natural topographic depression, man-made excavation, or impoundment composed primarily of earthen dikes (e.g., holding, storage, settling, or aeration pits, ponds, and lagoons) to be a surface impoundment. (40 C.F.R. § 260.10.)

2. Operating Requirements

Impoundment overtopping must be prevented, and dikes must be designed and maintained to preserve structural integrity. (40 C.F.R. § 264.221.) This structural integrity must be certified by a qualified engineer before a permit will issue. (40 C.F.R. § 264.226.) Adverse reactions from reactive, ignitable, or incompatible wastes must be avoided. (40 C.F.R. §§ 264.229, 264.230.)

All portions of the surface impoundment must be inspected during construction and installation. Weekly inspections are required subsequently to detect leaks and deterioration. (40 C.F.R. § 264.226.)

3. Liners and Leachate Collection Systems

New surface impoundments and replacements of or expansions to existing surface impoundments must have double liners and a leachate collection system between the liners. The upper liner must prevent migration of constituents into the liner through the post-closure period (i.e., the liner must be synthetic), and the lower liner must prevent migration of constituents through the liner for the same period. The lower liner requirement will be satisfied by a three-foot thick layer of recompacted clay with a permeability of less than 1×10^{-7} centimeters per second. (1984 RCRA Amendments § 202, amending RCRA § 3004, to be codified in the regulations at 40 C.F.R. § 264.221(c).) These requirements may be waived if the owner or operator can demonstrate that alternative design and operating practices and location characteristics will prevent migration of hazardous constituents into groundwater. A limited exemption is also provided for foundry monofills.

All liners must have appropriate chemical properties and sufficient strength and thickness to prevent liner failure. Liners must be placed on a foundation that provides sufficient support, and the liner must cover all surrounding earth likely to come into contact with the waste. (40 C.F.R. § 221(a).)

4. Emergency Repairs

A new or existing surface impoundment must be removed from service if its dikes leak or its liquid level suddenly drops. If the leak cannot be repaired by other means, the impoundment must be emptied. A repaired impoundment must be certified by a qualified engineer before service is resumed. (40 C.F.R. § 264.227.) If the impoundment is closed rather than repaired, normal closure procedures must be followed.

5. Closure and Post-Closure

At closure, treatment and storage surface impoundments must be decontaminated or have all wastes removed. If attempts to remove all contaminants from an impoundment fail, it must be closed as a disposal facility and will be subject to closure and post-closure obligations. The wastes in the impoundment must be stabilized to a bearing capacity sufficient to support a final cover. During the post-closure period, the cover must be maintained, groundwater monitoring (and response, if necessary) must continue, and run-on and run-off must be prevented. (40 C.F.R. § 264.228.)

D. Wastes Piles

1. Applicability

Waste piles are temporary accumulations of materials that must be managed in accordance with 40 C.F.R. Part 264, Subpart L. Waste permanently disposed of in a pile must be managed as a landfill under Subpart N. (40 C.F.R. § 264.250.)

2. Operating Requirements

New waste piles must contain leachate collection and removal systems operated to keep leachate depth under one foot. This requirement may be waived if the owner or operator demonstrates that design and operating practices and location will assure that no wastes will migrate into the environment. A waste pile must have a run-on control system, a run-off system, and particulate dispersal controls. (40 C.F.R. § 264.251.)

Waste pile liners must be inspected during and after installation, and the pile thereafter must be inspected weekly and after storms for proper operation. (40 C.F.R. § 264.254.)

3. Liners

New waste piles must have liners designed to prevent migration of wastes during the unit's active life (including the closure period). The liner may be clay and is expected to be removed at closure. The liner must have appropriate chemical properties and sufficient strength and thickness to prevent liner failure. The liner's foundation must provide sufficient support, and the liner must cover all surrounding earth likely to come in contact with the waste. (40 C.F.R. § 264.251(a).)

4. Enclosed Piles

Piles located inside a protective structure need not comply with the general waste pile design and operating requirements or with the groundwater monitoring and response requirements if they (a) receive no free liquids, (b) are protected from run-on, (c) disperse no particulates into the air, and (d) generate no leachate through decomposition or other reactions. (40 C.F.R. § 264.250(c).)

5. Closure and Post-Closure

At closure, all contaminated waste, system components, subsoil, and equipment must be removed or decontaminated. If this effort fails, the waste pile must be closed as a landfill. (40 C.F.R. § 264.258.)

E. Land Treatment Units

1. Applicability

Facilities at which hazardous waste is applied onto or incorporated into the soil surface are known as land treatment facilities. (40 C.F.R. § 260.10.)

2.   Design and Operating Requirements

New and existing land treatment units must be designed to ensure that hazardous wastes placed in the treatment zone are completely degraded, transformed, or immobilized. The details of this treatment program must be specified in the applicant's permit. (40 C.F.R. §§ 264.271, 264.273.)

Before treatment may begin, the owner or operator must demonstrate that hazardous waste constitutents in the treatment zone will be completely degraded, transformed, or immobilized by using field tests, laboratory analyses, available data, or operating data. If the required information is not available at the time of permit application, the owner or operator may apply for a two-phase permit that authorizes (a) a demonstration program, and (b) a final permit. (40 C.F.R. § 264.272.)

Food-chain crops may be grown in a land treatment unit only if the owner or operator can demonstrate that the hazardous waste constituents in the treatment zone will not be transferred into the food crop. Wastes containing cadmium are subject to additional requirements. (40 C.F.R. § 264.276.)

As with other hazardous waste facilities, run-on, run-off, and wind dispersal must be controlled. (40 C.F.R. § 264.273).

3. Unsaturated Zone Monitoring

The success of a treatment program must be monitored by soil core and soil pore liquid monitoring of either
(a) the Appendix VIII constituents reasonably expected at
the facility, or (b) principal hazardous constituents that
represent the most difficult constituents to be treated at
the facility. Soil pore monitoring is designed to detect
fast-moving, highly soluble constituents, and soil core monitoring to detect slow-moving constituents such as heavy
metals. Samples must be analyzed according to groundwater
monitoring program requirements (see pp. 177-80). If a
problem is detected, procedures expected to assure that
wastes will be completely degraded, transformed, or immobilized must be filed within 90 days. (40 C.F.R. § 264.278.)

4. Closure and Post-Closure

During the closure period, all operations necessary
to maximize degradation, transformation, or immobilization
of wastes must continue, and control systems must be maintained. Soil pore liquid monitoring of fast-moving constituents may be terminated 90 days after the last application
of waste, but soil core monitoring of slower-moving constituents must continue. These activities continue through the
post-closure period unless the owner or operator can
demonstrate that the soil in the treatment zone is no more
contaminated than background soil levels. If the owner can

make such a demonstration and in addition prove that no hazardous constituents have migrated beyond the treatment zone during the facility's active life, groundwater monitoring may cease. (40 C.F.R. § 264.280.)

F. Landfills

    1.   Applicability

       The term "landfill" is used as a catch-all for a facility at which waste is placed on or in the land and that is not a land treatment unit, surface impoundment, or injection well. (40 C.F.R. § 260.10.)

    2.   Operating Requirements

       The design and operating requirements for landfills are similar to those described above for surface impoundments. The double liner and leachate collection system requirements established by the 1984 RCRA Amendments, described above at pp. 202-03 for surface impoundments, apply equally to landfills. (40 C.F.R. § 264.301(a).) Landfills, again like the surface impoundments (see pp. 203-04), must have run-on, run-off, and wind dispersal controls, must conduct inspections during construction and thereafter, and must install a closure cap and conduct post-closure care (40 C.F.R. §§ 264.301, 264.310.)

3.   Special Requirements for Liquids and Containers

Under the 1984 RCRA Amendments, placement of bulk
or non-containerized liquid wastes in any landfill is prohibited as of May 8, 1985. (1984 RCRA Amendments § 201,
amending RCRA § 3004, to be codified in the regulations at
40 C.F.R. § 264.314.)

The 1984 Amendments also prohibit the placement of
nonhazardous liquid wastes in a landfill unless the owner or
operator of the landfill can demonstrate to EPA that (a)
the only reasonably available alternative to placement of
the waste in the landfill is placement in another landfill
or unlined surface impoundment that contains, or that may
reasonably be anticipated to contain, hazardous waste, and
(b) placement of the waste in the landfill will not present
a risk of contamination of any underground source of
drinking water.

Containers placed in landfills may not contain free
liquids unless the containers (1) are very small, (2) hold
free liquids that are solidified or mixed with absorbent, or
(3) are batteries, capacitors, or lab packs. (40 C.F.R.
§ 264.314.) Moreover, containers themselves may not be
landfilled unless they are (1) very small, (2) at least 90
percent full, or (3) crushed, shredded, or similarly reduced
in volume to the maximum extent possible. (40 C.F.R.
§ 264.315.)

By February 8, 1986, EPA must promulgate final regulations that minimize the presence of free liquids in containerized hazardous waste disposed in landfills. These regulations must prohibit the disposal in landfills of liquids that have been absorbed in materials that biodegrade or that release liquids when compressed, as might occur during routine landfill operations. (1984 RCRA Amendments § 201, amending RCRA § 3004.)

G. Additional Requirements for Incinerators

1. Applicability

EPA distinguishes on the basis of design criteria among regulated "incinerators," on the one hand, and "boilers" and "industrial furnaces," which temporarily are excluded from regulation. An "incinerator" is defined as any enclosed device using controlled flame combustion that neither meets the criteria for classification as a boiler nor is listed as an industrial furnace. (50 Fed. Reg. at 661, amending 40 C.F.R. § 260.10.)

2. Trial Burn

In order to demonstrate ability to comply with the incinerator regulations, a facility first must undergo a trial burn to test the contents of the waste and the efficiency of incineration. (40 C.F.R. § 270.62(b).)

3. Performance Standard

An incinerator must be designed, constructed, and
maintained to achieve a destruction and removal efficiency
("DRE") of 99.99 percent for each principal organic hazardous constituent ("POHC") designated in the facility permit.
(40 C.F.R. § 264.343.) The POHCs, selected from Part 261
Appendix VIII constituents (see Appendix C), are selected
by the permit writer as representative of the most difficult
wastes to incinerate at the particular facility. (40 C.F.R.
§ 264.342.)

4. Operating Requirements

The permit must specify which wastes may be burned
and the operating conditions under which they may be burned,
including carbon monoxide level, wastefeed rate, combustion
temperature, air-feed rate, allowable variations in
operating procedures, and control of fugitive emissions. In
addition, the incinerator must be operated with a system to
cut off waste feed automatically when operating conditions
deviate from established limits. (40 C.F.R. § 264.345.)

5. Monitoring and Inspections

The incinerator must be monitored to guarantee that
its operating requirements are being satisfied and must be
visually inspected at least daily for leaks, spills, fugitive emissions, and signs of tampering. The emergency waste
feed cutoff system must be tested weekly unless the Regional

Administrator approves less frequent inspection. Results of this monitoring must be placed in the operating log of the facility. (40 C.F.R. § 264.347.)

6.   Exemption

Waste that is hazardous only because of ignitability, corrosivity, or reactivity and that (i) does not contain any constituent listed in Appendix VIII to 40 C.F.R. Part 261 (set forth in Appendix D) and (ii) in the case of reactive waste, will not be burned when other hazardous wastes are present in the combustion zone, may be exempted from all incinerator requirements except waste analysis and closure requirements. (40 C.F.R. § 264.340.)

7.   Closure

At closure, all hazardous wastes must be removed from the incinerator site. (40 C.F.R. § 264.351.)

8.   Mobile Incinerators

Mobile incinerators are governed by EPA's general incinerator regulations. The Agency apparently has no plans to promulgate special rules for mobile units. However, the power to approve permits for mobile incinerators has been transferred from EPA's Regional Administrators to Headquarters. Thus, it is no longer necessary for the owner or operator of the incinerator to obtain approval from every region in which he would like to operate.

9. Ocean Incineration

EPA has proposed performance and operating standards for incinerator ships that burn hazardous wastes. (See 50 Fed. Reg. 8222 (Feb. 28, 1985).) The proposed regulations would impose standards equivalent to those governing land-based incinerators, unless the Convention on the Prevention of Marine Pollution by Dumping of Wastes and Other Matters (an international agreement implemented by the United States under the Marine Mammal Protection, Research and Sanctuaries Act) requires more stringent standards.

H. New and Innovative Treatment Technologies

The 1984 RCRA Amendments authorize EPA to issue special research, development, and demonstration permits for innovative and experimental technologies or processes. The purpose of this new provision is to encourage development of new hazardous waste treatment technologies. EPA may issue such permits without promulgating regulations establishing standards for the permits, and without regard to the substantive standards otherwise applicable to permitted or interim status facilities. (1984 RCRA Amendments § 214, amending RCRA § 3005, to be codified in the regulations at 40 C.F.R. § 270.65.) Permits issued under this new provision may provide for facility operation for one year, with a maximum renewal period of up to three years.

These permits will include terms and conditions necessary to protect human health and the environment, including, as necessary, standards in the following areas: monitoring, operations, insurance or bonding, financial responsibility, closure, remedial action, testing, and providing information requested by EPA.

PART 7: OTHER ENVIRONMENTAL OBLIGATIONS OF FACILITY
OWNERS AND OPERATORS

Beyond the RCRA hazardous waste management obligations imposed on facility owners and operators, as described
in Parts 5 and 6 of this Handbook, owners and operators of
all manufacturing, production, and operating facilities,
whether they are RCRA facilities or not, have additional
environmental obligations. For example, under Superfund,
owners and operators of facilities have liability and
reporting obligations in connection with the release of any
hazardous substance from the facility. In addition, under
the 1984 RCRA Amendments, owners and operators of facilities
that contain underground storage tanks will have notification, tank performance, and corrective action obligations
designed to prevent releases of regulated substances
(including most hazardous substances and petroleum products)
into the environment. Chapter XVII describes these additional Superfund obligations, and Chapter XVIII describes
the federal obligations regarding underground storage tanks.

CHAPTER XVII

FACILITY OWNERS' AND OPERATORS' SUPERFUND OBLIGATIONS

The Superfund obligations of owners and operators
of any facility that contains a hazardous substance are
similar to those of generators and transporters of hazardous
substances. This chapter briefly describes these obligations.

A. Responsibility for Cleanup

Like generators and transporters, facility owners
and operators may be held responsible under Superfund for
the costs of cleaning up spills and other releases or
threatened releases of hazardous substances from facilities.
A "facility" under Superfund includes any "site or area" at
which a hazardous substance has come to be located, and is
not limited to hazardous waste management or disposal facilities. (CERCLA § 101(9).) The owner's and operator's
liabilities are similar to the generator's liabilities,
described above in Chapter VII, and generally all generators
and transporters who use a site can be expected to be joined
with the owners and operators of the site in Superfund litigation.

It should be noted that Superfund explicitly
recognizes the potential responsibility of several sets of
owners and operators: those who own or operate a facility

at the time the release occurs; those who, at the time of hazardous waste disposal, owned or operated the facility; and, for an abandoned facility, anyone who owned, operated, or otherwise controlled activities at the facility immediately prior to the abandonment. (CERCLA § 107(a), 101(20).) The reader is referred to pp. 98-104 for a more complete discussion of those potential liabilities.

Superfund contains special provisions relating to the liability of the owner or operator of a hazardous waste disposal facility which has received a permit under Subtitle C of RCRA. All liability for these facilities under Superfund or otherwise is transferred to and assumed by a Post-closure Liability Trust Fund, in cases where the requirements of Subtitle C have been complied with, the facility closed, and the facility and surrounding area monitored up to five years to determine that there is no substantial likelihood of risk to public health or welfare. (CERCLA § 107(k).) However, because the statute does not indicate the role of the Fund where, for example, ground-water contamination is detected during the monitoring period, the extent to which the Fund will assume liability remains unclear.

B. Reporting Requirements

Any person in charge of a facility at which a spill or other release occurs must comply with the same reporting requirements applicable to hazardous waste generators and transporters. Specifically, see pp. 105-06. If a reportable quantity of a hazardous substance is released from the facility, the National Response Center (telephone: (800) 424-8802) and, in the case of serious spills that may cause injury, the local populace must be notified.

Owners and operators of hazardous waste facilites also were subject to the requirement that such facilities be reported to EPA by June 1981. This obligation is described more fully at p. 105.

CHAPTER XVIII

UNDERGROUND STORAGE TANKS

The 1984 RCRA Amendments established a comprehensive
new regulatory program to prevent leaks from underground
storage tanks (commonly referred to as the "LUST program").
(1984 RCRA Amendments § 601, adding RCRA §§ 9001-10.) In
response to reports that leakage from underground tanks had
become a major source of groundwater contamination (and that
contamination at over 50 Superfund sites had been caused, at
least in part, by leaking underground storage tanks),
Congress directed EPA to develop a new federal regulatory
scheme with three principal features: (1) notification to
the state by tank owners of the existence of tanks; (2)
compliance with standards for the detection, prevention, and
correction of releases from tanks; and (3) compliance with
tank performance standards. The program is expected to
cover well over two million tanks, and will be administered
by EPA or by states that adopt a program no less stringent
than the federal program.

The federal LUST program will be phased in over the
next several years as the statutory requirements of Section
601 of the 1984 RCRA Amendments are implemented through
regulations, the majority of which EPA plans to propose in
1986. The following chapter describes the broad regulatory
scheme mandated by the statute.

A. Regulated Underground Tanks

A tank will be subject to regulation if it meets two criteria: (1) its volume, including the volume of all underground pipes connected to it, is 10 percent or more beneath the surface of the ground; and (2) it contains a "regulated substance." (1984 RCRA Amendments § 601, adding RCRA § 9001(1).) Under this definition, a tank that ordinarily would be considered an above ground tank will be regulated if connecting underground pipes contain 10 percent of the volume of the tank. All such "underground tanks" are subject to LUST program requirements if they contain "regulated substances," which include liquid petroleum products and hazardous substances as defined under Superfund (see the definition of hazardous substance above in Chapter V) -- except for those substances already regulated as hazardous wastes under RCRA. (See Chapter IV.)

The following types of tanks (and their associated piping) will be exempt from regulation:

(1) septic tanks;

(2) storage tanks located above the floor in an underground area such as a basement or tunnel;

(3) small (1100 gallons or less) farm or residential tanks used for storing motor fuel for noncommercial purposes;

(4) oil or gas production liquid traps and associated gathering lines;

(5) flow-through process tanks;

(6) pipelines that already are regulated under
federal or state laws;

(7) surface impoundments;

(8) storm water or waste water collection
systems; and

(9) tanks storing heating oil for consumption on
the premises.

Until the LUST program regulations are promulgated, it is
unclear how broadly these exemptions will be defined. Key
exemptions for industry will be those for flow-through process tanks and for tanks storing heating oil used on the
premises.

B. Interim Prohibition

          Until the full regulatory LUST program takes effect,
Congress established an interim standard that took effect
automatically on May 8, 1985. (1984 RCRA Amendments § 601,
adding RCRA § 9003(g).) This so-called "interim prohibition"
is aimed primarily at preventing the installation of bare
steel tanks, but the statutory language implementing this
goal is broader. Each new underground storage tank
installed after May 8, 1985, and used to store regulated
substances:

(1) must prevent releases due to corrosion or structural failure for the operational life of the tank;

(2) ·must be cathodically protected against corrosion, constructed of noncorrosive material, steel-clad with a noncorrosive material, or designed in a manner to prevent any release of a stored substance; and

(3) must be constructed or lined with a material that is compatible with the substances to be stored. A tank will be exempt from the anticorrosion requirements of these interim standards only if the resistivity of the surrounding soil is at least 12,000 ohm/cm, which reduces the likelihood of corrosion (this has been called the "Arizona exemption"). A number of issues raised by the interim prohibition (e.g., at what point is a tank "installed," and what is the effect of the standard on installation and repair of piping) should be resolved when EPA issues guidance on this standard.

C. Tank Notification

The LUST program establishes notification requirements designed to assure that states become aware of the regulated underground tanks in their jurisdiction. (1984 RCRA Amendments § 601, adding RCRA § 9002.) Under RCRA § 9002 owners of regulated underground storage tanks currently in use must provide an agency designated by the state with notification of the tank's existence, including the following information, by May 8, 1986:

(1) the age of the tank;

(2) the type and size of the tank;

(3) the location of the tank; and

(4) the uses of the tank.

Any owner who brings a new tank into operation after May 8, 1986, must provide this information within 30 days.

Owners of tanks taken out of operation after January 1, 1974, are responsible also for notification, unless the owner knows that the tank was subsequently removed from the ground. This duty applies even if the tank has been sold. For tanks taken out of operation, notification must include:

(1) the date the tank was taken out of operation;

(2) the age of the tank when taken out of operation;

(3) the size and type of tank;

(4) the location of the tank; and

(5) the type and quantity of substances left stored in the tank when the tank was taken out of operation.

Owners of tanks taken out of operation on or before January 1, 1974, are exempt from any notification obligation. In addition, owners who have provided notice about a tank under

CERCLA § 103(c) (see pp. 105-06) are exempt from notification requirements.

By May 8, 1985, each state was required to designate an agency to receive notification forms from tank owners. On May 28, 1985, EPA proposed a notification form that essentially codified the information required by statute. EPA intends that its form, the final version of which is to be published by November 8, 1985, be used nationwide, but states will be allowed to substitute their own forms if those forms contain this minimum level of information.

Beginning one month after EPA prescribes the final form of notice, suppliers of regulated substances must inform the tank owners and operators whom they supply of the notification requirements. This responsibility will last for a period of 18 months. (1984 RCRA Amendments § 601, adding RCRA § 9002(a)(2)(B)(5).) In addition, when new tank performance standards (discussed below) are issued, tank sellers must inform any purchaser of a new tank of the notification requirements.

D. Basic Operating Standards for All Underground Storage Tanks

The 1984 RCRA Amendments direct EPA to promulgate regulations establishing operating standards for all underground storage tanks. At a minimum, these regulations must require (1) a leak detection system, either an inventory

control system together with tank testing or a comparable
method for identifying releases from tanks into the environment; (2) recordkeeping by owners and operators of monitoring or leak detection results; (3) reporting of tank
releases; (4) corrective action (and reporting of such
action) when releases are detected; and (5) provision for
the closure of tanks to prevent future releases of regulated
substances into the environment. (1984 RCRA Amendments
§ 601, adding RCRA § 9003(c).)

In drafting these regulations, EPA may distinguish
between types, classes, and ages of underground storage
tanks. Among the factors to be considered in drawing such
distinctions are: location, size, age, and uses of tanks;
soil and climate conditions; maintenance history; current
industry recommended practices and national consensus codes;
hydrogeology and water table; technical capability of owners
and operators; and the quantity of regulated substances
handled and the compatibility of these regulated substances
with the materials from which the tank is fabricated. The
regulations are scheduled to take effect by May 8, 1987, for
tanks containing petroleum products, and by November 8,
1988, for tanks containing other regulated substances.
(1984 RCRA Amendments § 601, adding RCRA §§ 9003(b), (f).)

In the spring of 1985, EPA released an internal
working document outlining the Agency's plans for implementing

the LUST program. In this document, EPA estimated that general performance standards for tank operation would be proposed in February or March 1986.

E. New Tank Performance Standards

In addition to the operating requirements described above, EPA must develop performance standards for new tanks, including standards for design, construction, installation, release detection, and compatibility. The 1984 RCRA Amendments require that these standards take effect May 7, 1987, for tanks containing petroleum products, and no later than November 8, 1987, for tanks containing other regulated substances. (1984 RCRA Amendments § 601, adding RCRA § 9003(c).) EPA has announced its intention to propose these standards along with the general tank operating standards in February or March 1986.

F. State Programs

Like the rest of the RCRA program, the LUST program is intended to be administered primarily by the states. The minimum tank standards will be federal, and the federal government will administer the program if a state does not take action. However, states are encouraged to administer the LUST program, and a state program will be effective in lieu of the federal program if the state adopts standards at least as stringent as the federal standards and provides for adequate enforcement of the program. (1984 RCRA Amendments § 601, adding RCRA § 9004.) In fact, most states have at least minimal standards for underground tanks, and several states have preceded the federal government in proposing comprehensive design and operating standards for tanks.

States that seek to administer the federal LUST program must promulgate regulations at least as stringent as the minimum federal standards in the following areas:

(1) leak detection;

(2) recordkeeping;

(3) corrective action;

(4) release and corrective action reporting;

(5) tank closure;

(6) financial responsibility for taking corrective action and compensating third parties for bodily injury and property damage;

(7) new tank performance standards; and

(8) tank notification.

No state program may be submitted to EPA for approval after May 8, 1987.

Once approved, the state program operates in lieu of the federal program, and EPA must notify the state if it plans any enforcement action within the state. If EPA finds, after public hearing, that a state program has not been effectively administered, EPA must give notice to the state and if appropriate action is not taken, EPA may withdraw approval of the state program. (1984 RCRA Amendments § 601, adding RCRA § 9006(a)(2), (e).)

G. Financial Responsibility Requirements

As discussed above, an authorized state LUST program must include regulations assuring the financial responsibility of tank owners. RCRA allows, but does not require, EPA to promulgate federal standards for these regulations. (1984 RCRA Amendments § 601, adding RCRA § 9003(d).) The statute authorizes use of insurance, guarantees, surety bonds, letters of credit, or self-insurance as proof of financial responsibility.

H. Enforcement

RCRA authorizes inspections of underground storage tanks by EPA or by officials of states with approved programs. Tank owners and operators must allow inspectors to gain access to the premises, to conduct sampling or testing, and to review records on the tank. EPA may also require tank owners or operators to conduct monitoring or testing. These inspections are to be "commenced and completed with reasonable promptness." Confidentiality may be requested for reports, records, or other information. (1984 RCRA Amendments § 601, adding RCRA § 9005.)

The statutes also authorizes EPA to issue administrative compliance orders or to file a civil action in a
U.S. district court for relief, including injunctive relief,
for violation of LUST program standards. If a state has an
approved state program to administer the LUST program, EPA
must give notice to the state prior to issuing an order or
commencing a civil action. Subjects of compliance orders
may request a public hearing within 30 days of the issuance
of the order. Violations of the requirements under the
program carry a maximum civil penalty of $10,000 per
tank per day. Violations of compliance orders may result in
civil penalties of up to $25,000 per day for each day of
continued noncompliance. (1984 RCRA Amendments § 601,
adding RCRA § 9006.)

Because there are millions of underground storage
tanks in the United States, a vast number of previously
unregulated tank owners and operators will become subject to
extensive reporting obligations, performance standards, and
regulatory oversight. This may put a considerable strain on
the capability of federal and state agencies to administer
and enforce these requirements.

PART 8: ENFORCEMENT

The RCRA statute arms EPA with a number of enforcement alternatives. Violations of RCRA regulations are punishable by administrative orders and judicial civil actions and, for certain knowing violators, by criminal prosecutions. The statute also authorizes suits by private citizens in certain circumstances. In contrast, Superfund primarily establishes principles of liability for cleanup and imposes the costs thereof on responsible parties. Chapters XIX and XX discuss the enforcement of these federal statutory and regulatory obligations.

The reader should be aware, however, that enforcement actions are generally not limited to charges of violating federal law. Instead, plaintiffs usually join with the federal counts various additional charges of violations of statutes and non-statutory "common law" theories of liability. The final chapter, therefore explores questions of hazardous waste generators', transporters', and facility owners' and operators' liability under these additional bases for liability for environmental harm. It concludes with a short discussion of the issues raised in connection with liability insurance for environmental harm.

CHAPTER XIX

RCRA ENFORCEMENT

Failure to comply with the RCRA hazardous waste
management obligations described in the previous chapters
subjects generators, transporters, and owners and operators
of hazardous waste management facilities to a range of
potential administrative penalties and judicial enforcement
actions. In addition, RCRA grants EPA broad authority to
inspect facilities and to order facility owners and operators to monitor, test, and take corrective action at their
sites. EPA also may take action under RCRA against imminent
hazards.

This chapter reviews the options available to EPA
for enforcement of RCRA hazardous waste management obligations and the rights of citizens to bring, or participate
in, enforcement actions. State RCRA programs authorized by
EPA must provide for adequate enforcement through comparable
mechanisms. Enforcement actions against tank owners and
operators under the underground storage tank program were
described in Chapter XVIII.

A. Facility Inspections

The 1984 RCRA Amendments create a new program of mandatory inspections of hazardous waste treatment storage and

disposal facilities. Beginning November 8, 1985, every permitted facility must be inspected at least once every two
years by EPA or the authorized state. The law directs EPA
to promulgate regulations governing the minimum frequency
and manner of such inspections, including the manner in
which records should be maintained and reports filed. EPA
may create different requirements for different categories
of facilities commensurate with the risks posed by each
category.

In addition, the RCRA Amendments direct EPA to
report to Congress on the potential for a private inspection
program to supplement federal and state inspections.

B. Administrative Orders

1. Compliance Orders

EPA may enforce RCRA regulations against generators, transporters, and facility owners and operators by
issuing an order requiring compliance immediately or within
a specified period. Violation of a compliance order may
result in civil penalties of up to $25,000 per day of non-
compliance, and suspension or revocation of any permits
issued to the violator.

Persons named in the compliance order are entitled
upon request to a hearing before EPA. This is the forum
provided for challenging assessed penalties. Failure to
request a hearing may be deemed a waiver of rights.

Procedural rules governing such hearings are set forth at 40 C.F.R. Part 22.

Penalties assessed under a compliance order must take into account the seriousness of the violation and any good faith efforts to comply with the applicable requirements. (RCRA § 3008.) EPA has implemented this directive in its RCRA Civil Penalty Policy (May 8, 1984). The penalty policy provides that the penalty is calculated by: (1) determining a "gravity-based" penalty for a particular violation (taking into account the potential for harm and the extent of deviation from a statutory or regulatory requirement; (2) calculating the amount of economic benefit of noncompliance where appropriate; and (3) adjusting the penalty for special circumstances, i.e., good faith efforts to comply, degree of willfulness or negligence, history of noncompliance, ability to pay or other unique factors.

2. Corrective Action

The 1984 RCRA Amendments authorize EPA to issue an administrative order requiring corrective action for releases of hazardous waste from interim status facilities. Prior to that legislation, EPA required corrective action only in the context of the permit program. The Agency's position was that it was infeasible to seek corrective action in any other fashion because the interim status rules are self-implementing. This new provision gives EPA the power to deal directly with an ongoing environmental problem caused by an interim status facility without awaiting issuance of a final permit. EPA may suspend or revoke a facility's interim status and assess civil penalties of up to $25,000 per day for noncompliance with a cleanup order. (1984 RCRA Amendments § 233, amending RCRA § 3008.)

3. Monitoring, Analysis, and Testing

EPA may order an owner or operator of a current or former waste management site, or the previous owner or operator, to conduct such monitoring, testing, analysis and reporting as EPA may deem reasonable to ascertain the nature and extent of a suspected substantial hazard to human health or the environment. Failure to comply with such an order may subject the recipient to civil penalties of $5,000 per day of violation. (RCRA § 3013.)

4. Imminent Hazards

EPA may issue an administrative order (or bring a civil lawsuit) requiring the taking of such actions as may be required with regard to any site that may present an immi-nent and substantial endangerment to health or the environ-ment. (RCRA § 7003.) Failure to comply with, or violation of, an administrative order may subject the recipient to civil penalties of up to $5,000 per day. Under the 1984 RCRA Amendments, whenever EPA receives information that a site presents an imminent hazard, the Agency must provide immediate notice to the local government and post a notice at the site. (1984 RCRA Amendments § 403, adding RCRA § 7003(c).)

It is noteworthy that this provision authorizes EPA action if a situation "may present" an imminent and substantial danger. The "may present" wording was substituted in 1980 for the previous statutory phrase "is presenting," with the clear congressional expectation that the government's burden of proof in these cases would be eased. Interestingly, the parallel provision of Superfund, enacted at approximately the same time as the 1980 RCRA Amendments, retains the "is presenting" language.

C. Civil Actions

Civil penalties assessed through the various administrative orders described in the previous section are collected, if contested, through a lawsuit brought in federal district court.

In addition to these penalty collection actions (or in conjunction with them), EPA also may bring a civil action in the federal district court for a temporary or permanent injunction, or for civil penalties of up to $25,000 for each day of violation of any RCRA Subtitle C requirement. (RCRA § 3008(a).) If a facility is insolvent or beyond the jurisdiction of the court, EPA may, under a provision of the 1984 Amendments, take direct action against guarantors of financial responsibility. The guarantor may invoke any defenses that would have been available to the owner or operator, and his liability is limited to the amount of his guarantee. (1984 RCRA Amendments § 205, adding RCRA § 3004(t).) In addition, as noted above, EPA may bring a civil lawsuit requiring the taking of such actions as may be necessary with regard to any site that may present an imminent and substantial endangerment to health or the environment. (RCRA § 7003.)

D. Criminal Actions

Unlike most environmental control statutes, RCRA contains several stiff criminal enforcement provisions, providing for substantial fines and multi-year jail terms. The 1984 RCRA Amendments increased these penalties beyond what had been previously authorized. (1984 RCRA Amendments § 232, amending RCRA § 3008(d).) The statute, as amended, currently authorizes penalties and imprisonment for the following knowing violations:

Any Person Who Knowingly:	Penalties and Imprisonment Authorized:
(1) transports or causes to be transported a listed or identified hazardous waste to an unpermitted facility	$50,000 per day, five years
(2) treats, stores or disposes of hazardous waste without a permit or in violation of the permit or any applicable interim status standards	$50,000 per day, five years

Any Person Who Knowingly:	Penalties and Imprisonment Authorized:
(3) omits material information or makes a false material statement or misrepresentation in any application, label, manifest, record, report, permit, or other document filed, maintained, or used for purposes of compliance with the hazardous waste regulations	$50,00 per day, two years
(4) handles any hazardous waste and destroys, alters, or conceals any record required to be maintained	$50,000 per day, two years
(5) transports or causes to be transported any hazardous waste without the required manifest	$50,000 per day two years
(6) exports hazardous waste in violation of the statute	$50,000 per day, two years

It should be emphasized that Congress did not intend that these criminal provisions be invoked for minor technical violations of RCRA requirements. As the Conference Report on the 1980 RCRA Amendments (which significantly toughened the criminal provisions) stated:

> This Section is intended to prevent abuses of the permit system by those who obtain and then knowingly disregard them. It is not aimed at punishing minor or technical variations from permit regulations or conditions if the facility operator is acting responsibility [sic]. The Department of Justice has exercised its prosecutorial discretion responsibly under similar provisions in other statutes and the conferees assume that, in light of the upgrading of the penalties from misdemeanor to felony,

> similar care will be used in decid-
> ing when a particular permit vio-
> lation may warrant criminal prosecu-
> tion under this Act.

H.R. Rep. No. 172, 96th Cong., 1st Sess. 37, <u>reprinted in</u>

1980 U.S. Code Cong. & Ad. News 5036 (emphasis added).

In addition, the 1980 Amendments to RCRA added a

unique crime to the statute known as "knowing endangerment."

This offense may be penalized by fines of up to $1 million,

and imprisonment of fifteen years. As redefined by the 1984

RCRA Amendments, the offense consists of any of the six crim-

inal violations listed above, if committed by a person who

knows at the time that he is placing another person in

imminent danger of death or serious bodily injury. (1984

RCRA Amendments § 232, amending RCRA § 3008(e).) The stat-

ute defines in detail what constitutes "knowing" that

another person is endangered. (RCRA § 3008(f).)

The provision authorizing "knowing endangerment"

prosecutions was drafted in such detail to avoid a misun-

derstanding of the role that Congress intended the provision

to play. As the Conference Report explained:

> The purpose of this new section is to provide
> enhanced felony penalties for certain life-
> threatening conduct. At the same time, <u>the</u>
> <u>new offense is drafted in a way intended to</u>
> <u>assure to the extent possible that persons</u>
> <u>are not prosecuted or convicted unjustly for</u>
> <u>making difficult business judgments where such</u>
> <u>judgments are made without the necessary</u>
> <u>scienter</u> . . . . [T]he endangerment offense
> depends upon a showing that a natural person
> actually knew that his conduct at that time

placed another person in imminent danger of
death or serious bodily injury . . . .
The Department of Justice has expressed its
belief that this provision is necessary to
protect the public from knowing and unjusti-
fied conduct which threatens life or serious
bodily harm. Because no concrete harm need
actually result for a person to be prosecuted
under this section, however, the conferees
as well as responsible members of the business community believe that it is necessary
to make the offense as precise and carefully
drawn as possible. There is also general
recognition that <u>serious criminal charges are
not an appropriate vehicle for second-guessing
the wisdom of judgments that are made on the
basis of what was known at the time</u> where
the person acted without the necessary element of scienter. In this light, the
concept of "reckless endangerment" embodied
in the House amendment has been rejected in
favor of a knowing endangerment provision
that is specifically molded to the activities and risks covered by the Solid Waste
Disposal Act.

H.R. Rep. No. 172, 96th Cong., 1st Sess. 37-39, <u>reprinted in</u>
1980 U.S. Code Cong. & Ad. News 5036-38 (emphasis added).

E. <u>Citizen Suits</u>

The statute authorizes any person to bring a
lawsuit on his own behalf against any other person
(including the United States or any other government in-
strumentality, to the extent permitted by the Eleventh
Amendment) who is alleged to be in violation of any permit,
standard, regulation, condition, requirement, or order under
RCRA. (RCRA § 7002.) A citizen may also sue EPA for
failure to perform any nondiscretionary duty under the statute. In addition, the 1984 RCRA Amendments authorize citizen

suits in cases where any past or present hazardous waste
management practice is alleged to present an imminent and
substantial endangerment to health or the environment.
(1984 RCRA Amendments § 401, amending RCRA § 7002.) A
citizen plaintiff must give notice to EPA, to the state, and
to the prospective defendant 60 days before bringing suit to
enforce a RCRA requirement, or 90 days before bringing an
imminent hazard suit.

Citizen suits are not permitted where EPA or a
state is diligently prosecuting a civil or criminal
action to enforce RCRA. In addition, under the 1984 RCRA
Amendments, citizen imminent hazard suits are barred when
EPA or a state is prosecuting an imminent hazard action
under RCRA or Superfund, and when EPA is proceeding with a
remedial action, or has entered into a consent decree with
the responsible parties under Superfund. The 1984 RCRA
Amendments also prohibit citizen suits with respect to
siting and issuance of permits for hazardous waste facilities. (1984 RCRA Amendments § 401, amending RCRA § 7002.)

The statute grants citizens certain rights to
intervention. As amended in 1984, the statute permits a
person to intervene as a matter of right in any citizen suit
brought to enforce RCRA. A citizen also may intervene in an
imminent hazard suit brought by another citizen when he
claims an interest relating to the subject of the action,

and is so situated that the disposition of the action may, as a practical matter, impair or impede his ability to protect that interest, unless EPA or the state shows that his interest is adequately represented by existing parties. (1984 RCRA Amendments § 401, amending RCRA § 7002.) It should be noted that these provisions supplement, rather than replace, the general rules of intervention under the Federal Rules of Civil Procedure. Under those rules, the citizen seeking to intervene has the burden of proof of showing that his interest is not adequately represented by existing parties.

The 1984 RCRA Amendments also added a new provision for public participation in settlements of RCRA imminent hazard suits. Whenever EPA proposes to settle such a suit, the Agency must give notice and an opportunity for comment on the proposed settlement prior to its entry. The Agency also must offer the opportunity for a public meeting in the affected area. (1984 RCRA Amendments § 401, amending RCRA § 7003.)

CHAPTER XX

SUPERFUND ENFORCEMENT

Superfund authorizes EPA to respond to spills or
other releases or substantial threat of releases of a hazardous substance, or of any pollutant that might imminently and
substantially endanger public health or welfare. EPA
generally first must attempt to secure voluntary cleanup by
responsible parties. If this effort fails, EPA may perform
the cleanup work itself and then seek reimbursement.

Unlike RCRA and most other environmental statutes,
Superfund does not include a typical enforcement provision
guiding the management of wastes or handling of pollutants.
This is a consequence of the fundamental nature of
Superfund, which is to establish rules of liability for
cleanup costs resulting from releases of hazardous substances rather than a complex regulatory scheme to prevent
such releases. Basically, the "penalties" that may arise
out of Superfund are the costs of the litigation and cleanup
that may be imposed on targets of Superfund litigation.
(For additional discussion of Superfund liabilities, see pp.
98-104, and Appendix H.)

However, Superfund does contain one enforcement
provision with penalties. As noted above, if an imminent
and substantial danger to health or the environment exists,

EPA may compel responsible parties to clean up a site by means of a court injunction or an administrative order. Willful violation or refusal to comply with an administrative order can result in fines of up to $5,000 per day and -- unique among the environmental statutes -- punitive damages of up to three times the cost of the government's cleanup.

A Superfund enforcement action typically begins with EPA's issuance of "notice letters" to all known potentially liable parties, informing them of the Agency's intent to compel private cleanup or to undertake governmental cleanup and sue responsible parties for the goverment's costs. EPA's issuance of these notice letters stems from its statutory obligation to determine whether cleanup action will be performed properly by responsible parties before expending Superfund monies. (CERCLA § 104(a)(1).)

Because of high litigation costs and uncertain liability exposure in cases that typically involve numerous parties, fragmentary records, and complex issues of causation and injury, a number of Superfund cases have been settled, rather than litigated. Because all generators, transporters, and owners and operators involved with a Superfund site are potentially liable, settlement negotiations frequently include dozens of parties. However, because of the possibility that responsible parties

may be jointly and severally liable for the costs of Superfund cleanup, a settling party cannot be certain that a
settlement signed by less than all responsible parties will
fully insulate the signers from further liability. Moreover, because the scope of potential remedial action at a
site frequently cannot be determined by the time of settlement, responsible parties cannot rid themselves of the
threat of future liability unless the government provides a
release from all liability.

In response to these issues, a number of mechanisms
have been incorporated into settlements reached to date in
an effort to protect settling parties from further litigation. For example, settling parties in several cases have
obtained the government's promise not to sue non-settling
parties for more than their fair share of costs incurred at
the site. The purpose of such a commitment is to blunt
later claims that litigating (non-settling) defendants might
assert against the settling parties, by eliminating any
argument that the litigating defendants were being asked to
pay more than their fair share. The government also typically provides at least limited releases as to further liability for work covered in a settlement.

In addition to these prior settlement agreements as a reflection of government policy, EPA also has
issued a formal interim Superfund settlement policy which

provides guidance on the Agency's general principles for settling Superfund cases with private parties. EPA's current settlement policy is published at 50 Fed. Reg. 5034 (Feb. 6, 1985) and is reprinted as Appendix J. One important element of the policy is that EPA has backed off its previous requirement that private parties collectively agree to settle for at least 80 percent of the anticipated cleanup costs at a site. The Agency's prior insistence on the 80 percent figure stood in the way of settlement where, for example, generators that accounted for more than 20 percent of the waste at a site refused to settle or were insolvent. In this regard, the Agency also has indicated for the first time that Superfund monies will be used to make up any shortfall when the government settles for less than 100 percent of the cleanup costs and no financially viable parties remain to be sued.

EPA also has indicated its intention to continue to provide settling parties protection against contribution suits from non-settling parties. In addition, the Agency will be more flexible in providing settling parties broad releases from further liability at the site, depending on the anticipated effectiveness of the remedy agreed upon as part of the settlement. In all settlements, however, EPA will insist on "reopener clauses" to be applied in the event that future conditions at the site pose an imminent and substantial danger.

Although EPA's policy reflects a new flexibility toward achieving settlements, the true impact of the policy will not be known until EPA, and especially the EPA Regional offices (which continue to have primary responsibility for initiating Superfund cleanup) apply it in particular cases. Furthermore, despite the attractions of settlement agreements, many Superfund lawsuits have been filed, and many more may be anticipated in the future. Some hazardous waste generators singled out by the government on the basis of weak evidence may choose to litigate their liability and put the government to its proof rather than cut litigation costs by joining in a settlement.

Hazardous waste managers also should be aware that other federal environmental statutes authorize enforcement activities, and claims based upon these statutes often are joined to Superfund claims. The major statutes cited include the Safe Drinking Water Act, the imminent hazard provisions of RCRA, the Toxic Substances Control Act, the Clean Air Act, and the Clean Water Act. EPA published a notice listing these provisions at 47 Fed. Reg. 20664 (May 13, 1982).

CHAPTER XXI

STATE RESPONSIBILITIES, COMMON LAW LIABILITIES, AND LIABILITY INSURANCE ISSUES

The previous chapters of this book have reviewed the obligations imposed on generators, transporters, and facility owners and operators by RCRA and Superfund. To a certain extent, as explained in Chapter II, each of these federal programs gives the states a significant role in the regulatory process. However, the prudent environmental manager must recognize that these federally authorized activities do not necessarily mark the end of state attention to waste management matters. Nor do these programs constitute a complete list of potential legal problems that companies might face as a result of hazardous waste management activity. In this chapter, we briefly review these additional considerations and conclude with a brief discussion of liability insurance issues.

A. State RCRA Programs and Superfund Statutes

As more fully explained in Chapter II, states may obtain "interim" or "final" authorization from the federal government to take over administration of the hazardous waste management program mandated by RCRA. Authorized state programs must be "equivalent to" and "consistent with" the federal program. (RCRA § 3006.) That language, taken alone, might appear to limit the latitude of states to design their

own programs. However, as noted in Chapter II, at pp. 8-9,
RCRA explicitly provides that state programs may be more
stringent than the federal program. (RCRA § 3009.) EPA has
resolved the tension between these potentially contradictory
sections in favor of allowing states to design more
stringent programs. In practical terms, this means that a
state may be authorized to administer its RCRA program even
if the program does not include all of the exceptions and
exclusions from regulation provided in the federal program.
For example, some states have not adopted the so-called small
quantity generator exemption in the federal program, yet
they have obtained interim and final authorization from the
federal government.

A number of states also have passed their own
"Superfund" laws. Some, like New Jersey's and New York's,
impose significant additional tax burdens on chemical manufacturers and waste disposers. (N.J. Spill Compensation &
Control Act, N.J. Stat. Ann. § 58:10-23.11h (West 1982); N.Y.
State Fin. Law § 97-b (McKinney 1982).) These statutes also
may establish standards of liability different from those
set forth in the federal laws. (See N.Y. Envtl. Conserv.
Law § 27-1313(3) and N.Y. Pub. Health Law § 1389-b(3)
(McKinney 1982).) Some states also have developed programs
to control the siting of hazardous waste management facilities, which may have a significant effect on some plant
location decisions.

(See, e.g., Massachusetts Hazardous Waste Facility Siting Regulations, Mass. Admin. Code tit. 990, reprinted at 2 [State Solid Waste -- Land Use] Env't Rep. (BNA) 1206:0581.)

B. Common Law Liabilities

In addition to the statutory and regulatory obligations described earlier in this book, companies also may be subject to certain non-statutory "common law" duties, arising out of the judicial development of principles involving liability for torts. The nature and extent of these obligations is uncertain at present, largely for three reasons.

First, hazardous waste management issues only recently have begun to receive extensive judicial attention. Thus, the development of "common law" in this area is in its infancy.

Second, the increasing degree of direct regulation imposed under RCRA and Superfund raises the possibility that these historic common law obligations may be held by the courts to have been preempted. This conclusion seems possible in light of two 1981 decisions of the Supreme Court. In City of Milwaukee v. Illinois, 451 U.S. 304 (1981), the Court held that the Clean Water Act preempted the federal common law of nuisance as it pertained to water pollution. Two months later, the Court held that the Marine Mammal Protection, Research, and Sanctuaries Act also preempted

the federal common law of nuisance as applied to the pollution of coastal water. (Middlesex County Sewerage Authority
v. National Sea Clammers Association, 453 U.S. 1 (1981).)
Indeed, two federal district courts have held that RCRA and
Superfund together preempt the federal common law of
nuisance in the area of hazardous waste disposal. (City of
Philadelphia v. Stepan Chemical Co., 544 F. Supp. 1135 (E.D.
Pa. 1982); United States v. Price, 523 F. Supp. 1055 (D.N.J.
1981), aff'd, 688 F.2d 204 (3d Cir. 1982).)

Third, the fact that the common law varies from the
federal to state level and from state to state further
complicates "common law" analysis. Even if the common law
is allowed to develop in the courts, it may take differing
paths among varying jurisdictions.

Nonetheless, decisions in this area indicate a
growing trend of judicial activism in using the common law
to redress environmental problems caused by hazardous waste
management practices. It is clear that corporate environmental managers must be aware of the possibility that common
law obligations may be imposed upon them, particularly by
the state courts, and must evaluate these considerations in
developing compliance strategies.

The common law obligations of principal concern in
the hazardous waste context arise under five historic
theories of liability: public or private nuisance,

trespass, negligence, and strict liability for "abnormally dangerous activity." These theories have been cited by courts in general discussions of potential generator liability (see, e.g., City of Philadelphia v. Stepan Chemical Co., supra), and used by state courts as a basis for holding liable owners and operators of hazardous waste management facilities. For example, the Illinois Supreme Court affirmed an order directing that a fully permitted chemical waste disposal facility, which was operating in compliance with its permits, be closed because it created a public nuisance. (Village of Wilsonville v. SCA Services, Inc., 86 Ill. 2d 1, 426 N.E.2d 824 (1981).)

This book will not present a detailed analysis of these highly technical legal theories. However, a very brief overview of each should provide a basis for environmental managers to recognize potential problems that may exist. For more detailed discussions, the reader might consult the October 1982 Report to Congress pursuant to Section 301(e) of Superfund, entitled Injuries and Damages from Hazardous Wastes -- Analysis and Improvement of Legal Remedies, or one of several articles and law review notes. (E.g., DiBenedetto, General Liability Under the Common Law and Federal and State Statutes, 39 Bus. Law. 611 (1984); Note, Liability for Generators of Hazardous Waste: The Failure of Existing Enforcement Mechanisms, 69 Geo. L.J.

1047 (1981); Note, Allocating the Costs of Hazardous Waste
Disposal, 94 Harv. L. Rev. 584 (1981); or Note, Strict
Liability for Generators, Transporters, and Disposers of
Hazardous Wastes, 64 Minn. L. Rev. 949 (1980).)

1.   Public Nuisance

The common law liability theory probably most
likely to be relevant to hazardous waste management is
creation of a public nuisance. Under this theory, the person who has caused a substantial problem to exist is
responsible for its remedy if the problem represents an
unreasonable interference with the rights of the general
public. Thus, for example, the court in Village of
Wilsonville v. SCA Services, Inc., noted above, upheld an
injunction against a sanitary landfill despite its
compliance with applicable environmental permits. The site
was found to be a nuisance because it emitted dust and
odors, required transport of hazardous materials through
town, and posed an ultimate threat to groundwater. Another
hazardous waste disposal facility owner and operator was
enjoined from further operations and ordered to finance a
cleanup based on both public and private nuisance grounds in
Wood v. Picillo, 443 A.2d 1244 (R.I. 1982).

One New York case, State v. Schenectady Chemicals,
Inc., 117 Misc. 2d 960, 459 N.Y.S.2d 971 (Sup. Ct. 1983),
aff'd, 103 A.D.2d 33, 479 N.Y.S.2d 1010 (3d Dep't 1984),

raises the possibility that generators may be found liable in public nuisance. In Schenectady Chemicals, the state sued a generator who had hired an independent contractor to transport and dispose of its hazardous wastes during the 1950s and 1960s. The contractor allegedly disposed of the wastes on its property by pouring them into the surface water or on the ground, or by dumping or burying biodegradable containers. The chemicals allegedly contaminated underlying groundwater. The state sought from the generator partial payment of the cleanup costs, claiming that the generator had contributed to the creation and maintenance of a public nuisance. The court refused to dismiss the public nuisance claims, noting that the common law must evolve to deal with the new and unforeseen problems engendered by chemical waste disposal. In addition, the court rejected Schenectady Chemical's motion to dismiss based on a "state of the art" defense, stating that compliance with the latest industry standards is not a defense to an action to abate a nuisance. Fault was not an issue, the court said, because the inquiry is limited to whether the condition, not the conduct creating it, is causing damage to the public.

2.   Private Nuisance

In some situations, managers of hazardous waste also may be subject to suit under a private nuisance theory. Like the public nuisance theory, a cause of action for private nuisance arises when the defendant's actions have substantially interfered with another person's use and enjoyment of land. However, to maintain a private nuisance action, the plaintiff must have a property interest in the land at issue. This requirement restricts the number of potential plaintiffs for private nuisance claims. To prevail, a claimant in a private nuisance action must show that the severity of his harm outweighs the benefits derived from the defendant's conduct, and the defendant's compliance with environmental permits thus may be of greater weight in avoiding liability for private nuisance than in cases involving public nuisance.

Private nuisance was one of the grounds for injunction and damages in Wood v. Picillo, noted above. In another case, Amax, Inc. v. Sohio Industrial Products Co., 121 Misc. 2d 814, 469 N.Y.S.2d 282 (Sup. Ct. 1983), the court denied a motion to dismiss an action for private nuisance brought by the present owner of property against the previous owner, alleging that the previous owner's burial of radioactive wastes contaminated the property.

3.   Trespass

The third theory, trespass, also requires that the plaintiff have an interest in the exclusive possession of the land at issue. Furthermore, physical invasion of the plaintiff's property is required for an action to succeed.

This theory has not been widely used in cases brought to date. However, in City of Philadelphia v. Stepan Chemical Co., noted above, the court refused to dismiss a complaint in trespass against hazardous waste generators. Although the generators did not themselves enter upon the property in dispute, the court said, they could be found liable in trespass if they knew or had reason to know that their independent waste disposal contractors would trespass on another's land.

4.   Negligence

The fourth theory, negligence, is likely to be more generally available than either the private nuisance or trespass claims. As classically stated, a person is negligent if he violates his duty to exercise reasonable care and, by so doing, injures another person. However, several key questions must be resolved to establish a negligence claim in the hazardous waste context. It is uncertain, for example, what duties are or were owed by waste managers to any given party or set of parties. Indeed, these duties may vary among waste generators, transporters, treaters, or disposers. A second important question is whether the actions of any or all of these parties, even if dangerous, constitute the "proximate," i.e., immediate, cause of another's injury. For example, where a third party transporter has deposited a generator's wastes at a disposal site that eventually poses an environmental threat, it simply is not clear whether it is fair or reasonable to attribute current or potential problems to the generator. Third, proving that actual injury has resulted from waste management activities, rather than some intervening cause, may be quite difficult.

The leading case concerning negligence in a hazardous waste context is Ewell v. Petro Processors of Louisiana, Inc., 364 So. 2d 604 (La. App. 1978), cert. denied, 366 So. 2d 575 (La. 1979). The plaintiffs in Ewell, who owned an interest in land adjacent to an industrial waste disposal facility, sought damages from both the facility's owners and its customers, the generators. The appellate court readily affirmed the lower court's finding that the defendant negligently permitted toxic waste materials to leak over onto the plaintiffs' property from an improperly constructed disposal pit. With respect to the generators, the court looked to see whether they were aware of the leakage at the pits when they dumped hazardous material at the site. The court found liable one generator whose employees had dumped hazardous material into the pits prior to the discovery of the leakage as well as after the lawsuit was filed.

5. Abnormally Dangerous Activity

The fifth common law theory of potential application is that of strict liability for "abnormally dangerous activity." In brief, the theory is that certain activities are so inherently dangerous that no party involved with them can escape strict liability for such problems as may arise. This theory has been applied to such matters as transportation of hazardous chemicals (see Indiana Harbor Belt Railroad v. American Cyanamid Co., 517 F. Supp. 314 (N.D. Ill. 1981)) and has been touted by those who seek to broaden the common law basis for liability arising from hazardous waste management activities. In one case, the New Jersey Supreme Court explicitly found that the toxic waste disposal is an abnormally dangerous activity, carrying an unavoidable risk of harm. (State Department of Environmental Protection v. Ventron Corp., 94 N.J. 254, 463 A.2d 893 (1983).) The court therefore imposed strict liability on the owners of a mercury processing facility who had dumped untreated mercury wastes onto a tract of land, from which the wastes migrated into a river estuary.

Finally, as mentioned above, the development of these common law theories is made more complicated because we do not have a unitary court system. The common law varies between the federal and state courts and between the states. On the federal level, it is uncertain whether these

common law theories may be asserted as a matter of federal
common law for hazardous waste management activities, since
(as discussed above) several courts (although not yet the
United States Supreme Court) have held that RCRA and
Superfund preempt the further development and application
of any federal common law.

On the state level, the common law may continue to
develop and be applied in many widely-varying circumstances.
Varying standards for liability may emerge in different
states. This development may be particularly troubling for
companies that operate in numerous states and seek to maintain coherent, coordinated management controls on their
activities.

C. Liability Insurance Issues

In conjunction with evaluating its potential liabilities under common law, a company may wish to assess the
extent of coverage available under its insurance policies.
There are three common forms of insurance policies that may
provide coverage for environmental claims: pollution liability policies, environmental impairment liability policies,
and comprehensive general liability ("CGL") policies.
Unlike the others, the CGL policy was not designed especially to provide for these types of claims. CGL policies
have, however, often been held to provide coverage and
should not be overlooked by a company facing potential

liability for an environmental problem. Case law concerning environmental claims made under CGL policies is complex and is evolving rapidly. Therefore, applicable state law should be consulted closely whenever a claim against a company is made.

A discussion of several important issues in hazardous waste insurance cases follows. Other issues, often unique to the insured, may also arise.

1. <u>Coverage Trigger</u>

The continuous seepage of hazardous wastes presents a peculiar fact situation, requiring a determination of the applicable date of damage in order to identify the policy of insurance that applies. A variety of theories for determining the date on which coverage is triggered in such circumstances exists.

2. <u>Damage Expected or Intended by the Insured</u>

Generally, property damage must be the intentional result of the insured's intentional act to be excluded from coverage. For coverage to apply, at the very least, there must be a high degree of uncertainty that damage will result from the insured's acts. In one case, a court found that there was no "occurrence" within the meaning of a company's general liability policies by relying, in part, on the absence of any suggestion that the insured's dumping was accidental, and on the fact that the dumping was a continuous activity. (<u>See</u> <u>America States Insurance Co. v. Maryland Casualty Co.</u>, 587 F. Supp. 1549 (E.D. Mich. 1984).)

3. Pollution Exclusion Clause

The question whether a pollution exclusion clause formed a part of the policy, particularly when policies were issued in the early 1970s, has surfaced repeatedly in hazardous waste cases. When it is a part of the policy, its applicability is a critical issue.

In many cases where property damage resulted from regular business activity of the insured, the insured has been deemed an active polluter and the pollution exclusion clause has been applied. In other contexts, however, such as where the insured was a generator of wastes, the pollution exclusion clause has sometimes been construed narrowly and found inapplicable. Recently, the insurance industry has moved towards a more expansive pollution exclusion that does not contain the exception for sudden and accidental discharges. CGL policies issued in January 1986 and thereafter are therefore unlikely to provide coverage for environmental claims.

4. Absence of Adjudicatory Proceedings Against
    the Insured

In some states, environmental agencies are empowered to levy fines and order cleanup of hazardous waste sites without instituting adjudicatory proceedings against the insured. Comprehensive general liability policies usually create an obligation for the carrier to defend "suits" against the insured. It is unclear whether such an obligation arises when there are no formal adjudicating proceedings against the insured.

5. Duty to Give Prompt Notification of Claims

Because federal and state officials often proceed informally with claims regarding responsibility for cleanup, the question of when an insured should notify the carrier about a claim related to cleanup obligations has arisen frequently in hazardous waste cases. It is often wise to consider early notification of environmental claims in order to facilitate settlement.

6. Coverage for Preventive Measures

Voluntary measures undertaken by the insured to prevent or mitigate damage resulting from a release of a hazardous substance present difficult insurance coverage issues. Most policies exclude coverage where the insured voluntarily assumes any obligations or incurs any expenses. For this reason, a company must be cautious about taking steps to prevent or mitigate damage when not compelled to do so if it wishes to recover the costs of such measures from its insurer. At the same time, many CGL policies oblige the insured to take reasonable steps to mitigate damage immediately after an occurrence. Whether the insured has taken appropriate steps following a known release of hazardous waste may therefore be an issue in insurance litigation. Because of the difficulty of reconciling these provisions, as well as the strong public policy reasons to encourage preventative actions, insureds sometimes have succeeded in gaining coverage for the costs of preventive actions.

7. <u>Damage to Insured's Property</u>

The CGL policy typically excludes coverage for damage to property owned, occupied, or used by the insured. For this reason, it is often unclear whether the costs of on-site cleanup (as opposed to off-site cleanup) will be covered.

APPENDIX A

DEFINITION OF SOLID WASTE
(40 C.F.R. § 261.2)

The following definition of "solid waste" was
published on January 4, 1985 (50 Fed. Reg. 664) and will be
codified in the regulations at 40 C.F.R. § 261.2. See
discussion of this revised definition beginning at p. 37 in
the text.

TABLE 1

	Use constituting disposal (261.2(c)(1)) (1)	Energy recovery/ fuel (261.2(c)(2)) (2)	Reclamation (261.2(c)(3)) (3)	Speculative accumulation (261.2(c)(4)) (4)
Spent Materials	(*)	(*)	(*)	(*)
Sludges (listed in 40 CFR Part 261.31 or .32)	(*)	(*)	(*)	(*)
Sludges exhibiting a characteristic of hazardous waste	(*)	(*)		(*)
By-products (listed in 40 CFR Part 261.31 or 261.32)	(*)	(*)	(*)	(*)
By-products exhibiting a characteristic of hazardous waste	(*)	(*)		(*)
Commercial chemical products listed in 40 CFR § 261.33	(*)	(*)		
Scrap metal	(*)	(*)	(*)	(*)

Note.—The terms "spent materials", "sludges", "by-products," and "scrap metal" are defined in § 261.1.

§ 261.2 Definition of solid waste.

(a)(1) A *solid waste* is any discarded material that is not excluded by § 261.4(a) or that is not excluded by variance granted under §§ 260.30 and 260.31.

(2) A *discarded material* is any material which is:

(i) *Abandoned,* as explained in paragraph (b) of this section; or

(ii) *Recycled,* as explained in paragraph (c) of this section; or

(iii) Considered *inherently waste-like,* as explained in paragraph (d) of this section.

(b) Materials are solid waste if they are *abandoned* by being:

(1) Disposed of; or

(2) Burned or incinerated; or

(3) Accumulated, stored, or treated (but not recycled) before or in lieu of being abandoned by being disposed of, burned, or incinerated.

(c) Materials are solid wastes if they are *recycled*—or accumulated, stored, or treated before recycling—as specified in paragraphs (c)(1) through (c)(4) of this section.

(1) *Used in a manner constituting disposal.* (i) Materials noted with a "*" in Column 1 of Table I are solid wastes when they are:

(A) Applied to or placed on the land in a manner that constitutes disposal; or

(B) Contained in products that are applied to the land (in which case the product itself remains a solid waste).

(ii) However, commercial chemical products listed in § 261.33 are not solid wastes if they are applied to the land and that is their ordinary manner of use.

(2) *Burning for energy recovery.* (i) Materials noted with a "*" in column 2 of Table 1 are solid wastes when they are:

(A) Burned to recover energy;

(B) Used to produce a fuel;

(C) Contained in fuels (in which case the fuel itself remains a solid waste).

(ii) However, commercial chemical products listed in § 261.33 are not solid wastes if they are themselves fuels.

(3) *Reclaimed.* Materials noted with a "*" in column 3 of Table 1 are solid wastes when reclaimed.

(4) *Accumulated speculatively.* Materials noted with a "*" in column 4 of Table 1 are solid wastes when accumulated speculatively.

(d) *Inherently waste-like materials.* The following materials are solid wastes when they are recycled in any manner:

(1) Hazardous Waste Nos. F020, F021 (unless used as an ingredient to make a product at the site of generation), F022, F023, F026, and F028.

(2) The Administrator will use the following criteria to add wastes to that list:

(i)(A) The materials are ordinarily disposed of, burned, or incinerated; or

(B) The materials contain toxic constituents listed in Appendix VIII of Part 261 and these constituents are not ordinarily found in raw materials or products for which the materials substitute (or are found in raw materials or products in smaller concentrations) and are not used or reused during the recycling process; and

(ii) The material may pose a substantial hazard to human health and the environment when recycled.

(e) *Materials that are not solid waste when recycled.* (1) Materials are not solid wastes when they can be shown to be recycled by being:

(i) Used or reused as ingredients in an industrial process to make a product, provided the materials are not being reclaimed; or

(ii) Used or reused as effective substitutes for commercial products; or

(iii) Returned to the original process from which they are generated, without first being reclaimed. The material must be returned as a substitute for raw material feedstock, and the process must use raw materials as principal feedstocks.

(2) The following materials are solid wastes, even if the recycling involves use, reuse, or return to the original process (described in paragraphs (e)(1) (i)–(iii) of this section:

(i) Materials used in a manner constituting disposal, or used to produce products that are applied to the land; or

(ii) Materials burned for energy recovery, used to produce a fuel, or contained in fuels; or

(iii) Materials accumulated speculatively; or

(iv) Materials listed in paragraph (d)(1) of this section.

(f) *Documentation of claims that materials are not solid wastes or are conditionally exempt from regulation.* Respondents in actions to enforce regulations implementing Subtitle C of RCRA who raise a claim that a certain material is not a solid waste, or is conditionally exempt from regulation, must demonstrate that there is a known market or disposition for the material, and that they meet the terms of the exclusion or exemption. In doing so, they must provide appropriate documentation (such as contracts showing that a second person uses the material as an ingredient in a production process) to demonstrate that the material is not a waste, or is exempt from regulation. In addition, owners or operators of facilities claiming that they actually are recycling materials must show that they have the necessary equipment to do so.

APPENDIX B

LISTS OF HAZARDOUS WASTES FROM NONSPECIFIC SOURCES, FROM SPECIFIC SOURCES, AND FROM DISCARDED CHEMICAL PRODUCTS (40 C.F.R. §§ 261.31-.33)

Wastes listed in 40 C.F.R. §§ 261.31 and 261.32 are considered hazardous wastes subject to RCRA regulation. See pp. 38-45 in the text. Discarded commercial chemical products, off-specification species, container residues, and spill residues listed in 40 C.F.R. § 261.33 also are subject to regulation as hazardous wastes. See pp. 45-48 in the text.

§ 261.31 Hazardous wastes from non-specific sources.

Industry and EPA hazardous waste No.	Hazardous waste	Hazard code
Generic:		
F001	The following spent halogenated solvents used in degreasing: tetrachloroethylene, trichloroethylene, methylene chloride, 1,1,1-trichloroethane, carbon tetrachloride, and chlorinated fluorocarbons; and sludges from the recovery of these solvents in degreasing operations.	(T)
F002	The following spent halogenated solvents: tetrachloroethylene, methylene chloride, trichloroethylene, 1,1,1-trichloroethane, chlorobenzene, 1,1,2-trichloro-1,2,2-trifluoroethane, ortho-dichlorobenzene, and trichlorofluoromethane; and the still bottoms from the recovery of these solvents.	(T)
F003	The following spent non-halogenated solvents: xylene, acetone, ethyl acetate, ethyl benzene, ethyl ether, methyl isobutyl ketone, n-butyl alcohol, cyclohexanone, and methanol; and the still bottoms from the recovery of these solvents.	(I)
F004	The following spent non-halogenated solvents: cresols and cresylic acid, and nitrobenzene; and the still bottoms from the recovery of these solvents.	(T)
F005	The following spent non-halogenated solvents: toluene, methyl ethyl ketone, carbon disulfide, isobutanol, and pyridine; and the still bottoms from the recovery of these solvents.	(I, T)
F006	Wastewater treatment sludges from electroplating operations except from the following processes: (1) sulfuric acid anodizing of aluminum; (2) tin plating on carbon steel; (3) zinc plating (segregated basis) on carbon steel; (4) aluminum or zinc-aluminum plating on carbon steel; (5) cleaning/stripping associated with tin, zinc and aluminum plating on carbon steel; and (6) chemical etching and milling of aluminum.	(T)
F019	Wastewater treatment sludges from the chemical conversion coating of aluminum.	(T)
F007	Spent cyanide plating bath solutions from electroplating operations (except for precious metals electroplating spent cyanide plating bath solutions).	(R, T)
F008	Plating bath sludges from the bottom of plating baths from electroplating operations where cyanides are used in the process (except for precious metals electroplating plating bath sludges).	(R, T)
F009	Spent stripping and cleaning bath solutions from electroplating operations where cyanides are used in the process (except for precious metals electroplating spent stripping and cleaning bath solutions).	(R, T)
F010	Quenching bath sludge from oil baths from metal heat treating operations where cyanides are used in the process (except for precious metals heat-treating quenching bath sludges).	(R, T)
F011	Spent cyanide solutions from salt bath pot cleaning from metal heat treating operations (except for precious metals heat treating spent cyanide solutions from salt bath pot cleaning).	(R, T)
F012	Quenching wastewater treatment sludges from metal heat treating operations where cyanides are used in the process (except for precious metals heat treating quenching wastewater treatment sludges).	(T)
F024	Wastes, including but not limited to, distillation residues, heavy ends, tars, and reactor clean-out wastes from the production of chlorinated aliphatic hydrocarbons, having carbon content from one to five, utilizing free radical catalyzed processes. [This listing does not include light ends, spent filters and filter aids, spent dessicants, wastewater, wastewater treatment sludges, spent catalysts, and wastes listed in § 261.32.]	(T)

Industry and EPA hazardous waste No.	Hazardous waste	Hazard code
K039	Filter cake from the filtration of diethylphosphorodithioic acid in the production of phorate.	(T)
K040	Wastewater treatment sludge from the production of phorate	(T)
K041	Wastewater treatment sludge from the production of toxaphene	(T)
K098	Untreated process wastewater from the production of toxaphene	(T)
K042	Heavy ends or distillation residues from the distillation of tetrachlorobenzene in the production of 2,4,5-T.	(T)
K043	2,6-Dichlorophenol waste from the production of 2,4-D	(T)
K099	Untreated wastewater from the production of 2,4-D	(T)
Explosives:		
K044	Wastewater treatment sludges from the manufacturing and processing of explosives	(R)
K045	Spent carbon from the treatment of wastewater containing explosives	(R)
K046	Wastewater treatment sludges from the manufacturing, formulation and loading of lead-based initiating compounds.	(T)
K047	Pink/red water from TNT operations	(R)
Petroleum refining:		
K048	Dissolved air flotation (DAF) float from the petroleum refining industry	(T)
K049	Slop oil emulsion solids from the petroleum refining industry	(T)
K050	Heat exchanger bundle cleaning sludge from the petroleum refining industry	(T)
K051	API separator sludge from the petroleum refining industry	(T)
K052	Tank bottoms (leaded) from the petroleum refining industry	(T)
Iron and steel:		
K061	Emission control dust/sludge from the primary production of steel in electric furnaces.	(T)
K062	Spent pickle liquor from steel finishing operations	(C, T)
Secondary lead:		
K069	Emission control dust/sludge from secondary lead smelting	(T)
K100	Waste leaching solution from acid leaching of emission control dust/sludge from secondary lead smelting.	(T)
Veterinary pharmaceuticals:		
K084	Wastewater treatment sludges generated during the production of veterinary pharmaceuticals from arsenic or organo-arsenic compounds.	(T)
K101	Distillation tar residues from the distillation of aniline-based compounds in the production of veterinary pharmaceuticals from arsenic or organo-arsenic compounds.	(T)
K102	Residue from the use of activated carbon for decolorization in the production of veterinary pharmaceuticals from arsenic or organo-arsenic compounds.	(T)
Ink formulation: K086	Solvent washes and sludges, caustic washes and sludges, or water washes and sludges from cleaning tubs and equipment used in the formulation of ink from pigments, driers, soaps, and stabilizers containing chromium and lead.	(T)
Coking:		
K060	Ammonia still lime sludge from coking operations	(T)
K067	Decanter tank tar sludge from coking operations	(T)

§ 261.32 Hazardous wastes from specific sources.

Industry and EPA hazardous waste No.	Hazardous waste	Hazard code
Wood preservation: K001	Bottom sediment sludge from the treatment of wastewaters from wood preserving processes that use creosote and/or pentachlorophenol.	(T)
Inorganic pigments:		
K002	Wastewater treatment sludge from the production of chrome yellow and orange pigments.	(T)
K003	Wastewater treatment sludge from the production of molybdate orange pigments	(T)
K004	Wastewater treatment sludge from the production of zinc yellow pigments	(T)
K005	Wastewater treatment sludge from the production of chrome green pigments	(T)
K006	Wastewater treatment sludge from the production of chrome oxide green pigments (anhydrous and hydrated).	(T)
K007	Wastewater treatment sludge from the production of iron blue pigments	(T)
K008	Oven residue from the production of chrome oxide green pigments..............................	(T)
Organic chemicals:		
K009	Distillation bottoms from the production of acetaldehyde from ethylene	(T)
K010	Distillation side cuts from the production of acetaldehyde from ethylene	(T)
K011	Bottom stream from the wastewater stripper in the production of acrylonitrile.................	(R, T)
K013	Bottom stream from the acetonitrile column in the production of acrylonitrile..............	(R, T)
K014	Bottoms from the acetonitrile purification column in the production of acrylonitrile	(T)
K015	Still bottoms from the distillation of benzyl chloride	(T)
K016	Heavy ends or distillation residues from the production of carbon tetrachloride.............	(T)
K017	Heavy ends (still bottoms) from the purification column in the production of epichlorohydrin.	(T)
K018	Heavy ends from the fractionation column in ethyl chloride production.........................	(T)
K019	Heavy ends from the distillation of ethylene dichloride in ethylene dichloride production.	(T)
K020	Heavy ends from the distillation of vinyl chloride in vinyl chloride monomer production.	(T)
K021	Aqueous spent antimony catalyst waste from fluoromethanes production	(T)
K022	Distillation bottom tars from the production of phenol/acetone from cumene	(T)
K023	Distillation light ends from the production of phthalic anhydride from naphthalene	(T)
K024	Distillation bottoms from the production of phthalic anhydride from naphthalene............	(T)
K093	Distillation light ends from the production of phthalic anhydride from ortho-xylene	(T)
K094	Distillation bottoms from the production of phthalic anhydride from ortho-xylene	(T)
K025	Distillation bottoms from the production of nitrobenzene by the nitration of benzene.....	(T)
K026	Stripping still tails from the production of methy ethyl pyridines	(T)
K027	Centrifuge and distillation residues from toluene diisocyanate production....................	(R, T)
K028	Spent catalyst from the hydrochlorinator reactor in the production of 1,1,1-trichloroethane.	(T)
K029	Waste from the product steam stripper in the production of 1,1,1-trichloroethane	(T)
K095	Distillation bottoms from the production of 1,1,1-trichloroethane	(T)
K096	Heavy ends from the heavy ends column from the production of 1,1,1-trichloroethane.	(T)
K030	Column bottoms or heavy ends from the combined production of trichloroethylene and perchloroethylene.	(T)
K083	Distillation bottoms from aniline production	(T)
K103	Process residues from aniline extraction from the production of aniline.........................	(T)
K104	Combined wastewater streams generated from nitrobenzene/aniline production	(T)
K085	Distillation or fractionation column bottoms from the production of chlorobenzenes.........	(T)
K105	Separated aqueous stream from the reactor product washing step in the production of chlorobenzenes.	(T)
Inorganic chemicals:		
K071	Brine purification muds from the mercury cell process in chlorine production, where separately prepurified brine is not used.	(T)
K073	Chlorinated hydrocarbon waste from the purification step of the diaphragm cell process using graphite anodes in chlorine production.	(T)
K106	Wastewater treatment sludge from the mercury cell process in chlorine production......	(T)
Pesticides:		
K031	By-product salts generated in the production of MSMA and cacodylic acid	(T)
K032	Wastewater treatment sludge from the production of chlordane...................................	(T)
K033	Wastewater and scrub water from the chlorination of cyclopentadiene in the production of chlordane.	(T)
K034	Filter solids from the filtration of hexachlorocyclopentadiene in the production of chlordane.	(T)
K097	Vacuum stripper discharge from the chlordane chlorinator in the production of chlordane.	(T)
K035	Wastewater treatment sludges generated in the production of creosote........................	(T)
K036	Still bottoms from toluene reclamation distillation in the production of disulfoton...........	(T)
K037	Wastewater treatment sludges from the production of disulfoton.................................	(T)
K038	Wastewater from the washing and stripping of phorate production...............................	(T)

B-3

§ 261.33 Discarded commercial chemical products, off-specification species, container residues, and spill residues thereof.

~~The following~~ materials or items ~~are~~ hazardous ~~wastes if and~~ when they are ~~discarded~~ or intended to be ~~discarded:~~

(a) Any commercial chemical product, or manufacturing chemical intermediate having the generic name listed in paragraph (e) or (f) of this section.

(b) Any off-specification commercial chemical product or manufacturing chemical intermediate which, if it met specifications, would have the generic name listed in paragraph (e) or (f) of this section.

(c) Any container or inner liner removed from a container that has been used to hold any commercial chemical product or manufacturing chemical intermediate having the generic names listed in paragraph (e) of this section, or any container or inner liner removed from a container that has been used to hold any off-specification chemical product and manufacturing chemical intermediate which, if it met specifications, would have the generic name listed in paragraph (e) of this section, unless the container is empty as defined in § 261.7(b)(3) of this chapter.

[Comment: Unless the residue is being beneficially used or reused, or legitimately recy-

*

*This paragraph was amended as follows on January 4, 1985, 50 Fed. Reg. 665.

The following materials or items are hazardous wastes when they are discarded or intended to be discarded as described in § 261.2(a)(2)(i), when they are burned for purposes of energy recovery in lieu of their original intended use, when they are used to produce fuels in lieu of their original intended use, when they are applied to the land in lieu of their original intended use, or when they are contained in products that are applied to the land in lieu of their original intended use.

*   *   *   *   *

cied or reclaimed; or being accumulated, stored, transported or treated prior to such use, re-use, recycling or reclamation. EPA considers the residue to be intended for discard, and thus a hazardous waste. An example of a legitimate re-use of the residue would be where the residue remains in the container and the container is used to hold the same commerical chemical product or manufacturing chemical product or manufacturing chemical intermediate it previously held. An example of the discard of the residue would be where the drum is sent to a drum reconditioner who reconditions the drum but discards the residue.]

(d) Any residue or contaminated soil, water or other debris resulting from the cleanup of a spill into or on any land or water of any commercial chemical product or manufacturing chemical intermediate having the generic name listed in paragraph (e) or (f) of this section, or any residue or contaminated soil, water or other debris resulting from the cleanup of a spill, into or on any land or water, of any off-specification chemical product and manufacturing chemical intermediate which, if it met specifications, would have the generic name listed in paragraph (e) or (f) of this section.

[Comment: The phrase "commercial chemical product or manufacturing chemical intermediate having the generic name listed in . . ." refers to a chemical substance which is manufactured or formulated for commercial or manufacturing use which consists of the commercially pure grade of the chemical, any technical grades of the chemical that are produced or marketed, and all formulations in which the chemical is the sole active ingredient. It does not refer to a material, such as a manufacturing process waste, that contains any of the substances listed in paragraphs (e) or (f). Where a manufacturing process waste is deemed to be a hazardous waste because it contains a substance listed in paragraphs (e) or (f), such waste will be listed in either §§ 261.31 or 261.32 or will be identified as a hazardous waste by the characteristics set forth in Subpart C of this part.]

(e) The commercial chemical products, manufacturing chemical intermediates or off-specification commercial chemical products or manufacturing chemical intermediates referred to in paragraphs (a) through (d) of this section, are identified as acute hazardous wastes (H) and are subject to be the small quantity exclusion defined in § 261.5(e).

[Comment: For the convenience of the regulated community the primary hazardous properties of these materials have been indicated by the letters T (Toxicity), and R (Reactivity). Absence of a letter indicates that the compound only is listed for acute toxicity.]

These wastes and their corresponding EPA Hazardous Waste Numbers are:

Hazardous waste No.	Substance
P023	Acetaldehyde, chloro-
P002	Acetamide, N-(aminothioxomethyl)-
P057	Acetamide, 2-fluoro-
P058	Acetic acid, fluoro-, sodium salt
P066	Acetimidic acid, N-[(methylcarbamoyl)oxy]thio-, methyl ester
P001	3-(alpha-Acetonylbenzyl)-4-hydroxycoumarin and salts, when present at concentrations greater than 0.3%
P002	1-Acetyl-2-thiourea
P003	Acrolein
P070	Aldicarb
P004	Aldrin
P005	Allyl alcohol
P006	Aluminum phosphide
P007	5-(Aminomethyl)-3-isoxazolol
P008	4-aAminopyridine
P009	Ammonium picrate (R)
P119	Ammonium vanadate
P010	Arsenic acid
P012	Arsenic (III) oxide
P011	Arsenic (V) oxide
P011	Arsenic pentoxide
P012	Arsenic trioxide
P038	Arsine, diethyl-
P054	Aziridine
P013	Barium cyanide
P024	Benzenamine, 4-chloro-
P077	Benzenamine, 4-nitro-
P028	Benzene, (chloromethyl)-
P042	1,2-Benzenediol, 4-[1-hydroxy-2-(methylamino)ethyl]-
P014	Benzenethiol
P028	Benzyl chloride
P015	Beryllium dust
P016	Bis(chloromethyl) ether
P017	Bromoacetone
P018	Brucine
P021	Calcium cyanide
P123	Camphene, octachloro-
P103	Carbamimidoselenoic acid
P022	Carbon bisulfide
P022	Carbon disulfide
P095	Carbonyl chloride
P033	Chlorine cyanide
P023	Chloroacetaldehyde
P024	p-Chloroaniline
P026	1-(o-Chlorophenyl)thiourea
P027	3-Chloropropionitrile
P029	Copper cyanides
P030	Cyanides (soluble cyanide salts), not elsewhere specified
P031	Cyanogen
P033	Cyanogen chloride
P036	Dichlorophenylarsine
P037	Dieldrin
P038	Diethylarsine

B-5

Hazardous waste No.	Substance
P039	O,O-Diethyl S-[2-(ethylthio)ethyl] phosphoro-dithioate
P041	Diethyl-p-nitrophenyl phosphate
P040	O,O-Diethyl O-pyrazinyl phosphorothioate
P043	Diisopropyl fluorophosphate
P044	Dimethoate
P045	3,3-Dimethyl-1-(methylthio)-2-butanone, O-[(methylamino)carbonyl] oxime
P071	O,O-Dimethyl O-p-nitrophenyl phosphoro-thioate
P082	Dimethylnitrosamine
P046	alpha, alpha-Dimethylphenethylamine
P047	4,6-Dinitro-o-cresol and salts
P034	4,6-Dinitro-o-cyclohexylphenol
P048	2,4-Dinitrophenol
P020	Dinoseb
P085	Diphosphoramide, octamethyl-
P039	Disulfoton
P049	2,4-Dithiobiuret
P109	Dithiopyrophosphoric acid, tetraethyl ester
P050	Endosulfan
P088	Endothall
P051	Endrin
P042	Epinephrine
P046	Ethanamine, 1,1-dimethyl-2-phenyl-
P084	Ethenamine, N-methyl-N-nitroso-
P101	Ethyl cyanide
P054	Ethylenimine
P097	Famphur
P056	Fluorine
P057	Fluoroacetamide
P058	Fluoroacetic acid, sodium salt
P065	Fulminic acid, mercury(II) salt (R,T)
P059	Heptachlor
P051	1,2,3,4,10,10-Hexachloro-6,7-epoxy-1,4,4a,5,6,7,8,8a-octahydro-endo,endo-1,4:5,8-dimethanonaphthalene
P037	1,2,3,4,10,10-Hexachloro-6,7-epoxy-1,4,4a,5,6,7,8,8a-octahydro-endo,endo-1,4:5,8-demethanonaphthalene
P060	1,2,3,4,10,10-Hexachloro-1,4,4a,5,8,8a-hexahydro-1,4:5,8-endo, endo-dimeth- an-onaphthalene
P004	1,2,3,4,10,10-Hexachloro-1,4,4a,5,8,8a-hexahydro-1,4:5,8-endo,exo-dimethanonaphthalene
P060	Hexachlorohexahydro-exo,exo-dimethanonaphthalene
P062	Hexaethyl tetraphosphate
P116	Hydrazinecarbothio_mide
P068	Hydrazine, methyl-
P063	Hydrocyanic acid
P063	Hydrogen cyanide
P096	Hydrogen phosphide
P064	Isocyanic acid, methyl ester
P007	3(2H)-Isoxazolone, 5-(aminomethyl)-
P092	Mercury, (acetato-O)phenyl-
P065	Mercury fulminate (R,T)
P016	Methane, oxybis(chloro-
P112	Methane, tetranitro- (R)
P118	Methanethiol, trichloro-
P059	4,7-Methano-1H-indene, 1,4,5,6,7,8,8-hep-tachloro-3a,4,7,7a-tetrahydro-
P066	Methomyl
P067	2-Methylaziridine
P068	Methyl hydrazine
P064	Methyl isocyanate
P069	2-Methyllactonitrile
P071	Methyl parathion
P072	alpha-Naphthylthiourea
P073	Nickel carbonyl
P074	Nickel cyanide

Hazardous waste No.	Substance
P074	Nickel(II) cyanide
P073	Nickel tetracarbonyl
P075	Nicotine and salts
P076	Nitric oxide
P077	p-Nitroaniline
P078	Nitrogen dioxide
P076	Nitrogen(II) oxide
P078	Nitrogen(IV) oxide
P081	Nitroglycerine (R)
P082	N-Nitrosodimethylamine
P084	N-Nitrosomethylvinylamine
P050	5-Norbornene-2,3-dimethanol, 1,4,5,6,7,7-hex-achloro, cyclic sulfite
P085	Octamethylpyrophosphoramide
P087	Osmium oxide
P087	Osmium tetroxide
P088	7-Oxabicyclo[2.2.1]heptane-2,3-dicarboxylic acid
P089	Parathion
P034	Phenol, 2-cyclohexyl-4,6-dinitro-
P048	Phenol, 2,4-dinitro-
P047	Phenol, 2,4-dinitro-6-methyl-
P020	Phenol, 2,4-dinitro-6-(1-methylpropyl)-
P009	Phenol, 2,4,6-trinitro-, ammonium salt (R)
P036	Phenyl dichloroarsine
P092	Phenylmercuric acetate
P093	N-Phenylthiourea
P094	Phorate
P095	Phosgene
P096	Phosphine
P041	Phosphoric acid, diethyl p-nitrophenyl ester
P044	Phosphorodithioic acid, O,O-dimethyl S-[2-(methylamino)-2-oxoethyl] ester
P043	Phosphorofluoric acid, bis(1-methylethyl)-ester
P094	Phosphorothioic acid, O,O-diethyl S-(ethylthio)methyl ester
P089	Phosphorothioci acid, O,O-diethyl O-(p-nitro-phenyl) ester
P040	Phosphorothioic acid, O,O-diethyl O- pyrazinyl ester
P097	Phosphorothioic acid, O,O-dimethyl O-[p-((di-methylamino)-sulfonyl)phenyl]ester
P110	Plumbane, tetraethyl-
P098	Potassium cyanide
P099	Potassium silver cyanide
P070	Propanal, 2-methyl-2-(methylthio)-, O-[(methylamino)carbonyl]oxime
P101	Propanenitrile
P027	Propanenitrile, 3-chloro-
P069	Propanenitrile, 2-hydroxy-2-metl yl-
P081	1,2,3-Propanetriol, trinitrate- (R)
P017	2-Propanone, 1-bromo-
P102	Propargyl alcohol
P003	2-Propenal
P005	2-Propen-1-ol
P067	1,2-Propylenimine
P102	2-Propyn-1-ol
P008	4-Pyridinamine
P075	Pyridine, (S)-3-(1-methyl-2-pyrrolidinyl)-, and salts
P111	Pyrophosphoric acid, tetraethyl ester
P103	Selenourea
P104	Silver cyanide
P105	Sodium azide
P106	Sodium cyanide
P107	Strontium sulfide
P108	Strychnidin-10-one, and salts
P018	Strychnidin-10-one, 2,3-dimethoxy-
P108	Strychnine and salts
P115	Sulfuric acid, thallium(I) salt
P109	Tetraethyldithiopyrophosphate

Hazardous waste No	Substance	Hazardous Waste No	Substance
P110	Tetraethyl lead	U006	Acetyl chloride (C,R,T)
P111	Tetraethylpyrophosphate	U007	Acrylamide
P112	Tetranitromethane (R)	U008	Acrylic acid (I)
P062	Tetraphosphoric acid, hexaethyl ester	U009	Acrylonitrile
P113	Thallic oxide	U150	Alanine, 3-[p-bis(2-chloroethyl)amino] phenyl-, L-
P113	Thallium(III) oxide	U011	Amitrole
P114	Thallium(I) selenite	U012	Aniline (I,T)
P115	Thallium(I) sulfate	U014	Auramine
P045	Thiofanox	U015	Azaserine
P049	Thioimidodicarbonic diamide	U010	Azirino(2',3':3,4)pyrrolo(1,2-a)indole-4,7-dione, 6-amino-8-[((aminocarbonyl) oxy)methyl]-1,1a,2,8,8a,8b-hexahydro-8a-methoxy-5-methyl-,
P014	Thiophenol	U157	Benz[j]aceanthrylene, 1,2-dihydro-3-methyl-
P116	Thiosemicarbazide	U016	Benz[c]acridine
P026	Thiourea, (2-chlorophenyl)-	U016	3,4-Benzacridine
P072	Thiourea, 1-naphthalenyl-	U017	Benzal chloride
P093	Thiourea, phenyl-	U018	Benz[a]anthracene
P123	Toxaphene	U018	1,2-Benzanthracene
P118	Trichloromethanethiol	U094	1,2-Benzanthracene, 7,12-dimethyl-
P119	Vanadic acid, ammonium salt	U012	Benzenamine (I,T)
P120	Vanadium pentoxide	U014	Benzenamine, 4,4'-carbonimidoylbis(N,N-dimethyl-
P120	Vanadium(V) oxide	U049	Benzenamine, 4-chloro-2-methyl-
P001	Warfarin, when present at concentrations greater than 0.3%	U093	Benzenamine, N,N'-dimethyl-4-phenylazo-
P121	Zinc cyanide	U158	Benzenamine, 4,4'-methylenebis(2-chloro-
P122	Zinc phosphide, when present at concentrations greater than 10%	U222	Benzenamine, 2-methyl-, hydrochloride
		U181	Benzenamine, 2-methyl-5-nitro
		U019	Benzene (I,T)
		U038	Benzeneacetic acid, 4-chloro-alpha-(4-chlorophenyl)-alpha-hydroxy, ethyl ester
		U030	Benzene, 1-bromo-4-phenoxy-
		U037	Benzene, chloro-
		U190	1,2-Benzenedicarboxylic acid anhydride
		U028	1,2-Benzenedicarboxylic acid, [bis(2-ethylhexyl)] ester
		U069	1,2-Benzenedicarboxylic acid, dibutyl ester
		U088	1,2-Benzenedicarboxylic acid, diethyl ester
		U102	1,2-Benzenedicarboxylic acid, dimethyl ester
		U107	1,2-Benzenedicarboxylic acid, di-n-octyl ester
		U070	Benzene, 1,2-dichloro-
		U071	Benzene, 1,3-dichloro-
		U072	Benzene, 1,4-dichloro-
		U017	Benzene, (dichloromethyl)-
		U223	Benzene, 1,3-diisocyanatomethyl- (R,T)
		U239	Benzene, dimethyl-(I,T)
		U201	1,3-Benzenediol
		U127	Benzene, hexachloro-
		U056	Benzene, hexahydro- (I)
		U188	Benzene, hydroxy-
		U220	Benzene, methyl-
		U105	Benzene, 1-methyl-1-2,4-dinitro-
		U106	Benzene, 1-methyl-2,6-dinitro-
		U203	Benzene, 1,2-methylenedioxy-4-allyl-
		U141	Benzene, 1,2-methylenedioxy-4-propenyl-
		U090	Benzene, 1,2-methylenedioxy-4-propyl-
		U055	Benzene, (1-methylethyl)- (I)
		U169	Benzene, nitro- (I,T)
		U183	Benzene, pentachloro-
		U185	Benzene, pentachloro-nitro-
		U020	Benzenesulfonic acid chloride (C,R)
		U020	Benzenesulfonyl chloride (C,R)
		U207	Benzene, 1,2,4,5-tetrachloro-
		U023	Benzene, (trichloromethyl)-(C,R,T)
		0234	Benzene, 1,3,5-trinitro- (R,T)
		U021	Benzidine
		U202	1,2-Benzisothiazolin-3-one, 1,1-dioxide
		U120	Benzo[j,k]fluorene
		U022	Benzo[a]pyrene
		U022	3,4-Benzopyrene
		U197	p-Benzoquinone

(f) The commercial chemical products, manufacturing chemical intermediates, or off-specification commercial chemical products referred to in paragraphs (a) through (d) of this section, are identified as toxic wastes (T) unless otherwise designated and are subject to the small quantity exclusion defined in § 261.5 (a) and (f).

[Comment: For the convenience of the regulated community, the primary hazardous properties of these materials have been indicated by the letters T (Toxicity), R (Reactivity), I (Ignitability) and C (Corrosivity). Absence of a letter indicates that the compound is only listed for toxicity.]

These wastes and their corresponding EPA Hazardous Waste Numbers are:

Hazardous Waste No.	Substance
U001	Acetaldehyde (I)
U034	Acetaldehyde, trichloro-
U187	Acetamide, N-(4-ethoxyphenyl)-
U005	Acetamide, N-9H-fluoren-2-yl-
U112	Acetic acid, ethyl ester (I)
U144	Acetic acid, lead salt
U214	Acetic acid, thallium(I) salt
U002	Acetone (I)
U003	Acetonitrile (I,T)
U248	3-(alpha-Acetonylbenzyl)-4-hydroxycoumarin and salts, when present at concentrations of 0.3% or less
U004	Acetophenone
U005	2-Acetylaminofluorene

Hazardous Waste No.	Substance	Hazardous Waste No.	Substance
U023	Benzotrichloride (C,R,T)	U063	Dibenz[a,h]anthracene
U050	1,2-Benzphenanthrene	U063	1,2:5,6-Dibenzanthracene
U085	2,2'-Bioxirane (I,T)	U064	1,2:7,8-Dibenzopyrene
U021	(1,1'-Biphenyl)-4,4'-diamine	U064	Dibenz[a,i]pyrene
U073	(1,1'-Biphenyl)-4,4'-diamine, 3,3'-dichloro-	U066	1,2-Dibromo-3-chloropropane
U091	(1,1'-Biphenyl)-4,4'-diamine, 3,3'-dimethoxy-	U069	Dibutyl phthalate
U095	(1,1'-Biphenyl)-4,4'-diamine, 3,3'-dimethyl-	U062	S-(2,3-Dichloroallyl) diisopropylthiocarbamate
U024	Bis(2-chloroethoxy) methane	U070	o-Dichlorobenzene
U027	Bis(2-chloroisopropyl) ether	U071	m-Dichlorobenzene
U244	Bis(dimethylthiocarbamoyl) disulfide	U072	p-Dichlorobenzene
U028	Bis(2-ethylhexyl) phthalate	U073	3,3'-Dichlorobenzidine
U246	Bromine cyanide	U074	1,4-Dichloro-2-butene (I,T)
U225	Bromoform	U075	Dichlorodifluoromethane
U030	4-Bromophenyl phenyl ether	U192	3,5-Dichloro-N-(1,1-dimethyl-2-propynyl) benzamide
U128	1,3-Butadiene, 1,1,2,3,4,4-hexachloro-		
U172	1-Butanamine, N-butyl-N-nitroso-	U060	Dichloro diphenyl dichloroethane
U035	Butanoic acid, 4-[Bis(2-chloroethyl)amino] benzene-	U061	Dichloro diphenyl trichloroethane
		U078	1,1-Dichloroethylene
U031	1-Butanol (I)	U079	1,2-Dichloroethylene
U159	2-Butanone (I,T)	U025	Dichloroethyl ether
U160	2-Butanone peroxide (R,T)	U081	2,4-Dichlorophenol
U053	2-Butenal	U082	2,6-Dichlorophenol
U074	2-Butene, 1,4-dichloro- (I,T)	U240	2,4-Dichlorophenoxyacetic acid, salts and esters
U031	n-Butyl alchohol (I)		
U136	Cacodylic acid	U083	1,2-Dichloropropane
U032	Calcium chromate	U084	1,3-Dichloropropene
U238	Carbamic acid, ethyl ester	U085	1,2:3,4-Diepoxybutane (I,T)
U178	Carbamic acid, methylnitroso-, ethyl ester	U108	1,4-Diethylene dioxide
U176	Carbamide, N-ethyl-N-nitroso-	U086	N,N-Diethylhydrazine
U177	Carbamide, N-methyl-N-nitroso-	U087	O,O-Diethyl-S-methyl-dithiophosphate
U219	Carbamide, thio-	U088	Diethyl phthalate
U097	Carbamoyl chloride, dimethyl-	U089	Diethylstilbestrol
U215	Carbonic acid, dithallium(I) salt	U148	1,2-Dihydro-3,6-pyradizinedione
U156	Carbonochloridic acid, methyl ester (I,T)	U090	Dihydrosafrole
U033	Carbon oxyfluoride (R,T)	U091	3,3'-Dimethoxybenzidine
U211	Carbon tetrachloride	U092	Dimethylamine (I)
U033	Carbonyl fluoride (R,T)	U093	Dimethylaminoazobenzene
U034	Chloral	U094	7,12-Dimethylbenz[a]anthracene
U035	Chlorambucil	U095	3,3'-Dimethylbenzidine
U036	Chlordane, technical	U096	alpha,alpha-Dimethylbenzylhydroperoxide (R)
U026	Chlornaphazine	U097	Dimethylcarbamoyl chloride
U037	Chlorobenzene	U098	1,1-Dimethylhydrazine
U039	4-Chloro-m-cresol	U099	1,2-Dimethylhydrazine
U041	1-Chloro-2,3-epoxypropane	U101	2,4-Dimethylphenol
U042	2-Chloroethyl vinyl ether	U102	Dimethyl phthalate
U044	Chloroform	U103	Dimethyl sulfate
U046	Chloromethyl methyl ether	U105	2,4-Dinitrotoluene
U047	beta-Chloronaphthalene	U106	2,6-Dinitrotoluene
U048	o-Chlorophenol	U107	Di-n-octyl phthalate
U049	4-Chloro-o-toluidine, hydrochloride	U108	1,4-Dioxane
U032	Chromic acid, calcium salt	U109	1,2- Diphenylhydrazine
U050	Chrysene	U110	Dipropylamine (I)
U051	Creosote	U111	Di-N-propylnitrosamine
U052	Cresols	U001	Ethanal (I)
U052	Cresylic acid	U174	Ethanamine, N-ethyl-N-nitroso-
U053	Crotonaldehyde	U067	Ethane, 1,2-dibromo-
U055	Cumene (I)	U076	Ethane, 1,1-dichloro-
U246	Cyanogen bromide	U077	Ethane, 1,2-dichloro-
U197	1,4-Cyclohexadienedione	U114	1,2-Ethanediylbiscarbamodithioic acid
U056	Cyclohexane (I)	U131	Ethane, 1,1,1,2,2,2-hexachloro-
U057	Cyclohexanone (I)	U024	Ethane, 1,1'-[methylenebis(oxy)]bis[2-chloro-
U130	1,3-Cyclopentadiene, 1,2,3,4,5,5-hexa- chloro-	U003	Ethanenitrile (I, T)
U058	Cyclophosphamide	U117	Ethane,1,1'-oxybis- (I)
U240	2,4-D, salts and esters	U025	Ethane, 1,1'-oxybis[2-chloro-
U059	Daunomycin	U184	Ethane, pentachloro-
U060	DDD	U208	Ethane, 1,1,1,2-tetrachloro-
U061	DDT	U209	Ethane, 1,1,2,2-tetrachloro-
U142	Decachlorooctahydro-1,3,4-metheno-2H- cyclobuta[c,d]-pentalen-2-one	U218	Ethanethioamide
		U247	Ethane, 1,1,1,-trichloro-2,2-bis(p-methoxy-phenyl).
U062	Diallate		
U133	Diamine (R,T)	U227	Ethane, 1,1,2-trichloro-
U221	Diaminotoluene	U043	Ethene, chloro-

Hazardous Waste No.	Substance	Hazardous Waste No.	Substance
U042	Ethene, 2-chloroethoxy-	U068	Methane, dibromo-
U078	Ethene, 1,1-dichloro-	U080	Methane, dichloro-
U079	Ethene, trans-1,2-dichloro-	U075	Methane, dichlorodifluoro-
U210	Ethene, 1,1,2,2-tetrachloro-	U138	Methane, iodo-
U173	Ethanol, 2,2'-(nitrosoimino)bis-	U119	Methanesulfonic acid, ethyl ester
U004	Ethanone, 1-phenyl-	U211	Methane, tetrachloro-
U006	Ethanoyl chloride (C,R,T)	U121	Methane, trichlorofluoro-
U112	Ethyl acetate (I)	U153	Methanethiol (I,T)
U113	Ethyl acrylate (I)	U225	Methane, tribromo-
U238	Ethyl carbamate (urethan)	U044	Methane, trichloro-
U038	Ethyl 4,4'-dichlorobenzilate	U121	Methane, trichlorofluoro-
U114	Ethylenebis(dithiocarbamic acid)	U123	Methanoic acid (C,T)
U067	Etylene dibromide	U036	4,7-Methanoindan, 1,2,4,5,6,7,8,8-octa-chloro-3a,4,7,7a-tetrahydro-
U077	Ethylene dichloride		
U115	Ethylene oxide (I,T)	U154	Methanol (I)
U116	Ethylene thiourea	U155	Methapyrilene
U117	Ethyl ether (I)	U247	Methoxychlor.
U076	Ethylidene dichloride	U154	Methyl alcohol (I)
U118	Ethylmethacrylate	U029	Methyl bromide
U119	Ethyl methanesulfonate	U186	1-Methylbutadiene (I)
U139	Ferric dextran	U045	Methyl chloride (I,T)
U120	Fluoranthene	U156	Methyl chlorocarbonate (I,T)
U122	Formaldehyde	U226	Methylchloroform
U123	Formic acid (C,T)	U157	3-Methylcholanthrene
U124	Furan (I)	U158	4,4'-Methylenebis(2-chloroaniline)
U125	2-Furancarboxaldehyde (I)	U132	2,2'-Methylenebis(3,4,6-trichlorophenol)
U147	2,5-Furandione	U068	Methylene bromide
U213	Furan, tetrahydro- (I)	U080	Methylene chloride
U125	Furfural (I)	U122	Methylene oxide
U124	Furfuran (I)	U159	Methyl ethyl ketone (I,T)
U206	D-Glucopyranose, 2-deoxy-2(3-methyl-3-nitro-soureido)-	U160	Methyl ethyl ketone peroxide (R,T)
		U138	Methyl iodide
U126	Glycidylaldehyde	U161	Methyl isobutyl ketone (I)
U163	Guanidine, N-nitroso-N-methyl-N'nitro-	U162	Methyl methacrylate (I,T)
U127	Hexachlorobenzene	U163	N-Methyl-N'-nitro-N-nitrosoguanidine
U128	Hexachlorobutadiene	U161	4-Methyl-2-pentanone (I)
U129	Hexachlorocyclohexane (gamma isomer)	U164	Methylthiouracil
U130	Hexachlorocyclopentadiene	U010	Mitomycin C
U131	Hexachloroethane	U059	5,12-Naphthacenedione, (8S-cis)-8-acetyl-10-[(3-amino-2,3,6-trideoxy-alpha-L-lyxo-hexopyranosyl)oxyl]-7,8,9,10-tetrahydro-6,8,11-trihydroxy-1-methoxy-
U132	Hexachlorophene		
U243	Hexachloropropene		
U133	Hydrazine (R,T)		
U086	Hydrazine, 1,2-diethyl-	U165	Naphthalene
U098	Hydrazine, 1,1-dimethyl-	U047	Naphthalene, 2-chloro-
U099	Hydrazine, 1,2-dimethyl-	U166	1,4-Naphthalenedione
U109	Hydrazine, 1,2-diphenyl-	U236	2,7-Naphthalenedisulfonic acid, 3,3'-[(3,3'-di-methyl-(1,1'-biphenyl)-4,4'-diyl)]-bis (azo)bis(5-amino-4-hydroxy)-,tetrasodium salt
U134	Hydrofluoric acid (C,T)		
U134	Hydrogen fluoride (C,T)		
U135	Hydrogen sulfide		
U096	Hydroperoxide, 1-methyl-1-phenylethyl- (R)	U166	1,4-Naphthaquinone
U136	Hydroxydimethylarsine oxide	U167	1-Naphthylamine
U116	2-Imidazolidinethione	U168	2-Naphthylamine
U137	Indeno[1,2,3-cd]pyrene	U167	alpha-Naphthylamine
U139	Iron dextran	U168	beta-Naphthylamine
U140	Isobutyl alcohol (I,T)	U026	2-Naphthylamine, N,N'-bis(2-chloromethyl)-
U141	Isosafrole	U169	Nitrobenzene (I,T)
U142	Kepone	U170	p-Nitrophenol
U143	Lasiocarpine	U171	2-Nitropropane (I)
U144	Lead acetate	U172	N-Nitrosodi-n-butylamine
U145	Lead phosphate	U173	N-Nitrosodiethanolamine
U146	Lead subacetate	U174	N-Nitrosodiethylamine
U129	Lindane	U111	N-Nitroso-N-propylamine
U147	Maleic anhydride	U176	N-Nitroso-N-ethylurea
U148	Maleic hydrazide	U177	N-Nitroso-N-methylurea
U149	Malononitrile	U178	N-Nitroso-N-methylurethane
U150	Melphalan	U179	N-Nitrosopiperidine
U151	Mercury	U180	N-Nitrosopyrrolidine
U152	Methacrylonitrile (I,T)	U181	5-Nitro-o-toluidine
U092	Methanamine, N-methyl- (I)	U193	1,2-Oxathiolane, 2,2-dioxide
U029	Methane, bromo-	U058	2H-1,3,2-Oxazaphosphorine, 2-[bis(2-chloro-ethyl)amino]tetrahydro-, oxide 2-
U045	Methane, chloro- (I,T)		
U046	Methane, chloromethoxy-	U115	Oxirane (I,T)

Hazardous Waste No.	Substance	Hazardous Waste No.	Substance
U041	Oxirane, 2-(chloromethyl)-	U205	Sulfur selenide (R,T)
U182	Paraldehyde	U232	2,4,5-T
U183	Pentachlorobenzene	U207	1,2,4,5-Tetrachlorobenzene
U184	Pentachloroethane	U208	1,1,1,2-Tetrachloroethane
U185	Pentachloronitrobenzene	U209	1,1,2,2-Tetrachloroethane
U242	Pentachlorophenol	U210	Tetrachloroethylene
U186	1,3-Pentadiene (I)	U212	2,3,4,6-Tetrachlorophenol
U187	Phenacetin	U213	Tetrahydrofuran (I)
U188	Phenol	U214	Thallium(I) acetate
U048	Phenol, 2-chloro-	U215	Thallium(I) carbonate
U039	Phenol, 4-chloro-3-methyl-	U216	Thallium(I) chloride
U081	Phenol, 2,4-dichloro-	U217	Thallium(I) nitrate
U082	Phenol, 2,6-dichloro-	U218	Thioacetamide
U101	Phenol, 2,4-dimethyl-	U153	Thiomethanol (I,T)
U170	Phenol, 4-nitro-	U219	Thiourea
U242	Phenol, pentachloro-	U244	Thiram
U212	Phenol, 2,3,4,6-tetrachloro-	U220	Toluene
U230	Phenol, 2,4,5-trichloro-	U221	Toluenediamine
U231	Phenol, 2,4,6-trichloro-	U223	Toluene diisocyanate (R,T)
U137	1,10-(1,2-phenylene)pyrene	U222	O-Toluidine hydrochloride
U145	Phosphoric acid, Lead salt	U011	1H-1,2,4-Triazol-3-amine
U087	Phosphorodithioic acid, 0,0-diethyl-, S-methyl-lester	U226	1,1,1-Trichloroethane
		U227	1,1,2-Trichloroethane
U189	Phosphorous sulfide (R)	U228	Trichloroethene
U190	Phthalic anhydride	U228	Trichloroethylene
U191	2-Picoline	U121	Trichloromonofluoromethane
U192	Pronamide	U230	2,4,5-Trichlorophenol
U194	1-Propanamine (I,T)	U231	2,4,6-Trichlorophenol
U110	1-Propanamine, N-propyl- (I)	U232	2,4,5-Trichlorophenoxyacetic acid
U066	Propane, 1,2-dibromo-3-chloro-	U234	sym-Trinitrobenzene (R,T)
U149	Propanedinitrile	U182	1,3,5-Trioxane, 2,4,6-trimethyl-
U171	Propane, 2-nitro- (I)	U235	Tris(2,3-dibromopropyl) phosphate
U027	Propane, 2,2'oxybis[2-chloro-	U236	Trypan blue
U193	1,3-Propane sultone	U237	Uracil, 5[bis(2-chloromethyl)amino]-
U235	1-Propanol, 2,3-dibromo-, phosphate (3:1)	U237	Uracil mustard
U126	1-Propanol, 2,3-epoxy-	U043	Vinyl chloride
U140	1-Propanol, 2-methyl- (I,T)	U248	Warfarin, when present at concentrations of 0.3% or less
U002	2-Propanone (I)		
U007	2-Propenamide	U239	Xylene (I)
U084	Propene, 1,3-dichloro-	U200	Yohimban-16-carboxylic acid, 11,17-dimethoxy-18-[(3,4,5-trimethoxy-benzoyl)oxy]-, methyl ester
U243	1-Propene, 1,1,2,3,3,3-hexachloro-		
U009	2-Propenenitrile		
U152	2-Propenenitrile, 2-methyl- (I,T)		
U008	2-Propenoic acid (I)	U249	Zinc phosphide, when present at concentrations of 10% or less
U113	2-Propenoic acid, ethyl ester (I)		
U118	2-Propenoic acid, 2-methyl-, ethyl ester		
U162	2-Propenoic acid, 2-methyl-, methyl ester (I,T)		
U233	Propionic acid, 2-(2,4,5-trichlorophenoxy)-		
U194	n-Propylamine (I,T)		
U083	Propylene dichloride		
U196	Pyridine		
U155	Pyridine, 2-[(2-(dimethylamino)-2-thenyla-mino]-		
U179	Pyridine, hexahydro-N-nitroso-		
U191	Pyridine, 2-methyl-		
U164	4(1H)-Pyrimidinone, 2,3-dihydro-6-methyl-2-thioxo-		
U180	Pyrrole, tetrahydro-N-nitroso-		
U200	Reserpine		
U201	Resorcinol		
U202	Saccharin and salts		
U203	Safrole		
U204	Selenious acid		
U204	Selenium dioxide		
U205	Selenium disulfide (R,T)		
U015	L-Serine, diazoacetate (ester)		
U233	Silvex		
U089	4,4'-Stilbenediol, alpha,alpha'-diethyl-		
U206	Streptozotocin		
U135	Sulfur hydride		
U103	Sulfuric acid, dimethyl ester		
U189	Sulfur phosphide (R)		

[45 FR 78529, 78541, Nov. 25, 1980, as amended at 46 FR 27477, May 20, 1981; 49 FR 19923, May 10, 1984]

APPENDIX C

LIST OF HAZARDOUS WASTE CONSTITUENTS
(40 C.F.R. PART 261, APPENDIX VIII)

The presence of the following constituents in a waste may lead EPA in the future to list a waste as hazardous. In addition, if concentrations of these constituents exceed background concentrations, facilities must undertake corrective action. See pp. 41-42 in the text.

APPENDIX VII—BASIS FOR LISTING HAZARDOUS WASTE

EPA hazardous waste No.	Hazardous constituents for which listed
F001	Tetrachloroethylene, methylene chloride trichloroethylene, 1,1,1-trichloroethane, carbon tetrachloride, chlorinated fluorocarbons.
F002	Tetrachloroethylene, methylene chloride, trichloroethylene, 1,1,1-trichloroethane, chlorobenzene, 1,1,2-trichloro-1,2,2-trifluoroethane, ortho-dichlorobenzene, trichlorofluoromethane.
F003	N.A.
F004	Cresols and cresylic acid, nitrobenzene.
F005	Toluene, methyl ethyl ketone, carbon disulfide, isobutanol, pyridine.
F006	Cadmium, hexavalent chromium, nickel, cyanide (complexed).
F007	Cyanide (salts).
F008	Cyanide (salts).
F009	Cyanide (salts).
F010	Cyanide (salts).
F011	Cyanide (salts).
F012	Cyanide (complexed).
F019	Hexavalent chromium, cyanide (complexed).
F024	Chloromethane, dichloromethane, trichloromethane, carbon tetrachloride, chloroethylene, 1,1-dichloroethane, 1,2-dichloroethane, trans-1-2-dichloroethylene, 1,1-dichloroethylene, 1,1,1-trichloroethane, 1,1,2-trichloroethane, trichloroethylene, 1,1,1,2-tetra-chloroethane, 1,1,2,2-tetrachloroethane, tetrachloroethylene, pentachloroethane, hexachloroethane, allyl chloride (3-chloropropene), dichloropropane, dichloropropene, 2-chloro-1,3-butadiene, hexachloro-1,3-butadiene, hexachlorocyclopentadiene, hexachlorocyclohexane, benzene, chlorobenzene, dichlorobenzenes, 1,2,4-trichlorobenzene, tetrachlorobenzene, pentachlorobenzene, hexachlorobenzene, toluene, naphthalene.

EPA hazardous waste No.	Hazardous constituents for which listed
K001	Pentachlorophenol, phenol, 2-chlorophenol, p-chloro-m-cresol, 2,4-dimethylphenyl, 2,4-dinitrophenol, trichlorophenols, tetrachlorophenols, 2,4-dinitrophenol, cresosote, chrysene, naphthalene, fluoranthene, benzo(b)fluoranthene, benzo(a)pyrene, indeno(1,2,3-cd)pyrene, benz(a)anthracene, dibenz(a)anthracene, acenaphthalene.
K002	Hexavalent chromium, lead
K003	Hexavalent chromium, lead.
K004	Hexavalent chromium.
K005	Hexavalent chromium, lead.
K006	Hexavalent chromium.
K007	Cyanide (complexed), hexavalent chromium.
K008	Hexavalent chromium.
K009	Chloroform, formaldehyde, methylene chloride, methyl chloride, paraldehyde, formic acid.
K010	Chloroform, formaldehyde, methylene chloride, methyl chloride, paraldehyde, formic acid, chloroacetaldehyde.
K011	Acrylonitrile, acetonitrile, hydrocyanic acid.
K013	Hydrocyanic acid, acrylonitrile, acetonitrile.
K014	Acetonitrile, acrylamide.
K015	Benzyl chloride, chlorobenzene, toluene, benzotrichloride.
K016	Hexachlorobenzene, hexachlorobutadiene, carbon tetrachloride, hexachloroethane, perchloroethylene.
K017	Epichlorohydrin, chloroethers [bis(chloromethyl) ether and bis (2-chloroethyl) ethers], trichloropropane, dichloropropanols.
K018	1,2-dichloroethane, trichloroethylene, hexachlorobutadiene, hexachlorobenzene.
K019	Ethylene dichloride, 1,1,1-trichloroethane, 1,1,2-trichloroethane, tetrachloroethanes (1,1,2,2-tetrachloroethane and 1,1,1,2-tetrachloroethane), trichloroethylene, tetrachloroethylene, carbon tetrachloride, chloroform, vinyl chloride, vinylidene chloride.
K020	Ethylene dichloride, 1,1,1-trichloroethane, 1,1,2-trichloroethane, tetrachloroethanes (1,1,2,2-tetrachloroethane and 1,1,1,2-tetrachloroethane), trichloroethylene, tetrachloroethylene, carbon tetrachloride, chloroform, vinyl chloride, vinylidene chloride.
K021	Antimony, carbon tetrachloride, chloroform.
K022	Phenol, tars (polycyclic aromatic hydrocarbons).
K023	Phthalic anhydride, maleic anhydride.
K024	Phthalic anhydride, 1,4-naphthoquinone.
K025	Meta-dinitrobenzene, 2,4-dinitrotoluene.
K026	Paraldehyde, pyridines, 2-picoline.
K027	Toluene diisocyanate, toluene-2, 4-diamine.
K028	1,1,1-trichloroethane, vinyl chloride.

EPA hazardous waste No.	Hazardous constituents for which listed
K029	1,2-dichloroethane, 1,1,1-trichloroethane, vinyl chloride, vinylidene chloride, chloroform.
K030	Hexachlorobenzene, hexachlorobutadiene, hexachloroethane, 1,1,1,2-tetrachloroethane, 1,1,2,2-tetrachloroethane, ethylene dichloride.
K031	Arsenic.
K032	Hexachlorocyclopentadiene.
K033	Hexachlorocyclopentadiene.
K034	Hexachlorocyclopentadiene.
K035	Creosote, chrysene, naphthalene, fluoranthene benzo(b) fluoranthene, benzo(a)pyrene, indeno(1,2,3-cd) pyrene, benzo(a)anthracene, dibenzo(a)anthracene, acenaphthalene.
K036	Toluene, phosphorodithioic and phosphorothioic acid esters.
K037	Toluene, phosphorodithioic and phosphorothioic acid esters.
K038	Phorate, formaldehyde, phosphorodithioic and phosphorothioic acid esters.
K039	Phosphorodithioic and phosphorothioic acid esters.
K040	Phorate, formaldehyde, phosphorodithioic and phosphorothioic acid esters.
K041	Toxaphene.
K042	Hexachlorobenzene, ortho-dichlorobenzene.
K043	2,4-dichlorophenol, 2,6-dichlorophenol, 2,4,6-trichlorophenol.
K044	N.A.
K045	N.A.
K046	Lead.
K047	N.A.
K048	Hexavalent chromium, lead.
K049	Hexavalent chromium, lead.
K050	Hexavalent chromium.
K051	Hexavalent chromium, lead.
K052	Lead.
K060	Cyanide, napthalene, phenolic compounds, arsenic.
K061	Hexavalent chromium, lead, cadmium.
K062	Hexavalent chromium, lead.
K069	Hexavalent chromium, lead, cadmium.
K071	Mercury.
K073	Chloroform, carbon tetrachloride, hexachloroethane, trichloroethane, tetrachloroethylene, dichloroethylene, 1,1,2,2-tetrachloroethane.
K083	Aniline, diphenylamine, nitrobenzene, phenylenediamine.
K084	Arsenic.
K085	Benzene, dichlorobenzenes, trichlorobenzenes, tetrachlorobenzenes, pentachlorobenzene, hexachlorobenzene, benzyl chloride.
K086	Lead, hexavalent chromium.
K087	Phenol, naphthalene.
K093	Phthalic anhydride, maleic anhydride.
K094	Phthalic anhydride.
K095	1,1,2-trichloroethane, 1,1,1,2-tetrachloroethane, 1,1,2,2-tetrachloroethane.
K096	1,2-dichloroethane, 1,1,1-trichloroethane, 1,1,2-trichloroethane.
K097	Chlordane, heptachlor.
K098	Toxaphene.
K099	2,4-dichlorophenol, 2,4,6-trichlorophenol.
K100	Hexavalent chromium, lead, cadmium.
K101	Arsenic.
K102	Arsenic.
K103	Aniline, nitrobenzene, phenylenediamine.
K104	Aniline, benzene, diphenylamine, nitrobenzene, phenylenediamine.

EPA hazardous waste No.	Hazardous constituents for which listed
K105	Benzene, monochlorobenzene, dichlorobenzenes, 2,4,6-trichlorophenol.
K106	Mercury.

N.A.—Waste is hazardous because it fails the test for the characteristic of ignitability, corrosivity, or reactivity.

[46 FR 4619, Jan. 16, 1981, as amended at 46 FR 27477, May 20, 1981; 49 FR 5312, Feb. 10, 1984]

EFFECTIVE DATE NOTE: At 49 FR 5312, Feb. 10, 1984, the entry identified by EPA hazardous waste no. F024, was added to the table in Appendix VII, effective August 10, 1984.

APPENDIX VIII—HAZARDOUS CONSTITUENTS

Acetonitrile (Ethanenitrile)
Acetophenone (Ethanone, 1-phenyl)
3-(alpha-Acetonylbenzyl)-4-hydroxycoumarin and salts (Warfarin)
2-Acetylaminofluorene (Acetamide, N-(9H-fluoren-2-yl)-)
Acetyl chloride (Ethanoyl chloride)
1-Acetyl-2-thiourea (Acetamide, N-(aminothioxomethyl)-)
Acrolein (2-Propenal)
Acrylamide (2-Propenamide)
Acrylonitrile (2-Propenenitrile)
Aflatoxins
Aldrin (1,2,3,4,10,10-Hexachloro-1,4,4a,5,8,8a,8b-hexahydro-endo,exo-1,4:5,8-Dimethanonaphthalene)
Allyl alcohol (2-Propen-1-ol)
Aluminum phosphide
4-Aminobiphenyl ([1,1'-Biphenyl]-4-amine)
6-Amino-1,1a,2,8,8a,8b-hexahydro-8-(hydroxymethyl)-8a-methoxy-5-methylcarbamate azirino[2',3':3,4]pyrrolo[1,2-a]indole-4,7-dione, (ester) (Mitomycin C) (Azirino[2'3':3,4]pyrrolo(1,2-a)indole-4,7-dione, 6-amino-8-[((aminocarbonyl)oxy)methyl]-1,1a,2,8,8a,8b-hexahydro-8amethoxy-5-methy-)
5-(Aminomethyl)-3-isoxazolol (3(2H)-Isoxazolone, 5-(aminomethyl)-) 4-Aminopyridine (4-Pyridinamine)
Amitrole (1H-1,2,4-Triazol-3-amine)
Aniline (Benzenamine)
Antimony and compounds, N.O.S.*
Aramite (Sulfurous acid, 2-chloroethyl-, 2-[4-(1,1-dimethylethyl)phenoxy]-1-methylethyl ester)

* The abbreviation N.O.S. (not otherwise specified) signifies those members of the general class not specifically listed by name in this appendix.

Arsenic and compounds, N.O.S.*
Arsenic acid (Orthoarsenic acid)
Arsenic pentoxide (Arsenic (V) oxide)
Arsenic trioxide (Arsenic (III) oxide)
Auramine (Benzenamine, 4,4'-carbonimidoylbis[N,N-Dimethyl-, monohydrochloride)
Azaserine (L-Serine, diazoacetate (ester))
Barium and compounds, N.O.S.*
Barium cyanide
Benz[c]acridine (3,4-Benzacridine)
Benz[a]anthracene (1,2-Benzanthracene)
Benzene (Cyclohexatriene)
Benzenearsonic acid (Arsonic acid, phenyl-)
Benzene, dichloromethyl- (Benzal chloride)
Benzenethiol (Thiophenol)
Benzidine ([1,1'-Biphenyl]-4,4'diamine)
Benzo[b]fluoranthene (2,3-Benzofluoranthene)
Benzo[j]fluoranthene (7,8-Benzofluoranthene)
Benzo[a]pyrene (3,4-Benzopyrene)
p-Benzoquinone (1,4-Cyclohexadienedione)
Benzotrichloride (Benzene, trichloromethyl)
Benzyl chloride (Benzene, (chloromethyl)-)
Beryllium and compounds, N.O.S.*
Bis(2-chloroethoxy)methane (Ethane, 1,1'-[methylenebis(oxy)]bis[2-chloro-])
Bis(2-chloroethyl) ether (Ethane, 1,1'-oxybis[2-chloro-])
N,N-Bis(2-chloroethyl)-2-naphthylamine (Chlornaphazine)
Bis(2-chloroisopropyl) ether (Propane, 2,2'-oxybis[2-chloro-])
Bis(chloromethyl) ether (Methane, oxybis[chloro-])
Bis(2-ethylhexyl) phthalate (1,2-Benzenedicarboxylic acid, bis(2-ethylhexyl) ester)
Bromoacetone (2-Propanone, 1-bromo-)
Bromomethane (Methyl bromide)
4-Bromophenyl phenyl ether (Benzene, 1-bromo-4-phenoxy-)
Brucine (Strychnidin-10-one, 2,3-dimethoxy-)
2-Butanone peroxide (Methyl ethyl ketone, peroxide)
Butyl benzyl phthalate (1,2-Benzenedicarboxylic acid, butyl phenylmethyl ester)
2-sec-Butyl-4,6-dinitrophenol (DNBP) (Phenol, 2,4-dinitro-6-(1-methylpropyl)-)
Cadmium and compounds, N.O.S.*
Calcium chromate (Chromic acid, calcium salt)
Calcium cyanide
Carbon disulfide (Carbon bisulfide)
Carbon oxyfluoride (Carbonyl fluoride)
Chloral (Acetaldehyde, trichloro-)
Chlorambucil (Butanoic acid, 4-[bis(2-chloroethyl)amino]benzene)
Chlordane (alpha and gamma isomers) (4,7-Methanoindan, 1,2,4,5,6,7,8,8-octachloro-3,4,7,7a-tetrahydro-) (alpha and gamma isomers)
Chlorinated benzenes, N.O.S.*
Chlorinated ethane, N.O.S.*
Chlorinated fluorocarbons, N.O.S.*

Chlorinated naphthalene, N.O.S.*
Chlorinated phenol, N.O.S.*
Chloroacetaldehyde (Acetaldehyde, chloro-)
Chloroalkyl ethers, N.O.S.*
p-Chloroaniline (Benzenamine, 4-chloro-)
Chlorobenzene (Benzene, chloro-)
Chlorobenzilate (Benzeneacetic acid, 4-chloro-alpha-(4-chlorophenyl)-alpha-hydroxy-, ethyl ester)
2-Chloro-1,3-butadiene (chloroprene)
p-Chloro-m-cresol (Phenol, 4-chloro-3-methyl)
1-Chloro-2,3-epoxypropane (Oxirane, 2-(chloromethyl)-)
2-Chloroethyl vinyl ether (Ethene, (2-chloroethoxy)-)
Chloroform (Methane, trichloro-)
Chloromethane (Methyl chloride)
Chloromethyl methyl ether (Methane, chloromethoxy-)
2-Chloronaphthalene (Naphthalene, beta-chloro-)
2-Chlorophenol (Phenol, o-chloro-)
1-(o-Chlorophenyl)thiourea (Thiourea, (2-chlorophenyl)-)
3-Chloropropene (allyl chloride)
3-Chloropropionitrile (Propanenitrile, 3-chloro-)
Chromium and compounds, N.O.S.*
Chrysene (1,2-Benzphenanthrene)
Citrus red No. 2 (2-Naphthol, 1-[(2,5-dimethoxyphenyl)azo]-)
Coal tars
Copper cyanide
Creosote (Creosote, wood)
Cresols (Cresylic acid) (Phenol, methyl-)
Crotonaldehyde (2-Butenal)
Cyanides (soluble salts and complexes), N.O.S.*
Cyanogen (Ethanedinitrile)
Cyanogen bromide (Bromine cyanide)
Cyanogen chloride (Chlorine cyanide)
Cycasin (beta-D-Glucopyranoside, (methyl-ONN-azoxy)methyl-)
2-Cyclohexyl-4,6-dinitrophenol (Phenol, 2-cyclohexyl-4,6-dinitro-)
Cyclophosphamide (2H-1,3,2,-Oxazaphosphorine, [bis(2-chloroethyl)amino]-tetrahydro-, 2-oxide)
Daunomycin (5,12-Naphthacenedione, (8S-cis)-8-acetyl-10-[(3-amino-2,3,6-trideoxy)-alpha-L-lyxo-hexopyranosyl)oxy]-7,8,9,10-tetrahydro-6,8,11-trihydroxy-1-methoxy-)
DDD (Dichlorodiphenyldichloroethane) (Ethane, 1,1-dichloro-2,2-bis(p-chlorophenyl)-)
DDE (Ethylene, 1,1-dichloro-2,2-bis(4-chlorophenyl)-)
DDT (Dichlorodiphenyltrichloroethane) (Ethane, 1,1,1-trichloro-2,2-bis(p-chlorophenyl)-)
Diallate (S-(2,3-dichloroallyl) diisopropylthiocarbamate)
Dibenz[a,h]acridine (1,2,5,6-Dibenzacridine)
Dibenz[a,j]acridine (1,2,7,8-Dibenzacridine)

Dibenz[a,h]anthracene (1,2,5,6-Dibenzanthracene)

7H-Dibenzo[c,g]carbazole (3,4,5,6-Dibenzcarbazole)

Dibenzo[a,e]pyrene (1,2,4,5-Dibenzpyrene)

Dibenzo[a,h]pyrene (1,2,5,6-Dibenzpyrene)

Dibenzo[a,i]pyrene (1,2,7,8-Dibenzpyrene)

1,2-Dibromo-3-chloropropane (Propane, 1,2-dibromo-3-chloro-)

1,2-Dibromoethane (Ethylene dibromide)

Dibromomethane (Methylene bromide)

Di-n-butyl phthalate (1,2-Benzenedicarboxylic acid, dibutyl ester)

o-Dichlorobenzene (Benzene, 1,2-dichloro-)

m-Dichlorobenzene (Benzene, 1,3-dichloro-)

p-Dichlorobenzene (Benzene, 1,4-dichloro-)

Dichlorobenzene, N.O.S.* (Benzene, dichloro-, N.O.S.*)

3,3'-Dichlorobenzidine ([1,1'-Biphenyl]-4,4'-diamine, 3,3'-dichloro-)

1,4-Dichloro-2-butene (2-Butene, 1,4-dichloro-)

Dichlorodifluoromethane (Methane, dichlorodifluoro-)

1,1-Dichloroethane (Ethylidene dichloride)

1,2-Dichloroethane (Ethylene dichloride)

trans-1,2-Dichloroethene (1,2-Dichloroethylene)

Dichloroethylene, N.O.S.* (Ethene, dichloro-, N.O.S.*)

1,1-Dichloroethylene (Ethene, 1,1-dichloro-)

Dichloromethane (Methylene chloride)

2,4-Dichlorophenol (Phenol, 2,4-dichloro-)

2,6-Dichlorophenol (Phenol, 2,6-dichloro-)

2,4-Dichlorophenoxyacetic acid (2,4-D), salts and esters (Acetic acid, 2,4-dichlorophenoxy-, salts and esters)

Dichlorophenylarsine (Phenyl dichloroarsine)

Dichloropropane, N.O.S.* (Propane, dichloro-, N.O.S.*)

1,2-Dichloropropane (Propylene dichloride)

Dichloropropanol, N.O.S.* (Propanol, dichloro-, N.O.S.*)

Dichloropropene, N.O.S.* (Propene, dichloro-, N.O.S.*)

1,3-Dichloropropene (1-Propene, 1,3-dichloro-)

Dieldrin (1,2,3,4,10,10-hexachloro-6,7-epoxy-1,4,4a,5,6,7,8,8a-octa-hydro-endo,exo-1,4:5,8-Dimethanonaphthalene)

1,2:3,4-Diepoxybutane (2,2'-Bioxirane)

Diethylarsine (Arsine, diethyl-)

N,N-Diethylhydrazine (Hydrazine, 1,2-diethyl)

O,O-Diethyl S-methyl ester of phosphorodithioic acid (Phosphorodithioic acid, O,O-diethyl S-methyl ester

O,O-Diethylphosphoric acid, O-p-nitrophenyl ester (Phosphoric acid, diethyl p-nitrophenyl ester)

Diethyl phthalate (1,2-Benzenedicarboxylic acid, diethyl ester)

O,O-Diethyl O-2-pyrazinyl phosphorothioate (Phosphorothioic acid, O,O-diethyl O-pyrazinyl ester

Diethylstilbesterol (4,4'-Stilbenediol, alpha,alpha-diethyl, bis(dihydrogen phosphate, (E)-)

Dihydrosafrole (Benzene, 1,2-methylene-dioxy-4-propyl-)

3,4-Dihydroxy-alpha-(methylamino)methyl benzyl alcohol (1,2-Benzenediol, 4-[1-hydroxy-2-(methylamino)ethyl]-)

Diisopropylfluorophosphate (DFP) (Phosphorofluoridic acid, bis(1-methylethyl) ester)

Dimethoate (Phosphorodithioic acid, O,O-dimethyl S-[2-(methylamino)-2-oxoethyl] ester

3,3'-Dimethoxybenzidine ([1,1'-Biphenyl]-4,4'diamine, 3-3'-dimethoxy-)

p-Dimethylaminoazobenzene (Benzenamine, N,N-dimethyl-4-(phenylazo)-)

7,12-Dimethylbenz[a]anthracene (1,2-Benzanthracene, 7,12-dimethyl-)

3,3'-Dimethylbenzidine ([1,1'-Biphenyl]-4,4'-diamine, 3,3'-dimethyl-)

Dimethylcarbamoyl chloride (Carbamoyl chloride, dimethyl-)

1,1-Dimethylhydrazine (Hydrazine, 1,1-dimethyl-)

1,2-Dimethylhydrazine (Hydrazine, 1,2-dimethyl-)

3,3-Dimethyl-1-(methylthio)-2-butanone, O-[(methylamino) carbonyl]oxime (Thiofanox)

alpha,alpha-Dimethylphenethylamine (Ethanamine, 1,1-dimethyl-2-phenyl-)

2,4-Dimethylphenol (Phenol, 2,4-dimethyl-)

Dimethyl phthalate (1,2-Benzenedicarboxylic acid, dimethyl ester)

Dimethyl sulfate (Sulfuric acid, dimethyl ester)

Dinitrobenzene, N.O.S.* (Benzene, dinitro-, N.O.S.*)

4,6-Dinitro-o-cresol and salts (Phenol, 2,4-dinitro-6-methyl-, and salts)

2,4-Dinitrophenol (Phenol, 2,4-dinitro-)

2,4-Dinitrotoluene (Benzene, 1-methyl-2,4-dinitro-)

2,6-Dinitrotoluene (Benzene, 1-methyl-2,6-dinitro-)

Di-n-octyl phthalate (1,2-Benzenedicarboxylic acid, dioctyl ester)

1,4-Dioxane (1,4-Diethylene oxide)

Diphenylamine (Benzenamine, N-phenyl-)

1,2-Diphenylhydrazine (Hydrazine, 1,2-diphenyl-)

Di-n-propylnitrosamine (N-Nitroso-di-n-propylamine)

Disulfoton (O,O-diethyl S-[2-(ethylthio)ethyl] phosphorodithioate)

2,4-Dithiobiuret (Thioimidodicarbonic diamide)

Endosulfan (5-Norbornene, 2,3-dimethanol, 1,4,5,6,7,7-hexachloro-, cyclic sulfite)

Endrin and metabolites (1,2,3,4,10,10-hexachloro-6,7-epoxy-1,4,4a,5,6,7,8,8a-octahydro-endo,endo-1,4:5,8-dimethanonaphthalene, and metabolites)

Ethyl carbamate (Urethan) (Carbamic acid, ethyl ester)

Ethyl cyanide (propanenitrile)

Ethylenebisdithiocarbamic acid, salts and esters (1,2-Ethanediylbiscarbamodithioic acid, salts and esters

Ethyleneimine (Aziridine)

Ethylene oxide (Oxirane)

Ethylenethiourea (2-Imidazolidinethione)

Ethyl methacrylate (2-Propenoic acid, 2-methyl-, ethyl ester)

Ethyl methanesulfonate (Methanesulfonic acid, ethyl ester)

Fluoranthene (Benzo[j,k]fluorene)

Fluorine

2-Fluoroacetamide (Acetamide, 2-fluoro-)

Fluoroacetic acid, sodium salt (Acetic acid, fluoro-, sodium salt)

Formaldehyde (Methylene oxide)

Formic acid (Methanoic acid)

Glycidylaldehyde (1-Propanol-2,3-epoxy)

Halomethane, N.O.S.*

Heptachlor (4,7-Methano-1H-indene, 1,4,5,6,7,8,8-heptachloro-3a,4,7,7a-tetrahydro-)

Heptachlor epoxide (alpha, beta, and gamma isomers) (4,7-Methano-1H-indene, 1,4,5,6,7,8,8-heptachloro-2,3-epoxy-3a,4,7,7-tetrahydro-, alpha, beta, and gamma isomers)

Hexachlorobenzene (Benzene, hexachloro-)

Hexachlorobutadiene (1,3-Butadiene, 1,1,2,3,4,4-hexachloro-)

Hexachlorocyclohexane (all isomers) (Lindane and isomers)

Hexachlorocyclopentadiene (1,3-Cyclopentadiene, 1,2,3,4,5,5-hexachloro-)

Hexachloroethane (Ethane, 1,1,1,2,2,2-hexachloro-)

1,2,3,4,10,10-Hexachloro-1,4,4a,5,8,8a-hexahydro-1,4:5,8-endo,endo-dimethanonaphthalene (Hexachlorohexahydro-endo,endo-dimethanonaphthalene)

Hexachlorophene (2,2'-Methylenebis(3,4,6-trichlorophenol))

Hexachloropropene (1-Propene, 1,1,2,3,3,3-hexachloro-)

Hexaethyl tetraphosphate (Tetraphosphoric acid, hexaethyl ester)

Hydrazine (Diamine)

Hydrocyanic acid (Hydrogen cyanide)

Hydrofluoric acid (Hydrogen fluoride)

Hydrogen sulfide (Sulfur hydride)

Hydroxydimethylarsine oxide (Cacodylic acid)

Indeno(1,2,3-cd)pyrene (1,10-(1,2-phenylene)pyrene)

Iodomethane (Methyl iodide)

Iron dextran (Ferric dextran)

Isocyanic acid, methyl ester (Methyl isocyanate)

Isobutyl alcohol (1-Propanol, 2-methyl-)

Isosafrole (Benzene, 1,2-methylenedioxy-4-allyl-)

Kepone (Decachlorooctahydro-1,3,4-Methano-2H-cyclobuta[cd]pentalen-2-one)

Lasiocarpine (2-Butenoic acid, 2-methyl-, 7-[(2,3-dihydroxy-2-(1-methoxyethyl)-3-methyl-1-oxobutoxy)methyl]-2,3,5,7a-tetrahydro-1H-pyrrolizin-1-yl ester)

Lead and compounds, N.O.S.*

Lead acetate (Acetic acid, lead salt)

Lead phosphate (Phosphoric acid, lead salt)

Lead subacetate (Lead, bis(acetato-O)tetrahydroxytri-)

Maleic anhydride (2,5-Furandione)

Maleic hydrazide (1,2-Dihydro-3,6-pyridazinedione)

Malononitrile (Propanedinitrile)

Melphalan (Alanine, 3-[p-bis(2-chloroethyl)amino]phenyl-, L-)

Mercury fulminate (Fulminic acid, mercury salt)

Mercury and compounds, N.O.S.*

Methacrylonitrile (2-Propenenitrile, 2-methyl-)

Methanethiol (Thiomethanol)

Methapyrilene (Pyridine, 2-[(2-dimethylamino)ethyl]-2-thenylamino-)

Metholmyl (Acetimidic acid, N-[(methylcarbamoyl)oxy]thio-, methyl ester

Methoxychlor (Ethane, 1,1,1-trichloro-2,2'-bis(p-methoxyphenyl)-)

2-Methylaziridine (1,2-Propylenimine)

3-Methylcholanthrene (Benz[j]aceanthrylene, 1,2-dihydro-3-methyl-)

Methyl chlorocarbonate (Carbonochloridic acid, methyl ester)

4,4'-Methylenebis(2-chloroaniline) (Benzenamine, 4,4'-methylenebis-(2-chloro-)

Methyl ethyl ketone (MEK) (2-Butanone)

Methyl hydrazine (Hydrazine, methyl-)

2-Methyllactonitrile (Propanenitrile, 2-hydroxy-2-methyl-)

Methyl methacrylate (2-Propenoic acid, 2-methyl-, methyl ester)

Methyl methanesulfonate (Methanesulfonic acid, methyl ester)

2-Methyl-2-(methylthio)propionaldehyde-o-(methylcarbonyl) oxime (Propanal, 2-methyl-2-(methylthio)-, O-[(methylamino)carbonyl]oxime)

N-Methyl-N'-nitro-N-nitrosoguanidine (Guanidine, N-nitroso-N-methyl-N'-nitro-)

Methyl parathion (O,O-dimethyl O-(4-nitrophenyl) phosphorothioate)

Methylthiouracil (4-1H-Pyrimidinone, 2,3-dihydro-6-methyl-2-thioxo-)

Mustard gas (Sulfide, bis(2-chloroethyl)-)

Naphthalene

1,4-Naphthoquinone (1,4-Naphthalenedione)

1-Naphthylamine (alpha-Naphthylamine)

2-Naphthylamine (beta-Naphthylamine)

1-Naphthyl-2-thiourea (Thiourea, 1-naphthalenyl-)

Nickel and compounds, N.O.S.*

Nickel carbonyl (Nickel tetracarbonyl)

Nickel cyanide (Nickel (II) cyanide)

Nicotine and salts (Pyridine, (S)-3-(1-methyl-2-pyrrolidinyl)-, and salts)
Nitric oxide (Nitrogen (II) oxide)
p-Nitroaniline (Benzenamine, 4-nitro-)
Nitrobenzine (Benzene, nitro-)
Nitrogen dioxide (Nitrogen (IV) oxide)
Nitrogen mustard and hydrochloride salt (Ethanamine, 2-chloro-, N-(2-chloroethyl)-N-methyl-, and hydrochloride salt)
Nitrogen mustard N-Oxide and hydrochloride salt (Ethanamine, 2-chloro-, N-(2-chloroethyl)-N-methyl-, and hydrochloride salt)
Nitroglycerine (1,2,3-Propanetriol, trinitrate)
4-Nitrophenol (Phenol, 4-nitro-)
4-Nitroquinoline-1-oxide (Quinoline, 4-nitro-1-oxide-)
Nitrosamine, N.O.S.*
N-Nitrosodi-n-butylamine (1-Butanamine, N-butyl-N-nitroso-)
N-Nitrosodiethanolamine (Ethanol, 2,2'-(nitrosoimino)bis-)
N-Nitrosodiethylamine (Ethanamine, N-ethyl-N-nitroso-)
N-Nitrosodimethylamine (Dimethylnitrosamine)
N-Nitroso-N-ethylurea (Carbamide, N-ethyl-N-nitroso-)
N-Nitrosomethylethylamine (Ethanamine, N-methyl-N-nitroso-)
N-Nitroso-N-methylurea (Carbamide, N-methyl-N-nitroso-)
N-Nitroso-N-methylurethane (Carbamic acid, methylnitroso-, ethyl ester)
N-Nitrosomethylvinylamine (Ethenamine, N-methyl-N-nitroso-)
N-Nitrosomorpholine (Morpholine, N-nitroso-)
N-Nitrosonornicotine (Nornicotine, N-nitroso-)
N-Nitrosopiperidine (Pyridine, hexahydro-, N-nitroso-)
Nitrosopyrrolidine (Pyrrole, tetrahydro-, N-nitroso-)
N-Nitrososarcosine (Sarcosine, N-nitroso-)
5-Nitro-o-toluidine (Benzenamine, 2-methyl-5-nitro-)
Octamethylpyrophosphoramide (Diphosphoramide, octamethyl-)
Osmium tetroxide (Osmium (VIII) oxide)
7-Oxabicyclo[2.2.1]heptane-2,3-dicarboxylic acid (Endothal)
Paraldehyde (1,3,5-Trioxane, 2,4,6-trimethyl-)
Parathion (Phosphorothioic acid, O,O-diethyl O-(p-nitrophenyl) ester
Pentachlorobenzene (Benzene, pentachloro-)
Pentachloroethane (Ethane, pentachloro-)
Pentachloronitrobenzene (PCNB) (Benzene, pentachloronitro-)
Pentachlorophenol (Phenol, pentachloro-)
Phenacetin (Acetamide, N-(4-ethoxyphenyl)-)
Phenol (Benzene, hydroxy-)
Phenylenediamine (Benzenediamine)
Phenylmercury acetate (Mercury, acetatophenyl-)
N-Phenylthiourea (Thiourea, phenyl-)
Phosgene (Carbonyl chloride)
Phosphine (Hydrogen phosphide)
Phosphorodithioic acid, O,O-diethyl S-[(ethylthio)methyl] ester (Phorate)
Phosphorothioic acid, O,O-dimethyl O-[p-((dimethylamino)sulfonyl)phenyl] ester (Famphur)
Phthalic acid esters, N.O.S.* (Benzene, 1,2-dicarboxylic acid, esters, N.O.S.*)
Phthalic anhydride (1,2-Benzenedicarboxylic acid anhydride)
2-Picoline (Pyridine, 2-methyl-)
Polychlorinated biphenyl, N.O.S.*
Potassium cyanide
Potassium silver cyanide (Argentate(1-), dicyano-, potassium)
Pronamide (3,5-Dichloro-N-(1,1-dimethyl-2-propynyl)benzamide)
1,3-Propane sultone (1,2-Oxathiolane, 2,2-dioxide)
n-Propylamine (1-Propanamine)
Propylthiouracil (Undecamethylenediamine, N,N'-bis(2-chlorobenzyl)-, dihydrochloride)
2-Propyn-1-ol (Propargyl alcohol)
Pyridine
Reserpine (Yohimban-16-carboxylic acid, 11,17-dimethoxy-18-[(3,4,5-trimethoxybenzoyl)oxy]-, methyl ester)
Resorcinol (1,3-Benzenediol)
Saccharin and salts (1,2-Benzoisothiazolin-3-one, 1,1-dioxide, and salts)
Safrole (Benzene, 1,2-methylenedioxy-4-allyl-)
Selenious acid (Selenium dioxide)
Selenium and compounds, N.O.S.*
Selenium sulfide (Sulfur selenide)
Selenourea (Carbamimidoselenoic acid)
Silver and compounds, N.O.S.*
Silver cyanide
Sodium cyanide
Streptozotocin (D-Glucopyranose, 2-deoxy-2-(3-methyl-3-nitrosoureido)-)
Strontium sulfide
Strychnine and salts (Strychnidin-10-one, and salts)
1,2,4,5-Tetrachlorobenzene (Benzene, 1,2,4,5-tetrachloro-)
2,3,7,8-Tetrachlorodibenzo-p-dioxin (TCDD) (Dibenzo-p-dioxin, 2,3,7,8-tetrachloro-)
Tetrachloroethane, N.O.S.* (Ethane, tetrachloro-, N.O.S.*)
1,1,1,2-Tetrachlorethane (Ethane, 1,1,1,2-tetrachloro-)
1,1,2,2-Tetrachlorethane (Ethane, 1,1,2,2-tetrachloro-)
Tetrachloroethane (Ethene, 1,1,2,2-tetrachloro-)
Tetrachloromethane (Carbon tetrachloride)
2,3,4,6,-Tetrachlorophenol (Phenol, 2,3,4,6-tetrachloro-)
Tetraethyldithiopyrophosphate (Dithiopyrophosphoric acid, tetraethyl-ester)

Tetraethyl lead (Plumbane, tetraethyl-)
Tetraethylpyrophosphate (Pyrophosphoric acide, tetraethyl ester)
Tetranitromethane (Methane, tetranitro-)
Thallium and compounds, N.O.S.*
Thallic oxide (Thallium (III) oxide)
Thallium (I) acetate (Acetic acid, thallium (I) salt)
Thallium (I) carbonate (Carbonic acid, dithallium (I) salt)
Thallium (I) chloride
Thallium (I) nitrate (Nitric acid, thallium (I) salt)
Thallium selenite
Thallium (I) sulfate (Sulfuric acid, thallium (I) salt)
Thioacetamide (Ethanethioamide)
Thiosemicarbazide (Hydrazinecarbothioamide)
Thiourea (Carbamide thio-)
Thiuram (Bis(dimethylthiocarbamoyl) disulfide)
Toluene (Benzene, methyl-)
Toluenediamine (Diaminotoluene)
o-Toluidine hydrochloride (Benzenamine, 2-methyl-, hydrochloride)
Tolylene diisocyanate (Benzene, 1,3-diisocyanatomethyl-)
Toxaphene (Camphene, octachloro-)
Tribromomethane (Bromoform)
1,2,4-Trichlorobenzene (Benzene, 1,2,4-trichloro-)
1,1,1-Trichloroethane (Methyl chloroform)
1,1,2-Trichloroethane (Ethane, 1,1,2-trichloro-)
Trichloroethene (Trichloroethylene)
Trichloromethanethiol (Methanethiol, trichloro-)
Trichloromonofluoromethane (Methane, trichlorofluoro-)
2,4,5-Trichlorophenol (Phenol, 2,4,5-trichloro-)
2,4,6-Trichlorophenol (Phenol, 2,4,6-trichloro-)
2,4,5-Trichlorophenoxyacetic acid (2,4,5-T) (Acetic acid, 2,4,5-trichlorophenoxy-)
2,4,5-Trichlorophenoxypropionic acid (2,4,5-TP) (Silvex) (Propionoic acid, 2-(2,4,5-trichlorophenoxy)-)
Trichloropropane, N.O.S.* (Propane, trichloro-, N.O.S.*)
1,2,3-Trichloropropane (Propane, 1,2,3-trichloro-)
O,O,O-Triethyl phosphorothioate (Phosphorothioic acid, O,O,O-triethyl ester)
sym-Trinitrobenzene (Benzene, 1,3,5-trinitro-)
Tris(1-aziridinyl) phosphine sulfide (Phosphine sulfide, tris(1-aziridinyl-)
Tris(2,3-dibromopropyl) phosphate (1-Propanol, 2,3-dibromo-, phosphate)
Trypan blue (2,7-Naphthalenedisulfonic acid, 3,3'-[(3,3'-dimethyl(1,1'-biphenyl)-4,4'-diyl)bis(azo)]bis(5-amino-4-hydroxy-, tetrasodium salt)
Uracil mustard (Uracil 5-[bis(2-chloroethyl)amino]-)

Vanadic acid, ammonium salt (ammonium vanadate)
Vanadium pentoxide (Vanadium (V) oxide)
Vinyl chloride (Ethene, chloro-)
Zinc cyanide
Zinc phosphide

[46 FR 27477, May 20, 1981; 46 FR 29708, June 3, 1981; 49 FR 5312, Feb. 10, 1984]

EFFECTIVE DATE NOTE: At 49 FR 5312, Feb. 10, 1984, the entries for 2-Chloro-1, 3-butadiene (chloroprene), and 3-Chloropropene (allyl chloride), were added to the table in Part 261, App. VIII, effective August 10, 1984.

APPENDIX D

CONCENTRATION LEVELS DESIGNATED IN TABLE I OF THE GROUNDWATER PROTECTION REGULATIONS
(40 C.F.R. § 264.94)

If the concentrations of the following hazardous constituents exceed the levels listed, facilities must undertake corrective action. See p. 178 in the text. These concentration levels are listed in the National Interim Primary Drinking Water Standards, 40 C.F.R. §§ 141.11 and 141.12.

Maximum Concentration of Constituents for Groundwater Protection

Constituent	Maximum concentration*
Arsenic	0.05
Barium	1.0
Cadmium	0.01
Chromium	0.05
Lead	0.05
Mercury	0.002
Selenium	0.01
Silver	0.05
Endrin (1,2,3,4,10,10-hexachloro-1, 7-epoxy-1,4,4a,5,6,7,8,9a-octahydro-1, 4-endo, endo-5,8-dimethano naphthalene)	0.0002
Lindane (1,2,3,4,5,6-hexachlorocyclohexane, gamma isomer)	0.004
Methoxychlor (1,1,1-Trichloro-2,2-bis (p-methoxyphenylethane)	0.1
Toxaphene ($C_{10}C_{10}Cl6$ Technical chlorinated camphene, 67-69 percent chlorine)	0.005
2,4-D (2,4-Dichlorophenoxyacetic acid)	0.1
2,4,5-TP Silvex (2,4,5-Trichlorophenoxy-propionic acid)	0.01

*Milligrams per liter.

APPENDIX E

PROPOSED REVISION TO THE NATIONAL CONTINGENCY PLAN

On February 12, 1985, EPA proposed revisions to the National Contingency Plan designed to streamline response mechanisms, ensure prompt, cost-effective response, and clarify responsibilities in the Plan. 50 Fed. Reg. 5862.

ENVIRONMENTAL PROTECTION AGENCY

40 CFR Part 300

[SWH-FRL 2671-8]

National Oil and Hazardous Substances Pollution Contingency Plan

AGENCY: Environmental Protection Agency.

ACTION: Proposed rule.

SUMMARY: Pursuant to section 105 of the Comprehensive Environmental Response, Compensation, and Liability Act of 1980 (CERCLA) and Executive Order 12316, the Environmental Protection Agency (EPA) is proposing revisions to the National Oil and Hazardous Substances Pollution Contingency Plan (NCP). This revision of the NCP reflects experience gained over the past two years since the NCP was last revised. The purpose of the revisions is to streamline the response mechanisms; to ensure prompt, cost-effective response; to respond to issues raised in the litigation pertaining to the current NCP; and to clarify responsibilities and authorities contained in the NCP. CERCLA provides that actions taken in response to releases of hazardous substances shall be in accordance with the NCP. Section 311 of the Clean Water Act (CWA) provides that actions taken to remove oil discharges shall, to the greatest extent possible, be in accordance with the NCP. The revised NCP, proposed today, shall be applicable to response actions taken pursuant to CERCLA and section 311 of the CWA.

In addition, the EPA is proposing a policy concerning the extent to which response actions taken pursuant to CERCLA will be consistent with other pertinent Federal and State environmental and public health standards.

DATES: Comments on § 300.66(b)(4) only may be submitted on or before March 14, 1985. Comments on the remainder of the revisions to the NCP may be submitted on or before April 15, 1985.

ADDRESSES: The public docket for the NCP is located in Room S398, U.S. Environmental Protection Agency, 401 M Street, SW., Washington, D.C. 20460, and is available for viewing from 9:00 a.m. to 4:00 p.m. Monday through Friday, excluding holidays.

FOR FURTHER INFORMATION CONTACT: Douglas Cohen, Office of Emergency and Remedial Response (WH-548D). U.S. Environmental Protection Agency, 401 M Street SW., Washington, D.C.

20460, (800) 424-9346, or in the Washington, D.C. area (202) 382-3000.

SUPPLEMENTARY INFORMATION: The contents of today's preamble are listed in the following outline:

I. Introduction
II. Major Revisions
III. Other Revisions
IV. Economic Inpacts of Proposed NCP Revisions
V. Summary of Supporting Analyses
　A. Classification Under E.O. 12991
　B. Regulatory Flexibility Act
　C. Paperwork Reduction Act
VI. List of Subjects in 40 CFR Part 300

I. Introduction

Pursuant to section 105 of the Comprehensive Environmental Response, Compensation, and Liability Act of 1980, Pub. L. 96-510 ("CERCLA" or "the Act") and Executive Order 12316, the Environmental Protection Agency ("EPA" or "the Agency") is proposing revisions to the National Oil and Hazardous Substances Pollution Contingency Plan ("NCP" or "the Plan"). Revisions to the NCP were last promulgated on July 16, 1982 (47 FR 31180). In today's revision, the Agency has reprinted Subparts A–G and Appendix A of the NCP in their entirety for the reader's convenience. However, comment is only requested on new or changed parts of the Plan as indicated. The Agency has not reprinted Subpart H. Changes in Subpart H are so indicated. In addition, the Agency is not reprinting Appendix B which is the National Priorities List. The Agency is also proposing a policy which addresses in detail the extent to which response actions taken pursuant to CERCLA should be consistent with pertinent Federal or State environmental or public health standards. This policy can be found as a appendix to this Preamble and is entitled "Draft Policy on CERCLA Compliance With the Requirements of Other Environmental Laws". Finally, EPA is providing a shortened comment period only for § 300.66(b)4). The comment period for this section only will be 30 days.

In developing the revisions proposed today, the Agency reviewed and evaluated program operations under the current NCP to identify areas requiring clarification, modification or streamlining based on the early years of program experience. Many of the changes to subpart F, pertaining to CERCLA response operations are a result of this evaluation. In addition, most of the proposed revisions to the other subparts were recommended by the National Response Team (NRT). The 12 member Federal agencies of the NRT undertook and comprehensive review of

the national response mechanism and its operations (included in Subparts B, C and D of the Plan) as well as oil and hazardous substances response operations under Subparts E and F and made many recommendations to clarify and streamline the Plan. Finally, some of the revisions reflect agreements reached in settlement of a lawsuit brought by the Environmental Defense Fund (EDE) and the State of New Jersey (*EDF* v. *US EPA*, No. 82-2234, D.C. Cir., Febraury 1, 1984; *State of New Jersey* v. U.S. EPA No. 82-2238, D.C. Cir., Feb. 1, 1984.) The Agency agreed to the following in the settlement.

• EPA will propose amendments to the NCP to require that (1) relevant quantitative health and environmental standards and criteria developed by EPA under other programs be used in determining the extent of remedy, and (2) if such standard or criteria are substantially adjusted (e.g., for risk level or exposure factors), then the lead agency must explain the basis for this adjustment.

• EPA will propose amendments to the NCP to allow facilities presently owned by the United States or its agencies to be included in future revisions to the National Priorities List (NPL).

• EPA will propose amendments to the NCP to (a) require development of Community Relations plans for all Fund-financed response actions, (b) require public review of feasibility studies for all Fund-financed response measures and (c) provide comparable public participation for private-party response measures taken pursuant to enforcement actions.

• EPA will promulgate a rule addressing the issue of whether response activities must comply with other Federal, State or local environmental laws.

The proposed NCP revision address all of the settlement agreement provisions.

Section II of this preamble discusses the major proposed revisions to the NCP. All of the major revisions to this Plan are in Subpart F. These revisions pertain to hazardous substance response activities under CERCLA. Section III of the preamble discusses other modifications made to each subpart of the Plan, including Subpart F. In developing the revisions to the Plan, the Agency did not believe it was necessary to modify the basic formulation of the Plan or the national response structure. EPA has left the response structure intact so that the proven national and regional response mechanisms may continue to be used for response operations under CERCLA and the CWA. The Plan continues to be structured as follows:

Subpart A—definitions
Subparts B, C, D—Assignment of responsibilities under the NCP, national response organization and response planning
Subpart E—Oil Removal
Subpart F—Hazardous Substance Response
Subpart G—National Resource Trustees
Subpart H—Use of Dispersants

II. Major Revisions

The major revisions to the Plan are all in subpart F. The first revision restructures the criteria for undertaking removal action under CERCLA. The second streamlines the remedial response process and more specifically identifies the level of clean up to be achieved during CERCLA cleanups. The third modifies and expands the rules pertaining to listing and deleting of releases on the National Priorities List (NPL). The fourth emphasizes the use of alternative and innovative technology, and recycling or reuse as alternatives to conventional technology and practices. The last clarifies and elaborates on roles and responsibilities of non-lead agency parties, including responsible parties, under CERCLA.

CERCLA authorizes two general types of response to hazardous substance releases: Removal and remedial action. Removal actions generally are actions to clean up or remove hazardous substances or pollutants or contaminants from the environment. Remedial action includes measures consistent with permanent remedy taken alone or in addition to removal action to prevent or minimize the release of hazardous substances or pollutants or contaminants.

A. Removal Action

Discussion

Section 104 of CERCLA authorizes the performance of removal activities, as defined in section 101(23) of the Act, whenever there is a release or substantial threat of release of a hazardous substance, or of any pollutant or contaminant which may present an imminent and substantial danger to public health or welfare. The term "removal" is broadly defined in section 101(23) to include a wide variety of activities. The major statutory limitation on removal activities is set forth in section 104(c)(1), which provides that removal activities [other than activities described in section 104(b)] shall not continue after $1,000,000 has been obligated or 6 months has elapsed from date of initial response, unless certain findings are made. The effect of this

statutory provision is to limit removal activities to short-term, relatively inexpensive activities unless there is an emergency situation which presents an immediate risk to public health, welfare, or the environment.

For purposes of the current Plan, EPA established two categories of situations in which removal activities were authorized. First, the lead agency is authorized under § 300.65 to conduct "immediate removal" activities when it determines that action is necessary to prevent or mitigate an immediate and significant risk of harm to human life or health or to the environment. Several examples of situations which would pose such risks are included in this section. The authority to undertake immediate removal activities is not dependent on whether the release is included on the NPL. Second, under § 300.67, the lead agency is authorized to undertake "planned removal" actions when it determines either that continuation of an immediate removal will result in a substantial cost savings, or, that the public or environment will be at risk from exposure to hazardous substances, if response is delayed at a release not on the NPL. Again, as with § 300.65, the Plan cites examples of factors the Agency will use in determining whether a planned removal is warranted. Approval of planned removal activities is conditioned upon, among other things, assurances that the affected State would share the costs of the activity; no such State cost-share is required for immediate removal activities.

The Agency had believed that the distinction between immediate and planned removal would result in better management of the Fund. In addition, the Agency believed that under the existing removal provisions, the lead agency would have the flexibility to ensure that Fund money would be used effectively to protect public health and the environment.

Based on its experience with the removal program over the past two years, EPA believes that the existing removal provisions tend to complicate and interfere with expeditious responses to situations which present threats to public health or the environment, and do not provide significant Fund-management benefits.

First, the distinction between sites that are eligible for immediate removal action and those situations which are eligible only for planned removal treatment is often difficult to define in practice. Although some situations are obviously within the immediate removal category, for others the question is more difficult. Time spent in properly

classifying actions, and documenting the "immediacy" and "significance" of the risk to health or the environment in immediate removals can delay necessary response and consume significant amounts of staff and decisionmakers' energies. This not only may delay necessary response, but can also result in an unproductive expenditure of Fund resources.

Second, the present removal provisions in many cases have not provided an effective mechanism for addressing threats which are not "immediate and significant," especially at sites which are neither listed nor eligible for listing on the NPL. Although the Agency had anticipated that the planned removal mechanism would provide an effective means of dealing with such situations, this has often not been the case. While some planned removal actions have been taken expeditiously, the administrative requirements imposed on planned removals, especially the requirement that the affected State provide a cost-share, have delayed some responses, and have the potential for creating such delay in the future. Perhaps more significantly, until recently, few planned removal activities have been undertaken at all, perhaps in part because of the same administrative and funding complications. The failure to undertake removal action, or the undue delay in undertaking such action at sites can result in an increase in the problem posed by a site, which, in turn, can result in an increase in the cost of response actions which may be required at a later date.

Third, the existing removal provisions do not provide the Fund management benefits EPA had expected. To the extent that necessary removal efforts are delayed and site conditions deteriorate, the present provisions may lead to a long-term increase in expenditures from the Fund.

Because of these concerns with the removal authorities in the current Plan, EPA is proposing to eliminate the distinction between immediate and planned removals and to establish a single standard which must be satisfied before removal activity can be authorized under the Plan. The standard would apply to all releases and threatened releases without regard to whether the site was included on the NPL. The proposed revisions are described below.

Proposed § 300.65(b)(1) would authorize the lead agency to undertake removal action where there was a release or threat of release of (1) a hazardous substance; or, (2) of a pollutant or contaminant (which is defined for purposes of Subpart F so as to incorporate the criteria of 104(a) concerning imminent and substantial danger), where there was a threat to public health, welfare, or the environment, whether or not the release had been included on the NPL. Section 300.65(b)(2) includes a list of the type of factors which would be considered in determining that a threat to public health, welfare or the environment exists.

This single, simplified standard would replace the various distinct standards which now must be applied by the lead agency in determining whether a short-term, relatively low cost action should be undertaken as an "immediate removal", a "planned removal" or an "initial remedial measure (IRM)." The standard is intended to be broad enough to authorize removal action in any of the circumstances which can now be addressed under any of these authorities in the existing Plan.

Under the proposed removal provisions, no removal activities, except removals at sites owned by the State at the time of disposal (50 percent cost-sharing sites), would be subject to administrative restrictions (including State cost-sharing requirements) currently imposed upon planned removals and IRMs. Elimination of these requirements is not inconsistent with the statute. Although the Agency has the discretion to require cost-sharing for removal actions, section 104(c)(3) generally *requires* such cost-sharing only with respect to *remedial* actions. In addition, with respect to activities now addressed under the IRM authority, there is nothing in CERCLA which limits the taking of removal activities at sites where further remedial activity is contemplated. In fact, the definition of "remedy" in section 101(24) of CERCLA indicates that remedial activities may be taken in addition to removal actions in the event of a release.

EPA does not expect that the revision of the removal authority will result in any significant increase in the type of activities which are now being routinely implemented under the removal authority.

Agency experience has indicated that certain types of response actions are, as a general rule, appropriately conducted as part of a removal action. Based on this experience, EPA proposes to specify, in § 300.65(c), particular types of actions that are appropriate removal responses to commonly encountered situations. Specification of situations commonly encountered at removal sites and appropriate responses to such situations, is not intended to limit the

lead agency from addressing other types of situations under its removal authority, or from implementing different responses to any of the listed situations, or from deferring response action to other appropriate Federal or State enforcement or response authorities. However, EPA believes that specification of appropriate response activities will streamline the process of selecting and implementing removal activities by among other things, helping to limit evaluations to determine the appropriate response. EPA also believes that specification of appropriate responses will assist OSC's in recommending actions (or selecting actions to the extent they have been delegated authority) and the reviewing official in selecting appropriate responses. Finally, listing of such general responses will also help focus discussion between the Agency and potentially responsible parties who may have some ability or interest in implementing response measures.

As mandated by section 104(c)(1) of CERCLA, § 300.65(b)(3) of the proposed revision provides that all removal action will be terminated after 6 months have elapsed from the date of initial response at the site, or $1 million has been obligated, unless there is an immediate risk at the site, continued-response actions are immediately required to address an emergency, and such assistance will not otherwise be provided in a timely manner. Section 300.65(b)(4) provides that the lead agency shall make the 6 month or $1 million determination at the earliest possible time. This limitation on removal actions was also imposed on both immediate and planned removals in the existing NCP.

The above discussed removal provisions in proposed 300.65 apply only to removals undertaken pursuant to section 104(a) of CERCLA. Activities authorized by 104(b) of CERCLA, while included within the statutory definition of removals, are subject to different requirements. Section 104(b) activities include investigations, monitoring, surveys, testing, and planning, legal, fiscal, economic, engineering, architectural or other studies. In particular, 104(b) actions may be taken whenever the criteria of 104(b) are met. In addition, 104(b) activities are not subject to the limitations of 104(c)(1).

Finally, § 300.65 (f) and (g) address the issue of CERCLA removal actions compliance with the requirements of other public health and environmental laws.

Section 300.65(f) provides that removal actions shall, to the greatest extent practicable considering the

exigencies of the circumstances, attain or exceed applicable or relevant Federal, public health or environmental standards. Federal criteria guidance and advisories and State standards also should be considered in formulating the removal action. This requires the OSC to attempt to *use* those requirements where appropriate. However, because removal actions often involve situations requiring expeditious action to protect public health, welfare, and the environment, it may not always be feasible to fully meet these standards and criteria, guidance or advisories. In those circumstances where it is necessary to deviate from applicable or relevant standards or criteria, guidance or advisories, the decision documents, OSC report, or subsequent documents should specify the reasons for these deviations.

Section 300.65(g) requires permits or authorization for the off-site storage treatment or disposal of hazardous substances. In addition, disposal of the hazardous substances must be in compliance with all applicable and relevant Federal public health and environmental standards.

B. Remedial Response

Section 300.68 of the current NCP provides methods and criteria for determining the appropriate extent of remedial action. These provisions are organized to reflect the normal sequence for taking remedial action at a site, including discussion of how to plan remedial actions, how to array alternatives, and how to select the cost-effective alternative from among these alternatives.

EPA's experience with the remedial progam has shown that the basic remedial response structure of the current Plan works. This proposal, therefore, retains that basic structure, but makes a number of changes within it. In general, these changes include amendments designed to streamline the process, and changes reflecting current Agency practices and policies.

The most significant changes are discussed in the following section, "Overview of Changes." A discussion of "Specific Changes" follows which details how these significant changes fit within the remedial response structure, and explains the additional proposed amendments.

Overview of Changes

Section 300.68 of the NCP currently authorizes phased remedial actions. Specifically, the existing Plan provides for IRMs to stabilize conditions at the site and to mitigate the immediate public health or environmental threat. Subsequent remedial actions are then classified as either "source control" or "off-site" remedial action. Each of these classifications contains different criteria for triggering and carrying out remedial actions.

These classifications are largely eliminated in this proposal, in favor of a more straightforward approach. First, the proposal eliminates IRMs as a distinct category. As discussed earlier, EPA is proposing amendments designed to eliminate certain restrictions for taking removal actions. With that added flexibility, IRMs should no longer be necessary; that is, removal actions will be able to address actions that normally should begin prior to initiating longer-term remedial responses. A possible exception are removal actions that cannot be completed within 6 months or $1 million dollars, as required by section 104(c)(3) of the statute. To the extent an immediate threat remains, those removal actions could be continued under the statutory exception allowing waiver of these limitations. If no immediate threat remained, continued response would appropriately be addressed by a remedial action.

Similarly, the proposal eliminates the formal distinctions between "source control" and "off-site" actions since the appropriate response to either type of problem is often the same. The Plan will still refer to source control measures and "management of migration" actions, but will not attempt to categorize the response actions that are appropriate to respond to each classification.

The proposed changes introduce the concept of "operable units." An operable unit is a discrete response measure that is consistent with a permanent remedy, but is not the permanent remedy in and of itself. This change codifies the practice of phasing remedial action at sites that present complex cleanup problems. For example, it is often appropriate first to conduct a surface cleanup of a site, and then, after additional analysis of more complex hydrogeological factors, to select and implement remedial measures addressing ground water contamination. Some of the more extensive actions now addressed under the current IRM authority may be addressed as preliminary "operable units."

As discussed earlier in this preamble, the Agency agreed to address in this proposed rulemaking the extent to which response actions are required to comply with other Federal, State and local laws. Several changes in section 300.68 reflect the draft policy EPA has developed to address this issue. The proposed rule is discussed in greater

detail in an appendix to this document, entitled "Draft Policy on CERCLA Compliance With the Requirements of Other Environmental Laws."

As part of the development of a policy on compliance with other environmental laws, the Agency recognized that some potential CERCLA actions may more appropriately be taken under other environmental laws. Therefore, changes in the scoping and analysis sections allow the consideratiuon of the extent to which response or enforcement mechanisms under other Federal or State laws may adequately address the problem.

EPA has concluded that CERCLA cleanups need not comply with other environmental standards, as a matter of law, but that as a matter of sound practice, they should, except in certain circumstances. CERCLA contains criteria for responding to releases that may differ sharply from the considerations underlying other regulatory programs. For example, another environmental statute might require that standards be set at a level without regard to costs, while CERCLA requires that the selected Fund-financed remedial alternative take into account Fund-balancing cost considerations. As another example, extensive and potentially protracted permitting procedures under an environmental statute could impede rapid cleanups at CERCLA sites.

Nonetheless, other environmental requirements often provide critical guidance in determining the appropriate level of cleanup at a CERCLA site, directly or indirectly. Directly, an environmental regulation might define the level of protection that is "adequate" to protect health, welfare or the environment, which is a necessary element of determining the appropriate level of cleanup under CERCLA. Indirectly, an environmental criterion, although not specifically applicable to the activity at a CERCLA site, might provide useful information about the level of risk presented by exposure to known quantities of hazardous substances, or on appropriate treatment technologies.

This proposal attempts to reconcile these sometimes competing concerns, by providing that EPA will attain the substantive provisions of other Federal public health and environmental standards except in certain circumstances. These circumstances are designed to address situations when other environmental requirements are likely to conflict with CERCLA's goals. The proposal divides environmental requirements into two categories: Those *standards* that are "applicable or

relevant," which must be *met* unless one of five circumstances exists, and other Federal and State standards, criteria, advisories and guidance which are to be *used* in developing that remedy. Generally, "applicable'" standards are those that would otherwise be legally applicable if the actions were not undertaken pursuant to CERCLA section 104 or section 106. "Relevant" standards are those designed to apply to problems sufficiently similar to those encountered at CERCLA sites that their application is appropriate, although not legally required. Standards are also relevant if they would be legally applicable to the CERCLA cleanup but for jurisdictional restrictions associated with the requirement. For example, while RCRA site closure regulations might not be legally applicable to a "typical" RCRA facility which ceased operations prior to the effective date of RCRA subtitle C regulations, these regulations would generally be relevant to a determination of what type of capping or monitoring would be necessary to adequately protect health and the environment. Similarly, RCRA treats facilities different depending on whether they are "interim status" (prior to issuances of permit) or operating under a permit. If they are interim status they must comply with 40 CFR Part 265 standards and if they are permitted, they must comply with 40 CFR Part 264 standards. To the extent that the standards differ, EPA will generally be consistent with the often stricter standards of Part 264, where relevant, in determining the appropriate response at CERCLA sites because the 264 standards represent the ultimate RCRA compliance standards and are consistent with CERCLA's goals of long-term protection of public health and the environment. Printed as an appendix to this preamble is a memorandum entitled "Draft Policy on CERCLA Compliance With the Requirements of Other Environmental Laws" which includes a non-binding, advisory list of environmental requirements that EPA believes generally should fall into the "applicable or relevant" category.

The Agency specifically requests comment on applying applicable or relevant RCRA ground water protection and closure requirements to CERCLA actions.

A process, to be developed by the Agency, to assess the public health impacts of chemicals present at CERCAL remedial sites, may be used to set Alternative Concentration Limits (ACLs) pursuant to the RCRA ground water protection requirements (40 CFR 264.94). This process will identify the most toxic and persistent 40 CFR Part 261 Appendix VIII chemicals present at a specific site and set ACLs for those chemicals. Setting ACLs for the most toxic and persistent chemicals should ensure that the cost-effective remedy will prevent present or potential hazard to human health or the environment.

In determining the appropriate extent of remedy as it relates to other Federal standards, the first step is to consider the extent to which the standard is in fact applicable or relevant to the unique circumstances at the site. For example, some Superfund sites involve situations that RCRA *did not "intend to address."* In those situations, the RCRA regulations would not be applicable per se, but may be relevant on a case-by-case basis. As an example, RCRA was not designed to cover the subsequent management of waste indiscriminantly disposed over 200 miles of roadway, or the subsequent management of contaminated river beds. In such situations, RCRA standards would not be applicable, but parts of the RCRA standards may be relevant.

The following are situations which define circumstances in which applicable or relevant standards are not required to be met by CERCAL remedial actions:

• *Interim measures:* If the selected remedy is not the final remedy for the site, it might be impractical or inappropriate to apply other environmental standards. For example, it might be appropriate to treat contaminated drinking water at the tap as an interim measure, pending final decisions on the appropriate extent of cleanup in the contaminated aquifer itself.

• *Fund-balancing:* As provided in section 104(c)(4) of CERCAL, for Fund-finance actions only, the lead agency will balance the need for protection of public health, welfare and the environment at the site against the amount of money available in the Fund to respond to other sites. Thus, the decisionmaker could select a remedy that does not meet an othewise applicable or relevant public health or environmental standard if complying with that standard would be disproportionately costly, and Fund monies could be more productively used at another site where a response was necessary.

• *Unacceptable Environmental Impacts:* In some cases, it might be possible to meet applicable or relevant Federal standards, but compliance might result in significant adverse environmental impacts. This might be the case, for example, when dredging contaminants from the bottom of a body of water to levels required by environmental standards would result in more harm to the ecosystem than an alternative remedial response.

• *Technical Impracticality:* This situation could occur when it is technically impractical, from an engineering perspective, to achieve the standard at the specific site. For example, although the environmental standard may require that contaminated ground water attain background levels, this may be impractical because of the unique hydrogeologic conditions. Another example is a situation where the site is characterized by a steep slope and the standard would require a cap. While the placement of a cap on a steep slope could be technically feasible, it would not be practical because of long-term problems with maintaining the integrity of the cap. The Agency does not intend that this determination be based on a cost benefit determination.

• For enforcement actions under section 106 of CERCLA only, the decisionmaker could choose not to meet an otherwise applicable or relevant standard if the fund is unavailable, there is a strong public interest in expedited clean up, and the litigation probably would not result in the desired remedy. For example, this situation could occur where the defendant lacks sufficient resources to pay for a complete remedy or where liability is in question, the Fund is unavailable and the public interest is served by expeditous cleanup. One situation where the Fund is unavailable is where the State does not have sufficient funds to make the necessary State cost-share match.

Three important qualifications apply to these situations. First, in EPA's experience they will only occur infrequently. That is, most remedial action *will* conform to applicable or relevant Federal public health and environmental standards. Second, when these circumstances exist, they will not result in selection of a remedy that disregards health and environment concerns rather, the decisionmaker will select the alternative that most closely approaches the level of protection provided by the applicable or relevant standard, considering the circumstances which prevented meeting the standard. Third and finally, the basis for not meeting the standard will be fully documented and explained in the appropriate decision documents.

EPA will use Federal health and environmental criteria, advisories, or guidance or State standards in developing the appropriate remedial response at a site, especially where there are no applicable or relevant Federal standards. If EPA determines that these criteria, advisories, or guidance or State standards are relevant, but are not used in the selected remedial alternative or are substantially adjusted, the decision documents will indicate the basis for adjusting or not using them.

In additon, for reason discussed earlier, CERCLA cleanup will generally not be subject to procedural and administrative requirements of other environmental programs, such as permitting. EPA will ensure public participation in these actions through community relations plans, discussed later in this preamble. However, remedial actions that involve storage, treatment or disposal of hazardous substances, pollutants or contaminants at off-site facilities shall only occur at facilities that are operating under appropriate Federal or State permits or authorization.

The final major change proposed in § 300.68 is to clarify the meaning of the term "cost-effective" in the context of selection of the appropriate extent of remedy. Section 300.68(j) in the current NCP provides that the Agency shall select the alternative which is "cost-effective (i.e., the lowest cost alternative that is technologically feasible and reliable and which effectively mitigates and minimizes damage to and provides adequate protection of public health, welfare, or the environment)." Unfortunately, this language has given many observers the erroneous impression that EPA was required in all cases to select the *lowest cost* remedy that provided *minimally adequate* protection of public health, welfare and the environment. EPA did not intend, nor does it believe that CERCLA requires, that cost effectiveness be defined in such narrow terms.

Therefore, to address this issue, EPA is proposing in 300.68(i) to eliminate the reference to selection of the "lowest cost alternative." Instead, 300.68(i) would simply provide that the appropriate extent of remedy shall be determined by selection of a cost effective remedial alternative which effectively mitigates or minimizes the threat to and provides adequate protection of public health, welfare, and the environment. Under the proposed revisions, this requires the selection of a remedy which at a minimum, attains or exceeds applicable or relevant Federal public health or environmental standards. This amendment would also clarify EPA's position that cost effectiveness does not mean simply the selection of the lowest cost minimally adequate remedy. EPA considered replacing this "lowest cost" language with a more sophisticated decision rule that clearly reflected the concern that cost be taken into account in remedial selection, while providing the flexibility to select a remedy which is more reliable and protective than the least expensive minimally adequate alternative. Development of such a decision rule, however, is very difficult at this stage of the Superfund program.

Pending development of such a decision rule, EPA proposes to use the following general approach in selecting the cost-effective alternative from among remedies which provide what is considered to be at least minimally adequate protection. First, it is clear that among remedies which are *equally* feasible, reliable, and provide the same level of protection, EPA will select the least expensive remedy. Second, where all factors are not equal, EPA must evaluate the cost of each alternative and the level of protection provided by each alternative. Of course, in evaluating the cost of remedial alternatives, EPA must consider not only immediate capital costs, but the cost of dealing with the waste over the entire period that it would be expected to pose a threat to health and the environment. To give an example, EPA might select a treatment or destruction technology with a higher capital cost than long-term containment because the treatment/destruction offered a permanent solution to the problem. The reliability of various alternatives will be taken into account to the maximum extent possible, including the cost of such factors as the long-term operations and maintenance and the integrity of physical structures.

Finally, EPA clearly would not always pick the most protective option, regardless of cost. Instead, EPA would consider costs, technology, reliability, administrative and other concerns and their relevant effects on public health, welfare and the environment. This would allow the decisionmaker to select that alternative which, *at the specific site* in question, was most appropriate from a cost, technology, reliability and administrative perspective, considering public health, welfare, and environmental impacts.

Specific Changes

Section 300.68 generally follows the order in which a remedial action is planned and implemented. Several changes are proposed throughout the section. Some of these implement the major changes discussed above; others are designed to streamline the remedial program, to remove ambiguities, or to codify current EPA practice. These will be discussed in the order in which they appear in the section, using, for ease of

reference, the letters and headings that begin each subsection.

(a) *Introduction.* This subsection has been revised to clarify the circumstances under which remedial actions may be taken. The language in the existing NCP indicates that remedial actions can only be taken at sites on the NPL. The purpose of this restriction was to ensure that the limited Fund monies were only used for remedial action at NPL sites, which had been identified as posing the greatest potential threats to human health and the environment, *not* to make the NPL the exclusive list of necessary remedial or enforcement actions. The purpose of the change is to clarify the purpose of the NPL. It provides that remedial action may be taken at any site; however, *Fund-financed* remedial action is available only for sites on the NPL. This allows parties to conduct remedial actions at non-NPL sites and to seek recovery of their costs from those responsible for the release through section 107 of CERCLA.

Other proposed revisions to this subsection include: introduction of the term "Remedial Project Manager" (RPM) to describe the remedial action counterpart of the "On-Scene Coordinator" (OSC) in removal actions; and, a provision that Federal, State, and local environmental permits or authorization are not required for Fund-financed remedial action, or for remedial action taken pursuant to section 106 of CERCLA except for storage, treatment or disposal of wastes at an off-site facility; implementing this portion of the policy discussed under "Overview of Changes," above.

(b) *State Involvement.* Among the proposed changes to this subsection is the statement that a State participating in a Fund-financed remedial action must meet the requirements of section 104(c)(3) of CERCLA; i.e., requirements that the State will assure future operation and maintenance of the remedial measure, that it will assure the availability of an off-site facility that meets RCRA requirements, and that it will share in the costs of remedial actions. These requirements are currently found in §§ 300.62 and 300.67(b) of the NCP.

Another change clarifies EPA's interpretation that planning activities taken pursuant to section 104(b) of CERCLA generally do not require a State cost-share. Thus these planning costs, such as RI/FS and design work, are not subject to the State cost-share requirement unless the site was owned at the time of any hazardous substance disposal by the State or political

subdivision. The absence of the cost-share requirements for these activities has enabled EPA to move ahead more rapidly with remedial planning activities at NPL sites.

(c) *Scoping of Response Actions.* This section has been greatly expanded to reflect the early planning that precedes implementation of remedial action. The proposal requires examination of what types of actions may be necessary to remedy a release: Removal action, source control measures and actions to manage migration, or some combination of those measures. Because IRM's have been eliminated as a special category of remedial actions, removal actions would be considered in scoping the response action. This should foster an integrated process that allows rapid implementation of actions necessary to protect public health and the environment, consistent with longer term remedial actions.

The factors to consider in the scoping process, currently located in § 300.68(e)(2), have been moved to the scoping section and expanded to reflect factors that the lead agency should consider when approaching a response action. The proposal adds several new factors in § 300.68(c)(2), including:

• Paragraph (ii)—The proposed addition of a "routes of exposure" factor reflects sound environmental and is intended to assure that all actual and potential routes of exposure are considered.

• Paragraph (iii)—The proposal adds considerations relevant to off-site versus on-site disposal and the use of permanent destruction or immobilization for certain chemicals. In addition, EPA believes that the persistence, mobility and ability to bioaccumulate should be considered in determining how to handle substances. Where substances are persistent, mobile or bioaccumulate readily, the Agency believes that additional measures may be necessary to prevent future environmental or public health threats. Permanent destruction, neutralization, or immobilization will be preferred in treating or disposing of these wastes.

• Paragraph (iv)—The proposal adds floodplain and wetlands proximity as a factor to assure analysis of floodplains and wetlands in accordance with the requirements of Eexecutive Orders 11988 and 11990.

• Paragraph (vii)—Recycle/reuse of certain substances may be available as a way of permanently abating future threats of release. Recycle/reuse also has the added benefit of helping to conserve the capacity of RCRA permitted disposal facilities.

• Paragraph (xi)—Consistent with the proposed requirement regarding compliance with other environmental laws, among the factors proposed to be considered during scoping is the extent to which the contamination levels exceed applicable or relevant State and Federal environmental standards, advisories and criteria.

• Paragraph (xiii)—Where the remedial action may be carried out by responsible parties, the Agency proposes to assess the ability of the responsible parties to implement and maintain the remedial measure until the threat is abated. When responsible parties may not be able to support long-term monitoring or otherwise implement or maintain the remedy, it might be appropriate to require responsible parties to consider higher capital construction cost remedies that abate the threat more quickly and certainly.

(d) *Operable Unit.* As discussed earlier, the proposal reflects EPA's practice of dividing complex response actions into operable units. Operable units must be cost-effective and consistent with permanent remedial action and may be carried out as either removal or remedial actions.

(e) *Remedial Investigation/Feasibility Study.* As provided in the current NCP, the proposal requires evaluation of alternative remedial responses through a remedial investigation and feasibility study. This subsection also indicates that during remedial planning the analysis should assess the need for a removal action in lieu of or in addition to the remedial action.

(f) *Development of Alternatives.* This subparagraph addresses the first step of the cost-effectiveness analysis in the feasibility study and requires the development of alternative remedial responses. The proposed changes spell out in greater detail the range of alternatives that should be developed. These include off-site treatment or disposal alternatives and the no-action alternative, as well as alternatives designed to implement the proposed requirement regarding compliance with other environmental requirements. In this last category, the feasibility study should develop alternatives that attain, exceed, and fall short of other environmental requirements, to aid the decisionmaker in determining the alternative that best fits within the framework of that policy. In addition, the decisionmaker should take into account alternatives which consider relevant criteria, guidance or advisories, especially where there are no relevant or applicable standards. Finally, where appropriate, the feasibility study should take into account alternative

technologies, such as waste minimization, destruction, and recycling.

(g) *Initial Screening of Alternatives.* Once alternatives are developed, section 300.68(g) requires screening of alternatives on the basis of cost, effectiveness, and engineering feasibility. In substance, this subsection remains largely unchanged. One change is to specify that an alternative that would otherwise be eliminated because of disproportionate costs should nonetheless be considered if there is no other remedy that adequately protects human health and the environment by meeting applicable and relevant standards, advisories, or criteria. Since these applicable and relevant requirements often define the minimally adequate level of public health and environmental protection, the decisionmaker normally should consider (although not necessarily select) the alternative incorporating applicable or relevant requirements, irrespective of costs.

A second change proposed in this subsection is to specify that the feasibility study should document any alternatives eliminated on the basis of cost. Finally, an expanded paragraph on "effectiveness" would replace the current paragraph on "Effects of the Alternative," and would clarify when ineffective alternatives should be eliminated. Two types of alternatives should generally be screened out: those that do not effectively contribute to the level of protection, and those with significant adverse effects and limited environmental benefits.

However, the fact that an alternative does not meet "applicable or relevant" standards would not necessarily be a reason to eliminate it, since under EPA's proposed requirement regarding compliance with other environmental laws, such an alternative might be selected under appropriate circumstances, indicated in 300.68(i).

(h) *Detailed Analysis of Alternatives.* This subsection requires a detailed analysis of those alternatives remaining after the initial screening, in terms of cost, engineering, and environmental and public health protection. Two substantive changes are proposed in this subsection.

The first explains how the proposed requirement regarding compliance with other environmental laws applies to the analysis of alternatives. Specifically, the analysis should consider the extent to which the alternative meets or exceeds applicable or relevant requirements. For management of migration actions, i.e., where contaminants have moved or are likely to move off-site, when no applicable or relevant requirements

apply, the lead agency should evaluate the risks of exposure projected to remain after implementation of the alternative in those circumstances. This evaluation of risks is unnecessary for alternatives attaining or exceeding applicable or relevant requirements since those requirements generally establish the appropriate level of cleanup without further analysis of the residual risk.

An assessment of the risk posed by the source-control remedial measures likewise is not required, since the goal of these measures is to prevent future releases into the environment. In additions, these source control situations pose difficulty in modeling risks. For source control remedial measures, therefore, EPA will use a technology-based approach to determine the appropriate alternative for preventing further releases.

The second proposed change in this subsection is to require an analysis of whether recycle/reuse, waste minimization, destruction, or other advanced and innovative or alternative technologies are appropriate to remedy the release. This change parallels modifications proposed in paragraphs (d)(2)(vii) and (f)(2), discussed earlier.

(i) *Selection of Remedy.* This final step in the remedial process is the selection by the decisionmaker of the appropriate remedial alternative. There are two important changes in the proposal. First, as discussed earlier, the selected remedy must meet the substantive requirements of applicable or relevant Federal standards unless one of the enumerated circumstances is present. The applicable and relevant standards define the adequate level of protection of public health and the environment. One of these circumstances, "Fund-balancing," is the subject of § 300.68(k) of the current NCP. Accordingly, that subsection would be subsumed in the new subsection (i).

Second, also discussed earlier, the proposal clarifies that EPA is not required to select the lowest cost remedy that provides minimally adequate protection.

(j) *Appropriate Actions.* This new subsection would set out certain remedial actions that, in EPA's experience, are appropriate in specific circumstances. The subsection details appropriate remedial responses that are, in general, an appropriate response to contaminated ground water, contaminated surface water, contaminated soil or waste, and the threat of direct contact with hazardous substances. As with removals, Agency experience has indicated that certain types of actions are generally appropriate to address situations commonly found at remedial sites. This specification is not intended to limit the lead agency from employing responses which are different than those listed or from responding to more than just the listed circumstances. The Agency retains the ability to develop the most appropriate response, considering the individual site and other characteristics.

(k) *Remedial Site Sampling.* Finally, another new subsection would specify those circumstances in which sampling performed in support of remedial action is presumed adequate. This subsection codifies current EPA practice on conducting site sampling.

Section 300.68(k) provides for a written plan for sampling performed pursuant to remedial action. This plan will specify the nature and extent of sampling. A written plan which meets the criteria of § 300.68(k) will be considered adequate. Section 300.68(k)(2) requires that this remedial quality assurance site sampling plan be reviewed and approved by the appropriate EPA Regional or Headquarters Quality Assurance Officer.

C. Site Evaluation Phase and NPL Determination

Introduction

Section 300.66 currently serves two purposes. First, it establishes criteria to determine the appropriate action when a preliminary site assessment indicates a need for further response, or when the OSC and lead Agency concur that further response should follow an immediate removal action. Second, it outlines the process and criteria for placing sites on the NPL.

Several changes are proposed in this section. In general, these changes call for the development of more detailed information in the site evaluation phrase. Additionally, the proposed modifications delete the prohibition against listing Federal facilities on the NPL, and include providing additional bases for including sites on the NPL, and provisions for deleting sites from the NPL. The effect of these latter changes will be increase EPA's flexibility to take remedial actions at problem sites, and to provide a more formal mechanism for removing sites from the NPL.

The NPL has been promulgated separately from this rulemaking. The promulgated NPL can be found at 49 FR 37070, September 21, 1984, and the most recent proposed revisions to the NPL can be found at 49 FR 40320, October 15, 1984.

Specific Changes

Subsection (a)—Site Evaluation. These provisions consolidate the substance of the material found in subsections (a)-(c) in the existing NCP. Subsection (a) discusses the site evaluation phase, which extends from the time of discovery of a release through preliminary assessment and site inspection. The proposal clarifies that the purpose of site evaluation is to determine the nature of potential threats occasioned by a release and to collect data for determining whether a release should be included on the NPL. To provide greater flexibility, paragraph (a)(2) of the proposal expands authorized activity to include preliminary assessments in addition to site inspections, and removes the requirements that response officials and enforcement officials conduct these activities jointly. Paragraph (a)(3) establishes that in remedial situations, preliminary assessments consist of review of existing data and may include off-site reconnaissance. The preliminary assessment is intended to eliminate further consideration of releases which do not pose threats to public health and the environment, to determine potential danger to those living or working in the vicinity of the releases, and to establish priority for scheduling site inspections.

Proposed paragraph (a)(4) would further elaborate the purposes for a site inspection: To determine whether a release poses no actual or potential threat to public health and the environment; to determine whether there is immediate potential danger to those living or working in the vicinity of the release; and to collect data to determine whether a release should be placed on the NPL.

Subsections (b)-(c)-NPL. The principal changes proposed in these provisions are intended to provide EPA with additional flexibility to place sites on the NPL. Since a site must be on the NPL to be eligible for Fund-financed remedial action, this increased flexibility provides greater opportunities to take remedial actions at sites, when appropriate. For the reasons stated below, EPA is providing for a somewhat shortened comment period on the proposal to add a new basis for listing a site on the NPL.

Proposed subsection (a) generally addresses the ways in which a release can be included on the NPL. In general, the NCP currently requires that a site satisfy one of two tests to be eligible for inclusion on the NPL: The release must score above a threshold level using the Hazard Ranking System (HRS), or the release must be designated by the State

as its highest priority release. The proposal retains these provisions (the HRS has not been changed since July 1982).

Pursuant to CERCLA section 105(8)(B), the State may designate a top priority site for inclusion on the NPL. EPA will allow each State to designate *one* top priority site over the life of the NPL.

Proposed paragraph (b)(4) would add a new mechanism for including a release on the NPL irrespective of its HRS score, based on a determination that a site poses a significant threat to public health. Specifically, EPA may base that determination on whether the Department of Health and Human Services has issued a health advisory as a consequence of the release. This might, for example, make eligible for remedial action a site at which a small number of people are seriously threatened, although scoring on the HRS would not necessarily exceed the threshold level.

CERCLA does not require that a site be on the NPL to be eligible for Fund-financed remedial responses. That restriction is one EPA voluntarily imposed in the existing NCP, for reasons of Fund-management and to alert the public to the significance of a site being included among the priority releases. The Agency believes that the restriction still serves these important functions and should be retained. However, the restriction has led to instances in which remedial action, although seemingly appropriate, was unavailable because the site did not receive a sufficiently high HRS score. The above criteria attempt to address this problem by broadening the bases for inclusion on the NPL. EPA will continue to propose and solicit comments on revisions of the NPL, so that interested parties will have an opportunity to address the extent to which a particular site warrants being included on the list.

EPA is providing for a 30 day comment period on this proposal to provide an additional basis for inclusion of a site on the NPL, rather than the 60 day comment period provided for the remainder of the proposed revisions of the NCP. The Agency intends to review the comments on this proposal in an expedited fashion, and depending on the nature of the comments may finalize this change prior to a final decision on the remainder of the proposed amendments.

The Agency is identifying this particular issue for expedited comment for several reasons. First, EPA is now considering appropriate response measures at several sites which are not eligible for inclusion on the NPL based on the existing NCP criteria, but which could be listed on the basis of the proposed new criteria. Addition of these new criteria for NPL listing could allow expedited addition of such sites to the NPL. As a result, EPA would be able to select remedial measures at these sites, if appropriate, such as where remedial measures are more cost-effective than taking removal actions at these sites.

Second, EPA has previously solicited comment on the general issue of alternative criteria for listing sites on the NPL (48 FR 40675–76, September 8, 1983), including the possible use of health advisories as a basis for listing sites which do not receive a sufficiently high HRS score. Third, EPA believes that the issue of adding a new listing criteria is a relatively discrete and narrow one. Thus, EPA believes that utilizing a 30 day comment period on this particular issue would not impose an undue burden on persons who would be interested in commenting on this issue.

Another proposed modification would delete the prohibition which limits sites currently owned by the Federal Government from being included on the NPL. EPA is soliciting comments on different ways of advising the public of the status of Federal Government clean-up efforts. One approach would be the listing on the NPL on the NPL of sites currently owned by the Federal Government. Other approaches the Agency can consider for Federal facilities include the periodic publishing of the list of each Agency's priorities through the A–106 process under Executive Order 12088, or the publishing of a list of each Federal agency's facility cleanup priorities independent of the NPL.

The proposal addresses when sites may be deleted from the NPL. Sites may be deleted where no further response is appropriate, based on the following criteria:

(1) If the responsible parties or other parties have completed all appropriate response actions;

(2) If all appropriate Fund-financed response under CERCLA has been completed and no further cleanup by responsible parties is appropriate; or

(3) If EPA has determined that the release poses no significant threats so that taking response action is not appropriate at the time.

Notwithstanding deletion from the NPL, a previously listed site will remain eligible for Fund-financed remedial action if future conditions warrant that action.

Other, less significant changes to the NPL provisions include: Reiteration of the statutory criteria that the NPL contain at least 400 releases and potential releases, and that the list be updated annually; clarification that inclusion on the NPL is a precondition to eligibility for *Fund-financed* remedial action, not a precondition to liability under section 106 of CERCLA (enforcement actions) nor to action under section 107 for non-Fund-financed costs or Fund-financed non-remedial expenditure; and a requirement that States include appropriate documentation with HRS score sheets (as is currently done). EPA is not proposing to modify the HRS in this rulemaking and is not soliciting comments on the HRS.

D. Other Party Responses

The former § 300.71, concerning worker health and safety has been moved to § 300.38. The new § 300.71 addresses the requirements the NCP imposes on parties other than the lead agency (including responses by responsible parties, other private parties and Federal and State governments).

Discussion

Proposed § 300.71(a) recognizes that *parties* other than the lead agency may undertake response actions and specifies the roles the lead agency and other parties play in the different types of responses: Enforcement actions under CERCLA section 106 and response actions and recovery of costs by other parties pursuant to section 107.

Enforcement Actions

Section 300.71(a) clarifies the lead agency's responsibility in reviewing actions undertaken pursuant to § 106 of CERCLA. Proposed § 300.71(a) directs that the lead agency, *in specific limited circumstances*, evaluate the adequacy of the response action proposed by the responsible party and approve those actions, taking into consideration the factors discussed in §§ 300.65 (for removal actions) and 300.68 paragraphs (c) through (i) (for remedial actions). In enforcement remedial actions, the lead agency, however, will not apply the Fund-balancing considerations discussed in § 300.68(i).

Other Non-Lead Agency Responses and Recovery of Costs Pursuant to CERCLA Section 107

When a private party seeks to recover response costs from a responsible party under CERCLA section 107(a)(1–4)(B), that party must demonstrate that its response actions were *consistent with the NCP.* (States and the Federal Government must show that other actions were "not inconsistent" with the NCP.) To clarify what "consistent with the NCP" for this purpose means, § 300.71(a) has been added to the NCP.

First, § 300.71(a) (3) and (5) state that the lead agency does *not* have to evaluate and approve a response action for those costs to be recovered from a responsible party pursuant to CERCLA section 107. Instead, § 300.71(a)3) states that only response actions undertaken pursuant to section 106 actions instituted by the Federal Government and actions involving preauthorization of Fund moneys under 300.25(d) of the NCP require advance Federal government approval of a response action. Furthermore, § 300.71(a)(5) goes on to spell out the requirements a private party must meet to be consistent with the NCP. These requirements are as follows:

A. *Removal Actions:*
—take removal in circumstances as specified in § 300.65

B. *Remedial Actions:*
—consider factors as enumerated in § 300.68(c)–(i)
—provide for an appropriate analysis of alternatives
—selection of the cost-effective response.

The private party may choose a more costly response, but the responsible party is only responsible for the costs of the "cost-effective" remedy.

When a private party intends to take a response action and wishes to seek reimbursement from the Fund it must first become preauthorized [See § 300.25(d) for the preauthorization requirements].

Section 300.71(c) addresses the process of certification for individuals or organizations. Certification is a method for establishing engineering, scientific, or other technical expertise necessary to undertake remedial actions, safely and effectively. Demonstrating this technical expertise is one of the requirements for requesting preauthorization [See § 300.25(d)(5)]. Certification, however, is not necessary for fund preauthorization. To receive certification, the organization must submit a written request for certification that demonstrates that the organization has the qualifications necessary for implementing response action.

The advantage of certification is that the organization need only submit the written request demonstrating its qualifications one time rather than each time it requests preauthorization. Thus, an organization which becomes certified will administratively speed up the preauthorization process.

Section 300.71(c)(4) specifies that the Administrator will respond to certification requests within 180 days. The 180 days start when a complete certification request is received by the Administrator. Once certification is granted, the individual or organization will be considered to be generally qualified, but the certification shall not constitute advance approval of all response work.

Section 300.71(e) states that response completed by any party does not release parties from liability to the government under CERCLA.

III. Other Revisions

In addition to the major revisions discussed in section II, the following minor revisions to all the subparts are proposed (including revisions to subpart F not discussed in the previous section). These revisions are presented below by subpart.

Subpart A

Section 300.5 Abbreviations.

The Agency proposes to add the abbreviation "RPM" meaning "Remedial Project Manager" to the list of abbreviations. This corresponds to other changes proposed in today's rulemaking that define the role and responsibilities of this Federal official.

Section 300.6 Defintions.

Discussion

A number of changes to this section are proposed. The first is the addition of definitions for terms used in the present Plan but not previously defined. These terms are "activation," "coastal waters," "CERCLA," "feasibility study," "inland waters," "specified ports and harbors," "size classes for releases," "first Federal official," "remedial investigation," and "source control." The intent of these additions is to address questions that have been raised concerning the defintion of these terms as used in the Plan. The second change is the addition of some new terms and the deletion of an existing term used in the Plan. The new terms added to the Plan are "managment of migration," "operable unit," "project plan" and "remedial project manager." The terms deleted from the Plan are "off-site remedial measures" and "responsible official." The final change is the revison of definitions for "OSC" and "lead agency." These definitions have been modified to correspond to present practice and to reflect changes proposed to other sections of the Plan.

Specific Changes

"Activation" has been defined to clarify that the entire RRT or NRT must not necessarily be assembled to consider issues raised during a response. There are many situations

where the expertise of only a portion of the RRT or NRT membership is necessary to provide advice or assistance to the OSC/RPM, thus not requiring the participation of all members. The proposed definition states this position and provides the RRT or NRT charimen with the discretion to assemble the appropriate RRT or NRT members to carry out their responsiblities.

Definitions have been added for the terms "inland waters" and "coastal waters" as used to classify size of discharges for oil spills. These terms were not meant to correspond to the waters within the inland zone and coastal zone, but there were different interpretations as to what was the correct definiton. The definition of these terms should resolve inconsistencies between EPA and USCG OSCs when classifying oil spills on inland rivers.

"CERCLA" or "Superfund" has been defined. "Feasibility Study" and "Remedial Investigation," two key parts of remedial action have been defined. The term "specified ports and harbors" has been defined to mean port and harbor areas on inland rivers, and land areas immediately adjacent to those waters, where the U.S. Coast Guard (USCG) acts as predesignated OSC. Questions have been raised whether there were specific locations where the USCG should be OSC. The Agency's opinion, as indicated by the definition, is that exact locations where the USCG acts as OSC should be negotiated between USCG districts and EPA regions on a regional basis and identified in Regional Contingency Plans. Negotiations at this level can best account for resource availability of the two agencies.

A definition has also been added for the term "first Federal official" to clarify the roles and authorities of this individual. In many areas of the country, representatives of NRT member agencies may arrive at the scene of a discharge or release before the predesignated OSC. This definition clarifies that this official is authorized to coordinate response activities under this Plan and initiate actions normally performed by the OSC until their arrival. This new definition corresponds to an additional revision to 300.33 proposed today concerning the scope of authority for these officials.

The final definition added involves size classes for releases of hazardous substances, pollutants, or contaminants into the environment. Size classes are generally meant to be triggers for actions and report requirements under this Plan, and may not directly relate to the severity of a release. Thus, the

Agency did not include a size classification for hazardous substance releases in the 1982 revision to the Plan. Since that time, there has been some confusion on whether hazardous substance releases should be classified in the same manner as oil spills. The Agency intended that releases be classified by the OSC taking into account the many factors that effect the impact of a release (e.g., quantity, environmental; medium affected, location). The Agency considered the use of a factor such as reportable quantity to classify releases, but does not feel that using this quantity, which relates only to reporting requirements, would account for all the variables that influences the impact of a release on public health or welfare or the environment. Thus the definition for size classification requires OSCs to classify a release based on their assessment of its threat to public health or welfare or the environment, taking into account the many variables that influence this potential threat.

The Agency also proposes to add another new term, "remedial project manager (RPM)," and delete the existing definition of "responsible official." These changes are ment to clarify who is responsible for coordinating Federal remedial actions resulting from releases of hazardous substances, pollutants, or contaminants. As a matter of practice, predesignated OSCs are generally involved only in oil response under subpart E and removals under subpart F. The Term "OSC" has not been widely used for the lead agency personnel managing remedial actions. The term RPM is added as the remedial action counterpart to the OSC to distinguish between the OSC and the RPM since the activities they are responsible for implementing under the Plan are different in scope, nature, and duration. This new definition complements definitional changes for OSC and lead agency. This change necessitates changes in subparts A, B, C, D, and F to reflect the role and responsibilities of the RPM. These changes will be cited throughout this preamble. EPA has reviewed each citation of the term "OSC" in the present Plan, and added the term "RPM" where appropriate.

The term "RPM" was not added in sections where only removal actions were indicated. EPA intends to designate RPMs for each remedial action undertaken under subpart F of this Plan. In addition, by agreement, the USCG will predesignate an RPM for any remedial actions involving vessels in the coastal zone. The definition of RPM for remedial actions on the Department of

Defense (DOD) facilities indicates the Federal official designated by DOD. This accounts for those situations where DOD may designate EPA to act as RPM for a remedial action involving their facilities, based on an EPA/DOD Memorandum of Understanding. Interested public may obtain copies of this MOU from EPA or DOD. The roles and responsibilities of an RPM are discussed in greater detail in the discussion of changes to 300.33 later in today's preamble.

The definitions for two terms presently included in 300.6 have been modified. These are "OSC" and "lead agency." The definition of OSC has been modified by deleting any reference to States acting under cooperative agreements under CERCLA, by limiting OSC responsibilities to responses under subpart E and removals under subpart F of the PLAN (to complement the new RPM responsibilities for remedial actions), and by adding language to clarify DOD predesignated OSC responsibilities. The deletion of States acting under cooperative agreements is meant to clarify the respective roles of the Federal Government and the States in removal actions. As redefined, the terms OSC and RPM will only apply to Federal officials, since this person is responsible for coordinating the response of Federal agencies under this Plan. As is discussed later in today's preamble, States acting as lead agency for a response under CERCLA will still carry out the responsibilities of the Federal OSC/RPM. The language concerning DOD has been clarified to indicate that DOD acts as predesignated OSC only for releases of hazardous substances from their vessels and facilities. For discharges of oil from DOD vessels and facilities, EPA or USCG OSCs will provide advice and oversight of response actions as they do for incidents involving other Federal agencies. This change is discussed in more detail later in today's preamble in the section covering proposed changes to §300.33. The definition of "lead agency" has also been modified to clarify the relationship of this term to "OSC" and the new "RPM" proposed today. As indicated above, the OSC and RPM are Federal officials. In the case of a State-lead response under subpart F of this Plan, the State will carry out the responsibilities of the OSC or RPM, but will not replace that Federal official. This change, combined with the change in the definition of OSC and the addition of the new term RPM, should help clarify any confusion over the respective roles of the OSC and lead agency as used in the Plan.

The Agency has reviewed the use of the terms OSC, RPM, and lead agency throughout the Plan. OSC or RPM is proposed where this individual is authorized to take action under the Plan; lead agency is proposed where the authority does not necessarily rest with the individual OSC/RPM (but the lead agency could internally delegate such authority as it sees fit). "OSC" is used in subpart E to reflect the vesting of authority in the lead Federal official on-scene due to the emergency nature of spill responses. "Lead agency" is used most frequently in subpart F to reflect vesting of authority with the agency since many actions in CERCLA responses (particularly remedial actions) require the OSC/RPM to consult and clear actions with other officials.

Subpart B

Section 300.22 Coordination among and by Federal agencies.

Discussion

An editorial change has been made to (d)(2) to correct a typographical error. The word "of" on line 3 is replaced by "or."

Also, although there has been no change in the language, the Agency would like to clarify existing language in paragraph (f) concerning coordination of responses to spills involving Outer Continental Shelf Lands Act (OCSLA) operations. There have been some inquiries concerning the status of a Department of Transportation/ Department of Interior (DOI) Memorandum of Understanding that addresses response to OCS incidents. This MOU, which outlines the roles of the DOI representative and the USCG on-scene coordinator for discharges in connection with OCS operations, was signed on August 16, 1971 and remains in effect. The Agency does not believe it is necessary to refer to this MOU in the Plan since it serves only to clarify overlapping jurisdiction of the agencies under OCSLA and the Clean Water Act and does not affect the Federal OCS response. Interested public may obtain copies of the MOU from DOI or the USCG.

Section 300.23 Other assistance by Federal agencies.

Discussion

The Agency proposes to add a description of capabilities of NRT member agencies to support OSCs/ RPMs during a response action. These capability statements were deleted in the 1982 revisions to the Plan. Since that

time, the Agency has reconsidered this issue and feels that it is appropriate to include a brief description of Federal agency capabilities to increase the public's understanding of the respective capabilities of the various agencies that support an OSC or RPM during a response. References to the new term RPM are proposed in §§ 300.23(b) and 300.23(c)(1).

Section 300.24 State and local participation.

Discussion

The Agency proposes to add language to this section concerning the roles of State and local governments in protecting the public health and welfare during an initial response to a discharge or release and to clarify a State's use of the titles OSC and RPM.

Specific Changes

A new paragraph (e) is proposed to address the role of the State and local governments in protecting public health and welfare during a response. In most instances where a Federal response is necessary for a discharge of oil or release of a hazardous substance, pollutant, or contaminant, State and local officials are on scene before the OSC. The proposed addition reflects this first responder role to initiate public safety actions (roadblocks, crowd control, etc.) to protect the public health and welfare pending the arrival of the OSC. It also recognizes that it is a State and local responsibility, as a practical matter rather than Federal law, which will direct any evacuation necessary because of a discharge or release. The Agency believes that these officials are the most capable to carry out these actions, both because of their police powers and since most evacuations are time critical in nature. A similar change is also proposed to § 300.62 for responses under subpart F.

The Agency also proposes to add language to clarify that States may use the titles OSC and RPM for their response personnel without such use carrying the legal meanings for Federal officials in this Plan. This change is necessary since the OSC and RPM have been redefined as Federal officials. However, States acting as lead agency through a contract or cooperative agreement must carry out the same responsibilities as the Federal OSC/ RPM (except coordinating and directing Federal agency response actions).

Section 300.25   Non-Government participation.

Discussion

The Agency proposes to add language at the end of paragraph (b) of this section to clarify the role of the scientific support coordinator (SSC) in coordinating technical and scientific information from non-government sources. Existing language in the Plan does not indicate who is responsible for coordinating these efforts. While this information is helpful in carrying out a response, the participation must be coordinated to ensure the OSC is not overburdened with this assistance. The SSC is the appropriate person to coordinate this non-government participation in technical and scientific issues. Also a reference to RPM is proposed in § 300.25(b).

Pursuant to section 111(a)(2) of CERCLA, § 300.25(d) requires that a person other than the Federal Government or a State or person operating under contract or cooperative agreement with the United States who takes response action and wishes to seek reimbursement from the Fund must first obtain prior approval from EPA of the response action and the submission of a claim against the Fund. This preauthorization requirement was intended to ensure that private responses for which Fund reimbursement is sought are cost-effective and otherwise in accordance with this Plan. In addition, the preauthorization requirement is necessary for proper Fund management, to ensure that Fund monies be available for the most urgent priorities.

This proposal would add paragraphs (2), (3), (4), and (5) to § 300.25(d). Fund preauthorization will be considered only for (1) releases warranting removal action pursuant to § 300.65; (2) 104(b) actions where the agency believes the site will be or is listed on the NPL; and (3) remedial actions at NPL sites. Preauthorization will be subject to Fund balancing considerations. The factors considered for determining priority are competing uses of the Fund, listing on the NPL, determination of potential threat to public health and the qualifications of the requester. Payment of a claim under section 112 will be conditioned on the lead agency certifying that costs incurred were necessary and consistent with the preauthorization. The Agency is currently in the process of developing separate regulations that will specifically address the preauthorization process.

Subpart C

Section 300.31   Organization.

Discussion

The Agency proposes to add a diagram outlining the NCP concepts, and maps showing the 10 Standard Federal Regions and 12 USCG Districts. These were included in the 1980 Plan and deleted in the 1982 revisions. The Agency feels that the addition of these items will increase the public's understanding of the national response mechanism and provide information on the EPA region or USCG district with jurisdiction over specific geographic locations in the U.S.

Section 300.32   Planning and coordination.

Discussion

Eight changes or additions to this section are proposed. The intent of all these modifications is to reflect present practices and to better define the roles of the NRT and RRT in the national response mechanism. Each proposed change is discussed below.

Specific Changes

The first set of changes apply to the designation of NRT or RRT chairmen during a responsive activation. Existing language in (a)(2) of this section and in 300.34(f)(2) indicates that the chairman for an activation is the representative of the Federal lead agency for the response. This has caused some confusion over whether DOD would act as chairman for responses involving releases of hazardous substances, pollutants, or contaminants from their vessels and facilities. The Agency believes, with DOD concurrence, that for continuity of organization, the EPA or USCG should act as chairman for the NRT or RRT during a response to an incident involving DOD. Thus, the Agency proposes to change the last sentence in (a)(2) and to add a sentence to (b)(1) indicating that the NRT or RRT chairman during an activation is the EPA or USCG representative, based on whether the discharge or release occurs in the inland zone or coastal zone, or as otherwise agreed upon by the USCG and EPA representatives. There could be situations, such as a DOD remedial action in the coastal zone, where the USCG would defer to EPA to act as chairman.

The second set of changes relate to the role of the NRT in providing advice to the RRTs. The existing language in (a)(8) indicates that the NRT may consider matters referred to it by an RRT for settlement. This has resulted in some concern since the word

"settlement" seems to imply that there must be a dispute within the RRT before NRT involvement is appropriate. EPA did not intend this to be the case. RRTs are encouraged to refer matters to the NRT whenever necessary. To clarify this, EPA proposes to change (a)(8) to indicate that the NRT will consider any matters referred to it by RRTs for resolution of outstanding issues or to provide advice. Also, there has been some confusion since the present Plan does not address when it is appropriate for an RRT to refer matters to the NRT. To clarify this, a new paragraph (b)(7) is proposed. This language indicates that RRTs may refer matters to the NRT whenever there is insufficient national policy guidance, a technical issue requiring solution, a question concerning interpretation of language in the Plan, or a disagreement on discretionary actions between RRT members that cannot be resolved on a regional level. Note that disagreements at the RRT level must involve discretionary actions of the RRT. Actions of an RRT that are not discretionary in nature, although they may be disagreeable to some RRT members, would not be appropriate for referral to the NRT.

The third change to this section involves the addition of specific responsibility for the NRT to monitor response related research and development activities of Federal agencies. Many agencies have research and development (R&D) projects underway that support response activities. The Agency intends that the NRT monitor R&D activities of NRT agencies to ensure that the appropriate coordination occurs between agencies and that duplication of effort is minimized. The NRT will be in a position to identify areas requiring R&D, and to provide recommendations for future efforts to the appropriate agencies. The language proposed for a new (a)(7)(v) will task the NRT with this specific role.

The forth change to this section involves the role of the NRT and RRT in training and preparedness for response. Existing language in the Plan in (a)(6) authorizes the NRT to consider and make recommendations to appropriate agencies. While this has occurred, the Agency believes that the NRT and RRTs should take a more direct role in training and prepardness for response. To implement this, the Agency proposes to task the NRT and RRT with specific responsibilities in this area. The language proposed for a new (a)(7)(vi) under direct planning and preparedness responsibilities of the NRT adds the responsibility for monitoring response training to encourage coordination of available training resources between member agencies. This should result in less duplication and better coordination of response training by Federal agencies with responsibilities under this Plan. In addition to the NRT role, RRTs will also have responsibility for training and preparedness at the regional level. The Agency proposes to task the RRTs specifically with encouraging the State and local response community with improving their response preparedness and to conduct training exercises as necessary within the region to ensure that members of the response community within the region are prepared to carry out their respective roles. The Agency does not see this as a significant change from present practice, since most RRTs are already involved in training exercises on a recurring basis. the New language proposed for (b)(6)(x) formalizes this role. The language proposed for (b)(6)(ix) also formalizes existing practices. With limits on the availability of Federal resources, State and local agencies are relied on extensively to provide initial response, assessment, and monitoring support for the OSC. The Agency intends that RRTs become involved in encouraging the improvement of State and local Response preparedness.

The fifth change to this section addresses training for OSCs, RPMs, and their on scene representatives. Existing language in the Plan does not address training of OSCs and RPMs. There has always been an implicit responsibility for the Federal agency providing the OSC to train those persons to carry out their responsibilities under the Plan. The proposed language added at (c)(1) formalizes this implicit responsibility. The Agency also proposes to add a new (c)(2) addressing training of on scene representatives of the OSC or RPM. A change proposed today in 300.33 authorizes the OSC or RPM to designate capable representatives of other Federal, State, and local government agencies to act as their on scene representatives at a response. The language added in (c)(2) tasks the OSC or RPM to ensure, to the extent practicable, that persons they designate to act as their on scene representatives are adequately trained and prepared to carry out actions they will be tasked with, such as monitoring cleanups, etc.

The sixth change to this section revises the description of the role of the RRT as described in paragraph (b) to clarify the makeup of an RRT. The existing language does not specifically address the structuring of RRTs. As a result, some RRTs are based on the

Standard Federal Region while others have subdivided within a region to account for differences in geographic jurisdiction of member agencies. The proposed revision to paragraph (b) and (b)(6) and the addition to (b)(2) reflects the Agency's opinion that RRTs be based on the Standard Federal Regions. The revisions provide for a network of 10 standing RRTs to carry out the planning, coordination, training, evaluation, and preparedness within the region while preserving the incident-specific nature of the RRT to correspond with differences in geographic jurisdictions for member agencies. This structuring recognizes that "regional" boundaries of all RRT members do not correspond to the Standard Federal Regions and provides the flexibility for representation on the incident-specific team based on the geographic location of the incident. Agencies with regional boundaries that do not correspond to the Standard Federal Region, such as the USCG, will be authorized to designate additional representatives to the standing RRT to ensure that their agency is represented for all locations within the region. Participation for a particular incident will involve only those representatives with jurisdiction over the area affected by the release.

The seventh change addresses RRT responsibilities required by the recent rulemaking on subpart H of the Plan. A new sentence (b)(c)(i) is added to ensure that RRTs conduct advance planning on the use of dispersants and other chemical and biological agents. The current § 300.32(b)(6)(1)–(vii) are accordingly renumbered as (b)(6)(ii)–(viii).

The final change to this section deletes the reference in paragraph (d) to DOI providing SSCs for inland areas. As a matter of practice, the SSC for inland areas is normally provided by EPA. This change reflects this practice, but the language still provides for obtaining SSCs from other agencies if determined to be appropriate by the RRT.

Section 300.33   Response operations.

Discussion

Nine changes or additions are proposed to this section. the intent of these revision is to better reflect existing jurisdiction, authorities, and responsibilities of OSCs, to correspond to present practice, and to incorporate the roles and responsibilities of the remedial project manager (RPM). Specific references to the new term RPM are proposed where appropriate in each subparagraph in 300.33(b) except in 300.33(b)(1) and 300.33(b)(12) (as proposed renumbered), which are

applicable only to removal actions. Changes to this section also correspond to revised sections being added in subpart C convering public information and worker health and safety. Each proposed change is discussed below.

Specific Change

The first change to this section is the revision of paragraph (a) to reflect the addition of remedial project managers (RPM), to clarify DOD's role as predesignated OSC for hazardous substance, pollutant, or contaminant releases only with respect to their vessels and facilities, and to specify the USCG role at waste sites in the coastal zone. As discussed earlier, the Agency proposes to disignate RPMs for remedial actions, and the existing language in the beginning of (a) has been changed to reflect this proposal. In addition, the language has been modified to reflect DOD's role as predesignated OSC and RPM for hazardous substance, pollutant, or contaminant release from their vessels and facilities. Finally, paragraph (a) has been revised to reflect the role of the USCG OSC in initial response to releases from hazardous waste sites in the coastal zone and to address the transition between the USCG OSC and EPA RPM for remedial actions at facilities in the coastal zone. This change incorporates provisions of the DOT/EPA Instrument of Redelegation of October 1981. This agreement was published in the **Federal Register** on December 31, 1981 at 46 FR 63294.

The second change to this section expands the authority of the first Federal official at the scene of a discharge or release. Existing language in (b)(i) tasks the first official of an agency with responsibilities under this Plan arriving on scene to coordinate activities under the Plan until arrival of the OSC. The Agency proposes to amend this paragraph to authorize this official to initiate necessary actions pending the arrival of the OSC. This authority includes initiating Federal Fund-financed cleanup actions if such actions are required prior to the arrival of the OSC on scene. This will allow for rapid emergency containment or mitigation measures in those situations where the predesignated OSC is not able to get to the scene of an incident immediately. It should be noted that the authority to initiate Fund-financed actions has been limited by requiring authorization by the OSC or an authorized representative of the lead agency before comitting funds. The first Federal official will normally not be familiar with the cirteria or restrictions for use of the applicable Fund, so any initiation of action requiring funding must be approved by the OSC or other designated agency official before it occurs. This change should allow for rapid action when necessary, yet ensure that any actions taken before the arrival of the OSC are consistent with policies and procedures required by the CERCLA or 311(k) Fund manager.

The third change to this section adds language to (b)(3) authorization the OSC or RPM to designate capable persons from government agencies to act as their on scene representatives at a response. As a practical matter, because of limited resources, the OSC or RPM is not able to be on scene throughout a response. As a result, they rely on representatives from their own or from other agencies to monitor response actions when they are not present. This change formalizes this existing practice. It should be noted, however, that these designated representative are only acting on behalf of and may take actions only as authorized by the predesignated OSC or RPM, not assuming the full authorities and responsibilities of this person. In addition, State and local representatives are not authorized to act in responses funded by CERCLA or the 311(k) Fund unless the appropriate contract or cooperative agreement has been established.

The fourth change modifies existing language in (b)(8) concerning the responsibilities of Federal agencies for discharges of oil or releases of hazardous substances, pollutants, or contaminants from vessels or facilities under their jurisdiction. Existing language in this paragraph seems to limit hazardous substance responsibility to the 297 hazardous substances designated by EPA under section 311(b)(2) of the Clean Water Act. The Agency proposes to delete this limitation and to add additional responsibility for pollutant or contaminant releases. This change expands agency responsibility to include all releases covered by CERCLA. An additional change expands Federal agency responsibility to include contiguous lands under their jurisdiction. There has also been some confusion over the role of the OSC at a discharge or release involving a Federal agency. The existing language authorizes the OSC to conduct appropriate response activities if, in their opinion, the responsible agency does not act promptly or take appropriate action. There has been some concern that the responsible Federal agency may not have the expertise necessary to carry out a proper and timely response, or the OSC would act

independently without providing sufficient opportunity for the Federal agency to respond. The Agency believes that it is implicit that the OSC will consult with the Federal agency before acting, but to clarify this, the language has been changed to require the OSC, or in the case of a remedial action the lead agency, to consult with and coordinate all response activities with the responsible agency. In addition, language has been added to indicate that the OSC or RPM is available to provide advice or assistance as requested by the responsible agency throughout that agency's response. In any case, involvement by the OSC or RPM will be limited by restrictions on the use of the 311(k) Fund and CERCAL Trust Fund at incidents involving Federal Facilities and vessels. The final change to (b)(8) clarifies that DOD designates OSCs or RPMs only for releases of hazardous substances, pollutants, or contaminants with respect to their vessels or facilities. DOD will still be responsible for discharges of oil from their vessels or facilities, but the predesignated EPA or USCG OSC will have an oversight role as they do for incidents involving other Federal agencies.

The fifth change modifies existing language in (b)(9) concerning the OSC's or RPM's relationship with the land managing agency or natural resource trustee. The existing language provides for the OSC to notify the land managing agency or natural resource trustee of a discharge or release affecting Federal resources under its jurisdiction. While this has occurred, questions have been raised concerning to what extent the OSC or RPM should consult with the affected agency or trustee. The Agency believes that the OSC or RPM should consult with and coordinate all response activities that may affect Federal resources with the appropriate land manager or resource trustee. The language added to (b)(9) reflects this opinion.

The sixth change to this section is the addition of an OSC/RPM responsibility to consult with DOI or DOC in those cases where a discharge or release may adversely affect any endangered or threatened species or result in destruction or adverse modification of their habitats. This responsibility was deleted in the 1982 revision to the Plan. As a result, there has been some confusion over the applicability of the Endangered Species Act and the other statutes that protect endangered or threatened species. The Agency feels that there has always been an implicit responsibility for the OSC to consider

impacts on these species. In order to clear up any confusion which may exist, reference to this need to consult with either DOI or Department of Commerce has been added as (b)(10).

The seventh change involves the reference to addressing worker health and safety concerns in the existing (b)(10). As part of today's rulemaking, the Agency proposes to consolidate the worker health and safety provisions presently in 300.57 and 300.71 in a new section 300.38. The reasoning behind this consolidation is discussed later in today's preamble. the existing (b)(10) has been renumbered as (b)(11), and the reference to the applicable section of the Plan has been amended to reflect this change.

The eighth change involves the addition of an OSC/RPM responsibility as a new paragraph (b)(13) for ensuring that the appropriate public and private interests are both kept informed and their concerns considered throughout a response. This change relates to the proposed addition of a new section 300.39 addressing public information during a response. There has always been an implicit responsibility for OSCs to address public information concerns; this change merely formalizes this responsibility.

The ninth change to this section involves the addition of specific responsibilities for the RPM in remedial actions as a new § 300.33(b)(14).

Section 300.34 Special forces and teams.

Discussion

Six changes to this section are proposed. These changes are necessary to correspond to proposed revisions in other sections of the Plan and to reflect present practices. Each proposed change is discussed below.

Specific Changes

The first change to this section is the incorporation of the new term RPM. References to RPM are proposed for 300.34 (a), (a)(2), (c)(2), (c)(4), (e), (f)(4)(i), (f)(4)(iii), (f)(4)(iv), and (h)(i). (Note that the current 300.34(f)(5) is proposed for renumbering as 300.34(f)(4)—see below.)

The second change to this section relates to the description of USCG Strike Team capabilities in paragraph (a)(1). The reference to ship salvage capability has been deleted since the U.S. Navy is the Federal agency most knowledgeable and experienced in ship salvage. This change corresponds with a proposed addition to 300.37, discussed later in today's preamble, addressing marine salvage. Also, reference to U.S. Navy capability is included in the DOD agency capability statement added to 300.23(b). In addition, the word "shipboard" has been added in front of "damage control" to avoid any confusion with the term "damages" as defined in CERCLA.

The third change to this section is an editorial correction to paragraph (c)(1). The correct name of the ERT is the "Environmental Response Team", not "Emergency Response Team".

The fourth change to this section is a general update of the language in paragraph (d) describing the roles of the SSC. Reference to RPMs has been added and other minor changes have been made to reflect current practices. In addition, a reference to the agency that provides the SSC has been added.

The fifth change to this section clarifies language in paragraph (e) concerning the availability of the USCG Public Information Assist Team (PIAT) and EPA Public Affairs Assist Team (PAAT) to support OSCs and RPMs during a response. Existing language indicates that these teams are available during major responses. The Agency did not intend to limit use of these teams to major incidents only. To clarify this, changes are proposed to clearly indicate that these teams are available to the OSC or RPM any time outside public affairs support is necessary.

The final change to this section deletes paragraph (f)(2) which refers to what agency acts as chairman of the RRT during activation for a response. As discussed earlier in this preamble, this information has been moved to 300.32(b)(1).

Section 300.35 Multiregional responses.

Discussion

Three changes are proposed to incorporate the new term "RPM" in this section. In 300.35(b), "/RPM" is added after each of the three OSC references.

Section 300.36 Communications.

Discussion

One change is proposed to incorporate the new term "RPM" in this section. In 300.36(a), "/RPM" is added after the second OSC reference only.

Section 300.37 Special considerations.

Discussion

The Agency proposes to rename this section from "Response equipment" to "Special Considerations" and add a new paragraph (b) to address marine salvage. In 1982, the Marine Board of the

Commission on Engineering and Technical Systems, National Research Council completed a study of marine salvage in the United States. One of the recommendations of this committee was that the NCP be amended to address marine salvage. This change adds a brief description of marine salvage activities. In addition, because marine salvage activities are complex, the language added encourages OSCs to request technical assistance from DOD to draw on their salvage expertise when involved in a response where marine salvage activities are undertaken.

Section 300.38 (Proposed New) Worker health and safety.

Discussion

The Agency proposes to replace § 300.71 of the current NCP, Worker Health and Safety, and § 300.57(a), Special Considerations, with a new § 300.38, Worker Health and Safety, to reflect the recommendations of an interagency work group which has studied the issue of providing for the protection of the health and safety of employees involved in response actions. The Agency also proposes that § 300.33(b)(10) be revised accordingly (see previous discussion). This amendment is not intended to preempt the Occupational Safety and health Administration (OSHA) from exercising its authority at response sites.

A. Introduction. In December of 1980, a Memorandum of Understanding was signed by the EPA, USCG, OSHA and the National Institute for Occupational Safety and Health, which set up a work group to deal with the health and safety of employees involved in hazardous waste site investigations, clean-up and hazardous substance emergencies. The conclusions of the Work Group form the basis for this revision to the NCP.

B. Conclusions and Recommendations fo the Work Group. The work group concluded that the greatest employee safety and health protection currently available can best be provided by OSHA applying its safety and health regulations to hazardous substance response activities. The work group recommended that this approach be supplemented by the technical advice and assistance of qualified government and non-government personnel as needed, and by the comprehensive training of both workers and supervisors involved in hazardous substance response actions.

The work group recommended that continuing research should be conducted by both Government and

nongovernment sources in the areas of open environment air monitoring technology, industrial hygiene and instrumentation, engineering controls and personal protective equipment, and in any related areas which serve to improve the safety and health protection of workers involved in hazardous substance response activities. It further recommended that the results of this research be made available to Federal, State, and local agencies as it is developed. The work group noted that the on-going effort to improve the protection afforded workers involved in hazardous substance response actions must not preclude the use of currently established methods for their protection.

The work group is preparing a "Occupational Safety and Health Guidance Manual for Superfund Activities." This guidance manual will provide governmental agency and private organization officials with the best information that the four Agencies have available on the subject of protecting workers involved in hazardous substance response actions. As new information becomes available, the manual will be updated to reflect relevant findings.

C. EPA Analysis and Conclusions. EPA believes that the work group's conclusions are sound as they apply to CERCLA response actions involving private sector employees and working conditions covered by the Occupational Safety and Health Act (OSH Act, 29 U.S.C. 651 *et seq.*). OSHA has promulgated safety and health regulations covering a wide variety of working conditions. These include the Occupational Safety and Health Standards (29 CFR Part 1910), commonly known as the General Industry Standards, the Safety and Health Regulations for Construction (29 CFR Part 1926) and, where applicable, the Shipyard and Longshoring Standards (29 CFR Parts 1915 and 1918) and OSHA Marine Terminal Regulations (29 CFR Part 1917). Many of the occupational safety and health hazards at response actions can be addressed effectively through application of OSHA standards. OSHA also has recordkeeping, reporting, and related regulations (29 CFR Part 1904). Moreover, OSHA enforcement expertise and available sanctions can be effective in encouraging compliance with these standards during response actions.

For purposes of the NCP, OSHA standards and policies will form the basis for worker safety and health protection; however, other safety and health rules may apply. These include the following:

(1) As of February, 1984, 24 States operate OSHA-approved programs (State Plans) for occupational safety and health, pursuant to section 18 of the OSH Act. These operations, with respect to whether response actions in such States would need to comply with the State occupational safety and health requirements, would be subject to inspections by State OSH inspectors. (The State may choose not to cover CERCLA response activities, in which case jurisdiction reverts to Federal OSHA.)

(2) Federal agencies other than OSHA regulate worker safety and health for certain working conditions. Where an agency other then OSHA has statutory authority for regulating occupational safety and health and exercises that authority, OSHA is preempted under section 4(b)(1) of the OSH Act from applying its authorities to those working conditions. In some cases safety and health requirements of these other agencies could apply at sites of CERCLA response actions. For example, the Department of Transportation (DOT) has issued regulations requiring motor carriers to immobilize unattended motor vehicles. OSHA is precluded from issuing citations for hazards covered by these DOT standards.

The NCP modification recognizes these other Federal requirements and does not exclude their application and enforcement. This amendment is not intended to preempt OSHA from exercising its authority with respect to response actions.

(3) The occupational safety and health of Federal employees is provided for by their individual agencies. Section 19(a)(1) of the OSH Act requires these agencies to provide working conditions for their employees which are consistent with OSHA standards for private sector employees, and specific requirements with which Federal agencies must comply are set forth in Executive Order 12196 (45 FR 12769–12772, February 27, 1980) and 29 CFR Part 1960. OSHA evaluates the working conditions of Federal employees and Federal agencies' occupational safety and health programs.

(4) State and local government employees are not subject to Federal enforcement under the OSH Act; however, in the twenty-four States that have Federal OSHA-approved plans, States must ensure that State and local employees are provided working conditions consistent with the level of safety provided for private sector employees. Where such State plans exist, States have the right to inspect the

working conditions of these employees and issue citations. In all non-plan States, State and local government workers are protected by whatever general provisions the State or local government has, if any, for the health and safety of its employees.

There may be hazardous situations at response actions that are not directly or completely covered by OSHA or other occupational safety and health standards. Nevertheless, under section (5)(a)(1) of the OSH Act employers have the general duty to furnish employees with a place of employment "* * * free from recognized hazards that are causing or are likely to cause death or serious physical harm." Under this provision of the OSH Act, OSHA may issue citations for hazards that may or may not be directly covered by an OSHA standard but which should not be allowed to continue.

Specific Changes

The Agency proposes to delete the existing language in §§ 300.57 and 300.71 addressing worker health and safety and to consolidate these requirements in a new § 300.38. This is being done to clarify the responsibilities of the OSC and RPM at a response. Differences in the language in §§ 300.57 and 300.71 of the present Plan has resulted in some confusion over the role of the OSC in ensuring worker health and safety in responses under subparts E and F. The Agency feels that the worker health and safety provisions apply equally to both oil and hazardous substance responses under the Plan, and consolidation of the worker health and safety provisions in one section should resolve this confusion.

The revisions also should clarify any confusion that exists concerning the responsibility of the OSC and RPM for the health and safety of workers at the response site. The revision makes it clear that each governmental agency and private employer is responsible for the health and safety of their own personnel. In a Federal Fund-financed response, the lead agency will be responsible for ensuring that a program to protect workers is made available and that workers at the scene of a response are apprised of the response site hazards and the provisions of the safety and health program at the scene, but responsibility for compliance with the program will rest with the government agency or private employer at the site. This is no different from present Agency guidance that requires a site safety plan for hazardous substance responses. The Federal Government is not assuming responsibility for individual workers.

Paragraph (b) of this new section tasks responsible parties at a non-Federal Fund-financed response with ensuring that response actions that they take include provisions for a safety and health program for their workers. The Agency believes that failure of a responsible party to ensure such measures could be considered an improper cleanup and allow action, including possible assumption of the cleanup, by the lead agency monitoring the response.

Section 300.39 (Proposed New) Public information.

Discussion

The Agency proposes to add a new § 300.39 to address public information at a response. Although public information has always been an OSC's responsibility, specific reference to this was deleted in the 1982 revision to the Plan. Since public information is such an important part of a response, the Agency feels that this general information should be included in the Plan and apply to responses under both subparts E and F. This change corresponds to revisions to subpart F also being proposed in today's rulemaking that address community relations at hazardous substance responses.

Paragraph (a) of this new section tasks OSCs, RPMs, and agency community relations personnel with ensuring that all appropriate public and private interests are kept informed and their concerns considered throughout a response. The Agency believes that it is essential to provide the public prompt, accurate information on the nature of an incident and the actions underway to mitigate any damage.

Paragraph (b) of this new section addresses the coordination of media relations. This paragraph outlines the establishment of an on-scene news office to coordinate media relations and issue official Federal information. During a large response, there may be a need for participating Federal agencies to make their own press releases or respond to media inquiries. It is essential that these actions be coordinated with the OSC or RPM, thus a requirement has been added that all Federal press releases or statements be cleared through the OSC or RPM. Regional Attorneys should also clear such releases or statements when EPA is the lead Agency. EPA OSC/RPMs have easy access to Regional Attorneys and usually have had experience working with these attorneys. Coast Guard or other non-EPA OSC/RPMs do not have to clear such releases or statements through the Regional Attorneys. This is consistent with previous guidance in the Plan that was deleted in the 1982 revision.

Section 300.40 (Proposed New) OSC reports.

Discussion

The Agency proposes to create a new § 300.40 titled "OSC Reports" to move the report requirements presently in § 300.56 to this new section, and to revise this section to apply to both discharges of oil and releases of hazardous substances, pollutants, or contaminants. A change in the title of the section from "Pollution reports" to "OSC reports" is proposed to reflect the common name of these reports. The term "pollution reports" or "polreps" usually refers to frequent status reports filed by the OSC during the course of an incident.

Existing language in § 300.69 of the Plan has provisions for documenting incidents involving hazardous substances, but no specific format is required. This change will standardize the report format requirements for both subparts E and F. Reports will be required for all incidents classified as major by the OSC and for any other incident when requested by the RRT. In addition, changes proposed to 300.69 in today's rulemaking will require the completion of an OSC report for all CERCLA Fund-financed removal actions.

In addition to this significant change, six minor changes are proposed to the report format. Three changes add the terms "release" or "hazardous substance, pollutant, or contaminant" to account for the applicability to subpart F. The other three changes add requirements for documenting State participation, impacts of the discharge or release on natural resources, and public information/community relations activities.

Subpart D

Section 300.42 Regional contingency plans.

One change is proposed to incorporate the new term "RPM" in subpart D. In § 300.42(b), "RPM" is added after OSC.

Subpart E

Section 300.51 Phase I—Discovery and notification.

Discussion

The Agency proposed one change to subsection (b) concerning reporting of oil discharges. This change parallels a proposed change to § 300.63 discussed

later in today's preamble concerning reporting of hazardous substance releases. Existing language in subsection (b) indicates that reports of oil discharges should be made to either the NRC or to the nearest USCG or EPA office. Any report not made directly to the NRC must be relayed to the NRC if not previously reported to the predesigned OSC. This language is based on regulations in 33 CFR Part 153 for reporting of oil discharges as required by the Clean Water Act. These provisions have resulted in a significant number of reports being received at locations other than the NRC. While in most cases this does not delay Federal response actions, it has been difficult for the USCG and EPA to determine the actual number of discharges that have occurred. In many cases, responsible parties notify both the NRC and the predesignated OSC, thus resulting in duplication of effort. The proposed regulations require reporting to the NRC unless direct reporting is impractical. In such cases, reports can be made to the predesignated USCG or EPA OSC, any USCG unit, or a USCG district office. The Agency believes that direct reporting to the NRC is the most effective and efficient means of facilitating government response action. With existing communications systems, OSCs are normally notified of discharge reports within 15 minutes of their receipt by the NRC.

The Agency proposed to amend subsection (b) to require all reports be made to the NRC unless direct reporting is impractical. An example of such a situation would be a vessel at sea, where a telephone is not available. In such cases, reporting to the nearest USCG unit or a predesignated OSC at the nearest EPA regional office will be authorized, and these locations will relay the information to the NRC. This should result in all discharge reports being recorded at the NRC. The Agency believes that direct reporting to the NRC is the best means of ensuring that the appropriate USCG or EPA OSC is rapidly notified of a discharge. Reports to any other locations may result in delays in relaying the information to the OSC. In addition, collecting all reports at the NRC will provide the USCG and EPA with accurate statistics on the frequency and location of oil discharges and allow for efficient allocation of resources to address such incidents.

The Coast Guard intends to amend the reporting regulations in 33 CFR Part 153 to reflect these revisions if this proposal is adopted. The Agency solicits comments on this proposed modification to reporting procedures.

Section 300.52 Phase II—Preliminary assessment and initiation of action.

Discussion

The Agency proposes one change to paragraph (d) concerning notification of natural resource trustees. These trustees require early notification of incidents that may have affected natural resources. In many instances, there may be impacts that are not readily apparent to the OSC, but could be determined by using the expertise of the resource trustee. This change encourages OSCs to consult with the natural resource trustee when practical for assistance in determining if resources have been damaged by an oil discharge.

Section 300.54 Documentation and cost recovery.

Discussion

Two changes are proposed to this section. The first change adds a requirement in paragraph (b) for OSCs to submit OSC reports. This corresponds to the previous discussion on moving the report requirements to 300.40.

The second change concerns the availability of documentation to natural resource trustees. Existing language in (b) states that documentation should be made available where practicable. The Agency did not intend to limit the trustee's access to this documentation. To clarify this, the words "where practicable" have been deleted.

Section 300.56 [Reserved]

Discussion

As discussed above, the Agency proposes to move the OSC report requirements to a new § 300.40 in subpart C. This new section will apply to both oil and hazardous substance incidents. The specific requirement for OSC reports for oil discharges has been added to 300.54. As a result, § 300.56 will be designated as "Reserved."

Section 300.57 Waterfowl conservation.

Discussion

As discussed above, the Agency proposes to consolidate the worker health and safety considerations in a new § 300.38. In conjunction with this change, paragraph (a) of this section will be deleted, § 300.57 renamed "Waterfowl Conservation", and the current lettering and title of the remaining paragraph (i.e., (b) Waterfowl Conservation) will be deleted.

Section 300.58   Funding.

Discussion

The Agency proposes to add language to paragraph (b) addressing reimbursement of Federal agencies for OSC support. Federal agencies have been called upon by the OSC in many situations to provide support that goes beyond program authorities for these agencies. In addition, some of this assistance results in the Federal agency incurring expenses that should be reimbursable. The Agency agrees with this. Procedures already exist in 33 CFR Part 153 for reimbursement to Federal agencies from the 311(k) Fund for certain costs incurred while providing assistance requested by the OSC. The change proposed to paragraph (b) will add specific reference to this procedures.

Subpart F

Section 300.61   General.

Discussion

This section describes various principles generally applicable to subpart F of the plan. The modifications proposed to this section are minor and are intended to clarify certain provisions and make them consistent with the rest of the Plan. Major modifications to subpart F are discussed in section II.

Specfic Changes

CERCLA section 104(a)(1) authorizes response unless the Agency determines that the response action be done properly by a responsible party. The Agency considers the timeliness of the response to be an important factor in determining whether the response will be conducted properly. Therefore, in § 300.61(b), EPA proposes stating that the responsible party response must be conducted in a timely fashion, or Fund-financed response action may be authorized. This clarifies existing EPA policy that the reponsible party seeking to conduct the site response must initiate and complete the response in a timely fashion or the Fund may be engaged to remedy the threats posed by the site.

In § 300.61(c) the Agency has added two additional factors to help coordinate and speed site response. These include involving the Regional Response Team (RRT) and encouraging the establishment of private organizations to aid in site response. As stated previously, the Agency believes that the RRT can help coordinate response measures when several Federal agencies are involved in the response and wants to advocate the use of the group. Private organizations, as

outlined in § 300.71 of this proposal, may provide useful services in accelerating site response. In addition, § 300.61(c) allows the response personnel to consider alternative or innovative technology in developing the cost-effective response.

Section 300.61(d) has been amended to specify that the lead agency will provide surveillance of responsible party actions, where practicable. This codifies existing operating procedures under which the lead agency will generally oversee response actions, which will tend to assure adequate protection of public health, welfare and the environment.

Where surveillance indicates that necessary and proper response actions are not being taken, the lead agency may complete the remaining response actions. The responsible parties will be liable for any response costs resulting from surveillance and/or completion of response actions.

Finally, an important addition is being proposed in § 300.61(e). CERCLA section 107 states that persons may bring actions for recovery of costs incurred consistent with the NCP. (The Federal and State governments may recover for costs incurred "not consistent" with the Plan.) Section 107 does not limit such liability to only those costs incurred at those sites listed on the NPL. However, some question has arisen whether a site must be listed on the NPL for an action to be consistent with the NCP for purposes of recovery of costs by private parties and States. EPA proposes to clarify this issue and other issues in subsection (e). This subsection states that subpart F does not establish any preconditions to any enforcement action; nor does it limit the rights of any person to seek recovery of non Fund-financed response costs from responsible parties pursuant to CERCLA §107, except as provided in § 300.71. In addition, the subsection states that actions in implementing subpart F are discretionary and that subpart F does not create any rights to any Federal actions.

Section 300.62   State role.

Discussion

Several minor additions and clarifications are proposed in this section. The procedures and requirements outlined in this section require little modification.

Section 300.62(a)(1) has been amended to clarify that various agencies of the Federal Government may enter into contracts and cooperative agreements. The prior omission of the USCG, FEMA & HHS which have such

authority, from this subsection was an oversight.

Proposed subsection (a)(2) specifies that cooperative agreements are unnecessary for State response and other actions that are not Fund-financed. Coordination with EPA or USCG is encouraged, however. Superfund State contracts and cooperative agreements are intended to facilitate coordination between the Federal and State governments. Where a Federal role is not required because the Fund is not involved, a contract or agreement is unnecessary. Likewise, the subsection clarifies that for any other party actions, such Superfund State contracts and agreements are not required.

However, if a State wants its expenditures for response actions taken at a site to count as part of its required cost-share match, a cooperative agreement or contract must be executed for this purpose.

The Agency is aware that some confusion may exist concerning the implications of State cooperative agreements or contracts. In subsection (c) language has been added to clarify that State cooperative agreements or contracts are not a precondition to enforcement action or cost-recovery pursuant to CERCLA section 107. This language reinforces the new proposed language in § 300.61(e) and § 300.71.

Section 300.62(d) has been changed to require that the State provide a firm commitment and funding only prior to *remedial action*. This reflects Agency policy not to require these commitments for remedial design and remedial planning activities.

Proposed subsection (h) recognizes the roles that State and local safety organizations currently play in response actions. Such organizations are expected to initiate public safety measures deemed necessary to protect public health and welfare of local populations. This language reflects the role State and local governments perform at this time, in undertaking evacuation and limiting public access when necessary.

Section 300.63   Discovery and notification.

Discussion

Three changes are proposed to revise subsections (b) and (c) concerning reporting of hazardous substance releases. This proposed revision will establish consistent reporting requirements for both oil discharges and hazardous substance releases and parallels a proposed revision to 300.51

discussed earlier in today's preamble. Existing language in subsection (b) requires all reports of hazardous substance releases be made to the NRC. In addition, EPA's soon to be promulgated Superfund Notification Rule, 40 CFR Part 302, provides that all reporting of releases pursuant to CERCLA section 103 (a) and (b) be made to the NRC. Since the requirement to provide notice only to the NRC was adopted in the NCP in 1982, EPA has received several requests to consider alternate reporting provision to account for situations when direct reporting to the NRC may not be practicable, such as releases from ships at sea. The Agency considered modifying the Superfund Notification Rule, 40 CFR Part 302 to provide for reporting to other than the NRC in some limited circumstances, but decided to defer consideration of such a change until this rulemaking in order to allow additional public comment and to assure that if such a change were adopted, appropriate mechanisms were in place so that even when initial notice was provided to other than the NRC, the NRC would receive notification in a timely manner. This requirement is based on the statutory language in section 103(a) of CERCLA that notice be provided to the NRC.

The Agency proposes to amend subsection (b) to require all reports be made to the NRC unless direct reporting is impractical. In such cases, reporting to a predesignated OSC at the nearest USCG office or EPA Regional Office will be authorized, and these officials are given the responsibility to relay the information to the NRC.

The Agency believes that authorizing initial reporting to the OSC is consistent with the intent of 103(a), as long as there is assurance that the report is subsequently relayed to the NRC, and that making the report to the OSC does not delay any necessary response. EPA believes that providing for initial notice to the OSC as discussed above would be consistent with this intent, yet would provide additional flexibility in those situations where reporting directly to the NRC is impractical. These situations will be limited, so most reports will still be made directly to the NRC.

The Agency intends to amend the reporting regulations in 40 CFR Parts 117 and 302 to reflect these revisions if this proposal is adopted and solicits comments on this proposed modification to reporting procedures. Pending adoption of this proposal to allow reporting to the OSC, in some limited circumstances, the requirement in § 300.63 and in the Superfund

Notification Rule, 40 CFR Part 302 remain in effect.

A second change proposed to this section involves notification to States. Existing language in subsection (b) indicates that the NRC shall notify the Governor of a State affected by a release. This conflicts with existing procedures where reports to the States are made by the OSC or the lead agency. The Agency believes that the OSC or lead agency is in the best position to be familiar with State organizations that require notification. Revisions are proposed to subsection (c) to reflect that notifications to States will be made by the OSC or lead agency.

A third change proposed is the addition of a new subsection (d). The purpose of this addition is to clarify who should conduct further analysis of the release, based on the level of threat posed. If the notification indicates that a release may require response action under § 300.65, a preliminary assessment pursuant to § 300.64 should be initiated as soon as possible. If such response action is not likely to be required, a less detailed preliminary assessment pursuant to section 300.66 should be conducted. The Agency believes that this language will aid in clarifying confusion over the degree of preliminary assessment to be conducted, and when such assessments should be conducted.

Section 300.64   Preliminary assessment for removal actions.

Discussion

There are two types of preliminary assessment: One for removal actions and one for remedial responses. The preliminary assessment for remedial action is at times less comprehensive than the preliminary assessment for removal since less immediate threats will be more comprehensively evaluated during a site investiagion.

This section clarifies some confusion that has arisen over the level of preliminary assessment to be conducted. The title of this section has been changed to clarify that it applies only to removal preliminary assessment.

Specific Changes

In subsection (a), the statement that "Other releases shall be assessed as soon as practicable" has been deleted. This sentence was deleted so that the section would only apply to releases that may present a problem needing a removal, consistent with the title change.

The existing section does not address when it is appropriate to request input from HHS on public health issues.

Proposed subsection (a) clarifies that the OSC may request HHS to evaluate the public health threat posed by the release if it would be helpful in determining the need for removal action.

The revised language includes a provision for notification of the natural resource trustee if resources may have been damaged. A new subsection (d) has been added that requires the OSC to notify the trustee if the preliminary assessment indicates that natural resources damage may have occurred. This seciton has been added to ensure that the trustee is award of possible damage at an early stage in the investigation and is able to initiate appropriate action.

The section also recognizes that damage may not be readily apparent to the OSC/RPM and encourages the OSC/RPM to seek the expertise of the natural resource trustee in determining if any damage exists. A complementary section on notification of trustees has also been inserted in § 300.69. Section 300.65 and § 300.66 were discussed in Section II.

Section 300.67   Community Relations.

Discussion

Section 300.67 is a new section. Experience gained during the early years of the program has shown that a strong community relations component is an important aspect of a successful cleanup program. The purpose of the community relations program is to provide communities with accurate information about problems posed by releases of hazardous substances, and give local officials and citizens the opportunity to comment on the technical solutions to the site problems.

Specific Changes

Subsection (a) requires that all removal actions pursuant to 300.65 and all remedial actions at NPL sites including enforcement actions, must have a formal community relations plan, except for short term or urgent removal actions or urgent enforcement actions. A formal plan will not be required for remedial response actions not listed on the NPL. This reflects current operating procedures and may encourage and expedite private and responsible parties responses to releases not listed on the NPL. In addition, because most USCG spill responses are removal situations, USCG will rarely be required to prepare a formal plan. Current USCG procedures will continue to be followed for spill incidents. The Agency's community relations guidance provides guidance in determining whether or not a plan is necesssary for other removals or urgent enforcement actions. The Office of Emergency and Remedial Response may be contacted for copies of the guidance and propose updates.

The formal plan, based on discussions with citizens in the community, should include the following: A description of the site location and history; a thorough discussion of the history of community relations activities and a summary of recent citizen issues; site specific community relations objectives and communication activities; and a community relations workplan, staffing plan, budget and mailing list. Such plans should be reviewed by the public. The use of the RRT to assist community relations activities should be considered in developing such plans.

Subsection (b) states that in the case of actions posing a threat pursuant to § 300.65(b), or enforcement actions to compel response analogous to § 300.65 or other short term action to abate a threat to public health, welfare or the environment, a spokesperson will be designated to provide the community with information on the release and the response. This reflects current operating procedures in emergency situations. No new method of operation or procedures is contemplated by this section.

Subsection (c) is directed to the timing of the community relations plan for remedial actions at NPL releases including, Fund-financed and enforcement actions. This section reflects EPA's community relations guidance document and states that plans should be developed and implementation begun prior to field activities. This subsection also states that, in certain cases, the responsible party may develop and implement specific parts of the community relations plan with lead agency oversight. This will conserve Agency resources and may result in more responsible parties coming forward to correct past hazardous waste releases.

Section (d) states that the minimum public comment period allowed for review of feasibility studies for remedial actions at NPL releases shall be 21 calendar days. The comment period is to be held prior to final selection of the remedy and allows for effective community and responsible party input into the decision-making process. The public may also have the opportunity to comment during the development of the feasibility study. This will provide the public with advance warning as to possible remedial alternatives.

This public involvement is an important component of the administrative record development by the Agency in support of the remedy

selected. For this reason, the Agency expects that all concerns regarding the cleanup be raised during this period by all affected parties.

Subsection (e) requires that a responsiveness summary be included in the record of decision, addressing the major issues raised by the community. The Agency believes a summary of major comments will be helpful in explaining how the Agency has taken the comments into account in reaching its final decision.

As noted earlier, the consent decree reached in the litigation with the Environmental Defense Fund concerning the NCP requires EPA to propose amendments to the NCP to . . . (c) provide comparable public participation for private-party response measures taken pursuant to enforcement actions. Thus, the provisions for public review of RI/FS in enforcement actions are comparable to those required for Fund-financed cleanup, and responsiveness summaries are required for enforcement actions as well as Fund-financed actions.

The lead agency in appropriate circumstances may schedule additional meetings involving potentially responsible parties and a limited number of representatives of the public, where these representatives have adequate legal and technical capability and can provide appropriate assurances concerning any confidential information that may arise during the discussions, if in the judgment of the lead Agency such meetings may facilitate resolution of issues involving the appropriate remedy at the site.

Two revisions are proposed to § 300.69. The first adds a requirement for the completion of OSC reports for all major releases and all Fund-financed removals. The second change adds language addressing the reimbursement of Federal agencies for costs incurred during a response.

Revisions of § 300.68 and § 330.71 were discussed in section II of this preamble.

Subpart G

Section 300.72   Designation of Federal Trustees.

The Agency proposes one minor change to correct a typographical error in subparagraph (b)(1) of this section. The word "in" at the end of line 4 is replaced by "or."

Section 300.73   State Trustee.

The change proposed in the first sentence is to simplify and consolidate the several references to CERCLA

sections into a single general reference to CERCLA provisions for State trustees.

CERCLA Section 111 provides that:

(h)(1) In accordance with regulations promulgated under section 301(c) of this Act, damages for injury to, destruction of, or loss of natural resources resulting from a release of a hazardous substance, for the purposes of this Act and section 311(f) (4) and (5) of the Federal Water Pollution Control Act, shall be assessed by Federal officials designated by the President under the National Contingency Plan published under section 105 of the Act, and such officials shall act for the President as trustee under this section and section 311(f)(5) of the Federal Water Pollution Control Act.

(2) Any determination or assessment of damages for injury to, destruction of, or loss of natural resources for the purposes of this Act and section 311(f) (4) and (5) of the Federal Water Pollution Control Act shall have the force and effect of a rebuttable presumption on behalf of any claimant (including a trustee under section 107 of this Act or a Federal agency) in any judicial or adjudicatory administrative proceeding under this Act or section 311 of the Federal Water Pollution Control Act.

The Agency is considering whether to adopt one of three possible approaches with respect to the assessment of damages for injury to, destruction or loss of any State natural resources within its borders, belonging to, managed by or appertaining to such State.

The first approach is to amend this section to designate Federal officials who, as appropriate, could perform assessments of State natural resource damages at the request of State trustees. States could also perform assessments, however, only Federal assessments, performed in accordance with the regulations required by section 301(c) of CERCLA, would be entitled to the rebuttable presumption established in section 111(h)(2) of CERCLA.

The second approach would be that only States would perform assessments of damages for injury to, destruction or loss of any State natural resources and such assessments would be entitled to the rebuttable presumption in § 111(h)(2).

The final approach would be that only States would perform assessments of damages for injury to, destruction or loss of any State natural resources. Such assessments however, would be entitled to the rebuttable presumption in § 111(h)(2) only where they are performed in accordance with regulations promulgated under section 301(c) of CERCLA.

The Agency requests on these various approaches.

Subpart H

Use of Dispersants and Other Chemicals.

Discussion

The Agency is proposing several changes to subpart H as promulgated in the **Federal Register** on July 18, 1984 (49 FR 29192).

In the preamble to the current subpart H, the statement was made that the SSC in inland areas was generally the DOI. Although the NCP, as promulgated on July 16, 1982 (47 FR 31208 stated that generally the SSC for the inland areas will be provided by EPA or DOI today's proposed revisions delete the reference to DOI. As a matter of practice, the SSC for inland areas is normally provided by EPA. This change reflects current practice, although SSCs may be obtained from other agencies if determined to be appropriate by the RRT.

The Agency would also like to clarify its position on the authorization and consultation process for using dispersants, surface collecting agents, burning agents, or biological additives on oil discharged into navigable waters. Under § 300.84 (a) and (b) of the current subpart H (49 FR 20197, July 18, 1984), the OSC must obtain the concurrence of the EPA representative to the RRT and the concurrence of the States with jurisdiction over the navigable waters polluted by the oil discharge prior to authorizing the use of a product on the NCP Product Schedule. This provision will remain unchanged. However, a statement is proposed as an addition to subsections (a) and (b) to indicate that the OSC should consult with appropriate Federal agencies as practicable when considering the use of such products on an oil discharge. A similar change to § 300.84(b), burning agents will be made.

Section 300.84(e) which permits the OSC to authorize the use of such products without obtaining the concurrence of the EPA RRT representatives or the States if the RRT and the States with jurisdiction over the waters of the area approve in advance the use of certain products on the schedule. An addition is proposed to the last sentence in § 300.84(e) to allow use under such circumstances without consultation with other appropriate Federal agencies.

IV. Economic Impacts of Proposed NCP Revisions

The incremental economic effect of each of the proposed revisions is defined as the economic changes that may result from the revision compared to the current Superfund program without the revision. Some of the revisions have already been instituted as policy changes in the Superfund program and are being proposed as changes to the NCP for the purposes of consistency. These revisions can thus be considered not to result in economic effects when compared to the current NCP.

There are four major proposed revisions to the NCP. They are as follows:

• Eliminate planned removals and initial remedial measures as distinct response categories. Revise the provisions to establish one category of removal action to be accomplished in response to a threat to public health, welfare, or environment;

• Add explicit requirements for community relations programs and public comment at Fund-financed and enforcement responses;

• Explicitly require use of existing Federal public health and environmental standards, where applicable or relevant in selecting the appropriate remedy;

• Provide for listing of releases on the NPL which, while not meeting HRS criteria pose significant public health threats.

The anticipated effects and the proposed revisions are listed below:

1. In the current NCP, §§ 300.65 and 300.67 authorize two categories of removal action: immediate and planned. Section 300.68 authorizes IRMs to be taken as a part of a remedial action. The criteria for taking IRMs are similar to those for planned removals except that IRMs must be cost-effective. Both planned removals and IRMs require State cost-sharing. The proposed revisions eliminate planned removal and IRM categories and expand the category of removals and modify the standard for taking action.

The anticipated effects of this proposed revision are as follows:

The State costs will be reduced, with a corresponding increase in demand on the Fund. With 60 projected planned removals and 104 projected IRMs expected to be reclassified as removals over a 6-year period, cost savings to States will be about $4.9 million (undiscounted FY 84 dollars). Increased demand of $4.9 million on the Fund could reduce funds available at one remedial response that might otherwise have been conducted. The revision may

accelerate removal and remedial activity, thereby increasing costs to responsible parties and reducing health and environmental risks of exposure to hazardous substances and possibly reduce the longer term costs because of quicker response. States will also save the costs of preparing cooperative agreements in the case of reclassified removal actions.

2. In the current NCP, § 300.61(c)(3) states that, to the extent practicable, response personnel should be sensitive to local community concerns in accordance with applicable guidance.

The proposed revisions define major Superfund community relations program requirements and require response personnel to conduct a public comment period on draft feasibility studies.

The anticipated effects are minor. Full compliance may increase response costs slightly, particularly administrative costs to EPA and local governments, with a corresponding increase in costs to responsible parties. Greater public involvement may expedite response process in some cases, thereby offsetting any costs caused by delays.

3. In the current NCP use of existing EPA or other Federal standards is not explicitly discussed, except in the preamble.

The proposed revisions explicitly require the use of existing Federal public health and environmental standards in selecting the appropriate remedy, where such standards are applicable or relevant, with limited exceptions. Risk assessments are required where no standards are applicable or relevant. Under current operating procedures, we are generally meeting standards because we believe they generally define adequate protection of health and the environment.

The anticipated effects of this revision are as follows:

Some additional costs may be incurred by EPA in making necessary determinations and performing analyses. The magnitude of these effects will be estimated as guidance or policy is developed.

4. In the current NCP § 300.66 establishes the listing process for the NPL. Currently, EPA policy requires an HRS score of 28.50 to be added to the NPL.

The proposed revisions allow releases for which an HHS health advisory has been issued to be listed on the NPL.

The anticipated effects of this revision are as follows:

The effects depend upon the number of sites listed using the criteria. Costs to States and responsible parties will increase, but the magnitude of this increase cannot be estimated accurately. Because sites so listed will have potentially major public health impacts, the proposed changes will give the Agency broader authority to undertake remedial action to protect public health and the environment. Given limited Fund size, listing of these sites will replace, rather than supplement, funds spent on other sites, resulting in no net economic impacts.

The anticipated effects of all of the revisions are as follows:

State costs will be reduced, with a corresponding increase in demands on the Fund. With a total of 356 Fund-financed RI/FS (320 at private sites), projected over FY 84–89 period, and 247 Fund-financed remedial designs projected over the same period (222 at private facilities), total cost savings to States will be about $30 million (FY 84 dollars). Increased demand of $30 million on the Fund could decrease by about 4 the number of sites that might otherwise receive remedial response. The policy change may accelerate remedial activities by removing the State cost-share requirement, resulting in earlier reduced risks of exposure to hazardous substances.

V. Summary of Supporting Analyses

A. Classification Under E.O. 12291

Proposed regulations must be classified as major or nonmajor to satisfy the rulemaking protocol established by Executive Order 12291. E.O. 12291 establishes the following criteria for a regulation to qualify as a major rule:

1. An annual effect on the economy of $100 million or more;

2. A major increase in costs or prices for consumers, individual industries, Federal, State, or local government agencies or geographic regions; or

3. Significant adverse effects on competition, employment, investment, productivity, innovation, or on the ability of United States-based enterprises to compete with foreign-based enterprises in domestic or export markets.

The proposed NCP is a nonmajor rule because it would have no significant incremental economic effects. To the extent that economic impacts do occur, they are likely to be positive.

This regulation was submitted to OMB for review under Executive Order 12291.

B. Regulatory Flexibility Act

In accordance with the Regulatory Flexibility Act of 1980, Agencies must evaluate the effects of a proposed

regulation on "small entities." That Act recognizes three types of such entities:

1. Small businesses (specified by Small Business Administration regulations);

2. Small organizations (independently owned, nondominant in their field, nonprofit); and

3. Small governmental jurisdictions (serving communities with fewer than 5,000 people).

If the proposed rule is likely to have a "significant impact on a substantial number of small entities," the Act requires that a Regulatory Flexibility Analysis be performed. EPA certifies that the NCP will not have a significant impact on a substantial number of small entities. To the extent that impacts on small entities occur, they are likely to be positive.

Small businesses and small organizations will generally be affected only by the proposed changes that address enforcement actions. These changes in the NCP generally codify existing enforcement policies (e.g., proposed changes to require enforcement responses to comply with applicable or relevant federally enforceable environmental standards) and therefore modifying the NCP will not impose any additional burden on small entities subject to enforcement actions. Although requiring community relations plans (CRPs) at most enforcement responses will increase responsible party costs, these costs are small (averaging $6,000) relative to response costs and may save costs by expediting the response process. Moreover, it is a matter of Agency discretion whether to proceed with enforcement actions against small entities that may be significantly affected by such actions. Therefore there are no necessary adverse impacts on small businesses and organizations directly associated with the NCP.

The proposed changes may affect some small government jurisdictions, but most of the effects are likely to be positive. For example, the proposed change to mandate CRPs may reduce the burden on small government jurisdictions by providing an efficient vehicle for the local government involvement.

C. Paperwork Reduction Act

Today's proposed rule does not impose any regulatory burden on parties outside of EPA, including any reporting or information collection requirements.

VI. Lists of Subjects in 40 CFR Part 300

Air pollution control, Chemicals, Hazardous materials, Hazardous substances, Intergovernmental relations,

National resources, Occupational safety and health, Oil pollution, Reporting and record keeping requirements, Superfund, Waste treatment and disposal, Water pollution control, Water supply.

For the reasons set forth in the preamble, Part 300, Subpart J, Chapter I of Title 40, Code of Federal Regulations, is amended as follows:

1. The authority citation for Part 300 reads as follows:

Authority: Sec. 105 Pub. L. 96–510, 94 Stat. 2764, 42 U.S.C. 9605; Sec. 311(c)(2), Pub. L. 92–500 as amended, 86 Stat. 865, 33 U.S.C. 1321 (c)(2); E.O. 12316, 46 FR 42237; E.O. 11735, 38 FR 21243.

Dated: January 25, 1985.

Lee M. Thomas,
Acting Administrator.

1. 40 CFR Part 300 (Subparts A–G) is revised as follows (Appendix A is republished without change for reader convenience):

PART 300—NATIONAL OIL AND HAZARDOUS SUBSTANCES POLLUTION CONTINGENCY PLAN

Subpart A—Introduction

Authority: Sec. 105. Pub. L. 96–510. 94 Stat. 2764. 42 U.S.C. 9605 and sec. 311(c)(2), Pub. L. 92–500, as amended: 86 Stat. 865, 33 U.S.C. 1321(c)(2): Executive Order 12316, 47 FR 42237 (August 20, 1981); Executive Order 11735, 38 FR 21243 (August 1873).

Subpart A—Introduction

§ 300.1 Purpose and objectives.

The purpose of the National Oil and Hazardous Substances Pollution Contingency Plan (Plan) is to effectuate the response powers and responsibilities created by the Comprehensive Environmental Response, Compensation, and Liability Act of 1980 (CERCLA) and the authorities established by section 311 of the Clean Water Act (CWA), as amended.

§ 300.2 Authority.

The Plan is required by section 105 of CERCLA, 42 U.S.C. 9605, and by section 311(c)(2) of the CWA, as amended, 33 U.S.C. 1321(c)(2). In Executive Order 12316 (46 FR 42237) the President delegated to the Environmental Protection Agency the responsibility for the amendment of the NCP and all of the other functions vested in the President by section 105 of CERCLA. Amendments to the NCP shall be coordinated with members of the National Response Team prior to publication for notice and comment including the Federal Emergency Management Agency and the Nuclear Regulatory Commission in order to avoid inconsistent or duplicative requirements in the emergency planning responsibilities of those agencies.

§ 300.3 Scope.

(a) The Plan applies to all Federal agencies and is in effect for:

(1) The navigable waters of the United States and adjoining shorelines, for the contiguous zone, and the high seas beyond the contiguous zone in connection with activities under the Outer Contintental Shelf Lands Act or the Deep Water Port Act of 1974, or which may affect natural resources belonging to, appertaining to, or under the exclusive management authority of the United States (including resources under the Fishery Conservation and Management Act of 1976). (See sections 311(b)(1) and 502(7) of the Clean Water Act.)

(2) Releases or substantial threats of releases of hazardous substances into the environment, and releases or substantial threats of releases of pollutants or contaminants which may present an imminent and substantial danger to public health or welfare.

(b) The Plan provides for efficient, coordinated and effective response to discharge of oil and releases of hazardous substances, pollutants and contaminants in accordance with the authorities of CERCLA and the CWA. It provides for:

(1) Division and specification of responsibilities among the Federal, State, and local governments in response actions, and appropriate roles for private entities.

(2) The national response organization that may be brought to bear in response actions, including description of the organization, response personnel and resources that are available to respond.

(3) The establishment of requirements for Federal regional and Federal local contingency Plans, and encouragement of preplanning for response by other levels of government.

(4) Procedures for undertaking removal operations pursuant to section 311 of the Clean Water Act.

(5) Procedures for undertaking response operations pursuant to CERCLA.

(6) Designation of trustees for natural resources for purposes of CERCLA.

(7) National policies and procedures for the use of dispersants and other chemicals in removal and response actions.

(c) In implementing this Plan, consideration shall be given to the Joint Canada/U.S. Contingency Plan; the U.S./Mexico Joint Contingency Plan and international assistance plans and agreements, security regulations and responsibilities based on international agreements, Federal statutes and executive orders. Actions taken pursuant to this Plan shall conform to the provisions of international joint contingency Plans, where they are applicable. The Department of State should be consulted prior to taking any action which may affect its activities.

§ 300.4 Application.

The Plan is applicable to response taken pursuant to the authorities under CERCLA and section 311 of the CWA.

§ 300.5 Abbreviations.

(a) Department and Agency Title Abbreviations.

DOC—Department of Commerce
DOD—Department of Defense
DOE—Department of Energy
DOI—Department of the Interior
DOJ—Department of Justice
DOL—Department of Labor
DOS—Department of State
DOT—Department of Transportation
EPA—Environmental Protection Agency
FEMA—Federal Emergency Management Agency
HHS—Department of Health and Human Services
NIOSH—National Institute for Occupational Safety and Health
NOAA—National Oceanic and Atmospheric Administration
USCG—U.S. Coast Guard

(1) Operational Title Abbreviations.

ERT—Environmental Response Team
FCO—Federal Coordinating Officer
NRC—National Response Center
NRT—National Response Team
NSF—National Strike Force
OSC—On-Scene Coordinator
PATT—Public Affairs Assist Team
PIAT—Public Information Assist Team
RPM—Remedial Project Manager
RRC—Regional Response Center
RRT—Regional Response Team
SSC—Scientitic Support Coordinator

§ 300.6 Definitions.

Terms not defined in this section have the meaning given by CERCLA or the CWA.

Activation means notification by telephone or other expeditious manner or, when required, the assembly of some or all appropriate members of the RRT or NRT.

Claim, as defined by section 101(4) of CERCLA, means a demand in writing for a sum certain.

CERCLA or "Superfund", is the Comprehensive Environmental Response, Compensation and Liability Act of 1980.

Coastal waters, for the purposes of classifying the size of discharges, means the waters of the coastal zone except for the Great Lakes and specified ports and harbors on inland rivers.

Coastal zone, as defined for the purpose of this Plan, means all U.S. waters subject to the tide, U.S. waters of the Great Lakes, specified ports and harbors on the inland rivers, waters of the contiguous zone, other waters of the high seas subject to this Plan, and the land surface or land substrata, ground waters, and ambient air proximal to those waters. The term coastal zone delineates an area of Federal responsibility for response action. Precise boundaries are determined by EPA/USCG agreements and identified in Federal regional contingency plans.

Contiguous zone means the zone of the high seas, established by the United States under Article 24 of the Convention on the Territorial Sea and Contiguous Zone, which is contiguous to the territorial sea and which extends nine miles seaward from the outer limit of the territorial sea.

Discharge, as defined by section 311(a)(2) of CWA, includes, but is not limited to, any spilling, leaking, pumping, pouring, emitting, emptying or dumping of oil. For purposes of this Plan, discharge shall also mean substantial threat or discharge.

Drinking water supply, as defined by section 101(7) of CERCLA, means any raw or finished water source that is or may be used by a public water system (as defined in the Safe Drinking Water Act) or as drinking water by one or more individuals.

Environment, as defined by section 101(8) of CERCLA, means (a) the navigable waters, the waters of the contiguous zone, and the ocean waters of which the natural resources are under the exclusive management authority of the U.S. under the Fishery Conservation and Management Act of 1976, and (b) any other surface water, ground water, drinking water supply, land surface and subsurface strata, or ambient air within the United States or under the jurisdiction of the United States.

Facility, as defined by section 101(9) of CERCLA, means (a) any building, structure, installation, equipment, pipe or pipeline (including any pipe into a sewer or publicly owned treatment works), well, pit, pond, lagoon, impoundment, ditch, landfill, storage container, motor vehicle, rolling stock, or aircraft, or (b) any site or area where a hazardous substance has been deposited, stored, disposed of, or placed, or otherwise come to be located; but does not include any consumer product in consumer use or any vessel.

Feasibility study, is a process undertaken by the lead agency (or responsible party if the responsible party will be developing a clean-up proposal) for developing, evaluating and selecting remedial actions which emphasizes data analysis. The feasibility study is generally performed concurrently and in an interdependent fashion with the Remedial Investigation. In certain situations, the Agency may require potential responsible parties to conclude initial phases of the remedial investigation prior to initiation of the feasibility study. The Feasibility study process uses data gathered during the remedial investigation. This data is used to define the objectives of the response action and to broadly develop remedial action alternatives. Next, an initial screening of these alternatives is required to reduce the number of alternatives to a workable number. Finally, the feasibility study involves a detailed analysis of a limited number of alternatives which remain after the initial screening stage. The factors that are considered in screening and analyzing the alternatives are public health, economics, engineering practically, environmental impacts and institutional issues.

Federally permitted release, as defined by section 101(10) of CERCLA, means (a) discharges in compliance with a permit under section 402 of the Federal Water Pollution Control Act; (b) discharges resulting from circumstances identified and reviewed and made part of the public record with respect to a permit issued or modified under section 402 of the Federal Water Pollution Control Act and subject to a condition of such permit; (c) continuous or anticipated intermittent discharges from a point source, identified in a permit or permit application under section 402 of the Federal Water Pollution Control Act, which are caused by events occurring within the scope of relevant operating or treatment systems; (d) discharges in compliance with a legally enforceable permit under section 404 of the Federal Water Pollution Control Act; (e) releases in compliance with a legally enforceable final permit issued pursuant to section 3005(a) through (d) of the Solid Waste Disposal Act from a hazardous waste treatment, storage, or disposal facility when such permit specifically identifies the hazardous substances and makes such substances subject to a standard of practice, control procedure or bioassay limitation or condition, or other control on the hazardous substances in such releases; (f) any release in compliance with a legally enforceable permit issued under section 102 or section 103 of the Marine Protection, Research and Sanctuaries Act of 1972; (g) any injection of fluids authorized under Federal underground injection control programs or State programs submitted for Federal approval (and not disapproved by the Administrator of EPA) pursuant to part C of the Safe Drinking Water Act; (h) any emission into the air subject to a permit or control regulation under section 111, section 112, title 1 part C, title 1 part D, or State implementation plans submitted in accordance with section 110 of the Clean Air Act (and not disapproved by the Administrator of EPA), including any schedule or waiver granted, promulgated, or approved under these sections; (i) any injection or fluids or other materials authorized under applicable State law (1) for the purpose of stimulating or treating wells for the production of crude oil, natural gas, or water, (2) for the purpose of secondary, tertiary, or other enhanced recovery of crude oil or natural gas, or (3) which are brought to the surface in conjunction with the production of crude oil or natural gas and which are reinjected; (j) the introduction of any pollutant into a publicly owned treatment works when such pollutant is specified in and in compliance with applicable pretreatment standards of section 307 (b) or (c) of the CWA and enforceable requirements in a pretreatment program submitted by a State or municipality for Federal approval under section 402 of such Act, and (k) any release of source, special nuclear, or by-product material, as those terms are defined in the Atomic Energy Act of 1954, in compliance with a legally enforceable license, permit, regulation, or order issued pursuant to the Atomic Act of 1954.

First Federal official, means the first representative of a Federal agency, with responsibility under this Plan, to arrive at the scene of a discharge or release. This official coordinates activities under this Plan and is authorized to initiate necessary actions normally carried out by the OSC, until arrival of the predesignated OSC.

Fund or Trust Fund means the Hazardous Substance Response Trust Fund established by section 221 of CERCLA.

Ground water, as defined by section 101(12) of CERCLA, means water in a saturated zone or stratum beneath the surface of land or water.

Hazardous substance, as defined by section 101(14) of CERCLA, means (a) any substance designated pursuant to section 311(b)(2)(A) of the CWA; (b) any element, compound, mixture, solution, or substance designated pursuant to section 102 of CERCLA; (c) any hazardous waste having the characteristics identified under or listed pursuant to section 3001 of the Solid

Waste Disposal Act (but not including any waste the regulation of which under the Solid Waste Disposal Act has been suspended by Act of Congress); (d) any toxic pollutant listed under section 307(a) of the CWA; (e) any hazardous air pollutant listed under section 112 of the Clean Air Act; and (f) any imminently hazardous chemical substance or mixture with respect to which the Administration has taken action pursuant to section 7 of the Toxic Substances Control Act. The term does not include petroleum, including crude oil or any fraction thereof which is not otherwise specifically listed or designated as a hazardous substance under subparagraphs (a) through (f) of this paragraph, and the term does not include natural gas, natural gas liquids, liquified natural gas or synthetic gas usable for fuel (or mixtures of natural gas and such synthetic gas).

Inland waters, for the purposes of classifying the size of discharges, means those waters of the U.S. in the inland zone, waters of the Great Lakes, and specified ports and harbors on inland rivers.

Inland zone means the environment inland of the coastal zone excluding the Great Lakes and specified ports and harbors of inland rivers. The term inland zone delineates the area of Federal responsibility for response action. Precise boundaries are determined by EPA/USCG agreement and identified in Federal regional contingency plans.

Lead agency means the Federal agency (or State agency operating pursuant to a contract or cooperative agreement executed pursuant to a contract or cooperative agreement executed pursuant to section 104(d)(1) of CERCLA) that has primary responsibility for coordinating response action under this Plan. A Federal lead agency is the agency that provides the OSC or RPM as specified elsewhere in this Plan. In the case of a State as lead agency, the State shall carry out the same responsibilities delineated for OSCs/RPMs in this Plan (except coordinating and directing Federal agency response actions).

Management of Migration, means actions that are taken to minimize and mitigate the migration of hazardous substances or pollutants or contaminants and the effects of such migration. Management of migration actions may be appropriate where the hazardous substances or pollutants or contaminants are no longer at or near the area where they were originally located or situations where a source cannot be adequately identified or characterized. Measures may include, but are not limited to, provision of

alternative water supplies, management of a plume of contamination or treatment of drinking water aquifer.

Natural Resources, as defined by section 101(16) of CERCLA, means land, fish, wildlife, biota, air water, ground water, drinking water supplies, and other such resources belonging to, managed by, held in trust by, appertaining to, or otherwise controlled by the United States (including the resources of fishery conservation zones established by the fishery Conservation and Management Act of 1976), any State or local government or any foreign government.

Offshore facility, as defined by section 101(17) of CERCLA and section 311(a)(11) of the CWA, means any facility of any kind located in, on, or under any of the navigable waters of the U.S. and any facility of any kind which is subject to the jurisdiction of the U.S. and is located in, on, or under any other waters, other than a vessel or a public vessel.

Oil, as defined by section 311(a)(1) of CWA, means oil of any kind or in any form, including, but not limited to, petroleum, fuel oil, sludge, oil refuse, and oil mixed with wastes other than dredged spoil.

Oil pollution fund means the fund established by section 311(k) of the CWA.

Onshore Facility, (a) as defined by section 101(18) of CERCLA, means any facility (including, but not limited to, motor vehicles and rolling stock) of any kind located in, on, or under any land or non-navigable waters within the United States; and (b) as defined by section 311(a)(10) of CWA means any facility (including, but not limited to, motor vehicles and rolling stock) of any kind located in, on, or under any land within the United States other than submerged land.

On-Scene Coordinator (OSC) means the Federal official predesignated by the EPA or USCG to coordinate and direct Federal responses under Subpart E and removals under Subpart F of this Plan; or the DOD official designated to coordinate and direct the removal actions from releases of hazardous substances, pollutants, or contaminants from DOD vessels and facilities.

Operable Unit, is a discrete part of the entire response action that decreases a release, threat or release, or pathway of exposure.

Person, as defined by section 1012(21) or CERCLA, means an individual, firm, cooperation, association, partnership, consortium, joint venture, commercial entity, U.S. Government, State municipality, commission, political

subdivision of a State, or any interstate body.

Plan means the National Oil and Hazardous Substances Pollution Contingency Plan published under section 311(c) of the CWA and revised pursuant to section 105 of CERCLA.

Pollutant or containment, as defined by section 104(a)(2) of CERCLA, shall include, but not be limited to, any element, substance, compound, or mixture, including disease causing agents, which after release into the environment and upon exposure, ingestion, inhalation, or assimilation into any organism, either directly from the environment or indirectly by ingesting through food chains, will or may reasonably be anticipated to cause death, disease, behavioral abnormalities, cancer, genetic mutation, physiological malfunctions (including malfunctions in reproduction) or physical deformation, in such organisms or their offspring. The term does not include petroleum, including crude oil and any fraction thereof which is not otherwise specifically listed or designated as a hazardous substance under section 101(14)(A) through (F) of CERCLA, nor does it include natural gas, liquified natural gas, or synthetic gas of pipeline quality (or mixture of natural gas and synthetic gas). For purposes of subpart F of this plan, the term pollutant or contaminant means any pollutant or contaminant whch may present an imminent and substantial danger to public health, or welfare.

Release, as defined by section 101(22) of CERCLA, means any spilling, leaking, pumping, pouring, emitting, emptying, discharging, injection, escaping, leaching, dumping, or disposing into the environment, but excludes (a) any release which results in exposure to persons solely within a workplace, with respect to a claim which such persons may assert against the employer of such persons (b) emissions from the engine exhaust of a motor vehicle, rolling stock, aircraft, vessel, or pipeline pumping station engine; (c) release of source, by-product or special nuclear material from a nuclear incident, as those terms are defined in the Atomic Energy Act of 1954, if such release is subject to requirements with respect to financial protection established by the Nuclear Regulatory Commission under section 170 of such act, or, for the purpose of section 104 of CERCLA or any other response action, any release of source, byproduct, or special nuclear material from any processing site designated under section 122(a)(1) or 302(a) of the Uranium Mill Tailings Radiation Control Act of 1978; and (d) the normal application of fertilizer. For the purpose of this Plan, release also means substantial threat of release.

Remedial Investigation is a process undertaken by the lead agency (or responsible party if the responsible party will be developing a clean-up proposal) which emphasizes data collection and site characterization. The remedial investigation is generally performed concurrently and in an interdependent fashion with the feasibility study. However, in certain situations the Agency may require potential responsible parties to conclude initial phases of the remedial investigation prior to initiation of the feasibility study. A remedial investigation is undertaken to determine the nature and extent of the problem presented by the release. This includes sampling and monitoring, as necessary, and includes the gathering of sufficient information to determine the necessity for and proposed extent of remedial action. Part of the remedial investigation involves assessing whether the threat can be mitigated or minimized by controlling the source of the contamination at or near the area where the hazardous substances or pollutants or contaminants were originally located (source control remedial actions) or whether additional actions will be necessary because the hazardous substances or pollutants or contaminants have migrated from the area of their original location (management of migration).

Remedial Project Manager (RPM) means the Federal official designated by EPA (or the USCG for vessels) to coordinate, monitor, or direct remedial activities under Subpart F of this Plan; or the Federal official DOD designates to coordinate and direct Federal remedial actions resulting from releases of hazardous substances, pollutants, or contaminants from DOD facilities or vessels.

Remedy or remedial action, as defined by section 101(24) of CERCLA, means those actions consistent with permanent remedy taken instead of, or in addition to, removal action in the event of a release of threatened release of a hazardous substances so that they do not migrate to cause substantial danger to present or future public health or welfare or the environment. The term includes, but is not limited to, such actions at the location of the release as storage, confinement, perimeter protection using dikes, trenches, or ditches, clay cover, neutralization, clean-up or released hazardous substances or contaminated materials recycling or reuse, diversion,

destruction, segregation of reactive wastes, dredging or excavations, repair or replacement of leaking containers, collection of leachate and runoff, on-site treatment or incineration, provision of alternative water supplies, and any monitoring reasonably required to assure that such actions protect the public health and welfare and the environment. The term includes the costs of permanent relocation of residents and businesses and community facilities where the President determines that, along or in combination with other measures, such relocation is more cost-effective than and environmentally preferable to the transportation, storage, treatment, destruction, or secure disposition off-site of such hazardous substances or may otherwise be necessary to protect the public health or welfare. The term does not include off-site transport of hazardous substances or contaminated materials unless the President determines that such actions (a) are more cost-effective than other remedial actions; (b) will create new capacity to manage in compliance with subtitle C of the Solid Waste Disposal Act, hazardous substances in addition to those located at the affected facility; or (c) are necessary to protect public health or welfare or the environment from a present or potential risk which may be created by further exposure to the continued presence of such substances or materials.

Remove or removal, as defined by section 311(a)(8) of CWA refers to removal of oil or hazardous substances from the water and shorelines or the taking of such other actions as may be necessary to minimize or mitigate damage to the public health, welfare, or the environment. As defined by section 101(23) of CERCLA, remove or removal means the clean-up or removal of released hazardous substances from the environment; such actions as may be necessary to prevent, minimize, or mitigate damage to the public health or welfare or the environment, which may otherwise result from such release or threat of release. The term includes, in addition, without being limited to, security fencing or other measures to limit access, provision of alternative water supplies, temporary evacuation and housing of threatened individuals not otherwise provided for, action taken under section 104(b) of CERCLA, and any emergency assistance which may be provided under the Disaster Relief Act of 1974.

Respond or response, as defined by section 101(25) of CERCLA, means

remove, removal, remedy, or remedial action.

Site Quality Assurance and Sampling Plan, is a written document, associated with site sampling activities, which presents in specific terms the organization (where applicable), objectives, functional activities, and specific quality assurance (OA) and quality control (OC) activities designed to achieve the data quality goals of a specific project(s) or continuing operation(s). The OA Project Plan is prepared for each specific project or continuing operation (or group of similar projects of continuing operations). The OA Project Plan will be prepared by the responsible Program Office, Regional Office, Laboratory, contractor, recipient of an assistance agreement or other organization.

Size classes of discharges refers to the following size classes of oil discharges which are provided as guidance to the OSC and serve as the criteria for the actions delineated in Subpart E. They are not meant to imply associated degrees of hazard to public health or welfare, nor are they a measure of environmental damage. Any oil discharge that poses a substantial threat to the public health or welfare or results in critical public concern shall be classified as a major discharge regardless of the following quantitative measures;

(a) _Minor discharge_ means a discharge to the inland waters of less than 1,000 gallons of oil or a discharge to the coastal waters of less than 10,000 gallons of oil.

(b) _Medium discharge_ means a discharge of 1,000 to 10,000 gallons of oil to the inland waters or a discharge of 10,000 to 100,000 gallons of oil to the coastal waters.

(c) _Major discharge_ means a discharge of more than 10,000 gallons of oil to the inland waters or more than 100,000 gallons of oil to the coastal waters.

Size classes of releases refers to the following size classifications which are provided as guidance to the OSC for meeting pollution report requirements in Subpart C. The final determination of the appropriate classification of a release will be made by the OSC based on consideration of the particular release (e.g., size, location, impact, etc.).

(a) _Minor release_ means a release of a quantity of hazardous substance, pollutant, or contaminant that posed minimal threat to public health or welfare or the environment.

(b) _Medium release_ means all releases not meeting the criteria for classification as a minor or major release.

(c) *Major release* means a release of any quantity of hazardous substances, pollutant, or contaminant that posts a substantial threat to public health or welfare or the environment or results in significant public concern.

Source control remedial action means measures that are intended to contain the hazardous substances or pollutants or contaminants where they are located or eliminate potential contamination by transporting the hazardous substances or pollutants or contaminants to a new location. Source control remedial actions may be appropriate if a substantial concentration or amount of hazardous substances or pollutants or contaminants remain at or near the area where they are originally located and inadequate barriers exist to retard migration of hazardous substances or pollutants or contaminants into the environment. Source control remedial actions may not be appropriate if most hazardous substances or pollutants or contaminants have migrated from the area where originally located or if the lead agency determines that the hazardous substances or pollutants or contaminants are adequately contained.

Specified ports and harbors means those port and harbor areas on inland rivers, and land areas immediately adjacent to those waters, where the USCG acts as predesignated on-scene coordinator. Precise locations are determined by EPA/USCG regional agreements and identified in Federal regional contingency plans.

Trustee means any Federal natural resources management agency designated in Subpart G of this plan, and any State agency which may prosecute claims for damages under section 107(f) of CERCLA.

United States, as defined by section 311(2)(5) of CWA, refers to the States, the District of Columbia, the Commonwealth of Puerto Rico, Guam, American Samoa, the Virgin Islands, and the Trust Territory of the Pacific Islands. As defined by section 101(27) of CERCLA, *United States* and *State* include the several States of the United States, the District of Columbia, the Commonwealth of Puerto Rico, Guam, American Samoa, the United States Virgin Islands, the Commonwealth of the Northern Marianas and any other territory or possession over which the U.S. has jurisdiction.

Volunteer means any individual accepted to perform services by a Federal agency which has authority to accept volunteer services (examples: see 16 U.S.C. 742f(c)). A volunteer is subject to the provisions of the authorizing statute, and § 300.25 of this Plan.

Subpart B—Responsibility

§ 300.21 Duties of President delegated to Federal agencies.

(a) In Executive Order 11735 and Executive Order 12316, the President delegated certain functions and responsibilities vested to him by the CWA and CERCLA, respectively. Responsibilities so delegated shall be responsibilities of Federal agencies under this Plan unless:

(1) Responsibility is redelegated pursuant to section 8(f) of Executive Order 12316, or

(2) Executive Order 11735 or Executive Order 12316 is amended or revoked.

§ 300.22 Coordination among and by Federal agencies.

(a) Federal agencies should coordinate their planning and response activities through the mechanisms described in Subpart C of this Plan and other means as may be appropriate.

(b) Federal agencies should coordinate planning and response action with affected State and local government and private entities.

(c) Federal agencies with facilities or other resources which may be useful in a Federal response situation should make those facilities or resources available consistent with agency capabilities and authorities.

(d) When the Administrator of EPA or the Secretary of the Department in which the Coast Guard is operating determines:

(1) That there is an imminent and substantial endangerment to the public health or welfare or the environment because of a release or threatened release of a hazardous substance from a facility; he/she may request the Attorney General to secure the relief necessary to abate the threat. The action described here is in addition to any actions taken by a State or local government for the same purpose.

(e) In accordance with section 311(d) of CWA, whenever a marine disaster in or upon the navigable waters of the United States has created a substantial threat of a pollution hazard to the public health or welfare because of a discharge or an imminent discharge from a vessel of large quantities of oil or hazardous substances designated pursuant to section 311(b)(2)(A) of CWA, the United States may:

(1) Coordinate and direct all public and private efforts to abate the threat;

(2) Summarily remove and, if necessary, destroy the vessel by whatever means are available without regard to any provisions of law governing the employment of personnel

or the expenditure of appropriated funds. The authority for these actions has been delegated under Executive Order 11735 to the Administrator of EPA and the Secretary of the Department in which the Coast Guard is operating, respectively, for the waters for which each designates the OSC under this Plan.

(f) Response actions to remove discharges originating from the Outer Continental Shelf Lands Act operations shall be in accordance with this Plan.

(g) Where appropriate, discharges of radioactive materials shall be handled pursuant to the appropriate Federal radiological plan. For purposes of this Plan, the Federal Radiological Emergency Response Plan (49 FR 35896, Sept. 12, 1984) is the appropriate response plan.

§ 300.23 Other assistance by Federal agencies.

(a) Each of the Federal agencies listed in paragraph (b) of this section has duties established by statute, executive order, or Presidential directive which may be relevant to Federal response action following or in prevention of a discharge of oil or a release of a hazardous substance, pollutant or contaminant. These duties may also be relevant to the rehabilitation, restoration, and replacement of damaged or lost natural resources. Federal regional contingency plans should call upon agencies to carry out these duties in a coordinated manner.

(b) The following Federal agencies may be called upon by an OSC/RPM during the planning or implementation of a response to provide assistance in their respective areas of expertise as indicated below, consistent with agency capabilities and legal authorities:

(1) The Department of Agriculture (USDA) provides expertise in managing agricultural, forest, and wilderness areas. The Soil Conservation Service can provide to the OSC/RPM predictions of the effects of pollutants on soil and their movements over and through soil.

(2) The Department of Commerce (DOC), through NOAA, provides scientific expertise on living marine resources for which it is responsible and their habitats, including endangered species and marine mammals; coordinates scientific support for responses and contingency planning in coastal and marine areas, including assessments of the hazards that may be involved, predictions of movement and dispersion of discharged oil and released hazardous substance releases; provides information on actual and

predicted meteorological, hydrologic, ice, and oceanographic conditions for marine, coastal, and inland waters; furnishes charts and maps, including tide and circulation information for coastal and territorial waters and for the Great Lakes.

(3) The Department of Defense (DOD), consistent with its operational requirements, may provide assistance to other Federal agencies on request. The United States Army Corps of Engineers has specialized equipment and personnel for maintaining navigation channels, for removing navigation obstructions, for accomplishing structural repairs, and performing maintenance to hydropower electric generating equipment. The Corps can also provide design services, perform construction, and can provide contract writing and contract administration services for other Federal agencies. The United States Navy (USN), as a result of its mission and Pub. L. 80-513 (Salvage Act), is the Federal agency most knowledgeable and experienced in ship salvage, shipboard damage control, and diving. The USN has an extensive array of specialized equipment and personnel available for use in these areas as well as specialized containment, collection, and removal equipment specifically designed for salvage-related and open sea pollution incidents. Also, upon request of the OSC, locally deployed USN oil spill equipment may be provided. These services and equipment are available on a reimbursable basis to Federal agencies upon request when commercial equipment is not available. As described elsewhere in the Plan, DOD officials serve as OSCs for removal action and as RPMs for remedial actions resulting from releases of hazardous substances, pollutants, or contaminants from DOD vessels and facilities.

(4) The Department of Energy (DOE) provides advice to the OSC/RPM when assistance is required in identifying the source and extent of radioactive releases, and in the removal and disposal of radioactive contamination.

(5) The Department of Health and Human Services (HHS) is responsible for providing assistance on all matters related to the assessment of health hazards at a response, and protection of both response worker's and the public's health.

(6) The Federal Emergency Management Agency (FEMA) will provide advice and assistance to the OSC/RMP on coordinating civil emergency planning and mitigation efforts with other Executive agencies, State and local governments, and the private sector. In the event of a major

disaster declaration or emergency determination by the President at a hazardous materials response site, FEMA will coordinate all disaster or emergency actions with the OSC/RPM.

(7) The Department of the Interior (DOI) should be contacted through Regional Environmental Officers (REO), who are the designated members of RRTs. Department land managers have jurisdiction over the National Park System, National Wildlife Refuges and Fish Hatcheries, the public lands, and certain water projects in western States. In addition, bureaus and offices have relevant expertise as follows: *Fish and Wildlife Service:* fish and wildlife, including endangered and threatened species, migratory birds, certain marine mammals; habitats, resource contaminants; laboratory research facilities. *Geological Survey:* geology, hydrology (ground water and surface), and natural hazards. *Bureau of Land Management:* Minerals, soils, vegetation, wildlife, habitat, archaeology, wilderness; hazardous materials; etc. *Minerals Management Services:* manned facilities for Outer Continental Shelf (OCS) oversight. *Bureau of Mines:* analysis and identification of inorganic hazardous substances. *Office of Surface Mining:* coal mine wastes, land reclamation. *National Park Service* biological and general natural resources expert personnel at Park units. *Bureau of Indian Affairs:* assistance in implementing NCP in American Samoa, Guam, the Trust Territory of the Pacific Islands, and the Virgin Islands.

(8) The Department of Justice (DOJ) can provide expert advice on complicated legal questions arising from discharge or releases and Federal agency responses. In addition, the DOJ represents the Federal Government, including its agencies, in litigation.

(9) The Department of Labor (DOL), through the Occupational Safety and Health Administration (OSHA), will provide the OSC/RPM with advice, guidance, and assistance regarding hazards to persons involved in removal or control or oil discharges and hazardous substance releases, and in the precautions necessary to prevent hazards to their health and safety.

(10) The Department of Transportation (DOT) provides expertise on all modes of transporting oil and hazardous substances. Through the USCG, DOD offers expertise in domestic/international fields of port safety and security, maritime law enforcement, ship navigation and construction, and the manning, operation, and safety of vessels and marine facilities. The USCG also

maintains continuously manned facilities which can be used for command, control, and surveillance of oil discharges and hazardous substance releases occurring in the coastal zone. The USCG provides predesignated OSCs for the coastal zone.

(11) The Department of State (DOS) will lead in the development of joint international contingency plans. It will also help to coordinate an international response when discharges or releases cross international boundaries or involve foreign flag vessels. Additionally, this Department will coordinate requests for assistance from foreign governments and U.S. proposals for conducting research at incidents that occur in waters of other countries.

(12) The Environmental Protection Agency (EPA) provides expertise on environmental effects of oil discharges or releases of hazardous substances, pollutants, or contaminants and environmental pollution control techniques. EPA provides predesignated OSCs for the inland zone and RPMs for all remedial actions, unless otherwise agreed. EPA also will generally provide the SSC for responses in inland areas. EPA may enter into a contract or cooperative agreement with the appropriate State in order to implement a remedial action.

(c) In addition to their general responsibilities under paragraph (a) of this section, Federal agencies should:

(1) Make necessary information available to the NRT, RRTs, and OSCs RPMs.

(2) Inform the NRT and RRTs (consistent with national security considerations) of changes in the availability of resources that would affect the operations of the Plan.

(3) Provide representatives as necessary to the NRT and RRTs and assist RRTs and OSCs in formulating Federal regional and Federal local contingency plans.

(d) All Federal agencies are responsible for reporting releases of hazardous substances and discharges of oil from facilities or vessels which are under their jurisdiction or control in accordance with section 104 (a) and (b) and 101(24) of CERCLA subject to the following:

(1) HHS is delegated all authorities under section 104(b) of CERCLA relating to a determination that illness, disease or complaints thereof may be attributable to exposure to a hazardous substance, pollutant or contaminant. (In addition, section 104(i) of CERCLA calls upon HHS to: establish appropriate disease/exposure registries; conduct appropriate testing for exposed

individuals; develop maintain and provide information on health effects of toxic substances; and maintain a list of areas restricted or closed because of toxic substance contamination.)

(2) FEMA is delegated the authorities vested in the President by section 104(a) of CERCLA to the extent they require permanent relocation of residents, businesses, and community facilities or temporary evacuation and housing of threatened individuals not otherwise provided for. (FEMA is also delegated authority under section 101(24) of CERCLA to the extent they require a determination by the President that "permanent relocation of residents and businesses and community facilities" is included within the terms "remedy" and "remedial action" as defined in section 101(24) of CERCLA.)

(3) DOD is delegated all authority of section 104 (a) and (b) of CERCLA with respect to releases from DOD facilities or vessels, including vessels owned or bareboat chartered and operated.

(e) If the situation is beyond the capability of State and local governments and the statutory authority of Federal agencies, the President, acting upon a request by the Government, may declare a major disaster or emergency and appoint a Federal Coordinating Officer to assume responsibility for direction and control of the Federal response.

§ 300.24 State and local participation.

(a) Each State governor is requested to assign an office or agency to represent the State on the appropriate RRT. Local governments are invited to participate in activities on the appropriate RRT as may be provided by State law or arranged by the State's representative. The State's representative may participate fully in all facets of activities of the appropriate RRT and is encouraged to designate the element of the State government that will direct State supervised response operations.

(b) State and local government agencies are encouraged to include contingency planning for response, consistent with this Plan and Regional Contingency Plans, in all emergency and disaster planning.

(c) States are encouraged to use State authorities to compel potentially responsible parties to undertake response actions, or to themselves undertake response actions which are not eligible for Federal funding.

(d) States may enter into contract or cooperative agreements pursuant to section 104(c)(3) and (d) of CERCLA or

section 311(c)(2)(H) of the CWA, as appropriate, to undertake actions authorized under Subparts E and F of this Plan. Requirements for entering into these agreements are included in § 300.58 and § 300.62 of this Plan. While the terms "On-Scene Coordinator," "OSC," Remedial Project Manager," and "RPM" are reserved for Federal officials for the purpose of this Plan, a State agency may choose to use these titles for its response personnel without such use connoting the definitions, responsibilities, and authorities for these titles for Federal officials under this Plan. In the case of a State as lead agency, the State shall carry out the same responsibilities delineated for OSCs/RPMs in this Plan (except coordinating and directing Federal agency response actions).

(e) Since State and local public safety organizations would normally be the first government representatives at the scene of a discharge or release, they would be expected to initiate public safety measures necessary to protect public health and welfare, and are responsible for directing evacuations pursuant to existing State/local procedures.

§ 300.25 Nongovernment participation.

(a) Industry groups, academic organizations, and others are encouraged to commit resources for response operations. Specific commitments should be listed in Federal regional and Federal local contingency plans.

(b) It is particularly important to use the valuable technical and scientific information generated by the non-government local community along with those from Federal and State Government to assist the OSC/RPM in devising cleanup strategies where effective standard techniques are unavailable, and to ensure that pertinent research will be undertaken to meet national needs. The SSC shall act as liaison between the OSC/RPM and such interested organizations.

(c) Federal local contingency plans shall establish procedures to allow for well-organized, worthwhile, and safe use of volunteers. Local plans should provide for the direction of volunteers by the OSC, or by other Federal, State of local officials knowledgeable in contingency operations and capable of providing leadership. Local plans also should identify specific areas in which volunteers can be used, such as beach surveillance, logistical support, and bird and wildlife treatment. Unless specifically requested by the OSC,

volunteer generally should not be used for physical removal or remedial activities. If, in the judgment of the OSC or an appropriate participating agency, dangerous conditions exist, volunteers shall be restricted from on-scene operations.

(d) (1) If any person other than the Federal Government or a State or person operating under contract or cooperative agreement with the United States, takes response action and intends to seek reimbursement from the Fund, such actions to be in conformity with this Plan for purposes of section 111(a)(2) of CERCLA may only be reimbursed if such person notifies the administrator of EPA or his/her designee prior to taking such action and receives prior approval to take such action.

(2) The process of prior approval of Fund reimbursement requests is preauthorization. Fund-preauthorization will be considered only for:

(i) Releases warranting a removal action pursuant to § 300.65;

(ii) 104(b) activities; and

(iii) Remedial actions on the National Priorities List.

(3) All requests for preauthorization will be reviewed to determine whether the request should receive priority for funding.

(4) Preauthorization does not obligate the Fund. For purposes of payment of a claim under CERCLA section 112, the responsible Federal official must certify that costs incurred were necessary and consistent with the Fund preauthorization.

(5) All persons requesting preauthorization must demonstrate the technical and other capabilities to respond safely and effectively to releases of hazardous substances, or pollutants or contaminants.

Subpart C—Organization

§ 300.31 Organizational concepts.

Three fundamental kinds of activity are performed pursuant to the Plan: Planning and coordination, operations at the scene of a discharge and/or release, and communications. The organizational elements created to perform these activities are discussed below in the context of their roles in these activities. The organizational concepts of this Plan are depicted in Figure 1. The Standard Federal Regional boundaries are shown in Figure 2 and the U.S. Coast Guard District boundaries are shown in Figure 3.

BILLING CODE 6560-50-M

National Contingency Plan Concepts

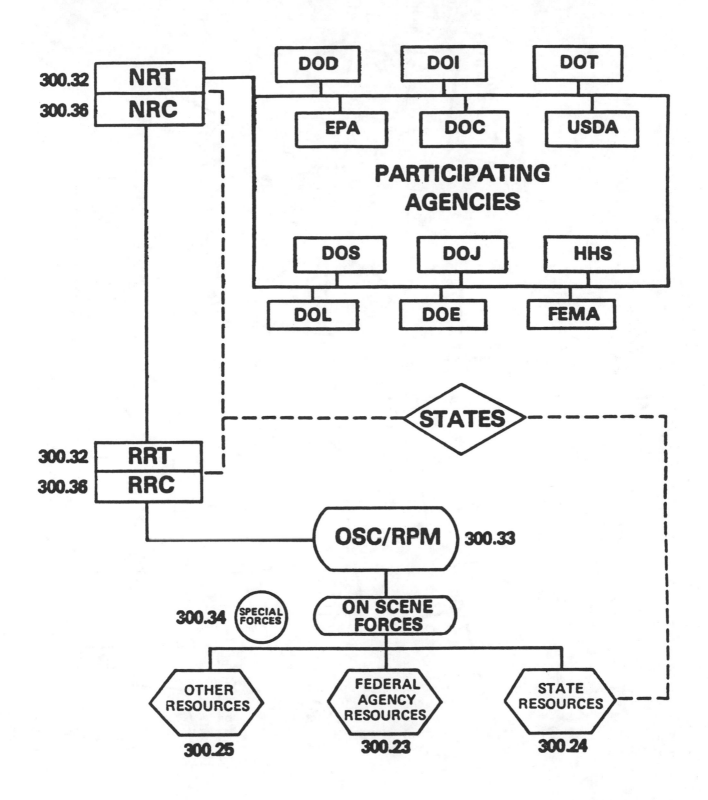

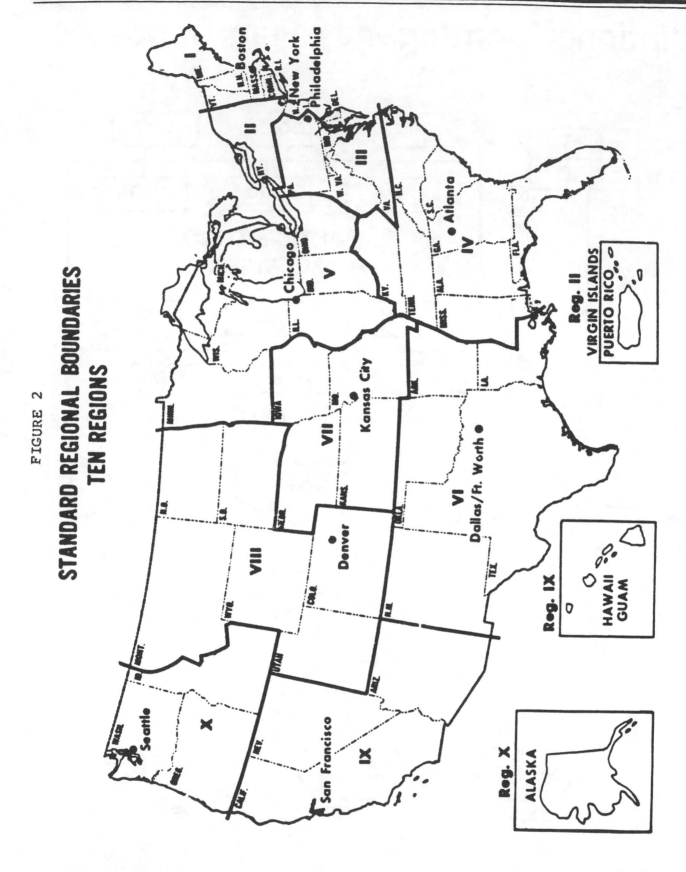

FIGURE 2

STANDARD REGIONAL BOUNDARIES
TEN REGIONS

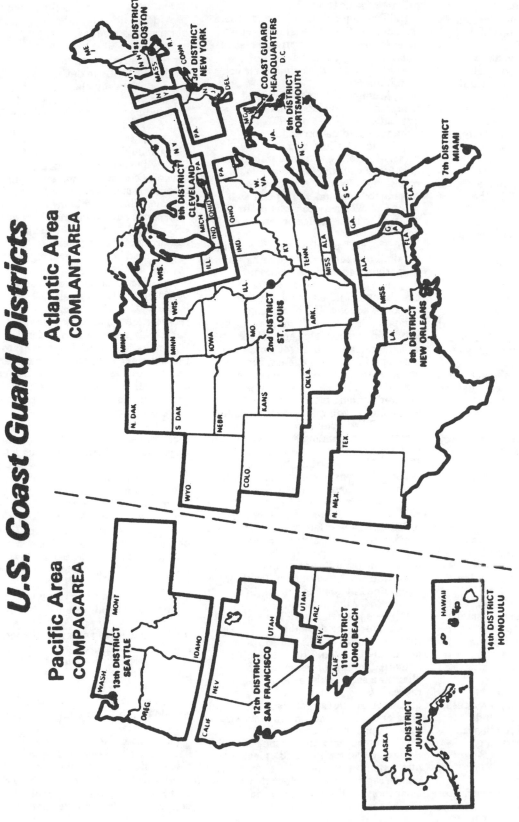

FIGURE 3

U.S. Coast Guard Districts

Atlantic Area COMLANTAREA

Pacific Area COMPACAREA

BILLING CODE 6560-50-C

§ 300.32 Planning and coordination.

(a) National planning and coordination is accomplished through the National Response Team (NRT).

(1) The NRT consists of representatives from the agencies named in § 300.23. Each agency shall designate a member to the team and sufficient alternates to ensure representation, as agency resources permit. Other agencies may request membership on the NRT by forwarding such requests to the chairman of the NRT.

(2) Except for periods of activation because of a response action, the representative of EPA shall be the chairman and the representative of USCG shall be the vice chairman of the NRT. The vice chairman shall maintain records of NRT activities along with national, regional, and local plans for response actions. When the NRT is activated for response actions, the chairman shall be the EPA or USCG representative, based on whether the discharge or release occurs in the inland zone or coastal zone, unless otherwise agreed upon by the chairman and vice chairman.

(3) While the NRT desires to achieve a consensus on all matters brought before it, certain matters may prove unresolvable by this means. In such cases, each cabinet, department or agency serving as a participating agency on the NRT may be accorded one vote in NRT proceedings.

(4) The NRT may establish such by-laws and committees as it deems appropriate to further the purposes for which it is established.

(5) When the NRT is not activated for a response action, it shall serve as a standing committee to evaluate methods of responding to discharges or releases, to recommend needed changes in the response organization and to recommend revisions to this Plan.

(6) The NRT may consider and make recommendations to appropriate agencies on the training, equipping and protection of response teams and necessary research, development, demonstration, and evaluation to improve response capabilities.

(7) Direct planning and preparedness responsibilities of the NRT include:

(i) Maintaining national readiness to respond to a major discharge of oil or release of a hazardous substance or pollutant or contaminant which is beyond regional capabilities.

(ii) Monitoring incoming reports from all RRTs and activating when necessary;

(iii) Reviewing regional responses to oil discharges and hazardous substance releases, including an evaluation of equipment readiness and coordinate among responsible public agencies and private organizations;

(iv) Developing procedures to ensure the coordination of Federal, State, and local governments and private response to oil discharges and releases of hazardous substances, pollutants or contaminants;

(v) Monitoring response-related research and development, testing, and evaluation activities of NRT agencies to enhance coordination and avoid duplication of effort; and

(vi) Monitoring response training to encourage coordination of available resources between agencies with responsibilities under this plan.

(8) The NRT may consider matters referred to it for advice or resolution by an RRT.

(b) The RRT provides the appropriate regional mechanism for planning and preparedness activities before a response action is taken and for coordination and advice during such response actions. The two principal components of the RRT mechanism are a standing team, which consists of designated representatives from each participating Federal agency, State governments, and local governments (as agreed upon by the States): And incident-specific teams where participation will relate to the technical nature of the incident and its geographic location. The standing team jurisdiction will correspond with the Standard Federal Regions and will include communications, planning, coordination, training, evaluation, preparedness, and other such matters on a Region-wide basis. The incident-specific team jurisdiction will relate to the operational requirements of discharge or release response. Appropriate levels of activation, including participation by State and local governments, shall be determined by the designated RRT chairman for the incident.

(1) Except when the RRT is activated for a removal incident, the representatives of EPA and USCG shall act as co-chairmen. When the RRT is activated for response actions, the chairman shall be the EPA or USCG representative, based on whether the discharge or release occurs in the inland zone or coastal zone, unless otherwise agreed upon by the co-chairmen.

(2) Each participating agency should designate one member and at least one alternate member to the RRT. Agencies whose regional subdivisions do not correspond to the standard Federal Regions may designate additional representatives to the standing RRT to ensure appropriate coverage of the standard Federal Region. Participating States may also designate one member and at least one alternate member to the Team. All agencies and States may also provide additional representatives as observers to meetings of the RRT.

(3) RRT members should designate representatives from their agencies to work with OSCs in developing Federal local contingency plans, providing for the use of agency resources, and in responding to discharges and releases [see § 300.43].

(4) Federal regional and Federal local plans should adequately provide the OSC with assistance from the Federal agencies commensurate with agencies' resources, capabilities, and responsibilities within the region. During a response action, the members of the RRT should seek to make available the resources of their agencies to the OSC as specified in the Federal regional and Federal local contingency plans.

(5) Affected States are encouraged to participate actively in all RRT activities [see § 300.24(a)], to designate representatives to work with the RRT and OSCs in developing Federal regional and Federal local plans, to plan for and make available State resources, and to serve as the contact point for coordination of response with local government agencies whether or not represented on the RRT.

(6) The standing RRT will serve to recommend changes in the regional response organization as needed, to revise the regional plan as needed, and to evalute the preparedness of the agencies and the effectiveness of local plans for the Federal response to discharge and releases. The RRT should:

(i) Conduct advance planning for use of dispersants, surface collection agents, burning agents, biological additives, or other chemical agents in accordance with § 300.84(e) of this Plan.

(ii) Make continuing review of regional and local responses to discharges or releases, considering available legal remedies, equipment readiness and coordination among responsible public agencies and private organizations.

(iii) Based on observations of response operations, recommend revisions of the National Contingency Plan to the NRT.

(iv) Consider and recommend necessary changes based on continuing review of response actions in the region.

(v) Review OSC actions to help ensure that Federal regional and Federal local contingency plans are developed satisfactorily.

(vi) Be prepared to respond to major discharges or releases outside the region.

(vii) Meet at least semiannually to review response actions carried out during the preceding period, and consider changes in Federal regional and Federal local contingency plans.

(viii) Provide letter reports on their activities to the NRT twice a year, no later than January 31 and July 31. At a minimum, reports should summarize recent activities, organizational changes, operational concerns, and efforts to improve State and local coordination.

(ix) Encourage the State and local response community to improve their preparedness for response.

(x) Conduct training exercises as necessary to ensure preparedness of the response community within the region.

(7) Whenever there is insufficient national policy guidance on a matter before the RRT, a technical matter requiring solution, a question concerning interpretation of the Plan, or there is a disagreement on discretionary actions between RRT members that cannot be resolved at the regional level, it may be referred to the NRT for advice or resolution.

(c) The OSC is responsible for developing any Federal local contingency plans for the Federal response in the area of the OSC's responsibility. This may be accomplished in cooperation with the RRT and designated State and local representatives [see § 300.43]. Boundaries for Federal local contingency plans shall coincide with those agreed upon between EPA, DOD and the USCG (subject to Executive Order 12316) to determine OSC areas of responsibility and should be clearly indicated in the regional contingency plan. Where practicable, consideration should be given to jurisdictional boundaries established by State and local plans.

(1) The lead agency should provide appropriate training for its OSCs, RPMs, and other response personnel to carry out their responsibilities under this Plan.

(2) To the extent practicable, OSCs/RPMs should ensure that persons designated to act as their on-scene representatives are adequately trained and prepared to carry out actions under this Plan.

(d) Scientific support for the development of regional and local plans is organized by appropriate agencies to provide special expertise and assistance. Generally, the Scientific Support Coordinator (SSC) for plans encompassing the coastal area will be provided by NOAA, and the SSC for inland areas will generally be provided by EPA. SSCs may be obtained from other agencies if determined to be appropriate by the RRT.

§ 300.33 Response operations.

(a) EPA and USCG shall designate OSCs/RPMs for all areas in each region provided, however, that DOD shall designate OSCs/RPMs responsible for taking all actions resulting from releases of hazardous substances, pollutants, or contaminants from DOD facilities and vessels. DOD will be the removal response authority with respect to incidents involving DOD military weapons and munitions. Removal actions involving nuclear weapons should be conducted in accordance with the joint Department of Defense, Department of Energy, and Federal Emergency Management Agency agreement for Response to Nuclear Incidents and Nuclear Weapons Significant Incidents of January 8, 1981. The USCG will furnish or provide OSCs for oil discharges and for the immediate removal of hazardous substances, pollutants, or contaminants into or threatening the coastal zone except that the USCG will not provide predesignated OSCs for discharges and releases from hazardous waste management facilities or in similarly chronic incidents. EPA shall furnish or provide OSCs for discharges and releases into or threatening the inland zone and shall furnish or provide RPMs for federally funded remedial actions except as otherwise agreed. The USCG will provide an initial response to hazardous waste management facilities within the coastal zone in accordance with the DOT/EPA Instrument of Redelegation (46 FR 63294). EPA will also assume all remedial actions resulting from removals initiated by the USCG in the coastal zone except those involving vessels. The USCG OSC shall contact the cognizant EPA RPM as soon as it is evident that a removal may require a follow-up remedial action to ensure that the required planning can be initiated and an orderly transition to EPA lead can occur.

(b) The OSC/RPM directs Federal Fund-financed response efforts and coordinates all other Federal efforts at the scene of a discharge or release subject to Executive Order 12316. As part of the planning and preparation for response, the OSCs/RPMs shall be predesignated by the regional or district head of the lead agency.

(1) The first Federal official to arrive at the scene of a discharge or release should coordinate activities under this Plan and is authorized to initiate necessary actions normally carried out by the OSC until the arrival of the predesignated OSC. This official may initiate Federal Fund-financed actions only as authorized by the OSC or (if the OSC is unavailable) the authorized representative of the lead agency.

(2) The OSC/RPM shall, to the extent practicable under the circumstances, collect pertinent facts about the discharge or release, such as its source and cause; the existence of potentially responsible parties; the nature, amount, and location of discharged or released materials; the probable direction and time of travel of discharged or released materials; the pathways to human and environmental exposure; potential impact on human health, welfare, environment, and safety; the potential impact on natural resources and property which may be affected; priorities for protecting human health, welfare and the environment; and appropriate cost documentation.

(3) The OSC/RPM shall direct response operations [see Subparts E and F for descriptive details]. The OSC's/RPM's effort shall be coordinated with other appropriate Federal, State, local and private response agencies. OSC/RPMs may designate capable persons from Federal, State, or local agencies to act as their on-scene representative. State and local representatives, however, are not authorized to take actions under Subparts E and F that involve expenditures of CWA 311(k) or CERCLA funds unless an appropriate contract or cooperative agreement has been established.

(4) The OSC (and when the RRT has been activated for a remedial action, the RPM) should consult regularly with the RRT in carrying out this Plan and will keep the RRT informed of activities under this Plan.

(5) The OSC/RPM shall advise the appropriate State agency (as agreed upon with each State) as promptly as possible of reported discharges and releases.

(6) The OSC/RPM shall evaluate incoming information and immediately advise FEMA of potential major disaster situations. In the event of a major disaster or emergency, under the Disaster Relief Act of 1974 (Pub. L. 93-288), the OSC/RPM will coordinate any response activities with the Federal Coordinating Officer designated by the President. In addition, the OSC/RPM should notify FEMA of situations potentially requiring evacuation, temporary housing, and permanent relocation.

(7) In those instances where a possible public health emergency exists, the OSC/RPM should notify the HHS representative to the RRT. Throughout response actions, the OSC/RPM may call upon the HHS representative for assistance in determining public health

threats and for advice on worker health safety problems.

(8) All Federal agencies should plan for emergencies and develop procedures for dealing with oil discharges and releases of hazardous substances, pollutants, or contaminants from vessels and facilities under their jurisdiction. All Federal agencies, therefore, are responsible for designating the office that coordinates response to such incidents in accordance with this Plan and applicable Federal regulations and guidelines. The OSC/RPM should provide advice and assistance as requested by Federal agencies for incidents involving vessels or facilities under their jurisdiction. At the request of the Federal agency, or if, in the opinion of the OSC (or in a remedial action, the lead agency,) the responsible Federal agency does not act promptly or take appropriate action to respond to a discharge or release occurring on a vessel or facility, including contiguous lands under its jurisdiction, the OSC (or in a remedial action, the lead agency) designated to respond in the area where the discharge or release occurs may conduct appropriate response activities. If this occurs, the OSC (or in a remedial action, the lead agency) shall consult with and coordinate all response activities taken with the responsible Federal agency. With respect to release of hazardous substances, pollutants, or contaminants from DOD facilities or vessels, DOD designates the OSC/RPM.

(9) The OSC/RPM should advise the affected land managing agency and trustees of natural resources, as promptly as possible, of releases and discharges affecting Federal resources under its jurisdiction. The OSC or RPM should consult with and coordinate all response activities with the affected land managing agency or resource trustee to the extent practicable.

(10) Where the OSC/RPM becomes aware that a discharge or release may adversely affect any endangered or threatened species, or result in destruction or adverse modification of the habitat of such species, the OSC/RPM should consult with the DOI or DOC (NOAA).

(11) The OSC/RPM is responsible for addressing worker health and safety concerns at a response scene, in accordance with § 300.38 of this Plan.

(12) The OSC shall submit reports to the RRT and appropriate agencies as significant developments occur during removal actions.

(13) OSCs/RPMs should ensure that all appropriate public and private interests are kept informed and that their concerns are considered

throughout a response in accordance with § 300.39 to the extent practicable.

(14) The RPM is the prime contact for remedial actions being taken (or needed to be taken) at sites on the proposed or promulgated National Priorities List (NPL). These actions include:

(i) *Fund Financed Cleanup/Federal Lead*—The RPM coordinates, directs and reviews the work of all EPA, State and local governments, U.S. Army Corps of Engineers, and all other agencies and contractors to assure compliance with this Plan. Based upon the reports of these parties, the RPM recommends action for decisions by lead agency officials. The RPM's period of responsibility begins prior to initiation of the Remedial Investigation/Feasibility Study (RI/FS) [described in § 300.68(e)] and continues through design, construction, deletion of the site from the NPL, and in some cases, the CERCLA cost recovery activity. The RPM should coordinate with the OSC to ensure an orderly transition from OSC response activities of a State-lead remedial activities.

(ii) *Fund Financed Cleanup/State Lead*—The RPM serves in an oversight capacity during the planning, design and cleanup activities of a State-lead remedial action, offering both technical and programmatic guidance.

(iii) The RPM should be involved in all decisionmaking processes necessary to ensure compliance with this Plan and the cooperative agreement between the EPA and the State.

300.34 Special forces and teams.

(a) The National Strike Force (NSF) consists of the Strike Teams established by the USCG on the Atlantic, Pacific and Gulf coasts and includes emergency task forces to provide assistance to the OSC/RPM.

(1) The Strike Teams can provide communication support, advice and assistance for oil and hazardous substances removal. These teams also have knowledge of shipboard damage control and diving. Additionally, they are equipped with specialized containment and removal equipment, and have rapid transportation available. When possible, the Strike Teams will train the emergency task forces and assist in the development of regional and local contingency plans.

(2) The OSC/RPM may request assistance from the Strike Teams. Requests for a team may be made directly to the Commanding Officer of the appropriate team, the USCG member of the RRT, the appropriate USCG Area Commander, or the Commandant of the USCG through the NRC.

(b) Each USCG OSC manages emergency task forces trained to evaluate, monitor, and supervise pollution responses. Additionally, they have limited "initial aid" response capability to deploy equipment prior to the arrival of a clean-up contractor, or other response personnel.

(c)(1) The Environmental Response Team (ERT) is established by EPA in accordance with its disaster and emergency responsibilities. The ERT includes expertise in biology, chemistry, hydrology, geology and engineering.

(2) It can provide access to special decontamination equipment for chemical releases and advice to the OSC/RPM in hazard evaluation; risk assessment; multimedia sampling and analysis program; on-site safety, including development and implementation plans; clean-up techniques and priorities; water supply decontamination and protection; application of dispersants; environmental assessment; degree of clean-up required; and disposal of contaminated material.

(3) The ERT also provides both introductory and intermediate level training courses to prepare response personnel.

(4) OSC/RPM or RRT requests for ERT support should be made to the EPA representative on the RRT; the EPA Headquarters, Director, Office of Emergency and Remedial Response; or the appropriate EPA regional emergency coordinator.

(d) Scientific Support Coordinators (SSCs) are available, at the request of OSCs/RPMs, to assist with actual or potential responses to discharges of oil or releases of hazardous substances, pollutants, or contaminants. Generally, SSCs are provided by the National Oceanic and Atmospheric Administration (NOAA) in coastal and marine areas, and by the Environmental Protection Agency (EPA) in inland regions.

(1) During a response, the SSC serves under the direction of the OSC/RPM and is responsible for providing scientific support for operational decisions and to coordinate on-scene scientific activity. Depending on the nature of the incident, the SSC can be expected to provide certain specialized scientific skills and to work with governmental agencies, universities, community representatives, and industry to compile information that would assist the OSC/RPM in assessing the hazards and potential effects of discharges and releases and in developing response strategies.

(2) If requested by the OSC/RPM, the SSC will serve as the principal liaison for scientific information and will facilitate communications to and from the scientific community on response issues. The SSC, in this role, will attempt to reach a consensus on scientific issues surrounding the response but will also ensure that any differing opinions within the community are communicated to the OSC/RPM.

(3) The SSC will assist the OSC/RPM in responding to requests for assistance from the State and Federal agencies regarding scientific studies and environmental assessments. Details on access to scientific support shall be included in regional contingency plans.

(e) The USCG Public Information Assist Team (PIAT) and the EPA Public Affairs Assist Team (PAAT) are available to assist OSCs/RPMs and regional or district offices meet the demands for public information and participation. Their use is encouraged any time the OSC/RPM requires outside public affairs support. Requests for these teams may be made through the NRC.

(f)(1) The RRT may be activated by the Chairman as an emergency response team when a discharge or release:

(i) Exceeds the response capability available to the OSC in the place where it occurs;

(ii) Transects regional boundaries; or

(iii) May pose a substantial threat to the public health, welfare or to the environment, or to regionally significant amounts of property. Regional contingency plans shall specify detailed criteria for activation of RRTs.

(2) The RRT may be activated during any pollution emergency by a request from any RRT representative to the chairman of the Team. Request for RRT activation shall later be confirmed in writing. Each representative, or an appropriate alternate, should be notified immediately when the RRT is activated.

(3) During prolonged removal or remedial action, the RRT may not need to be activated or may need to be activated only in a limited sense, or have available only those members of the RRT who are directly affected or can provide direct response assistance.

(4) When the RRT is activated for a discharge or release, agency representatives shall meet at the call of the chairman and may:

(i) Monitor and evaluate reports from the OSC/RPM. The RRT may advise the OSC/RPM on the duration and extent of Federal response and may recommend to the OSC/RPM specific actions to respond to the discharge or release.

(ii) Request other Federal, State or local government, or private agencies to

provide resources under their existing authorities to respond to a discharge or release or to monitor response operations.

(iii) Help the OSC/RPM prepare information releases for the public and for communication with the NRT.

(iv) If the circumstances warrant, advise the regional or district head of the agency providing the OSC/RPM that a different OSC/RPM should be designated.

(v) Submit Pollution Reports (POLREPS) to the NRC as significant developments occur.

(5) When the RRT is activated, affected States may participate in all RRT deliberations. State government representatives participating in the RRT have the same status as any Federal member of the RRT.

(6) The RRT can be deactivated by agreement between the EPA and USCG team members. The time of deactivation should be included in the POLREPS.

(g) The NRT should be activated as an emergency response team when an oil discharge or hazardous substance release:

(1) Exceeds the response capability of the regions in which it occurs;

(2) Transects regional boundries;

(3) Involves significant population threat or national policy issues, substantial amounts of property, or substantial threats to natural resources; or

(4) Is requested by any NRT member.

(h) When activated for a response action, the NRT shall meet at the call of the chairman and may:

(1) Monitor and evaluate reports from the OSC/RPM. The NRT may recommend to the OSC/RPM, through the RRT, actions to combat the discharge or release.

(2) Request other Federal, State and local governments, or private agencies, to provide resources under their existing authorities to combat a discharge or release or to monitor response operations.

(3) Coordinate the supply of equipment, personnel, or technical advice to the affected region from other regions or districts.

§ 300.35 Multi-regional responses.

(a) If a discharge or release moves from the area covered by one Federal local or Federal regional contingency plan into another area, the authority for removal or response actions should likewise shift. If a discharge or release or substantial threat of discharge or release affects areas covered by two or more regional plans, the response mechanisms of both may be activated. In this case, removal or response actions

of all regions concerned shall be fully coordinated as detailed in the regional plans.

(b) There shall be only one OSC/RPM at any time during the course of a response operation. Should a discharge or release affect two or more areas, the EPA, DOD and USCG, as appropriate, shall give prime consideration to the area vulnerable to the greatest threat. The RRT shall designate the OSC/RPM if EPA, DOD and USCG members are unable to agree on the designation. The NRT shall designate the OSC/RPM if members of one RRT to two adjacent RRTs are unable to agree on the designation.

(c) Where the USCG has provided the OSC for emergency response to a release from hazardous waste management facilities located in the coastal zone, responsibility for response action shall shift to EPA, in accordance with EPA/USCG agreements.

§ 300.36 Communications.

(a) The NRC is the national communications center for activities related to response actions. It is located at USCG Headquarters in Washington, D.C. The NRC receives and relays notices of discharges or releases to the appropriate OSC, disseminates OSC/RPM and RRT reports to the NRT when appropriate, and provides facilities for the NRT to use in coordinating a national response action when required.

(b) The commandant, USCG, will provide the necessary communications, plotting facilities, and equipment for the NRC.

(c) Notice of an oil discharge or release of a hazardous substance in an amount equal to or greater than the reportable quantity must be made immediately in accordance with 33 CFR Part 153, Subpart B and section 103(a) of CERCLA, respectively. Notification shall be made to the NRC Duty Officer, HQ USCG, Washington, D.C. telephone (800) 424-8802 (or current local telephone number). All notices of discharges or releases received at the NRC shall be relayed immediately by telephone to the OSC or lead agency.

(d) The RRC provides facilities and personnel for communications, information storage, and other requirements for the RRC.

§ 300.37 Speical considerations.

(a) *Response Equipment*—The Spill Cleanup Inventory (SKIM) system is available to help OSCs and RRTs and private parties gain rapid information as to the location of response and support equipment. This inventory is accessible through the NRC and USCG's OSCs. The inventory includes private and commercial equipment, as well as government resources. The RRTs and OSCs shall ensure that data in the system are current and accurate. The USCG is responsible for maintaining and updating the system with RRT and OSC input.

(b) *Marine salvage.* (1) Marine salvage operations generally fall into five categories: Afloat salage; offshore salvage; river and harbor clearance; cargo salvage; and rescue towing. Each category requires different knowledge and specialized types of equipment. The complexity of such operations may be further compounded by local environmental and geographic conditions.

(2) The nature of marine salvage and the conditions under which it occurs combine to make such operations imprecise, difficult, hazardous, and expensive. Thus, responsible parties or other persons attempting to perform such operations without adequate knowledge, equipment, and experience could aggrevate, rather than relieve, the situation. OSCs with responsibility for monitoring, evaluating, or supervising these activities should request technical assistance from DOD as necessary to ensure that proper actions are taken.

§ 300.38 Worker health and safety.

(a) Requirements under the Occupational Safety and Health Act of 1970 (29 U.S.C. 651 et seq.) (OSH Act) and under the laws of States with plans approved under Section 18 of the OSH Act (State OSH laws), as well as other applicable safety and health requirements, will be applied to response activities under this Plan. These requirements are subject to enforcement by the appropriate Federal and State agencies. Federal OSHA requirements include, among other things, all OSHA General Industry (29 CFR Part 1910), Construction (29 CFR Part 1926), Shipyard (29 CFR Part 1915), and Longshorning (29 CFR Part 1918), standards wherever they are relevant, as well as OSHA recordkeeping and reporting regulations. Employers at response actions under this Plan will also be subject to the general duty requirement of section 5(a)(1) of the OSH Act, 29 U.S.C. 654(a)(1). No action by the lead agency with respect to response activities under this Plan constitutes an exercise of statutory authority within the meaning of section 4(b)(1) of the OSH Act. All governmental agencies and private employers are directly responsible for the health and safety of their own employees.

(b) Under a response action taken by a responsible party, the responsible party must assure that an occupational health and safety program is made available for the protection of workers at the response site, and that workers entering the response site are apprised of the response site hazards and provisions of the safety and health program.

(c) Under a Federal Fund-financed response, the lead agency must assure that a program for occupational safety and health is made available for the protection of workers at the response site, and that workers entering the response site are apprised of the response site hazards and provisions of the safety and health program. Any contract relating to a Federal Fund-financed response action under this Plan shall require the contractor at the response site to comply with this program and with any applicable provision of the OSH Act and State OSH laws as defined in § 300.38(a).

§ 300.39 Public information.

(a) When an incident occurs, it is imperative to give the public prompt, accurate information on the nature of the incident and the actions underway to mitigate the damage. OSCs/RPMs and community relations personnel should ensure that all appropriate public and private interests are kept informed and that their concerns are considered throughout a response. They should coordinate with available public affairs/ community relations resources to carry out this responsibility.

(b) An on-scene news office may be established to coordinate media relations and to issue official Federal information on an incident. Whenever possible, it will be headed by a representative of the lead agency. The OSC/RPM determines the location of the on-scene news office, but every effort should be made to locate it near the scene of the incident. If a participating agency believes public interest warrants the issuance of statements and an on-scene news office has not been established, the affected agency should recommend its establishment. All Federal news releases or statements by participating agencies should be cleared through the OSC/RPM.

§ 300.40 OSC reports.

(a) Within 60 days after the conclusion of a major discharge of oil, a major hazardous substance, pollutant, or contaminant release, or when requested by the RRT, the EPA or USCG OSC shall submit to the RRT a complete report on the response operation and the actions

taken. The OSC shall at the same time send a copy of the report to the NRT. The RRT shall review the OSC's report and prepare an endorsement to the NRT for review. This shall be accomplished within 30 days after the report has been received.

(b) The OSC's report shall accurately record the situation as it developed, the actions taken, the resources committed and the problems encountered. The OSC's recommendations are a source for new procedures and policy.

(c) the format for the OSC's report shall be as follows:

(1) Summary of Events—a chronological narrative of all events, including:

(i) The cause of discharge of release;

(ii) The initial situation;

(iii) Efforts to obtain response by responsible parties;

(iv) The organization of the response, including State participation;

(v) The resources committed;

(vi) The location [waterbody (if applicable), State, city, latitude and longitude] of the hazardous substance, pollutant, or contaminant release or oil discharge. For oil discharges, indicate whether the discharge was in connection with activities regulated under the Outer Continental Shelf Lands Act (OCSLA), the Trans-Alaska Pipeline Authority Act or Deepwater Port Act;

(vii) Comments on whether the discharge or release might have or actually did affect natural resources;

(viii) Comments on Federal or State damage assessment activities and efforts to replace or restore damaged natural resources;

(ix) Details of any threat abatement action taken under CERCLA or under section 311 (c) or (d) of the CWA; and

(x) Public information/community relations activities.

(2) Effectiveness of Removal Actions—A candid and thorough analysis of the effectiveness of removal actions taken by:

(i) The responsible party;

(ii) State and local forces;

(iii) Federal agencies and special forces; and

(iv) [If applicable] contractors, private groups and volunteers.

(3) Problems Encountered—A list of problems affecting response with particular attention to problems of intergovernmental coordination.

(4) Recommendations—OSC recommendations, including at a minimum:

(i) Means to prevent a recurrence of the discharge or release;

(ii) Improvement of response actions;

(iii) Any recommended changes in the National Contingency Plan or Federal regional plan.

Subpart D—Plans

§ 300.41 Regional and local plans.

(a) In addition to the National Contingency Plan (NCP), a Federal regional plan shall be developed for each standard Federal region and, where practicable, a Federal local plan shall be developed.

(b) These plans will be available for inspection at EPA Regional Offices or USCG district offices. Addresses and telephone numbers for these offices may be found in the United States Government Manual (issued annually) or in local telephone directories.

§ 300.42 Regional contingency plans.

(a) The RRTs, working with the States, shall develop Federal regional plans for each standard Federal region. The purpose of these plans is coordination of a timely, effective response by various Federal agencies and other organizations to discharges of oil and releases of hazardous substances, pollutants and contaminants in order to protect public health, welfare and the environment. Regional contingency plans should include information on all useful facilities and resources in the region, from government, commercial, academic and other sources. To the greatest extent possible, regional plans will follow the format of the National Contingency Plan.

(b) SSCs shall organize and coordinate the contributions of scientists of each region to the response activities of the OCS/RPM and RRT to the greatest extent possible. SSCs, with advice from RRT members, shall also develop the parts of the regional plan that relate to scientific support.

(c) Regional plans shall contain lines of demarcation between the inland and coastal zones, as mutually agreed upon by USCG and EPA.

§ 300.43 Local contingency plans.

(a) Each OSC shall maintain a Federal local plan for response in his or her area of responsibility, where practicable. In areas in which the USCG provides the OSC, such plans shall be developed in all cases. The plan should provide for a well-coordinated response that is integrated and compatible with the pollution response, fire, emergency and disaster plans of local, State and other non-Federal entities. The plan should identify the probable locations of discharges or releases, the available resources to respond to multi-media incidents, where such resources can be obtained, waste disposal methods and facilities consistent with local and State plans developed under the Resource Conservation and Recovery Act (42 U.S.C. 6901 et seq.), and a local structure for responding to discharges or releases.

(b) While the OSC is responsible for developing Federal local plans, a successful planning effort will depend upon the full cooperation of all the agencies' representatives and the development of local capabilities to respond to discharges or releases. Particular attention should be given, during the planning process, to developing a multi-agency local response team for coordinating on-scene efforts. The RRT should ensure proper liaison between the OSC and local representatives.

Subpart E—Operational Response Phases for Oil Removal

§ 300.51 Phase I—Discovery and notification.

(a) A discharge of oil may be discovered through:

(1) A report submitted by the person in charge of the vessel or facility in accordance with statutory requirements;

(2) Deliberate search by patrols; and

(3) Random or incidental observation by government agencies or the public.

(b) All reports of discharges should be made to the NRC. If direct reporting to the NRC is not practicable, reports may be made to the predesignated OSC at the nearest USCG or EPA office. All reports shall be promptly relayed to the NRC. Federal regional and Federal regional and Federal local plans shall provide for prompt reporting to the NRC, RRC, and appropriate State agency (as agreed upon with the State).

(c) Upon receipt of a notification of discharge, the NRC shall promptly notify the OSC. The OSC shall proceed with the following phases as outlined in Federal regional and Federal local plans.

§ 300.52 Phase II—Preliminary assessment and initiation of action.

(a) The OSC for a particular area is responsible for promptly initiating preliminary assessment.

(b) The preliminary assessment shall be conducted using available information, supplemented where necessary and possible by an on-scene inspection. The OSC shall undertake actions to:

(1) Evaluate the magnitude and severity of the discharge or threat to public health, welfare, or the environment;

(2) Assess the feasibility of removal;

(3) Determine the existence of potential responsible parties; and

(4) Ensure that authority exists for undertaking additional response actions.

(c) The OSC, in consultation with legal authorities when appropriate, shall make a reasonable effort to have the discharger voluntarily and promptly perform removal actions. The OSC shall ensure adequate surveillance over whatever actions are initiated. If effective actions are not being taken to eliminate the threat, or if removal is not being properly done, the OSC shall, to the extent practicable under the circumstances, so advise the responsible party. If the responsible party does not take proper removal actions, or is unknown, or is otherwise unavailable, the OSC shall, pursuant to section 311(c)(1) of the CWA, determine whether authority for a Federal response exists, and, if so, take appropriate response actions. Where practicable, continuing efforts should be made to encourage response by responsible parties.

(d) The OSC should ensure that the trustees of affected natural resources are notified, in order that the trustees may initiate appropriate actions when natural resources have been or are likely to be damaged (see Subpart G of Part 300). Where practicable, the OSC should consult with trustees in such determinations.

§ 300.53 Phase III—Containment, countermeasures, clean-up, and disposal.

(a) Defensive actions should begin as soon as possible to prevent, minimize, or mitigate threat to the public health or welfare or the environment. Actions may include: analyzing water samples to determine the source and spread of the oil; controlling the source of discharge; measuring and sampling; source and spread control or salvage operations; placement of physical barriers to deter the spread of the oil or to protect endangered species; control of the water discharged from upstream impoundment; and the use of chemicals and other materials in accordance with Subpart H, to restrain the spread of the oil and mitigate its effects.

(b) Appropriate actions should be taken to recover the oil or mitigate its effects. Of the numerous chemical physical methods that may be used, the chosen methods should be the most consistent with protecting the public health and welfare and the environment. Sinking agents shall not be used.

(c) Oil and contaminated materials recovered in cleanup operations shall be disposed of in accordance with Federal regional and Federal local contingency plans.

§ 300.54 Phase IV—Documentation and cost recovery.

(a) Documentation shall be collected and maintained to support all actions taken under the CWA and to form the basis for cost recovery. In general, documentation should be sufficient to prove the source and circumstances of the incident, the responsible party or parties, and impact and potential impacts to the public health and welfare and the environment. When appropriate, documentation should also be collected for scientific understanding of the environment and for the research and development of improved response methods and technology. Damages to private citizens (including loss of earnings) are not addressed by this Plan. Evidentiary and cost documentation procedures and requirements are specified in the USCG Marine Safety Manual (Commandant Instruction M16000.3) and 33 CFR Part 153.

(b) OSCs shall submit OSC reports to the RRT as required by § 300.40.

(c) The OSC shall ensure the necessary collection and safeguarding of information, samples, and reports. Samples and information must be gathered expeditiously during the response to ensure an accurate record of the impacts incurred. Documentation materials shall be made available to the trustees of affected natural resources.

(d) Information and reports obtained by the EPA or USCG OSC shall be transmitted to the appropriate offices responsible for follow-up actions.

§ 300.55 General pattern of response.

(a) When the OSC receives a report of a discharge, actions normally should be taken in following sequence:

(1) Immediately notify the RRT and NRC when the reported discharge is an actual or potential major discharge.

(2) Investigate the report to determine pertinent information such as the threat posed to public health or welfare, or the environment, the type and quantity of polluting material, and the source of the discharge.

(3) Officially classify the size of the discharge and determine the course of action to be followed.

(4) Determine whether a discharger or other person is properly carrying out removal. Removal is being done properly when:

(i) The clean-up is fully sufficient to minimize or mitigate threat to the public health, welfare, and the environment (removal efforts are "improper" to the extent that Federal efforts are necessary

to further minimize or mitigate those threats).

(ii) The removal efforts are in accordance with applicable regulations including this Plan.

(5) Determine whether a State or political subdivision has the capability to carry out response actions and a contract or cooperative agreement has been established with the appropriate fund administrator for this purpose.

(6) Notify the RRT (including the affected State), SSC, and the trustees of affected natural resources in accordance with the applicable regional plan.

(b) The preliminary inquiry will probably show that the situation falls into one of the five classes. These classes and the appropriate response to each are outlined below:

(1) If the investigation shows that no discharge exists, the case shall be considered a false alarm and should be closed.

(2) If the investigation shows a minor discharge with the responsible party taking proper removal action, contact should be established with the party. The removal action should be monitored to ensured continued proper action.

(3) If the investigation shows a minor discharge with improper removal action being taken, the following measures shall be taken:

(i) An immediate effort should be made to stop further pollution and remove past and on-going contamination.

(ii) The responsible party shall be advised of what action will be considered appropriate.

(iii) If the responsible party does not properly respond, he shall be notified of his potential liability for Federal response performed under the CWA. This liability includes all costs of removal and may include the costs of assessing and restoring damaged natural resources and other actual or necessary costs of a Federal response.

(iv) The OSC shall notify appropriate State and local officials, keep the RRT advised and initiate Phase III operations as conditions warrant.

(v) Information shall be collected for possible recovery of response costs in accordance with § 300.54.

(4) When the investigation shows that an actual or potential medium oil discharge exists, the OSC shall follow the same general procedures as for a minor discharge. If appropriate, the OSC shall recommend activation of the RRT.

(5) When the investigation shows an actual or potential major oil discharge, the OSC shall follow the same procedures as for minor and medium discharges.

§ 300.56 [Reserved]

§ 300.57 Waterfowl conservation.

The DOI representatives and the State liaison to the RRT shall arrange for the coordination of professional and volunteer groups permitted and trained to participate in waterfowl dispersal, collection, cleaning, rehabilitation and recovery activities (consistent with 16 U.S.C. 703–712 and applicable State laws). Federal regional and Federal local plans will, to the extent practicable, identify organizations or institutions that are permitted to participate in such activities and operate such facilities. Waterfowl conservation activities will normally be included in Phase III response actions (§ 300.53 of this subpart).

§ 300.58 Funding.

(a) If the person responsible for the discharge does not act promptly including timely actions, or take proper removal actions, or if the person responsible for the discharge is unknown, Federal discharge removal actions may begin under section 311(c)(1) of the CWA. The discharger, if known, is liable for the costs of Federal removal in accordance with section 311(f) of the CWA and other Federal laws.

(b) Actions undertaken by the participating agencies in response to pollution shall be carried out under existing programs and authorities when available. This Plan intends that Federal agencies will make resources available, expend funds, or participate in response to oil discharges under their existing authority. Authority to expend resources will be in accordance with agencies' basic statutes and, if required, through interagency agreements. Where the OSC requests assistance from a Federal agency, that agency may be reimbursed in accordance with the provisions of 33 CFR 153.407. Specific interagency reimbursement agreements may be signed when necessary to ensure that the Federal resources will be available for a timely response to a discharge of oil. The ultimate decisions as to the appropriateness of expending funds rests with the agency that is held accountable for such expeditures.

(c) The OSC shall exercise sufficient control over removal operation to be able to certify that reimbursement from the following funds is appropriate:

(1) The oil pollution fund, administered by the Commandant, USCG, has been established pursuant to section 311(k) of the CWA. Regulations governing the administration and use of

the fund are contained in 33 CFR Part 153.

(2) The fund authorized by the Deepwater Port Act is administered by the Commandant, USCG. Governing regulations are contained in 33 CFR Parts 136 and 150.

(3) The fund authorized by the Outer Continental Shelf Lands Act, as amended, is administered by the Commandant, USCG. Governing regulations are contained in 33 CFR Parts 136 and 150.

(4) The fund authorized by the Trans-Alaska Pipeline Authorization Act is administered by a Board of Trustees under the purview of the Secretary of the Interior. Governing regulations are contained in 43 CFR Part 29.

(d) Response actions other than removal, such as scientific investigations not in support of removal actions or law enforcement, shall be provided by the agency with legal responsibility for those specific actions:

(e) The funding of a response to a discharge from a Federally operated or supervised facility or vessel is the responsiblity of the operating or supervising agency.

(f) The following agencies have funds available for certain discharge removal actions:

(1) EPA may provide funds to begin timely discharge removal actions when the OSC is an EPA representative.

(2) The USCG pollution control efforts are funded under "operating expenses." These funds are used in accordance with agency directives.

(3) The Department of Defense has two specific sources of funds which may be applicable to an oil discharge under appropriate circumstances. (This does not consider military resources which might be made available under specific conditions.)

(i) Funds required for removal of a sunken vessel or similar obstruction of navigation are available to the Corps of Engineers through Civil Works Appropriations, Operations and Maintenance, General.

(ii) The U.S. Navy may conduct salvage operations contingent on defense operational commitments, when funded by the requesting agency. Such funding may be requested on a direct cite basis.

(4) Pursuant to section 311(c)(2)(H) of the CWA, the State or States affected by a discharge of oil, may act where necessary to remove such discharge and may, pursuant to 33 CFR Part 153, be reimbursed from the pollution revolving fund for the reasonable costs incurred in such a removal.

(i) Removal by a State is necessary within the meaning of section 311(c)(2)(H) of the CWA when the OSC determines that the owner or operator of the vessel, onshore facility, or offshore facility from which the discharge occurs does not affect removal properly, or is unknown, and that:

(A) State action is required to minimize or mitigate significant threat to the public health or welfare which Federal action cannot minimize or mitigate, or

(B) Removal or partial removal can be done by the State at a cost which is less than or not significantly greater than the cost which would be incurred by the Federal departments or agencies.

(ii) State removal actions must be in compliance with this Plan in order to qualify for reimbursement.

(iii) State removal actions are considered to be Phase III actions, under the same definitions applicable to Federal agencies.

(iv) Actions taken by local governments in support of Federal discharge removal operations are considered to be actions of the State for purposes of this section. Federal regional and Federal local plans shall show what funds and resources are available from participating agencies under various conditions and cost arrangements. Interagency agreements may be necessary to specify when reimbursement is required.

Subpart F—Hazardous Substances Response

§ 300.61 General.

(a) This subpart establishes methods and criteria for determining the appropriate extent of response authorized by CERCLA: (1) When there is a release of a hazardous substance or there is a substantial threat of such a release into the environment; or, (2) when there is a release or substantial threat of a release into the environment of any pollutant or contaminant which may present an imminent and substantial danger to the public health or welfare.

(b) Section 104(a)(1) of CERCLA authorizes removal or remedial action unless it is determined that such removal or remedial action will be done properly by the owner or operator of the vessel or facility from which the release or threat of release emanates, or by any other responsible party. If appropriate response actions are not being taken or executed properly, including in a timely manner, the lead agency may initiate proper action, terminate any improper actions and should so advise any known responsible party, and complete response activities.

(c) In determining the need for and in planning or undertaking Fund-financed action, the lead agency should, to the extent practicable:

(1) Engage in prompt response.

(2) Encourage State participation in response actions (see § 300.62).

(3) Conserve Fund monies by encouraging private party clean-up.

(4) Be sensitive to local community concerns (see § 300.67).

(5) Rely on established technology, but also consider alternative and innovative technology when feasible and cost-effective.

(6) Involve the RRT in both removal and remedial response actions at appropriate decision-making stages.

(7) Encourage the involvement and sharing of technology by industry and other experts.

(8) Encourage the involvement of organizations to coordinate responsible party actions, foster site cleanup and provide technical advice to the public, Federal and State Government and industry.

(d) The lead agency should, as practicable, provide surveillance over actions taken by responsible parties to ensure that a response is conducted consistent with this Plan.

(e) (1) This subpart does not establish any preconditions to enforcement action by either the Federal or State Governments to compel response actions by responsible parties.

(2) While some of this subpart is oriented toward federally funded response actions, this subpart may be used as guidance concerning methods and criteria for response actions by other parties under other funding mechanisms. Except as provided in § 300.71 nothing in this part limits the rights of any person to seek recovery of response costs from responsible parties pursuant to CERCLA section 107.

(3) Activities by the Federal and State Governments in implementing this subpart are discretionary governmental functions. This subpart does not create in any private party a right to Federal response or enforcement action. This subpart does not create any duty of the Federal Government to take any response action at any particular time.

§ 300.62 State role.

(a)(1) States are encouraged to undertake actions authorized under this subpart. Section 104(d)(1) of CERCLA authorizes the Federal Government to enter into contracts or cooperative agreements with the State to take Fund-financed response actions authorized under CERCLA, when the Federal government determines that the State has the capability to undertake such actions.

(2) Cooperative agreements or State Superfund contracts are unnecessary for response actions that are not fund-financed, including any State or other party actions. Coordination with EPA or USCG is encouraged in such situations, however.

(b) EPA will provide assistance from the Fund to States pursuant to a contract or cooperative agreement. The cooperative agreement can authorize States to undertake most actions specified in this Subpart.

(c) Contracts and cooperative agreements between the State(s) and Federal Government for Fund-financed remedial action are subject to section 104(c)(3) of CERCLA. Such agreements are not a precondition to access, information gathering, investigations, studies or liability pursuant to section 106 and 107 of CERCLA.

(d) Prior to remedial action as defined in section 101(24) of CERCLA, the State must make a firm commitment, through either a new or amended cooperative agreement or State contract, to provide funding for remedial implementation by:

(1) Authorizing the reduction of a State credit to cover its share of costs;

(2) Identifying currently available funds earmarked for remedial implementation; or

(3) Submitting a plan with milestones for obtaining necessary funds.

(e) State credits allowed under section 104(c)(3) of CERCLA must be documented on a site-specific basis for State out-of-pocket, non-Federal eligible response costs between January 1, 1978, and December 11, 1980. Prior to remedial investigation activity at a site, the State must submit its estimate of these costs as a part of the cooperative agreement application, or as a part of the EPA State agreement. State credits will be applied against State cost shares for federally funded remedial actions. A State cannot be reimbursed from the Fund for credit in excess of its matching share nor may the credit be applied to any other site.

(f) Pursuant to section 104(c)(2) of CERCLA, prior to determining any appropriate remedial action, the lead agency shall consult with the affected State or States.

(g) States are encouraged to participate in all RRT planning and response activities.

(h) State and local public safety organizations are normally expected to initiate public safety measures (e.g., actions to limit public access to site) and are responsible for directing evacuations pursuant to existing State/local procedures.

§ 300.63 Discovery or notification.

(a) A release may be discovered through:

(1) Notification in accordance with sections 103 (a) or (c) of CERCLA;

(2) Investigation by government authorities conducted in accordance with section 104(e) of CERCLA or other statutory authority;

(3) Notification of a release by a Federal or State permit holder when required by its permit;

(4) Inventory efforts or random or incidental observation by government agencies or the public;

(5) Other sources.

(b) All reports of releases should be made to the NRC. If direct reporting to the NRC is not practicable, reports may be made to the predesignated OSC at the nearest USCG or EPA office. All such reports shall be promptly relayed to the NRC.

(c) Upon receipt of a notification of a release, the NRC shall promptly notify the appropriate OSC or lead agency. The OSC or lead agency shall notify the Governor of the State affected by the release.

(d) (1) When the OSC is notified of a release which may require response pursuant to § 300.65(b), a preliminary assessment should be undertaken by the OSC pursuant to § 300.64.

(2) When notification indicates that action pursuant to § 300.65(b) is not required, site evaluation should be undertaken by the lead agency pursuant to § 300.66.

§ 300.64 Preliminary assessment for removal actions.

(a) A preliminary assessment of a release or threat of a release identified for possible CERCLA response pursuant to § 300.65 should be undertaken by the OSC as promptly as possible. The OSC should base the assessment on readily available information. This assessment may include but is not limited to:

(1) Identification of the source and nature of the release or threat of release;

(2) Evaluation of the threat to public health by HHS;

(3) Evaluation of the magnitude of the potential threat;

(4) Evaluation of factors necessary to make the determination of whether a removal is necessary; and

(5) Determination if a non-Federal party is undertaking proper response.

(b) A preliminary assessment of releases or threats of releases from hazardous waste management facilities may include collection or review of data such as site management practices, information from generators, photographs, analysis of historical photographs, literature searches, and

personal interviews conducted as appropriate. In addition, a perimeter (off-site) inspection may be necessary to determine the potential for a release. Finally, if more information is needed, a site visit may be performed, if conditions are such that it may be performed safely.

(c) A preliminary assessment should be terminated when the OSC or lead agency determines:

(1) There is no release or threat of release;

(2) The source is neither a vessel nor a facility;

(3) The release does not involve a hazardous substance, nor a pollutant or contaminant;

(4) The amount, quantity and concentration released does not warrant Federal response;

(5) A party responsible for the release, or any other person, is providing appropriate response, and on-scene monitoring by the government is not required; or

(6) The assessment is completed.

(d) If it is determined during the assessment that natural resources have been, or are likely to be damaged, the OSC or lead agency should ensure that the trustees of the affected natural resources are notified in order that the trustees may initiate appropriate actions. Where practicable, the OSC should consult with trustees in making such determinations.

(e) If the preliminary assessment indicates that removal action under § 300.65 is not required, but that remedial actions under § 300.68 may be necessary, the lead agency should initiate site evaluation pursuant to § 300.66.

§ 300.65 Removals.

(a) (1) In determining the appropriate extent of action to be taken at a given release, the lead agency shall first review the preliminary assessment and the current site conditions to determine if removal action is appropriate.

(2) Where the responsible parties are known, an effort initially should be made, to the extent practicable considering the exigencies of the circumstances, to have them perform the necessary removal actions. Where responsible parties are unknown an effort initially should be made, to the extent practicable considering the exigencies of the circumstances, to locate them and have them perform the necessary removal action.

(3) This section does not apply to removal actions taken pursuant to section 104(b) of CERCLA. The criteria

for such actions are set forth in section 104(b).

(b) (1) At any release, regardless of whether it is included on the National Priorities List, where the lead agency determines that there is a threat to public health, welfare or the environment, based on the factors in subsection (b)(2), the lead agency may take any appropriate action to abate, minimize, stabilize, mitigate or eliminate the release or threat of release, or the threat resulting from that release or threat of release.

(2) The following factors shall be considered in determining the apropriateness of a removal action pursuant to this subsection:

(i) Actual or potential exposure to hazardous substances or pollutants or contaminants by nearby populations, animals or food chain;

(ii) Actual or potential contamination of drinking water supplies or sensitive ecosystems;

(iii) Hazardous substances or pollutant or contaminants in drums, barrels, tanks, or other bulk storage containers, that may pose a threat of release;

(iv) High levels of hazardous substances or pollutants or contaminants in soils largely at or near the surface, that may migrate.

(v) Weather conditions that may cause hazardous substances or pollutants or contaminants to migrate or be released;

(vi) Threat of fire or explosion;

(vii) The availability of other appropriate Federal or State response and enforcement mechanisms to respond to the release;

(viii) Other situations or factors which may pose similar threats to public health, welfare or the environment.

(3) Removal actions, other than those authorized under section 104(b) of CERCLA, shall be terminated after $1 million has been obligated for the action or 6 months have elapsed from the date of initial response unless the lead agency determines that: (i) there is an immediate risk to public health, welfare or the environment, (ii) continued response actions are immediately required to prevent, limit, or mitigate an emergency, and (iii) such assistance will not otherwise be provided on a timely basis.

(4) If the lead agency determines that a removal action pursuant to this subsection is appropriate, actions should begin as soon as possible to prevent, minimize or mitigate the threat to public health, welfare or the environment. The lead agency should, at the earliest possible time, also make any

necessary determinations contained in paragraph (b)(3) of this section.

(c) The following removal actions are as a general rule appropriate in the following situations; however, this list does not limit the lead agency from taking any other actions deemed necessary in response to any situation or preclude the lead agency from deferring response action to other appropriate Federal or State enforcement or response authorities.

(1) Fences, warning signs, or other security or site control precautions— where humans or animals have access to the release;

(2) Drainage controls (e.g. run-off or run-on diversion)—where precipitation or run-off from other sources (e.g. flooding) may enter the release area from other areas;

(3) Stabilization of berms, dikes, or impoundments—where needed to maintain the integrity of the structures;

(4) Capping of contaminated soils or sludges—where needed to reduce migration of hazardous substances, or pollutants or contaminants into soil, ground water or air.

(5) Using chemicals and other materials to retard the spread of the release or to mitigate its effects—where the use of such chemicals will reduce the spread of the release;

(6) Removal of highly contaminated soils from drainage areas—where removal will reduce the spread of contamination;

(7) Removal of drums, barrels, tanks or other bulk containers containing or that may contain hazardous substances or pollutants or contaminants—where it will reduce the likelihood of spillage, leakage, exposure to humans, animals or food chain, or fire or explosion.

(8) Provison of alernative water supply—where it will reduce the likelihood of exposure of humans or animals to contaminated water.

(d) Where necessary to protect public health or welfare, the lead agency may request that FEMA conduct a temporary relocation or evacuation.

If the lead agency determines that the removal action will not fully address the threat or potential threat posed by the release and the release may require remedial action, the OSC should coordinate with the RPM to ensure an orderly transition from removal to remedial response activities.

(f) Although Fund-financed removal actions and removal actions pursuant to CERCLA section 106 are not required to comply with other Federal, State and local laws governing the removal activity, including permit requirements, such removal actions shall, to the greatest extent practicable considering

the exigencies of the circumstances, attain or exceed applicable or relevant Federal public health or environmental standards. Applicable standards are those standards that would be legally applicable if the actions were not undertaken pursuant to CERCLA section 104 or section 106. Relevant standards are those designed to apply to circumstances sufficiently similar to those encountered at CERCLA sites that their application would be appropriate, although not legally required. Federal criteria, guidance and advisories and State standards also should be considered in formulating the removal action.

(g) Fund-financed removal actions and removal actions pursuant to section 106 of CERCLA involving the storage, treatment, or disposal of hazardous substances or pollutants or contaminants at off-site facilities shall involve only such off-site facilities that are operating under appropriate Federal or State permits or authorization.

§ 300.66 Site evaluation phase and national priorities list determination.

(a) (1) *The Site Evaluation Phase.* This phase of response includes activities beginning with discovery of a release and extends through the initial evaluaton (preliminary assessment and site inspection—see § 300.64). The purpose of the site evaluation phase is to further categorize the nature of any releases and potential threats to public health, welfare, and the environment and to collect data as required to determine whether a release should be included on the National Priorities List (NPL). (See § 300.66 (b) and (c) below.)

(2) Pursuant to section 104 (b) and (e) of CERCLA and other authorities, the lead agency may undertake preliminary assessments and site inspections to gather appropriate information to determine if a release warrants response, and if so, its priority for response.

(3) For response actions that may be taken pursuant to § 300.68, a preliminary assessment consists of a review of existing data and may include an off-site reconnaissance. The purposes of such a preliminary assessment are:

(i) To eliminate from further consideration those releases where available data indicates no threat or potential threat to public health or the environment exists;

(ii) To determine if there is any potential need for removal action;

(iii) To establish priority for scheduling a site inspection.

(4) A site inspection consists of a visual inspection of the site and

routinely includes collection of samples. There are several major purposes for a site inspection:

(i) To determine which releases pose no threat or potential threat to public health and the environment;

(ii) To determine if there is any immediate threat to persons living or working near the release;

(iii) To collect data, where appropriate, to determine whether a release should be included on the NPL.

(b) *Methods for Establishing Priorities.* (1) Section 105(8)(A) of CERCLA requires the President to include as part of the Plan criteria for establishing priorities among releases and potential releases. Three mechanisms are set forth here for that purpose: The Hazard Ranking System (HRS); designation by the States of their top priority releases; and determination that a site poses a significant threat to public health, welfare or the environment as indicated in paragraph (b)(4) of this section. These criteria will be used to establish and amend the NPL (see § 300.66(c)).

(2) The primary mechanism for identifying releases for inclusion on the NPL will be scores calculated by applying the HRS (Appendix A).

(3) Each State may designate a release as the State's highest priority release by certifying in writing, signed by the Governor or the Governor's designee, that the release presents the greatest danger to public health, welfare or the environment among known releases in the State. Each State may designate one top priority site over the life of the NPL.

(4) In addition to those releases identified by their HRS scores as candidates for the NPL, EPA may identify for inclusion on the NPL any other release that the Agency determines is a significant threat to public health, welfare or the environment. EPA may make such a determination when the Department of Health and Human Services has issued a health advisory as a consequence of the release.

(c) (1) The National Priorities List. Section 105(8)(B) of CERCLA requires the President to establish a list of at least 400 releases and potential releases, based upon the criteria developed pursuant to section 105(8)(A) of the Act. CERCLA also requires the States to identify their priorities at least annually and requires that each State's designated top priority releases be included among the one hundred (100) highest priority releases, to the degree practicable. The process for establishing the NPL is set forth below.

(2) The NPL serves as a basis to guide the allocation of Fund resources among

releases. Only those releases included on the NPL will be considered eligible for Fund-financed remedial action.

Inclusion on the NPL is not a precondition to liability pursuant to Agency action under CERCLA section 106 or to action under CERCLA 107, for recovery of non-Fund-financed costs or Fund-financed costs other than remedial construction costs.

(3) States that wish to submit candidates for the NPL must use the HRS (Appendix A of this part) to score the releases and furnish EPA with appropriate documentation for the scores.

(4) EPA will notify the States at least thirty days prior to the deadline for submitting candidate releases for the NPL or any revisions.

(5) EPA will review the States' HRS scoring documents and revise the application of the hazard ranking criteria when appropriate. EPA will add any additional priority releases known to the Agency after consultation with the States. Taking into account the HRS scores, the States' top priority releases, and the criteria specified in (b)(4) of this section, EPA will compile the NPL.

(6) Ranking of Releases. Minor differences in HRS scores among releases may not accurately differentiate among threats represented by the releases. Thus, releases having similar scores may be presented in groups on the NPL.

(7) Sites may be deleted from the NPL where no further response is appropriate. In deleting sites the Agency will consider whether any of the following criteria have been met:

(i) EPA in consultation with the State has determined that responsible or other parties have completed all appropriate response actions required at that time;

(ii) All appropriate Fund-financed response under CERCLA has been completed, and EPA has determined that no further cleanup by responsible parties is appropriate at that time; or

(iii) Based on a remedial investigation, EPA has determined that the release poses no significant threat to public health or the environment and, therefore, taking of remedial measures is not appropriate at that time.

(8) All releases deleted from the NPL are eligible for further Fund-financed remedial actions should future conditions warrant such action.

(9) EPA will submit the recommended NPL to the NRT for review and comment. EPA will publish any proposed revisions to the NPL for public comment.

(10) EPA will revise and publish the NPL at least annually.

§ 300.67 Community relations.

(a) A formal community relations plan must be developed and implemented for removal actions taken pursuant to 300.65 and for remedial action at NPL sites, including enforcement actions, except as provided for in subsection (b). Such plans must specify the communication activities which will be undertaken during the response and shall include provision for a public comment period on the alternatives analysis undertaken pursuant to § 300.68. The use of the RRT to assist community relations activities should be considered in developing community relations plans.

(b) In the case of actions taken pursuant to 300.65 or enforcement action to compel response analogous to section 300.65, or other short term action needed to abate a threat to public health, welfare, or the environment, a spokesperson will be designated by the lead agency. The spokesperson will inform the community of actions taken, respond to inquiries, and provide information concerning the release. In such cases, if the action is of short duration, or if response is needed immediately, a formal plan is not necessary. However, if the removal action extends over 45 days, a formal plan must be developed and implemented.

(c) For all remedial actions at NPL sites including Fund-financed and enforcement actions, a community relations plan must be developed, and approved, prior to initiation of field activities and implemented during the course of the action. In enforcement actions a responsible party may be permitted with lead agency oversight to develop and implement appropriate parts of the community relations plan.

(d) In remedial actions at NPL sites including Fund-financed and enforcement actions, feasibility studies that outline alternative remedial measures must be provided to the public for review and comment for a period of not less than 21 calendar days. Such review and comment shall precede selection of the remedial response. Public meeting(s) should, as a general rule, be held during the comment period. The lead agency may also provide the public with an opportunity to comment during the development of the feasibility study.

(e) A document which summarizes the major issues raised by the public and how they are addressed must be included in the decision document approving the remedy.

(f) In enforcement actions in litigation under CERCLA section 106, the community relations plan, including provision for public review of any feasibility study prepared for source control or management of migration measures, may be modified or adjusted at the direction of the court of jurisdiction or to accommodate the court calendar.

(g) Where parties agree to implement the permanent site remedy pursuant to an administrative order on consent, the lead agency shall provide public notice and a 30-day period for public comment, including comment on remedial measures. Where settlement is embodied in a consent decree, public notice and opportunity for public comment shall be provided in accordance with 28 CFR 50.7. A document summarizing the major issues raised by the public and how they are addressed will be prepared.

§ 300.68 Remedial action.

(a) (1) *Introduction.* Remedial actions are those responses to releases that are consistent with permanent remedy to prevent or minimize the release of hazardous substances or pollutants or contaminants so that they do not migrate to cause substantial danger to present or future public health, welfare, or the environment [CERCLA section 101(24)]. Fund-financed remedial action may be taken only at those releases on the NPL.

(2) The Remedial Project Manager (RPM) shall carry out responsibilities in a remedial action as delineated in § 300.33(b).

(3) Federal, State and local public health or environmental permits are not required for Fund-financed remedial action or remedial actions taken pursuant to Federal action under section 106 of CERCLA. However, remedial actions that involve storage, treatment, or disposal of hazardous substances, pollutants or contaminants at off-site facilities shall involve only such off-site facilities that are operating under appropriate Federal or State permits or authorization.

(b) (1) *State Involvement.* States are encouraged to undertake Fund-financed remedial response in accordance with § 300.62 of this Plan.

(2) States must meet the requirements of CERCLA section 104(c)(3) prior to undertaking Fund-financed remedial action.

(3) Planning activities associated with remedial actions taken pursuant to CERCLA section 104(b) shall not require a State cost share unless the facility was owned at the time of any disposal of hazardous substances therein by the State or a political subdivision thereof. such planning activities include, but are not limited to, remedial investigations,

feasibility studies, and design of the proposed remedy. For sites owned by a State or its political subdivision, cost sharing commitment is required prior to remedial action.

(c) (1) *Scoping of Response Actions.* The lead agency, in cooperation with State(s), will examine available information and determine, based on the factors indicated in paragraph (c)(2) of this section, the type of response that may be needed to remedy the release. This scoping will serve as a basis for requesting funding for a necessary removal action, remedial investigation or feasibility study. Initial analysis should indicate the extent to which the release or threat of release may pose a threat to public health, welfare or the environment, the types of removal measures and/or remedial measures suitable to abate the threat, and set priorities for implementation of the measures.

(2) The following should be assessed in determining whether and what type of remedial and/or removal actions should be considered:

(i) Population, environmental, and welfare concerns at risk;

(ii) Routes of exposure;

(iii) Amount, concentration, hazardous properties, environmental fate (e.g. ability to bio-accumulate, persistence, mobility, etc), and form of the substance(s) present;

(iv) Hydrogeological factors (e.g., soil permeability, depth to saturated zone, hydrologic gradients, proximity to a drinking water aquifer, floodplains and wetlands proximity);

(v) Climate (rainfall, etc.);

(vi) The extent to which the source can be adequately identified and characterized;

(vii) Whether substances at the site may be reused or recycled;

(viii) The likelihood of future releases if the substances remain on-site;

(ix) The extent to which natural or man-made barriers currently contain the substances and the adequacy of the barriers;

(x) The extent to which the substances have migrated or are expected to migrate from the area of their original location or new location if relocated and whether future migration may pose a threat to public health, welfare, or the environment;

(xi) Extent to which contamination levels exceed applicable or relevant Federal or State public health or environmental standards, advisories and criteria and the extent to which there are applicable or relevant standards for the storage, treatment, or disposal of materials of the type present at the release;

(xii) Contribution of the contamination to an air, land or water pollution problem;

(xiii) Ability of responsible party to implement and maintain the remedy until the threat is permanently abated;

(xiv) The availability of other appropriate Federal or State response and enforcement mechanisms to respond to the release;

(xv) Other appropriate matters may be considered.

(3) As a remedial investigation progresses, the project may be modified if the lead agency determines that, based on the factors in subparagraph (2) of this section, such modifications would be appropriate.

(d) *Operable Unit.* Response action may be conducted in operable units. Operable units may be conducted as remedial and/or removal actions.

(1) Response actions may be separated into operable units consistent with achieving a permanent remedy. These operable units may include removal actions pursuant to § 300.65(b), and/or remedial actions involving source controls, and/or management of migration.

(2) The RPM should recommend whether or not operable units should be implemented prior to selection of the appropriate final remedial measure.

(3) In some instances, implementation of operable units can and should begin before selection of an appropriate final remedial action if such measures are cost-effective and consistent with a permanent remedy. Compliance with § 300.68(b) is a prerequisite to implementing remedial operable units.

(e) *Remedial Investigation/Feasibility Study* (RI/FS). A RI/FS should be undertaken by the lead agency conducting the remedial action to determine the nature and extent of the threat presented by the release and evaluate proposed remedies. This includes sampling, monitoring, and exposure assessment, as necessary, and includes the gathering of sufficient information to determine the necessity for and proposed extent of remedial action. Part of the RI/FS may involve assessing whether the threat can be prevented or minimized by controlling the source of the contamination at or near the area where the hazardous substances were originally located (source control measures) and/or whether additional actions will be necessary because the hazardous substances have migrated from the area of or near their original location (management of migration). Planning for remedial action at these releases should also assess the need for removals.

During the remedial investigation, the original scoping of the project may be modified based on the factors in ¾ 300.68(c).

(f) *Development of Alternatives.* (1) A reasonable number of alternatives must be developed including:

(i) Alternatives for treatment or disposal at an off-site facility, as appropriate;

(ii) Alternatives which attain applicable or relevant Federal public health or environmental standards;

(iii) As appropriate, alternatives which exceed applicable or relevant Federal public health or environmental standards;

(iv) Alternatives which do not attain applicable or relevant public health or environmental standards but will reduce the likelihood of present or future threat from the hazardous substances and which provide significant protection to public health, welfare, and the environment. This must include an alternative which most closely approaches the level of protection provided by the applicable or relevant standards.

(v) No action alternative.

(2) These alternatives should be developed based upon the analysis conducted under paragraphs (c), (d) and (e) of this section. The alternatives should consider and integrate waste minimization, destruction, and recycling where appropriate. This must include an alternative which most closely approaches the level of protection provided by the applicable or relevant standards.

(g) *Initial Screening of Alternatives.* The alternatives developed under paragraph (f) of this section will be subject to an initial screening to narrow the list of potential remedial actions for further detailed analysis. When an alternative is eliminated in screening, the rationale should be documented in the feasibility study. Three broad criteria should be used in the initial screening of alternatives:

(1) *Cost.* For each alternative, the cost of implementing the remedial action must be considered including operation and maintenance costs. An alternative that far exceeds the costs of other alternatives evaluated and that does not provide substantially greater public health or environmental protection, or technical reliability should usually be excluded from further consideration unless there is no other remedy which meets applicable or relevant Federal public health or environmental standards.

(2) *Acceptable Engineering Practices.* Alternatives must be feasible for the location and conditions of the release,

applicable to the problem, and represent a reliable means of addressing the problem.

(3) *Effectiveness.* Those alternatives that do not effectively contribute to the protection of public health, welfare, and the environment should not be considered further. If an alternative has significant adverse effects, and very limited environmental benefits, it should also be excluded from further consideration.

(h) *Detailed Analysis of Alternatives.* (1) A more detailed evaluation will be conducted of the limited number of alternatives that remain after the initial screening in paragraph (g).

(2) The detailed analysis of each alternative should include:

(i) Refinement and specification of alternatives in detail, with emphasis on use of established technology. Innovative or advanced technology should be evaluated as an alternative to conventional technology;

(ii) Detailed cost estimation, including operation and maintenance costs, and distribution of costs over time;

(iii) Evaluation in terms of engineering implementation, reliability, and constructability;

(IV) An assessment of the extent to which the alternative is expected to effectively prevent, mitigate, or minimize threats to, and provide adequate protection of, public health, welfare, and the environment. This shall include an evaluation of the extent to which the alternative attains or exceeds applicable or relevant Federal public health or environmental standards advisories and criteria. Where the analysis determines that Federal public health or environmental standards are not applicable or relevant, the analysis should evaluate the risks of the various exposure levels projected or remaining after implemention of the alternative under consideration.

(V) An analysis of whether recycle/reuse, waste minimization or destruction or other advanced, innovative or alternative technologies is appropriate to reliably minimize present or future threats to public health, welfare or the environment.

(VI) An analysis of any adverse environmental impacts, methods for mitigating these impacts, and costs of mitigation.

(3) In performing the detailed analysis of alternatives, it may be necessary to gather additional data to complete the analysis.

(i) *Selection of Remedy.* (1) The appropriate extent of remedy shall be determined by the lead agency's selection of a cost-effective remedial alternative which effectively mitigates

and minimizes threats to and provides adequate protection of public health, welfare and the environment. This will require selection of a remedy which attains or exceeds applicable or relevant Federal public health or environmental standards. In making this determination, the lead agency will consider the extent to which the Federal standard(s) are applicable or relevant to the specific circumstances at the site.

(2) In selecting the appropriate extent of remedy from among the alternatives which will achieve adequate protection of public health, welfare and the environment in accordance with (1) of this subsection, the lead agency will consider cost, technology, reliability, administrative and other concerns, and their relevant effects on public health, welfare and the environment.

(3) If there are no applicable or relevant Federal public health or environmental standards, the lead agency will select that cost-effective alternative which effectively mitigates and minimizes threats to and provides adequate protection of public health, welfare, and the environment, considering cost, technology, and the reliability of the remedy.

(4) Applicable or relevant Federal public health and environmental criteria and advisories and State standards shall be used, with appropriate adjustment, in determining the appropriate action.

(5) Notwithstanding paragraph (1)(i) of this section, the lead agency may select an alternative that does not meet applicable or relevant Federal public health or environmental standards in one of the following circumstances:

(i) The selected alternative is not the final remedy and will become part of a more comprehensive remedy.

(ii) All of the alternatives which meet applicable or relevant Federal standards fall into one or more of the following categories:

(A) *Fund-Balancing:* For Fund-financed responses only, considering the amount of money available in the Fund, the need for protection of public health, welfare and the environment at the facility under consideration is outweighed by the need for action at other sites which may present a threat to public health, welfare or the environment. Fund-balancing is not a consideration in determining the appropriate extent of remedy when the response will be performed or funded by a responsible party.

(B) *Technical Impracticality:* No alternative that attains or exceeds applicable or relevant Federal public health or environmental standards is technically practical to implement;

(C) *Unacceptable Environmental Impacts:* The alternatives that attain or exceed applicable or relevant Federal public health or environmental standards, if implemented, will result in significant adverse environmental impacts; or

(iii) Where the remedy is to be carried out pursuant to Federal action under CERCLA section 106, the Fund is unavailable, there is a strong public interest in expedited clean up, and the litigation probably would not result in the desired remedy.

(6) In the event that one of the circumstances in subsection (5) of this section applies, the lead agency shall select that alternative which most closely approaches the level of protection provided by applicable or relevant Federal public health or environmental standards.

(7) (i) If a factor under subsection (i)(5) is used in eliminating an alternative or in scaling down the extent of remedy it must be explained and documented in the appropriate decision document.

(ii) If relevant Federal public health or environmental criteria, advisories or guidance or State standards are not used or are adjusted, the decision documents must explain and document the reasons. The rationale for not using such standards, criteria, advisories or guidance may include one or more of the circumstances enumerated in § 300.68(i)(5).

(j) *Appropriate Actions:* The following remedial actions are as a general rule appropriate in the following situations; however, this list does not limit the lead agency from taking any other actions deemed necessary in response to any situation.

(1) In response to contaminated ground water—elimination or containment of the contamination to prevent further contamination, treatment and/or removal of such ground water to reduce or eliminate the contamination, physical containment of such ground water to reduce or eliminate potential exposure to such contamination, and/or restrictions on use of the ground water to eliminate potential exposure to the contamination.

(2) In response to contaminated surface water—elimination or containment of the contamination to prevent further pollution, and/or treatment of the contaminated water to reduce or eliminate its hazard potential;

(3) In response to contaminated soil or waste—actions to remove, treat, or contain the soil or waste to reduce or eliminate the potential for hazardous substances or pollutants or contaminants to contaminate other

media (ground water, surface water, or air) and to reduce or eliminate the potential for such substances to be inhaled, absorbed, or ingested;

(4) In response to the threat of direct contact with hazardous substances or pollutants or contaminants—any of the actions listed in § 300.65(c) to reduce the likelihood of such contact or the severity of any effects from such contact.

(k) *Remedial Site Sampling:* (1) Sampling performed pursuant to Fund-financed remedial action must have written quality assurance site sampling plan. Sampling performed pursuant to the written quality assurance site sampling plan will be adequate if the quality assurance site sampling plan includes, at a minimum, the following elements:

(i) A description of the objectives of the sampling efforts with regard to both the phase of the sampling and the ultimate use of the data;

(ii) Sufficient specification of sampling protocol and procedures;

(iii) Sufficient sampling to adequately characterize the source of the release, likely transport pathways, and/or potential receptor exposure; and,

(iv) Specifications of the types, locations, and frequency of samples taken, taking into account the unique properties of the site, including the appropriate hydrological, geological, hydrogeological, physiographical, and meteorological properties of the site.

(2) In Fund-financed actions or actions under CERCLA section 106, the quality assurance site sampling plan must be reviewed and approved by the appropriate EPA Regional or Headquarters quality assurance office.

§ 300.69 Documentation and cost recovery.

(a) During all phases of response, documentation shall be collected and maintained to support all actions taken under this Plan, and to form the basis for cost recovery. In general, documentation should be sufficient to provide the source and circumstances of the condition, the identity of responsible parties, accurate accounting of Federal or private party costs incurred, impacts and potential impacts to the public health, welfare and environment. Where applicable, documentation should also include when the National Response Center received notification of a release of a reportable quantity and should clarify when Fund-balancing has been used to limit the Federal response.

(b) The information and reports obtained by the lead agency for Fund-financed response action should be transmitted to the RRC. Copies can then be forwarded to the NRT, members of

the RRT, and others as appropriate. In addition, OSCs shall report as required by § 300.40 for all major releases and all Fund-financed removal actions taken.

(c) Information and documentation of actual or potential natural resource damages shall be made available to the trustees of affected natural resources.

(d) Actions undertaken by the participating agencies in response shall be carried out under existing programs and authorities when available. This plan intends that Federal agencies will make resources available, expend funds, or participate in responses to releases under their existing authority. Authority to expend resources will be in accordance with Agencies' statutes and, if required, through interagency agreements. Where the lead agency requests assistance from a Federal agency, that agency may be reimbursed. Specific interagency reimbursement agreements may be signed when necessary to ensure that the Federal resources will be available for a timely response to a release. The ultimate decision as to the appropriateness of expended funds rests with the agency that is held accountable for such expenditures.

§ 300.70 Methods of remedying releases.

(a) The following section lists methods for remedying releases that may be considered by the lead agency in taking response action. This list of methods should not be considered inclusive of all possible methods of remedying releases.

(b) Engineering Methods for On-Site Actions—(1)(i) *Air emissions control*—The control of volatile gaseous compounds should address both lateral movements and atmospheric emissions. Before gas migration controls can be properly installed, field measurements to determine gas concentrations, pressures, and soil permeabilities should be used to establish optimum design for control. In addition, the types of hazardous substances present, the depth to which they extend, the nature of the gas and the subsurface geology of the release area should, if possible, be determined. Typical emission control techniques include the following:

(A) Pipe vents;
(B) Trench vents;
(C) Gas barriers;
(D) Gas collection;
(E) Overpacking.

(ii) *Surface water controls*—These are remedial techniques designed to reduce water infiltration and to control runoff at release areas. They also serve to reduce erosion and to stabilize the surface of covered sites. These types of

control technologies are usually
implemented in conjunction with other
types of control include the following:

(A) Surface seals;

(B) Surface water diversions and
collection systems;

(1) Dikes and berms;

(2) Ditches, diversions, waterways;

(3) Chutes and downpipes;

(4) Levees;

(5) Seepage basins and ditches;

(6) Sedimentation basins and ditches;

(7) Terraces and benches;

(C) Grading;

(D) Revegetation.

(iii) *Ground water controls*—Ground
water pollution is a particularly serious
problem because, once an aquifer has
been contaminated, the resource cannot
usually be cleaned without the
expenditure of great time, effort and
resources. Techniques that can be
applied to the problem with varying
degrees of success are as follows:

(A) Impermeable barriers;

(1) Slurry walls;

(2) Grout curtains;

(3) Sheet pilings;

(B) Permeable treatment beds;

(C) Ground water pumping;

(1) Water table adjustment;

(2) Plume containment.

(D) Leachate control—Leachate
control systems are applicable to control
of surface seeps and seepage of leachate
to ground water. Leachate collection
systems consist of a series of drains
which intercept the leachate and
channel it to a sump, wetwell, treatment
system, or appropriate surface discharge
point. Technologies applicable to
leachate control include the following:

(1) Subsurface drains;

(2) Drainage ditches;

(3) Liners.

(iv) *Contaminated water and sewer
lines*—Sanitary sewers and municipal
water mains located down gradient from
hazardous waste disposal sites may
become contaminated by infiltration of
leachate or polluted ground water
through cracks, ruptures, or poorly
sealed joints in piping. Technologies
applicable to the control of such
contamination to water and sewer lines
include:

(A) Grouting;

(B) Pipe relining and sleeving;

(C) Sewer relocation.

(2) Treatment technologies.

(i) *Gaseous emissions treatment*—
Gases from waste disposal sites
frequently contain malodorous and toxic
substances, and thus require treatment
before release to the atmosphere. There
are two basic types of gas treatment
systems:

(A) Vapor phase adsorption

(B) Thermal oxidation.

(ii) *Direct waste treatment methods*—
In most cases, these techniques can be
considered long-term permanent
solutions. Many of these direct
treatment methods are not fully
developed and the applications and
process reliability are not well
demonstrated. Use of these techniques
for waste treatment may require
considerable pilot plant work.
Technologies applicable to the direct
treatment of wastes are:

(A) Biological methods:

(1) Treatment via modified
conventional wastewater treatment
techniques;

(2) Anaerobic, aerated and facultative
lagoons;

(3) Supported growth biological
reactors.

(B) Chemical methods;

(1) Chlorination;

(2) Precipitation, flocculation,
sedimentation;

(3) Neutralization;

(4) Equalization;

(5) Chemical oxidation.

(C) Physical methods:

(1) Air stripping;

(2) Carbon absorption;

(3) Ion exchange;

(4) Reverse osmosis;

(5) Permeable bed treatment;

(6) Wet air oxidation;

(7) Incineration.

(iii) *Contaminated soils and
sediments*—In some cases where it can
be shown to be cost-effective,
contaminated sediments and soils will
be treated on the site. Technologies
available include:

(A) Incineration;

(B) Wet air oxidation;

(C) Solidification;

(D) Encapsulation;

(E) In site treatment:

(1) Solution mining (soil washing or
soil flushing);

(2) Neutralization/detoxification;

(3) Microbiological degradation.

(c) Offsite Transport for Storage,
Treatment, Destruction or Secure
Disposition.

(1) General—Offsite transport or
storage, treatment, destruction, or
secure disposition offsite may be
provided in cases where EPA
determines that such actions:

(i) Are most cost-effective than other
forms of remedial actions;

(ii) Will create new capacity to
manage, in compliance with Subtitle C
of the Solid Waste Disposal Act,
hazardous substances in addition to
those located at the affected facility; or

(iii) Are necessary to protect public
health, welfare, or the environment from
a present or potential risk which may be
created by further exposure to the

continued presence of such substances
or materials.

(2) Contaminated soils and sediments
may be removed from the site.
Technologies used to remove
contaminated sediments on soils
include:

(i) Excavation;

(ii) Hydraulic dredging;

(iii) Mechanical dredging.

(d) Provision of Alternative water
supplies can be provided in several
ways.

(1) Provision of individual treatment
units;

(2) Provision of water distribution
system;

(3) Provision of new wells in a new
location or deeper wells;

(4) Provision of cisterns;

(5) Provision of bottled or treated
water;

(6) Provision of upgraded treatment
for existing distribution systems.

(e) *Relocation*—Permanent relocation
of residents, businesses, and community
facilities may be provided where it is
determined that human health is in
danger and that, alone or in combination
with other measures, relocation would
be cost-effective and environmentally
preferable to other remedial response.
Temporary relocation may also be taken
in appropriate circumstances.

§ 300.71 Other party responses.

(a) (1) As an alternative or in addition
to any Fund-financed response, the lead
agency may seek to have those persons
responsible for the release respond to
the release pursuant to CERCLA section
106 and other authorities.

(2) In addition, any person may
undertake a response action to reduce
or eliminate the release or threat of
release of hazardous substances, or
pollutants or contaminants. Section 107
of CERCLA authorizes persons to
recover certain response costs
consistent with this Plan from
responsible parties.

(3) When a person (including a
responsible party) other than the lead
agency takes the response, the lead
agency shall evaluate and approve the
adequacy of proposals submitted when
the response is:

(i) action taken pursuant to
enforcement action under section 106 of
CERCLA; or

(ii) action involving preauthorization
of Fund expenditures, pursuant to
§ 300.25 (d) of this Plan.

(4) In evaluating proposed response
actions specified in (a)(3) above, the
lead agency shall consider the factors
discussed in paragraphs (c) through (i)
of § 300.68 for remedial actions and the

factors discussed in § 300.65(b) for removal actions. The lead agency will not, however, apply the Fund balancing considerations set forth in paragraph (i)(5)(B)(ii)(A) of section 300.68 to determine the appropriate extent of remedy provided by parties under paragraph (a)(3)(i) of this section.

(5) When a responsible party or other person takes a response action in a circumstance other than that specified in (a)(3) above, to be consistent with the NCP for purposes of recovering their costs pursuant to CERCLA section 107 (or for a State or Federal government response, to be not inconsistent), that person must:

(i) Where the action is a removal action, act in circumstances warranting removal and implement removal action consistent with § 300.65.

(ii) Where the action is a remedial action:

(A) Provide for an appropriate analysis of remedial alternatives;

(B) Consider the factors discussed in paragraphs (c) through (i) of § 300.68; and

(C) Select the cost-effective response;

(6) Persons performing response actions which are neither fund-financed nor pursuant to enforcement action under section 106 of CERCLA shall comply with all otherwise legally applicable Federal, State and local requirements, including permit requirements as appropriate.

(b) *Organizations.* Pursuant to CERCLA section 105(9) organizations may assist or conduct site response by:

(1) organizing responsible parties,

(2) initiating negotiation or other cooperative efforts,

(3) apportioning costs among liable parties,

(4) recommending appropriate settlements to the lead agency,

(5) conducting the RI/FS in accordance with this plan,

(6) evaluating and recommending appropriate remedies to the lead agency,

(7) implementing and overseeing response actions

(8) obtaining assurances for continued site maintenance from responsible parties and/or,

(9) recommending sites for deletion after completion of all appropriate response action.

(c) *Certification.* Organizations may be certified to conduct site response actions. Certification is not necessary for, but may facilitate, Fund preauthorization under § 300.25(d) and lead agency evaluation of the adequacy of responsible party proposals.

(1) An organization may request certification by submitting a written request to the Administrator or designee establishing that the requesting organization has engineering, scientific, or other technical expertise necessary to evaluate the appropriate extent of remedy, oversee the design of remedial actions, and/or implement those actions.

(2) For each specific release being addressed, the certified organization must:

(i) Meet the requirements of § 300.25(d) if requesting preauthorization;

(ii) Have established procedures to recuse members of the organization that may have a conflict of interest with a party potentially responsible for the release.

(3) The Administrator will respond to a request for certification within 180 days of receipt of the request. The Administrator may grant certification, request further information relating to the requested certification or deny certification.

(4) Certification is effective for 2 years from the date of latest certification. If certification is not renewed at that time it automatically expires.

(5) Certification is not to be construed as approval by the lead agency of response actions undertaken by that organization. Certification does not authorize that organization to act on behalf of, or as an agent for the lead agency.

(6) Certification may be revoked at the discretion of the Administrator for failure to comply with this Plan or the requirements of CERCLA.

(d) *Releases from Liability.* Implementation of response measures by responsible parties, certified organizations or other persons does not release those parties from liability.

Subpart G—Trustees for Natural Resources

§ 300.72　Designation of Federal Trustees.

When natural resources are lost or damaged as a result of a discharge of oil release of a hazardous substance, the following officials are designated to act as Federal trustees pursuant to section 111(h)(1) of CERLA for purposes of sections 111(h)(1), 111(b) and 107(f) of CERCLA:

(a) (1) *Natural Resource Loss.* Damage to resources of any kind loclated on, over or under land subject to the management or protection of a Federal land managing agency, other than land or resources in or under United States waters that are navigable by deep draft vessels, including waters of the contiguous zone and parts of the high seas to which the National Contingency Plan is applicable and other waters subject to tidal influence.

(2) *Trustee.* The head of the Federal land managing agency, or the head of any other single entity designated by it to act as trustee for a specific resource.

(b) (1) *Natural Resource Loss.* Damage to fixed or non-fixed resources subject to the management or protection of a Federal agency, other than land or resources in or under United States waters that are navigable by deep draft vessels, including waters of the contiguous zone and parts of the high seas to which the National Contingency Plan is applicable and other waters subject to tidal influence.

(2) *Trustee.* The head of the Federal agency authorized to manage or protect these resources by statute, or the head of any other single entity designated by it to act as trustee for a specific resource.

(c) (1) *Natural Resource Loss.* Damage to a resource of any kind subject to the management or protection of a Federal agency and lying in or under United States waters that are navigable by deep draft vessels, including waters of the contiguous zone and parts of the high seas to which the National Contingency Plan is applicable and other waters subject to tidal influence, and upland areas serving as habitat for marine mammals and other species subject to the protective jurisdiction of NOAA.

(2) *Trustee.* The Secretary of Commerce or the head of any other single Federal entity designated by it to act as trustee for a specific resource; provided, however, that where resources are subject to the statutory authorities and jurisdictions of the Secretaries of the Departments of Commerce or the Interior, they shall act as co-trustees.

(d) (1) *National Resource Loss.* Damages to natural resources protected by treaty (or other authority pertaining to Native American tribes) or located on lands held by the United States in trust for Native American communities or individuals.

(2) *Trustee.* The Secretary of the Department of the Interior, or the head of any other single Federal entity disignated by it to act as trustee for specific resources.

§ 300.73　State trustees.

States may act as trustee for natural resouces within the boundary of a State belonging to, managed by, controlled by or appertaining to such State as provided by CERCLA.

§ 300.74　Responsibilities of trustees.

(a) The Federal trustees for natural resources shall be responsible for assessing damages to the resource in accordance with regulations promulgated under section 301(c) of

CERCLA, seeking recovery for the losses from the person resonsible or from the Fund, and devising and carring out restoration, rehabilitation and replacement plans pursuant to CERCLA.

(b) Where there are multiple trustees, because of co-existing or contiguous natural resources or concurrent jurisdictions, they shall coordinate and cooperate in carrying out these responsibilities.

* * * * *

Appendix A—Uncontrolled Hazardous Waste Site Ranking System: A Users Manual (Federal Register Version; July 16, 1982)

Table of Contents

1.0 Introduction

The Comprehensive Environmental Response, Compensation and Liability Act of 1980 (CERCLA) (Pub. L. 96–510) requires the President to identify the 400 facilities in the nation warranting the highest priority for remedial action. In order to set the priorities, CERCLA requires that criteria be established based on relative risk or danger, taking into account the population at risk; the hazardous potential of the substances at a facility; the potential for contamination of drinking water supplies, for direct human contact, and for destruction of sensitive ecosystems; and other appropriate factors.

This document describes the Hazard Ranking System (HRS) to be used in evaluating the relative potential of uncontrolled hazardous substance facilities to cause human health or safety problems, or ecological or environmental damage. Detailed instructions for using the HRS are given in the following sections. Uniform application of the ranking system in each State will permit EPA to identify those releases of hazardous substances that pose the greatest hazard to humans or the environment. However, the HRS by itself cannot establish priorities for the allocation of funds for remedial action. The HRS is a means for applying uniform technica judgement regarding the potential ha :ards presented by a facility relative to other facilities. It does not address the feasibility, desirability, or degree of cleanup required. Neither does it deal with the readiness or ability of a State to carry out such remedial action as may be indicated, or to meet other conditions prescribed in CERCLA.

The HRS assigns three scores to a hazardous facility:

• S_M reflects the potential for harm to humans or the environment from migration of a hazardous substance away from the facility by routes involving ground water, surface water, or air. It is a composite of separate scores for each of the three routes.

• S_{FE} reflects the potential for harm from substances that can explode or cause fires.

• S_{DC} reflects the potential for harm from direct contact with hazardous substances at the facility (i.e., no migration need be involved).

The score for each hazard mode (migration, fire and explosion and direct contact) or route is obtained by considering a set of

factors that characterize the potential of the facility to cause harm (Table 1). Each factor is assigned a numerical value (on a scale of 0 to 3, 5 or 8) according to prescribed guidelines. This value is then multiplied by a weighting factor yielding the factor score. The factor scores are then combined: scores within a factor category are added; when the total scores for each factor category are multiplied together to develop a score for ground water, surface water, air, fire and explosion, and direct contact.

In computing S_{FE} or S_{DC}, or an individual migration route score, the product of its factor category scores is divided by the maximum possible score, and the resulting ratio is multiplied by 100. The last step puts all scores on a scale of 0 to 100.

S_M is composite of the scores for the three possible migration routes;

$$S_M = \frac{1}{1.73}\sqrt{s_{gw}^2 + s_{sw}^2 + s_a^2}$$

where: S_{gw} = ground water route score
S_{sw} = surface water route score
S_a = air route score

The effect of this means of combining the route scores is to emphasize the primary (highest scoring) route in aggregating route scores while giving some additional consideration to the secondary or tertiary routes if they score high. The factor 1/1.73 is used simply for the purpose of reducing S_M scores to a 100-point scale.

The HRS does not quantify the probability of harm from a facility or the magnitude of the harm that could result, although the factors have been selected in order to approximate both those elements of risk. It is a procedure for ranking facilities in terms of the potential threat they pose by describing:

• The manner in which the hazardous substances are contained.

• The route by which they would be released.

• The characteristics and amount of the harmful substances, and

• The likely targets.

The multiplicative combination of factor category scores is an approximation of the more rigorous approach in which one would express the hazard posed by a facility as the product of the probability of a harmful occurrence and the magnitude of the potential damage.

The ranking of facilities nationally for remedial action will be based primarily on S_M. S_{FE} and S_{DC} may be used to identify facilities requiring emergency attention.

2.0 Using the Hazard Ranking System— General Considerations

Use of the HRS requires considerable information about the facility, its surroundings, the hazardous substances present, and the geological character of the area down to the aquifers that may be at risk. Figure 1 illustrates a format for recording general information regarding the facility being evaluated. It can also serve as a cover sheet for the work sheets used in the evaluation.

Where there are no data for a factor, it should be assigned a value of zero. However, if a factor with no data is the only factor in a category (e.g., containment), then the factor is given a score of 1. If data are lacking for more than one factor in connection with the evaluation of either S_{gw}, S_{sw}, S_a, S_{FE} or S_{DC}, that route score is set at zero.

The following sections give detailed instructions and guidance for rating a facility. Each section begins with a work sheet designed to conform to the sequence of steps required to perform the rating. Guidance for evaluating each of the factors then follows. Using the guidance provided, attempt to assign a score for each of the three possible migration routes. Bear in mind that if data are missing for more than one factor in connection with the evaluation of a route, then you must set that route score at 0 (i.e., there is no need to assign scores to factors in a route that will be set at 0).

3.0 Ground Water Migration Route

3.1 Observed Release. If there is direct evidence of release of a substance of concern from a facility to ground water, enter a score of 45 on line 1 of the work sheet for the ground water route (Figure 2); then you need not evaluate route characteristics and containment factors (lines 2 and 3). Direct evidence of release must be analytical. If a contaminant is measured (regardless of frequency) in ground water or in a well in the vicinity of the facility at a significantly (in terms of demonstrating that a release has occurred, not in terms of potential effects) higher level than the background level, then quantitative evidence exists, and a release has been observed. Qualitative evidence of release (e.g., an oily or otherwise objectionable taste or smell in well water) constitutes direct evidence only if it can be confirmed that it results from a release at the facility in question. If a release has been observed, proceed to "3.4 Waste Characteristics" to continue scoring. If direct evidence is lacking, enter a value of 0 on line 1 and continue the scoring procedure by evaluating Route Characteristics.

3.2 Route Characteristics. Depth to aquifer of concern is measured vertically from the lowest point of the hazardous substances to the highest seasonal level of the saturated zone of the aquifer of concern (Figure 3). This factor is one indicator of the ease with which a pollutant from the facility could migrate to ground water. Assign a value as follows:

Distance	Assigned value
>150 feet	0
76 to 150 feet	1
21 to 75 feet	2
0 to 20 feet	3

Net precipitation (precipitation minus evaporation) indicates the potential for leachate generation at the facility. Use net seasonal rainfall (seasonal rainfall minus seasonal evaporation) data if available. If net precipitation is not measured in the region in which the facilty is located, calculate it by subtracting the mean annual lake evaporation for the region (obtained from Figure 4) from the normal annual precipitation for the region (obtained from Figure 5). EPA Regional Offices will have maps for areas outside the continental U.S. Assign a value as follows:

Net precipitation	Assigned value
−10 inches	0
−10 to +5 inches	1
+5 to +15 inches	2
+15 inches	3

Permeability of unsaturated zone (or intervening geological formations) is an indicator of the speed at which a contaminant could migrate from a facility. Assign a value from Table 2.

Physical state refers to the state of the hazardous substances at the time of disposal, except that gases generated by the hazardous substances in a disposal area should be considered in rating this factor. Each of the hazardous substances being evaluated is assigned a value as follows:

Physical state	Assigned value
Solid, consolidated or stabilized	0
Solid, unconsolidated or unstabilized	1
Powder or fine material	2
Liquid, sludge or gas	3

3.3 Containment. Containment is a measure of the natural or artificial means that have been used to minimize or prevent a contaminant from entering ground water. Examples include liners, leachate collection systems, and sealed containers. In assigning a value to this rating factor (Table 3), consider all ways in which hazardous substances are stored or disposed at the facility. If the facility involves more than one method of storage or disposal, assign the highest from among all applicable values (e.g., if a landfill has a containment value of 1, and, at the same location, a surface impoundment has a value of 2, assign containment a value of 2).

3.4 Waste Characteristics. In determining a waste characteristics score, evaluate the most hazardous substances at the facility that could migrate (i.e., if scored, containment is not equal to zero) to ground water. Take the substance with the highest score as representative of the potential hazard due to waste characteristics. Note that the substance that may have been observed in the release category can differ from the substance used in rating waste characteristics. Where the total inventory of substances in a facility is known, only those present in amounts greater than the reportable quantity (see CERCLA section 102 for definition) may be evaluated.

Toxicity and Persistence have been combined in the matrix below because of their important relationship. To determine the overall value for this combined factor, evaluate each factor individually as discussed below. Match the individual values assigned with the values in the matrix for the combined rating factor. Evaluate several of the most hazardous substances at the facility independently and enter only the highest score in the matrix on the work sheet.

Value for toxicity	Value for persistence			
	0	1	2	3
0	0	0	0	0
1	3	6	9	12
2	6	9	12	15
3	9	12	15	18

Persistence of each hazardous substance is evaluated on its biodegradability as follows:

Substance	Assigned value
Easily biodegradable compounds	0
Straight chain hydrocarbons	1
Substituted and other ring compounds	2
Metals, polycyclic compounds and halogenated hydrocarbons	3

More specific information is given in Tables 4 and 5.

Toxicity of each hazardous substance being evaluated is given a value using the rating scheme of Sax (Table 6) or the National Fire Protection Association (NFPA) (Table 7) and the following guidance:

Toxicity	Assigned value
Sax level 0 or NFPA level 0	0
Sax level 1 or NFPA level 1	1
Sax level 2 or NFPA level 2	2
Sax level 3 or NFPA level 3 or 4	3

Table 4 presents values for some common compounds.

Hazardous waste quantity includes all hazardous substances at a facility (as received) except that with a containment value of 0. Do not include amounts of contaminated soil or water; in such cases, the amount of contaminating hazardous substance may be estimated.

On occasion, it may be necessary to convert data to a common unit to combine them. In such cases, 1 ton = 1 cubic yard = 4 drums and for the purposes of converting bulk storage, 1 drum = 50 gallons. Assign a value as follows:

Tons/cubic yards	Number of drums	Assigned value
0	0	0
1 to 10	1 to 40	1
11 to 62	41 to 250	2
63 to 125	251 to 500	3
126 to 250	501 to 1,000	4
251 to 625	1,001 to 2,500	5
626 to 1,250	2,501 to 5,000	6
1,251 to 2,500	5,001 to 10,000	7
>2,500	>10,000	8

3.5 Targets. Ground water use indicates the nature of the use made of ground water drawn from the aquifer of concern within 3 miles of the hazardous substance, including the geographical extent of the measurable concentration in the aquifer. Assign a value using the following guidance:

Ground water use	Assigned value
Unusable (e.g., extremely saline aquifer, extremely low yield, etc.)................................	0
Commercial, industrial or irrigation and another water source presently available; not used, but usable	1
Drinking water with municipal water from alternate unthreatened sources presently available (i.e., minimal hookup requirements); or commercial, industrial or irrigation with no other water source presently available	2
Drinking water; no municipal water from alternate unthreatened sources presently available	3

Distance to nearest well and population served have been combined in the matrix below to better reflect the important relationship between the distance of a population from hazardous substances and the size of the population served by ground water that might be contaminated by those substances. To determine the overall value for this combined factor, score each individually as discussed below. Match the individual values assigned with the values in the matrix for the total score.

Value for population served	Value for distance to nearest well				
	0	1	2	3	4
0	0	0	0	0	0
1	0	4	6	8	10
2	0	8	12	16	20
3	0	12	18	24	30
4	0	16	24	32	35
5	0	20	30	35	40

Distance to nearest well is measured from the hazardous substance (not the facility boundary) to the nearest well that draws water from the aquifer of concern. If the actual distance to the nearest well is unknown, use the distance between the hazardous substance and the nearest occupied building not served by a public water supply (e.g., a farmhouse). If a discontinuity in the aquifer occurs between the hazardous substance and all wells, give this factor a score of 0, except where it can be shown that the contaminant is likely to migrate beyond the discontinuity. Figure 6 illustrates how the distance should be measured. Assign a value using the following guidance:

Distance	Assigned value
>3 miles	0
2 to 3 miles	1
1 to 2 miles	2
2,000 feet to 1 mile	3
<2,000 feet	4

Population served by ground water is an indicator of the population at risk, which includes residents as well as others who would regularly use the water such as workers in factories or offices and students. Include employees in restaurants, motels, or campgrounds but exclude customers and travelers passing through the area in autos, buses, or trains. If aerial photography is used, and residents are known to use ground water, assume each dwelling unit has 3.8 residents. Where ground water is used for irrigation, convert to population by assuming 1.5

persons per acre of irrigated land. The well or wells of concern must be within three miles of the hazardous substances, including the area of known aquifer contamination, but the "population served" need not be. Likewise, people within three miles who do not use water from the aquifer of concern are not to be counted. Assign a value as follows:

Population	Assigned value
0	0
1 to 100	1
101 to 1,000	2
1,001 to 3,000	3
3,001 to 10,000	4
>10,000	5

4.0 Surface Water Route

4.1 *Observed Release.* Direct evidence of release to surface water must be quantitative evidence that the facility is releasing contaminants into surface water. Quantitative evidence could be the measurement of levels of contaminants from a facility in surface water, either at the facility or downhill from it, that represents a significant (in terms of demonstrating that a release has occurred, not in terms of potential effects) increase over background levels. If direct evidence of release has been obtained (regardless of frequency), enter a value of 45 on line 1 of the work sheet (Figure 7) and omit the evaluation of the route characteristics and containment factors. If direct evidence of release is lacking, enter a value of 0 on line 1 and continue with the scoring procedure.

4.2 *Route characteristics. Facility slope and intervening terrain* are indicators of the potential for contaminated runoff or spills at a facility to be transported to surface water. The facility slope is an indicator of the potential for runoff or spills to leave the facility. Intervening terrain refers to the average slope of the shortest path which would be followed by runoff between the facility boundary and the nearest downhill surface water. This rating factor can be assessed using topographic maps. Table 8 shows values assigned to various facility conditions.

One-year 24-hour rainfall (obtained from Figure 8) indicates the potential for area storms to cause surface water contamination as a result of runoff, erosion, or flow over dikes. Assign a value as follows:

Amount of rainfall (inches)	Assigned value
<1.0	0
1.0 to 2.0	1
2.1 to 3.0	2
>3.0	3

Distance to the nearest surface water is the shortest distance from the hazardous substance, (not the facility or property boundary) to the nearest downhill body of surface water (e.g., lake or stream) that is on the course that runoff can be expected to follow and that at least occasionally contains water. Do not include man-made ditches which do not connect with other surface water bodies. In areas having less than 20 inches of normal annual precipitation (see

Figure 5), consider intermittent streams. This factor indicates the potential for pollutants flowing overland and into surface water bodies. Assign a value as follows:

Distance	Assigned value
>2 miles	0
1 to 2 miles	1
1,000 feet to 1 mile	2
<1,000 feet	3

Physical state is assigned a value using the procedures in Section 3.2.

4.3 *Containment. Containment* is a measure of the means that have been taken to minimize the likelihood of a contaminant entering surface water either at the facility or beyond the facility boundary. Examples of containment are diversion structures and the use of sealed containers. If more than one type of containment is used at a facility, evaluate each separately (Table 9) and assign the highest score.

4.4 *Waste Characteristics.* Evaluate waste characteristics for the surface water route with the procedures described in Section 3.4 for the ground water route.

4.5 *Targets. Surface water use* brings into the rating process the use being made of surface water downstream from the facility. The use or uses of interest are those associated with water taken from surface waters within a distance of three miles from the location of the hazardous substance. Assign a value as follows:

Surface water use (fresh or salt water)	Assigned value
Not currently used	0
Commercial or industrial	1
Irrigation, economically important resources (e.g., shellfish), commercial food preparation, or recreation (e.g., fishing, boating, swimming)	2
Drinking water	3

Distance to a sensitive environment refers to the distance from the hazardous substance (not the facility boundary) to an area containing an important biological resource or to a fragile natural setting that could suffer an especially severe impact from pollution. Table 10 provides guidance on assigning a value to this rating factor.

Population served by surface water with water intake within 3 miles downstream from facility (or 1 mile in static surface water such as a lake) is a rough indicator of the potential hazard exposure of the nearby population served by potentially contaminated surface water. Measure the distance from the probable point of entry to surface water following the surface flow (stream miles). The population includes residents as well as others who would regularly use the water such as workers in factories or offices and students. Include employees in restaurants, motels, or campgrounds but exclude customers and travelers passing through the area in autos, buses and trains. The distance is measured from the hazardous substance, including observations in stream or sediment samples, regardless of facility boundaries. Where only residential houses can be counted (e.g., from an aerial photograph), and residents are known to be using surface water, assume 3.8 individuals per dwelling unit. Where surface water is used for irrigation, convert to population by assuming 1.5 persons per acre of land irrigated. Assign a value as follows:

DISTANCE TO SURFACE WATER

Population	>3 miles	2 to 3 miles	1 to 2 miles	2,001 feet to 1 mile	0 to 2,000 feet
0	0	0	0	0	0
1 to 100	0	4	6	8	10
101 to 1,000	0	8	12	16	20
1,001 to 3,000	0	12	18	24	30
3,001 to 10,000	0	16	24	32	35
>10,000	0	20	30	35	40

5.0 Air Route

5.1 *Observed Release.* The only acceptable evidence of release for the air route is data that show levels of a contaminant at or in the vicinity of the facility that significantly exceed background levels, regardless of the frequency of occurrence. If such evidence exists, enter a value of 45 on line 1 of the work sheet (Figure 9); if not, assign line 1 a 0 value and then $S_a=0$. Record the date, location, and the sampling protocol for monitoring data on the work sheet. Data based on transitory conditions due to facility disturbance by investigative personnel are not acceptable.

5.2 *Waste Characteristics.* The hazardous substance that was observed for scoring the release category may be different from the substance used to score waste characteristics.

Reactivity and incompatibility, measures of the potential for sudden release of concentrated air pollutants, are evaluated independently, and the highest value for either is recorded on the work sheet.

Reactivity provides a measure of the fire/explosion threat at a facility. Assign a value based on the reactivity classification used by NFPA (see Table 11). Reactivity ratings for a number of common compounds are given in Table 4.

Incompatibility provides a measure of the increased hazard when hazardous substances are mixed under uncontrolled conditions, leading to production of heat, pressure, fire, explosion, violent reaction, toxic dusts, mists, fumes or gases, or flammable fumes or gases. Table 12 provides examples of incompatible combinations of materials. Additional information can be obtained from *A Method for Determining the Compatibility of Hazardous Wastes,* H. K. Hatayama, *et al.,* EPA-600/2-80-076 (1980). Assign a value using the following guidance:

Incompatibility	Assigned value
No incompatible substances are present	0
Present but do not pose a hazard	1
Present and may pose a future hazard	2
Present and posing an immediate hazard	3

Toxicty should be rated for the most toxic of the substances that can reasonably be expected to be transported away from the facility via the air route. Using the

information given in Tables 4, 6, and 7, assign values as follows:

Toxicity	Assigned value
Sax Level 0 or NFPA level 0	0
Sax Level 1 or NFPA level 1	1
Sax Level 2 or NFPA level 2	2
Sax Level 3 or NFPA level 3 or 4	3

Hazardous Waste Quantity. Assign hazardous waste quantity a value as described in Section 3.4.

5.3 *Targets. Population within a four-mile radius* is an indicator of the population which may be harmed should hazardous substances be released to the air.

The distance is measured from the location of the hazardous substances, not from the facility boundary. The population to be counted includes persons residing within the four-mile radius as well as transients such as workers in factories, offices, restaurants, motels, or students. It excludes travelers passing through the area. If aerial photography is used in making the count, assume 3.8 individuals per dwelling unit. Select the highest value for this rating factor as follows:

DISTANCE TO POPULATION FROM HAZARDOUS SUBSTANCE

Population	1 to 4 miles	½ to 1 mile	¼ to ½ mile	0 to ¼ mile
0	0	0	0	0
1 to 100	9	12	15	18
101 to 1,000	12	15	18	21
1,001 to 3,000	15	18	21	24
3,001 to 10,000	18	21	24	27
>10,000	21	24	27	30

Distance to sensitive environment is an indicator of the likelihood that a region that contains important biological resources or that is a fragile natural setting would suffer serious damage if hazardous substances were to be released from the facility. Assign a value from Table 10.

Land use indicates the nature and level of human activity in the vicinity of a facility. Assign highest applicable value from Table 13.

6.0 Computing the Migration Hazard Mode Score, S_M

To compute S_M, complete the work sheet (Figure 10) using the values of S_{gw}, S_{sw}, and S_{as} obtained from the sections.

7.0 Fire and Explosion

Compute a score for the fire and explosion hazard mode, S_{FE}, when either a state or local fire marshall has certified that the facility presents a significant fire or explosion threat to the public or to sensitive environments or there is a demonstrated fire and explosion threat based on filed observations (e.g., combustible gas indicator readings). Document the threat.

7.1 *Containment. Containment* is an indicator of the measures that have been taken to minimize or prevent hazardous substances at the facility from catching fire or exploding. Normally it will be given a value of 3 on the work sheet (Figure 11). If no

hazardous substances that are individually ignitable or explosive are present and those that may be hazardous in combination are segregated and isolated so that they cannot come together to form incompatible mixtures, assign this factor a value of 1.

7.2 *Waste Characteristics. Direct evidence* of ignitability or explosion potential may exist in the form of measurements with appropriate instruments. If so, assign this factor a value of 3; if not, assign a value of 0.

Ignitability is an indicator of the threat of fire at a facility and the accompanying potential for release of air contaminants. Assign this rating factor a value based on the NEPA classification scheme (Table 14). Table 4 gives values for a number of common compounds. Assign values as follows:

Ignitability	Assigned value
Flashpoint 200 °F. or NEPA level 0	0
Flashpoint 140 °F to 200 °F or NEPA level 1	1
Flashpoint 80 °F to 140 °F or NEPA level 2	2
Flashpoint <80 °F or NEPA levels 3 or 4	3

Reactivity. Assign values as in Section 5.2.

Incompatibility. Assign values as in Section 5.2.

Hazardous Waste Quantity. Assign values as in Section 3.4.

7.3 *Targets. Distance to nearest population* is the distance from the hazardous substance to the nearest building or area in which one or more persons are likely to be located either for residential, educational, business, occupational, or recreational purposes. It is an indicator of the potential for harm to humans from fire and explosion. The building or area need not be off-site. Assign values as follows:

Distance	Assigned value
>2 miles	0
1 mile to 2 miles	1
½ mile to mile	2
210 feet to ½ mile	3
51 feet to 200 feet	4
0 to 50 feet	5

Distance to nearest building is and indicator of the potential for property damage as a result of fire or explosion. Assign a value as follows:

Distance	Assigned value
>½ mile	0
201 feet to ½ mile	1
51 to 200 feet	2
0 to 50 feet	3

Distance to nearest sensitive environment is measured from the hazardous substances, not from the facility boundary. It is an indicator of potential harm to a sensitive environment from fire or explosion at the facility. Select the highest value using the guidance provided in Table 15 *except* assign a value of 3 where fire could be expected to spread to a sensitive environment even though that environment is more than 100 feet from the hazardous substance.

Land Use. Assign values as in section 5.3.

Population within two-mile radius (measured from the location of the hazardous substance, not from the facility boundary) is a rough indicator of the population at risk in the event of fire or explosion at a facility. The population to be counted includes those residing within the two-mile radius as well as people regularly in the vicinity such as workers in factories, offices, or students. It does not include travelers passing through the area. If aerial photography is used in making the count, assume 3.8 individuals per dwelling. Assign values as follows:

Population	Assigned value
0	0
1 to 100	1
101 to 1,000	2
1,001 to 3,000	3
3,001 to 10,000	4
>10,000	5

Number of buildings within two mile radius (measured from the hazardous substance, not from the facility boundary) is a rough indicator of the property damage that could result from fire and explosion at a facility. Assign values to this factor as follows:

Number of buildings	Assigned value
0	0
1 to 26	1
27 to 260	2
261 to 790	3
791 to 2,600	4
>2,600	5

8.0 Direct Contact

The direct contact hazard mode refers to the potential for injury by direct contact with hazardous substances at the facility.

8.1 *Observed Incident.* If there is a confirmed instance in which contact with hazardous substances at a facility has caused injury, illness, or death to humans or domestic or wild animals, enter a value of 45 on line 1 of the work sheet (Figure 12) and proceed to line 4 (toxicity). Document the incident giving the date, location and pertinent details. If no such instance is known, enter "0" on line 1 and proceed to line 2.

8.2 *Accessibility. Accessibility to hazardous substance* refers to the measures taken to limit access by humans or animals to hazardous substances. Assign a value using the following guidance:

Barrier	Assigned value
A 24-hour surveillance system (e.g., television monitoring or surveillance by guards or facility personnel) which continuously monitors and controls entry onto the facility; or an artificial or nautral barrier (e.g., a fence combined with a cliff), which completely surrounds the facility; and a means to control entry, at all times, through the gates or other entrances to the facilitiy (e.g., an attendant, television monitors, locked entrances, or controlled roadway access to the facility)	0
Security guard, but no barrier	1
A barrier, but no separate means to control entry	2
Barriers do not completely surround the facility	3

8.3 *Containment. Containment* indicates whether the hazardous substance itself is accessible to direct contact. For example, if the hazardous substance at the facility is in surface impoundments, containers (sealed or unsealed), piles, tanks, or landfills with a cover depth of less than 2 feet, or has been spilled on the ground or other surfaces easily contacted (e.g., the bottom of shallow pond or creek), assign this rating factor a value of 15. Otherwise, assign a value of 0.

8.4 *Waste Characteristics. Toxicity.* Assign a value as in section 3.4.

8.5 *Targets. Population within one-mile radius* is a rough indicator of the population that could be involved in direct contact incidents at an uncontrolled facility. Assign a value as follows:

Population	Assigned value
0	0
1 to 100	1
101 to 1,000	2
1,001 to 3,000	3
3,001 to 10,000	4
>10,900	5

Distance to a critical habitat (of an endangered species) is a rough measure of the probability of harm to members of an endangered species by direct contact with hazardous substance. Assign a value as follows:

Distance	Assigned value
>1 mile	0
½ to 1 mile	1
¼ to ½ mile	2
<¼ mile	3

TABLE 1

COMPREHENSIVE LIST OF RATING FACTORS

HAZARD MODE	FACTOR CATEGORY	FACTORS		
		GROUND WATER ROUTE	SURFACE WATER ROUTE	AIR ROUTE
Migration	Route Characteristics	• Depth to Aquifer of Concern • Net Precipitation • Permeability of Unsaturated Zone • Physical State	• Facility Slope and Intervening Terrain • One-Year 24-Hour Rainfall • Distance to Nearest Surface Water • Physical State	
	Containment	• Containment	• Containment	
	Waste Characteristics	• Toxicity/Persistence • Hazardous Waste Quantity	• Toxicity/Persistence • Hazardous Waste Quantity	• Reactivity/Incompatibility • Toxicity • Hazardous Waste Quantity
	Targets	• Ground Water Use • Distance to Nearest Well/ Population Served	• Surface Water Use • Distance to Sensitive Environment • Population Served/Distance to Water Intake Downstream	• Land Use • Population Within 4-Mile Radius • Distance to Sensitive Environment
Fire and Explosion	Containment	• Containment		
	Waste Characteristics	• Direct Evidence • Ignitability • Reactivity • Incompatibility • Hazardous Waste Quantity		
	Targets	• Distance to Nearest Population • Distance to Nearest Building • Distance to Nearest Sensitive Environment • Land Use • Population Within 2-Mile Radius • Number of Buildings Within 2-Mile Radius		
Direct Contact	Observed Incident	• Observed Incident		
	Accessibility	• Accessibility of Hazardous Substances		
	Containment	• Containment		
	Toxicity	• Toxicity		
	Targets	• Population Within 1-Mile Radius • Distance to Critical Habitat		

TABLE 2.— PERMEABILITY OF GEOLOGIC MATERIALS*

Type of material	Aproximate range of hydraulic conductivity	Assigned value
Clay, compact till, shale; unfractured metamorphic and igneous rocks.	<10⁻⁷ cm/sec......	0
Silt, loess, silty clays, silty loams, clay loams; less permeable limestone, dolomites, and sandstone; moderately permeable till.	<10⁻⁵>10⁻⁷ cm/ sec.	1
Fine sand and silty sand; sandy loams; loamy sands; moderately permeable limestone, dolomites, and sandstone (no karst); moderately fractured igneous and metamorphic rocks, some coarse till.	<10⁻³>10⁻⁵ cm/ sec.	2
Gravel, sand; highly fractured igneous and metamorphic rocks; permeable basalt and lavas; karst limestone and dolomite.	>10⁻³ cm/sec......	3

* Derived from:

Davis, S.N., *Porosity and Permeability of Natural Materials in Flow-Through Porous Media*, R.J.M. DeWest ed., Academic Press, New York, 1969.
Freeze, R.A. and J.A. Cherry, *Groundwater*, Prentice-Hall, Inc., New York, 1979.

TABLE 3.—CONTAINMENT VALUES FOR GROUND WATER ROUTE

[Assign containment a value of 0 if: (1) All the hazardous substances at the facility are underlain by an essentially non permeable surface (natural or artificial) and adequate leachate collection systems and diversion systems are present; or (2) there is no ground water in the vicinity. The value "0" does not indicate no risk. Rather, it indicates a significantly lower relative risk when compared with more serious sites on a national level. Otherwise, evaluate the containment for each of the different means of storage or disposal at the facility using the following guidance]

	Assigned value
A. Surface Impoundment	
Sound run-on diversion structure, essentially non permeable liner (natural or artificial) compatible with the waste, and adequate leachate collection system	0
Essentially non permeable compatible liner with no leachate collection system; or inadequate freeboard	1

TABLE 3.—CONTAINMENT VALUES FOR GROUND WATER ROUTE—Continued

[Assign containment a value of 0 if: (1) All the hazardous substances at the facility are underlain by an essentially non permeable surface (natural or artificial) and adequate leachate collection systems and diversion systems are present; or (2) there is no ground water in the vicinity. The value "0" does not indicate no risk. Rather, it indicates a significantly lower relative risk when compared with more serious sites on a national level. Otherwise, evaluate the containment for each of the different means of storage or disposal at the facility using the following guidance]

	Assigned value
Potentially unsound run-on diversion structure; or moderately permeable compatible liner	2
Unsound run-on diversion structure; no liner; or incompatible liner	3
B. Containers	
Containers sealed and in sound condition, adequate liner, and adequate leachate collection system	0
Containers sealed and in sound condition, no liner or moderately permeable liner	1
Containers leaking, moderately permeable liner	2

TABLE 3.—CONTAINMENT VALUES FOR GROUND WATER ROUTE—Continued

[Assign containment a value of 0 if: (1) All the hazardous substances at the facility are undertain by an essentially non permeable surface (natural or artificial) and adequate leachate collection systems and diversion systems are present; or (2) there is no ground water in the vicinity. The value "0" does not indicate no risk. Rather, it indicates a significantly lower relative risk when compared with more serious sites on a national level. Otherwise, evaluate the containment for each of the different means of storage or disposal at the facility using the following guidance.]

	Assigned value
Containers leaking and no liner or incompatible liner	3
C. Piles	
Piles uncovered and waste stabilized; or piles covered, waste unstabilized, and essentially non permeable liner	0
Piles uncovered, waste unstabilized, moderately permeable liner, and leachate collection system	1
Piles uncovered, waste unstabilized, moderately permeable liner, and no leachate collection system	2
Piles uncovered, waste unstabilized, and no liner ...	3
D. Landfill	
Essentially non permeable liner, liner compatible with waste, and adequate leachate collection system	0
Essentially non permeable compatible liner, no leachate collection system, and landfill surface precludes ponding..........	1
Moderately permeable, compatible liner, and landfill surface precludes ponding	2
No liner or incompatible liner; moderately permeable compatible liner; landfill surface encourages ponding; no run-on control	3

TABLE 4.—WASTE CHARACTERISTICS VALUES FOR SOME COMMON CHEMICALS

Chemical/ Compound	Tox- icity[1]	Persist- ence[2]	Ignit- ability[3]	Reac- tivity[3]	Vola- tility[1]
Acetalde- hyde..........	3	0	3	2	*3
Acetic acid	3	0	2	1	1
Acetone	2	0	3	0	3
Aldrin	3	3	1	0	*0
Ammonia, anhydrous...	3	0	1	0	3
Aniline	3	1	2	0	1
Benzene	3	1	3	0	3
Carbon tetrachlo- ride	3	3	0	0	3
Chlordane.....	3	3	*0	*0	*0
Chloroben- zene..........	2	2	3	0	1
Chloroform.....	3	3	0	0	3
Cresol-O	3	1	2	0	1
Cresol-M&P ...	3	1	1	0	1
Cyclohexane ...	2	2	3	0	3
Endrin..........	3	3	1	0	*0
Ethyl benzene	2	1	3	0	1
Formalde- hyde..........	3	0	2	0	*3
Fromic acid ...	3	0	2	0	2
Hydrochloric acid..........	3	0	0	0	3
Isopropyl ether..........	3	1	3	1	3
Lindane..........	3	3	1	0	0
Methane..........	1	1	3	0	*3
Methyl ethyl ketone	2	0	3	0	2
Methyl parathion in kylene solution	3	3	3	2	*2

TABLE 4.—WASTE CHARACTERISTICS VALUES FOR SOME COMMON CHEMICALS—Continued

Chemical/ Compound	Tox- icity[1]	Persist- ence[2]	Ignit- ability[3]	Reac- tivity[3]	Vola- tility[1]
Naphthalene...	2	1	2	0	1
Nitric acid	3	0	0	0	*3
Parathion	3	3	1	2	*0
PCB	3	3	Δ0	Δ0	Δ0
Petroleum Kerosene (fuel oil No. 1)	3	1	2	0	*1
Phenol..........	3	1	2	0	1
Sulfuric Acid ...	3	0	0	2	1
Toluene..........	2	1	3	0	2
Trichloroben- zene..........	2	3	1	0	1
α- Trichlor- oethane..........	2	2	1	0	3
Xylene..........	2	1	3	0	1

[1] Sax, N.I., *Dangerous Properties of Industrial Materials*, Van Nostrand Rheinhold Co., New York, 4th ed., 1975. The highest rating listed under each chemical is used.

[2] JRB Associates, Inc., *Methodology for Rating the Hazard Potential of Waste Disposal Sites*, May 5, 1980.

[3] National Fire Protection Association, National Fire Codes, Vol. 13, No. 49, 1977.

* Professional judgment based on information contained in the U.S. Coast Guard CHRIS Hazardous Chemical Data, 1978.

Δ Professional judgment based on existing literature.

TABLE 5.—PERSISTENCE (BIODEGRADABILITY) OF SOME ORGANIC COMPOUNDS *

Value—3 Highly Persistent Compounds

aldrin	heptachlor
benzopyrene	heptachlor epoxide
benzothiazole	1,2,3,4,5,7,7- heptachloronoronorbornene
benzothiophene	hexachlorobenzene
benzyl butyl phthalate	hexachloror-1,3,-butadiene
bromochlorobenzene	hexachlorocyclohexane
bromoform butanol	hexachloroethane
bromophenyl phyntl ether	methyl benzothiazole
chlordane	pentachlorobiphenyl
chlorohydroxy benzophenone	pentachlorophenol
bis-chloroisoprophyl ether	1,1,3,3-tetrachloroacentone
m-chloronitrobenzene	tetrachlorobiphenyl
DDE	thiomethylbenzothiazole
DDT	trichlorobenzene
dibromobenzene	trichlorobiphenyl
dibutyl phthalate	trichlorofluoromethane
1,4-dichlorobenzene	2,4,6-trichlorophenol
dichlorodifluoroethane	triphenyl phosphate
dieldrin	bromodichloromethane
diethyl phtalate	bromoform
di (2-ethylhexyl) phthalate	carbon tetrachloride
dihexyl phthalate	chloroform
di-isobutyl phthalate	chloromochloromethane
dimethyl phthalate	dibromodichloroethane
4,6-dinitro-2-aminophenol	tetrachloroethane
dipropyl phthalate	1,1,2-trichloroethane
endrin	

Value—2 Highly Persistent Compounds

acenaphthylene	cis-2-ethyl-4-methyl-1,3- dioxolane
atrazine	trans-2-ehtyl-4-methyl-1,3- dioxolane
(diethyl) atrazine	guaiacol
barbital	2-hydroxyadiponitrile
borneol	isophorone
bromobenzene	indene
camphor	isoborneol
chlorobenzene	isopropenyl-r-isopropyl ben- zene
1,2,-bis-chloroethoxy ethane	2-methoxy biphenyl
b-chloroethyl methyl ether	methyl biphenyl
chloromethyl ether	methyl chloride
chloromethyl ethyl ether	methylidene
3-chloropyridine	methylene chloride
di-t-butyl-p-benzoquinone	nitroanisole

TABLE 5.—PERSISTENCE (BIODEGRADABILITY) OF SOME ORGANIC COMPOUNDS *—Continued

dichloroethyl ether	nitrobenzene
dihyrocarvone	1,1,2,-trichloroethylene
dimethyl sulfoxide	tnmethyl-trioxo-hexahydro- traizine isomer
2,6-dinitrototuene	

Value—1 Somewhat Persistent Compounds

acetylene dichloride	limonene
behenic acid, methyl ester	methyl ester of lignocenc acid
benzene	methane
benzene sulfonic acid	2-methyl-5-ethyl-pyridine
butyl benzene	methyl naphtalene
butyl bromide	methyl palmitate
e-caprolactam	methyl phenyl carbinol
carbon-disulfide	methyl stearate
o-cresol	naphthalene
decane	nonane
1,2-dichloroethane	octane
1,2-dimethoxy benzene	octyl chloride
1,3-dimethyl naphthalene	pentane
1,4-dimethyl phenol	phenyl benzoate
dioctyl adipate	phtalic andhydride
n-dodecane	propylbenzene
ethyl benzene	1-terpinnel
2-ethyl-n-hexane	toluene
o-ethyltoluene	vinly benzene
isodecane	xylene
isoprophyl benzene	

Value—0 Highly Nonpersistent Compounds

acetaldehyde	methyl benzoate
acetic acid	3-methyl butanol
acetone	methyl ethyl ketone
acetophenone	2-methylpropanol
benzoic acid	octadecane
di-isobutyl carbinol	pentadecane
docosane	pentanol
eicosane	propanol
ethanol	propylamines
ethylamine	tetradecane
hexadecane	n-tridecane
methanol	n-undecane

* JRB Associates, Inc., *Methodology for Rating the Hazard Potential for Waste Disposal Sites*, May 5, 1980.

TABLE 6.—SAX TOXICITY RATINGS*

0 = No Toxicity

This designation is given to materials which fall into one of the following categories:

(a) Materials which cause no harm under any conditions of normal use.

(b) Materials which produce toxic effects on humans only under the most unusual conditions or by overwhelming dosage.

1 = Slight Toxicity

(a) *Acute local.* Materials which on single exposures lasting seconds, minutes, or hours cause only slight effects on the skin or mucuous membranes regardless of the extent of the exposure.

(b) *Acute systemic.* Materials which can be absorbed into the body by inhalation, ingestion, or through the skin and which produce only slight effects following single exposures lasting seconds, minutes, or hours, or following ingestion of a single dose, regardless of the quantity absorbed or the extent of exposure.

(c) *Chronic local.* Materials which on continuous or repeated exposures extending over periods of days, months, or years cause only slight and usually reversible harm to the skin or mucous membranes. The extent of exposure may be great or small.

(d) *Chronic systemic.* Materials which can be absorbed into the body by inhalation, ingestion, or through the skin and which produce only slightly usually reversible effects extending over days, months, or years. The extent of the exposure may be great or small.

In general, those substances classified as having "slight toxicity" produce changes in the human body which are readily reversible and which will disappear following termination of exposure, either with or without medical treatment.

TABLE 6.—SAX TOXICITY RATINGS*—Continued

2 = Moderate Toxicity

(a) *Acute local.* Materials which on single exposure lasting seconds, minutes, or hours cause moderate effects on the skin or mucous membranes. These effect may be the result of intense exposure for a matter or seconds or moderate exposure for a matter of hours.

(b) *Acute systemic.* Materials which can be absorbed into the body by inhalation, ingestion, or through the skin and produce moderate effects following single exposures lasting seconds, minutes, or hours, or following ingestion of a single dose.

(c) *Chronic local.* Materials which on continuous or repeated exposures extending over periods of days, months, or years cause moderate harm to the skin or mucous membranes.

(d) *Chronic systemic.* Materials which can be absorbed into the body by inhalation, ingestion, or through the skin and which produce moderate effects following continuous or repeated exposure extending over periods of days, months, or years.

Those substances classified as having "moderate toxicity" may produce irreversible as well as reversible changes in the human body. Those changes are not of such severity as to threaten life or to produce serious physical impairment.

3 = Severe Toxicity

(a) *Acute local.* Materials which on single exposure lasting seconds or minutes cause injury to skin or mucous membranes or sufficient severity to threaten life or the cause permanent physical impairment or disfigurement.

(b) *Acute systemic.* Materials which can be absorbed into the body by inhalation, ingestion, or through the skin and which can cause injury of sufficient severity to threaten life following a single exposure lasting seconds, minutes, or hours, or following ingestion of a single dose.

(c) *Chronic local.* Materials which on continuous or repeated exposures extending over periods of days, months, or years can cause injury to skin or mucous membranes of sufficient severity to threaten life or cause permanent impairment, which disfigurement, or irreversible change.

(d) *Chronic systemic.* Materials which can be absorbed into the body by inhalation, ingestion, or through the skin and which can cause death or serious physical impairment following continuous or repeated exposures to small amounts extending over periods of days, months, or years.

*Sax, N.I., *Dangerous Properties of Industrial Materials*, Van Nostrand Rheinhold Company, New York, 4th Edition, 1975.

TABLE 7.—NFPA TOXICITY RATINGS*

0	Materials which on exposure under fire conditions would offer no health hazard beyond that of ordinary combustible material.
1	Materials only slightly hazardous to health. It may be desirable to wear self-contained breathing apparatus.
2	Materials hazardous to health, but areas may be entered freely with self-contained breathing apparatus.
3	Materials extremely hazardous to health, but areas may be entered with extreme care. Full protective clothing, including self-contained breathing apparatus, rubber gloves, boots and bands around legs, arms and waist should be provided. No skin surface should be exposed.
4	A few whiffs of the gas or vapor could cause death, or the gas, vapor, or liquid could be fatal on penetrating the fire fighters' normal full protective clothing which is designed for resistance to heat. For most chemicals having a Health 4 rating, the normal full protective clothing available to the average fire department will not provide adequate protection against skin contact with these materials. Only special protective clothing designed to protect against the specific hazard should be worn.

* National Fire Protection Association. *National Fire Codes*, Vol. 13, No. 49, 1977.

TABLE 8.—VALUES FOR FACILITY SLOPE AND INTERVENING TERRAIN

Facility slope	Terrain average slope <3%; or site separated from water body by areas of higher elevation	Terrain average slope 3 to 5%	Terrain average slope 5 to 8%	Terrain average slope >8%	Site in surface water
Facility is closed basin	0	0	0	0	3
Facility has average slope <3%	0	1	1	2	3
Average slope 3 to 5%	0	1	2	2	3
Average slope 5 to 8%	0	2	2	3	3
Average slope >8%	0	2	3	3	3

TABLE 9.—CONTAINMENT VALUES FOR SURFACE WATER ROUTE

[Assign containment a value of 0 if: (1) All the waste at the site is surrounded by diversion structures that are in sound condition and adequate to contain all runoff, spills, or leaks from the waste; or (2) intervening terrain precludes runoff from entering surface water. Otherwise, evaluate the containment for each of the different means of storage of disposal at the site and assign a value as follows]

	Assigned value
A. Surface Impoundment	
Sound diking or diversion structure, adequate freeboard, and no erosion evident	0
Sound diking or diversion structure, but inadequate freeboard	1

TABLE 9.—CONTAINMENT VALUES FOR SURFACE WATER ROUTE—Continued

[Assign containment a value of 0 if: (1) All the waste at the site is surrounded by diversion structures that are in sound condition and adequate to contain all runoff, spills, or leaks from the waste; or (2) intervening terrain precludes runoff from entering surface water. Otherwise, evaluate the containment for each of the different means of storage of disposal at the site and assign a value as follows]

	Assigned value
Diking not leaking, but potentially unsound	2
Diking unsound, leaking, or in danger of collapse	3
B. Containers	
Containers sealed, in sound condition, and surrounded by sound diversion or containment system	0
Containers sealed and in sound condition, but not surrounded by sound diversion or containment system	1
Containers leaking and diversion or containment structures potentially unsound	2
Containers leaking, and no diversion or containment structures or diversion structures leaking or in danger of collapse	3
C. Waste Piles	
Piles are covered and surrounded by sound diversion or containment system	0
Piles covered, wastes unconsolidated, diversion or containment system not adequate	1
Piles not covered, wastes unconsolidated, and diversion or containment system potentially unsound	2
Piles not covered, wastes unconsolidated, and no diversion or containment of diversion system leaking or in danger of collapse	3
D. Landfill	
Landfill slope precludes runoff, landfill surrounded by sound diversion system, or landfill has adequate cover material	0
Landfill not adequately covered and diversion system sound	1
Landfill not covered and diversion system potentially unsound	2
Landfill not covered and no diversion system present, or diversion system unsound	3

TABLE 10.—Values for Sensitive Environment (Surface Water)

Assigned value =	0	1	2	3
Distance to wetlands* (5 acre minimum):				
Coastal	>2 miles	1 to 2 miles	½ to 1 mile	< ½ mile
Fresh Water	>1 mile	¼ to 1 mile	100 feet to ¼ mile	< 100 feet
Distance to critical habitat (of endangered species)** or National Wildlife Refuge.	>1 mile	½ to 1 mile	¼ to ½ mile	< ¼ mile

* Wetland is defined by EPA in the Code of Federal Regulations 40 CFR Part 230, Appendix A, 1980.
** Endangered species are designated by the U.S. Fish and Wildlife Service.

TABLE 11.—NFPA REACTIVITY RATINGS

NFPA level	Assigned value
0	Materials which are normally stable even under fire exposure conditions and which are not reactive with water	0
1	Materials which in themselves are normally stable but which may become unstable at elevated temperatures and pressures or which may react with water with some release of energy but not violently	1
2	Materials which in themselves are normally unstable and readily undergo violent chemical change but do not detonate.	

TABLE 11.—NFPA REACTIVITY RATINGS—Continued

NFPA level	Assigned value
Includes materials which can undergo chemical change with rapid release of energy at normal temperatures and pressures or which can undergo violent chemical changed at elevated temperatures and pressures. Also includes those materials which may react violently with water or which may form potentially explosive mixtures with water	2

TABLE 11.—NFPA REACTIVITY RATINGS—Continued

NFPA level		Assigned value
3	Materials which in themselves are capable of detonation or of explosive decomposition or of explosive reaction but which requires a strong initiating source or which must be heated under confinement before initiation. Includes materials which are sensitive to thermal or mechanical shock at elevated temperatures and pressures or which react explosively with water without requiring heat or confinement	3
4	Materials which in themselves are readily capable of detonation or of explosive decomposition or explosive reaction at normal temperatures and pressures. Includes materials which are sensitive to mechanical or localized thermal shock	3

TABLE 12.—INCOMPATIBLE MATERIALS

[In the lists below, the mixing of a Group A material with a Group B material may have the potential consequence as noted]

Group 1-A	Group 1-B
Acetylene sludge	Acid sludge
Alkaline caustic liquids	Acid and water
Alkaline cleaner	Battery acid
Alkaline corrosive liquids	Chemical cleaners
Alkaline corrosive battery fluid	Electrolyte acid
Caustic wastewater	Etching acid liquid or solvent
Lime sludge and other corrosive alkalies	Pickling liquor and other corrosive acids
Lime wastewater	Spent acid
Lime and water	Spent mixed acid
Spent caustic	Spent sulfuric acid

Potential consequences: Heat generation; violent reaction.

Group 2-A	Group 2-B
Aluminum	Any waste in Group 1-A or 1-B
Berylium	
Calcium	
Lithium	
Potassium	
Sodium	
Zinc Powder	
Other reactive metals and metal hydrides	

Potential consequences: Fire or explosion; generation of flammable hydrogen gas.

Group 3-A	Group 3-B
Alcohols	Any concentrated waste in Groups 1-A or 1-B
Water	Calcium
	Lithium
	Metal hydrides
	Potassium
	SO_2Cl_2, $SOCl_2$, PCl_3, CH_3, $SiCl_4$
	Other water-reactive waste

Potential consequences: Fire, explosion, or heat generation; generation of flammable or toxic gases.

TABLE 12.—INCOMPATIBLE MATERIALS—Continued

[In the lists below, the mixing of a Group A material with a Group B material may have the potential consequence as noted]

Group 4-A	Group 4-B
Alcohols	Concentrated Group 1-A or 1-B wastes
Aldehydes	Group 2-A wastes
Halogenated hydrocarbons	
Nitrated hydrocarbons	
Unsaturated hydrocarbons	
Other reactive organic compounds and solvents	

Potential consequences: Fire, explosion, or violent reaction.

Group 5-A	Group 5-B
Spent cyanide and sulfide solutions	Group 1-B wastes

Potential consequences: Generation of toxic hydrogen cyanide or hydrogen sulfide gas.

TABLE 12.—INCOMPATIBLE MATERIALS—Continued

In the lists below, the mixing of a Group A material with a Group B material may have the potential consequence as noted]

Group 6-A	Group 6-B
Chlorates	Acetic acid and other organic acids
Chlorine	Concentrated mineral acids
Chlorites	Group 2-A wastes
Chromic acid	Group 4-A wastes
Hypochlorities	Other flammable and combustible wastes
Nitrates	
Nitric acid, fuming	
Perchlorates	
Permanganates	
Peroxides	
Other strong oxidizers	

Potential consequences: Fire, explosion, or violent reaction.

Source: Hazardous Waste Management Law, Regulations, and Guidelines for the Handling of Hazardous Waste. California Department of Health, Sacramento, California, February 1975.

TABLE 13.—VALUES FOR LAND USE (AIR ROUTE)

Assigned value =	0	1	2	3
Distance to Commercial-Industrial.	>1 mile	½ to 1 mile	¼ to ½ mile	< ¼ mile
Distance to National/State Parks, Forests, Wildlife Reserves, and Residential Areas.	>2 miles	1 to 2 miles	¼ to 1 mile	< ¼ mile
Distance to Agricultural Lands (in Production within 5 years):				
Ag Land	>1 mile	½ to 1 mile	¼ to ½ mile	< ¼ mile
Prime Ag Land *	2 miles	1 to 2 miles	½ to 1 mile	< ½ mile
Distance to Historic/Landmark Sites (National Register of Historic Places and National Natural Landmarks).				Within view of site or if site is subject to significant impacts

* Defined in the Code of Federal Regulations, 7 CFR 657.5, 1981.

TABLE 14.—NFPA IGNITABILITY LEVELS AND ASSIGNED VALUES

NFPA level	Assigned value
4 Very flammable gases, very volatile flammable liquids, and materials that in the form of dusts or mists readily form explosive mixtures when dispersed in air	3
3 Liquids which can be ignited under all normal temperature conditions. Any materials that ignites spontaneously at normal temperatures in air	
2 Liquids which must be moderately heated before ignition will occur and solids that readily give off flammable vapors	2
1 Materials that must be preheated before ignition can occur. Most combustible solids have a flammability rating of 1	1
0 Materials that will not burn	0

TABLE 15.—VALUES FOR SENSITIVE ENVIRONMENTS (FIRE AND EXPLOSION)

Assigned value =	0	1	2	3
Distance to Wetlands*	>100 feet			<100 feet
Distance to critical habitat**	> ½ mile	1,000 feet to ½ mile	100 to 1,000 feet	<100 feet

* Wetland is defined by EPA in the Code of Federal Regulations 40 CFR Part 230, Appendix A, 1980.
** Designated by the U.S. Fish and Wildlife Service.

BILLING CODE 6560-50-M

GROUND WATER ROUTE WORK SHEET

	Rating Factor	Assigned Value (Circle One)	Multiplier	Score	Max. Score	Ref. (Section)
1	OBSERVED RELEASE	0 45	1		45	3.1
	If observed release is given a score of 45, proceed to line [6].					
	If observed release is given a score of 0, proceed to line [2].					
2	ROUTE CHARACTERISTICS					3.2
	Depth to Aquifer of Concern	0 1 2 3	2		6	
	Net Precipitation	0 1 2 3	1		3	
	Permeability of the Unsaturated Zone	0 1 2 3	1		3	
	Physical State	0 1 2 3	1		3	
	Total Route Characteristics Score				15	
3	CONTAINMENT	0 1 2 3	1		3	3.3
4	WASTE CHARACTERISTICS					3.4
	Toxicity/Persistence	0 3 6 9 12 15 18	1		18	
	Hazardous Waste Quantity	0 1 2 3 4 5 6 7 8	1		8	
	Total Waste Characteristics Score				26	
5	TARGETS					3.5
	Ground Water Use	0 1 2 3	3		9	
	Distance to Nearest Well/Population Served	0 4 6 8 10 12 16 18 20 24 30 32 35 40	1		40	
	Total Targets Score				49	
6	If line [1] is 45, multiply [1] x [4] x [5]					
	If line [1] is 0, multiply [2] x [3] x [4] x [5]				57,330	
7	Divide line [6] by 57,330 and multiply by 100				S_{gw} =	

Figure 2

Ground Water Route Work Sheet

41

Facility Name: _____

Location: _____

EPA Region: _____

Person(s) in Charge of the Facility: _____

Name of Reviewer: _____ Date: _____

General Description of the Facility:

(For example: landfill, surface impoundment, pile, container; types of hazardous substances; location of the facility; contamination route of major concern; types of information needed for rating; agency action, etc.)

_____

_____

_____

_____

Scores: S_M = _____ (S_{gw} = _____ S_{sw} = _____ S_a = _____)

S_{FE} = _____

S_{DC} = _____

Figure 1

HRS COVER SHEET

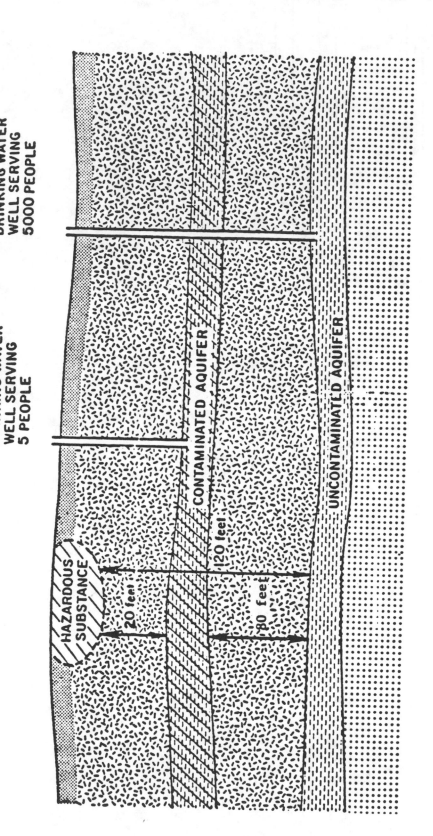

FIGURE 3.   DEPTH TO AQUIFER OF CONCERN*

*Treat target and route characteristics factors consistently. For example, if the upper aquifer is the aquifer of concern, then the "depth to aquifer of concern" is 20 feet and the "population served" is 5 persons. If the lower aquifer is "of concern", the "depth" is 120 feet (assuming no known contamination below the indicated "hazardous substance") and the "population" is 5000 persons. If the upper aquifer is contaminated and the lower aquifer is "of concern", the "depth" would be 80 feet (vertical distance between hazardous substance and aquifer of concern) and the population would be 5000 persons.

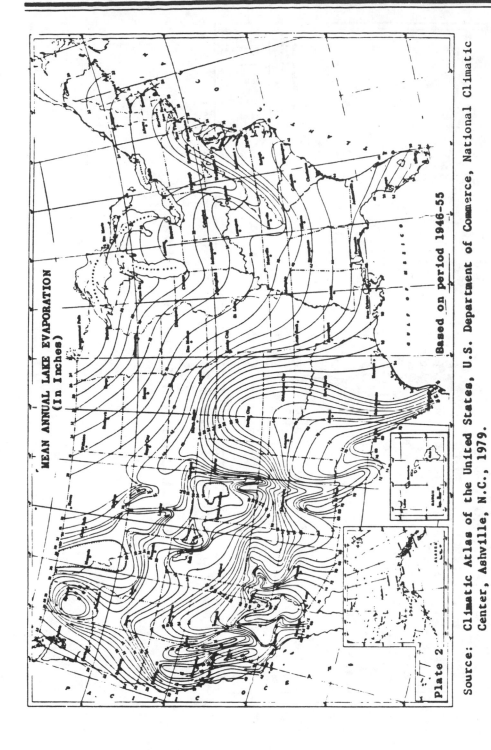

Source: Climatic Atlas of the United States, U.S. Department of Commerce, National Climatic
Center, Ashville, N.C., 1979.

FIGURE 4
MEAN ANNUAL LAKE EVAPORATION
(IN INCHES)

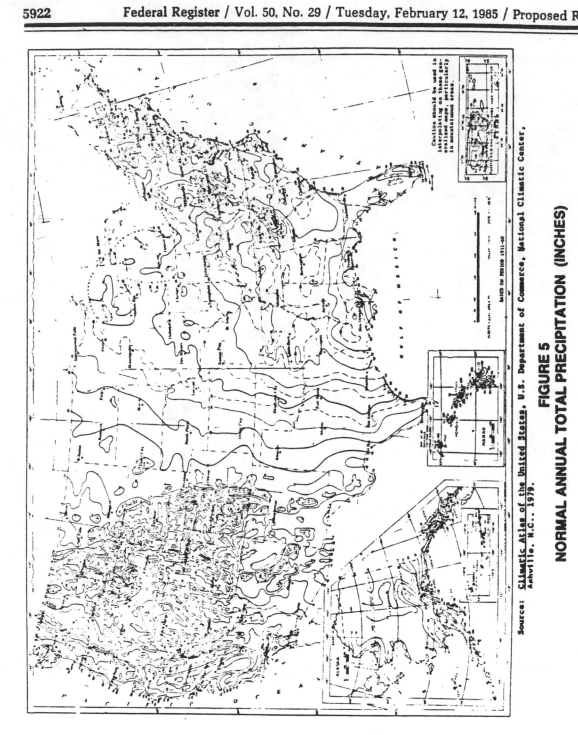

FIGURE 5
NORMAL ANNUAL TOTAL PRECIPITATION (INCHES)

Source: Climatic Atlas of the United States, U.S. Department of Commerce, National Climatic Center, Asheville, N.C., 1979.

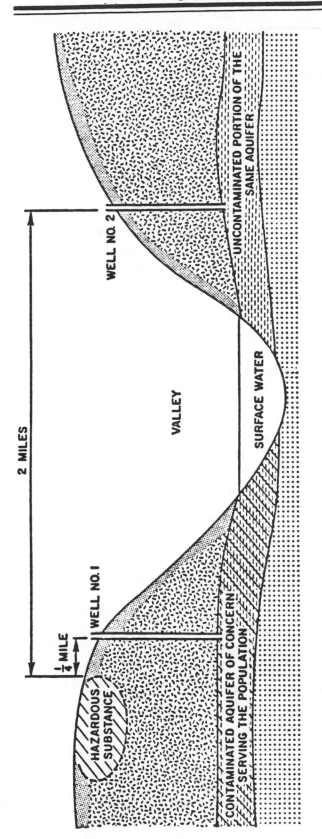

FIGURE 6

Distance to Nearest Well

In the situation depicted above, the distance between the hazardous substance and the nearest well (No. 1) is ¼ mile. If well No. 1 did not exist, the distance to well No. 2 would be immaterial since there is a discontinuity in the aquifer (surface water) between it and the hazardous substance. Under such circumstances, the factor score would be "0". However, if it could be demonstrated that the contaminant had migrated beyond the discontinuity, then the distance to the nearest well would be 2 miles (assuming well No. 1 does not exist).

SURFACE WATER ROUTE WORK SHEET

Rating Factor	Assigned Value (Circle One)	Multi-plier	Score	Max. Score	Ref. (Section)
① OBSERVED RELEASE	0 45	1		45	4.1

If observed release is given a value of 45, proceed to line ④.
If observed release is given a value of 0, proceed to line ②.

② ROUTE CHARACTERISTICS					4.2
Facility Slope and Intervening Terrain	0 1 2 3	1		3	
1-yr. 24-hr. Rainfall	0 1 2 3	1		3	
Distance to Nearest Surface Water	0 1 2 3	2		6	
Physical State	0 1 2 3	1		3	
Total Route Characteristics Score				15	
③ CONTAINMENT	0 1 2 3	1		3	4.3
④ WASTE CHARACTERISTICS					4.4
Toxicity/Persistence	0 3 6 9 12 15 18	1		18	
Hazardous Waste Quantity	0 1 2 3 4 5 6 7 8	1		8	
Total Waste Characteristics Score				26	
⑤ TARGETS					4.5
Surface Water Use	0 1 2 3	3		9	
Distance to a Sensitive Environment	0 1 2 3	2		6	
Population Served/ Distance to Water Intake Downstream	0 4 6 8 10 12 16 18 20 24 30 32 35 40	1		40	
Total Targets Score				55	

⑥ If line ① is 45, multiply ① x ④ x ⑤ If line ① is 0, multiply ② x ③ x ④ x ⑤	64,350	

⑦ Divide line ⑥ by 64,350 and multiply by 100 $S_{sw} =$

Figure 7

Surface Water Route Work Sheet

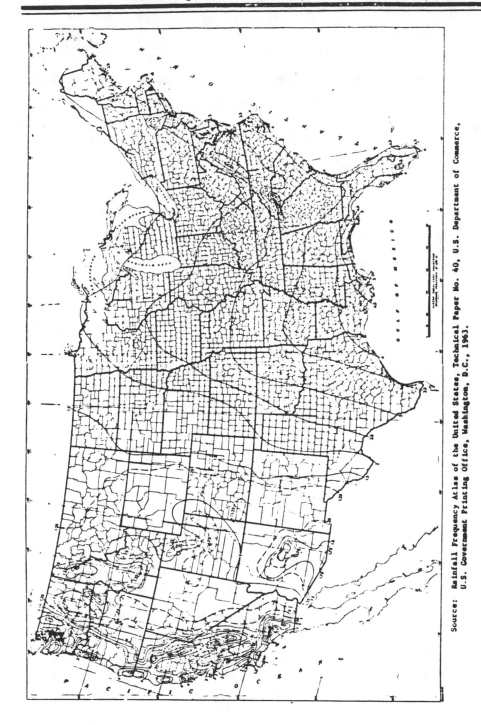

Source: Rainfall Frequency Atlas of the United States, Technical Paper No. 40, U.S. Department of Commerce, U.S. Government Printing Office, Washington, D.C., 1963.

FIGURE 8
1-YEAR 24-HOUR RAINFALL
(INCHES)

	s	s²
Groundwater Route Score (S_{gw})		
Surface Water Route Score (S_{sw})		
Air Route Score (S_a)		
$S_{gw}^2 + S_{sw}^2 + S_a^2$		
$\sqrt{S_{gw}^2 + S_{sw}^2 + S_a^2}$		
$\sqrt{S_{gw}^2 + S_{sw}^2 + S_a^2} \big/ 1.73$		$S_M =$

Figure 10

WORKSHEET FOR COMPUTING S_M

AIR ROUTE WORK SHEET

	Rating Factor	Assigned Value (Circle One)	Multiplier	Score	Max. Score	Ref. (Section)
[1]	OBSERVED RELEASE	0 45	1		45	5.1
	Date and Location:					
	Sampling Protocol:					
	If line [1] is 0, then S = 0. Enter on line [4].					
	If line [1] is 45, then proceed to line [2].					
[2]	WASTE CHARACTERISTICS					5.2
	Reactivity and Incompatibility	0 1 2 3	1		3	
	Toxicity	0 1 2 3	3		9	
	Hazardous Waste Quantity	0 1 2 3 4 5 6 7 8	1		8	
	Total Waste Characteristics Score				20	
[3]	TARGETS					5.3
	Population Within 4-Mile Radius	0 9 12 15 18 / 21 24 27 30	1		30	
	Distance to Sensitive Environment	0 1 2 3	2		6	
	Land Use	0 1 2 3	1		3	
	Total Targets Score				39	
					35,100	

[4] Multiply [1] x [2] x [3]

[5] Divide line [4] by 35,100 and multiply by 100   S =

Figure 9

Air Route Work Sheet

FIRE AND EXPLOSION WORK SHEET

Rating Factor	Assigned Value (Circle One)	Multi-plier	Score	Max. Score	Ref. (Section)
1 Containment	1 3	1		3	7.1
2 Waste Characteristics					7.2
Direct Evidence	0 3	1		3	
Ignitability	0 1 2 3	1		3	
Reactivity	0 1 2 3	1		3	
Incompatibility	0 1 2 3	1		3	
Hazardous Waste Quantity	0 1 2 3 4 5 6 7 8	1		8	
Total Waste Characteristics Score			20		
3 Targets					7.3
Distance to Nearest Population	0 1 2 3 4 5	1		5	
Distance to Nearest Building	0 1 2 3	1		3	
Distance to Sensitive Environment	0 1 2 3	1		3	
Land Use	0 1 2 3	1		·3	
Population Within 2-Mile Radius	0 1 2 3 4 5	1		5	
Buildings Within 2-Mile Radius	0 1 2 3 4 5	1		5	
Total Target Score			24		
4 Multiply [1] x [2] x [3] x [4]			1,440		
5 Divide line [5] by 1,440 and multiply by 100		S_{FE} =			

Figure 11

DIRECT CONTACT WORK SHEET

Rating Factor	Assigned Value (Circle One)	Multi-plier	Score	Max. Score	Ref. (Section)
1 Observed Incident	0 45	1		45	8.1
If line [1] is 45, proceed to line [4] If line [1] is 0, proceed to line [2]					
2 Accessibility	0 1 2 3	1		3	8.2
3 Containment	0 15	1		15	8.3
4 Waste Characteristics Toxicity	0 1 2 3	5		15	8.4
5 Targets					8.5
Population within a 1-mile radius	0 1 2 3 4 5	4		20	
Distance to a critical habitat	0 1 2 3	4		12	
Total Targets Score			32		
6 If line [1] is 45, multiply [1] x [4] x [5] If line [1] is 0, multiply [2] x [3] x [4] x [5]			21,600		
7 Divide line [6] by 21,600 and multiply by 100		S_{DC} =			

Figure 12
Direct Contact Work Sheet

2. 40 CFR Subpart H, § 300.84 is amended by revising paragraphs (a)–(e) as follows:

Subpart H—Use of Dispersants and Other Chemicals

§ 300.84 Authorization of use.

(a) The OSC, with the concurrence of the EPA representative to the RRT and the concurrence of the States with jurisdiction over the navigable waters polluted by the oil discharge, may authorize the use of dispersants, surface collecting agents, and biological additives on the oil discharge, provided that the dispersants, surface collecting agents, or additives are on the NCP Product Schedule. The OSC should consult with other appropriate Federal agencies as practicable when considering the use of such products.

(b) The OSC, with the concurrence of the EPA representative to the RRT and the concurrence of the States with jurisdiction over the navigable waters polluted by the oil discharge, may authorize the use of burning agents on a case-by-case basis. The OSC should consult with other appropriate Federal Agencies as practicable when considering the use of such products.

(c) The OSC may authorize the use of any dispersant, surface collecting agent, other chemical agent, burning agent, or biological additive (including products not on the NCP Product Schedule) without obtaining the concurrence of the EPA representative to the RRT or the States with jurisdiction over the navigable waters polluted by the oil discharge, when in the judgment of the OSC, the use of the product is necessary to prevent or substantially reduce a hazard to human life. The OSC is to inform the EPA RRT representative and the affected States of the use of a product as soon as possible and, pursuant to the provisions in paragraph (a) of this section, obtain their concurrence for its continued use once the threat to human life has subsided.

(d) Sinking agents shall not be authorized for application to oil discharges.

(e) RRTs should consider, as part of their planning activities, the appropriateness of using the dispersants, surface collecting agents, or biological additives listed on the NCP Products Schedule, and the appropriateness of using burning agents. Regional contingency plans should address the use of such products in specific contexts. If the RRT and the States with jurisdiction over the waters of the area to which a plan applies approve in advance the use of certain products as described in the plan, the

OSC may authorize the use of the products without obtaining the concurrence of the EPA representative to the RRT or of the States and without consultation with other appropriate Federal agencies.

Appendix

Note.—This is an Appendix to the document and will not appear in the Code of Federal Regulations.

Memorandum

Subject: CERCLA Compliance With Other Environmental Statutes

From: Lee M. Thomas, Assistant Administrator

To: Regional Administrator Regions I–X

This memorandum sets forth the Environmental Protection Agency (EPA) policy on the applicability of the standards, criteria, advisories, and guidance of other State and Federal environmental and public health statutes to actions taken pursuant to sections 104 and 106 of the Comprehensive Environmental Response, Compensation, and Liability Act of 1980 (CERCLA). This policy addresses considerations for on-site and off-site actions taken under CERCLA.

I. Discussion

The National Contingency Plan (NCP) establishes the process for determining appropriate removal and/or remedial actions at Superfund sites. In the course of this process, EPA will give primary consideration to the selection of those response actions that are effective in preventing or, where prevention is not practicable, minimizing the release of hazardous substances so that they do not migrate to cause substantial danger to present or future public health, welfare, or the environment. As a general rule, this can be accomplished by pursuing remedies that meet the standards of applicable or relevant Federal public health or environmental laws. However, because of the unique circumstances at particular sites, there may be alternatives that do not meet the standards of other laws, but which still provide protection of public health, welfare, and the environment.

Although response actions which prevent hazardous substances from migrating into the environment are seen as the most effective under CERCLA, actions which minimize migration must also be considered since CERCLA primarily addresses inadequate *past* disposal practices and resulting unique site conditions. At certain sites, it may be technically impracticable, environmentally unacceptable or excessively costly to implement a response action that prevents migration or restores the site to its original, uncontaminated condition.

II. Policy

Section 104 of CERCLA requires that for off-site remedial actions, storage, destruction, treatment or secure disposition be in compliance with subtitle C of Resource Conservation and Recovery Act (RCRA). CERCLA is silent, however, concerning the requirements of other laws with regard to all other response actions taken pursuant to sections 104 and 106. As a general rule, the Agency's policy is to attain or exceed applicable or relevant environmental and public health standards in CERCLA response actions unless one of the specifically enumerated situations is present. Where such a situation is present and a standard is not used, the Agency must document and explain the reasons in the decision documents. Federal criteria and advisories, and State standards also will be *considered* in fashioning CERCLA remedies and, if appropriate, relevant portions will be used. If EPA does not use a relevant part of these standards, criteria or advisories in the remedial action, the decision documents will state the reasons.

A. On-site Response Actions

(1) For removal actions, EPA's policy is to pursue actions that will meet applicable or relevant standards, and criteria of other Federal environmental and public health laws to the maximum extent practicable, considering the exigencies of the situation.

(2) For remedial actions, EPA's policy is to pursue remedies that attain or exceed applicable and relevant standards of other Federal public health and environmental laws, unless specific circumstances, identified below, exist.

CERCLA procedural and administrative requirements will be modified to provide safeguards similar to those provided under other laws. Application for and receipt of permits is not required for on-site response actions taken under the Fund-financed or enforcement authorities of CERCLA.

R. Off-Site Response Actions

CERCLA removal and remedial activities that involve the removal of hazardous substances from a CERCLA site to off-site facilities for proper storage, treatment or disposal must be in compliance with all applicable or relevant standards of Federal environmental and public health statutes.

Off-site facilities that are used for storage, treatment, or disposal of Superfund wastes must have all appropriate permits or authorizations.

If the facility or process that is being considered for receipt of the Superfund wastes has not been permitted or authorized, the State or responsible party will be required to obtain all appropriate permits. A State's responsibility for obtaining any appropriate Federal, State or local permits (e.g. RCRA, TSCA, NPDES, Clean Air, etc.) will be specified in a contract or cooperative agreement with the State as part of its assurances required under section 104(c) of CERCLA.

III. Federal and State Requirements That May Be Relevant or Applicable to Response Actions

Federal and State environmental standards, guidance and advisories fall into two categories:

• Federal standards that are relevant or applicable.
• Other standards, criteria, advisories or guidance to be considered.

A complete list of both categories of requirements is attached. This list is our initial effort. A revised and annotated list will be included in the forthcoming Guidance for Feasibility Studies.

A. Federal Standards That Are Relevant or Applicable

Applicable standards are those standards that would be specifically triggered by the circumstances associated with the proposed Superfund remedy except for the fact that the proposed action would be undertaken pursuant to CERCLA section 104 or section 106.

Relevant standards are those designed to apply to circumstances sufficiently similar to those encountered at CERCLA sites in which their application would be appropriate at a specific site although not legally required. Standards also are relevant if they would be legally applicable to CERCLA § 104 or § 106 actions but for legal technicalities such as trigger dates or definitions. For example, TSCA PCB standards would be relevant even though the PCBs were produced prior to January 1976, which triggers TSCA requirements.

B. Other Requirements, Advisories or Guidances To Be Considered

This category includes other standards, criteria, advisories and guidance that may be useful in developing Superfund remedies. These requirements, advisories and guidances were developed by EPA, other Federal Agencies and the States. The data underlying these requirements may be used at Superfund sites in an appropriate way.

IV. Implementation

A. Removal Actions

For both on and off-site removal actions, the On-Scene-Coordinator should consult with the Regional Response Team within the framework of the Regional Contingency Plan to determine the most effective action.

(1) *On-site.* For on-site removal actions, the OSC should attempt to *attain* all Federal applicable or relevant public health or environmental standards. The OSC also should *consider* other Federal criteria, guidance and advisories as well as State standards in formulating the removal action. However, because removal actions often involve situations requiring expeditous action to protect public health, welfare, or the environment, it may not always be feasible to fully meet them. In those circumstances where they cannot be attained, the decision documents, OSC reports, or other documents should specify the reasons.

(2) *Off-site.* Off-site facilities that are used for storage, treatment, or disposal of Superfund wastes must have all appropriate permits or authorizations.

B. Remedial Actions

1. *Presentation and Analysis of Alternatives.* As part of the feasibility study (FS), at least one alternative for each of the following must, at a minimum, be evaluated within the requirements of the feasibility study guidance and presented to the decision-maker.

(a) Alternatives for treatment or disposal in an off-site facility, as appropriate;[1]

(b) Alternativs which *attain* applicable and relevant Federal public health or environmental standards;

(c) As appropriate, alternatives which *exceed* applicable and relevent public health or environmental standards;

(d) Alternatives which do not attain applicable or relevant public health or environmental standards but will reduce the likelihood of present or future threat from the hazardous substances. This must include an alternative which closely approaches the level of protection provided by the applicable or relevant standards and meets CERCLA's objective of adequately protecting public health, welfare and environment;

(e) A no action alternative.

In some cases, there may be some overlap between these alternatives.

2. *Selection of Remedy.* The decision-maker will consider all of the alternatives arrayed in the feasibility study and will give primary consideration to remedies that attain or exceed applicable or relevant Federal public health and environmental standards. Where the selected remedy involves an EPA standard, criterion, or advisory, the decision-maker will ensure appropriate coordination with affected EPA programs.

In appropriate cases, the decision-maker may select a remedial action that includes both on and off-site components.

The decision-maker may select an alternative that does not attain applicable or relevant standards in one of the following circumstances, recognizing that a consideration in making this determination is the extent to which the standard was intended to apply to the specific circumstances present at the site.[2]

a. The selected alternative is not the final remedy and will become part of a more comprehensive remedy;

b. All of the alternatives which meet applicable or relevant standards fall into one or more of the following categories:

(i) *Fund-Balancing*—For Fund-financed actions only; exercise the Fund-balancing provisions of CERCLA section 104(c)(4);

(ii) *Technically impracticality*—It is technically impractical from an engineering perspective to achieve the standard at the specific site in question;

(iii) *Unacceptable environmental impacts*—All alternatives that attain or exceed standards would cause unacceptable damage to the environment; or

(c) Where the remedy is to be carried out pursuant to CERCLA section 106; the Hazardous Response Trust Fund is unavailable or would be used; there is a strong public interest in expedited clean up; and the litigation probably would not result in the desired remedy.

Where one of these situations is present, the decision-maker *may* select an alternative which does not attain or exceed applicable or relevant public health or environmental standards. The basis for not meeting the standard must be fully documented and explained in the appropriate decision documents.

The Agency anticipates that most of CERCLA remedial actions *will* attain or exceed applicable or relevant public health or environmental standards. However, where the specific circumstances discussed above preclude the selection of a remedy that attains standards, the decision-maker will select the alternative that *most closely approaches the level of protection* provided by the applicable or relevant standard, considering the reasons for not meeting that standard.

EPA also will use appropriate Federal public health and environmental criteria, advisories, and guidance and State standards in developing appropriate remedial alternatives. If the decision-maker determines that such

---

[1] These alternatives must be consistent with forthcoming guidance on "Procedures for Implementing CERCLA Delegations for Off-Site Response Actions." In some cases, off-site disposal or treatment may not be feasible and this alternative may be eliminated during initial screening of alternatives. The decision documents should reflect this screening.

[2] In determining whether a particular standard is applicable or relevant the decision-maker should refer to the attached list "Applicable or Relevant Requirements." For example, RCRA did not "contemplate" the regulation of the indiscriminant disposal of waste over 210 miles of roadway, or the contamination of a river bed with hazardous waste. In such situations, RCRA regulations would *not* be applicable per se, but on a case-by-case basis part of the regulation may be relevant.

standards, criteria, advisories or guideance are relevant, but are not used in the selected remedial alternative, the decision documents will indicate the basis for not using them.

For Fund-financed actions, where State standards are part of the cost-effective remedy, the Fund will pay to attain those standards. Where the cost-effective remedy does not include those State standards, the State may pay the difference to attain them.

3. *Administrative and Procedural Aspects.* The following modifications will be made to the Superfund community relations program to ensure that it provides a similar level of public involvement to that provided by the permitting programs of other environmental laws:

• A fact sheet should be included with the public notice and feasibility study which is provided to the public 2 weeks before the 3 week public comment period. The fact sheet will clearly summarize the feasibility study response alternatives and other issues, including which alternatives attain or exceed public health and environmental standards and criteria. For those alternatives that do not attain applicable and relevant standards of other public health and environmental laws, the fact sheet shall identify how they fail to attain the standards and explain how they nonetheless meet the goals of CERCLA. The public notice should include a timetable in which a decision will be reached, any tentative determinations which the Agency has made, the location where relevant documents can be obtained, identification of community involvement opportunities, the name of an Agency contact and other appropriate information.

• A public notice and updated fact sheet should be prepared upon (1) Agency selection of the final response action and (2) upon completion of the final engineering design. Prior to selecting the final engineering design, the Agency may hold a public meeting to inform the public of the design alternatives and solicit comments.

• If a remedy is identified that is different from those proposed during the feasibility study public comment period, a new 3 week public comment period may be required prior to amending the record of decision, taking into consideration the features of the alternatives addressed in the public comment period.

In addition, certain aspects of the CERCLA administrative process may be modified to assure comparability with the administrative requirements (i.e.

recordkeeping, monitoring) of the other environmental programs.

The CERCLA enforcement community relations program will also be modified to provide for an enhanced public participation program for both consent decrees and administrative orders. This program will be substantially equivalent to the revised program for Fund-financed actions. Furthermore, consent decrees and administrative orders will incorporate administrative requirements (i.e. recordkeeping, monitoring) similar to those mandated by other environmental programs.

V. Applicability of Policy

This policy applies to three different situations:

• A site specific FS has not yet been initiated.
• The FS has been initiated, but the remedy has not yet been selected.
• The FS is completed and the remedy has been selected.

All sites where the FS has not yet been initiated must meet all of the requirements of this policy.

Where the FS has been initiated and the remedy has not yet been selected, the requirements of this policy do not apply to Record of Decisions (RODs) signed before March 1, 1985. RODs signed before March 1, 1985, should present to the decision-maker at least one alternative that attains or exceeds applicable or relevant standards and, if it is not selected should indicate the reasons why it was not selected.

Where the FS is complete and the remedy has been selected, the decision-maker may on a case-by-case basis revise the selected remedy.

If you have any questions or comments, please contact Will am N. Hedeman, Director, Office of E nergency and Remedial Response (FTS 382–2180) or Douglas Cohen of his Policy Analysis Staff (FTS 382–3044).

Attachment

Applicable or Relevant Requirements

1. Office of Solid Waste

• Open Dump Criteria (RCRA Subtitle D, 40 CFR Part 257)

Note.—Only relevant to nonhazardous wastes. In most situations Superfund wastes will be handled in accordance with RCRA Subtitle C requirements.

• Hazardous Waste Regulations (RCRA Subtitle C, 40 CFR Part 264) including liner, cap, groundwater, and closure requirements under the following subparts:
F. Ground-Water Protection
G. Closure and Post Closure
H. Containers
I. Tanks

J. Surface Impoundments
K. Waste Piles
L. Land Treatment
M. Landfills
N. Incinerators

2. Office of Water

• Maximum Contaminant Levels (for *all* sources of drinking water exposure).
• Underground Injection Control Regulations.
• State Water Quality Standards (apply for surface water discharge).
• Requirements established pursuant to section 301 and section 403(c) of the Clean Water Act.
• Ocean Dumping Requirements including incineration at sea.
• Pretreatment standards for discharge into a publicly owned treatment works.

3. Office of Pesticides and Toxic Substances

• "PCB Requirements including Disposal and Marking Rule (43 FR 7150, 2–17–78); PCB Ban Rule (44 FR 31514, 5–31–79) PCB Electrical Equipment Rule (47 FR 37342, August 25, 1982); Uncontrolled PCBs Rule (49 FR 28172, July 10, 1984) and other related rulemakings."
• 40 CFR 775 Subpart J—Disposal of Waste Material Containing TCDD.

4. Office of External Affairs

• Guidelines for Specification of Disposal Sites for Dredged or Fill Material (section 404(b)(1) Guidelines, 40 CFR Part 230).
• Denial or Restriction of Disposal Site for Dredged Material: Final rule (section 404(c)).

5. Office of Air and Radiation

• Uranium mill tailing rules.
• National Ambient Air Quality Standards.
• High and low level radioactive waste rule.
• Asbestos disposal rules.

6. Other Federal Requirements

• OSHA requirements.
• Preservation of scientific, historical or archaeological data.
• D.O.T. Hazardous Materials Transport Rules.
• Regulation of activities in or affecting waters of the United States pursuant to 33 CFR 320–329.
• The following requirements are triggered by fund-financed actions:
—Preservation of rivers on the national inventory, Wild and Scenic Rivers Act, section 40 CFR 6.302(e).
—Protection of threatened or endangered species and their habitats.

—Conservation or Wildlife Resources.
—Executive Orders related to Floodplains (11988) and Wetlands (11990).
—Coastal Zone Management Act.

Other Requirements, Advisories and Guidance To Be Considered

1. Federal Requirements, Advisories and Procedures

• Recommended Maximum Concentration Limits (RMCLs).
• Health Advisories, EPA, Office of Water.
• Federal Water Quality Criteria.

Note.—Federal water quality criteria are not legally enforceable. State water quality standards, developed using appropriate aspects of Federal water quality criteria, are legally enforceable. In many cases, States water quality standards do not include specific numerical limitations on a large number of priority pollutants. When there are no numerical state standards for a given pollutant, Federal water quality criteria should be considered.

• Pesticide and Food additive tolerances and action levels data.

Note.—Germane portions of tolerances and action levels may be relevant in certain situations.

• Waste load allocation procedures, EPA Office of Water.
• Federal Sole Source Aquifer requirements.
• Public health basis in listing decisions under sec. 112 of the Clean Air Act.
• EPA's groundwater protection strategy.
• New Source Performance Standards for Storage Vessels for Petroleum Liquids.
• TSCA health data.
• Pesticide registration data.
• TSCA chemical advisories (2 or 3 issued to date).·
• Advisories issued by FWS and NWFS under the Fish and Wildlife Coordination Act.
• National Environmental Policy Act.
• Floodplain and Wetlands Executive Orders.
• TSCA Compliance Program Policy.

2. State Requirements

• State Requirements on Disposal and Transport of Radioactive wastes.
• State Approval of Water Supply System Additions or Developments.
• State Ground Water Withdrawal Approvals.
• Requirements of authorized (Subtitle C of RCRA) State hazardous waste programs.
• State Implementation Plans and Delegated Programs Under Clean Air Act.

• All other State requirements, not delegated through EPA authority.

Note.—Many other State and local requirements could be relevant. The guidance for feasibility studies will include a more comprehensive list.

3. USEPA RCRA Guidance Documents

A. EPA's RCRA Design Guidelines

(1) Surface Impoundments, Liners Systems, Final Cover and Freeboard Control.
(2) Waste Pile Design—Liner Systems.
(3) Land Treatment Units.
(4) Landfill Design—Liner Systems and Final Cover.

B. Permitting Guidance Manuals

(1) Permit Applicant's Guidance Manual of Hazardous Waste Land Treatment, Storage, Disposal Facilities.
(2) Permit Writer's Guidance Manual for Hazardous Waste Land Treatment, Storage, Disposal Facilities.
(3) Permit Writer's Guidance Manual for Subpart F.
(4) Permit Applicants Guidance Manual for the General Facility Standards.
(5) Waste Analysis Plan Guidance Manual.
(6) Permit Writer's Guidance Manual for Hazardous Waste Tanks.
(7) Model Permit Application for Existing Incinerators.
(8) Guidance Manual for Evaluating Permit Applications for the Operation of Hazardous Waste Incinerator Units.
(9) A Guide for Preparing RCRA Permit Applications for Existing Storage Facilities.
(10) Guidance Manual on closure and post-closure Interim Status Standards.

C. Technical Resource Documents (TRDs)

(1) Evaluating Cover Systems for Solid and Hazardous Waste.
(2) Hydrologic Simulation of Solid Waste Disposal Sites.
(3) Landfill and Surface Impoundment Performance Evaluation.
(4) Lining of Water Impoundment and Disposal Facilities.
(5) Management of Hazardous Waste Leachate.
(6) Guide to the Disposal of Chemically Stabilized and Solidified Waste.
(7) Closure of Hazardous Waste Surface Impoundments.
(8) Hazardous Waste Land Treatment.
(9) Soil Properties, Classification, and Hydraulic Conductivity Testing.

D. Test Methods for Evaluating Solid Waste

(1) Solid Waste Leaching Procedure Manual.

(2) Methods for the Prediction of Leachate Plume Migration and Mixing.
(3) Hydrologic Evaluation of Landfill Performance (HELP) Model Hydrologic Simulation on Solid Waste Disposal Sites.
(4) Procedures for Modeling Flow Through Clay Liners.
(5) Test Methods for Evaluating Solid Wastes.
(6) A Method for Determining the Compatibility of Hazardous Wastes.
(7) Guidance Manual on Hazardous Waste Compatibility.

4. USEPA Office of Water Guidance Documents

A. Pretreatment Guidance Documents

(1) 304(g) Guidance Document Revised Pretreatment Guidelines (3 Volumes).
Provides technical data describing priority pollutants and their effects on wastewater treatment processes to be used in developing local limits; describes technologies applicable to categorical industries.

B. Water Quality Guidance Documents

(1) Ecological Evaluation of Proposed Discharge of Dredged Material into Ocean Waters (1977).
(2) Technical Support Manual: Waterbody Surveys and Assessments for Conducting Use Attainability Analyses (1983).
Outlines methods for conducting use attainability analyses under the Clean Water Act.
(3) Water-Related Environmental Fate of 129 Priority Pollutants (1979).
Describe the transformation and transportation of priority pollutants.
(4) Water Quality Standards Handbook (1983).
Provides an overview of the Criteria Standards Program under the Clean Water Act and outlines methods for conducting criteria standards modification.
(5) Technical Support Document for Water Quality-based Toxics Control.

C. NPDES Guidance Documents

(1) NPDES Best Management Practices Guidance Manual (June 1981).
Provides a protocol for evaluating BMPs for controlling discharges of toxic and hazardous substances to receiving waters.
(2) Biomonitoring Guidance, July 1983, subsequent biomonitoring policy statements, and case studies on toxicity reduction evaluation (May 1983).

D. Ground Water/UIC Guidance Document

(1) Designation of a USDW.
(2) Elements of Aquifer Identification.

(3) Interim guidance for public participation.

(4) Definition of major facilities.

(5) Corrective action requirements.

(6) Requirements applicable to wells injecting into, through or above an aquifer which has been exempted pursuant to § 146.104(b)(4).

(7) Guidance for UIC implementation on Indian lands.

5. USEPA Manuals From the Office of Research and Development

(1) EW 846 methods—laboratory analytic methods.

(2) Lab protocols developed pursuant to Clean Water Act section 304(h).

[FR Doc. 85–2802 Filed 2–11–85; 8:45 am]

BILLING CODE 6560-60-M

APPENDIX F

SUPERFUND RELEASE REPORTING REGULATIONS
(40 C.F.R. Part 302)

ENVIRONMENTAL PROTECTION AGENCY

40 CFR Parts 117 and 302

[SW H-FRL 2665-6(b)]

Notification Requirements; Reportable Quantity Adjustments

AGENCY: Environmental Protection Agency (EPA).

ACTION: Final rule.

SUMMARY: Sections 103(a) and 103(b) of the Comprehensive Environmental Response, Compensation, and Liability Act of 1980 ("CERCLA") require that persons in charge of vessels or facilities from which hazardous substances have been released in quantities that are equal to or greater than the reportable quantities immediately notify the National Response Center of the release. Section 102(b) sets a reportable quantity of one pound for hazardous substances, except those for which reportable quantities have been established pursuant to section 311(b)(4) of the Clean Water Act ("CWA").

Section 102(a) authorizes the Environmental Protection Agency ("EPA") to adjust reportable quantities for hazardous substances and to designate as hazardous substances, substances which when released into the environment may present substantial danger to the public health or welfare or the environment. This final rule adjusts many of the reportable quantities established in section 102(b). These reportable quantity adjustments are intended to reduce the burdens of reporting on the regulated community, allow EPA to focus its resources on the most serious releases, and protect public health and welfare and the environment more effectively. This rule also designates, under section 102(a) all substances listed under the various statutory provisions referenced in section 101(14) of CERCLA. This rule also revises reportable quantities established pursuant to section 311(b)(4) of the Clean Water Act for discharges of hazardous substances into navigable waters, so that the CWA section 311 reportable quantities will be identical to and therefore consistent with those promulgated under CERCLA.

To help implement these changes, today's rule clarifies requirements for notifying the National Response Center of a release of a hazardous substance in a quantity equal to or greater than its reportable quantity. The toll-free telephone number of the National Response Center is listed under **"ADDRESSES."**

EFFECTIVE DATE: July 3, 1985.

CERCLA section 305 provides for a legislative veto of regulations promulgated under CERCLA. Although *INS* v. *Chadha*, 462 U.S. 919, 103 S. Ct. 2764 (1983), cast doubt on the validity of the legislative veto, EPA has transmitted a copy of this regulation to the Secretary of the Senate and the Clerk of the House of Representatives. If any action by Congress calls the effective date of this regulation into question, the Agency will publish a notice of clarification in the Federal Register.

ADDRESSES: The toll-free telephone number of the National Response Center is (800) 424-8802; in the Washington, D.C. metropolitan area (202) 426-2675.

The record supporting this rulemaking is available for public inspection at Room S-325, U.S. Environmental Protection Agency, 401 M Street SW, Washington, D.C. 20460 (Docket Number 102RQ). The docket may be inspected between 8:00 a.m. and 4:00 p.m. Monday through Friday. As provided in 40 CFR Part 2, a reasonable fee may be charged for copying services.

FOR FURTHER INFORMATION CONTACT:

Dr. K. Jack Kooyoomjian, Response Standards and Criteria Branch, Emergency Response Division (WH-548B), U.S. Environmental Protection Agency, 401 M Street, SW, Washington D.C. 20460,
or the

RCRA/Superfund Hotline (800) 424-9346, in Washington, D.C., (202) 382-3000.

SUPPLEMENTARY INFORMATION: The contents of today's preamble are listed in the following outline:

I. Introduction

A. *Statutory Authority*

The Comprehensive Environmental Response, Compensation, and Liability Act of 1980 [Pub. L. 96-510], 42 U.S.C. 9601 *et seq.*, enacted on December 11, 1980, establishes broad federal authority to deal with releases or threats of releases of hazardous substances from vessels and facilities. The Act defines a set of "hazardous substances" by reference to other environmental statutes (section 101(14)); this list currently contains 698 substances. The Environmental Protection Agency ("EPA") may designate additional hazardous substances (section 102).

The Act requires the person in charge of a vessel or facility to notify the National Response Center ("NRC") immediately when there is a release of a designated hazardous substance in an amount equal to or greater than the reportable quantity ("RQ") for that substance (sections 103(a) and (b)). Section 102(b) of CERCLA establishes RQs for releases of designated hazardous substances at one pound, unless other reportable quantities were assigned under section 311 of the Federal Water Pollution Control Act ("Clean Water Act" or "CWA"). Section 102 authorizes EPA to adjust all of these reportable quantities.

A major purpose of the section 103(a) and (b) notification requirements is to alert the appropriate government officials to releases of hazardous substances that may require rapid response to protect public health and welfare and the environment. Under the Act, the federal government may respond whenever there is a release or a substantial threat of a release into the environment of a hazardous substance or of other pollutants or contaminants which may present an imminent and substantial danger to public health or welfare (section 104). Response activities are to be taken, to the extent possible, in accordance with the National Contingency Plan (40 CFR Part 300), which was originally developed under the CWA and which has been revised to reflect the responsibilities and authority created by CERCLA. EPA emphasizes that notification based on reportable quantities is merely a trigger for informing the government of a release so that the appropriate federal personnel can evaluate the need for a federal response action and undertake any necessary response (removal or remedial action) in a timely fashion. Reportable quantities serve no other purpose; for example, a reportable quantity need not be released before a claim for damages or cleanup costs may be filed against the Hazardous Substance Response Trust Fund. Federal personnel will evaluate all reported releases, but will not necessarily initiate a removal or remedial action in response to all reported releases, because the release of a reportable quantity will not necessarily pose a hazard to public health or welfare or the environment. Government personnel will assess each release on a case-by-case basis.

B. Background of This Rulemaking

On May 25, 1983, EPA proposed a rule (48 FR 23552) to clarify procedures for reporting releases and to adjust reportable quantities for 387 of the 698 CERCLA hazardous substances. That Notice of Proposed Rulemaking (NPRM) also listed, for the first time, the "hazardous substances" designated by section 101(14) of CERCLA. The NPRM discussed in detail the CERCLA notification provisions (including the persons required to notify the NRC of a release, the substances for which notification is required, the types of releases subject to the notification requirements, and the exemptions from these requirements), the methodology and criteria used to adjust the reportable quantity levels, and the RQ adjustments proposed under section 102 of CERCLA and under section 311 of the CWA. That same day, EPA also published an Advance Notice of Proposed Rulemaking (ANPRM) concerning the designation of hazardous substances in addition to those specified in section 101(14) of the Act (48 FR 23602). In response to requests, and to increase the public's opportunity to express its opinion on the NPRM and ANPRM, the original 60-day comment period for both notices was extended by 30 days, so that the comment period closed on August 25, 1963. EPA received

136 comment letters totalling over 1,000 pages; these comments represent the first formal statements of public opinion on the methodology developed for adjusting RQs, the actual RQ adjustments proposed, and various issues relating to notification. A summary of the comments received, together with the Agency's responses, is contained in the Responses to Comments on the Notice of Proposed Rulemaking on the Adjustment of Reportable Quantities ["Responses to Comments"], which is available for inspection at Room S–325, U.S. Environmental Protection Agency, 401 M Street, SW, Washington, D.C. 20460.

Today, the Agency is promulgating RQ adjustments and clarifications of reporting procedures. The RQs of 340 CERCLA hazardous substances (including 21 hazardous waste streams) are adjusted in this final rule. Today's Federal Register also contains an NPRM proposing RQ adjustments for 105 of the remaining 358 hazardous substances. All of these adjustments apply not only to CERCLA RQs, but to RQs established pursuant to section 311(b)(4) of the CWA. In preparing the final rule, EPA has carefully considered all of the public comments submitted on the proposals made in the May 25, 1983 NPRM.

Section II of this preamble notes the significant differences between today's rule and the NPRM and refers the reader to the detailed discussion of each change elsewhere in the preamble. Section III presents issues raised in the NPRM that are not resolved in today's rule. Sections IV, V, and VI discuss the operation of the rule, major public comments, and the Agency's responses to these comments. Section VII provides a summary of the analyses supporting the rule.

As was stated in the preamble to the proposed rule, other provisions of the Act may be applicable even where notification is not required. Therefore, nothing in this preamble or final rule should be interpreted as reflecting Agency policy or the applicable law with respect to other provisions of the Act. For example, a party responsible for a release is liable for the costs of cleaning up that release and for any natural resource damages, even if the release is not subject to the notification requirements of sections 103 (a) and (b). Similarly, claims may be filed against the Hazardous Substance Response Trust Fund for cleanup costs and damages even if less than a reportable quantity has been released. Moreover, proper reporting of a release in accordance with sections 103 (a) and (b) does not preclude liability for cleanup

costs. The fact that a release of a hazardous substance is properly reported or that it is not subject to the notification requirements of sections 103 (a) and (b) will not prevent EPA or other governmental agencies from taking response actions under section 104, seeking reimbursement from responsible parties under section 107, or pursuing an enforcement action against responsible parties. Note also that this rule does not affect hazardous substance reporting requirements imposed by certain other regulations and statutes. (See, e.g., the discussion of MARPOL 73/78 and TSCA section 8(e) in section IV.G. below.)

This final rule formally designates those substances which are listed under the statutes referred to in section 101(14). Substances listed under the Solid Waste Disposal Act, commonly known as the Resource Conservation and Recovery Act ("RCRA"), will now be "hazardous substances" under CERCLA, regardless of whether they are hazardous wastes under RCRA. This final rule does not otherwise address the designation of hazardous substances which are not already designated under the statutes listed in CERCLA section 101(14). The Agency has conducted several preliminary economic and technical analyses on this subject (see 48 FR 23603), and the May 25, 1983 ANPRM invited public comment. EPA has carefully reviewed the comments received and is in the process of further developing its designation policy. The Agency's designation policy will be the subject of a separate rulemaking.

C. Organization of the Final Rule

Today's final rule amends 40 CFR by adding Part 302. Section 302.1 describes the fourfold purpose of the new regulation, including (1) listing those substances designated as hazardous under section 101(14) of CERCLA; (2) identifying reportable quantities for these substances; (3) describing the notification requirements for releases of these substances; and (4) identifying reportable quantities for hazardous substances that were previously assigned RQs under section 311(b)(4) of the Clean Water Act.

Section 302.2 explains the abbreviations used in the rule. Section 302.3 defines the following terms:

1. "The Act," "CERCLA," and "Superfund"
2. "Administrator"
3. "Consumer product"
4. "Environment"
5. "Facility"
6. "Hazardous substance"
7. "Hazardous waste"
8. "Navigable waters"

9. "Offshore facility"
10. "Onshore facility"
11. "Person"
12. "Release"
13. "Reportable quantity"
14. "United States"
15. "Vessel"

Section 302.4 includes Table 302.4, which lists the substances designated as hazardous under section 101(14) (and now section 102) of CERCLA together with the RQ established for each substance. Section 302.4 also denotes the conditions whereby a solid waste not specifically listed as a hazardous substance can still be a hazardous substance if it exhibits any of certain characteristics. Section 302.5 provides that each quantity listed as the "Final RQ" in Table 302.4 is the reportable quantity for that listed hazardous substance. Section 302.5 also presents the RQs for unlisted hazardous wastes. Section 302.6 incorporates the statutory requirement that any person in charge of a vessel or facility must immediately notify the NRC whenever he or she has knowledge of any release of a hazardous substance from the vessel or facility in a quantity equal to or greater than the RQ; it also provides rules for determining when notification is required for releases of (1) mixtures or solutions that contain hazardous substances, and (2) releases of massive forms of metals. Section 302.7 incorporates by reference the statutory penalties for failure to notify the NRC of hazardous substance releases that equal or exceed the RQs. Today's rule also has an appendix that lists each hazardous substance in Chemical Abstracts Service Registry Number (CASRN) order.

Finally, this rule revises 40 CFR 117.3 to make the CWA RQs equal to those shown in Table 302.4 of 40 CFR 302.4.

II. Summary of Changes From the Proposed Rule

EPA has made the following changes from the proposed rule. Each change is discussed in detail in the preamble section noted.

1. Wastes classified as hazardous under RCRA that are properly delisted, deleted, or exempted by a state pursuant to an approved state program shall not be considered hazardous substances for purposes of CERCLA notification requirements so long as they do not contain any other listed CERCLA substances (see section IV.D.1.b.).

2. A supplement to Table 302.4 that lists CERCLA hazardous substances in CASRN order has been added as an appendix to today's rule to help users identify hazardous substances (see section IV.D.1.d.).

3. The exemption from notification requirements of releases of metal where the diameter of the particles of metal equals or exceeds 100 micrometers (0.004 inches) now appears both as a footnote to Table 302.4 and as part of 40 CFR 302.6 (see section IV.D.1.f.).

4. Proper disposal of hazardous substances in interim status facilities or facilities with final permits under RCRA need not be reported under CERCLA (see section IV.D.2.a.).

5. The rule for determining when notification is required for releases of mixtures and solutions containing hazardous substances is now stated in 40 CFR 302.6 (see section IV.D.3.b.).

6. "[N]ormal application of pesticides" is no longer defined in 40 CFR 302.3; instead, the preamble interprets the statutory phrase "application of pesticides" (see section IV.E.).

7. The specific penalties imposed by CERCLA Section 103(b) no longer appear in 40 CFR 302.7(a); instead, the section incorporates the statutory penalties by reference (see section IV.H.).

8. Language has been added to the 40 CFR 302.5(b) discussion of "Unlisted Hazardous Substances" to emphasize: (1) that the 100-pound RQ for unlisted hazardous wastes applies only to substances which are wastes prior to their initial release; and (2) that the RQ given in Table 302.4 for unlisted wastes that exhibit EP toxicity applies to the waste itself, not merely to the toxic contaminant (see sections IV.D.1. and V.F.4.).

9. Various RQ changes have been made (see section V.G.).

10. Retention of statutory RQ for methyl isocyanate (see section V.H. .

11. Various other changes have been made in Table 302.4 (see sections V.G. through V.L.).

III. Issues Addressed in the NPRM But Not Resolved in This Rule

A. Continuous Releases

Section 103(f)(2) of CERCLA exempts certain releases from the general notification requirements of CERCLA if they are "continuous," "stable in quantity and rate," and notification has been given either under sections 103(a) and (b) "for a period sufficient to establish the continuity, quantity, and regularity" of the release or under section 103(c) (which relates to notification of the existence of certain facilities that are or have been used for storage, treatment, or disposal of hazardous wastes). Notification of continuous releases must be given "annually, or at such time as there is any statistically significant increase" in

the quantity of the hazardous substance being released.

In the May 25, 1983 NPRM, EPA requested comment on the types of releases that could qualify for the section 103(f)(2) exemption and on possible notification systems for such releases. Many comments on these issues were received. Due to the complexity of the issues involved, the Agency has decided to study the continuous release exemption further; today's rule does not resolve continuous release issues.

B. Federally Permitted Releases

One of the exemptions from section 103 reporting requirements is for "federally permitted releases." The definition of "federally permitted release" in CERCLA section 101(10) specifically identifies releases permitted under other environmental statutes.

In the NPRM, EPA explained the Agency's interpretation of each of the types of releases exempted by the definition of "federally permitted release." EPA received many comments on various aspects of the federally permitted release exemption, most of which urged a broader interpretation of one or more of the federally permitted releases. Due to the complexity of the issues involved, the Agency has decided to study the scope of this exemption further; today's rule does not resolve the "federally permitted release" issue.

C. Radionuclide RQs

Radionuclides are hazardous substances under CERCLA because they are designated as hazardous air pollutants under section 112 of the Clean Air Act. The NPRM noted that EPA is considering several issues for future adjustments to radionuclide RQs. Two major related issues are:

(1) The units the Agency should use to measure RQs; and

(2) Whether one RQ should be set for all radionuclides or whether different RQs for specific radionuclides should be used.

EPA received many comments on these issues. Today's final rule does not adjust the RQ for radionuclides; the issue is being evaluated for action in a future rulemaking. Until then, the one-pound (0.454 kilogram) RQ is applicable. As noted in the NPRM, the Agency recognizes that the pound or kilogram is not a suitable unit on which to base a notification requirement for radionuclides, because releases much smaller than one pound may pose a significant threat to public health or welfare or the environment. The Agency encourages releasers to report radionuclide releases of less than one pound.

D. Carcinogen RQs

The May 25, 1983 NPRM noted that the Agency has been collecting and evaluating data on the relative activity of substances as potential carcinogens. The methodology for adjusting RQs on the basis of potential carcinogenicity will be presented for public comment in a future rulemaking, and adjusted RQs for potentially carcinogenic substances will be proposed at that time. Until these substances receive final adjusted RQs, their statutory RQs will apply.

The NPRM published elsewhere in today's Federal Register proposes adjusted RQs for 12 substances that were evaluated as potential carcinogens but for which EPA's Carcinogen Assessment Group (CAG) did not find any sound evidence of potential carcinogenicity.

IV. Notification

A. Introduction

CERCLA sections 103 (a) and (b) require any person in charge of an offshore or onshore facility or a vessel to report to the National Response Center as soon as he or she has knowledge of any release of a hazardous substance that is equal to or greater than the reportable quantity. In the preamble to the May 25, 1983 NPRM, EPA elaborated on the notification requirements established by CERCLA, addressing such issues as the mechanics of notification, the persons required to notify the NRC of a release, the substances for which notification is required, the types of releases subject to the notification requirements, the exemptions from these requirements, and duplicate reporting. The following sections discuss comments received on these and other notification issues.

B. Purposes and Mechanics of Notification

Notification based on RQs serves as a trigger for informing the government of a release so that the need for response can be evaluated and any necessary response undertaken in a timely fashion. Federal personnel will evaluate all reported releases, although the government will not necessarily respond to all reported releases with a removal or remedial action. The reportable quantities do not themselves represent any determination that releases of a particular quantity are actually harmful to public health or welfare or the environment.

Reporting of releases pursuant to CERCLA sections 103 (a) and (b) is to be

made by telephone to the National Response Center. The toll-free number of the NRC is (800) 424–8802; in the Washington, D.C. metropolitan area the number is (202) 426–2675. Pursuant to the National Contingency Plan (NCP) (40 CFR Part 300), the duty officer at the NRC will record pertinent information about the release and relay this release information directly to an On-Scene Coordinator ("OSC") at either the relevant EPA regional office or the relevant U.S. Coast Guard district office. The OSC will then evaluate the circumstances of the release, give pertinent information to appropriate state and local officials, and decide whether and in what manner the federal government should respond to the release.

A few commenters stated that it is a misuse of time and money to report releases which do not result in a federal removal or remedial action; they argued that the probability of a federal response action should be an important consideration in designing the notification system. EPA disagrees. The government is not obligated to respond to every release to which it has authority to respond and therefore should not design a notification system on such a basis. Reportable quantities have been established so that the Agency is alerted promptly to situations that may warrant a government response. While EPA will not initiate a removal or remedial action for every release that is reported, EPA must obtain the information it needs to determine who has response authority, to assess whether there is a need for a federal response action, and to check that action is properly taken by others where appropriate.

C. Persons Covered by This Rule

The NPRM preamble considered the issue of which persons are required to notify the NRC of a release. In so doing, definitions of the key terms of the CERCLA notification requirements were presented. Responses to the major comments received are provided below.

1. Facility

Several commenters discussed the Agency's statement that "for notification purposes, EPA will consider the entire contiguous plant or installation and contiguous grounds under common ownership to be the reporting facility rather than each vent, pipe, or piece of equipment at such a plant" (48 FR 23553). Some of the commenters appeared to misinterpret EPA's intentions.

The Agency intended the statement to reflect its belief that numerous

concurrent releases (releases occurring within the same 24-hour period) of the same hazardous substance from one contiguous plant or installation need not be reported individually, but should be reported in a single notification. This policy will avoid unnecessary and burdensome calls where a plant is experiencing more than one reportable release, because it allows the regulated community to consider multiple concurrent releases of the same substance as one release for reporting purposes.

The comments received favored this policy, although a few commenters suggested that EPA expand the definition of facility to include outdoor areas within the boundary of a plant. In addition, some commenters questioned whether a releaser must aggregate the total volume of concurrent releases in order to determine if a reportable quantity has been met or exceeded.

The "facility" from which a release has entered or may enter into the environment does not include outdoor areas. Rather, the definition of "environment" includes all outdoor (i.e., not completely enclosed) areas surrounding and within a given facility. All concurrent releases of the same substance from a particular facility into the environment must be aggregated to determine if an RQ has been exceeded. Releases from separate facilities, however, need not be aggregated. EPA intends for multiple concurrent releases of the same substance from a single facility to be reported in a single notification as a single release. Where multiple concurrent RQ releases are occurring at various parts of a contiguous plant or installation on contiguous grounds under common ownership (e.g., at a chemical manufacturing plant or an oil refinery), the person in charge should also report these multiple concurrent releases in a single notification. The policy of consolidating notifications also applies to concurrent releases from separate storage facilities, so long as the releases are at the same location, i.e., located on contiguous grounds under common ownership.

2. Person In Charge

The NPRM preamble discussion of "person in charge" stated that EPA would not seek to designate the specific individuals or positions within business entities who would be responsible for reporting hazardous substance releases. The Agency indicated that such decisions are better made by the management of the affected organization. Two commenters argued that the lack of a clear definition of "person in charge" would result in responsible individuals being unaware of their duty to report releases and would lead to delayed reporting or failure to report. EPA was urged to define explicitly the term "person in charge."

EPA disagrees with these commenters. The proper assignment of reporting responsibilities depends on the specific operation involved, management structure, and other case-specific considerations. It would be unnecessary and unwise for the government to try to determine "persons in charge" at all entities affected by CERCLA.

D. Releases Covered by This Rule

The NPRM addressed the substances for which notification is required, the types of releases subject to the notification requirements, and the determination of when a reportable quantity has been released. Many comments were received on various topics under each of these issues.

1. Hazardous Substances Subject to This Rule

a. ICRE Substances. Any hazardous waste having the characteristics identified or listed pursuant to Section 3001 of the Solid Waste Disposal Act (commonly known as the Resource Conservation and Recovery Act, or "RCRA"), but not including any waste the regulation of which has been suspended by Act of Congress, is considered a hazardous substance under section 101(14)(C) of CERCLA. These characteristics are commonly known as ICRE: ignitability, corrosivity, reactivity and extraction procedure toxicity (see 40 CFR 261.21–261.24).

The obligation to report releases to the environment of substances exhibiting the characteristics of ignitability, corrosivity, or reactivity has been the subject of some confusion.[1] Under section 103(a) of CERCLA, persons in charge of a vessel or facility must notify the NRC of the release of a "hazardous substance." The term "hazardous substance" includes all substances designated in § 302.4 of today's rule as well as wastes exhibiting the ICR characteristics under RCRA. Therefore, the release of a non-designated substance exhibiting an ICR characteristic is the release of a hazardous substance only if the

substance is a waste. If a non-designated ICR substance is spilled and immediately cleaned up for repackaging, reprocessing, recycling, or reuse, it is not a waste and the spill need not be reported (see 45 FR 78540, Nov. 25, 1980). However, if the substance is not cleaned up, or is cleaned up for eventual disposal, it is then a waste (and thus a hazardous substance) which has been released to the environment and must be reported if it exceeds the RQ.

The Agency acknowledges that the proposed rulemaking may not have been clear on this point. Accordingly, we are publishing elsewhere in today's Federal Register a proposal to set the RQ at 100 pounds for non-designated substances which are not wastes prior to their initial release but which exhibit an ICR characteristic.

Pending completion of final rulemaking on that proposal, notice given to the NRC pursuant to 49 CFR 171.15, if required under that section, of the release of a non-designated substance that is not a waste prior to its initial release, will be deemed to satisfy the reporting requirements of section 103(a) of CERCLA. Note that this policy does not apply to the release of non-designated substances which exhibit an ICR characteristic and which are wastes prior to their initial release. Such releases must be reported if they are equal to or in excess of the 100-pound RQ. Section 302.5(b) of today's final rule has been clarified to show the distinction between substances that are wastes prior to their initial release and substances that become wastes after their initial release.

b. State Delisting under RCRA. Several commenters disagreed with EPA's statement in the NPRM that reporting is required even for releases of hazardous waste which the state has properly delisted, deleted, or exempted from the state's RCRA program pursuant to authority granted by EPA. Upon further review of the RCRA regulations governing "delisting" of RCRA hazardous wastes, EPA has decided to alter its policy. Under 40 CFR 260.22, a person may petition for a regulatory amendment to exclude a waste at a particular generating facility from the lists of hazardous wastes in §§ 261.30–261.33. The petitioner must demonstrate that the waste produced by the particular facility does not meet any of the criteria under which the waste type was listed or characterized as a hazardous waste. Moreover, if granted, the exclusion applies only to the waste generated at the individual facility covered by the petitioner's demonstration. State RCRA regulations

must be substantially equivalent to these federal regulations to obtain EPA approval of the state program.

Once a specific waste from a particular facility has been shown not to contain constituents or exhibit characteristics that are considered hazardous under RCRA, there appears to be no reason to require notification under CERCLA of a release of the exempted waste. By definition, exempted wastes lack the hazardous constituents or characteristics for which the waste type was listed as hazardous. Therefore, so long as a state-exempted waste does not contain any other listed CERCLA substances, EPA will not consider the exempted waste subject to CERCLA notification requirements.

c. Petroleum Exclusion. As defined in CERCLA section 101(14), the term "hazardous substance" under CERCLA does not include

petroleum, including crude oil or any fraction thereof which is not otherwise specifically listed or designated as a hazardous substance under subparagraphs (A) through (F) of this paragraph, and the term does not include natural gas, natural gas liquids, liquefied natural gas, or synthetic gas usable for fuel (or mixtures of natural gas and such synthetic gas).

Some commenters raised questions about the limits of the exclusion of petroleum from the definition of hazardous substance. EPA interprets the petroleum exclusion to apply to materials such as crude oil, petroleum feedstocks, and refined petroleum products, even if a specifically listed or designated hazardous substance is present in such products. However, EPA does not consider materials such as waste oil to which listed CERCLA substances have been added to be within the petroleum exclusion. Similarly, pesticides are not within the petroleum exclusion, even though the active ingredients of the pesticide may be contained in a petroleum distillate; when an RQ of a listed pesticide is released, the release must be reported.

d. Nomenclature. The May 25, 1983 NPRM requested comments on several options for a nomenclature system that would be most useful for the promulgated list of CERCLA hazardous substances. The first option was that actually employed in Table 302.4 as it appeared in the NPRM, i.e., the names of the substances as they appear in the environmental statutes (and implementing regulations) that are incorporated in the CERCLA definition of a hazardous substance. A second alternative presented was to use only the Chemical Abstracts Collective Index System name, and a third was to list the

---

[1] Substances exhibiting the characteristic of extraction procedure (EP) toxicity are not at issue here, because the chemicals at which the EP toxicity test is aimed are all specifically designated as hazardous under Section 302.4 of today's regulation.

major synonyms for each hazardous substance.

Five commenters recommended use of the names provided by the Chemical Abstracts Service (CAS) in the Chemical Abstracts Collective Index System. Although use of the Collective Index names would avoid much of the confusion involved with using synonyms and would serve as positive identification of the material, many of the individuals who may need to report releases will not have easy access to Collective Index names for the substances under their control. Even among professional chemists, CAS Collective Index names are not yet widely used. For example, the term "chloroform" remains widely preferred over the Collective Index name "methane, trichloro-."

Several commenters recommended listing the "major" synonyms for each substance, pointing out that most individuals who must report releases are not chemists and therefore are familiar with the substance only by the name provided by the supplier. The commenters stated that the potential releaser cannot be expected to determine whether the substance he is dealing with is a CERCLA hazardous substance unless the name provided is also on the CERCLA list.

The Agency recognizes that listing major synonyms would, in some respects, simplify determining whether a particular named chemical is a hazardous substance. However, as several commenters pointed out, the difficulties involved in making such a list would be great. For some of the substances, more than 80 synonyms might be necessary, making Table 302.4 very unwieldy. The length of the table would be increased by a factor of at least five, increasing the difficulty of finding a named material on the list. Moreover, the choice of synonyms to be included would still be subjective, and constant updates would be needed as omitted names were found.

The names of the CERCLA hazardous substances that appeared in Table 302.4 are those that are already familiar to the regulated community under other statutes. The Agency has therefore determined that, in today's final rule, Table 302.4 will contain the same names as were listed in the NPRM, plus any other names not previously discovered by which a substance is identified in the other statutes listed in section 101(14) and their implementing regulations. Several commenters suggested that in addition to the list of names in Table 302.4, a supplementary list in CAS Registry Number order be provided. EPA has adopted this suggestion. The

CAS Registry Number, when available, uniquely identifies the designated hazardous substance. Such a list appears as an appendix to the rule as a convenience to the regulated community.

e. Generic Classes of Organic and Metallic Compounds. EPA decided not to establish RQs for the many broad generic classes of organic and metallic compounds designated as toxic pollutants under section 307(a) of the Clean Water Act, such as "chlorinated phenols," "phthalate esters," "polynuclear aromatic hydrocarbons," and "zinc and compounds." The majority of the commenters who addressed this issue understood and supported this decision. It was recognized that to establish a single RQ for broad classes of hazardous substances would be inappropriate for many of the compounds within each class. Many of the generic classes of compounds encompass hundreds or even thousands of specific compounds. It would be virtually impossible for the Agency to develop a reportable quantity for a generic class of compounds that would take into account the varying characteristics of all of the specific compounds in the class. To establish reportable quantities for generic groups of chemicals would conflict with existing knowledge of individual chemicals and their properties.

Several commenters were unsure of the Agency's position on reporting and liability for generic classes. These commenters believed that if no other RQ is established for a generic class, then they must still use the statutory one pound RQ established under CERCLA section 102(b). EPA has determined that the notification requirements need apply only to those specific compounds for which RQs are listed in Table 302.4, rather than to the generic classes of compounds. However, as the Agency indicated in the NPRM preamble, this does not preclude liability with respect to releases of specific compounds which are within one of these generic listings but which are not listed in Table 302.4. In other words, a releaser is liable for the cleanup of releases of hazardous substances which fall under any of the broad, generic classes, but does not have to report such releases when the specific compounds, and hence the RQs, are not listed in Table 302.4.

f. Massive Forms of Metals. EPA proposed that it would not require notification of releases of massive forms of the twelve solid metals originally listed under CWA section 307(a) when the diameter of the pieces of metal released equals or exceeds 100 micrometers (0.004 inches). Eleven of

fourteen commenters supported this approach, while three commenters suggested a smaller cutoff level. One of these commenters suggested that the cutoff be set at 10 micrometers rather than 100 micrometers, consistent with standards developed pursuant to the Occupational Safety and Health Act.

The cutoff size was deliberately set ten times larger than the maximum size considered by EPA to be respirable dust to ensure that releases containing small particles of metals would result in notification to the NRC. The Agency has determined that the 100-micrometer cutoff is sufficiently small to be the particle size below which notification of release of an RQ is required. The primary purpose of notification is to ensure that releasers notify the government so that the government, pursuant to the NCP, can assess the need to respond to the release. Although it is extremely unlikely that a release of solid metal particles of 100 micrometers or larger would require a response, the Agency wants to be notified of releases of smaller particles because, under some circumstances, releases of metal particles in the 10- to 100-micrometer range may require a response.

One of the eleven commenters supporting the 100-micrometer cutoff level suggested that this policy be more prominently displayed in the wording of the final rule. (In the NPRM, the 100-micrometer limitation appeared only as a footnote to Table 302.4.) 40 CFR 302.6 now states:

Notification of the release of an RQ of solid particles of antimony, arsenic, beryllium, cadmium, chromium, copper, lead, nickel, selenium, silver, thallium, or zinc is not required if the mean diameter of the particles released is larger than 100 micrometers (0.004 inches).

A particle larger than 100 micrometers in diameter will not pass through an American Society for Testing and Materials standard 140-mesh sieve.

2. Definition of Releases Subject to This Rule

a. Disposal of Hazardous Substances in RCRA Facilities. The May 25, 1983 NPRM discussion of the term "release" did not specify whether the term included or excluded the proper disposal of hazardous substances at a disposal facility that has been accorded interim status or that has received a final permit under RCRA. Some commenters suggested clarification of the meaning of the term in this regard.

EPA agrees that disposal of hazardous substances at a disposal facility in accordance with EPA regulations is not subject to CERCLA notification provisions. Where the disposal of wastes into permitted or interim status facilities is properly documented through the RCRA manifest system and RCRA regulations are followed, notification under CERCLA does not provide a significant additional benefit, so long as the facility is in substantial compliance with all applicable regulations and permit conditions. Where the disposer knows that the facility is not in substantial compliance, disposal of an RQ of a hazardous substance must be reported to the NRC. Of course, spills and accidents occurring during disposal that result in releases of reportable quantities of hazardous substances must also be reported to the NRC.

b. *Releases "Into the Environment."* A key element of the definition of "release" is the phrase "into the environment." As defined in CERCLA section 101(22), a hazardous substance must be released "into the environment" in a reportable quantity before notification of the release is required under CERCLA. Thus, the distinction between the "facility" (or "vessel") from which a substance is released and the "environment" into which a substance passes is the determining factor in requiring notification.

Hazardous substances may be released "into the environment" even if they remain on plant or installation grounds. Examples of such releases are spills from tanks or valves onto concrete pads or into lined ditches open to the outside air, releases from pipes into open lagoons or ponds, or any other discharges that are not wholly contained within buildings or structures. Such a release, if it occurs in a reportable quantity (e.g., evaporation of an RQ into the air from a dike or concrete pad), must be reported under CERCLA. On the other hand, hazardous substances may be spilled at a plant or installation but not enter the environment, e.g., when the substance spills onto the concrete floor of an enclosed manufacturing plant. Such a spill would need to be reported only if the substance were in some way to leave the building or structure in a reportable quantity. (Note, however, that the federal government may still respond and recover costs where there is a *threatened* release into the environment.]

Most of the commenters on this issue agreed with EPA's position that the distinction between "facility" and "environment" is central to determining when notification is required and that a release "into the environment" is a reportable event, but they disagreed with EPA on when a release reaches the

environment. The most common suggestion was to exclude from the definition of "environment" all of the grounds surrounding a facility that are controlled by the facility's owners or operators. Several commenters suggested that reporting should not be required as long as the facility operators are in control of released substances and initiate swift and adequate response efforts to prevent the environment from being endangered, consistent with prudent management practices. It was also suggested that so long as a release remains on facility property it would be inaccessible to the public and thus would not be a public hazard.

While EPA recognizes and appreciates the caution exercised by the majority of handlers of hazardous substances, accepting this redefinition of "environment" would be inconsistent both with the broad definition of environment in CERCLA section 101(8) and with the purpose of reporting. A primary function of CERCLA is to ensure that the government is made aware of any potentially serious release of a hazardous substance, so that the government has the opportunity to determine whether and how it needs to act. To exclude releases occurring near handling and storage facilities from CERCLA notification requirements would keep the federal government unaware of a very common form of release that may require government action. Releases onto the grounds surrounding a plant can migrate off-site through ground water or through release into the air. Defining "environment" to begin at the property line of a manufacturing plant or other installation is thus unacceptable to the Agency.

Following this same reasoning, defining environment in terms of public access, as several commenters suggested, is also unacceptable. Lack of public access to the site of a release does not preclude adverse effects on public health or welfare or the environment from the release. The volatilization of substances or their migration via ground water are obvious examples of how releases can travel off-site and threaten adjacent areas. EPA does not believe a reinterpretation of when a release enters the environment is necessary. A release into the environment will be reportable whether or not it remains on the grounds of a facility site.

One commenter requested that EPA clarify the meaning of the term "ambient air" in the definition of "environment" provided in 40 CFR Section 302.3. For the purposes of CERCLA, "ambient air" shall refer to the air that is not

completely enclosed in a building or structure and that is over and around the grounds of a facility.[2] A release into the air of a building or structure that does not reach the ambient air (either directly or via a ventilation system) is not a reportable event under CERCLA.

c. *"Workplace Exposure" Exclusion.* CERCLA section 101(22) excludes from the definition of release "any release which results in exposure to persons solely within a workplace, with respect to a claim which such persons may assert against the employer of such persons." In the May 25, 1983 NPRM preamble, EPA stated that the workplace exclusion was apparently intended to restrict the potential scope of third-party actions for personal injuries under the Act and that the limitation of hazardous substance exposure to persons within a workplace is not relevant in determining whether notification is appropriate.

Several commenters argued that the workplace exposure exclusion should be applied to workplace releases for purposes of CERCLA notification requirements. EPA disagrees. By its terms, the exclusion applies only to claims compensable through workers' compensation. The availability of workers' compensation does not appear to have any relation to the need for reporting of hazardous substance releases that threaten public health or welfare or the environment. While Congress intended to bar payment of Superfund monies to persons covered by workers' compensation systems, the legislative history clearly indicates that Congress did not intend to exclude all workplace releases of hazardous substances from CERCLA reporting requirements and response authorities. "For example, if a release occurring solely within a workplace created a hazard of damage to human life or to the environment, it is contemplated that the Fund would have the authority to respond with all of its authorities except for compensating workers whose employers are liable for their injuries under worker's compensation law" (S. Rep. 848, 96th Cong., 2d Sess. 94 (1980)). Thus, the need for notification must be determined by whether or not a release from a CERCLA "facility" or "vessel"

[2] The Agency's interpretation of "ambient air" for CERCLA reporting purposes differs from the definition of ambient air in the regulations promulgated pursuant to the Clean Air Act (CAA). These regulations define ambient air with reference to public access (see 40 CFR 50.1(e)). EPA believes that the CAA definition is inappropriate for CERCLA purposes, because the point of release for some potentially serious releases may be inaccessible to the general public, e.g., on private property.

enters "into the environment." If a release does not remain wholly contained within a building or structure, then it is a release into the environment for CERCLA purposes, whether or not it occurs within a workplace.

3. Determination of When a Reportable Quantity Has Been Released

Once it has been determined that a hazardous substance release is covered by CERCLA, the releaser must determine if the release is in a quantity equal to or greater than the reportable quantity of that substance. Two critical issues in making this determination are the period of release and the application of RQs to mixtures and solutions. This section discusses EPA's positions on these issues and responds to comments received on the NPRM.

a. Period of Release. EPA proposed to use a 24-hour period for measuring whether the reportable quantity of a substance has been released, noting that the 24-hour period has been used successfully under regulations implementing the CWA section 311. As soon as the person in charge knows that the amount of a release within that period equals or exceeds the applicable reportable quantity, the NRC must be notified. Eleven commenters concurred with the Agency's decision to use the 24-hour period, citing the consistency of the decision with the CWA section 311 regulations.

Three commenters misinterpreted the purpose of the 24-hour period as the time a person has in which to establish the knowledge that a release has occurred. EPA wants to clarify that when the amount of a CERCLA hazardous substance release equals or exceeds the reportable quantity, the person in charge, once he or she knows of the release, must immediately notify the National Response Center. The 24-hour period refers to the period within which a reportable quantity of a hazardous substance must be released for the release to be considered reportable; it does not refer to the time available for a person to report a release. Such reporting must occur immediately.

b. Mixtures of Hazardous Substances. When determining if notification is required for releases of mixtures and solutions containing hazardous substances, the Agency intends to apply the mixture rule developed in connection with the CWA section 311 regulations. This rule provides that "[d]ischarges of mixtures and solutions are subject to these regulations only where a component hazardous substance of the mixture or solution is discharged in a quantity equal to or

greater than its RQ" (44 FR 50767, August 29, 1979). RQs of different substances are not additive under the mixture rule, so that spilling a mixture containing half an RQ of one hazardous substance and half an RQ of another hazardous substance does not require a report.

Most commenters supported using the CWA mixture rule. These commenters agreed with EPA that it is generally technically appropriate to consider the RQs of component hazardous substances of a mixture individually when determining if a report is required. They also note that applying the CWA mixture rule to CERCLA hazardous substances would allow the regulated community to continue with existing monitoring and notification procedures.

One commenter opposed use of the CWA mixture rule, arguing that EPA has no data to support the implicit assumption that toxic effects are not additive or synergistic. The commenter stated that additive or synergistic effects often occur.

EPA recognizes that the toxic effects of chemical mixtures may in some instances be additive, synergistic, or even antagonistic. Unfortunately, only limited data exist on the extent of such effects. Moreover, trying to incorporate such data into the mixture rule for CERCLA notification purposes would make the determination of whether an RQ had been released much more complex and confusing. The RQ would vary with each mixture, depending on whether the components of the mixture had additive, synergistic, or antagonistic effects. Thus, a different RQ would have to be determined for each potential release situation, a highly complex approach that EPA has consistently tried to avoid (see section V.C.2. below). To be effective, the CERCLA notification system must be simple to administer and apply. For this reason, the Agency will apply the CWA mixture rule—contained in § 302.6 of today's rule—to releases subject to CERCLA reporting requirements.

Several commenters were uncertain when to apply the mixture rule to the various RCRA regulated wastes (F and K lists) and to the unlisted ICRE wastes. The Agency emphasizes that, for CERCLA purposes, the CWA mixture rule applies to ICRE wastes and to the RCRA F and K waste streams (all of which tend to be mixtures), if the concentrations of all the hazardous substances in the waste are known. If the concentrations of the substances are unknown, the RQ of the waste stream or unlisted waste applies. In addition, if the person in charge knows that an RQ of a hazardous constituent of a waste has

been released before the RQ for the waste stream or unlisted waste has been exceeded, he or she must report the release. However, CERCLA does not itself impose any testing reqirements.

Some commenters objected to application of the CWA mixture rule to waste streams, arguing that under-reporting could result if the components of the waste were incorrectly identified. The Agency, however, maintains that if the concentrations of the hazardous substances contained in the mixture are known, waste streams should be treated like any other mixture. If the releaser does not know the composition of the listed waste stream, EPA agrees that applying the RQ of the entire waste stream is the only reasonably conservative alternative.

For example, a mixture of spent (used) cresols and nitrobenzene is identified in the RCRA regulations (40 CFR 261.31) as a hazardous waste from a non-specific source, F004. F004 has an RQ of 100 pounds, because the RQ for cresols is 100 pounds, the RQ for nitrobenzene is 1000 pounds, and the lowest RQ for any of the hazardous substances in the mixture applies. If the person in charge knows only that a waste material contains unspecified amounts of cresols and nitrobenzene, then he or she would have to report if 100 pounds or more of the waste were released. The person in charge may, however, if sufficient data are available, apply the CWA mixture rule. If he or she knows that the F004 waste contains 50 percent cresols and 50 percent nitrobenzene, the releaser would have to report only when the total release equalled or exceeded 200 pounds, because at that point the 100-pound RQ of the cresol component would be equalled or exceeded. Because the concentrations of the hazardous substances in the waste stream are known, there is no reason to restrict the releaser to the F004 waste RQ of 100 pounds. In this case, for notification purposes, the waste stream is no different than a known mixture of pure substances.

A few commenters questioned whether the mixture rule applies to products where the active chemical ingredient for which it is named is present in less than 100 percent concentration. While the NPRM discussion of the mixture rule did not explicitly mention "formulations of less than 100 percent strength," such formulations are indeed mixtures or solutions and are covered by the mixture rule. Two commenters wanted EPA to waive the CERCLA notification requirements for mixtures containing very low concentrations of hazardous substances. These commenters suggested assigning a concentration-value to each hazardous substance below which notification would not be required. This approach would, in effect result in two rules for each substance, making application of the mixture rule cumbersome for the regulated community. Moreover, determining each concentration value would require the use of specific release scenarios, a methodology that EPA has rejected (see 48 FR 23569 and Section V.C.3. of this preamble). For these reasons, EPA is retaining the mixture rule for all mixtures containing any concentration of a hazardous substance, no matter how low the concentration.

E. Exemptions From the CERCLA Notification Requirements

CERCLA provides four types of exemptions from the notification requirements applicable to releases of hazardous substances in reportable quantities. Each type of exemption was discussed in the May 25, 1983 NPRM preamble. Responses to major comments received on the exemption for the application of pesticide products registered under the Federal Insecticide, Fungicide, and Rodenticide Act (FIFRA) are provided below. Issues relating to the limited exemption for continuous releases and exemptions for "federally permitted releases" are not resolved in today's rule.

Section 103(e) of CERCLA exempts from the notification provisions of the Act "the application of a pesticide product registered under the Federal Insecticide, Fungicide, and Rodenticide Act (FIFRA) [and] the handling and storage of such a pesticide product by an agricultural producer." In the proposed rule, EPA interpreted the application of pesticides as the normal application of registered pesticides (and pesticides used in accordance with FIFRA section 5 experimental use permits or FIFRA section 18 emergency exemptions) in ways that are consistent with the labeling instructions.

Commenters objected to several aspects of EPA's pesticide exemption policy as stated in the NPRM. The first category of objections concerned the wording of the policy. Some commenters suggested that the phrase "pursuant to the label directions" as used in the definition of "normal application of pesticides" applies more to consumer goods than to industrial chemicals, because the label directions of the latter may not include complete application practices. Other commenters objected to the use of the term "normal" in the definition of "normal application of pesticides," because the term does not

appear in CERCLA section 103(e) and constitutes a potentially unnecessary restriction on the exemption.

EPA agrees that the definition of "normal application of pesticides" is unnecessary, and the definition does not appear in today's final rule. The legislative history of CERCLA suggests that Congress intended that the pesticide exemption apply to the application of a pesticide generally in accordance with its purpose. S. Rep. No. 848, 96th Cong., 2d Sess. 45 (July 13, 1980). While strict compliance with labeling direction is not a prerequisite for the exemption, the extent of compliance will be a critical factor in determining whether the application was generally in accordance with the pesticide's purpose. EPA does not consider a spill of a pesticide to be either an "application" of the pesticide or in accordance with the pesticide's purpose. Consequently, such spills must be reported. Note, moreover, that use of a pesticide inconsistent with its labeling is a violation of FIFRA that is potentially subject to both civil and criminal penalties.

F. Duplicate Reporting

1. General

EPA is seeking to minimize unnecessary duplication between CERCLA reporting requirements and the reporting requirements of other environmental statutes. However, some commenters complained of the duplicative reporting burden created by CERCLA and of a lack of coordination among federal, state, and local agencies. Eight of these commenters suggested that one report to the NRC should suffice for all government agencies. Currently, one call to the NRC fulfills the requirement to report releases of hazardous substances under CERCLA and several other regulatory programs, including the Clean Water Act, the Resource Conservation and Recovery Act, and the Hazardous Materials Transportation Act, which is administered by the Department of Transportation. The May 25, 1983 NPRM preamble discussed the equivalence of compliance with certain RCRA reporting requirements and CERCLA notification requirements. Section 103(f)(1) of CERCLA exempts from the notification requirements of sections 103 (a) and (b) releases that are subject to reporting requirements (or specifically exempted from such reporting) under Subtitle C of RCRA and have been reported to the National Response Center. The Agency has reviewed all other areas of duplicate reporting created by CERCLA and has found that the burden imposed by

CERCLA notification requirements is not great. At most, the duplication that exists may require that more than one telephone call concerning a release be made by the releaser and recorded by government agencies.

Today's final rule does not affect hazardous substance reporting requirements imposed by certain other regulations and statutes, as discussed in section IV.G. below.

2. Newspaper Notification Requirement

CERCLA section 111(g) requires that owners or operators of any vessel or facility "provide reasonable notice to potential injured parties by publication in local newspapers serving the affected area" of any release of a hazardous substance. One commenter asked whether RQ notification requirements revoke section 111(g). The newspaper notification requirement established by section 111(g) of CERCLA is not affected by any of the notification requirements in today's rule.

G. Regulatory Consistency

EPA has always made every effort to coordinate its regulations of hazardous substances with other government agencies. For example, EPA and the Department of Transportation (DOT) (which includes the U.S. Coast Guard) have cooperated over the years in a series of regulatory actions, including the establishment of the centralized toll-free telephone number for reporting spills of hazardous substances to the NRC. EPA recognizes that cooperation with other agencies is vital to the development of clear and consistent regulatory policies in areas of complementary or shared responsibility. The Agency has carefully reviewed comments from other government agencies on the NPRM and does not believe that the CERCLA RQs or notification requirements create regulatory inconsistencies.

Many commenters questioned the extent of EPA–DOT coordination concerning CERCLA RQ regulations and regulations pursuant to the Hazardous Materials Transportation Act (HMTA). EPA recognizes the need for consistency between the RQ regulations and DOT's Hazardous Material Regulations (HMR). The Agency believes that the cooperative efforts of EPA and DOT will result in an RQ adjustment regulatory approach that will be consistent with any related regulations promulgated by DOT. EPA has promoted and will continue to promote coordination between the RQ adjustment regulation and the HMR. EPA wishes to clarify, however, that while it strongly supports cooperation between EPA and DOT, it has no authority to revise the HMR. Any changes must be made by DOT.

The International Convention for the Prevention of Pollution from Ships (MARPOL 73/78), as implemented through the Act to Prevent Pollution from Ships (33 U.S.C. 1901 *et seq.*), currently imposes reporting requirements concerning releases of harmful substances from U.S. ships wherever located and from foreign ships within the navigable waters of the United States. Under 33 U.S.C. 1908, as soon as a person in charge of a ship has knowledge of an event involving the actual or probable release into the sea of a harmful substance (broadly defined), he or she must report the incident to the Secretary of the department in which the Coast Guard is operating (currently DOT). No reportable quantities are specified. Thus, MARPOL 73/78, as implemented by 33 U.S.C. § 1908, may require reporting even where CERCLA does not.

Annex II of MARPOL 73/78 prohibits discharges of noxious liquid substances within 12 miles from shore. Beyond 12 miles, discharges are either prohibited or limited, depending on the nature of the cargo and compliance with several criteria. Annex II, scheduled to take effect in October 1986, applies to all ships carrying noxious liquid substances in bulk and limits operational discharges of these substances by setting minimum or maximum numerical values for distance from shore, depth of water, ship speed, concentration of substance in ship's wake, and maximum quantity of cargo residues that may be discharged. To improve regulatory consistency and enhance coordination with the U.S. Coast Guard, EPA intends to investigate the scope and intent of MARPOL 73/78 Annex II regulations (including a Coast Guard ANPRM (48 FR 1519–1521, Jan. 13, 1983) dealing with certain types of hazardous substances that are intended to be regulated in accord with MARPOL) and to examine regulatory and technical concerns arising from coordination between CERCLA and MARPOL.

Section 8(e) of the Toxic Substances Control Act (TSCA) may also require reporting where CERCLA does not. Pursuant to a Statement of Interpretation published March 16, 1978, 43 FR 11110, all emergency incidents of environmental contamination that present a "substantial risk of injury to health or the environment" must be reported to EPA under TSCA section 8(e). Section 8(e) could require notification even where no CERCLA hazardous substances or RQs have been

released. Persons subject to the notification requirement include both natural persons and business entities engaged in the manufacturing, processing, or commercial distribution of chemical substances or mixtures. No notification is required if the manufacturer, processor, or distributor knows that EPA has been informed of the risk presented by the incident. For hazardous substance releases subject to CERCLA, a single notification to the NRC will satisfy both CERCLA and TSCA section 8(e) reporting requirements; the Agency will ensure that section 8(e) reports are passed to the proper authorities.

H. Penalties

Section 302.7(a) of the proposed rule set forth the penalties imposed by CERCLA Section 103(b) for failure to notify the NRC of a reportable release. Section 302.7(a) of today's final rule does not specify the penalties established by CERCLA section 103(b); rather, the rule incorporates the statutory penalties by reference. The regulation still informs responsible parties of the statutory sanctions for failure to notify, but the change will avoid the need to amend 40 CFR 302.7 should CERCLA section 103(b) be amended. Currently, CERCLA section 103(b) provides that any person in charge of a facility or vessel from which a hazardous substance is released, other than a federally permitted release, in a quantity equal to or greater than the reportable quantity, who fails to notify the appropriate federal agency as soon as he has knowledge of the release, shall upon conviction be fined not more than $10,000 or imprisoned for not more than one year, or both. Notifications received under sections 103(a) or 103(b) or information obtained by such notice cannot be used against any reporting person in any criminal case, except a prosecution for perjury or for giving a false statement.

V. Reportable Quantity Adjustments

A. Introduction

The primary purpose of the CERCLA notification requirements, discussed above in section IV, is to ensure that releasers notify the government so that the need for a federal response can be evaluated and any necessary response undertaken in a timely fashion.

With this purpose in mind, EPA proposed adjustments to the statutory RQs of CERCLA hazardous substances based on specific scientific and technical criteria that relate to the possibility of harm from the release of a hazardous substance in a reportable

quantity. The adjusted RQs do not reflect a determination that a release of a substance will be hazardous at the RQ level and not hazardous below that level. EPA has not attempted to make such a determination because the actual hazard will vary with the unique circumstances of the release, and extensive data and analysis would be necessary to determine the hazard presented by each substance in a number of possible circumstances. Instead, the RQs reflect the Agency's judgment of which releases should trigger mandatory notification to the federal government so that the government may assess to what extent, if any, a federal removal or remedial action may be necessary.

Over forty commenters supported both the methodology EPA used in determining RQs and the results of this methodology. These commenters agreed that the RQ adjustments will:

(1) Increase the efficiency and certainty of the Superfund program;

(2) Reduce burdens on the regulated community; and

(3) Improve EPA's ability to concentrate its attention and resources on the releases that are potentially most threatening to public health or welfare or the environment.

In addition, EPA received many comments on various specific topics relating to the RQ adjustments that were discussed in the NPRM. Some commenters also discussed issues that were not explicitly addressed in the proposed rule. Responses to both types of comments are presented below.

B. Number of Reportable Quantity Levels and Their Values

1. Five RQ Levels

For purposes of making RQ adjustments under CERCLA, EPA has adopted the five RQ levels of 1, 10, 100, 1000, and 5000 pounds originally established pursuant to CWA section 311 (see 40 CFR Part 117). The Agency adopted the CWA five-level system primarily because (1) it has been successfully used pursuant to the CWA, (2) the regulated community is already familiar with these five levels, and (3) it provides a relatively high degree of discrimination among the potential hazards posed by different CERCLA hazardous substances. Many commenters voiced general support of the five-level system; however, as the next section discusses, some commenters criticized the use of one pound as the lowest RQ level.

2. One-Pound RQs

Several comments were received on the one-pound RQ level. A few commenters argued that a one-pound RQ is too small for reporting purposes. They reasoned that a one-pound release of a hazardous substance would have an inconsequential impact on public health and welfare and the environment and that federal agencies would not respond to such small releases.

The one-pound RQ is consistent with prior regulation under the Clean Water Act (see 40 CFR Part 117). One pound was selected under the Clean Water Act as the lowest reporting level because one pound is typically the smallest container size used in commerce for transporting moderately or extremely hazardous substances 40 FR 59989, December 30, 1975. Moreover, the Agency interviewed a large cross-section of field response personnel, and all of those interviewed indicated that they want to be notified of most releases, even at the one-pound level. In the interviews, the field response personnel recognized that the government may not institute removal or remedial actions for many one-pound releases, but they emphasized that notification was a prerequisite for determining (1) the need for a response under the circumstances, (2) the adequacy of any cleanup efforts, and (3) the degree to which post-release monitoring may be required. Furthermore, many releases tend to be escalating events, and early notification helps ensure an effective response.

Six commenters criticized the one-pound RQ level for posing an unreasonable burden on the regulated community. One commenter indicated that the adoption of one-pound RQs will require many companies to do extensive testing of raw materials in order to assure compliance with this regulation. CERCLA does not require any testing, and EPA does not intend to require any further testing beyond that which is already required by other statutes and their implementing regulations.

C. Methodology Used To Adjust Reportable Quantities

1. The Methodology Chosen

The selected strategy for adjusting RQs begins with an evaluation of the intrinsic physical, chemical, and toxicological properties of each designated hazardous substance. The intrinsic properties examined—called "primary criteria"—are aquatic toxicity, mammalian toxicity (oral, dermal, and inhalation), ignitability, reactivity, and chronic toxicity. (For the purposes of this rule, chronic toxicity—referred to as

"other toxic effects" in the May 25, 1983 NPRM—is defined as toxicity resulting from repeated or continuous exposure to either a single release or multiple releases of a hazardous substance.) In addition, substances that were identified as potential carcinogens have been evaluated for their relative activity as potential carcinogens; the RQs for these substances will be proposed in a separate rulemaking, and the methodology for adjusting RQs on the basis of potential carcinogenicity will at that time be presented for public comment.

The Agency ranks each intrinsic property on a five-tier scale, associating a specified range of values on each scale with a particular RQ value. Thus, each substance receives several tentative RQ values based on its particular properties.[3] The lowest of all of the tentative RQs becomes the "primary criteria RQ" for that substance. (See Section V.D.1. below for further detail.)

After the primary criteria RQs are assigned, substances are further evaluated for their susceptibility to certain extrinsic degradation processes. These extrinsic processes (referred to as "secondary criteria" in the May 25, 1983 NPRM) are biodegradation, hydrolysis, and photolysis, or "BHP." If the analysis indicates that a substance degrades relatively rapidly to a less harmful compound through one or more of these processes when it is released into the environment, the primary criteria RQ is raised one level. (See section V.D.2. below for further detail.) The single RQ assigned to each substance on the basis of the primary criteria and BHP becomes the adjusted RQ for that substance.

2. Multiple RQs and Media-Specific RQs

Many commenters objected to the Agency's proposal to establish a single RQ for each hazardous substance. It was suggested that either (1) the Agency should develop several RQs for each hazardous substance, for example, one RQ for each of the various environmental media (air, water, soil) into which a release might occur, or (2) the Agency should base the adjusted RQ for each substance on the most likely medium of release rather than on the most sensitive environmental trigger (as is currently done).

Several of the objecting commenters believed that the RQs would be arbitrary if they did not reflect the

varying degrees of risk presented by releases into different environmental media. For similar reasons, they argued that the RQs should vary depending on the form of the substance released (i.e., whether it is a solid, a liquid, or a gas) and its ability to dissipate into the environment. The objecting commenters believed that if the RQs were to reflect more accurately the hazards of given releases, the overall reporting burden would be reduced, because reports would not have to be made in situations where the government would be unlikely to respond.

As has been stated, the RQs are not intended to represent judgments by the Agency as to the specific degree of hazard associated with certain releases. The actual hazard will vary with the circumstances of the particular release, and many factors other than the size of the release will influence the government's response. The single RQ approach was adopted to provide a relatively simple reporting system that does not unduly burden either EPA or the regulated community. Since releases into more than one medium often occur, the single RQ approach will prevent confusion. Section 102(a) of CERCLA expressly authorizes the Administrator to set a single quantity for each hazardous substance, and the legislative history emphasizes the virtues of simplicity and administrative convenience (see Sen. Rep. 848, 96th Cong., 2d Sess. 29 (1980)). Moreover, the Agency simply does not have the resources to obtain the vast quantity of technical data required to develop RQs that, on the one hand, are tailored to fit every release situation, and that, on the other hand, are consistent, equitable, and adequately protective of public health and welfare and the environment.

EPA will be able to refine the single-RQ approach over time as more information becomes available, without having to expend substantial resources to develop a massive technical data base and undertake other burdensome rulemaking support. Radionuclides, because of their unique characteristics, are the one category of substances for which the Agency is considering deviation from the single RQ approach. As noted in section III.C. of this preamble, radionuclide RQs will be addressed in a separate rulemaking.

A number of commenters expressed the opinion that the RQ adjustment criteria should take particular release circumstances into consideration. The suggested circumstances included release into a sewer system, release near a public drinking water supply, release near a residential area, and air

---

[3] If available evidence shows that a substance hydrolyzes into a reaction product that is more hazardous than the original substance, the primary criteria are applied to the reaction product rather than to the original substance to determine the primary criteria RQ values for the original substance.

emissions from elevated sources (tall stacks). One commenter even stated that "determinations of actual harm" should be made for all substances with one- and ten-pound RQs by examining release potential, release history, the degree of hazard or risk of particular releases in various environmental media, and the likelihood that such releases would require federal action. The Agency position is that particular circumstances should not affect the RQ level; instead, they may influence the government's decisions concerning whether and how it should respond to a particular release.

Many commenters focused on the appropriateness of a single RQ governing emissions into the air as well as releases into other media. They argued as follows:

• Because the government cannot respond to most air emissions by containing or cleaning up the emissions, and because other government responses (e.g., evacuation of the nearby populace) are required only infrequently, requiring routine reporting of air emissions under a single-RQ approach would be wasteful and burdensome.

• The impacts of emissions into ambient air are substantially less than releases of similar size to water or soil, and the photolysis and degradation of many air emissions tend to be relatively rapid.

• Relatively few substances would be eligible for separate air release RQs, and EPA would not have to devote a substantial amount of effort and resources to make the appropriate adjustments.

The Agency believes that an exception to the single-RQ approach for air releases could not be restricted to air releases alone under the above reasoning. Several other types of releases exhibit certain of the characteristics of air releases, such as releases into large bodies of rapidly moving water. If the circumstances of particular releases were taken into account in setting RQs, the entire process would place an intolerable burden on Agency resources. The process would also become potentially inconsistent, inequitable, and subject to

delay. Moreover, the resulting complexity in RQs would be likely to engender both confusion and further charges of arbitrariness.

One commenter believed that, for the most part, releases that would be affected by a separate air release RQ would be those which are "continuous" and released from facilities subject to Clean Air Act regulations. If an air release falls within the exemptions provided by CERCLA for "continuous" or "federally permitted" releases, of course, no notification is necessary (except as required for continuous releases); if many air releases are exempt, a separate air release RQ would provide very few benefits.

3. Alternative Methodologies Considered

In the May 25, 1983 NPRM, EPA described and solicited comments on three alternative methodologies for adjusting RQs: Hazard Index, Scenarios, and Fate and Effects. Most commenters agreed with the Agency that these methodologies would be impractical to implement and would introduce unnecessary complexities into the RQ adjustment process, although several commenters encouraged further research into the Hazard Index approach. No new data to facilitate a more complete evaluation of these methodologies have been submitted. Because these methodologies are complex and require much data that are unavailable at this time, EPA is not currently pursuing these methodologies further for RQ adjustment purposes.

D. Criteria Used To Adjust Reportable Quantities

1. Primary Criteria

a. Aquatic Toxicity. In adjusting RQs, EPA used the categories of aquatic toxicity that were established pursuant to section 311 of the CWA. As Exhibit 1 shows, each category is linked to one of the five RQ levels. The RQ value based on aquatic toxicity is identical to the RQ promulgated under the CWA section 311 except where the use of updated aquatic toxicity data has resulted in a different RQ (see section V.F.2. below).

EXHIBIT 1.—CATEGORIES FOR REPORTABLE QUANTITY ASSIGNMENTS PURSUANT TO CWA SECTION 311

RQ (pounds)	Aquatic toxicity	Category
1	LC₅₀* <0.1 mg/liter	X
10	0.1mg/liter <LC₅₀ <1 mg/liter	A
100	1 mg/liter <LC₅₀ <10 mg/liter	B
1000	10 mg/liter <LC₅₀ <100 mg/liter	C
5000	100 mg/liter <LC₅₀ <500 mg/liter	D

* "LC₅₀" refers to that concentration of material which is lethal to one-half of the test population of aquatic animals upon continuous exposure for 96 hours. (See 40 CFR 116.14).
Source: 43 FR 10492, March 13, 1978.

One commenter questioned the rationale for assigning one-pound RQs to substances in the highest aquatic toxicity category. The commenter indicated that an RQ of 10 pounds, or even 100 pounds, could be assigned just as easily. The five-level reportable quantity scale for aquatic toxicity was taken directly from section 311 of the Clean Water Act. The CWA section 311 reporting categories are being retained for CERCLA reporting purposes in order to ensure consistency between the two closely related acts. The aquatic toxicity RQ scale has been used successfully in implementing the Clean Water Act, and the regulated community is familiar with it. Moreover, as noted above in the section on one-pound RQs, many releases tend to be escalating events requiring prompt attention.

b. Mammalian Toxicity. EPA separately evaluated oral, dermal, and inhalation toxicity for the mammalian toxicity criterion. A five-level scale was devised for each type of toxicity. These scales are shown in Exhibit 2. The RQ chosen for mammalian toxicity represents the lowest of the values derived from the three scales. These scales were discussed in detail in the NPRM (48 FR 23562–23563).

One commenter believed that the Agency's mammalian toxicity scales assign RQs which are too high for some poisonous substances. The commenter therefore proposed new scales based on mammalian toxicity that would assign many more one-pound RQs than the Agency's scales. The Agency believes that the scales suggested by the commenter are overly broad and could lead to unnecessary reporting.

EXHIBIT 2.—CATEGORIES FOR REPORTABLE QUANTITY ADJUSTMENTS BASED ON MAMMALIAN TOXICITY *

RQ (pounds)	Mammalian toxicity (oral)	Mammalian toxicity (dermal)	Mammalian toxicity (inhalation)
1	LD₅₀* <0.1 mg/kg	LD₅₀ <0.04 mg/kg	LC₅₀* <0.4 ppm.
10	0.1 mg/kg <LD₅₀ <1 mg/kg	0.04 mg/kg <LD₅₀ <0.4 mg/kg	0.4 ppm <LC₅₀ <4 ppm.
100	1 mg/kg <LD₅₀ <10 mg/kg	0.4 mg/kg <LD₅₀ <4 mg/kg	4 ppm <LC₅₀ <40 ppm.
1000	10 mg/kg <LD₅₀ <100 mg/kg	4 mg/kg <LD₅₀ <40 mg/kg	40 ppm <LC₅₀ <400 ppm.
5000	100 mg/kg <LD₅₀ <500 mg/kg	40 mg/kg <LD₅₀ <200 mg/kg	400 ppm <LC₅₀ <2000 ppm.

* For a detailed explanation of the derivation of these categories, see Technical Background Document to Support Rulemaking Pursuant to CERCLA Section 102.
b "LD₅₀" refers to that dose of a substance expected to cause the death of 50 percent of a defined experimental mammalian population.
c "LC₅₀" refers to that concentration of a substance in the air that is expected to cause the death of 50 percent of a defined experimental mammalian population.

c. *Ignitability and Reactivity.* The Agency used a five-level scale to assign RQs based on ignitability. The NPRM discussed this scale in detail (48 FR 23563). Exhibit 3 shows the scale used. The Agency did not assign one-pound RQs based on ignitability because small releases of a flammable substance would generally be consumed so quickly that any federal government response action would be infeasible.

EXHIBIT 3.—CATEGORIES FOR REPORTABLE QUANTITY ADJUSTMENTS BASED ON IGNITABILITY [a]

RQ (pounds)	Ignitability (fire)
1	No 1-pound RQs on the basis of ignitability.
10	Pyrophoric or self-ignitable.
100	FP[b] <100°F. BP[c] <100°F.
1000	FP <100°F. BP >100°F.
5000	FP 100°F–140°F.

[a] For a detailed explanation of the derivation of these categories, see Technical Background Document to Support Rulemaking Pursuant to CERCLA Section 102.
[b] "FP" refers to the flash point, the temperature at which a substance forms an ignitable mixture with the air at the surface of the substance, measured using the closed cup test.
[c] "BP" refers to the boiling point, the temperature at which a liquid boils.

The Agency also used five-level scales for assigning RQs based on two types of reactivity: reactivity with water and self-reaction. For reactivity, as for ignitability, no one-pound RQs were assigned. The NPRM discussed the reactivity scales and their development. Exhibit 4 shows the scales used.

One commenter requested that the minimum RQ level for the ignitability and reactivity RQ scales be set at 100 pounds instead of 10 pounds. The Agency has decided to retain the 10-pound minimum RQ level. As a result of interviews with federal government field response personnel, the Agency decided to remove the one-pound RQ level from the ignitability and reactivity RQ scales. Government response personnel indicated that releases of less than 10 pounds of ignitable and reactive substances normally would be adequately handled by appropriate local or state response personnel, and they concurred with the Agency's proposal to raise to 10 pounds the minimum reporting level for the ignitability and reactivity RQ scales. Government response personnel, however, objected to raising the minimum reporting level any further. They believed that reporting levels should be kept low to ensure timely reporting of releases and timely government response, if necessary.

EXHIBIT 4—CATEGORIES FOR REPORTABLE QUANTITY ADJUSTMENTS BASED ON REACTIVITY [a]

RQ (pounds)	Reactivity [b]	
	With water	Self-reaction
1	No 1-pound RQs on the basis of reactivity	No 1-pound RQs on the basis of reactivity
10	Inflames (e.g., Na, CaC₂).	Extreme self-reaction; may cause explosion or detonation.
100	Extreme reaction (e.g., SO₃).	High; may polymerize; requires stabilizer.
1000	High reaction (e.g., oleum).	Moderate; contamination may cause polymerization; no inhibitor required.
5000	Moderate reaction (e.g., NH₃).	Slight; may polymerize with low heat release.

[a] For a detailed explanation of the derivation of these categories, see Technical Background Document to Support Rulemaking Pursuant to CERCLA section 102.
[b] Based on heat release.

d. *Chronic Toxicity.* The Agency used data on chronic toxicity (referred to as "other toxic effects" in the May 25, 1983 NPRM) to adjust the statutory RQs for some hazardous substances. For other hazardous substances, data on chronic toxicity were still being evaluated at the time of the May 25, 1983 NPRM. RQs were not adjusted for those substances undergoing evaluation; thus, the statutory RQ applies. In addition, there are a few substances for which an RQ was proposed in the NPRM but for which EPA subsequently determined that further evaluation was necessary. The statutory RQ applies for these substances until a final RQ is promulgated (see section V.F.2. below).

When analyzed for chronic toxicity, substances are assigned scores based on both the minimum effective dose (MED) levels for repeated exposures and the severity of the effects caused by repeated or continuous exposure. The scores are then used to assign RQs. The NPRM described the methodology used (48 FR 23564); Exhibit 5 shows the RQ levels based on chronic toxicity.

EXHIBIT 5.—CATEGORIES FOR REPORTABLE QUANTITY ADJUSTMENTS BASED ON CHRONIC TOXICITY [a]

RQ (pounds)	Composite score
1	81–100
10	41–80
100	21–40
1000	6–20
5000	1–5

[a] For a detailed explanation of the derivation of these categories, see Technical Background Document to Support Rulemaking Pursuant to CERCLA Section 102.

A number of commenters suggested that chronic toxicity should not be used to determine RQs or should be used only

with additional restrictions. These commenters believed that chronic toxicity, which is a function of prolonged exposure, should not be considered because the purpose of the RQ program is to monitor episodic releases. The Agency decided to use chronic toxicity as a criterion in setting RQs because episodic releases which are not rapidly and completely cleaned up may result in repeated or continuous exposure to a toxic substance. Moreover, CERCLA reporting requirements cover both episodic and continuous releases. Continuous releases may also lead to repeated or continuous exposure to toxic substances.

e. *Potential Carcinogenicity.* Today's rule does not use any measure of potential carcinogenicity to adjust RQs. EPA is in the process of developing adjusted RQs for substances which have been identified as potential carcinogens. The statutory RQs for these substances apply while they are being considered for RQ adjustment. Table 302.4 notes those substances which are being evaluated for their relative activity as potential carcinogens (but which may or may not be potential carcinogens).

2. Other Criteria Used to Adjust RQs (BHP)

a. *Use of BHP Criteria.* Twenty commenters supported the use of the natural degradation processes of biodegradation, hydrolysis, and photolysis ("BHP") as additional criteria for adjusting RQs. The BHP criteria are used, where appropriate, to raise RQ values one level from that suggested by the primary criteria analysis. Four commenters opposed the use of BHP to adjust RQs.

The supporting commenters agreed that the above degradation processes tend to reduce the relative potential for harm to public health and welfare and the environment of certain hazardous substance releases. It was seen that taking the environmental fate characteristics of particular substances into account in setting RQ levels was an appropriate method to reduce the overall reporting burden while still adequately protecting public health and welfare and the environment. However, one commenter emphasized that the BHP criteria are a useful RQ adjustment tool only where the associated analysis is not overly complex, expensive, or time-consuming.

Several commenters requested clarification of the methodology used in applying BHP. The Technical Background Document supporting this rulemaking sets forth in detail the relatively simple, yet scientifically conservative methodology used to apply these criteria. First, several elimination criteria are used to limit the number of substances eligible for the one-level increase based on BHP. The elimination criteria include the following: tendency to bioaccumulate, environmental persistence, the presence of unusual hazards (e.g., high reactivity), the existence of hazardous degradation or transformation products, or a primary criteria RQ already at the maximum assignable level of 5000 pounds. The remaining substances are evaluated for their susceptibility to biodegradation, hydrolysis, and photolysis. As discussed below, the Agency uses ranges of degradation rates sufficient to ensure that the substances selected for the one-level increase in RQ (27 in today's final rule) are in fact relatively degradable.

Two commenters believed that the Agency's evaluation pursuant to the BHP criteria should lead to a downward adjustment if the risk posed by the release of a hazardous substance is increased as a result of biodegradation, hydrolysis, or photolysis (i.e., if the natural degradation processes produce materials in the environment that are more hazardous than the original substance released). The Agency agrees that consideration must be given to the toxicity of the degradation products. Where reaction products more hazardous than the original substance are readily known and identified, the Agency has based the primary criteria RQ of the original substance on the characteristics of the more hazardous reaction products, effectively resulting in a "downward adjustment."

Application of the primary criteria to the reaction products rather than to the original substances occurred in ten cases for the substances assigned final adjusted RQs in this rule. For example, substances known to generate hydrogen sulfide or phosphine upon hydrolysis have been assigned primary criteria RQs on the basis of these reaction products.

The few commenters opposing the use of BHP felt that biodegradation, hydrolysis, and photolysis should be considered by the On-Scene Coordinator in determining the government's response after a release has been reported, but that EPA should not use such processes to alter the initial reporting level suggested by the primary criteria. For the reasons given below, the Agency disagrees.

First, the commenters asserted that biodegradation, hydrolysis, and photolysis should not be applied in the setting of RQs because these processes may not affect the immediate hazard posed by a given release and instead may only reduce the potential long-term dangers of the release. However, EPA has used degradation measures that address both short- and long-term potential hazards. The RQ of a substance is not raised unless (1) the reported biological oxygen demand of the substance over a five-day period at 20 degrees Celsius is at least fifty percent of the theoretical oxygen demand (the stoichiometric quantity of oxygen needed to oxidize a substance completely to carbon dioxide and water), or (2) when subjected to hydrolysis, photolysis, or either process in conjunction with biodegradation, the estimated half-life of the substance is equal to or less than five days.

The primary criteria RQs of four substances (allyl chloride, butylamine, diazinon, and ethyl acrylate) were adjusted upwards in the May 25, 1983 NPRM on the basis of degradation data involving periods greater than five days, because data for shorter periods were unavailable. The Agency has since decided to adjust RQs according to the criteria stated above (i.e., evidence of degradation within five days), to ensure that all substances selected for the one-level increase will tend to degrade rapidly once they are released. Therefore, allyl chloride, butylamine, diazinon, and ethyl acrylate are assigned their primary criteria RQs in today's final rule.

The second major argument raised by the commenters opposed to the use of BHP was that the methods for measuring the occurrence and rate of biodegradation, hydrolysis, and photolysis do not take into account the entire range of environmental cond tions that could potentially affect each process. The Agency acknowledges this limitation in its analysis. RQs cannot be designed to account for every environmental condition of each release of a hazardous substance. Instead, each RQ level represents the Agency's best judgment concerning the threshold at which the NRC should be notified.

Although environmental conditions are not considered in the RQ adjustment process, EPA has taken into account certain physical characteristics of substances in adjusting RQs on the basis of biodegradability. The test for biodegradability is performed using a closed container, which may provide misleading data for highly volatile substances that are unlikely to remain in microbe-bearing soil or water. The Agency has therefore elected not to apply the biodegradation criterion to any highly volatile substance (i.e., with a boiling point less than 100 degrees Fahrenheit) unless that substance is also highly water soluble. Highly water soluble substances will tend to be retained in water or in soil (by soil moisture). The primary criteria RQ of acetaldehyde was raised one level under these circumstances; even though the boiling point of acetaldehyde is less than 100 degrees Fahrenheit, the substance is also highly water soluble.

b. *Other Criteria Considered and Rejected.* In the NPRM preamble, EPA noted that it had considered using volatilization (the process by which a substance vaporizes into the air) as an additional criterion for adjusting RQs, but had rejected it because the hazard posed by a release of a hazardous substance does not necessarily decrease when the substance moves from soil or water into the air. One commenter disagreed with the Agency's decision not to use volatilization, arguing that where a compound is particularly volatile, no response action may be feasible. EPA maintains its earlier position that the movement of a substance between environmental media (from the soil or water into the air) does not necessarily affect the potential hazard. The feasibility of a response is a decision for the On-Scene Coordinator.

c. *Broadening the Scope of the BHP Criteria.* The NPRM noted, without discussion, that the criteria of biodegradation, hydrolysis, and photolysis were not used to raise RQs based on chronic toxicity, and it did not mention the application of BHP to substances being evaluated for potential carcinogenicity. Several commenters expressed the opinion that BHP should be applied to hazardous substances evaluated for chronic toxicity and/or potential carcinogenicity. They noted that the processes of biodegradation, hydrolysis, and photolysis may, in certain cases, reduce the potential hazard of such substances. EPA agrees that BHP should be applied to those hazardous substances evaluated for chronic toxicity, and the Agency is considering whether to apply BHP to substances evaluated for potential carcinogenicity.

In fact, the Agency has already evaluated BHP with respect to those substances that were analyzed for chronic toxicity. Two substances evaluted for chronic toxicity have had their primary criteria RQs increased one level on the basis of biodegradability: acetonitrile (1000 to 5000 pounds) and methyl ethyl ketone (1000 to 5000 pounds).

A number of commenters argued that RQs should be adjusted more than one RQ level on the basis of the BHP criteria to reflect the speed and completeness with which a substance degrades. In a related suggestion, several commenters requested that EPA develop formal ranking scales for these criteria.

The lack of extensive data and the uncertainty of much of the existing data concerning the environmental fate of various hazardous substances prevent adjustments of more than one level to reflect the speed and completeness with which a substance degrades. The Agency believes that an upward adjustment of one level adequately lessens the reporting burden on the regulated community regarding releases of the 27 substances involved and satisfactorily protects public health and welfare and the environment.

Similar data gaps hinder development of formal ranking scales for the BHP criteria. Moreover, even if adequate data were available, the BHP criteria could not be easily applied through a more formal multi-tier ranking system, for many of the same reasons a hazard index is currently impractical. For example, there is no objective way to determine the proper numerical weights for the different primary and BHP criteria that would be combined in a more formal ranking system. Therefore, the Agency has determined that more formal ranking scales for the application of BHP are not practical at this time. Further refinement of the use of BHP may be undertaken in connection with a future rulemaking.

For a more detailed discussion of the BHP criteria and the problems of combining different criteria ranking, see the discussion of hazard indices in the May 25, 1983 NPRM at 48 FR 23568–23569, and the Technical Background Document to Support Rulemaking Pursuant to CERCLA section 102, available for inspection at Room S-325, U.S. Environmental Protection Agency, 401 M Street, SW, Washington, D.C. 20460.

d. *Additional Data Suggested.* Some commenters suggested specific data sources for analysis of BHP. EPA used one of these sources in making the adjustments proposed in the May 25, 1983 NPRM. On the basis of data contained in the other available sources, the RQs of acetonitrile and furfural have each been raised one level to 5000 pounds.

3. Additional Criteria Considered but Not Currently Used To Adjust RQs

a. *Release History and Release Potential.* Several comments were received on the use of release history and release potential as criteria for adjusting RQs. EPA agrees with those commenters who stated that the manner in which releases have been handled in the past under different circumstances is not directly related to whether a particular release in the future will pose a threat to public health or welfare or the environment. The potential hazards of each release must be considered on a case-by-case basis. For this reason, and because of the data problems mentioned in the NPRM, the Agency has decided not to adjust RQs on the basis of release history and release potential at this time.

b. *Corrosivity.* Two commenters supported the use of corrosivity as a criterion for adjusting RQs. A major difficulty in applying corrosivity as a criterion is developing a scale relating corrosivity to RQs that is useful for all CERCLA hazardous substances. None of the comments included a scale that the Agency considered adequate, and EPA has not identified a corrosivity scale that would be generally practicable. Therefore, corrosivity will not be used at this time as a criterion for adjusting RQs.

E. *Future RQ Adjustments*

1. Interim RQs

As noted below in section V.G., adjusted RQs for 358 of the 698 CERCLA hazardous substances do not appear in today's rule. One commenter urged EPA to publish proposed RQs for these substances as quickly as possible. Today's Federal Register contains an NPRM proposing RQs for 105 of the 358 substances not receiving an adjusted RQ in today's rule. EPA will propose RQ adjustments for the remaining substances as soon as sound technical evaluations for them are complete.

Another commenter indicated that potential delays in performing such evaluations could result in an unfair reporting burden for many substances that will temporarily retain their present RQs. The commenter therefore recommended that EPA propose interim RQ adjustments for such substances based on existing information and scientific judgments.

EPA disagrees. Proposing new temporary RQs for hazardous substances would be time-consuming in itself, and, because the temporary RQs would be based on incomplete analysis, they would be unfair to the regulated community and the general public. Interim levels would still need to be changed when RQ evaluations are completed. EPA will move expeditiously to complete its evaluations of the remaining CERCLA substances, but will not establish a set of interim RQs.

2. New Data

One commenter requested that provisions be specified for allowing RQ changes when new information relating to the primary criteria or BHP becomes available. This commenter felt that EPA should acknowledge the role of interested parties in effecting appropriate revisions to the final RQs and should clarify procedures for the submission of new data.

EPA welcomes the submission of new data concerning the primary criteria and BHP at any time. RQs are based on the best data available at the time of promulgation, but they are subject to change on the basis of new information. The Agency will periodically review submitted data to ensure that RQs are not based on superseded information.

F. *Application of the Methodology and Criteria*

1. Introduction

Many commenters voiced general support for EPA's choice of methodology and the results of the methodology. These commenters stated that the proposed RQ adjustments would increase the efficiency of the Superfund program, reduce burdens on the regulated community, and allow EPA to concentrate its resources on the releases which pose the potentially greatest threat to public health or welfare or the environment.

The remainder of this section responds briefly to comments received by the Agency concerning the RQs of various specific substances and discusses in greater detail the comments received concerning PCBs and unlisted hazardous wastes.

2. Comments on RQs of Specific Substances

The Agency received comments from over 100 commenters concerning the RQs of 90 individual substances and 12 groups of waste streams. The majority of these comments suggested raising the RQs for specific substances.

One commenter recommended several RQ changes on the basis of aquatic toxicity data recently compiled by the U.S. Department of the Interior. The Agency has reevaluated the RQs of several hazardous substances in light of these new data, and four of the substances singled out by the commenter have received new adjusted RQs. In addition, the new data were used to alter the proposed adjusted RQs of 12 other substances. Exhibit 6 lists the 16 substances which received new adjusted RQs on the basis of the new aquatic toxicity data. Statements by the same commenter contributed to a reexamination of the mammalian toxicity data for phosgene and the lowering of the phosgene RQ from 1000 to 10 pounds.

EXHIBIT 6.—SUBSTANCES WHICH RECEIVED FINAL ADJUSTED RQS DIFFERENT FROM PROPOSED ADJUSTED RQS ON THE BASIS OF NEW AQUATIC TOXICITY DATA

Substance	Proposed RQ	Final RQ
Aldicarb	10	1
4-Bromophenyl phenyl ether	10	100
Butyl benzyl phthalate	5000	100
N-Butyl phthalate	100	10
Dichlobenil	1000	100
4,6-Dinitro-o-cresol and salts	100	10
Dinitrophenol (and 2,5- and 2,6-isomers)	100	10
2,4-Dinitrophenol	100	10
Diethyl phthalate	100	1000
Kelthane	5000	10
Methomyl	1000	100
Pyrethrins	1000	1
2,4,5-T	100	1000
2,4,5-T Amines	100	5000
2,4,5-T Esters	100	1000
2,4,5-T Salts	100	1000

Some commenters suggested RQ changes for particular substances on the basis of volatility or particular incidents. Similarly, one commenter proposed new RQs for several waste streams based on the public impact of past releases of these wastes. However, as discussed in previous sections, neither volatility nor release history are currently being used to adjust RQs. The RQs of these substances and waste streams will therefore not be changed.

Commenters suggested raising the RQs of four substances on the basis of biodegradability. Two of these substances—crotonaldehyde and pentachlorophenol—have already been examined for biodegradability and been found not to meet the criteria for an upward RQ adjustment. EPA has reexamined the third substance, ammonia, on the basis of both chronic toxicity and BHP (although ammonia is volatile, it is also highly water soluble) and has proposed for ammonia an adjusted RQ of 100 pounds in the NPRM published in today's Federal Register. EPA has adjusted the RQ of the fourth substance, methyl ethyl ketone, from 1000 pounds to 5000 pounds on the basis of biodegradability.

Several commenters suggested that the RQs of metals might be based on the metal compound RQs (for soluble salts) that were assigned under CWA section 311. However, solid metal powders do not necessarily have the same effects as their soluble salts, and, therefore, the same RQs would not necessarily apply.

Many commenters argued that the RQ of ammonia should be raised from its current level of 100 pounds under the CWA; they cited the volatility of ammonia, the fact that most ammonia releases occur into air, the fact that the aquatic toxicity of the ammonium ion is much lower than that of ammonia itself, and the biodegradability of ammonia. It was also suggested that the 100-pound RQ would create a burdensome reporting requirement. Ammonia has undergone reevaluation since the May 25, 1983 NPRM; based on this reevaluation, the NPRM in today's Federal Register proposes to retain the 100-pound RQ for ammonia under CERCLA. The 100-pound RQ established under the CWA applies until a final adjusted RQ is promulgated.

3. PCBs

In the May 25, 1983 NPRM, the Agency proposed to lower the RQ for PCBs to one pound from the original 10-pound level set under section 311 of the Clean Water Act. The lower RQ was based on more recent aquatic toxicity data. The Agency acknowledged that because of the ubiquitous use of PCBs, it was concerned about the increased notification burden that might result from this proposed reduction of the PCB RQ. Comments were requested on these issues.

All of the comments received on this issue objected to the Agency's proposal to reduce the PCB RQ to one pound. The major concern of the commenters was that the one-pound RQ would appreciably increase the number of reportable releases and the burden on the regulated community while negligibly improving the protection of public health or welfare or the environment. Most commenters argued that restrictions on the location of equipment containing PCBs, current PCB management regulations under TSCA, and existing industry good housekeeping practices with regard to PCBs make exposure to PCBs unlikely.

Several commenters also expressed concern that significant over-reporting may dramatically increase the government's administrative costs for the notification program. Other commenters suggested alternative methods for estimating the number of PCB releases of different quantities for the purpose of calculating the economic effects of changing the PCB RQ.

Several commenters questioned the validity of the aquatic toxicity data used by the Agency and the manner in which it was employed to set the proposed RQ. Also, two commenters cited data indicating that PCBs do not pose any serious threats to human health, even

though the Agency had explained that the proposed PCB RQ was based on aquatic toxicity.

After considering the comments received on the PCB RQ, the Agency has decided to defer any promulgation of a final PCB RQ until a future rulemaking. The Agency is currently evaluating PCBs to determine whether the RQ should be based on the primary criterion of potential carcinogenicity. Until a final RQ is promulgated for PCBs, the existing RQ of 10 pounds (established under the CWA) will remain in effect.

4. Unlisted RCRA Wastes (ICRE Wastes)

CERCLA section 101(14)(c) includes in the definition of hazardous substances "any hazardous waste having the characteristics identified under or listed pursuant to section 3001 of the Solid Waste Disposal Act. . . ." Therefore, solid wastes, as defined by RCRA, which exhibit one or more of the characteristics of ignitability, corrosivity, reactivity, or extraction procedure toxicity (ICRE) are considered CERCLA hazardous substances, even though they are not specifically listed under RCRA. The RQs of ICRE wastes are listed in Table 302.4 under "Unlisted Hazardous Wastes." These RQs apply only to substances that are wastes prior to being released (see section IV.D.1. above). The RQ for ignitable, corrosive, or reactive unlisted wastes is 100 pounds, and unlisted hazardous wastes that exhibit extraction procedure (EP) toxicity have the reportable quantities listed in Table 302.4.

Some commenters suggested changing the RQ established for ignitable, corrosive, or reactive wastes. The comments that suggested raising the RQ for ICR wastes were based mainly on the assumption that a government response would seldom be required for releases of these wastes smaller than 1000 pounds. However, each of these suggestions assumes some specific scenario and ignores the fact that an RQ only reflects the Agency's judgment that the federal government should be notified of releases to which a response might be necessary. Especially when releases are of unknown mixtures, conservatism is a sensible approach; therefore, the RQ is designed to cover all hazardous substances potentially present. With this in mind, the RQ for ICR wastes will remain as proposed at 100 pounds.

Two commenters suggested that the releaser be given the opportunity to report releases of reactive or ignitable wastes based on the primary criteria RQ scales of Exhibits 3 and 4 in the NPRM (48 FR 23563). However, simply testing for the reactivity or ignitability of the waste does not further identify the composition of the waste; therefore, the waste is still unlisted. The primary criteria are designed to apply only to specific substances. Moreover, the Agency has not determined that listed and unlisted wastes pose similar potential hazards.

If an unlisted ICRE waste is analyzed and the concentrations of all of its hazardous components are identified, the waste is no longer an unlisted waste, but one characterized by its components. The specific substances present will then determine the applicable RQ in accordance with the Clean Water Act mixture rule (see section IV.D.3.b. above). For example, if a waste is known to be corrosive because of its sulfuric acid content, and no other CERCLA hazardous substances or other ICRE characteristics are present, the RQ of the waste is reached when 1000 pounds of sulfuric acid is released. If the aforementioned waste is a 25 percent solution of sulfuric acid in water, the RQ of the waste is not reached until 4000 pounds of the waste is released.

Several commenters suggested that the RQ for an EP toxic waste should apply to the EP toxic constituents of the waste rather than to the waste itself. If the composition of the waste stream is completely known, the waste is no longer an unlisted waste, and the mixture rule will apply. If the hazardous constituents of the waste and their concentrations are not completely known, however, it is impossible to apply the mixture rule as these commenters suggested. Unlisted wastes that exhibit EP toxicity have the reportable quantities listed in Table 302.4 for the contaminant on which the characteristic of EP toxicity is based; the RQ given applies to the waste itself, not merely to the toxic constituent. A sentence has been added to § 302.5(b) to clarify this point.

G. Summary of RQ Changes From the May 25, 1983 NPRM

The May 25, 1983 NPRM proposed raising the RQs for 177 CERCLA substances (including 15 waste streams) and lowering the RQs for 28 substances, leaving the RQs of 182 substances (including 11 waste streams) at their previous levels. On the basis of new aquatic toxicity data located by a commenter, the proposed adjusted RQs of 16 substances have been changed. Exhibit 6 lists these 16 substances. Similarly, new data on BHP has led to a one-level increase in the adjusted RQ of

furfural, and a reevaluation of mammalian toxicity data has led to a decrease in the phosgene RQ from 1000 to 10 pounds. Applying BHP to substances exhibiting chronic toxicity has raised the adjusted RQs of two other substances. The decision not to apply BHP to substances for which five-day degradation rates are insufficient to justify a one-level increase in RQ has resulted in a lower RQ for four substances. The use of data overlooked at the time of the NPRM has affected the adjusted RQs of four additional substances.

The NPRM proposed adjusted RQs for 47 substances (including 8 waste streams) that were subsequently selected for chronic toxicity and/or potential carcinogenicity assessment; these 47 substances will therefore remain at their statutory RQ levels pending future RQ adjustments. Of these 47 substances, however, 23 (including 6 waste streams) already had RQs of one pound on the basis of one or more of the other primary criteria. Further evaluation of chronic toxicity or potential carcinogenicity is unlikely to change these one-pound RQs, because there is no RQ level less than one pound and the analysis of the other primary criteria indicates that a one-pound RQ is appropriate (although new data on the primary criteria or on BHP may suggest otherwise).

Table 302.4 in the May 25, 1983 NPRM incorrectly described eighteen substances as having one-pound statutory RQs under CERCLA; however, these substances had been assigned RQs under the Clean Water Act (40 CFR Parts 116 and 117.3). Exhibit 7 lists the eighteen substances and their correct statutory and (where appropriate) final RQs.

In sum, final adjusted RQs now appear for 319 of 608 specific substances and 21 of 90 waste streams. Statutory RQs appear for the remaining substances.[4]

For further information concerning these RQ changes, see the Technical Background Document to Support Rulemaking Pursuant to CERCLA Section 102, available for inspection at Room S–325, U.S. Environmental Protection Agency, 401 M Street, SW, Washington, D.C. 20460.

---

[4] Adjustments have been proposed for 105 of these substances in an NPRM that appears in today's Federal Register. These substances are noted by two number symbols (##) in the "Pounds (Kg)" column of Table 302.4.

H. Retention of Statutory RQ for Methyl Isocyanate

The December 4, 1984 release of methyl isocyanate (MIC) in Bhopal, India caused major loss of human life. This event pointed out the extraordinarily serious nature of MIC's acute toxicity. At this point, EPA is withdrawing its proposal to amend the RQ for MIC and is requesting further data on its toxicity.

The one-pound statutory reporting requirement will continue to apply to releases of this hazardous substance until a rule adjusting its RQ is promulgated.

EXHIBIT 7.—SUBSTANCES WITH RQs ASSIGNED UNDER THE CLEAN WATER ACT THAT THE MAY 25, 1983 NPRM LISTED AS HAVING ONE-POUND STATUTORY RQs UNDER CERCLA

Substance	Correct CWA section 311 RQ	Final RQ
Aroclor 1016	10	*10
Aroclor 1221	10	*10
Aroclor 1232	10	*10
Aroclor 1242	10	*10
Aroclor 1248	10	*10
Aroclor 1254	10	*10
Aroclor 1260	10	*10
o-Dichlorobenzene	100	100
p-Dichlorobenzene	100	100
1,2-Dichloropropane	5000	1000
1,3-Dichloropropene	5000	100
2,4-Dinitrophenol	1000	10
2,4-Dinitrotoluene	1000	*1000
2,6-Dinitrotoluene	1000	*1000
2-Nitrophenol	1000	100
4-Nitrophenol	1000	100
2,4,5-Trichlorophenol	10	*10
2,4,6-Trichlorophenol	10	*10

* These substances were selected for evaluation of chronic toxicity and/or potential carcinogenicity and adjusted RQs will be proposed for them in a future rulemaking.

I. Table 302.4

1. Introduction

Table 302.4 lists all of the CERCLA hazardous substances together with their adjusted and statutory RQs. The first part of the table lists the individual hazardous substances regulated under the statutes cited in CERCLA section 101(14). The generic groups of chemicals designated under CWA section 307(a), such as "SILVER AND COMPOUNDS," are printed in capital letters and have no RQ assigned to them. These generic groups of chemicals could potentially encompass hundreds of specific compounds with varying toxicities; it is therefore not appropriate to establish a single RQ for each generic group. Although CERCLA notification requirements apply only to specific compounds for which RQs are listed in Table 302.4, CERCLA liability may still attach to releases of specific compounds that are within one of the generic listings but not specifically listed in Table 302.4.

The second part of the table contains the 90 hazardous waste streams designated under 40 CFR 261.31 and 261.32 (RCRA F and K lists). The Agency designated many of these waste streams as hazardous under RCRA because of the presence of specific hazardous constituents in the waste streams as set forth in Appendix VII of 40 CFR Part 261. The Agency is assigning RQs for these waste streams based on these hazardous constituents. The primary criteria and BHP, discussed above, were applied to each hazardous constituent in order to derive an RQ value. If a waste stream in 40 CFR 261.31 and 261.32 has more than one hazardous constituent, the RQ assigned to the particular waste stream represents the lowest RQ associated with the hazardous constituents present in that waste stream.

2. Minor Changes

In addition to the changes in proposed RQs described above in Section G, the following minor changes in Table 302.4 have been made:

(1) The listing for Chromium D007, one of the constituents of the characteristic of EP toxicity under the "Unlisted Hazardous Wastes," will now be "total chromium" (although it may be changed to hexavalent chromium at some time in the future under proposed amendments to RCRA). It was listed incorrectly as hexavalent chromium (VI) in Table 302.4 in the NPRM.

(2) The RCRA waste numbers for the characteristics of ignitability (D001), corrosivity (D002), and reactivity (D003) are now included in Table 302.4. They were omitted from Table 302.4 in the NPRM. In addition, the waste identification numbers for the constituents of the characteristic of EP toxicity, and the waste identification numbers for wastes F001 through K106, which were also omitted in the NPRM, are now properly included in the column for RCRA Waste Numbers in Table 302.4.

(3) In response to the suggestion of a commenter, the Table now notes that the RQ for asbestos is limited to friable forms of the substance; reporting of releases of other forms is not required, although other CERCLA liabilities may attach.

VI. Reportable Quantity Adjustments Under Section 311 of the Clean Water Act

In the May 25, 1983 NPRM, EPA requested comments on its proposal to make RQs adjusted under CERCLA the applicable RQs for purposes of reporting discharges of hazardous substances pursuant to section 311 of the Clean Water Act. Making RQs the same for substances listed under both statutes would make the notification requirements for the substances involved consistent and less confusing for the regulated community.

Of nine comments received on the issue of adjusting CWA RQs, five were completely in favor of the Agency's proposal and agreed that it would alleviate much confusion. However, four comments indicated that such adjustment should proceed only for those substances for which CWA RQs would be raised. These commenters claimed that CWA RQs are based on aquatic toxicity, while CERCLA RQs must consider releases into other media. Thus, they reasoned, lowering CWA RQs based on criteria used to set CERCLA RQs would be unfair.

EPA does not feel that different RQs under the two statutes would serve any purpose. Even if the CWA RQs were not lowered, releases of CWA substances would still be reportable when released at CERCLA RQ levels because CERCLA's scope and jurisdiction fully encompass all hazardous substance discharges reportable under CWA. The primary purpose of equalizing RQs under CERCLA and the CWA is to make the task of reporting releases less confusing for the regulated community.

VII. Summary of Supporting Analyses

A. Classification and Regulatory Impact Analysis

Rulemaking protocol under Executive Order 12291 requires that proposed regulations be classified as "major" or "non-major" for purposes of review by the Office of Management and Budget. According to the E.O. 12291, major rules are regulations that are likely to result in:

(1) An annual effect on the economy of $100 million or more; or

(2) A major increase in costs or prices for consumers, individual industries, federal, state, or local government agencies, or geographic regions; or

(3) Significant adverse effects on competition, employment, investment, productivity, innovation, or the ability of United States-based enterprises to compete with foreign-based enterprises in domestic or export markets.

The Regulatory Impact Analysis, available for inspection at Room S-325, U.S. Environmental Protection Agency, 401 M Street, SW, Washington, D.C. 20460, shows that today's regulation is "non-major" because it results in a net cost savings of approximately $17 million annually, of which about $2.6 million annually will be saved by the regulated community (the remainder to be saved by the government).[5]

B. Regulatory Flexibility Analysis

The Regulatory Flexibility Act of 1980 requires that a Regulatory Flexibility Analysis be performed for all rules that are likely to have "significant impact on a substantial number of small entities." Chapter 7 of the Regulatory Impact Analysis estimates the potential impact of today's regulation on a model small chemical firm. The chapter first estimates an upper-bound total annual cost of compliance by a small firm at $5,604 (in 1983 dollars) and then compares this figure to other measures of a small firm's economic status. Even with this extremely conservative estimate, the total cost per year of compliance is a negligible percentage of both the pre-tax annual cash flow and equity of the model small firm—a fraction of one percent for both measures. EPA therefore certifies that this regulation will not have a significant impact on a substantial number of small entities, and thus no Regulatory Flexibility Analysis is needed.

C. Information Impact Analysis

EPA anticipates that RQ adjustments will change the paperwork burden imposed on the regulated community for information collection associated with reporting releases. As estimated in the Regulatory Impact Analysis, today's regulation will reduce the paperwork burden of notification and recordkeeping on private parties by almost 50,000 hours.

The information collection requirements contained in this rule are covered by the U.S. Coast Guard submission for information collection by the National Response Center. The requirements have been approved by the Office of Management and Budget (OMB) under the provisions of the Paperwork Reduction Act of 1980, 44 U.S.C. 3501 et seq., and have been assigned OMB control number 2115-0137.

List of Subjects in 40 CFR Part 302

Air pollution control, Chemicals, Hazardous materials, Hazardous materials transportation, Hazardous substances, Intergovernmental relations, Natural resources, Nuclear materials, Pesticides and pests, Radioactive materials, Reporting and recordkeeping

[5] These figures do not include the costs or benefits associated with the continuous release exemption.

requirements, Superfund, Waste treatment and disposal, Water pollution control.

Dated: February 13, 1985.

Lee M. Thomas,
Administrator.

1. 40 CFR is amended by adding Part 302 as follows:

PART 302—DESIGNATION, REPORTABLE QUANTITIES, AND NOTIFICATION

Sec.
302.1 Applicability.
302.2 Abbreviations.
302.3 Definitions.
302.4 Designation of hazardous substances.
302.5 Determination of reportable quantities.
302.6 Notification requirements.
302.7 Penalties.

Authority: Section 102 of the Comprehensive Environmental Response, Compensation, and Liability Act of 1980, 42 USC 9602; Sections 311 and 501(a) of the Federal Water Pollution Control Act, 33 USC 1321 and 1361.

§ 302.1 Applicability.

This regulation designates under section 102(a) of the Comprehensive Environmental Response, Compensation, and Liability Act of 1980 ("the Act") those substances in the statutes referred to in section 101(14) of the Act, identifies reportable quantities for these substances, and sets forth the notification requirements for releases of these substances. This regulation also sets forth reportable quantities for hazardous substances designated under section 311(b)(2)(A) of the Clean Water Act.

§ 302.2 Abbreviations.

CASRN = Chemical Abstracts Service Registry Number
RCRA = Resource Conservation and Recovery Act of 1976, as amended
lb = pound
kg = kilogram
RQ = reportable quantity

§ 302.3 Definitions.

As used in this part, all terms shall have the meaning set forth below:

"The Act", "CERCLA", or "Superfund" means the Comprehensive Environmental Response, Compensation, and Liability Act of 1980 (Pub. L. 96–510);

"Administrator" means the Administrator of the United States Environmental Protection Agency ("EPA");

"consumer product" shall have the meaning stated in 15 U.S.C. 2052;

"environment" means (1) the navigable waters, the waters of the contiguous zone, and the ocean waters

of which the natural resources are under the exclusive management authority of the United States under the Fishery Conservation and Management Act of 1976, and (2) any other surface water, ground water, drinking water supply, land surface or subsurface strata, or ambient air within the United States or under the jurisdiction of the United States;

"facility" means (1) any building, structure, installation, equipment, pipe or pipeline (including any pipe into a sewer or publicly owned treatment works), well, pit, pond, lagoon, impoundment, ditch, landfill, storage container, motor vehicle, rolling stock, or aircraft, or (2) any site or area where a hazardous substance has been deposited, stored, disposed of, or placed, or otherwise come to be located; but does not include any consumer product in consumer use or any vessel;

"hazardous substance" means any substance designated pursuant to 40 CFR 302;

"hazardous waste" shall have the meaning provided in 40 CFR 261.3;

"navigable waters" or "navigable waters of the United States" means waters of the United States, including the territorial seas;

"offshore facility" means any facility of any kind located in, on, or under, any of the navigable waters of the United States, and any facility of any kind which is subject to the jurisdiction of the United States and is located in, on, or under any other waters, other than a vessel or a public vessel;

"onshore facility" means any facility (including, but not limited to, motor vehicles and rolling stock) of any kind located in, on, or under, any land or non-navigable waters within the United States;

"person" means an individual, firm, corporation, association, partnership, consortium, joint venture, commercial entity, United States Government, State, municipality, commission, political subdivision of a State, or any interstate body;

"release" means any spilling, leaking, pumping, pouring, emitting, emptying, discharging, injecting, escaping, leaching, dumping, or disposing into the environment, but excludes (1) any release which results in exposure to persons solely within a workplace, with respect to a claim which such persons may assert against the employer of such persons, (2) emissions from the engine exhaust of a motor vehicle, rolling stock, aircraft, vessel, or pipeline pumping station engine, (3) release of source, byproduct, or special nuclear material from a nuclear incident, as those terms are defined in the Atomic Energy Act of

1954, if such release is subject to requirements with respect to financial protection established by the Nuclear Regulatory Commission under Section 170 of such Act, or for the purposes of Section 104 of the Comprehensive Environmental Response, Compensation, and Liability Act or any other response action, any release of source, byproduct, or special nuclear material from any processing site designated under section 102(a)(1) or 302(a) of the Uranium Mill Tailings Radiation Control Act of 1978, and (4) the normal application of fertilizer;

"reportable quantity" means that quantity, as set forth in this part, the release of which requires notification pursuant to this part;

"United States" include the several States of the United States, the District of Columbia, the Commonwealth of Puerto Rico, Guam, American Samoa, the United States Virgin Islands, the Commonwealth of the Northern Marianas, and any other territory or possession over which the United States has jurisdiction; and

"vessel" means every description of watercraft or other artificial contrivance used, or capable of being used, as a means of transportation on water.

§ 302.4 Designation of hazardous substances.

(a) *Listed hazardous substances.* The elements and compounds and hazardous wastes appearing in Table 302.4 are designated as hazardous substances under section 102(a) of the Act.

(b) *Unlisted hazardous substances.* A solid waste, as defined in 40 CFR 261.2, which is not excluded from regulation as a hazardous waste under 40 CFR 261.4(b), is a hazardous substance under section 101(14) of the Act if it exhibits any of the characteristics identified in 40 CFR 261.20 through 261.24.

Table 302.4—List of Hazardous Substances and Reportable Quantities

Note—The numbers under the column headed "CASRN" are the Chemical Abstracts Service Registry Numbers for each hazardous substance. Other names by which each hazardous substance is identified in other statutes and their implementing regulations are provided in the "Regulatory Synonyms" column. The "Statutory RQ" column lists the RQs for hazardous substances established by section 102 of CERCLA. The "Statutory Code" column indicates the statutory source for designating each substance as a CERCLA hazardous substance: "1" indicates that the statutory source is section 311(b)(4) of the Clean Water Act, "2" indicates that the source is section 307(a) of the Clean Water Act, "3" indicates that the source is section 112 of the Clean Air Act, and "4" indicates that the source is RCRA section 3001. The

"RCRA Waste Number" column provides the waste identification numbers assigned to various substances by RCRA regulations. The column headed "Category" lists the code letters "X," "A," "B," "C," and "D," which are associated with reportable quantities of 1, 10, 100, 1000, and 5000 pounds, respectively. The "Pounds (kg)" column provides the reportable quantity for each hazardous substance in pounds and kilograms.

TABLE 302.4 - LIST OF HAZARDOUS SUBSTANCES AND REPORTABLE QUANTITIES

Hazardous Substance	CASRN	Regulatory Synonyms	Statutory			Final RQ	
			RQ	Code †	RCRA Waste Number	Category	Pounds(Kg)
Acenaphthene	83329		1*	2		X	1## (0.454)
Acenaphthylene	208968		1*	2		X	1## (0.454)
Acetaldehyde	75070	Ethanal	1000	1,4	U001	C	1000 (454)
Acetaldehyde, chloro-	107200	Chloroacetaldehyde	1*	4	P023	C	1000 (454)
Acetaldehyde, trichloro-	75876	Chloral	1*	4	U034	X	1# (0.454)
Acetamide, N-(aminothioxomethyl)-	591082	1-Acetyl-2-thiourea	1*	4	P002	C	1000 (454)
Acetamide, N-(4-ethoxyphenyl)-	62442	Phenacetin	1*	4	U187	X	1# (0.454)
Acetamide, N-9H-fluoren-2-yl-	53963	2-Acetylaminofluorene	1*	4	U005	X	1# (0.454)
Acetamide, 2-fluoro-	640197	Fluoroacetamide	1*	4	P057	B	100(45.4)
Acetic acid	64197		1000	1		D	5000 (2270)
Acetic acid, ethyl ester	141786	Ethyl acetate	1*	4	U112	D	5000 (2270)
Acetic acid, fluoro-, sodium salt	62748	Fluoroacetic acid, sodium salt	1*	4	P058	A	10 (4.54)
Acetic acid, lead salt	301042	Lead acetate	5000	1,4	U144	D	5000# (2270)
Acetic acid, thallium(I) salt	563688	Thallium(I) acetate	1*	4	U214	X	1## (0.454)
Acetic anhydride	108247		1000	1		D	5000 (2270)
Acetimidic acid,N-[(methylcarbamoyl) oxy]thio-, methyl ester.	16752775	Methomyl	1*	4	P066	B	100 (45.4)
Acetone	67641	2-Propanone	1*	4	U002	D	5000 (2270)
Acetone cyanohydrin	75865	2-Methyllactonitrile Propanenitrile, 2-hydroxy-2-methyl-	10	1,4	P069	A	10 (4.54)
Acetonitrile	75058	Ethanenitrile	1*	4	U003	D	5000 (2270)
3-(alpha-Acetonylbenzyl)- 4-hydroxycoumarin and salts	81812	Warfarin	1*	4	P001	B	100 (45.4)
Acetophenone	98862	Ethanone, 1-phenyl-	1*	4	U004	D	5000 (2270)
2-Acetylaminofluorene	53963	Acetamide, N-9H-fluoren-2-yl-	1*	4	U005	X	1# (0.454)
Acetyl bromide	506967		5000	1		D	5000 (2270)
Acetyl chloride	75365	Ethanoyl chloride	5000	1 4	U006	D	5000 (2270)
1-Acetyl-2-thiourea	591082	Acetamide, N-(aminothioxomethyl)-	1*	1	P002	C	1000 (454)
Acrolein	107028	2-Propenal	1	1,..4	P003	X	1 (0.454)
Acrylamide	79061	2-Propenamide	1*	4	U007	D	5000 (2270)
Acrylic acid	79107	2-Propenoic acid	1*	4	U008	D	5000 (2270)
Acrylonitrile	107131	2-Propenenitrile	100	1,2,4	U009	B	100# (45.4)
Adipic acid	124049		5000	1		D	5000 (2270)
Alanine, 3-[p-bis(2-chloroethyl)amino]phenyl-,L-	148823	Melphalan	1*	4	U150	X	1# (0.454)
Aldicarb	116063	Propanal, 2-methyl-2-(methylthio)-, O-[(methylamino) carbonyl]oxime.	1*	4	P070	X	1 (0.454)
Aldrin	309002	1,2,3,4,10-10-Hexachloro-1,4,4a,5,8,8a-hexahydro- 1,4:5,8-endo, exo- dimethanonaphthalene.	1	1,2,4	P004	X	1# (0.454)
Allyl alcohol	107186	2-Propen-1-ol	100	1,4	P005	B	100 (45.4)
Allyl chloride	107051		1000			C	1000 (454)
Aluminum phosphide	20859738		1*	4	P006	B	100 (45.4)
Aluminum sulfate	10043013		5000	1		D	5000 (2270)
5-(Aminomethyl)-3-isoxazolol	2763964	3(2H)-Isoxazolone, 5-(aminomethyl)-	1*	4	P007	C	1000 (454)
4-Aminopyridine	504245	4-Pyridinamine	1*	4	P008	C	1000 (454)

TABLE 302.4 - LIST OF HAZARDOUS SUBSTANCES AND REPORTABLE QUANTITIES—Continued

Hazardous Substance	CASRN	Regulatory Synonyms	Statutory RQ	Code #	RCRA Waste Number	Category	Final RQ Pounds(Kg)
Amitrole	61825	1H-1,2,4-Triazol-3-amine	1*	4	U011	X	1# (0.454)
Ammonia	7664417		100	1		B	100## (45.4)
Ammonium acetate	631618		5000	1		D	5000 (2270)
Ammonium benzoate	1863634		5000	1		D	5000 (2270)
Ammonium bicarbonate	1066337		5000	1		D	5000 (2270)
Ammonium bichromate	7789095		1000	1		C	1000# (454)
Ammonium bifluoride	1341497		5000	1		D	5000## (2270)
Ammonium bisulfite	10192300		5000	1		D	5000 (2270)
Ammonium carbamate	1111780		5000	1		D	5000 (2270)
Ammonium carbonate	506876		5000	1		D	5000 (2270)
Ammonium chloride	12125029		5000	1		D	5000 (2270)
Ammonium chromate	7788989		1000	1		C	1000# (454)
Ammonium citrate, dibasic	3012655		5000	1		D	5000 (2270)
Ammonium fluoborate	13826830		5000	1		D	5000 (2270)
Ammonium fluoride	12125018		5000	1		B	100 (45.4)
Ammonium hydroxide	1336216		1000	1		C	1000 (454)
Ammonium oxalate	6009707 5972736 14258492		5000	1		D	5000 (2270)
Ammonium picrate	131748	Phenol, 2,4,6-trinitro-, ammonium salt	1*	4	P009	A	10 (4.54)
Ammonium silicofluoride	16919190		1000	1		C	1000 (454)
Ammonium sulfamate	7773060		5000	1		D	5000 (2270)
Ammonium sulfide	12135761		5000	1		B	100 (45.4)
Ammonium sulfite	10196040		5000	1		D	5000 (2270)
Ammonium tartrate	14307438 3164292		5000	1		D	5000 (2270)
Ammonium thiocyanate	1762954		5000	1		D	5000 (2270)
Ammonium thiosulfate	7783188		5000	1		D	5000 (2270)
Ammonium vanadate	7803556	Vanadic acid, ammonium salt	1*	4	P119	C	1000 (454)
Amyl acetate iso- sec- tert-	628637 123922 626380 625161		1000	1		D	5000 (2270)
Aniline	62533	Benzenamine	1000	1,4	U012	D	5000 (2270)
Anthracene	120127		1*	2		X	1## (0.454)
Antimony ††	7440360		1*	2		X	1## (0.454)
ANTIMONY AND COMPOUNDS			1*	2			**
Antimony pentachloride	7647189		1000	1		C	1000 (454)
Antimony potassium tartrate	28300745		1000	1		B	100 (45.4)
Antimony tribromide	7789619		1000	1		C	1000 (454)
Antimony trichloride	10025919		1000	1		C	1000(454)
Antimony trifluoride	7783564		1000	1		C	1000 (454)
Antimony trioxide	1309644		5000	1		C	1000 (454)
Aroclor 1016	12674112	Polychlorinated Biphenyls (PCBs)	10	1,2		A	10# (4.54)
Aroclor 1221	11104282	Polychlorinated Biphenyls (PCBs)	10	1,2		A	10# (4.54)
Aroclor 1232	11141165	Polychlorinated Biphenyls (PCBs)	10	1,2		A	10# (4.54)
Aroclor 1242	53469219	Polychlorinated Biphenyls (PCBs)	10	1,2		A	10# (4.54)

TABLE 302.4 - LIST OF HAZARDOUS SUBSTANCES AND REPORTABLE QUANTITIES—Continued

Hazardous Substance	CASRN	Regulatory Synonyms	Statutory RQ	Code †	RCRA Waste Number	Category	Final RQ Pounds(Kg)
Aroclor 1248	12672296	Polychlorinated Biphenyls (PCBs)	10	1,2		A	10# (4.54)
Aroclor 1254	11097691	Polychlorinated Biphenyls (PCBs)	10	1,2		A	10# (4.54)
Aroclor 1260	11096825	Polychlorinated Biphenyls (PCBs)	10	1,2		A	10# (4.54)
Arsenic ††	7440382		1*	2,3		X	1# (0.454)
Arsenic acid	1327522 7778394		1*	4	P010	X	1# (0.454)
ARSENIC AND COMPOUNDS			1*	2			**
Arsenic disulfide	1303328		5000	1		D	5000# (2270)
Arsenic(III) oxide	1327533	Arsenic trioxide	5000	1,4	P012	D	5000# (2270)
Arsenic(V) oxide	1303282	Arsenic pentoxide	5000	1,4	P011	D	5000# (2270)
Arsenic pentoxide	1303282	Arsenic(V) oxide	5000	1,4	P011	D	5000# (2270)
Arsenic trichloride	7784341		5000	1		D	5000# (2270)
Arsenic trioxide	1327533	Arsenic(III) oxide	5000	1,4	P012	D	5000# (2270)
Arsenic trisulfide	1303339		5000	1		D	1000# (2270)
Arsine, diethyl-	692422	Diethylarsine	1*	4	P038	X	1# (0.454)
Asbestos †††	1332214		1*	2,3		X	1# (0.454)
Auramine	492808	Benzenamine, 4,4'-carbonimidoylbis(N,N-dimethyl-	1*	4	U014	X	1# (0.454)
Azaserine	115026	L-Serine, diazoacetate (ester)	1*	4	U015	X	1# (0.454)
Aziridine	151564	Ethylenimine	1*	4	P054	X	1# (0.454)
Azirino(2',3':3,4)pyrrolo(1,2-a)indole-4,7-dione,6-amino-8-[((aminocarbonyl)oxy)methyl]-1,1a,2,8,8a,8b-hexahydro-8a-methoxy-5-methyl-.	50077	Mitomycin C	1*	4	U010	X	1# (0.454)
Barium cyanide	542621		10	1,4	P013	A	10 (4.54)
Benz[j]aceanthrylene, 1,2-dihydro-3-methyl-	56495	3-Methylcholanthrene	1*	4	U157	X	1# (0.454)
Benz[c]acridine	225514	3,4-Benzacridine	1*	4	U016	X	1# (0.454)
3,4-Benzacridine	225514	Benz[c]acridine	1*	4	U016	X	1# (0.454)
Benzal chloride	98873	Benzene, dichloromethyl-	1*	4	U017	D	5000 (2270)
Benz[a]anthracene	56553	1,2-Benzanthracene Benzo[a]anthracene	1*	2,4	U018	X	1# (0.454)
1,2-Benzanthracene	56553	Benz[a]anthracene Benzo[a]anthracene	1*	2,4	U018	X	1# (0.454)
1,2-Benzanthracene, 7,12-dimethyl-	57976	7,12-Dimethylbenz[a]anthracene	1*	4	U094	X	1# (0.454)
Benzenamine	62533	Aniline	1000	1,4	U012	D	5000 (2270)
Benzenamine, 4,4'-carbonimidoylbis(N,N-dimethyl-	492808	Auramine	1*	4	U014	X	1# (0.454)
Benzenamine, 4-chloro-	106478	p-Chloroaniline	1*	4	P024	C	1000 (454)
Benzenamine, 4-chloro-2-methyl-, hydrochloride	3165833	4-Chloro-o-toluidine, hydrochloride	1*	4	U049	X	1# (0.454)
Benzenamine, N,N-dimethyl-4-phenylazo-	60117	Dimethylaminoazobenzene	1*	4	U093	X	1# (0.454)
Benzenamine, 4,4'-methylenebis(2-chloro-	101144	4,4'-Methylenebis(2-chloroaniline)	1*	4	U158	X	1# (0.454)
Benzenamine, 2-methyl-, hydrochloride	636215	o-Toluidine hydrochloride	1*	4	U222	X	1# (0.454)
Benzenamine, 2-methyl-5-nitro-	99558	5-Nitro-o-toluidine	1*	4	U181	X	1# (0.454)
Benzenamine, 4-nitro-	100016	p-Nitroaniline	1*	4	P077	D	5000 (2270)
Benzene	71432		1000	1,2,3,4	U019	C	1000# (454)
Benzene, 1-bromo-4-phenoxy-	101553	4-Bromophenyl phenyl ether	1*	2,4	U030	B	100 (45.4)
Benzene, chloro-	108907	Chlorobenzene	100	1,2,4	U037	B	100 (45.4)
Benzene, chloromethyl-	100447	Benzyl chloride	100	1,4	P028	B	100# (45.4)
Benzene, 1,2-dichloro-	95501	1,2-Dichlorobenzene o-Dichlorobenzene	100	1,2,4	U070	B	100 (45.4)

TABLE 302.4 - LIST OF HAZARDOUS SUBSTANCES AND REPORTABLE QUANTITIES—Continued

Hazardous Substance	CASRN	Regulatory Synonyms	Statutory RQ	Code †	RCRA Waste Number	Category	Final RQ Pounds(Kg)
Benzene, 1,3-dichloro-	541731	1,3-Dichlorobenzene m-Dichlorobenzene	1°	2,4	U071	B	100 (45.4)
Benzene, 1,4-dichloro-	106467	1,4-Dichlorobenzene p-Dichlorobenzene	100	1,2,4	U072	B	100 (45.4)
Benzene, dichloromethyl-	98873	Benzal chloride	1°	4	U017	D	5000 (2270)
Benzene, 2,4-diisocyanatomethyl-	584849 91087 26471625	Toluene diisocyanate	1°	4	U223	B	100 (45.4)
Benzene, dimethyl m- o- p-	1330207 108383 95476 106423	Xylene m- o- p-	1000	1,4	U239	C	1000 (454)
Benzene, hexachloro-	118741	Hexachlorobenzene	1°	2,4	U127	X	1# (0.454)
Benzene, hexahydro-	110827	Cyclohexane	1000	1,4	U056	C	1000 (454)
Benzene, hydroxy-	108952	Phenol	1000	1,2,4	U188	C	1000## (454)
Benzene, methyl-	108883	Toluene	1000	1,2,4	U220	C	1000 (454)
Benzene, 1-methyl-2,4-dinitro-	121142	2,4-Dinitrotoluene	1000	1,2,4	U105	C	1000# (454)
Benzene, 1-methyl-2,6-dinitro-	606202	2,6-Dinitrotoluene	1000	1,2,4	U106	C	1000# (454)
Benzene, 1,2-methylenedioxy-4-allyl-	94597	Safrole	1°	4	U203	X	1# (0.454)
Benzene, 1,2-methylenedioxy-4-propenyl-	120581	Isosafrole	1°	4	U141	X	1# (0.454)
Benzene, 1,2-methylenedioxy-4-propyl-	94586	Dihydrosafrole	1°	4	U090	X	1# (0.454)
Benzene, 1-methylethyl-	98828	Cumene	1°	4	U055	D	5000 (2270)
Benzene, nitro-	98953	Nitrobenzene	1000	1,2,4	U169	C	1000 (454)
Benzene, pentachloro-	608935	Pentachlorobenzene	1°	4	U183	X	1## (0.454)
Benzene, pentachloronitro-	82688	Pentachloronitrobenzene	1°	4	U185	X	1# (0.454)
Benzene, 1,2,4,5-tetrachloro-	95943	1,2,4,5-Tetrachlorobenzene	1°	4	U207	D	5000 (2270)
Benzene, trichloromethyl-	98077	Benzotrichloride	1°	4	U023	X	1# (0.454)
Benzene, 1,3,5-trinitro-	99354	sym-Trinitrobenzene	1°	4	U234	X	1## (0.454)
Benzeneacetic acid, 4-chloro-alpha-(4-chlorophenyl)-alpha-hydroxy-, ethyl ester.	510156	Ethyl 4,4'-dichlorobenzilate	1°	4	U038	X	1# (0.454)
1,2-Benzenedicarboxylic acid anhydride	85449	Phthalic anhydride	1°	4	U190	D	5000 (2270)
1,2-Benzenedicarboxylic acid,[bis(2-ethylhexyl)] ester	117817	Bis(2-ethylhexyl)phthalate	1°	2,4	U028	X	1# (0.454)
1,2-Benzenedicarboxylic acid,dibutyl ester	84742	n-Butyl phthalate Dibutyl phthalate Di-n-butyl phthalate	100	1,2,4	U069	A	10 (4.54)
1,2-Benzenedicarboxylic acid,diethyl ester	84662	Diethyl phthalate	1°	2,4	U088	C	1000 (454)
1,2-Benzenedicarboxylic acid,dimethyl ester	131113	Dimethyl phthalate	1°	2,4	U102	D	5000 (2270)
1,2-Benzenedicarboxylic acid,di-n-octyl ester	117840	Di-n-octyl phthalate	1°	2,4	U107	D	5000 (2270)
1,3-Benzenediol	108463	Resorcinol	1000	1,4	U201	D	5000 (2270)
1,2-Benzenediol,4-[1-hydroxy-2-(methylamino)ethyl]-	51434	Epinephrine	1°	4	P042	C	1000 (454)
Benzenesulfonic acid chloride	98099	Benzenesulfonyl chloride	1°	4	U020	B	100 (45.4)
Benzenesulfonyl chloride	98099	Benzenesulfonic acid chloride	1°	4	U020	B	100 (45.4)
Benzenethiol	108985	Thiophenol	1°	4	P014	B	100 (45.4)
Benzidine	92875	(1,1'-Biphenyl)-4,4'diamine	1°	2,4	U021	X	1# (0.454)
1,2-Benzisothiazolin-3-one,1,1-dioxide, and salts	81072	Saccharin and salts	1°	4	U202	X	1# (0.454)
Benzo[a]anthracene	56553	Benz[a]anthracene 1,2-Benzanthracene	1°	2,4	U018	X	1# (0.454)
Benzo[b]fluoranthene	205992		1°	2		X	1# (0.454)
Benzo[k]fluoranthene	207089		1°	2		X	1# (0.454)

TABLE 302.4 - LIST OF HAZARDOUS SUBSTANCES AND REPORTABLE QUANTITIES—Continued

Hazardous Substance	CASRN	Regulatory Synonyms	Statutory RQ	Code †	RCRA Waste Number	Final RQ Category	Final RQ Pounds(Kg)
Benzo[j,k]fluorene	206440	Fluoranthene	1ᵈ	2,4	U120	X	1 ## (0.454)
Benzoic acid	65850		5000	1		D	5000 (2270)
Benzonitrile	100470		1000	1		D	5000 (2270)
Benzo[ghi]perylene	191242		1*	2		X	1 ## (0.454)
Benzo[a]pyrene	50328	3,4-Benzopyrene	1*	2,4	U022	X	1# (0.454)
3,4-Benzopyrene	50328	Benzo[a]pyrene	1*	2,4	U022	X	1# (0.454)
p-Benzoquinone	106514	1,4-Cyclohexadienedione	1*	4	U197	X	1 ## (0.454)
Benzotrichloride	98077	Benzene, trichloromethyl-	1*	4	U023	X	1# (0.454)
Benzoyl chloride	98884		1000	1		C	1000 (454)
1,2-Benzphenanthrene	218019	Chrysene	1*	2,4	U050	X	1# (0.454)
Benzyl chloride	100447	Benzene, chloromethyl-	100	1,4	P028	B	100# (45.4)
Beryllium ††	7440417	Beryllium dust	1*	2,3,4	P015	X	1# (0.454)
BERYLLIUM AND COMPOUNDS			1*	2			**
Beryllium chloride	7787475		5000	1		D	5000# (2270)
Beryllium dust	7440417	Beryllium	1*	2,3,4	P015	X	1# (0.454)
Beryllium fluoride	7787497		5000	1		D	5000# (2270)
Beryllium nitrate	13597994 7787555		5000	1		D	5000# (2270)
alpha - BHC	319846		1*	2		X	1# (0.454)
beta - BHC	319857		1*	2		X	1# (0.454)
gamma - BHC	58899	Hexachlorocyclohexane (gamma isomer) Lindane	1	1,2,4	U129	X	1# (0.454)
delta - BHC	319868		1*	2		X	1 ## (0.454)
2,2'-Bioxirane	1464535	1,2,3,4-Diepoxybutane	1*	4	U085	X	1# (0.454)
(1,1'-Biphenyl)-4,4'diamine	92875	Benzidine	1*	2,4	U021	X	1# (0.454)
(1,1'-Biphenyl)-4,4'diamine,3,3'dichloro-	91941	3,3'-Dichlorobenzidine	1*	2,4	U073	X	1# (0.454)
(1,1'-Biphenyl)-4,4'-diamine,3,3'dimethoxy-	119904	3,3'-Dimethoxybenzidine	1*	4	U091	X	1# (0.454)
(1,1'Biphenyl)-4,4'-diamine,3,3'-dimethyl-	119937	3,3'-Dimethylbenzidine	1*	4	U095	X	1# (0.454)
Bis(2-chloroethoxy) methane	111911	Ethane, 1,1'-[methylenebis(oxy)]bis[2-chloro-	1*	2,4	U024	C	1000 (454)
Bis (2-chloroethyl) ether	111444	Dichloroethyl ether Ethane, 1,1'-oxybis[2-chloro-	1*	2,4	U025	X	1# (0.454)
Bis(2-chloroisopropyl) ether	108601	Propane, 2,2'-oxybis[2-chloro-	1*	2,4	U027	C	1000 (454)
Bis(chloromethyl) ether	542881	Methane, oxybis[chloro-	1*	4	P016	X	1# (0.454)
Bis(dimethylthiocarbamoyl) disulfide	137268	Thiram	1*	4	U244	A	10 (4.54)
Bis(2-ethylhexyl)phthalate	117817	1,2-Benzenedicarboxylic acid, [bis(2-ethylhexyl)] ester	1*	2,4	U028	X	1# (0.454)
Bromine cyanide	506683	Cyanogen bromide	1*	4	U246	C	1000 (454)
Bromoacetone	598312	2-Propanone, 1-bromo-	1*	4	P017	C	1000 (454)
Bromoform	75252	Methane, tribromo-	1*	2,4	U225	B	100 (45.4)
4-Bromophenyl phenyl ether	101553	Benzene, 1-bromo-4-phenoxy-	1*	2,4	U030	B	100 (45.4)
Brucine	357573	Strychnidin-10-one, 2,3-dimethoxy-	1*	4	P018	B	100 (45.4)
1,3-Butadiene, 1,1,2,3,4,4-hexachloro-	87683	Hexachlorobutadiene	1*	2,4	U128	X	1# (0.454)
1-Butanamine, N-butyl-N-nitroso-	924163	N-Nitrosodi-n-butylamine	1*	4	U172	X	1# (0.454)
Butanoic acid, 4-[bis(2-chloroethyl)amino]benzene-	305033	Chlorambucil	1*	4	U035	X	1# (0.454)
1-Butanol	71363	n-Butyl alcohol	1*	4	U031	D	5000 (2270)
2-Butanone	78933	Methyl ethyl ketone	1*	4	U159	D	5000 (2270)

TABLE 302.4 - LIST OF HAZARDOUS SUBSTANCES AND REPORTABLE QUANTITIES—Continued

Hazardous Substance	CASRN	Regulatory Synonyms	Statutory			Final RQ	
			RQ	Code †	RCRA Waste Number	Category	Pounds(Kg)
2-Butanone peroxide	1338234	Methyl ethyl ketone peroxide	1*	4	U160	A	10 (4.54)
2-Butenal	123739 4170303	Crotonaldehyde	100	1,4	U053	B	100 (45.4)
2-Butene, 1,4-dichloro-	764410	1,4-Dichloro-2-butene	1*	4	U074	X	1 (0.454)
Butyl acetate iso- sec- tert-	123864 110190 105464 540885		5000	1		D	5000 (2270)
n-Butyl alcohol	71363	1-Butanol	1*	4	U031	D	5000 (2270)
Butylamine iso- sec- sec- tert-	109739 78819 513495 13952846 75649		1000	1		C	1000 (454)
Butyl benzyl phthalate	85687		1*	2		B	100 (45.4)
n-Butyl phthalate	84742	1,2-Benzenedicarboxylic acid,dibutyl ester Dibutyl phthalate Di-n-butyl phthalate	100	1,2,4	U069	A	10 (4.54)
Butyric acid iso-	107926 79312		5000	1		D	5000 (2270)
Cacodylic acid	75605	Hydroxydimethylarsine oxide	1*	4	U136	X	1# (0.454)
Cadmium ††	7440439		1*	2		X	1# (0.454)
Cadmium acetate	543908		100	1		B	100# (45.4)
CADMIUM AND COMPOUNDS			1*	2			**
Cadmium bromide	7789426		100	1		B	100# (45.4)
Cadmium chloride	10108642		100	1		B	100# (45.4)
Calcium arsanate	7778441		1000	1		C	1000# (454)
Calcium arsenite	52740166		1000	1		C	1000# (454)
Calcium carbide	75207		5000	1		A	10 (4.54)
Calcium chromate	13765190	Chromic acid, calcium salt	1000	1,4	U032	C	1000# (454)
Calcium cyanide	592018		10	1,4	P021	A	10 (4.54)
Calcium dodecylbenzene sulfonate	26264062		1000	1		C	1000 (454)
Calcium hypochlorite	7778543		100	1		A	10 (4.54)
Camphene, octachloro-	8001352	Toxaphene	1	2,4	P123	X	1# (0.454)
Captan	133062		10	1		A	10## (4.54)
Carbamic acid, ethyl ester	51796	Ethyl carbamate (Urethan)	1*	4	U238	X	1# (0.454)
Carbamic acid, methylnitroso-,ethyl ester	615532	N-Nitroso-N-methylurethane	1*	4	U178	X	1# (0.454)
Carbamide, N-ethyl-N-nitroso-	759739	N-Nitroso-N-ethylurea	1*	4	U176	X	1# (0.454)
Carbamide, N-methyl-N-nitroso-	684935	N-Nitroso-N-methylurea	1*	4	U177	X	1# (0.454)
Carbamide, thio-	62566	Thiourea	1*	4	U219	X	1# (0.454)
Carbamimidoselenoic acid	630104	Selenourea	1*	4	P103	X	1## (0.454)
Carbamoyl chloride, dimethyl-	79447	Dimethylcarbamoyl chloride	1*	4	U097	X	1# (0.454)
Carbaryl	63252		100	1		B	100 (45.4)
Carbofuran	1563662		10	1		A	10 (4.54)
Carbon bisulfide	75150	Carbon disulfide	5000	1,4	P022	D	5000## (2270)
Carbon disulfide	75150	Carbon bisulfide	5000	1,4	P022	D	5000## (2270)
Carbonic acid, dithallium (I) salt	6533739	Thallium(I) carbonate	1*	4	U215	X	1## (0.454)
Carbonochloridic acid, methyl ester	79221	Methyl chlorocarbonate	1*	4	U156	C	1000 (454)
Carbon oxyfluoride	353504	Carbonyl fluoride	1*	4	U033	C	1000 (454)

TABLE 302.4 - LIST OF HAZARDOUS SUBSTANCES AND REPORTABLE QUANTITIES—Continued

Hazardous Substance	CASRN	Regulatory Synonyms	Statutory RQ	Code †	RCRA Waste Number	Final RQ Category	Final RQ Pounds(Kg)
Carbon tetrachloride	56235	Methane, tetrachloro-	5000	1,2,4	U211	D	5000# (2270)
Carbonyl chloride	75445	Phosgene	5000	1,4	P095	A	10 (4.54)
Carbonyl fluoride	353504	Carbon oxyfluoride	1°	4	U033	C	1000 (454)
Chloral	75876	Acetaldehyde, trichloro-	1°	4	U034	X	1# (0.454)
Chlorambucil	305033	Butanoic acid, 4-[bis(2-chloroethyl)amino]benzene-	1°	4	U035	X	1# (0.454)
CHLORDANE (TECHNICAL MIXTURE AND METABOLITES).			1°	2			**
Chlordane	57749	Chlordane, technical. 4,7-Methanoindan, 1,2,4,5,6,7,8,8-octachloro- 3a,4,7,7a-tetrahydro-	1	1,2,4	U036	X	1# (0.454)
Chlordane, technical	57749	Chlordane. 4,7-Methanoindan, 1,2,4,5,6,7,8,8-octachloro- 3a,4,7,7a-tetrahydro-	1	1,2,4	U036	X	1# (0.454)
CHLORINATED BENZENES			1°	2			**
CHLORINATED ETHANES			1°	2			**
CHLORINATED NAPHTHALENE			1°	2			**
CHLORINATED PHENOLS			1°	2			**
Chlorine	7782505		10	1		A	10 (4.54)
Chlorine cyanide	506774	Cyanogen chloride	10	1,4	P033	A	10 (4.54)
Chlornaphazine	494031	2-Naphthylamine, N,N-bis(2-chloroethyl)-	1°	4	U026	X	1# (0.454)
Chloroacetaldehyde	107200	Acetaldehyde, chloro-	1°	4	P023	C	1000 (454)
CHLOROALKYL ETHERS			1°	2			**
p-Chloroaniline	106478	Benzenamine, 4-chloro-	1°	4	P024	C	1000 (454)
Chlorobenzene	108907	Benzene, chloro-	100	1,2,4	U037	B	100 (45.4)
4-Chloro-m-cresol	59507	p-Chloro-m-cresol Phenol, 4-chloro-3-methyl-	1°	2,4	U039	D	5000 (2270)
p-Chloro-m-cresol	59507	4-Chloro-m-cresol Phenol, 4-chloro-3-methyl-	1°	2,4	U039	D	5000 (2270)
Chlorodibromomethane	124481		1°	2		B	100 (45.4)
1-Chloro-2,3-epoxypropane	106898	Epichlorohydrin Oxirane, 2-(chloromethyl)-	1000	1,4	U041	C	1000# (454)
Chloroethane	75003		1°	2		X	1## (0.454)
2-Chloroethyl vinyl ether	110758	Ethene, 2-chloroethoxy-	1°	2,4	U042	C	1000 (454)
Chloroform	67663	Methane, trichloro-	5000	1,2,4	U044	D	5000# (2270)
Chloromethyl methyl ether	107302	Methane, chloromethoxy-	1°	4	U046	X	1# (0.454)
beta-Chloronaphthalene	91587	2-Chloronaphthalene Naphthalene, 2-chloro-	1°	2,4	U047	D	5000 (2270)
2-Chloronaphthalene	91587	beta-Chloronaphthalene Naphthalene, 2-chloro-	1°	2,4	U047	D	5000 (2270)
2-Chlorophenol	95578	o-Chlorophenol Phenol, 2-chloro-	1°	2,4	U048	B	100 (45.4)
o-Chlorophenol	95578	2-Chlorophenol Phenol, 2-chloro-	1°	2,4	U048	B	100 (45.4)
4-Chlorophenyl phenyl ether	7005723		1°	2		D	5000 (2270)
1-(o-Chlorophenyl)thiourea	5344821	Thiourea, (2-chlorophenyl)-	1°	4	P026	B	100 (45.4)
3-Chloropropionitrile	542767	Propanenitrile, 3-chloro-	1°	4	P027	C	1000 (454)
Chlorosulfonic acid	7790945		1000	1		C	1000 (454)
4-Chloro-o-toluidine, hydrochloride	3165933	Benzenamine, 4-chloro-2-methyl-, hydrochloride	1°	4	U049	X	1# (0.454)
Chlorpyrifos	2921882		1	1		X	1 (0.454)
Chromic acetate	1066304		1000	1		C	1000## (454)

TABLE 302.4 - LIST OF HAZARDOUS SUBSTANCES AND REPORTABLE QUANTITIES—Continued

Hazardous Substance	CASRN	Regulatory Synonyms	Statutory			Final RQ	
			RQ	Code †	RCRA Waste Number	Category	Pounds(Kg)
Chromic acid	11115745 7738945		1000	1		C	1000# (454)
Chromic acid, calcium salt	13765190	Calcium chromate	1000	1,4	U032	C	1000# (454)
Chromic sulfate	10101538		1000	1		C	1000## (454)
Chromium ††	7440473		1*	2		X	1# (0.454)
CHROMIUM AND COMPOUNDS			1*	2			**
Chromous chloride	10049055		1000	1		C	1000## (454)
Chrysene	218019	1,2-Benzphenanthrene	1*	2,4	U050	X	1# (0.454)
Cobaltous bromide	7789437		1000	1		C	1000(454)
Cobaltous formate	544183		1000	1		C	1000 (454)
Cobaltous sulfamate	14017415		1000	1		C	1000 (454)
Coke Oven Emissions	N.A.		1*	3		X	1# (0.454)
Copper ††	7440508		1*	2		X	1## (0.454)
COPPER AND COMPOUNDS			1*	2			**
Copper cyanide	544923		1*	4	P029	A	10 (4.54)
Coumaphos	56724		10	1		A	10 (4.54)
Creosote	8001589		1*	4	U051	X	1# (0.454)
Cresol(s) m- o- p-	1319773 108394 95487 106445	Cresylic acid	1000	1,4	U052	C	1000## (454)
Cresylic acid m- o- p-	1319773 108394 95487 106445	Cresol(s)	1000	1,4	U052	C	1000## (454)
Crotonaldehyde	123739 4170303	2-Butenal	100	1,4	U053	B	100 (45.4)
Cumene	98828	Benzene, 1-methylethyl-	1*	4	U055	D	5000 (2270)
Cupric acetate	142712		100	1		B	100 (45.4)
Cupric acetoarsenite	12002038		100	1		B	100# (45.4)
Cupric chloride	7447394		10	1		A	10## (4.54)
Cupric nitrate	3251238		100	1		B	100 (45.4)
Cupric oxalate	5893663		100	1		B	100 (45.4)
Cupric sulfate	7758987		10	1		A	10## (4.54)
Cupric sulfate ammoniated	10380297		100	1		B	100 (45.4)
Cupric tartrate	815827		100	1		B	100## (45.4)
CYANIDES			1*	2			**
Cyanides (soluble cyanide salts), not elsewhere specified.	57125		1*	4	P030	A	10 (4.54)
Cyanogen	460195		1*	4	P031	B	100 (45.4)
Cyanogen bromide	506683	Bromine cyanide	1*	4	U246	C	1000 (454)
Cyanogen chloride	506774	Chlorine cyanide	10	1,4	P033	A	10 (4.54)
1,4-Cyclohexadienedione	106514	p-Benzoquinone	1*	4	U197	X	1## (0.454)
Cyclohexane	110827	Benzene, hexahydro-	1000	1,4	U056	C	1000(454)
Cyclohexanone	108941		1*	4	U057	D	5000 (2270)
1,3-Cyclopentadiene, 1,2,3,4,5,5-hexachloro-	77474	Hexachlorocyclopentadiene	1	1,2,4	U130	X	1# (0.454)
Cyclophosphamide	50180	2H-1,3,2-Oxazaphosphorine,2-[bis(2-chloroethyl)amino] tetrahydro-2-oxide	1*	4	U058	X	1# (0.454)

TABLE 302.4 - LIST OF HAZARDOUS SUBSTANCES AND REPORTABLE QUANTITIES—Continued

Hazardous Substance	CASRN	Regulatory Synonyms	Statutory			Final RQ	
			RQ	Code †	RCRA Waste Number	Category	Pounds(Kg)
2,4-D Acid	94757	2,4-D, salts and esters. 2,4-Dichlorophenoxyacetic acid, salts and esters	100	1,4	U240	B	100 (45.4)
2,4-D Esters	94111 94791 94804 1320189 1928387 1928616 1929733 2971382 25168267 53467111		100	1.		B	100 (45.4)
2,4-D, salts and esters	94757	2,4-D Acid. 2,4-Dichlorophenoxyacetic acid, salts and esters	100	1,4	U240	B	100 (45.4)
Daunomycin	20830813	5,12-Naphthacenedione, (8S-cis)-8-acetyl-10-[3-amino-2,3,6-trideoxy- alpha-L-lyxo- hexopyranosyl)oxy]-7,8,9,10-tetrahydro- 6,8,11-trihydroxy- 1-methoxy-.	1°	4	U059	X	1# (0.454)
DDD	72548	4,4' DDD. Dichlorodiphenyl dichloroethane TDE	1	1,2,4	U060	X	1# (0.454)
4,4' DDD	72548	DDD. Dichlorodiphenyl dichloroethane TDE	.1	1,2,4	U060	X	1# (0.454)
DDE	72559	4,4' DDE	1°	2		X	1# (0.454)
4,4' DDE	72559	DDE	1°	2		X	1# (0.454)
DDT	50293	4,4' DDT. Dichlorodiphenyl trichloroethane	1	1,2,4	U061	X	1# (0.454)
4,4'DDT	50293	DDT. Dichlorodiphenyl trichloroethane	1	1,2,4	U061	X	1# (0.454)
DDT AND METABOLITES			1°	2			
Decachlorooctahydro-1,3,4-metheno-2H-cyclobuta[c,d]-pentalen-2-one.	143500	Kepone	1	1,4	U142	X	1# (0.454)
Diallate	2303164	S-(2,3-Dichloroallyl) diisopropylthiocarbamate	1°	4	U062	X	1# (0.454)
Diamine	302012	Hydrazine	1°	4	U133	X	1# (0.454)
Diaminotoluene	95807 25376458 496720 823405	Toluenediamine	1°	4	U221	X	1# (0.454)
Diazinon	5333415		1	1		X	1 (0.454)
Dibenz[a,h]anthracene	53703	1,2:5,6-Dibenzanthracene. Dibenzo[a,h]anthracene	1°	2,4	U063	X	1# (0.454)
1,2:5,6-Dibenzanthracene	53703	Dibenz[a,h]anthracene. Dibenzo[a,h]anthracene	1°	2,4	U063	X	1# (0.454)
Dibenzo[a,h]anthracene	53703	Dibenz[a,h]anthracene. 1,2:5,6-Dibenzanthracene	1°	2,4	U063	X	1# (0.454)
1,2:7,8-Dibenzopyrene	189559	Dibenz[a,i]pyrene	1°	4	U064	X	1# (0.454)
Dibenz[a,i]pyrene	189559	1,2:7,8-Dibenzopyrene	1°	4	U064	X	1# (0.454)
1,2-Dibromo-3-chloropropane	96128	Propane, 1,2-dibromo-3-chloro-	1°	4	U066	X	1# (0.454)
Dibutyl phthalate	84742	1,2-Benzenedicarboxylic acid,dibutyl ester. Di-n-butyl phthalate n-Butyl phthalate	100	1,2,4	U069	A	10 (4.54)
Di-n-butyl phthalate	84742	1,2-Benzenedicarboxylic acid,dibutyl ester. n-Butyl phthalate Dibutyl phthalate	100	1,2,4	U069	A	10 (4.54)
Dicamba	1918009		1000	1		C	1000 (454)
Dichlobenil	1194656		1000	1		B	100 (45.4)
Dichlone	117806		1	1		X	1 (0.454)
S-(2,3-Dichloroallyl) diisopropylthiocarbamate	2303164	Diallate	1°	4	U062	X	1# (0.454)
3,5-Dichloro-N-(1,1-dimethyl-2-propynyl)benzamide	23950585	Pronamide	1°	4	U192	D	5000 (2270)

TABLE 302.4 - LIST OF HAZARDOUS SUBSTANCES AND REPORTABLE QUANTITIES—Continued

Hazardous Substance	CASRN	Regulatory Synonyms	Statutory			Final RQ	
			RQ	Code #	RCRA Waste Number	Category	Pounds(Kg)
Dichlorobenzene (mixed)	25321226		100	1		B	100 (45.4)
1,2-Dichlorobenzene	95501	Benzene, 1,2-dichloro- o-Dichlorobenzene	100	1,2,4	U070	B	100 (45.4)
1,3-Dichlorobenzene	541731	Benzene, 1,3-dichloro- m-Dichlorobenzene	1*	2,4	U071	B	100 (45.4)
1,4-Dichlorobenzene	106467	Benzene, 1,4-dichloro- p-Dichlorobenzene	100	1,2,4	U072	B	100 (45.4)
m-Dichlorobenzene	541731	Benzene, 1,3-dichloro- 1,3-Dichlorobenzene	1*	2,4	U071	B	100 (45.4)
o-Dichlorobenzene	95501	Benzene, 1,2-dichloro- 1,2-Dichlorobenzene	100	1,2,4	U070	B	100 (45.4)
p-Dichlorobenzene	106467	Benzene, 1,4-dichloro- 1,4-Dichlorobenzene	100	1,2,4	U072	B	100 (45.4)
DICHLOROBENZIDINE			1*	2			**
3,3-Dichlorobenzidine	91941	(1,1'-Biphenyl)-4,4'diamine,3,3'dichloro-	1*	2,4	U073	X	1# (0.454)
Dichlorobromomethane	75274		1*	2		D	5000 (2270)
1,4-Dichloro-2-butene	764410	2-Butene, 1,4-dichloro-	1*	4	U074	X	1 (0.454)
Dichlorodifluoromethane	75718	Methane, dichlorodifluoro-	1*	4	U075	D	5000 (2270)
Dichlorodiphenyl dichloroethane	72548	DDD 4,4' DDD TDE	1	1,2,4	U060	X	1# (0.454)
Dichlorodiphenyl trichloroethane	50293	DDT 4,4'DDT	1	1,2,4	U061	X	1# (0.454)
1,1-Dichloroethane	75343	Ethane, 1,1-dichloro- Ethylidene dichloride	1*	2,4	U076	C	1000 (454)
1,2-Dichloroethane	107062	Ethane, 1,2-dichloro- Ethylene dichloride	5000	1,2,4	U077	D	5000# (2270)
1,1-Dichloroethylene	75354	Ethene, 1,1-dichloro- Vinylidene chloride	5000	1,2,4	U078	D	5000# (2270)
1,2-trans-Dichloroethylene	156605	Ethene, trans-1,2-dichloro-	1*	2,4	U079	C	1000 (454)
Dichloroethyl ether	111444	Bis (2-chloroethyl) ether Ethane, 1,1'-oxybis(2-chloro-	1*	2,4	U025	X	1# (0.454)
2,4-Dichlorophenol	120632	Phenol, 2,4-dichloro-	1*	2,4	U081	B	100 (45.4)
2,6-Dichlorophenol	87650	Phenol, 2,6-dichloro-	1*	4	U082	B	100 (45.4)
2,4-Dichlorophenoxyacetic acid, salts and esters	94757	2,4-D Acid 2,4-D, salts and esters	100	1,4	U240	B	100 (45.4)
Dichlorophenylarsine	696286	Phenyl dichloroarsine	1*	4	P036	X	1# (0.454)
Dichloropropane 1,1-Dichloropropane 1,3-Dichloropropane	26638197 78999 142289		5000	1		C	1000 (454)
1,2-Dichloropropane	78875	Propylene dichloride	5000	1,2,4	U083	C	1000 (454)
Dichloropropane - Dichloropropene (mixture)	8003198		5000	1		D	5000## (2270)
Dichloropropene 2,3-Dichloropropene	26952238 78886		5000	1		D	5000## (2270)
1,3-Dichloropropene	542756	Propene, 1,3-dichloro-	5000	1,2,4	U084	D	5000## (2270)
2,2-Dichloropropionic acid	75990		5000	1		D	5000 (2270)
Dichlorvos	62737		10	1		A	10 (4.54)
Dieldrin	60571	1,2,3,4,10,10-Hexachloro-6,7-epoxy- 1,4,4a,5,6,7,8,8a-octahydro-endo,exo- 1,4:5,8- dimethanonaphthalene.	1	1,2,4	P037	X	1# (0.454)
1,2:3,4-Diepoxybutane	1464535	2,2'-Bioxirane	1*	4	U085	X	1# (0.454)
Diethylamine	109897		1000	1		C	1000## (454)
Diethylarsine	692422	Arsine, diethyl-	1*	4	P038	X	1# (0.454)

TABLE 302.4 - LIST OF HAZARDOUS SUBSTANCES AND REPORTABLE QUANTITIES—Continued

Hazardous Substance	CASRN	Regulatory Synonyms	Statutory RQ	Code †	RCRA Waste Number	Final RQ Category	Final RQ Pounds(Kg)
1,4-Diethylene dioxide	123911	1,4-Dioxane	1*	4	U108	X	1# (0.454)
N,N'-Diethylhydrazine	1615801	Hydrazine, 1,2-diethyl-	1*	4	U086	X	1# (0.454)
O,O-Diethyl S-[2-(ethylthio)ethyl]phosphorodithioate	298044	Disulfoton	1	1,4	P039	X	1 (0.454)
O,O-Diethyl S-methyl dithiophosphate	3288582	Phosphorodithioic acid, O,O-diethyl S-methylester	1*	4	U087	D	5000 (2270)
Diethyl-p-nitrophenyl phosphate	311455	Phosphoric acid,diethyl p-nitrophenyl ester	1*	4	P041	B	100 (45.4)
Diethyl phthalate	84662	1,2-Benzenedicarboxylic acid,diethyl ester	1*	2,4	U088	C	1000 (454)
O,O-Diethyl O-pyrazinyl phosphorothioate	297972	Phosphorothioic acid, O,O-diethyl O-pyrazinyl ester	1*	4	P040	B	100 (45.4)
Diethylstilbestrol	56531	4,4'-Stilbenediol, alpha,alpha'-diethyl-	1*	4	U089	X	1# (0.454)
1,2-Dihydro-3,6-pyridazinedione	123331	Maleic hydrazide	1*	4	U148	D	5000 (2270)
Dihydrosafrole	94586	Benzene, 1,2-methylenedioxy-4-propyl-	1*	4	U090	X	1# (0.454)
Diisopropyl fluorophosphate	55914	Phosphorofluoridic acid,bis(1-methylethyl) ester	1*	4	P043	B	100 (45.4)
Dimethoate	60515	Phosphorodithioic acid,O,O-dimethyl S-[2(methylamino)-2-oxoethyl] ester.	1*	4	P044	A	10 (4.54)
3,3'-Dimethoxybenzidine	119904	(1,1'-Biphenyl)-4,4'diamine,3,3'dimethoxy-	1*	4	U091	X	1# (0.454)
Dimethylamine	124403	Methanamine, N-methyl-	1000	1,4	U092	C	1000## (454)
Dimethylaminoazobenzene	60117	Benzenamine, N,N-dimethyl-4-phenylazo-	1*	4	U093	X	1# (0.454)
7,12-Dimethylbenz[a]anthracene	57976	1,2-Benzanthracene, 7,12-dimethyl-	1*	4	U094	X	1# (0.454)
3,3'-Dimethylbenzidine	119937	(1,1'Biphenyl)-4,4'-diamine,3,3'-dimethyl-	1*	4	U095	X	1# (0.454)
alpha,alpha-Dimethylbenzylhydroperoxide	80159	Hydroperoxide, 1-methyl-1-phenylethyl-	1*	4	U096	A	10 (4.54)
3,3-Dimethyl-1-(methylthio)-2-butanone, O-[(methylamino)carbonyl] oxime.	39196184	Thiofanox	1*	4	P045	B	100 (45.4)
Dimethylcarbamoyl chloride	79447	Carbamoyl chloride, dimethyl-	1*	4	U097	X	1# (0.454)
1,1-Dimethylhydrazine	57147	Hydrazine, 1,1-dimethyl-	1*	4	U098	X	1# (0.454)
1,2-Dimethylhydrazine	540738	Hydrazine, 1,2-dimethyl-	1*	4	U099	X	1# (0.454)
O,O-Dimethyl O-p-nitrophenyl phosphorothioate	298000	Methyl parathion	100	1,4	P071	B	100## (45.4)
Dimethylnitrosamine	62759	N-Nitrosodimethylamine	1*	2,4	P082	X	1# (0.454)
alpha,alpha-Dimethylphenethylamine	122098	Ethanamine, 1,1-dimethyl-2-phenyl-	1*	4	P046	D	5000 (2270)
2,4-Dimethylphenol	105679	Phenol, 2,4-dimethyl-	1*	2,4	U101	B	100 (45.4)
Dimethyl phthalate	131113	1,2-Benzenedicarboxylic acid,dimethyl ester	1*	2,4	U102	D	5000 (2270)
Dimethyl sulfate	77781	Sulfuric acid, dimethyl ester	1*	4	U103	X	1# (0.454)
Dinitrobenzene (mixed)	25154545 99650 528290 100254		1000	1		B	100 (45.4)
4,6-Dinitro-o-cresol and salts	534521	Phenol, 2,4-dinitro-6-methyl-, and salts	1*	2,4	P047	A	10 (4.54)
4,6-Dinitro-o-cyclohexylphenol	131895	Phenol, 2-cyclohexyl-4,6-dinitro-	1*	4	P034	B	100 (45.4)
Dinitrophenol	25550587 329715 573568		1000	1		A	10 (4.54)
2,5-							
2,6-							
2,4-Dinitrophenol	51285	Phenol, 2,4-dinitro-	1000	1,2,4	P048	A	10 (4.54)
Dinitrotoluene	25321146 610399		1000	1,2		C	1000# (454)
3,4-Dinitrotoluene							
2,4-Dinitrotoluene	121142	Benzene, 1-methyl-2,4-dinitro-	1000	1,2,4	U105	C	1000# (454)
Dinoseb	88857	Phenol, 2,4-dinitro-6-(1-methylpropyl)-	1*	4	P020	C	1000 (454)
Di-n-octyl phthalate	117840	1,2-Benzenedicarboxylic acid,di-n-octyl ester	1*	2,4	U107	D	5000 (2270)
1,4-Dioxane	123911	1,4-Diethylene dioxide	1*	4	U108	X	1# (0.454)
DIPHENYLHYDRAZINE			1*	2			**
1,2-Diphenylhydrazine	122667	Hydrazine, 1,2-diphenyl-	1*	2,4	U109	X	1# (0.454)

TABLE 302.4 - LIST OF HAZARDOUS SUBSTANCES AND REPORTABLE QUANTITIES—Continued

Hazardous Substance	CASRN	Regulatory Synonyms	Statutory			Final RQ	
			HQ	Code †	RCRA Waste Number	Category	Pounds(Kg)
Diphosphoramide, octamethyl-	152169	Octamethylpyrophosphoramide	1*	4	P085	B	100 (45.4)
Dipropylamine	142847	1-Propanamine, N-propyl-	1*	4	U110	D	5000 (2270)
Di-n-propylnitrosamine	621647	N-Nitrosodi-n-propylamine	1*	2,4	U111	X	1# (0.454)
Diquat	85007 2764729		1000	1		C	1000 (454)
Disulfoton	298044	O,O-Diethyl S-[2-(ethylthio)ethyl] phosphorodithioate	1	1,4	P039	X	1 (0.454)
2,4-Dithiobiuret	541537	Thioimidodicarbonic diamide	1*	4	P049	B	100 (45.4)
Dithiopyrophosphoric acid, tetraethyl ester	3689245	Tetraethyldithiopyrophosphate	1*	4	P109	B	100 (45.4)
Diuron	330541		100	1		B	100 (45.4)
Dodecylbenzenesulfonic acid	27176870		1000	1		C	1000 (454)
Endosulfan	115297	5-Norbornene-2,3-dimethanol,1,4,5,6,7,7-hexachloro, cyclic sulfite.	1	1,2,4	P050	X	1 (0.454)
alpha - Endosulfan	959988		1*	2		X	1 (0.454)
beta - Endosulfan	33213659		1*	2		X	1 (0.454)
ENDOSULFAN AND METABOLITES			1*	2			**
Endosulfan sulfate	1031078		1*	2		X	1 (0.454)
Endothall	145733	7-Oxabicyclo[2,2,1]heptane-2,3-dicarboxylic acid	1*	4	P088	C	1000 (454)
Endrin	72208	1,2,3,4,10,10-Hexachloro-6,7-epoxy-1,4,4a,5,6,7,8,8a-octahydro-endo,endo- 1,4:5,8-dimethanonaphthalene.	1	1,2,4	P051	X	1 (0.454)
Endrin aldehyde	7421934		1*	2		X	1 (0.454)
ENDRIN AND METABOLITES			1*	2			**
Epichlorohydrin	106898	1-Chloro-2,3-epoxypropane Oxirane, 2-(chloromethyl)-	1000	1,4	U041	C	1000# (454)
Epinephrine	51434	1,2-Benzenediol, 4-[1-hydroxy-2-(methylamino)ethyl]-	1*	4	P042	C	1000 (454)
Ethanal	75070	Acetaldehyde	1000	1,4	U001	C	1000 (454)
Ethanamine, 1,1-dimethyl-2-phenyl-	122098	alpha,alpha-Dimethylphenethylamine	1*	4	P046	D	5000 (2270)
Ethanamine, N-ethyl-N-nitroso-	55185	N-Nitrosodiethylamine	1*	4	U174	X	1# (0.454)
Ethane, 1,2-dibromo-	106934	Ethylene dibromide	1000	1,4	U067	C	1000# (454)
Ethane, 1,1-dichloro-	75343	1,1-Dichloroethane Ethylidene dichloride	1*	2,4	U076	C	1000 (454)
Ethane, 1,2-dichloro-	107062	1,2-Dichloroethane Ethylene dichloride	5000	1,2,4	U077	D	5000# (2270)
Ethane, 1,1,1,2,2,2-hexachloro-	67721	Hexachloroethane	1*	2,4	U131	X	1# (0.454)
Ethane, 1,1'-[methylenebis(oxy)]bis(2-chloro-	111911	Bis(2-chloroethoxy) methane	1*	2,4	U024	C	1000 (454)
Ethane, 1,1'-oxybis-	60297	Ethyl ether	1*	4	U117	B	100 (45.4)
Ethane, 1,1'-oxybis(2-chloro-	111444	Bis (2-chloroethyl) ether Dichloroethyl ether	1*	2,4	U025	X	1# (0.454)
Ethane, pentachloro-	76017	Pentachloroethane	1*	4	U184	X	1## (0.454)
Ethane, 1,1,1,2-tetrachloro-	630206	1,1,1,2-Tetrachloroethane	1*	4	U208	X	1# (0.454)
Ethane, 1,1,2,2-tetrachloro-	79345	1,1,2,2-Tetrachloroethane	1*	2,4	U209	X	1# (0.454)
Ethane, 1,1,2-trichloro-	79005	1,1,2-Trichloroethane	1*	2,4	U227	X	1# (0.454)
Ethane, 1,1,1-trichloro-2,2-bis(p-methoxyphenyl)-	72435	Methoxychlor	1	1,4	U247	X	1 (0.454)
1,2-Ethanediylbiscarbamodithioic acid	111546	Ethylenebis(dithiocarbamic acid)	1*	4	U114	D	5000 (2270)
Ethanenitrile	75058	Acetonitrile	1*	4	U003	D	5000 (2270)
Ethanethioamide	62555	Thioacetamide	1*	4	U218	X	1# (0.454)

TABLE 302.4 - LIST OF HAZARDOUS SUBSTANCES AND REPORTABLE QUANTITIES—Continued

Hazardous Substance	CASRN	Regulatory Synonyms	Statutory RQ	Code †	RCRA Waste Number	Final RQ Category	Final RQ Pounds(Kg)
Ethanol, 2,2'-(nitrosoimino)bis-	1116547	N-Nitrosodiethanolamine	1*	4	U173	X	1# (0.454)
Ethanone, 1-phenyl-	98862	Acetophenone	1*	4	U004	D	5000 (2270)
Ethanoyl chloride	75365	Acetyl chloride	5000	1,4	U006	D	5000 (2270)
Ethenamine, N-methyl-N-nitroso-	4549400	N-Nitrosomethylvinylamine	1*	4	P084	X	1# (0.454)
Ethene, chloro-	75014	Vinyl chloride	1*	2,3,4	U043	X	1# (0.454)
Ethene, 2-chloroethoxy-	110758	2-Chloroethyl vinyl ether	1*	2,4	U042	C	1000 (454)
Ethene, 1,1-dichloro-	75354	1,1-Dichloroethylene Vinylidene chloride	5000	1,2,4	U078	D	5000# (2270)
Ethene, 1,1,2,2-tetrachloro-	127184	Tetrachloroethylene	1*	2,4	U210	X	1# (0.454)
Ethene, trans-1,2-dichloro-	156605	1,2-trans-Dichloroethylene	1*	2,4	U079	C	1000 (454)
Ethion	563122		10	1		A	10## (4.54)
Ethyl acetate	141786	Acetic acid, ethyl ester	1*	4	U112	D	5000 (2270)
Ethyl acrylate	140885	2-Propenoic acid, ethyl ester	1*	4	U113	C	1000 (454)
Ethylbenzene	100414		1000	1,2		C	1000 (454)
Ethyl carbamate (Urethan)	51796	Carbamic acid, ethyl ester	1*	4	U238	X	1# (0.454)
Ethyl cyanide	107120	Propanenitrile	1*	4	P101	A	10 (4.54)
Ethyl 4,4'-dichlorobenzilate	510156	Benzeneacetic acid, 4-chloro-alpha-(4-chlorophenyl)-alpha-hydroxy-, ethyl ester.	1*	4	U038	X	1# (0.454)
Ethylene dibromide	106934	Ethane, 1,2-dibromo-	1000	1,4	U067	C	1000# (454)
Ethylene dichloride	107062	1,2-Dichloroethane Ethane, 1,2-dichloro-	5000	1,2,4	U077	D	5000# (2270)
Ethylene oxide	75218	Oxirane	1*	4	U115	X	1# (0.454)
Ethylenebis(dithiocarbamic acid)	111546	1,2-Ethanediylbiscarbamodithioic acid	1*	4	U114	D	5000 (2270)
Ethylenediamine	107153		1000	1		D	5000 (2270)
Ethylenediamine tetraacetic acid (EDTA)	60004		5000	1		D	5000 (2270)
Ethylenethiourea	96457	2-Imidazolidinethione	1*	4	U116	X	1# (0.454)
Ethylenimine	151564	Aziridine	1*	4	P054	X	1# (0.454)
Ethyl ether	60297	Ethane, 1,1'-oxybis-	1*	4	U117	B	100 (45.4)
Ethylidene dichloride	75343	1,1-Dichloroethane Ethane, 1,1-dichloro-	1*	2,4	U076	C	1000 (454)
Ethyl methacrylate	97632	2-Propenoic acid, 2-methyl-, ethyl ester	1*	4	U118	C	1000 (454)
Ethyl methanesulfonate	62500	Methanesulfonic acid, ethyl ester	1*	4	U119	X	1# (0.454)
Famphur	52857	Phosphorothioic acid, O,O-dimethyl-O-[p-[(dimethylamino)- sulfonyl]phenyl] ester.	1*	4	P097	C	1000 (454)
Ferric ammonium citrate	1185575		1000	1		C	1000 (454)
Ferric ammonium oxalate	2944674 55488874		1000	1		C	1000 (454)
Ferric chloride	7705080		1000	1		C	1000 (454)
Ferric dextran	9004664	Iron dextran	1*	4	U139	X	1## (0.454)
Ferric fluoride	7783508		100	1		B	100 (45.4)
Ferric nitrate	10421484		1000	1		C	1000 (454)
Ferric sulfate	10028225		1000	1		C	1000 (454)
Ferrous ammonium sulfate	10045893		1000	1		C	1000 (454)
Ferrous chloride	7758943		100	1		B	100 (45.4)
Ferrous sulfate	7720787 7782630		1000	1		C	1000 (454)
Fluoroacetic acid, sodium salt	62748	Acetic acid, fluoro-, sodium salt	1*	4	P058	A	10 (4.54)

TABLE 302.4 - LIST OF HAZARDOUS SUBSTANCES AND REPORTABLE QUANTITIES—Continued

Hazardous Substance	CASRN	Regulatory Synonyms	Statutory RQ	Code †	RCRA Waste Number	Final RQ Category	Final RQ Pounds(Kg)
Fluoranthene	206440	Benzo[j,k]fluorene	1*	2,4	U120	X	1## (0.454)
Fluorene	86737		1*	2		X	1## (0.454)
Fluorine	7782414		1*	4	P056	A	10 (4.54)
Fluoroacetamide	640197	Acetamide, 2-fluoro-	1*	4	P057	B	100 (45.4)
Formaldehyde	50000	Methylene oxide	1000	1,4	U122	C	1000# (454)
Formic acid	64186	Methanoic acid	5000	1,4	U123	D	5000 (2270)
Fulminic acid, mercury(II)salt	628864	Mercury fulminate	1*	4	P065	X	1## (0.454)
Fumaric acid	110178		5000	1		D	5000 (2270)
Furan	110009	Furfuran	1*	4	U124	B	100 (45.4)
Furan, tetrahydro-	109999	Tetrahydrofuran	1*	4	U213	C	1000 (454)
2-Furancarboxaldehyde	98011	Furfural	1000	1,4	U125	D	5000 (2270)
2,5-Furandione	108316	Maleic anhydride	5000	1,4	U147	D	5000 (2270)
Furfural	98011	2-Furancarboxaldehyde	1000	1,4	U125	D	5000 (2270)
Furfuran	110009	Furan	1*	4	U124	B	100 (45.4)
D-Glucopyranose, 2-deoxy-2-(3-methyl-3-nitrosoureido)-	18883664	Streptozotocin	1*	4	U206	X	1# (0.454)
Glycidylaldehyde	765344	1-Propanal, 2,3-epoxy-	1*	4	U126	X	1# (0.454)
Guanidine, N-nitroso-N-methyl-N'-nitro-	70257	N-Methyl-N'-nitro-N-nitrosoguanidine	1*	4	U163	X	1# (0.454)
Guthion	86500		1	1		X	1 (0.454)
HALOETHERS			1*	2			**
HALOMETHANES			1*	2			**
Heptachlor	76448	4,7-Methano-1H-indene,1,4,5,6,7,8,8-heptachloro-3a,4,7,7a-tetrahydro-.	1	1,2,4	P059	X	1# (0.454)
HEPTACHLOR AND METABOLITES			1*	2			**
Heptachlor epoxide	1024573		1*	2		X	1# (0.454)
Hexachlorobenzene	118741	Benzene, hexachloro-	1*	2,4	U127	X	1# (0.454)
Hexachlorobutadiene	87683	1,3-Butadiene, 1,1,2,3,4,4-hexachloro-	1*	2,4	U128	X	1# (0.454)
HEXACHLOROCYCLOHEXANE (all isomers)	608731		1*	2			**
Hexachlorocyclohexane (gamma isomer)	58899	gamma - BHC Lindane	1	1,2,4	U129	X	1# (0.454)
Hexachlorocyclopentadiene	77474	1,3-Cyclopentadiene, 1,2,3,4,5,5-hexachloro-	1	1,2,4	U130	X	1# (0.454)
1,2,3,4,10,10-Hexachloro-6,7-epoxy-1,4,4a,5,6,7,8,8a-octahydro-endo,endo- 1,4:5,8-dimethanonaphthalene.	72208	Endrin	1	1,2,4	P051	X	1 (0.454)
1,2,3,4,10,10-Hexachloro-6,7-epoxy-1,4,4a,5,6,7,8,8a-octahydro-endo,exo- 1,4:5,8-dimethanonaphthalene.	60571	Dieldrin	1	1,2,4	P037	X	1# (0.454)
Hexachloroethane	67721	Ethane, 1,1,1,2,2,2-hexachloro-	1*	2,4	U131	X	1# (0.454)
Hexachlorohexahydro-endo,endo-dimethanonaphthalene	465736	1,2,3,4,10,10-Hexachloro-1,4,4a,5,8,8a-hexahydro-1,4,5,8-endo,endo- dimethanonaphthalene.	1*	4	P060	X	1 (0.454)
1,2,3,4,10,10-Hexachloro-1,4,4a,5,8,8a-hexahydro-1,4,5,8-endo,endo- dimethanonaphthalene.	465736	Hexachlorohexahydro-endo,endo-dimethanonaphthalene	1*	4	P060	X	1 (0.454)
1,2,3,4,10-10-Hexachloro-1,4,4a,5,8,8a-hexahydro-1,4:5,8- endo, exo-dimethanonaphthalene.	309002	Aldrin	1	1,2,4	P004	X	1# (0.454)
Hexachlorophene	70304	2,2'-Methylenebis(3,4,6-trichlorophenol)	1*	4	U132	X	1## (0.454)
Hexachloropropene	1888717	1-Propene, 1,1,2,3,3,3-hexachloro-	1*	4	U243	C	1000 (454)
Hexaethyl tetraphosphate	757584	Tetraphosphoric acid, hexaethyl ester	1*	4	P062	B	100 (45.4)
Hydrazine	302012	Diamine	1*	4	U133	X	1# (0.454)
Hydrazine, 1,2-diethyl-	1615801	N,N'-Diethylhydrazine	1*	4	U086	X	1# (0.454)
Hydrazine, 1,1-dimethyl-	57147	1,1-Dimethylhydrazine	1*	4	U098	X	1# (0.454)

TABLE 302.4 - LIST OF HAZARDOUS SUBSTANCES AND REPORTABLE QUANTITIES—Continued

Hazardous Substance	CASRN	Regulatory Synonyms	Statutory			Final RQ	
			RQ	Code †	RCRA Waste Number	Category	Pounds(Kg)
Hydrazine, 1,2-dimethyl-	540738	1,2-Dimethylhydrazine	1*	4	U099	X	1# (0.454)
Hydrazine, 1,2-diphenyl-	122667	1,2-Diphenylhydrazine	1*	2,4	U109	X	1# (0.454)
Hydrazine, methyl-	60344	Methyl hydrazine	1*	4	P068	A	10 (4.54)
Hydrazinecarbothioamide	79196	Thiosemicarbazide	1*	4	P116	B	100 (45.4)
Hydrochloric acid	7647010		5000	1		D	5000 (2270)
Hydrocyanic acid	74908	Hydrogen cyanide	10	1,4	P063	A	10 (4.54)
Hydrofluoric acid	7664393	Hydrogen fluoride	5000	1,4	U134	B	100 (45.4)
Hydrogen cyanide	74908	Hydrocyanic acid	10	1,4	P063	A	10 (4.54)
Hydrogen fluoride	7664393	Hydrofluoric acid	5000	1,4	U134	B	100 (45.4)
Hydrogen phosphide	7803512	Phosphine	1*	4	P096	B	100 (45.4)
Hydrogen sulfide	7783064	Hydrosulfuric acid Sulfur hydride	100	1,4	U135	B	100## (45.4)
Hydroperoxide, 1-methyl-1-phenylethyl-	80159	alpha,alpha-Dimethylbenzylhydroperoxide	1*	4	U096	A	10 (4.54)
Hydrosulfuric acid	7783064	Hydrogen sulfide Sulfur hydride	100	1,4	U135	B	100## (45.4)
Hydroxydimethylarsine oxide	75605	Cacodylic acid	1*	4	U136	X	1# (0.454)
2-Imidazolidinethione	96457	Ethylenethiourea	1*	4	U116	X	1# (0.454)
Indeno(1,2,3-cd)pyrene	193395	1,10-(1,2-Phenylene)pyrene	1*	2,4	U137	X	1# (0.454)
Iron dextran	9004664	Ferric dextran	1*	4	U139	X	1## (0.454)
Isobutyl alcohol	78831	1-Propanol, 2-methyl-	1*	4	U140	D	5000 (2270)
Isocyanic acid, methyl ester	624839	Methyl isocyanate	1*	4	P064	X	1### (0.454)
Isophorone	78591		1*	2		D	5000 (2270)
Isoprene	78795		1000	1		C	1000## (454)
Isopropanolamine dodecylbenzenesulfonate	42504461		1000	1		C	1000 (454)
Isosafrole	120581	Benzene, 1,2-methylenedioxy-4-propenyl-	1*	4	U141	X	1# (0.454)
3(2H)-Isoxazolone, 5-(aminomethyl)-	2763964	5-(Aminomethyl)-3-isoxazolol	1*	4	P007	C	1000 (454)
Kelthane	115322		5000	1		A	10 (4.54)
Kepone	143500	Decachlorooctahydro-1,3,4-metheno-2H-cyclobuta[c,d]-pentalen-2-one.	1	1,4	U142	X	1# (0.454)
Lasiocarpine	303344		1*	4	U143	X	1# (0.454)
Lead ††	7439921		1*	2		X	1## (0.454)
Lead acetate	301042	Acetic acid, lead salt	5000	1,4	U144	D	5000# (2270)
LEAD AND COMPOUNDS			1*	2			**
Lead arsenate	7784409 7645252 10102484		5000	1		D	5000# (2270)
Lead chloride	7758954		5000	1		D	5000## (2270)
Lead fluoborate	13814965		5000	1		D	5000## (2270)
Lead fluoride	7783462		1000	1		C	1000## (454)
Lead iodide	10101630		5000	1		D	5000## (2270)
Lead nitrate	10099748		5000	1		D	5000## (2270)
Lead phosphate	7446277	Phosphoric acid, lead salt	1*	4	U145	X	1# (0.454)
Lead stearate	7428480 1072351 56189094 52652592		5000	1		D	5000## (2270)
Lead subacetate	1335326		1*	4	U146	X	1# (0.454)

TABLE 302.4 - LIST OF HAZARDOUS SUBSTANCES AND REPORTABLE QUANTITIES—Continued

Hazardous Substance	CASRN	Regulatory Synonyms	Statutory			Final RQ	
			RQ	Code †	RCRA Waste Number	Category	Pounds(Kg)
Lead sulfate	15739807 7446142		5000	1		D	5000## (2270)
Lead sulfide	1314870		5000	1		D	5000## (2270)
Lead thiocyanate	592870		5000	1		D	5000## (2270)
Lindane	58899	gamma - BHC Hexachlorocyclohexane (gamma isomer)	1	1,2,4	U129	X	1# (0.454)
Lithium chromate	14307358		1000	1		C	1000# (454)
Malathion	121755		10	1		B	100 (45.4)
Maleic acid	110167		5000	1		D	5000 (2270)
Maleic anhydride	108316	2,5-Furandione	5000	1,4	U147	D	5000 (2270)
Maleic hydrazide	123331	1,2-Dihydro-3,6-pyridazinedione	1*	4	U148	D	5000 (2270)
Malononitrile	109773	Propanedinitrile	1*	4	U149	C	1000 (454)
Melphalan	148823	Alanine, 3-[p-bis(2-chloroethyl)amino]phenyl-,L-	1*	4	U150	X	1# (0.454)
Mercaptodimethur	2032657		100	1		A	10 (4.54)
Mercuric cyanide	592041		1	1		X	1 (0.454)
Mercuric nitrate	10045940		10	1		A	10## (4.54)
Mercuric sulfate	7783359		10	1		A	10## (4.54)
Mercuric thiocyanate	592858		10	1		A	10## (4.54)
Mercurous nitrate	10415755 7782867		10	1		A	10## (4.54)
Mercury	7439976		1*	2,3,4	U151	X	1 (0.454)
MERCURY AND COMPOUNDS			1*	2			**
Mercury, (acetato-O)phenyl-	62384	Phenylmercuric acetate	1*	4	P092	X	1## (0.454)
Mercury fulminate	628864	Fulminic acid, mercury(II) salt	1*	4	P065	X	1## (0.454)
Methacrylonitrile	126987	2-Propenenitrile, 2-methyl-	1*	4	U152	C	1000 (454)
Methanamine, N-methyl-	124403	Dimethylamine	1000	1,4	U092	C	1000## (454)
Methane, bromo-	74839	Methyl bromide	1*	2,4	U029	C	1000 (454)
Methane, chloro-	74873	Methyl chloride	1*	2,4	U045	X	1## (0.454)
Methane, chloromethoxy-	107302	Chloromethyl methyl ether	1*	4	U046	X	1# (0.454)
Methane, dibromo-	74953	Methylene bromide	1*	4	U068	C	1000 (454)
Methane, dichloro-	75092	Methylene chloride	1*	2,4	U080	C	1000 (454)
Methane, dichlorodifluoro-	75718	Dichlorodifluoromethane	1*	4	U075	D	5000 (2270)
Methane, iodo-	74884	Methyl iodide	1*	4	U138	X	1# (0.454)
Methane, oxybis(chloro-	542881	Bis(chloromethyl) ether	1*	4	P016	X	1# (0.454)
Methane, tetrachloro-	56235	Carbon tetrachloride	5000	1,2,4	U211	D	5000# (2270)
Methane, tetranitro-	509148	Tetranitromethane	1*	4	P112	A	10 (4.54)
Methane, tribromo-	75252	Bromoform	1*	2,4	U225	B	100 (45.4)
Methane, trichloro-	67663	Chloroform	5000	1,2,4	U044	D	5000# (2270)
Methane, trichlorofluoro-	75694	Trichloromonofluoromethane	1*	4	U121	D	5000 (2270)
Methanesulfonic acid, ethyl ester	62500	Ethyl methanesulfonate	1*	4	U119	X	1# (0.454)
Methanethiol	74931	Methylmercaptan Thiomethanol	100	1,4	U153	B	100 (45.4)
Methanesulfenyl chloride, trichloro-	594423	Trichloromethanesulfenyl chloride	1*	4	P118	B	100 (45.4)
4,7-Methano-1H-indene,1,4,5,6,7,8,8-heptachloro-3a,4,7,7a-tetrahydro-	76448	Heptachlor	1	1,2,4	P059	X	1# (0.454)
Methanoic acid	64186	Formic acid	5000	1,4	U123	D	5000 (2270)

TABLE 302.4 - LIST OF HAZARDOUS SUBSTANCES AND REPORTABLE QUANTITIES—Continued

Hazardous Substance	CASRN	Regulatory Synonyms	Statutory			Final RQ	
			RQ	Code †	RCRA Waste Number	Category	Pounds(Kg)
4,7-Methanoindan; 1,2,4,5,6,7,8,8-octachloro- 3a,4,7,7a-tetrahydro-.	57749	Chlordane Chlordane, technical	1	1,2,4	U036	X	1# (0.454)
Methanol	67561	Methyl alcohol	1*	4	U154	D	5000 (2270)
Methapyrilene	91805	Pyridine, 2-[(2-(dimethylamino)ethyl)-2-thenylamino]-	1*	4	U155	D	5000 (2270)
Methomyl	16752775	Acetimidic acid, N-[(methylcarbamoyl)oxy]thio-, methyl ester.	1*	4	P066	B	100 (45.4)
Methoxychlor	72435	Ethane, 1,1,1-trichloro-2,2-bis(p-methoxyphenyl)-	1	1,4	U247	X	1 (0.454)
Methyl alcohol	67561	Methanol	1*	4	U154	D	5000 (2270)
2-Methylaziridine	75558	1,2-Propylenimine	1*	4	P067	X	1# (0.454)
Methyl bromide	74839	Methane, bromo-	1*	2,4	U029	C	1000 (454)
1-Methylbutadiene	504609	1,3-Pentadiene	1*	4	U186	B	100 (45.4)
Methyl chloride	74873	Methane, chloro-	.1*	2,4	U045	X	1## (0.454)
Methyl chlorocarbonate	79221	Carbonochloridic acid, methyl ester	-1*	4	U156	C	1000 (454)
Methyl chloroform	71556	1,1,1-Trichloroethane	1*	2,4	U226	C	1000 (454)
4,4'-Methylenebis(2-chloroaniline)	101144	Benzenamine, 4,4'-methylenebis(2-chloro-	1*	4	U158	X	1# (0.454)
2,2'-Methylenebis(3,4,6-trichlorophenol)	70304	Hexachlorophene	1*	4	U132	X	1## (0.454)
3-Methylcholanthrene	56495	Benz[j]aceanthrylene, 1,2-dihydro-3-methyl-	1*	4	U157	X	1# (0.454)
Methylene bromide	74953	Methane, dibromo-	1*	4	U068	C	1000 (454)
Methylene chloride	75092	Methane, dichloro-	1*	2,4	U080	C	1000 (454)
Methylene oxide	50000	Formaldehyde	1000	1,4	U122	C	1000# (454)
Methyl ethyl ketone	78933	2-Butanone	1*	4	U159	D	5000 (2270)
Methyl ethyl ketone peroxide	1338234	2-Butanone peroxide	1*	4	U160	A	10 (4.54)
Methyl hydrazine	60344	Hydrazine, methyl-	1*	4	P068	A	10 (4.54)
Methyl iodide	74884	Methane, iodo-	1*	4	U138	X	1# (0.454)
Methyl isobutyl ketone	108101	4-Methyl-2-pentanone	1*	4	U161	D	5000 (2270)
Methyl isocyanate	624839	Isocyanic acid, methyl ester	1*	4	P064	X	1###(0.4>4)
2-Methyllactonitrile	75865	Acetone cyanohydrin Propanenitrile, 2-hydroxy-2-methyl-	10	1,4	P069	A	10 (4.54)
Methylmercaptan	74931	Methanethiol Thiomethanol	100	1,4	U153	B	100 (45.4)
Methyl methacrylate	80626	2-Propenoic acid, 2-methyl-, methyl ester	5000	1,4	U162	C	1000 (454)
N-Methyl-N'-nitro-N-nitrosoguanidine	70257	Guanidine, N-nitroso-N-methyl-N'-nitro-	1*	4	U163	X	1# (0.454)
Methyl parathion	298000	O,O-Dimethyl O-p-nitrophenyl phosphorothioate	100	1,4	P071	B	100## (45.4)
4-Methyl-2-pentanone	108101	Methyl isobutyl ketone	1*	4	U161	D	5000 (2270)
Methylthiouracil	56042	4(1H)-Pyrimidinone, 2,3-dihydro-6-methyl-2-thioxo-.	1*	4	U164	X	1# (0.454)
Mevinphos	7786347		1	1		A	10 (4.54)
Mexacarbate	315184		1000	1		C	1000 (454)
Mitomycin C	50077	Azirino(2',3':3,4)pyrrolo(1,2-a)indole-4,7-dione,6-amino-8-[((aminocarbonyl)oxy)methyl]- 1,1a,2,8,8a,8b- hexahydro-8a-methoxy- 5-methyl-.	1*	4	U010	X	1# (0.454)
Monoethylamine	75047		1000	1		C	1000## (454)
Monomethylamine	74895		1000	1		B	100 (45.4)
Naled	300765		10	1		A	10 (4.54)
5,12-Naphthacenedione, (8S-cis)-8-acetyl-10-[3-amino-2,3,6-trideoxy-alpha-L- lyxo-hexopyranosyl)oxy]-7,8,9,10-tetrahydro- 6,8,11-trihydroxy- 1-methoxy-.	20830813	Daunomycin	1*	4	U059	X	1# (0.454)
Naphthalene	91203		5000	1,2,4	U165	B	100 (45.4)

TABLE 302.4 - LIST OF HAZARDOUS SUBSTANCES AND REPORTABLE QUANTITIES—Continued

Hazardous Substance	CASRN	Regulatory Synonyms	Statutory			Final RQ	
			RQ	Code †	RCRA Waste Number	Category	Pounds(Kg)
Naphthalene, 2-chloro-	91587	beta-Chloronaphthalene. 2-Chloronaphthalene	1*	2,4	U047	D	5000 (2270)
1,4-Naphthalenedione	130154	1,4-Naphthoquinone	1*	4	U166	D	5000 (2270)
2,7-Naphthalenedisulfonic acid,3,3'-[(3,3'-dimethyl- (1,1'-biphenyl)-4,4'-diyl)- bis(azo)]bis(5-amino- 4-hydroxy)-tetrasodium salt.	72571	Trypan blue	1*	4	U236	X	1# (0.454)
Naphthenic acid	1338245		100	1		B	100 (45.4)
1,4-Naphthoquinone	130154	1,4-Naphthalenedione	1*	4	U166	D	5000 (2270)
1-Naphthylamine	134327	alpha-Naphthylamine	1*	4	U167	X	1# (0.454)
2-Naphthylamine	91598	beta-Naphthylamine	1*	4	U168	X	1# (0.454)
alpha-Naphthylamine	134327	1-Naphthylamine	1*	4	U167	X	1# (0.454)
beta-Naphthylamine	91598	2-Naphthylamine	1*	4	U168	X	1# (0.454)
2-Naphthylamine, N,N-bis(2-chloroethyl)-	494031	Chlornaphazine	1*	4	U026	X	1# (0.454)
alpha-Naphthylthiourea	86884	Thiourea, 1-naphthalenyl-	1*	4	P072	B	100 (45.4)
Nickel ††	7440020		1*	2		X	1# (0.454)
NICKEL AND COMPOUNDS			1*	2			**
Nickel ammonium sulfate	15699180		5000	1		D	5000# (2270)
Nickel carbonyl	13463393	Nickel tetracarbonyl	1*	4	P073	X	1# (0.454)
Nickel chloride	7718549 37211055		5000	1		D	5000# (2270)
Nickel cyanide	557197	Nickel(II) cyanide	1*	4	P074	X	1# (0.454)
Nickel(II) cyanide	557197	Nickel cyanide	1*	4	P074	X	1# (0.454)
Nickel hydroxide	12054487		1000	1		C	1000# (454)
Nickel nitrate	14216752		5000	1		D	5000# (2270)
Nickel sulfate	7786814		5000	1		D	5000# (2270)
Nickel tetracarbonyl	13463393	Nickel carbonyl	1*	4	P073	X	1# (0.454)
Nicotine and salts	54115	Pyridine, (S)-3-(1-methyl-2-pyrrolidinyl)-, and salts	1*	4	P075	B	100 (45.4)
Nitric acid	7697372		1000	1		C	1000 (454)
Nitric oxide	10102439	Nitrogen(II) oxide	1*	4	P076	A	10 (4.54)
p-Nitroaniline	100016	Benzenamine, 4-nitro-	1*	4	P077	D	5000 (2270)
Nitrobenzene	98953	Benzene, nitro-	1000	1,2,4	U169	C	1000 (454)
Nitrogen dioxide	10102440 10544726	Nitrogen(IV) oxide	1000	1,4	P078	A	10 (4.54)
Nitrogen(II) oxide	10102439	Nitric oxide	1*	4	P076	A	10 (4.54)
Nitrogen(IV) oxide	10102440 10544726	Nitrogen dioxide	1000	1,4	P078	A	10 (4.54)
Nitroglycerine	55630	1,2,3-Propanetriol, trinitrate-	1*	4	P081	A	10 (4.54)
Nitrophenol (mixed) m- o- p-	25154556 554847 88755 100027	2-Nitrophenol 4-Nitrophenol Phenol, 4-nitro-	1000	1		B	100 (45.4)
p-Nitrophenol	100027	4-Nitrophenol Phenol, 4-nitro-	1000	1,2,4	U170	B	100 (45.4)
2-Nitrophenol	88755	o-Nitrophenol	1000	1,2		B	100 (45.4)
4-Nitrophenol	100027	p-Nitrophenol Phenol, 4-nitro-	1000	1,2,4	U170	B	100 (45.4)
NITROPHENOLS			1*	2			**
2-Nitropropane	79469	Propane, 2-nitro-	1*	4	U171	X	1# (0.454)
NITROSAMINES			1*	2			**

TABLE 302.4 - LIST OF HAZARDOUS SUBSTANCES AND REPORTABLE QUANTITIES—Continued

Hazardous Substance	CASRN	Regulatory Synonyms	Statutory			Final RQ	
			RQ	Code †	RCRA Waste Number	Category	Pounds(Kg)
N-Nitrosodi-n-butylamine	924163	1-Butanamine, N-butyl-N-nitroso-	1*	4	U172	X	1# (0.454)
N-Nitrosodiethanolamine	1116547	Ethanol, 2,2'-(nitrosoimino)bis-	1*	4	U173	X	1# (0.454)
N-Nitrosodiethylamine	55185	Ethanamine, N-ethyl-N-nitroso-	1*	4	U174	X	1# (0.454)
N-Nitrosodimethylamine	62759	Dimethylnitrosamine	1*	2,4	P082	X	1# (0.454)
N-Nitrosodiphenylamine	86306		1*	2		B	100 (45.4)
N-Nitrosodi-n-propylamine	621647	Di-n-propylnitrosamine	1*	2,4	U111	X	1# (0.454)
N-Nitroso-N-ethylurea	759739	Carbamide, N-ethyl-N-nitroso-	1*	4	U176	X	1# (0.454)
N-Nitroso-N-methylurea	684935	Carbamide, N-methyl-N-nitroso-	1*	4	U177	X	1# (0.454)
N-Nitroso-N-methylurethane	615532	Carbamic acid, methylnitroso-,ethyl ester	1*	4	U178	X	1# (0.454)
N-Nitrosomethylvinylamine	4549400	Ethenamine, N-methyl-N-nitroso-	1*	4	P084	X	1# (0.454)
N-Nitrosopiperidine	100754	Pyridine, hexahydro-N-nitroso-	1*	4	U179	X	1# (0.454)
N-Nitrosopyrrolidine	930552	Pyrrole, tetrahydro-N-nitroso-	1*	4	U180	X	1# (0.454)
Nitrotoluene	1321126		1000	1		C	1000 (454)
m-	99081						
o-	88722						
p-	99990						
5-Nitro-o-toluidine	99558	Benzenamine, 2-methyl-5-nitro-	1*	4	U181	X	1# (0.454)
5-Norbornene-2,3-dimethanol,1,4,5,6,7,7-hexachloro, cyclic sulfite.	115297	Endosulfan	1	1,2,4	P050	X	1 (0.454)
Octamethylpyrophosphoramide	152169	Diphosphoramide, octamethyl-	1*	4	P085	B	100 (45.4)
Osmium oxide	20816120	Osmium tetroxide	1*	4	P087	C	1000 (454)
Osmium tetroxide	20816120	Osmium oxide	1*	4	P087	C	1000 (454)
7-Oxabicyclo[2.2.1]heptane-2,3-dicarboxylic acid	145733	Endothall	1*	4	P088	C	1000 (454)
1,2-Oxathiolane, 2,2-dioxide	1120714	1,3-Propane sultone	1*	4	U193	X	1# (0.454)
2H-1,3,2-Oxazaphosphorine,2-[bis(2-chloroethyl)amino] tetrahydro-2-oxide.	50180	Cyclophosphamide	1*	4	U058	X	1# (0.454)
Oxirane	75218	Ethyleneoxide	1*	4	U115	X	1# (0.454)
Oxirane, 2-(chloromethyl)-	106898	1-Chloro-2,3-epoxypropane Epichlorohydrin	1000	1,4	U041	C	1000# (454)
Paraformaldehyde	30525894		1000	1		C	1000 (454)
Paraldehyde	123637	1,3,5-Trioxane, 2,4,6-trimethyl-	1*	4	U182	C	1000 (454)
Parathion	56382	Phosphorothioic acid,O,O-diethyl O-(p-nitrophenyl) ester	1	1,	P089	X	1# (0.454)
Pentachlorobenzene	608935	Benzene, pentachloro-	1*	4	U183	X	1## (0.454)
Pentachloroethane	76017	Ethane, pentachloro-	1*	4	U184	X	1## (0.454)
Pentachloronitrobenzene	82688	Benzene, pentachloronitro-	1*	4	U185	X	1# (0.454)
Pentachlorophenol	87865	Phenol, pentachloro-	10	1,2,4	U242	A	10# (4.54)
1,3-Pentadiene	504609	1-Methylbutadiene	1*	4	U186	B	100 (45.4)
Phenacetin	62442	Acetamide, N-(4-ethoxyphenyl)-	1*	4	U187	X	1# (0.454)
Phenanthrene	85018		1*	2		X	1## (0.454)
Phenol	108952	Benzene, hydroxy-	1000	1,2,4	U188	C	1000## (454)
Phenol, 2-chloro-	95578	2-Chlorophenol o-Chlorophenol	1*	2,4	U048	B	100 (45.4)
Phenol, 4-chloro-3-methyl-	59507	4-Chloro-m-cresol p-Chloro-m-cresol	1*	2,4	U039	D	5000 (2270)
Phenol, 2-cyclohexyl-4,6-dinitro-	131895	4,6-Dinitro-o-cyclohexylphenol	1*	4	P034	B	100 (45.4)
Phenol, 2,4-dichloro-	120832	2,4-Dichlorophenol	1*	2,4	U081	B	100 (45.4)
Phenol, 2,6-dichloro-	87650	2,6-Dichlorophenol	1*	4	U082	B	100 (45.4)
Phenol, 2,4-dimethyl-	105679	2,4-Dimethylphenol	1*	2,4	U101	B	100 (45.4)

TABLE 302.4 - LIST OF HAZARDOUS SUBSTANCES AND REPORTABLE QUANTITIES—Continued

Hazardous Substance	CASRN	Regulatory Synonyms	Statutory RQ	Code †	RCRA Waste Number	Final RQ Category	Final RQ Pounds(Kg)
Phenol, 2,4-dinitro-	51285	2,4-Dinitrophenol	1000	1,2,4	P048	A	10 (4.54)
Phenol, 2,4-dinitro-6-(1-methylpropyl)-	88857	Dinoseb	1*	4	P020	C	1000 (454)
Phenol, 2,4-dinitro-6-methyl-, and salts	534521	4,6-Dinitro-o-cresol and salts	1*	2,4	P047	A	10 (4.54)
Phenol, 4-nitro-	100027	p-Nitrophenol / 4-Nitrophenol	1000	1,2,4	U170	B	100 (45.4)
Phenol, pentachloro-	87865	Pentachlorophenol	10	1,2,4	U242	A	10# (4.54)
Phenol, 2,3,4,6-tetrachloro-	58902	2,3,4,6-Tetrachlorophenol	1*	4	U212	A	10 (4.54)
Phenol, 2,4,5-trichloro-	95954	2,4,5-Trichlorophenol	10	1,4	U230	A	10# (4.54)
Phenol, 2,4,6-trichloro-	88062	2,4,6-Trichlorophenol	10	1,2,4	U231	A	10# (4.54)
Phenol, 2,4,6-trinitro-, ammonium salt	131748	Ammonium picrate	1*	4	P009	A	10 (4.54)
Phenyl dichloroarsine	696286	Dichlorophenylarsine	1*	4	P036	X	1# (0.454)
1,10-(1,2-Phenylene)pyrene	193395	Indeno(1,2,3-cd)pyrene	1*	2,4	U137	X	1# (0.454)
Phenylmercuric acetate	62384	Mercury, (acetato-O)phenyl-	1*	4	P092	X	1## (0.454)
N-Phenylthiourea	103855	Thiourea, phenyl-	1*	4	P093	B	100 (45.4)
Phorate	298022	Phosphorodithioic acid, O,O-diethyl S-(ethylthio), methyl ester	1*	4	P094	X	1## (0.454)
Phosgene	75445	Carbonyl chloride	5000	1,4	P095	A	10 (4.54)
Phosphine	7803512	Hydrogen phosphide	1*	4	P096	B	100 (45.4)
Phosphoric acid	7664382		5000	1		D	5000 (2270)
Phosphoric acid.diethyl p-nitrophenyl ester	311455	Diethyl-p-nitrophenyl phosphate	1*	4	P041	B	100 (45.4)
Phosphoric acid, lead salt	7446277	Lead phosphate	1*	4	U145	X	1# (0.454)
Phosphorodithioic acid, O,O-diethyl S-methylester	3288582	O,O-Diethyl S-methyl dithiophosphate	1*	4	U087	D	5000 (2270)
Phosphorodithioic acid, O,O-diethyl S-(ethylthio), methyl ester.	298022	Phorate	1*	4	P094	X	1## (0.454)
Phosphorodithioic acid,O,O-dimethyl S-[2(methylamino)-2-oxoethyl] ester.	60515	Dimethoate	1*	4	P044	A	10 (4.54)
Phosphorofluoridic acid,bis(1-methylethyl) ester	55914	Diisopropyl fluorophosphate	1*	4	P043	B	100 (45.4)
Phosphorothioic acid,O,O-diethyl O-(p-nitrophenyl) ester	56382	Parathion	1	1,4	P089	X	1# (0.454)
Phosphorothioic acid, O,O-diethyl O-pyrazinyl ester	297972	O,O-Diethyl O-pyrazinyl phosphorothioate	1*	4	P040	B	100 (45.4)
Phosphorothioic acid, O,O-dimethyl O-[p-[(dimethylamino)-sulfonyl]phenyl] ester.	52857	Famphur	1*	4	P097	C	1000 (454)
Phosphorus	7723140		1*	1		X	1 (0.454)
Phosphorus oxychloride	10025873		5000	1		C	1000 (454)
Phosphorus pentasulfide	1314803	Phosphorus sulfide / Sulfur phosphide	100	1,4	U189	B	100 (45.4)
Phosphorus sulfide	1314803	Phosphorus pentasulfide / Sulfur phosphide	100	1,4	U189	B	100 (45.4)
Phosphorus trichloride	7719122		5000	1		C	1000 (454)
PHTHALATE ESTERS			1*	2			**
Phthalic anhydride	85449	1,2-Benzenedicarboxylic acid anhydride	1*	4	U190	D	5000 (2270)
2-Picoline	109068	Pyridine,2-methyl-	1*	4	U191	D	5000 (2270)
Plumbane, tetraethyl-	78002	Tetraethyl lead	100	1,4	P110	B	100## (45.4)
POLYCHLORINATED BIPHENYLS (PCBs)	1336363	Aroclors	10	1,2		A	10# (4.54)
	12674112	Aroclor 1016					
	11104282	Aroclor 1221					
	11141165	Aroclor 1232					
	53469219	Aroclor 1242					
	12672296	Aroclor 1248					
	11097691	Aroclor 1254					
	11096825	Aroclor 1260					
POLYNUCLEAR AROMATIC HYDROCARBONS			1*	2			**

TABLE 302.4 - LIST OF HAZARDOUS SUBSTANCES AND REPORTABLE QUANTITIES—Continued

Hazardous Substance	CASRN	Regulatory Synonyms	Statutory			Final RQ	
			RQ	Code #	RCRA Waste Number	Category	Pounds(Kg)
Potassium arsenate	7784410		1000	1		C	1000# (454)
Potassium arsenite	10124502		1000	1		C	1000# (454)
Potassium bichromate	7778509		1000	1		C	1000# (454)
Potassium chromate	7789006		1000	1		C	1000# (454)
Potassium cyanide	151508		10.	1,4	P098	A	10 (4.54)
Potassium hydroxide	1310583		1000	1		C	1000 (454)
Potassium permanganate	7722647		100	1		B	100 (45.4)
Potassium silver cyanide	506616		1*	4	P099	X	1 (0.454)
Pronamide	23950585	3,5-Dichloro-N-(1,1-dimethyl-2-propynyl)benzamide	1*	4	U192	D	5000 (2270)
1-Propanal, 2,3-epoxy-	765344	Glycidylaldehyde	1*	4	U126	X	1# (0.454)
Propanal, 2-methyl-2-(methylthio)-,O-[(methylamino) carbonyl]oxime.	116063	Aldicarb	1*	4	P070	X	1 (0.454)
1-Propanamine	107108	n-Propylamine	1*	4	U194	D	5000 (2270)
1-Propanamine, N-propyl-	142847	Dipropylamine	1*	4	U110	D	5000 (2270)
Propane, 1,2-dibromo-3-chloro-	96128	1,2-Dibromo-3-chloropropane	1*	4	U066	X	1# (0.454)
Propane, 2-nitro-	79469	2-Nitropropane	1*	4	U171	X	1# (0.454)
Propane, 2,2'-oxybis(2-chloro-	108601	Bis(2-chloroisopropyl) ether	1*	2,4	U027	C	1000 (454)
1,3-Propane sultone	1120714	1,2-Oxathiolane, 2,2-dioxide	1*	4	U193	X	1# (0.454)
Propanedinitrile	109773	Malononitrile	1*	4	U149	C	1000 (4.54)
Propanenitrile	107120	Ethyl cyanide	1*	4	P101	A	10 (4.54)
Propanenitrile, 3-chloro-	542767	3-Chloropropionitrile	1*	4	P027	C	1000 (454)
Propanenitrile, 2-hydroxy-2-methyl-	75865	Acetone cyanohydrin 2-Methyllactonitrile	10	1,4	P069	A	10 (4.54)
1,2,3-Propanetriol, trinitrate-	55630	Nitroglycerine	1*	4	P081	A	10 (4.54)
1-Propanol, 2,3-dibromo-, phosphate (3:1)	126727	Tris(2,3-dibromopropyl) phosphate	1*	4	U235	X	1# (0.454)
1-Propanol, 2-methyl-	78831	Isobutyl alcohol	1*	4	U140	D	5000 (2270)
2-Propanone	67641	Acetone	1*	4	U002	D.	5000 (2270)
2-Propanone, 1-bromo-	598312	Bromoacetone	1*	4	P017	C	1000 (454)
Propargite	2312358		10	1		A	10 (4.54)
Propargyl alcohol	107197	2-Propyn-1-ol	1*	4	P102	C	1000 (454)
2-Propenal	107028	Acrolein	1	1,2,4	P003	X	1 (0.454)
2-Propenamide	79061	Acrylamide	1*	4	U007	D	5000 (2270)
Propene, 1,3-dichloro-	542756	1,3-Dichloropropene	5000	1,2,4	U084	D	5000## (2270)
1-Propene, 1,1,2,3,3,3-hexachloro-	1888717	Hexachloropropene	1*	4	U243	C	1000 (454)
2-Propenenitrile	107131	Acrylonitrile	100	1,2,4	U009	B	100# (45.4)
2-Propenenitrile, 2-methyl-	126987	Methacrylonitrile	1*	4	U152	C	1000 (454)
2-Propenoic acid	79107	Acrylic acid	1*	4.	U008	D.	5000 (2270)
2-Propenoic acid, ethyl ester	140885	Ethyl acrylate	1*	4	U113	C	1000 (454)
2-Propenoic acid, 2-methyl-, ethyl ester	97632	Ethyl methacrylate	1*	4	U118	C	1000 (454)
2-Propenoic acid, 2-methyl-, methyl ester	80626	Methyl methacrylate	5000	1,4	U162	C	1000 (454)
2-Propen-1-ol	107186	Allyl alcohol	100	1,4	P005	B	100 (45.4)
Propionic acid	79094		5000	1		D	5000 (2270)
Propionic acid, 2-(2,4,5-trichlorophenoxy)-	93721	Silvex 2,4,5-TP acid	100	1,4	U233	B	100 (45.4)
Propionic anhydride	123626		5000	1		D	5000 (2270)

TABLE 302.4 - LIST OF HAZARDOUS SUBSTANCES AND REPORTABLE QUANTITIES—Continued

Hazardous Substance	CASRN	Regulatory Synonyms	Statutory RQ	Code †	RCRA Waste Number	Category	Final RQ Pounds(Kg)
a-Propylamine	107108	1-Propanamine	1*	4	U194	D	5000 (2270)
Propylene dichloride	78875	1,2-Dichloropropane	5000	1,2,4	U083	C	1000 (454)
Propylene oxide	75569		5000	1		B	100 (45.4)
1,2-Propylenimine	75558	2-Methylaziridine	1*	4	P067	X	1# (0.454)
2-Propyn-1-ol	107197	Propargyl alcohol	1*	4	P102	C	1000 (454)
Pyrene	129000		1*	2		X	1## (0.454)
Pyrethrins	121299 121211 8003347		1000	1		X	1 (0.454)
4-Pyridinamine	504245	4-Aminopyridine	,1*	4	P008	C	1000 (454)
Pyridine	110861		1*	4	U196	X	1## (0.454)
Pyridine, 2-[(2-(dimethylamino)ethyl]-2-thenylamino]-	91805	Methapyrilene	1*	4	U155	D	5000 (2270)
Pyridine, hexahydro-N-nitroso-	100754	N-Nitrosopiperidine	1*	4	U179	X	1# (0.454)
Pyridine,2-methyl-	109068	2-Picoline	1*	4	U191	D	5000 (2270)
Pyridine, (S)-3-(1-methyl-2-pyrrolidinyl)-, and salts	54115	Nicotine and salts	1*	4	P075	B	100 (45.4)
4(1H)-Pyrimidinone, 2,3-dihydro-6-methyl-2-thioxo-	56042	Methylthiouracil	1*	4	U164	X	1# (0.454)
Pyrophosphoric acid, tetraethyl ester	107493	Tetraethyl pyrophosphate	100	1,4	P111	B	100## (45.4)
Pyrrole, tetrahydro-N-nitroso-	930552	N-Nitrosopyrrolidine	1*	4	U180	X	1# (0.454)
Quinoline	91225		1000	1		D	5000 (2270)
RADIONUCLIDES			1*	3		X	1# (0.454)
Reserpine	50555	Yohimban-16-carboxylic acid,11,17-dimethoxy-18-[(3,4,5- trimethoxybenzoyl)oxy]-, methyl ester.	1*	4	U200	D	5000 (2270)
Resorcinol	108463	1,3-Benzenediol	1000	1,4	U201	D	5000 (2270)
Saccharin and salts	81072	1,2-Benzisothiazolin-3-one,1,1-dioxide, and salts	1*	4	U202	X	1# (0.454)
Safrole	94597	Benzene, 1,2-methylenedioxy-4-allyl-	1*	4	U203	X	1# (0.454)
Selenious acid	7783008		1*	4	U204	X	1## (0.454)
Selenium ††	7782492		1*	2		X	1## (0.454)
SELENIUM AND COMPOUNDS			1*	2			**
Selenium dioxide	7446084	Selenium oxide	1000	1,4	U204	C	1000## (454)
Selenium disulfide	7488564	Sulfur selenide	1*	4	U205	X	1# (0.454)
Selenium oxide	7446084	Selenium dioxide	1000	1,4	U204	C	1000## (454)
Selenourea	630104	Carbamimidoselenoic acid	1*	4	P103	X	1## (0.454)
L-Serine, diazoacetate (ester)	115026	Azaserine	1*	4	U015	X	1# (0.454)
Silver ††	7440224		1*	2		C	1000 (454)
SILVER AND COMPOUNDS			1*	2			**
Silver cyanide	506649		1*	4	P104	X	1 (0.454)
Silver nitrate	7761888		1	1		X	1 (0.454)
Silvex	93721	Propanoic acid, 2-(2,4,5-trichlorophenoxy)- 2,4,5-TP acid	100	1,4	U233	B	100 (45.4)
Sodium	7440235		1000	1		A	10 (4.54)
Sodium arsenate	7631892		1000	1		C	1000# (454)
Sodium arsenite	7784465		1000	1		C	1000# (454)
Sodium azide	26628228		1*	4	P105	C	1000 (454)
Sodium bichromate	10588019		1000	1		C	1000# (454)
Sodium bifluoride	1333831		5000	1		D	5000## (2270)
Sodium bisulfite	7631905		5000	1		D	5000 (2270)

TABLE 302.4 - LIST OF HAZARDOUS SUBSTANCES AND REPORTABLE QUANTITIES—Continued

Hazardous Substance	CASRN	Regulatory Synonyms	Statutory			Final RQ	
			RQ	Code #	RCRA Waste Number	Category	Pounds(Kg)
Sodium chromate	7775113		1000	1		C	1000# (454)
Sodium cyanide	143339		10	1,4	P106	A	10 (4.54)
Sodium dodecylbenzene sulfonate	25155300		1000	1		C	1000 (454)
Sodium fluoride	7681494		5000	1		C	1000 (454)
Sodium hydrosulfide	16721805		5000	1		D	5000 (2270)
Sodium hydroxide	1310732		1000	1		C	1000 (454)
Sodium hypochlorite	7681529 10022705		100	1		B	100 (45.4)
Sodium methylate	124414		1000	1		C	1000 (454)
Sodium nitrite	7632000		100	1		B	100## (45.4)
Sodium phosphate, dibasic	7558794 10039324 10140655		5000	1		D	5000 (2270)
Sodium phosphate, tribasic	7601549 7785844 10101890 10361894 7758294 10124568		5000	1		D	5000 (2270)
Sodium selenite	10102188 7782823		1000	1		C	1000## (454)
4,4'-Stilbenediol, alpha,alpha'-diethyl-	56531	Diethylstilbestrol	1*	4	U089	X	1# (0.454)
Streptozotocin	18883664	D-Glucopyranose, 2-deoxy-2-(3-methyl-3-nitrosoureido)-	1*	4	U206	X	1# (0.454)
Strontium chromate	7789062		1000	1		C	1000# (454)
Strontium sulfide	1314961		1*	4	P107	B	100 (45.4)
Strychnidin-10-one, and salts	57249	Strychnine and salts	10	1,4	P108	A	10 (4.54)
Strychnidin-10-one, 2,3-dimethoxy-	357573	Brucine	1*	4	P018	A	10 (4.54)
Strychnine and salts	57249	Strychnidin-10-one, and salts	10	1,4	P108	A	10 (4.54)
Styrene	100425		1000	1		C	1000 (454)
Sulfur hydride	7783064	Hydrogen sulfide Hydrosulfuric acid	100	1,4	U135	B	100## (45.4)
Sulfur monochloride	12771083		1000	1		C	1000 (454)
Sulfur phosphide	1314803	Phosphorus pentasulfide Phosphorus sulfide	100	1,4	U189	B	100 (45.4)
Sulfur selenide	7488564	Selenium disulfide	1*	4	U205	X	1# (0.454)
Sulfuric acid	7664939 8014957		1000	1		C	1000 (454)
Sulfuric acid, dimethyl ester	77781	Dimethyl sulfate	1*	4	U103	X	1# (0.454)
Sulfuric acid, thallium(I) salt	7446186 10031591	Thallium(I) sulfate	1000	1,4	P115	C	1000## (454)
2,4,5-T	93765	2,4,5-T acid 2,4,5-Trichlorophenoxyacetic acid	100	1,4	U232	C	1000 (454)
2,4,5-T acid	93765	2,4,5-T 2,4,5-Trichlorophenoxyacetic acid	100	1,4	U232	C	1000 (454)
2,4,5-T amines	2008460 6369966 6369977 1319728 3813147		100	1		D	5000 (2270)
2,4,5-T esters	93798 2545597 61792072 1928478 25168154		100	1		C	1000 (454)
2,4,5-T salts	13560991		100	1		C	1000 (454)

TABLE 302.4 - LIST OF HAZARDOUS SUBSTANCES AND REPORTABLE QUANTITIES—Continued

Hazardous Substance	CASRN	Regulatory Synonyms	Statutory		RCRA Waste Number	Final RQ	
			RQ	Code †		Category	Pounds(Kg)
TDE	72548	DDD 4,4' DDD Dichlorodiphenyl dichloroethane	1	1,2,4	U060	X	1# (0.454)
1,2,4,5-Tetrachlorobenzene	95943	Benzene, 1,2,4,5-tetrachloro-	1*	4	U207	D	5000 (2270)
2,3,7,8-Tetrachlorodibenzo-p-dioxin(TCDD)	1746016		1*	2		X	1# (0.454)
1,1,1,2-Tetrachloroethane	630206	Ethane,1,1,1,2-tetrachloro-	1*	4	U208	X	1# (0.454)
1,1,2,2-Tetrachloroethane	79345	Ethane, 1,1,2,2-tetrachloro-	1*	2,4	U209	X	1# (0.454)
Tetrachloroethylene	127184	Ethene, 1,1,2,2-tetrachloro-	1*	2,4	U210	X	1# (0.454)
2,3,4,6-Tetrachlorophenol	58902	Phenol, 2,3,4,6-tetrachloro-	1*	4	U212	A	10 (4.54)
Tetraethyldithiopyrophosphate	3689245	Dithiopyrophosphoric acid, tetraethyl ester	1*	4	P109	B	100 (45.4)
Tetraethyl lead	78002	Plumbane, tetraethyl-	100	1,4	P110	B	100## (45.4)
Tetraethyl pyrophosphate	107493	Pyrophosphoric acid, tetraethyl ester	100	1,4	P111	B	100## (45.4)
Tetrahydrofuran	109999	Furan, tetrahydro-	1*	4	U213	C	1000 (454)
Tetranitromethane	509148	Methane, tetranitro-	1*	4	P112	A	10 (4.54)
Tetraphosphoric acid, hexaethyl ester	757584	Hexaethyl tetraphosphate	1*	4	P062	B	100 (45.4)
Thallic oxide	1314325	Thallium(III) oxide	1*	4	P113	X	1## (0.454)
Thallium ††	7440280		1*	2		X	1## (0.454)
THALLIUM AND COMPOUNDS			1*	2			**
Thallium(I) acetate	563688	Acetic acid, thallium(I) salt	1*	4	U214	X	1## (0.454)
Thallium(I) carbonate	6533739	Carbonic acid, dithallium (I) salt	1*	4	U215	X	1## (0.454)
Thallium(I) chloride	7791120		1*	4	U216	X	1## (0.454)
Thallium(I) nitrate	10102451		1*	4	U217	X	1## (0.454)
Thallium(III) oxide	1314325	Thallic oxide	1*	4	P113	X	1## (0.454)
Thallium(I) selenide	12039520		1*	4	P114	X	1## (0.454)
Thallium(I) sulfate	7446186 10031591	Sulfuric acid, thallium(I) salt	1000	1,4	P115	C	1000## (454)
Thioacetamide	62555	Ethanethioamide	1*	4	U218	X	1# (0.454)
Thiofanox	39196184	3,3-Dimethyl-1-(methylthio)-2-butanone,O-[(methylamino) carbonyl] oxime.	1*	4	P045	B	100 (45.4)
Thioimidodicarbonic diamide	541537	2,4-Dithiobiuret	1*	4	P049	B	100 (45.4)
Thiomethanol	74931	Methanethiol Methylmercaptan	100	1,4	U153	B	100 (45.4)
Thiophenol	108985	Benzenethiol	1*	4	P014	B	100 (45.4)
Thiosemicarbazide	79196	Hydrazinecarbothioamide	1*	4	P116	B	100 (45.4)
Thiourea	62566	Carbamide, thio-	1*	4	U219	X	1# (0.454)
Thiourea, (2-chlorophenyl)-	5344821	1-(o-Chlorophenyl)thiourea	1*	4	P026	B	100 (45.4)
Thiourea, 1-naphthalenyl-	86884	alpha-Naphthylthiourea	1*	4	P072	B	100 (45.4)
Thiourea, phenyl-	103855	N-Phenylthiourea	1*	4	P093	B	100 (45.4)
Thiram	137268	Bis(dimethylthiocarbamoyl) disulfide	1*	4	U244	A	10 (4.54)
Toluene	108883	Benzene, methyl-	1000	1,2,4	U220	C	1000 (454)
Toluenediamine	95807 25376458 496720 823405	Diaminotoluene	1*	4	U221	X	1# (0.454)
Toluene diisocyanate	584849 91087 26471625	Benzene, 2,4-diisocyanatomethyl-	1*	4	U223	B	100 (45.4)
o-Toluidine hydrochloride	636215	Benzenamine, 2-methyl-, hydrochloride	1*	4	U222	X	1# (0.454)
Toxaphene	8001352	Camphene, octachloro-	1	1,2,4	P123	X	1# (0.454)

TABLE 302.4 - LIST OF HAZARDOUS SUBSTANCES AND REPORTABLE QUANTITIES—Continued

Hazardous Substance	CASRN	Regulatory Synonyms	Statutory			Final RQ	
			RQ	Code †	RCRA Waste Number	Category	Pounds(Kg)
2,4,5-TP acid	93721	Propionic acid, 2-(2,4,5-trichlorophenoxy)- Silvex	100	1,4	U233	B	100 (45.4)
2,4,5-TP acid esters	32534955		100	1		B	100 (45.4)
1H-1,2,4-Triazol-3-amine	61825	Amitrole	1*	4	U011	X	1# (0.454)
Trichlorfon	52686		1000	1		C	1000## (454)
1,2,4-Trichlorobenzene	120821		1*	2		B	100 (45.4)
1,1,1-Trichloroethane	71556	Methyl chloroform	1*	2,4	U226	C	1000 (454)
1,1,2-Trichloroethane	79005	Ethane, 1,1,2-trichloro-	1*	2,4	U227	X	1# (0.454)
Trichloroethene	79016	Trichloroethylene	1000	1,2,4	U228	C	1000# (454)
Trichloroethylene	79016	Trichloroethene	1000	1,2,4	U228	C	1000# (454)
Trichloromethanesulfenyl chloride	594423	Methanesulfenyl chloride, trichloro-	1*	4	P118	B	100 (45.4)
Trichloromonofluoromethane	75694	Methane, trichlorofluoro-	1*	4	U121	D	5000 (2270)
Trichlorophenol	25167822		10	1		A	10# (4.54)
2,3,4-Trichlorophenol	15950660						
2,3,5-Trichlorophenol	933788						
2,3,6-Trichlorophenol	933755						
2,4,5-Trichlorophenol	95954	Phenol, 2,4,5-trichloro-					
2,4,6-Trichlorophenol	88062	Phenol, 2,4,6-trichloro-					
3,4,5-Trichlorophenol	609198						
2,4,5-Trichlorophenol	95954	Phenol, 2,4,5-trichloro-	10	1,4	U230	A	10# (4.54)
2,4,6-Trichlorophenol	88062	Phenol, 2,4,6-trichloro-	10	1,2,4	U231	A	10# (4.54)
2,4,5-Trichlorophenoxyacetic acid	93765	2,4,5-T 2,4,5-T acid	100	1,4	U232	C	1000 (454)
Triethanolamine dodecylbenzenesulfonate	27323417		1000	1		C	1000 (454)
Triethylamine	121448		5000	1		D	5000 (2270)
Trimethylamine	75503		1000	1		C	1000## (454)
sym-Trinitrobenzene	99354	Benzene, 1,3,5-trinitro-	1*	4	U234	X	1## (0.454)
1,3,5-Trioxane, 2,4,6-trimethyl-	123637	Paraldehyde	1*	4	U182	C	1000 (454)
Tris(2,3-dibromopropyl) phosphate	126727	1-Propanol, 2,3-dibromo-, phosphate (3:1)	1*	4	U235	X	1# (0.454)
Trypan blue	72571	2,7-Naphthalenedisulfonic acid,3,3'-[(3,3'-dimethyl- (1,1'-biphenyl)-4,4'-diyl)- bis(azo)]bis(5-amino-4- hydroxy)-tetrasodium salt.	1*	4	U236	X	1# (0.454)
Unlisted Hazardous Wastes			1*	4			
Characteristic of Ignitability			1*	4	D001	B	100 (45.4)
Characteristic of Corrosivity			1*	4	D002	B	100 (45.4)
Characteristic of Reactivity			1*	4	D003	B	100 (45.4)
Characteristic of EP Toxicity			1*	4			
Arsenic			1*	4	D004	X	1# (0.454)
Barium			1*	4	D005	C	1000 (454)
Cadmium			1*	4	D006	X	1# (0.454)
Chromium			1*	4	D007	X	1# (0.454)
Lead			1*	4	D008	X	1## (0.454)
Mercury			1*	4	D009	X	1 (0.454)
Selenium			1*	4	D010	X	1## (0.454)
Silver			1*	4	D011	X	1 (0.454)
Endrin			1	1,4	D012	X	1 (0.454)
Lindane			1	1,4	D013	X	1# (0.454)
Methoxychlor			1	1,4	D014	X	1 (0.454)
Toxaphene			1	1,4	D015	X	1# (0.454)

TABLE 302.4 - LIST OF HAZARDOUS SUBSTANCES AND REPORTABLE QUANTITIES—Continued

Hazardous Substance	CASRN	Regulatory Synonyms	Statutory			Final RQ	
			RQ	Code †	RCRA Waste Number	Category	Pounds(Kg)
2,4-D			100	1,4	D016	B	100 (45.4)
2,4,5-TP			100	1,4	D017	B	100 (45.4)
Uracil, 5-[bis(2-chloroethyl)amino]-	66751	Uracil mustard	1*	4	U237	X	1# (0.454)
Uracil mustard	66751	Uracil, 5-[bis(2-chloroethyl)amino]-	1*	4	U237	X	1# (0.454)
Uranyl acetate	541093		5000	1		D	5000## (2270)
Uranyl nitrate	10102064 36478769		5000	1		D	5000## (2270)
Vanadic acid, ammonium salt	7803556	Ammonium vanadate	1*	4	P119	C	1000 (454)
Vanadium(V) oxide	1314621	Vanadium pentoxide	1000	1,4	P120	C	1000## (454)
Vanadium pentoxide	1314621	Vanadium(V) oxide	1000	1,4	P120	C	1000## (454)
Vanadyl sulfate	27774136		1000	1		C	1000## (454)
Vinyl acetate	108054		1000	1		D	5000 (2270)
Vinyl chloride	75014	Ethene, chloro-	1*	2,3,4	U043	X	1# (0.454)
Vinylidene chloride	75354	1,1-Dichloroethylene Ethene, 1,1-dichloro-	5000	1,2,4	U078	D	5000# (2270)
Warfarin	81812	3-(alpha-Acetonylbenzyl)-4-hydroxycoumarin and salts	1*	4	P001	B	100 (45.4)
Xylene (mixed)	1330207 108383 95476 106423	Benzene,dimethyl- m- o- p-	1000	1,4	U239	C	1000 (454)
Xylenol	1300716		1000	1		C	1000 (454)
Yohimban-16-carboxylic acid,11,17-dimethoxy- 18- [(3,4,5- trimethoxybenzoyl)oxy]-, methylester.	50555	Reserpine	1*	4	U200	D	5000 (2270)
Zinc ††	7440666		1*	2		X	1## (0.454)
ZINC AND COMPOUNDS			1*	2			**
Zinc acetate	557346		1000	1		C	1000## (454)
Zinc ammonium chloride	52628258 14639975 14639986		5000	1		D	5000## (2270)
Zinc borate	1332076		1000	1		C	1000## (454)
Zinc bromide	7699458		5000	1		D	5000## (2270)
Zinc carbonate	3486359		1000	1		C	1000## (454)
Zinc chloride	7646857		5000	1		D	5000## (2270)
Zinc cyanide	557211		10	1,4	P121	A	10## (4.54)
Zinc fluoride	7783495		1000	1		C	1000## (454)
Zinc formate	557415		1000	1		C	1000## (454)
Zinc hydrosulfite	7779864		1000	1		C	1000## (454)
Zinc nitrate	7779886		5000	1		D	5000## (2270)
Zinc phenolsulfonate	127822		5000	1		D	5000## (2270)
Zinc phosphide	1314847		1000	1,4	P122	C	1000## (454)
Zinc silicofluoride	16871719		5000	1		D	5000## (2270)
Zinc sulfate	7733020		1000	1		C	1000## (454)
Zirconium nitrate	13746899		5000	1		D	5000 (2270)
Zirconium potassium fluoride	16923958		5000	1		C	1000 (454)
Zirconium sulfate	14644612		5000	1		D	5000 (2270)
Zirconium tetrachloride	10026116		5000	1		D	5000 (2270)
F001			1*	4	F001	X	1# (0.454)

TABLE 302.4 - LIST OF HAZARDOUS SUBSTANCES AND REPORTABLE QUANTITIES—Continued

Hazardous Substance	CASRN	Regulatory Synonyms	Statutory			Final RQ	
			RQ	Code †	RCRA Waste Number	Category	Pounds(Kg)
The following spent halogenated solvents used in degreasing and sludges from the recovery of these solvents in degreasing operations:							
(a) Tetrachloroethylene	127184					X	1# (0.454)
(b) Trichloroethylene	79016					C	1000# (454)
(c) Methylene chloride	75092					C	1000 (454)
(d) 1,1,1-Trichloroethane	71556					C	1000 (454)
(e) Carbon tetrachloride	56235					D	5000# (2270)
(f) Chlorinated fluorocarbons	(N.A.)					D	5000 (2270)
F002			1°	4	F002	X	1# (0.454)
The following spent halogenated solvents and the still bottoms from the recovery of these solvents:							
(a) Tetrachloroethylene	127184					X	1# (0.454)
(b) Methylene Chloride	75092					C	1000 (454)
(c) Trichloroethylene	79016					C	1000# (454)
(d) 1,1,1-Trichloroethane	71556					C	1000 (454)
(e) Chlorobenzene	108907					B	100 (45.4)
(f) 1,1,2-Trichloro-1,2,2-trifluoroethane	76131					D	5000 (2270)
(g) o-Dichlorobenzene	106467					B	100 (45.4)
(h) Trichlorofluoromethane	75694					D	5000 (2270)
F003			1°	4	F003	B	100 (45.4)
The following spent non-halogenated solvents and the still bottoms from the recovery of these solvents:							
(a) Xylene	1330207					C	1000 (454)
(b) Acetone	67641					D	5000 (2270)
(c) Ethyl acetate	141786					D	5000 (2270)
(d) Ethylbenzene	100414					C	1000 (454)
(e) Ethyl ether	60297					B	100 (45.4)
(f) Methyl isobutyl ketone	108101					D	5000 (2270)
(g) n-Butyl alcohol	71363					D	5000 (2270)
(h) Cyclohexanone	108941					D	5000 (2270)
(i) Methanol	67561					D	5000 (2270)
F004			1°	4	F004	X	1## (0.454)
The following spent non-halogenated solvents and the still bottoms from the recovery of these solvents:							
(a) Cresols/Cresylic acid	1319773					C	1000# (454)
(b) Nitrobenzene	98953					C	1000 (454)
F005			1°	4	F005	X	1## (0.454)
The following spent non-halogenated solvents and the still bottoms from the recovery of these solvents:							
(a) Toluene	108883					C	1000 (454)
(b) Methyl ethyl ketone	78933					D	5000 (2270)
(c) Carbon disulfide	75150					D	5000 (2270)
(d) Isobutanol	78831					D	5000 (2270)
(e) Pyridine	110861					X	1## (0.454)
F006			1°	4	F006	X	1# (0.454)
Wastewater treatment sludges from electroplating operations except from the following processes: (1) sulfuric acid anodizing of aluminum; (2) tin plating on carbon steel; (3) zinc plating (segregated basis) on carbon steel; (4) aluminum or zinc-aluminum plating on carbon steel; (5) cleaning/stripping associated with tin, zinc and aluminum plating on carbon steel; and (6) chemical etching and milling of aluminum							
F007			1°	4	F007	A	10 (4.54)
Spent cyanide plating bath solutions from electroplating operations (except for precious metals electroplating spent cyanide plating bath solutions)							
F008			1°	4	F008	A	10 (4.54)
Plating bath sludges from the bottom of plating baths from electroplating operations where cyanides are used in the process (except for precious metals electroplating plating bath sludges)							
F009			1°	4	F009	A	10 (4.54)
Spent stripping and cleaning bath solutions from electroplating operations where cyanides are used in the process (except for precious metals electroplating spent stripping and cleaning bath solutions)							
F010			1°	4	F010	A	10 (4.54)

TABLE 302.4 - LIST OF HAZARDOUS SUBSTANCES AND REPORTABLE QUANTITIES—Continued

Hazardous Substance	CASRN	Regulatory Synonyms	Statutory			Final RQ	
			RQ	Code †	RCRA Waste Number	Category	Pounds(Kg)
Quenching bath sludge from oil baths from metal heat treating operations where cyanides are used in the process (except for precious metals heat-treating quenching bath sludges)							
F011 Spent cyanide solutions from salt bath pot cleaning from metal heat treating operations (except for precious metals heat treating spent cyanide solutions from salt bath pot cleaning)			1°	4	F011	A	10 (4.54)
F012 Quenching wastewater treatment sludges from metal heat treating operations where cyanides are used in the process (except for precious metals heat treating quenching wastewater treatment sludges)			1°	4	F012	A	10 (4.54)
F019 Wastewater treatment sludges from the chemical conversion coating of aluminum			1°	4	F019	X	1# (0.454)
F024 Wastes, including but not limited to distillation residues, heavy ends, tars, and reactor cleanout wastes, from the production of chlorinated aliphatic hydrocarbons,having carbon content from one to five, utilizing free radical catalyzed processes. (This listing does not include light ends, spent filters and filter aids, spent dessicants(sic), wastewater, wastewater treatment sludges, spent catalysts,and wastes listed in Section 261.32.)			1°	4	F024	X	1# (0.454)
K001 Bottom sediment sludge from the treatment of wastewaters from wood preserving processes that use creosote and/or pentachlorophenol			1°	4	K001	X	1# (0.454)
K002 Wastewater treatment sludge from the production of chrome yellow and orange pigments			1°	4	K002	X	1# (0.454)
K003 Wastewater treatment sludge from the production of molybdate orange pigments			1°	4	K003	X	1# (0.454)
K004 Wastewater treatment sludge from the production of zinc yellow pigments			1°	4	K004	X	1# (0.454)
K005 Wastewater treatment sludge from the production of chrome green pigments			1°	4	K005	X	1# (0.454)
K006 Wastewater treatment sludge from the production of chrome oxide green pigments (anhydrous and hydrated)			1°	4	K006	X	1# (0.454)
K007 Wastewater treatment sludge from the production of iron blue pigments			1°	4	K007	X	1# (0.454)
K008 Oven residue from the production of chrome oxide green pigments			1°	4	K008	X	1# (0.454)
K009 Distillation bottoms from the production of acetaldehyde from ethylene			1°	4	K009	X	1# (0.454)
K010 Distillation side cuts from the production of acetaldehyde from ethylene			1°	4	K010	X	1# (0.454)
K011 Bottom stream from the wastewater stripper in the production of acrylonitrile			1°	4	K011	X	1# (0.454)
K013 Bottom stream from the acetonitrile column in the production of acrylonitrile			1°	4	K013	X	1# (0.454)
K014 Bottoms from the acetonitrile purification column in the production of acrylonitrile			1°	4	K014	D	5000 (2270)

TABLE 302.4 - LIST OF HAZARDOUS SUBSTANCES AND REPORTABLE QUANTITIES—Continued

Hazardous Substance	CASRN	Regulatory Synonyms	Statutory			Final RQ	
			RQ	Code †	RCRA Waste Number	Category	Pounds(Kg)
K015 Still bottoms from the distillation of benzyl chloride			1°	4	K015	X	1# (0.454)
K016 Heavy ends or distillation residues from the production of carbon tetrachloride			1°	4	K016	X	1# (0.454)
K017 Heavy ends (still bottoms) from the purification column in the production of epichlorohydrin			1°	4	K017	X	1# (0.454)
K018 Heavy ends from the fractionation column in ethyl chloride production			1°	4	K018	X	1# (0.454)
K019 Heavy ends from the distillation of ethylene dichloride in ethylene dichloride production			1°	4	K019	X	1# (0.454)
K020 Heavy ends from the distillation of vinyl chloride in vinyl chloride monomer production			1°	4	K020	X	1# (0.454)
K021 Aqueous spent antimony catalyst waste from fluoromethanes production			1°	4	K021	X	1# (0.454)
K022 Distillation bottom tars from the production of phenol/acetone from cumene			1°	4	K022	X	1# (0.454)
K023 Distillation light ends from the production of phthalic anhydride from naphthalene			1°	4	K023	D	5000 (2270)
K024 Distillation bottoms from the production of phthalic anhydride from naphthalene			1°	4	K024	D	5000 (2270)
K025 Distillation bottoms from the production of nitrobenzene by the nitration of benzene			1°	4	K025	X	1# (0.454)
K026 Stripping still tails from the production of methyl ethyl pyridines			1°	4	K026	X	1## (0.454)
K027 Centrifuge and distillation residues from toluene diisocyanate production			1°	4	K027	X	1# (0.454)
K028 Spent catalyst from the hydrochlorinator reactor in the production of 1,1,1-trichloroethane			1°	4	K028	X	1# (0.454)
K029 Waste from the product steam stripper in the production of 1,1,1-trichloroethane			1°	4	K029	X	1# (0.454)
K030 Column bottoms or heavy ends from the combined production of trichloroethylene and perchloroethylene			1°	4	K030	X	1# (0.454)
K031 By-product salts generated in the production of MSMA and cacodylic acid			1°	4	K031	X	1# (0.454)
K032 Wastewater treatment sludge from the production of chlordane			1°	4	K032	X	1# (0.454)
K033 Wastewater and scrub water from the chlorination of cyclopentadiene in the production of chlordane			1°	4	K033	X	1# (0.454)
K034 Filter solids from the filtration of hexachlorocyclopentadiene in the production of chlordane			1°	4	K034	X	1# (0.454)
K035 Wastewater treatment sludges generated in the production of creosote			1°	4	K035	X	1# (0.454)
K036			1°	4	K036	X	1 (0.454)

TABLE 302.4 - LIST OF HAZARDOUS SUBSTANCES AND REPORTABLE QUANTITIES—Continued

Hazardous Substance	CASRN	Regulatory Synonyms	Statutory			Final RQ	
			RQ	Code †	RCRA Waste Number	Category	Pounds(Kg)
Still bottoms from toluene reclamation distillation in the production of disulfoton							
K037 Wastewater treatment sludges from the production of disulfoton			1*	4	K037	X	1 (0.454)
K038 Wastewater from the washing and stripping of phorate production			1*	4	K038	X	1# (0.454)
K039 Filter cake from the filtration of diethylphosphorodithioic acid in the production of phorate			1*	4	K039	X	1## (0.454)
K040 Wastewater treatment sludge from the production of phorate			1*	4	K040	X	1# (0.454)
K041 Wastewater treatment sludge from the production of toxaphene			1*	4	K041	X	1# (0.454)
K042 Heavy ends or distillation residues from the distillation of tetrachlorobenzene in the production of 2,4,5-T			1*	4	K042	X	1# (0.454)
K043 2,6-Dichlorophenol waste from the production of 2,4-D			1*	4	K043	X	1# (0.454)
K044 Wastewater treatment sludges from the manufacturing and processing of explosives			1*	4	K044	A	10 (4.54)
K045 Spent carbon from the treatment of wastewater containing explosives			1*	4	K045	A	10 (4.54)
K046 Wastewater treatment sludges from the manufacturing, formulation and loading of lead-based initiating compounds			1*	4	K046	X	1## (0.454)
K047 Pink/red water from TNT operations			1*	4	K047	A	10 (4.54)
K048 Dissolved air flotation (DAF) float from the petroleum refining industry			1*	4	K048	X	1# (0.454)
K049 Slop oil emulsion solids from the petroleum refining industry			1*	4	K049	X	1# (0.454)
K050 Heat exchanger bundle cleaning sludge from the petroleum refining industry			1*	4	K050	X	1# (0.454)
K051 API separator sludge from the petroleum refining industry			1*	4	K051	X	1# (0.454)
K052 Tank bottoms (leaded) from the petroleum refining industry			1*	4	K052	X	1## (0.454)
K060 Ammonia still lime sludge from coking operations			1*	4	K060	X	1# (0.454)
K061 Emission control dust/sludge from the primary production of steel in electric furnaces			1*	4	K061	X	1# (0.454)
K062 Spent pickle liquor from steel finishing operations			1*	4	K062	X	1# (0.454)
K069 Emission control dust/sludge from secondary lead smelting			1*	4	K069	X	1# (0.454)
K071 Brine purification muds from the mercury cell process in chlorine production, where separately prepurified brine is not used			1*	4	K071	X	1 (0.454)

TABLE 302.4 - LIST OF HAZARDOUS SUBSTANCES AND REPORTABLE QUANTITIES—Continued

Hazardous Substance	CASRN	Regulatory Synonyms	Statutory			Final RQ	
			RQ	Code #	RCRA Waste Number	Catego-ry	Pounds(Kg)
K073 Chlorinated hydrocarbon waste from the purification step of the diaphragm cell process using graphite anodes in chlorine production			1*	4	K073	X	1# (0.454)
K083 Distillation bottoms from aniline extraction			1*	4	K083	B	100 (45.4)
K084 Wastewater treatment sludges generated during the production of veterinary pharmaceuticals from arsenic or organo-arsenic compounds			1*	4	K084	X	1# (0.454)
K085 Distillation or fractionation column bottoms from the production of chlorobenzenes			1*	4	K085	X	1# (0.454)
K086 Solvent washes and sludges, caustic washes and sludges, or water washes and sludges from cleaning tubs and equipment used in the formulation of ink from pigments, driers, soaps, and stabilizers containing chromium and lead			1*	4	K086	X	1# (0.454)
K087 Decanter tank tar sludge from coking operations			1*	4	K087	X	1# (0.454)
K093 Distillation light ends from the production of phthalic anhydride from ortho-xylene			1*	4	K093	D	5000 (2270)
K094 Distillation bottoms from the production of phthalic anhydride from ortho-xylene			1*	4	K094	D	5000 (2270)
K095 Distillation bottoms from the production of 1,1,1-trichloroethane			1*	4	K095	X	1# (0.454)
K096 Heavy ends from the heavy ends column from the production of 1,1,1-trichloroethane			1*	4	K096	X	1# (0.454)
K097 Vacuum stripper discharge from the chlordane chlorinator in the production of chlordane			1*	4	K097	X	1# (0.454)
K098 Untreated process wastewater from the production of toxaphene			1*	4	K098	X	1# (0.454)
K099 Untreated wastewater from the production of 2,4-D			1*	4	K099	X	1# (0.454)
K100 Waste leaching solution from acid leaching of emission control dust/sludge from secondary lead smelting (Components of this waste are identical with those of K069).			1*	4	K100	X	1# (0.454)
K101 Distillation tar residues from the distillation of aniline-based compounds in the production of veterinary pharmaceuticals from arsenic or organo-arsenic compounds			1*	4	K101	X	1# (0.454)
K102 Residue from the use of activated carbon for decolorization in the production of veterinary pharmaceuticals from arsenic or organo-arsenic compounds			1*	4	K102	X	1# (0.454)
K103 Process residues from aniline extraction from the production of aniline			1*	4	K103	B	100 (45.4)
K104 Combined wastewater streams generated from nitrobenzene/aniline chlorobenzenes			1*	4	K104	X	1# (0.454)
K105 Separated aqueous stream from the reactor product washing step in the production of chlorobenzenes			1*	4	K105	X	1# (0.454)
K106 Wastewater treatment sludge from the mercury cell process in chlorine production			1*	4	K106	X	1 (0.454)

See footnotes on following page.

† - indicates the statutory source as defined by 1, 2, 3, or 4 below
1 - indicates that the statutory source for designation of this hazardous substance under CERCLA is CWA Section 311(b)(4)
2 - indicates that the statutory source for designation of this hazardous substance under CERCLA is CWA Section 307(a)
3 - indicates that the statutory source for designation of this hazardous substance under CERCLA is CAA Section 112
4 - indicates that the statutory source for designation of this hazardous substance under CERCLA is RCRA Section 3001
†† - no reporting of releases of this hazardous substance is required if the diameter of the pieces of the solid metal released is equal to or exceeds 100 micrometers (0.004 inches)
††† - the RQ for asbestos is limited to friable forms only
§ - the Agency may adjust the RQ for radionuclides in a future rulemaking; until then the statutory 1-pound RQ applies
1° - indicates that the 1-pound RQ is a CERCLA statutory RQ
** - indicates that no RQ is being assigned to the generic or broad class
# - indicates that the RQ is subject to change when the assessment of potential carcinogenicity and/or chronic toxicity is completed
- indicates that an adjusted RQ is proposed in a separate NPRM in today's Federal Register
- the Agency may adjust the RQ for methyl isocyanate in a future rulemaking; until then the statutory 1-pound RQ applies

APPENDIX A - SEQUENTIAL CAS REGISTRY NUMBER LIST OF CERCLA HAZARDOUS SUBSTANCES

CASRN	Hazardous Substance
50000	Formaldehyde Methylene oxide
50077	Azirino(2',3':3,4)pyrrolo(1,2-a)indole-4,7-dione,6-amino-8- [((aminocarbonyl)oxy)methyl]-1,1a,2,8,8a,8b-hexahydro-8a-methoxy-5-methyl- Mitomycin C
50180	Cyclophosphamide 2H-1,3,2-Oxazaphosphorine,2-[bis(2-chloroethyl)amino]tetrahydro-2-oxide
50293	DDT 4,4' DDT Dichlorodiphenyl trichloroethane
50328	Benzo[a]pyrene 3,4-Benzopyrene
50555	Reserpine Yohimban-16-carboxylic acid,11,17-dimethoxy-18-[(3,4,5-trimethoxybenzoyl)oxy]-,methyl ester
51285	2,4-Dinitrophenol Phenol, 2,4-dinitro-
51434	1,2-Benzenediol,4-[1-hydroxy-2-(methylamino)ethyl]- Epinephrine
51796	Carbamic acid, ethyl ester Ethyl carbamate (Urethan)
52686	Trichlorfon
52857	Famphur Phosphorothioic acid, O,O-dimethyl-O-[p-[(dimethylamino)-sulfonyl]phenyl] ester
53703	Dibenz[a,h]anthracene 1,2:5,6-Dibenzanthracene Dibenzo[a,h]anthracene
53963	Acetamide, N-9H-fluoren-2-yl- 2-Acetylaminofluorene
54115	Nicotine and salts Pyridine, (S)-3-(1-methyl-2-pyrrolidinyl)-,and salts
55185	Ethanamine, N-ethyl-N-nitroso- N-Nitrosodiethylamine
55630	Nitroglycerine 1,2,3-Propanetriol, trinitrate-
55914	Diisopropyl fluorophosphate Phosphorofluoridic acid,bis(1-methylethyl) ester
56042	Methylthiouracil 4(1H)-Pyrimidinone, 2,3-dihydro-6-methyl-2-thioxo-
56235	Carbon tetrachloride Methane, tetrachloro-
56382	Parathion Phosphorothioic acid,O,O-diethyl O-(p-nitrophenyl)ester
56495	Benz[j]aceanthrylene, 1,2-dihydro-3-methyl- 3-Methylcholanthrene
56531	Diethylstilbestrol 4,4'-Stilbenediol, alpha,alpha'-diethyl-

APPENDIX A - SEQUENTIAL CAS REGISTRY NUMBER LIST OF CERCLA HAZARDOUS SUBSTANCES—Continued

CASRN	Hazardous Substance
56553	Benz[a]anthracene 1,2-Benzanthracene Benzo[a]anthracene
56724	Coumaphos
57125	Cyanides (soluble cyanide salts), not elsewhere specified
57147	1,1-Dimethylhydrazine Hydrazine, 1,1-dimethyl-
57249	Strychnidin-10-one, and salts Strychnine and salts
57749	Chlordane Chlordane, technical 4,7-Methanoindene, 1,2,4,5,6,7,8,8-octachloro-3a,4,7,7a-tetrahydro-
57976	1,2-Benzanthracene, 7,12-dimethyl- 7,12-Dimethylbenz[a]anthracene
58899	gamma - BHC Hexachlorocyclohexane (gamma isomer) Lindane
58902	Phenol, 2,3,4,6-tetrachloro- 2,3,4,6-Tetrachlorophenol
59507	4-Chloro-m-cresol p-Chloro-m-cresol Phenol, 4-chloro-3-methyl-
60004	Ethylenediamine tetraacetic acid (EDTA)
60117	Benzenamine, N,N-dimethyl-4-phenylazo- Dimethylaminoazobenzene
60297	Ethane, 1,1'-oxybis- Ethyl ether
60344	Hydrazine, methyl- Methyl hydrazine
60515	Dimethoate Phosphorodithioic acid,O,O-dimethyl S-[2(methylamino)-2-oxoethyl] ester
60571	Dieldrin 1,2,3,4,10,10-Hexachloro-6,7-epoxy-1,4,4a,5,6,7,8,8a-octahydro-endo,exo-1,4:5,8-dimethanonaphthalene
61825	Amitrole 1H-1,2,4-Triazol-3-amine
62384	Mercury, (acetato-O)phenyl- Phenylmercuric acetate
62442	Acetamide, N-(4-ethoxyphenyl)- Phenacetin
62500	Ethyl methanesulfonate Methanesulfonic acid, ethyl ester
62533	Aniline Benzenamine
62555	Ethanethioamide Thioacetamide
62566	Carbamide, thio- Thiourea

APPENDIX A - SEQUENTIAL CAS REGISTRY NUMBER LIST OF CERCLA HAZARDOUS SUBSTANCES—Continued

CASRN	Hazardous Substance
62737	Dichlorvos
62748	Acetic acid, fluoro-, sodium salt Fluoroacetic acid, sodium salt
62759	Dimethylnitrosamine N-Nitrosodimethylamine
63252	Carbaryl
64186	Formic acid Methanoic acid
64197	Acetic acid
65850	Benzoic acid
66751	Uracil, 5-[bis(2-chloroethyl)amino]- Uracil mustard
67561	Methanol Methyl alcohol
67641	Acetone 2-Propanone
67663	Chloroform Methane, trichloro-
67721	Ethane, 1,1,1,2,2,2-hexachloro- Hexachloroethane
70257	Guanidine, N-nitroso-N-methyl-N'-nitro- N-Methyl-N'-nitro-N-nitrosoguanidine
70304	Hexachlorophene 2,2'-Methylenebis(3,4,6-trichlorophenol)
71363	1-Butanol n-Butyl alcohol
71432	Benzene
71556	Methyl chloroform 1,1,1-Trichloroethane
72208	Endrin 1,2,3,4,10,10-Hexachloro-6,7-epoxy-1,4,4a,5,6,7,8,8a-octahydro-endo,endo-1,4:5,8-dimethanonaphthalene
72435	Ethane, 1,1,1-trichloro-2,2-bis(p-methoxyphenyl)- Methoxychlor
72548	DDD 4,4' DDD Dichlorodiphenyl dichloroethane TDE
72559	DDE 4,4' DDE
72571	2,7-Naphthalenedisulfonic acid,3,3'-[(3,3'-dimethyl-(1,1'-biphenyl)-4,4'-diyl)-bis(azo))bis(5-amino-4-hydroxy)-tetrasodium salt Trypan blue
74839	Methane, bromo- Methyl bromide
74873	Methane, chloro- Methyl chloride
74884	Methane, iodo- Methyl iodide

APPENDIX A - SEQUENTIAL CAS REGISTRY NUMBER LIST OF CERCLA HAZARDOUS SUBSTANCES—Continued

CASRN	Hazardous Substance
74895	Monomethylamine
74908	Hydrocyanic acid Hydrogen cyanide
74931	Methanethiol Methylmercaptan Thiomethanol
74953	Methane, dibromo- Methylene bromide
75003	Chloroethane ,
75014	Ethene, chloro- Vinyl chloride
75047	Monoethylamine
75058	Acetonitrile Ethanenitrile
75070	Acetaldehyde Ethanal
75092	Methane, dichloro- Methylene chloride
75150	Carbon bisulfide Carbon disulfide
75207	Calcium carbide
75218	Ethylene oxide Oxirane
75252	Bromoform Methane, tribromo-
75274	Dichlorobromomethane
75343	1,1-Dichloroethane Ethane, 1,1-dichloro- Ethylidene dichloride
75354	1,1-Dichloroethylene Ethene, 1,1-dichloro- Vinylidene chloride
75365	Acetyl chloride Ethanoyl chloride
75445	Carbonyl chloride Phosgene
75503	Trimethylamine
75558	2-Methylaziridine 1,2-Propylenimine
75569	Propylene oxide
75605	Cacodylic acid Hydroxydimethylarsine oxide
75649	tert-Butylamine
75694	Methane, trichlorofluoro- Trichloromonofluoromethane
75718	Dichlorodifluoromethane Methane, dichlorodifluoro-
75865	Acetone cyanohydrin 2-Methyllactonitrile Propanenitrile, 2-hydroxy-2-methyl-
75876	Acetaldehyde, trichloro- Chloral
75990	2,2-Dichloropropionic acid
76017	Ethane, pentachloro- Pentachloroethane
76448	Heptachlor 4,7-Methano-1H-indene,1,4,5,6,7,8,8-heptachloro- 3a,4,7,7a-tetrahydro-

CASRN	Hazardous Substance
77474	1,3-Cyclopentadiene, 1,2,3,4,5,5-hexachloro- Hexachlorocyclopentadiene
77781	Dimethyl sulfate Sulfuric acid, dimethyl ester
78002	Plumbane, tetraethyl- Tetraethyl lead
78591	Isophorone
78795	Isoprene
78819	iso-Butylamine
78831	Isobutyl alcohol 1-Propanol, 2-methyl-
78875	1,2-Dichloropropane Propylene dichloride
78886	2,3-Dichloropropene
78933	2-Butanone Methyl ethyl ketone
78999	1,1-Dichloropropane
79005	Ethane, 1,1,2-trichloro- 1,1,2-Trichloroethane
79016	Trichloroethene Trichloroethylene
79061	Acrylamide 2-Propenamide
79094	Propionic acid
79107	Acrylic acid 2-Propenoic acid
79196	Hydrazinecarbothioamide Thiosemicarbazide
79221	Carbonochloridic acid, methyl ester Methyl chlorocarbonate
79312	iso-Butyric acid
79345	Ethane, 1,1,2,2-tetrachloro- 1,1,2,2-Tetrachloroethane
79447	Carbamoyl chloride, dimethyl- Dimethylcarbamoyl chloride
79469	2-Nitropropane Propane, 2-nitro-
80159	alpha,alpha-Dimethylbenzylhydroperoxide Hydroperoxide, 1-methyl-1-phenylethyl-
80626	Methyl methacrylate 2-Propenoic acid, 2-methyl-, methyl ester
81072	1,2-Benzisothiazolin-3-one,1,1-dioxide, and salts Saccharin and salts
81812	3-(alpha-Acetonylbenzyl)-4-hydroxycoumarin and salts Warfarin
82688	Benzene, pentachloronitro- Pentachloronitrobenzene
83329	Acenaphthene
84662	1,2-Benzenedicarboxylic acid,diethyl ester Diethyl phthalate
84742	1,2-Benzenedicarboxylic acid,dibutyl ester n-Butyl phthalate Dibutyl phthalate Di-n-butyl phthalate

CASRN	Hazardous Substance
85007	Diquat
85018	Phenanthrene
85449	1,2-Benzenedicarboxylic acid anhydride Phthalic anhydride
85687	Butyl benzyl phthalate
86306	N-Nitrosodiphenylamine
86500	Guthion
86737	Fluorene
86884	alpha-Naphthylthiourea Thiourea, 1-naphthalenyl-
87650	2,6-Dichlorophenol Phenol, 2,6-dichloro-
87683	1,3-Butadiene, 1,1,2,3,4,4-hexachloro- Hexachlorobutadiene
87865	Pentachlorophenol Phenol, pentachloro-
88062	Phenol, 2,4,6-trichloro- 2,4,6-Trichlorophenol
88722	o-Nitrotoluene
88755	o-Nitrophenol 2-Nitrophenol
88857	Dinoseb Phenol, 2,4-dinitro-6-(1-methylpropyl)-
91087	Benzene, 2,4-diisocyanatomethyl- Toluene diisocyanate
91203	Naphthalene
91225	Quinoline
91587	beta-Chloronaphthalene 2-Chloronaphthalene Naphthalene, 2-chloro-
91598	2-Naphthylamine beta-Naphthylamine
91805	Methapyrilene Pyridine, 2-[(2-(dimethylamino)ethyl)-2-thenyla- mino]-
91941	(1,1'-Biphenyl)-4,4'diamine,3,3'dichloro- 3,3'-Dichlorobenzidine
92875	Benzidine (1,1'-Biphenyl)-4,4'diamine
93721	Propionic acid, 2-(2,4,5-trichlorophenoxy)- Silvex 2,4,5-TP acid
93765	2,4,5-T 2,4,5-T acid 2,4,5-Trichlorophenoxyacetic acid
93798	2,4,5-T esters
94111	2,4-D Esters
94586	Benzene, 1,2-methylenedioxy-4-propyl- Dihydrosafrole
94597	Benzene, 1,2-methylenedioxy-4-allyl- Safrole
94757	2,4-D Acid 2,4-D, salts and esters 2,4-Dichlorophenoxyacetic acid, salts and esters

APPENDIX A - SEQUENTIAL CAS REGISTRY
NUMBER LIST OF CERCLA HAZARDOUS
SUBSTANCES—Continued

CASRN	Hazardous Substance
94791	2,4-D Esters
94804	2,4-D Esters
95476	Benzene, o-dimethyl- o-Xylene
95487	o-Cresol o-Cresylic acid
95501	Benzene, 1,2-dichloro- 1,2-Dichlorobenzene o-Dichlorobenzene
95578	2-Chlorophenol o-Chlorophenol Phenol, 2-chloro-
95807	Diaminotoluene Toluenediamine
95943	Benzene, 1,2,4,5-tetrachloro- 1,2,4,5-Tetrachlorobenzene
95954	Phenol, 2,4,5-trichloro- 2,4,5-Trichlorophenol
96128	1,2-Dibromo-3-chloropropane Propane, 1,2-dibromo-3-chloro-
96457	Ethylenethiourea 2-Imidazolidinethione
97632	Ethyl methacrylate 2-Propenoic acid, 2-methyl-, ethyl ester
98011	2-Furancarboxaldehyde Furfural
98077	Benzene, trichloromethyl- Benzotrichloride
98099	Benzenesulfonic acid chloride Benzenesulfonyl chloride
98828	Benzene, 1-methylethyl- Cumene
98862	Acetophenone Ethanone, 1-phenyl-
98873	Benzal chloride Benzene, dichloromethyl-
98884	Benzoyl chloride
98953	Benzene, nitro- Nitrobenzene
99081	m-Nitrotoluene
99354	Benzene, 1,3,5-trinitro- sym-Trinitrobenzene
99558	Benzenamine, 2-methyl-5-nitro- 5-Nitro-o-toluidine
99650	m-Dinitrobenzene
99990	p-Nitrotoluene
100016	Benzenamine, 4-nitro- p-Nitroaniline
100027	p-Nitrophenol 4-Nitrophenol Phenol, 4-nitro-
100254	p-Dinitrobenzene
100414	Ethylbenzene
100425	Styrene
100447	Benzene, chloromethyl- Benzyl chloride

APPENDIX A - SEQUENTIAL CAS REGISTRY
NUMBER LIST OF CERCLA HAZARDOUS
SUBSTANCES—Continued

CASRN	Hazardous Substance
100470	Benzonitrile
100754	N-Nitrosopiperidine Pyridine, hexahydro-N-nitroso-
101144	Benzenamine, 4,4'-methylenebis(2-chloro- 4,4'-Methylenebis(2-chloroaniline)
101553	Benzene, 1-bromo-4-phenoxy- 4-Bromophenyl phenyl ether
103855	N-Phenylthiourea Thiourea, phenyl-
105464	sec-Butyl acetate
105679	2,4-Dimethylphenol Phenol, 2,4-dimethyl-
106423	Benzene, p-dimethyl- p-Xylene
106445	p-Cresol p-Cresylic acid
106467	Benzene, 1,4-dichloro- 1,4-Dichlorobenzene p-Dichlorobenzene
106478	Benzenamine, 4-chloro- p-Chloroaniline
106514	p-Benzoquinone 1,4-Cyclohexadienedione
106898	1-Chloro-2,3-epoxypropane Epichlorohydrin Oxirane, 2-(chloromethyl)-
106934	Ethane, 1,2-dibromo- Ethylene dibromide
107028	Acrolein 2-Propenal
107051	Allyl chloride
107062	1,2-Dichloroethane Ethane, 1,2-dichloro- Ethylene dichloride
107108	1-Propanamine n-Propylamine
107120	Ethyl cyanide Propanenitrile
107131	Acrylonitrile 2-Propenenitrile
107153	Ethylenediamine
107186	Allyl alcohol 2-Propen-1-ol
107197	Propargyl alcohol 2-Propyn-1-ol
107200	Acetaldehyde, chloro- Chloroacetaldehyde
107302	Chloromethyl methyl ether Methane, chloromethoxy-
107493	Pyrophosphoric acid, tetraethyl ester Tetraethyl pyrophosphate
107926	Butyric acid
108054	Vinyl acetate
108101	Methyl isobutyl ketone 4-Methyl-2-pentanone
108247	Acetic anhydride
108316	2,5-Furandione Maleic anhydride

APPENDIX A - SEQUENTIAL CAS REGISTRY
NUMBER LIST OF CERCLA HAZARDOUS
SUBSTANCES—Continued

CASRN	Hazardous Substance
108383	Benzene, m-dimethyl- m-Xylene
108394	m-Cresol m-Cresylic acid
108463	1,3-Benzenediol Resorcinol
108601	Bis(2-chloroisopropyl) ether Propane, 2,2'-oxybis(2-chloro-
108883	Benzene, methyl- Toluene
108907	Benzene, chloro- Chlorobenzene
108941	Cyclohexanone
108952	Benzene, hydroxy- Phenol
108985	Benzenethiol Thiophenol
109068	2-Picoline Pyridine, 2-methyl-
109739	Butylamine
109773	Malononitrile Propanedinitrile
109897	Diethylamine
109999	Furan, tetrahydro- Tetrahydrofuran
110009	Furan Furfuran
110167	Maleic acid
110178	Fumaric acid
110190	iso-Butyl acetate
110758	2-Chloroethyl vinyl ether Ethene, 2-chloroethoxy-
110827	Benzene, hexahydro- Cyclohexane
110861	Pyridine
111444	Bis(2-chloroethyl) ether Dichloroethyl ether Ethane, 1,1'-oxybis(2-chloro-
111546	1,2-Ethanediylbiscarbamodithioic acid Ethylenebis(dithiocarbamic acid)
111911	Bis(2-chloroethoxy) methane Ethane, 1,1'-[methylenebis(oxy)]bis(2-chloro-
115026	Azaserine L-Serine, diazoacetate (ester)
115297	Endosulfan 5-Norbornene-2,3-dimethanol,1,4,5,6,7,7-hexachloro,cyclic sulfite
115322	Kelthane
116063	Aldicarb Propanal, 2-methyl-2-(methylthio)-,O-[(methylamino)carbonyl]oxime
117806	Dichlone
117817	1,2-Benzenedicarboxylic acid,[bis(2-ethylhexyl)] ester Bis(2-ethylhexyl)phthalate
117840	1,2-Benzenedicarboxylic acid,di-n-octyl ester Di-n-octyl phthalate

CASRN	Hazardous Substance
118741	Benzene, hexachloro- Hexachlorobenzene
119904	(1,1'-Biphenyl)-4,4'diamine,3,3'dimethoxy- 3,3'-Dimethoxybenzidine
119937	(1,1'Biphenyl)-4,4'-diamine,3,3'-dimethyl- 3,3'-Dimethylbenzidine
120127	Anthracene
120581	Benzene, 1,2-methylenedioxy-4-propenyl- Isosafrole
120821	1,2,4-Trichlorobenzene
120832	2,4-Dichlorophenol Phenol, 2,4-dichloro-
121142	Benzene, 1-methyl-2,4-dinitro- 2,4-Dinitrotoluene
121211	Pyrethrins
121299	Pyrethrins
121448	Triethylamine
121755	Malathion
122098	alpha,alpha-Dimethylphenethylamine Ethanamine, 1,1-dimethyl-2-phenyl-
122667	1,2-Diphenylhydrazine Hydrazine, 1,2-diphenyl-
123331	1,2-Dihydro-3,6-pyridazinedione Maleic hydrazide
123626	Propionic anhydride
123637	Paraldehyde 1,3,5-Trioxane, 2,4,6-trimethyl-
123739	2-Butenal Crotonaldehyde
123864	Butyl acetate
123911	1,4-Diethylene dioxide 1,4-Dioxane
123922	iso-Amyl acetate
124049	Adipic acid
124403	Dimethylamine Methanamine, N-methyl-
124414	Sodium methylate
124481	Chlorodibromomethane
126727	1-Propanol, 2,3-dibromo-, phosphate (3:1) Tris(2,3-dibromopropyl) phosphate
126987	Methacrylonitrile 2-Propenenitrile, 2-methyl-
127184	Ethene, 1,1,2,2-tetrachloro- Tetrachloroethylene
127822	Zinc phenolsulfonate
129000	Pyrene
130154	1,4-Naphthalenedione 1,4-Naphthoquinone
131113	1,2-Benzenedicarboxylic acid,dimethyl ester Dimethyl phthalate
131748	Ammonium picrate Phenol, 2,4,6-trinitro-, ammonium salt
131895	4,6-Dinitro-o-cyclohexylphenol Phenol, 2-cyclohexyl-4,6-dinitro-

CASRN	Hazardous Substance
133062	Captan
134327	1-Naphthylamine alpha-Naphthylamine
137268	Bis(dimethylthiocarbamoyl) disulfide Thiram
140885	Ethyl acrylate 2-Propenoic acid, ethyl ester
141786	Acetic acid, ethyl ester Ethyl acetate
142289	1,3-Dichloropropane
142712	Cupric acetate
142847	Dipropylamine 1-Propanamine, N-propyl-
143339	Sodium cyanide
143500	Decachlorooctahydro-1,3,4-metheno-2H- cyclobuta[c,d]-pentalen-2-one Kepone
145733	Endothall 7-Oxabicyclo[2,2,1]heptane-2,3-dicarboxylic acid
148823	Alanine, 3-[p-bis(2-chloroethyl)amino]phenyl-,L- Melphalan
151508	Potassium cyanide
151564	Aziridine Ethylenimine
152169	Diphosphoramide, octamethyl- Octamethylpyrophosphoramide
156605	1,2-trans-Dichloroethylene Ethene, trans-1,2-dichloro-
189559	1,2:7,8-Dibenzopyrene Dibenz[a,i]pyrene
191242	Benzo[ghi]perylene
193395	Indeno(1,2,3-cd)pyrene 1,10-(1,2-Phenylene)pyrene
205992	Benzo[b]fluoranthene
206440	Benzo[j,k]fluorene Fluoranthene
207089	Benzo[k]fluoranthene
208968	Acenaphthylene
218019	1,2-Benzphenanthrene Chrysene
225514	Benz[c]acridine 3,4-Benzacridine
297972	O,O-Diethyl O-pyrazinyl phosphorothioate Phosphorothioic acid, O,O-diethyl, O-pyrazinyl ester
298000	O,O-Dimethyl O-p-nitrophenyl phosphorothioate Methyl parathion
298022	Phorate Phosphorodithioic acid, O,O-diethyl S- (ethylthio),methyl ester
298044	O,O-Diethyl S-[2-(ethylthio)ethyl] phosphorodith- ioate Disulfoton
300765	Naled
301042	Acetic acid, lead salt Lead acetate
302012	Diamine Hydrazine

CASRN	Hazardous Substance
303344	Lasiocarpine
305033	Butanoic acid, 4-[bis(2-chloroethyl)amino] ben- zene- Chlorambucil
309002	Aldrin 1,2,3,4,10,10-Hexachloro-1,4,4a,5,8,8a- hexahydro-1,4:5,8-endo,exo- dimethanonaphthalene
311455	Diethyl-p-nitrophenyl phosphate Phosphoric acid,diethyl,p-nitrophenyl ester
315184	Mexacarbate
319846	alpha - BHC
319857	beta - BHC
319868	delta - BHC
329715	2,5-Dinitrophenol
330541	Diuron
333415	Diazinon
353504	Carbon oxyfluoride Carbonyl fluoride
357573	Brucine Strychnidin-10-one, 2,3-dimethoxy-
460195	Cyanogen
465736	Hexachlorohexahydro-endo,endo- dimethanonaphthalene 1,2,3,4,10,10-Hexachloro-1,4,4a,5,8,8a- hexahydro-1,4:5,8-endo,endo- dimethanonaphthalene
492808	Auramine Benzenamine, 4,4'-carbonimidoylbis (N,N-dimeth- yl-
494031	Chlornaphazine 2-Naphthylamine, N,N-bis(2-chloroethyl)-
496720	Diaminotoluene Toluenediamine
504245	4-Aminopyridine 4-Pyridinamine
504609	1-Methylbutadiene 1,3-Pentadiene
506616	Potassium silver cyanide
506649	Silver cyanide
506683	Bromine cyanide Cyanogen bromide
506774	Chlorine cyanide Cyanogen chloride
506876	Ammonium carbonate
506967	Acetyl bromide
509148	Methane, tetranitro- Tetranitromethane
510156	Benzeneacetic acid, 4-chloro-alpha-(4-chloro- phenyl)-alpha-hydroxy-,ethyl ester Ethyl 4,4'-dichlorobenzilate
513495	sec-Butylamine
528290	o-Dinitrobenzene
534521	4,6-Dinitro-o-cresol and salts Phenol,2,4-dinitro-6-methyl-, and salts
540738	1,2-Dimethylhydrazine Hydrazine, 1,2-dimethyl-

APPENDIX A - SEQUENTIAL CAS REGISTRY NUMBER LIST OF CERCLA HAZARDOUS SUBSTANCES—Continued

CASRN	Hazardous Substance
540885	tert-Butyl acetate
541093	Uranyl acetate
541537	2,4-Dithiobiuret Thioimidodicarbonic diamide
541731	Benzene, 1,3-dichloro- 1,3-Dichlorobenzene m-Dichlorobenzene
542621	Barium cyanide
542756	1,3-Dichloropropene Propene, 1,3-dichloro-
542767	3-Chloropropionitrile Propanenitrile, 3-chloro-
542881	Bis(chloromethyl) ether Methane, oxybis(chloro-
543908	Cadmium acetate
544183	Cobaltous formate
544923	Copper cyanide
554847	m-Nitrophenol
557197	Nickel cyanide Nickel(II) cyanide
557211	Zinc cyanide
557346	Zinc acetate
557415	Zinc formate
563122	Ethion
563688	Acetic acid, thallium(I) salt Thallium(I) acetate
573568	2,6-Dinitrophenol
584849	Benzene, 2,4-diisocyanatomethyl- Toluene diisocyanate
591082	Acetamide, N-(aminothioxomethyl)- 1-Acetyl-2-thiourea
592018	Calcium cyanide
592041	Mercuric cyanide
592858	Mercuric thiocyanate
592870	Lead thiocyanate
594423	Methanesulfenyl chloride, trichloro- Trichloromethanesulfenyl chloride
598312	Bromoacetone 2-Propanone, 1-bromo-
606202	Benzene, 1-methyl-2,6-dinitro- 2,6-Dinitrotoluene
608935	Benzene, pentachloro- Pentachlorobenzene
609198	3,4,5-Trichlorophenol
610399	3,4-Dinitrotoluene
615532	Carbamic acid, methylnitroso-,ethyl ester N-Nitroso-N-methylurethane
621647	Di-n-propylnitrosamine N-Nitrosodi-n-propylamine
624839	Isocyanic acid, methyl ester Methyl isocyanate

APPENDIX A - SEQUENTIAL CAS REGISTRY NUMBER LIST OF CERCLA HAZARDOUS SUBSTANCES—Continued

CASRN	Hazardous Substance
625161	tert-Amyl acetate
626380	sec-Amyl acetate
628637	Amyl acetate
628864	Fulminic acid, mercury(II)salt Mercury fulminate
630104	Carbamimidoselenoic acid Selenourea
630206	Ethane, 1,1,1,2-tetrachloro- 1,1,1,2-Tetrachloroethane
631618	Ammonium acetate
636215	Benzenamine, 2-methyl-, hydrochloride o-Toluidine hydrochloride
640197	Acetamide, 2-fluoro- Fluoroacetamide
684935	Carbamide, N-methyl-N-nitroso- N-Nitroso-N-methylurea
692422	Arsine, diethyl- Diethylarsine
696286	Dichlorophenylarsine Phenyl dichloroarsine
757584	Hexaethyl tetraphosphate Tetraphosphoric acid, hexaethyl ester
759739	Carbamide, N-ethyl-N-nitroso- N-Nitroso-N-ethylurea
764410	2-Butene, 1,4-dichloro- 1,4-Dichloro-2-butene
765344	Glycidylaldehyde 1-Propanal, 2,3-epoxy-
815827	Cupric tartrate
823405	Diaminotoluene Toluenediamine
924163	1-Butanamine, N-butyl-N-nitroso- N-Nitrosodi-n-butylamine
930552	N-Nitrosopyrrolidine Pyrrole, tetrahydro-N-nitroso-
933755	2,3,6-Trichlorophenol
933788	2,3,5-Trichlorophenol
959988	alpha - Endosulfan
1024573	Heptachlor epoxide
1031078	Endosulfan sulfate
1066304	Chromic acetate
1066337	Ammonium bicarbonate
1072351	Lead stearate
1111780	Ammonium carbamate
1116547	Ethanol, 2,2'-(nitrosoimino)bis- N-Nitrosodiethanolamine
1120714	1,2-Oxathiolane, 2,2-dioxide 1,3-Propane sultone
1185575	Ferric ammonium citrate
1194656	Dichlobenil
1300716	Xylenol
1303282	Arsenic(V) oxide Arsenic pentoxide

APPENDIX A - SEQUENTIAL CAS REGISTRY NUMBER LIST OF CERCLA HAZARDOUS SUBSTANCES—Continued

CASRN	Hazardous Substance
1303328	Arsenic disulfide
1303339	Arsenic trisulfide
1309644	Antimony trioxide
1310583	Potassium hydroxide
1310732	Sodium hydroxide
1314325	Thallic oxide Thallium(III) oxide
1314621	Vanadium(V) oxide Vanadium pentoxide
1314803	Phosphorus pentasulfide Phosphorus sulfide Sulfur phosphide
1314847	Zinc phosphide
1344870	Lead sulfide
1314961	Strontium sulfide
1319728	2,4,5-T amines
1319773	Cresol(s) Cresylic acid
1320189	2,4-D Esters
1321126	Nitrotoluene
1327522	Arsenic acid
1327533	Arsenic(III) oxide Arsenic trioxide
1330207	Benzene, dimethyl- Xylene
1332076	Zinc borate
1332214	Asbestos
1333831	Sodium bifluoride
1335326	Lead subacetate
1336216	Ammonium hydroxide
1336363	POLYCHLORINATED BIPHENYLS (PCBs) Aroclors
1338234	2-Butanone peroxide Methyl ethyl ketone peroxide
1338245	Naphthenic acid
1341497	Ammonium bifluoride
1464535	2,2'-Bioxirane 1,2:3,4-Diepoxybutane
1563662	Carbofuran
1615801	N,N'-Diethylhydrazine Hydrazine, 1,2-diethyl-
1746016	2,3,7,8-Tetrachlorodibenzo-p-dioxin(TCDD)
1762954	Ammonium thiocyanate
1863634	Ammonium benzoate
1888717	Hexachloropropene 1-Propene, 1,1,2,3,3,3-hexachloro-

APPENDIX A - SEQUENTIAL CAS REGISTRY NUMBER LIST OF CERCLA HAZARDOUS SUBSTANCES—Continued

CASRN	Hazardous Substance
1918009	Dicamba
1928387	2,4-D Esters
1928478	2,4,5-T esters
1928616	2,4-D Esters
1929733	2,4-D Esters
2008460	2,4,5-T amines
2032657	Mercaptodimethur
2303164	Diallate S-(2,3-Dichloroallyl) diisopropylthiocarbamate
2312358	Propargite
2545597	2,4,5-T esters
2763964	5-(Aminomethyl)-3-isoxazolol 3(2H)-Isoxazolone, 5-(aminomethyl)-
2764729	Diquat
2921882	Chlorpyrifos
2944674	Ferric ammonium oxalate
2971382	2,4-D Esters
3012655	Ammonium citrate, dibasic
3164292	Ammonium tartrate
3165933	Benzenamine, 4-chloro-2-methyl-,hydrochloride 4-Chloro-o-toluidine, hydrochloride
3251238	Cupric nitrate
3288582	O,O-Diethyl S-methyl dithiophosphate Phosphorodithioic acid, O,O-diethyl S-methylester
3486359	Zinc carbonate
3689245	Dithiopyrophosphoric acid,tetraethyl ester Tetraethyldithiopyrophosphate
3813147	2,4,5-T amines
4170303	2-Butenal Crotonaldehyde
4549400	Ethenamine, N-methyl-N-nitroso- N-Nitrosomethylvinylamine
5344821	1-(o-Chlorophenyl)thiourea Thiourea, (2-chlorophenyl)-
5893663	Cupric oxalate
5972736	Ammonium oxalate
6009707	Ammonium oxalate
6369966	2,4,5-T amines
6369977	2,4,5-T amines
6533739	Carbonic acid, dithallium (I) salt Thallium(I) carbonate
7005723	4-Chlorophenyl phenyl ether
7421934	Endrin aldehyde

CASRN	Hazardous Substance
7428480	Lead stearate
7439921	Lead
7439976	Mercury
7440020	Nickel
7440224	Silver
7440235	Sodium
7440280	Thallium
7440360	Antimony
7440382	Arsenic
7440417	Beryllium Beryllium dust
7440439	Cadmium
7440473	Chromium
7440508	Copper
7440666	Zinc
7446084	Selenium dioxide Selenium oxide
7446142	Lead sulfate
7446186	Sulfuric acid, thallium(I) salt Thallium(I) sulfate
7446277	Lead phosphate Phosphoric acid, lead salt
7447394	Cupric chloride
7488564	Selenium disulfide Sulfur selenide
7558794	Sodium phosphate, dibasic
7601549	Sodium phosphate, tribasic
7631892	Sodium arsenate
7631905	Sodium bisulfite
7632000	Sodium nitrite
7645252	Lead arsenate
7646857	Zinc chloride
7647010	Hydrochloric acid
7647189	Antimony pentachloride
7664382	Phosphoric acid
7664393	Hydrofluoric acid Hydrogen fluoride
7664417	Ammonia
7664939	Sulfuric acid
7681494	Sodium fluoride
7681529	Sodium hypochlorite

CASRN	Hazardous Substance
7697372	Nitric acid
7699458	Zinc bromide
7705080	Ferric chloride
7718549	Nickel chloride
7719122	Phosphorus trichloride
7720787	Ferrous sulfate
7722647	Potassium permanganate
7723140	Phosphorus
7733020	Zinc sulfate
7738945	Chromic acid
7758294	Sodium phosphate, tribasic
7758943	Ferrous chloride
7758954	Lead chloride
7758987	Cupric sulfate
7761888	Silver nitrate
7773060	Ammonium sulfamate
7775113	Sodium chromate
7778394	Arsenic acid
7778441	Calcium arsenate
7778509	Potassium bichromate
7778543	Calcium hypochlorite
7779864	Zinc hydrosulfite
7779886	Zinc nitrate
7782414	Fluorine
7782492	Selenium
7782505	Chlorine
7782630	Ferrous sulfate
7782823	Sodium selenite
7782867	Mercurous nitrate
7783008	Selenious acid
7783064	Hydrogen sulfide Hydrosulfuric acid Sulfur hydride
7783188	Ammonium thiosulfate
7783359	Mercuric sulfate
7783462	Lead fluoride
7783495	Zinc fluoride
7783508	Ferric fluoride
7783564	Antimony trifluoride

APPENDIX A - SEQUENTIAL CAS REGISTRY NUMBER LIST OF CERCLA HAZARDOUS SUBSTANCES—Continued

CASRN	Hazardous Substance
7784341	Arsenic trichloride
7784409	Lead arsenate
7784410	Potassium arsenate
7784465	Sodium arsenite
7785844	Sodium phosphate, tribasic
7786347	Mevinphos
7786814	Nickel sulfate
7787475	Beryllium chloride
7787497	Beryllium fluoride
7787555	Beryllium nitrate
7788989	Ammonium chromate
7789006	Potassium chromate
7789062	Strontium chromate
7789095	Ammonium bichromate
7789426	Cadmium bromide
7789437	Cobaltous bromide
7789619	Antimony tribromide
7790945	Chlorosulfonic acid
7791120	Thallium(I) chloride
7803512	Hydrogen phosphide Phosphine
7803556	Ammonium vanadate Vanadic acid, ammonium salt
8001352	Camphene, octachloro- Toxaphene
8001589	Creosote
8003198	Dichloropropane - Dichloropropene (mixture)
8003347	Pyrethrins
8014957	Sulfuric acid
9004864	Ferric dextran Iron dextran
10022705	Sodium hypochlorite
10025873	Phosphorus oxychloride
10025919	Antimony trichloride
10026116	Zirconium tetrachloride
10026225	Ferric sulfate
10031591	Sulfuric acid, thallium(I) salt Thallium(I) sulfate
10039324	Sodium phosphate, dibasic
10043013	Aluminum sulfate
10045893	Ferrous ammonium sulfate

CASRN	Hazardous Substance
10045940	Mercuric nitrate
10049055	Chromous chloride
10099748	Lead nitrate
10101538	Chromic sulfate
10101630	Lead iodide
10101890	Sodium phosphate, tribasic
10102064	Uranyl nitrate
10102188	Sodium selenite
10102439	Nitric oxide Nitrogen(II) oxide
10102440	Nitrogen dioxide Nitrogen(IV) oxide
10102451	Thallium(I) nitrate
10102484	Lead arsenate
10108642	Cadmium chloride
10124502	Potassium arsenite
10124568	Sodium phosphate, tribasic
10140655	Sodium phosphate, dibasic
10192300	Ammonium bisulfite
10196040	Ammonium sulfite
10361894	Sodium phosphate, tribasic
10380297	Cupric sulfate ammoniated
10415755	Mercurous nitrate
10421484	Ferric nitrate
10544726	Nitrogen dioxide Nitrogen(IV) oxide
10588019	Sodium bichromate
11096825	Aroclor 1260 Polychlorinated Biphenyls (PCBs)
11097691	Aroclor 1254 Polychlorinated Biphenyls (PCBs)
11104282	Aroclor 1221 Polychlorinated Biphenyls (PCBs)
11115745	Chromic acid
11141165	Aroclor 1232 Polychlorinated Biphenyls (PCBs)
12002038	Cupric acetoarsenite
12039520	Thallium(I) selenide
12054487	Nickel hydroxide
12125018	Ammonium fluoride
12125029	Ammonium chloride
12135761	Ammonium sulfide
12672296	Aroclor 1248 Polychlorinated Biphenyls (PCBs)
12674112	Aroclor 1016 Polychlorinated Biphenyls (PCBs)
12771083	Sulfur monochloride
13463393	Nickel carbonyl Nickel tetracarbonyl

CASRN	Hazardous Substance
13560991	2,4,5-T salts
13597994	Beryllium nitrate
13746899	Zirconium nitrate
13765190	Calcium chromate Chromic acid, calcium salt
13814965	Lead fluoborate
13826830	Ammonium fluoborate
13952846	sec-Butylamine
14017415	Cobaltous sulfamate
14216752	Nickel nitrate
14258492	Ammonium oxalate
14307358	Lithium chromate
14307438	Ammonium tartrate
14639975	Zinc ammonium chloride
14639986	Zinc ammonium chloride
14644612	Zirconium sulfate
15699180	Nickel ammonium sulfate
15739807	Lead sulfate
15950660	2,3,4-Trichlorophenol
16721805	Sodium hydrosulfide
16752775	Acetimidic acid, N-[(methylcarbamoyl)oxy]thio-, methyl ester Methomyl
16871719	Zinc silicofluoride
16919190	Ammonium silicofluoride
16923958	Zirconium potassium fluoride
18883664	D-Glucopyranose, 2-deoxy-2-(3-methyl-3-nitrosoureido)- Streptozotocin
20816120	Osmium oxide Osmium tetroxide
20830813	Daunomycin 5,12-Naphthacenedione, (8S-cis)-8-acetyl-10-[3-amino-2,3,6-trideoxy-alpha-L-lyxo-hexopyranosyl)oxy]-7,8,9,10-tetrahydro-6,8,11-trihydroxy-1-methoxy-
20859738	Aluminum phosphide
23950585	3,5-Dichloro-N-(1,1-dimethyl-2-propynyl)benzamide Pronamide
25154545	Dinitrobenzene (mixed)
25154556	Nitrophenol (mixed)
25155300	Sodium dodecylbenzene sulfonate
25167822	Trichlorophenol
25168154	2,4,5-T esters
25168267	2,4-D Esters
25321146	Dinitrotoluene
25321226	Dichlorobenzene (mixed)
25376458	Diaminotoluene Toluenediamine

APPENDIX A - SEQUENTIAL CAS REGISTRY NUMBER LIST OF CERCLA HAZARDOUS SUBSTANCES—Continued

CASRN	Hazardous Substance
25550587	Dinitrophenol
26264062	Calcium dodecylbenzene sulfonate
26471625	Benzene, 2,4-diisocyanatomethyl-Toluene diisocyanate
26628228	Sodium azide
26638197	Dichloropropane
26952238	Dichloropropene
27176870	Dodecylbenzenesulfonic acid
27323417	Triethanolamine dodecylbenzene sulfonate
27774136	Vanadyl sulfate
28300745	Antimony potassium tartrate
30525894	Paraformaldehyde
32534955	2,4,5-TP acid esters
33213659	beta - Endosulfan
36478769	Uranyl nitrate
37211055	Nickel chloride
39196184	3,3-Dimethyl-1-(methylthio)-2-butanone,O-[(methylamino)carbonyl] oxime Thiofanox
42504461	Isopropanolamine dodecylbenzene sulfonate
52628258	Zinc ammonium chloride
52652592	Lead stearate
52740166	Calcium arsenite
53467111	2,4-D Esters
53469219	Aroclor 1242 Polychlorinated Biphenyls (PCBs)
55488874	Ferric ammonium oxalate
56189094	Lead stearate
61792072	2,4,5-T esters

§ 302.5 Determination of reportable quantities.

(a) *Listed hazardous substances.* The quantity listed in the column "Final RQ" for each substance in Table 302.4 is the reportable quantity for that substance.

(b) *Unlisted hazardous substances.* Unlisted hazardous substances designated by 40 CFR 302.4(b), which substances are wastes prior to their initial release into the environment, have the reportable quantity of 100 pounds, except for those unlisted hazardous wastes exhibiting the characteristic of extraction procedure (EP) toxicity identified in 40 CFR 261.24. Unlisted hazardous wastes which exhibit EP toxicity have the reportable quantities listed in Table 302.4 for the contaminant on which the characteristic of EP toxicity is based. The reportable quantity applies to the waste itself, not merely to the toxic contaminant. If an unlisted hazardous waste exhibits EP toxicity on the basis of more than one contaminant, the reportable quantity for that waste shall be the lowest of the reportable quantities listed in Table 302.4 for those contaminants. If an unlisted hazardous waste exhibits the characteristic of EP toxicity and one or more of the other characteristics referenced in 40 CFR 302.4(b), the reportable quantity for that waste shall be the lowest of the applicable reportable quantities.

§ 302.6 Notification requirements.

(a) Any person in charge of a vessel or an offshore or an onshore facility shall, as soon as he has knowledge of any release (other than a federally permitted release or application of a pesticide) of a hazardous substance from such vessel or facility in a quantity equal to or exceeding the reportable quantity determined by this part in any 24-hour period, immediately notify the National Response Center ((800) 424-8802; in Washington, D.C. (202) 426-2675).

(b) Releases of mixtures and solutions are subject to these notification requirements only where a component hazardous substance of the mixture or solution is released in a quantity equal to or greater than its reportable quantity.

(c) Notification of the release of an RQ of solid particles of antimony, arsenic, beryllium, cadmium, chromium, copper, lead, nickel, selenium, silver, thallium, or zinc is not required if the mean diameter of the particles released is larger than 100 micrometers (0.004 inches).

(Approved by the Office of Management and Budget under the control number 2115-0137)

§ 302.7 Penalties.

(a) Any person

(1) In charge of a vessel from which a hazardous substance is released, other than a federally permitted release, into or upon the navigable waters of the United States, adjoining shorelines, or into or upon the waters of the contiguous zone,

(2) In charge of a vessel from which a hazardous substance is released, other than a federally permitted release, which may affect natural resources belonging to, appertaining to, or under the exclusive management authority of the United States (including resources under the Fishery Conservation and Management Act of 1976), and who is otherwise subject to the jurisdiction of the United States at the time of the release, or

(3) In charge of a facility from which a hazardous substance is released, other than a federally permitted release, in a quantity equal to or greater than that reportable quantity determined under this part who fails to notify immediately the National Response Center as soon as he has knowledge of such release shall be subject to all of the sanctions, including criminal penalties, set forth in section 103 of the Act with respect to such failure to notify.

(b) Notification received pursuant to this section or information obtained by the exploitation of such notification shall not be used against any such person in any criminal case, except a prosecution for perjury or for giving a false statement.

(c) This section shall not apply to the application of a pesticide product registered under the Federal Insecticide, Fungicide, and Rodenticide Act or to the handling and storage of such a pesticide product by an agricultural producer.

PART 117—[AMENDED]

2. 40 CFR Part 117 is amended by revising § 117.3 to read as follows:

§ 117.3 Determination of reportable quantities.

Each substance in Table 117.3 that is listed in Table 302.4, 40 CFR Part 302, is assigned the reportable quantity listed in Table 302.4 for that substance.

[FR Doc. 85-4238 Filed 4-3-85; 8:45 am]
BILLING CODE 6560-50-M

APPENDIX G

UNIFORM HAZARDOUS WASTE MANIFEST

Please print or type. (Form designed for use on elite (12-pitch) typewriter.)

Form Approved OMB No. 2000-0404 Expires 7-31-86

UNIFORM HAZARDOUS WASTE MANIFEST

1. Generator's US EPA ID No.

Manifest Document No.

2. Page 1 of

Information in the shaded areas is not required by Federal law.

3. Generator's Name and Mailing Address

A. State Manifest Document Number

B. State Generator's ID

4. Generator's Phone ( )

5. Transporter 1 Company Name

6. US EPA ID Number

C. State Transporter's ID

D. Transporter's Phone

7. Transporter 2 Company Name

8. US EPA ID Number

E. State Transporter's ID

F. Transporter's Phone

9. Designated Facility Name and Site Address

10. US EPA ID Number

G. State Facility's ID

H. Facility's Phone

GENERATOR

11. US DOT Description *(Including Proper Shipping Name, Hazard Class, and ID Number)*	12. Containers No.	12. Containers Type	13. Total Quantity	14. Unit Wt/Vol	I. Waste No.
a.					
b.					
c.					
d.					

J. Additional Descriptions for Materials Listed Above

K. Handling Codes for Wastes Listed Above

15. Special Handling Instructions and Additional Information

16. **GENERATOR'S CERTIFICATION:** I hereby declare that the contents of this consignment are fully and accurately described above by proper shipping name and are classified, packed, marked, and labeled, and are in all respects in proper condition for transport by highway according to applicable international and national governmental regulations.

Printed/Typed Name | Signature | Date: *Month Day Year*

TRANSPORTER

17. Transporter 1 Acknowledgement of Receipt of Materials

Printed/Typed Name | Signature | Date: *Month Day Year*

18. Transporter 2 Acknowledgement or Receipt of Materials

Printed/Typed Name | Signature | Date: *Month Day Year*

FACILITY

19. Discrepancy Indication Space

20. Facility Owner or Operator: Certification of receipt of hazardous materials covered by this manifest except as noted in Item 19.

Printed/Typed Name | Signature | Date: *Month Day Year*

EPA Form 8700-22 (3-84)

BILLING CODE 6560-50-C

APPENDIX H

AN OVERVIEW OF SUPERFUND LEGISLATION

On December 11, 1980, President Carter signed into law the Comprehensive Environmental Response, Compensation, and Liability Act of 1980 ("CERCLA"), Public Law 96-510, which is commonly known as the "Superfund" legislation. Superfund authorizes the federal government to clean up toxic contaminants, principally in hazardous waste dumps, with funds from a "superfund" generated primarily by a tax on the chemical industry. The Act also allows the government to recover the cost of cleanup and other damages caused by the contaminants by suing the parties responsible.

This appendix is intended as an overview of the major provisions of the Superfund legislation. Determination of the potential liability and obligations thereunder of a particular person or entity, however, will require a more focused analysis, with particular attention to the Act's definitions and various exceptions.

I. Response Authorities

The broad "response authority" the Act provides the government reflects the perception prompting the legislation: that the government lacked effective means to combat the danger posed by the release into the environment of a wide range of toxic substances. Thus the government[1] is

authorized to take action in response to the "release or

substantial threat of release into the environment" of "any

hazardous substance," regardless of the effect of such re-

lease on the environment, or the release of "any pollutant

or contaminant which may present an imminent and substantial

danger to the public health or welfare." (CERCLA § 104(a)(1).)

A "hazardous substance" includes any substance

designated or listed under Sections 311(b)(2)(A) and 307(a)

of the Federal Water Pollution Control Act, Section 3001 of

the Solid Waste Disposal Act (commonly known as the Resource

Conservation and Recovery Act, or RCRA), Section 112 of the

Clean Air Act, and Section 7 of the Toxic Substances Control

Act, (CERCLA § 101(14)), as well as any substance that EPA

designates as hazardous because when released into the

environment it "may present substantial danger to the public

health or welfare or the environment." (CERCLA § 102.) The

term "hazardous substance" -- and similarly "pollutant or

contaminant" -- expressly excludes petroleum or natural gas,

so that, in contrast to an earlier House bill, the Act pro-

vides no authority to take action in response to an oil

spill.

_____

[1] The Act speaks in terms of the "President" performing
     various functions. However, Section 115 of the Act
     authorizes the President to delegate his duties or
     powers under the Act and, by Executive Order, most of
     the powers have been delegated to EPA. Executive Order
     12316, 46 Fed. Reg. 42237 (Aug. 20, 1981).

The terms "release" and "environment" are defined broadly: a release into the environment includes, with limited exceptions, "any spilling, leaking, pumping, pouring, emitting, emptying, discharging, injecting, escaping, leaching, dumping, or disposing" into waters (also broadly defined), land surface or subsurface strata, or ambient air. Two notable exceptions are releases confined to a workplace, and releases from a nuclear incident that are covered by the Atomic Energy Act of 1954. (CERCLA §§ 101(22), 101(8).)

EPA's options for responding to a release are to "remove" or clean up the released substances, or to provide more permanent "remedial action" relating to the substance, including, for example, dredging or excavation, on-site treatment or incineration, and provision of alternative water supplies. (CERCLA §§ 101(23), 101(24).) The actions taken must be consistent with the "national contingency plan," originally published pursuant to the Federal Water Pollution Control Act. (CERCLA § 105.) The plan has been revised to implement the Act's broader scope by, for example, establishing criteria for determining priorities among releases for the purpose of removal or remedial action.

Further, to help determine the need for response to a release, EPA may request records, reports, or other information from parties possessing hazardous substances; make on-site inspections; and inspect and obtain samples of the substances. (CERCLA § 104(e)(1).)

Finally, EPA may take emergency abatement action when it determines that "there may be an imminent and substantial endangerment to the public health or welfare or the environment because of an actual or threatened release." Specifically, EPA may require the Justice Department to secure in federal district court the necessary equitable relief; or, alternatively, EPA may issue "such orders as may be necessary to protect public health and welfare and the environment." (CERCLA § 106(a).)

II. Hazardous Substance Response Trust Fund

The Act establishes a $1.6 billion "Superfund" to be used primarily to pay (a) governmental response costs as described above, and (b) certain "claims," including claims for response costs incurred by others as a result of carrying out the national contingency plan and claims by the federal government or by any state for injury to natural resources resulting from a release of a hazardous substance. The fund may not be used to pay claims for damages to natural resources, however, where the release and the resulting injury occurred wholly before the enactment of the Act. (CERCLA § 111.) Although the Senate bill allowed persons sustaining personal injury to submit claims for reimbursement of medical expenses and lost income from the fund, the legislation as enacted does not.

Any claim that may be asserted against the fund must first be presented to all parties who may be liable under the Act. If the claim is not satisfied within sixty days thereafter, the claimant may present the claim to the fund for payment, or alternatively, elect to sue the party liable in the court. If the claim is presented to the fund, EPA first must attempt to arrange a settlement between the parties; but if 45 days pass with no agreement, EPA may pay the claim from the fund. If EPA declines to make an award, the claim against the fund is submitted to a Board of Arbitrators, whose decision may be appealed to federal district court. The United States acquires by subrogation the rights of any claimant paid by the fund to recover the amount so paid from the party responsible or liable for the hazardous substance's release. (CERCLA § 112.)

The Hazardous Substance Response Trust Fund is derived primarily from three sources. (CERCLA § 221(a)-(b).) First, a petroleum tax contributes $.0079 for each barrel of "crude oil received at a United States refinery" and "petroleum products entered into the United States for consumption, use, or warehousing." Second, the fund receives monies from a tax, of varying amounts per ton, on 42 listed chemicals if sold or used by the manufacturer, producer, or

importer thereof. Methane and butane used as a fuel,
substances used in the production of fertilizer, sulfuric
acid produced as a by-product of air pollution, and substances derived from coal are specially exempt from the
chemical tax. Both the petroleum and chemical taxes became
effective on April 1, 1981, and terminate on September 30,
1985. Finally, the remainder of the $1.6 billion fund con-
sists of $220 million to be appropriated from general tax
revenues during fiscal years 1981 through 1985. (CERCLA
§§ 211, 221, adding Sections 4611, 4612, 4661, 4662 to the
Internal Revenue Code of 1954.)

III. Liability

        Although the centerpiece of the legislation is the
creation of a Superfund supported primarily by taxes on
industry to provide the government with necessary funds to
clean up environmental damage, the purpose of the Act is not
to spread the cost of environmental damages where the party
responsible is identifiable.

        To the contrary, the Act imposes liability for re-
leases -- or threatened releases that cause the incurrence
of response costs -- of a hazardous substance on several
types of parties. Specifically, the owner and operator of
a vessel or facility from which there is a release or threatened release are liable. The Act defines "vessel" to include
any water craft; and defines "facility" broadly to include,

for example, any building, structure, or equipment, or any
site where a hazardous substance has been deposited or
stored. In the case of an abandoned facility, the owner and
operator for purposes of the Act are the parties holding
those positions immediately prior to the abandonment.
(CERCLA §§ 101(28), 101(9), 101(20).)

In addition, the following parties are also liable
under the Act: any party who owned or operated a facility
at the time of "disposal" there of the hazardous substance;
any party who arranges for "disposal" or "treatment" of
hazardous substances at another party's facility; and any
party who accepts any hazardous substance for transport to a
disposal or treatment facility selected by that party.[2]

Each of these parties is liable for three types of
costs or damages: the costs of removal or remedial action
-- e.g., the response costs -- incurred by the federal government or the state; other necessary costs incurred by others
consistent with the national contingency plan; and damages
to natural resources owned or controlled by the federal
government, any state or local government, or any foreign
government. (CERCLA § 107(a).)

_____

[2]   The Act defines "disposal" and "treatment" with
      reference to Section 1004 of the Solid Waste Disposal
      Act. (CERCLA § 101(29).)

The standard of liability to be applied is that established by Section 311 of the Federal Water Pollution Control Act. 3/ · (CERCLA § 101(32).) The defenses to liability under the Act are restricted to proof that an act of God, an act of war, or certain acts or omissions of third parties caused the release or threat of release of the hazardous substance. (CERCLA § 107(b).)

The Act does, however, provide certain important limitations on liability for the costs and damages described. The liability for each release of a hazardous substance is limited in many cases to the costs of response action plus $50 million for any damages to natural resources. Liability is not limited, however, if the release was the result of willful misconduct or willful negligence, or was caused by a violation of applicable regulations, or where the responsible party did not cooperate with public officials in connection with response actions. Further, any party liable for a release or threat of release who fails to provide removal or remedial action upon order of EPA may be liable for punitive damages. (CERCLA § 107(c).)

There is no liability under the Act to the federal government or any state for damages to natural resources where the injury was, in effect, approved by a governmental

---

3/ The courts have interpreted the standard under the Federal Water Pollution Control Act to be strict liability.

authority; i.e., where "an irreversible and irretrievable commitment of natural resources" was "specifically identified" in "an environmental impact statement, or other comparable analysis," the decision to grant a permit or license "authorizes such commitment of natural resources," and the facility or project was otherwise operating within the terms of its permit or license. Nor is there liability for damages to natural resources where the damages and the release of a hazardous substance causing the damages occurred wholly before enactment of the legislation. (CERCLA § 107(f).)

As an exception to this liability scheme, the Act provides that existing law, and not the liability provisions of the Act, governs liability for response costs or damages resulting from a federally permitted release. (CERCLA § 107(j).) A "federally permitted release" includes, most notably, discharges in compliance with permits issued under the specified sections of the Federal Water Pollution Control Act, the Solid Waste Disposal Act, the Clean Air Act, and the Atomic Energy Act of 1954. (CERCLA § 101(10).)

Finally, the Act contains financial responsibility requirements to ensure recovery from the appropriate parties. The owner or operator of a large vessel is required to demonstrate financial responsibility of $300 per gross ton by obtaining insurance, a guarantee, or a surety bond, or qualifying as a self-insurer; the requirements for facilities are not specified, however, and cannot take effect for at least five years. (CERCLA § 108.)

IV. Post-closure Liability Fund

The Act contains special provisions relating to the liability of the owner or operator of a hazardous waste disposal facility that has received a permit under Subtitle C of the Solid Waste Disposal Act. The liability provided under the Act or any other law is transferred to and assumed by a Post-closure Liability Fund, in cases where the requirements of Subtitle C have been complied with, the facility closed, and the facility and surrounding area monitored to determine that there is no substantial likelihood of risk to public health or welfare. (CERCLA § 107(k).)

The Post-closure Liability Fund consists of funds generated from a tax on "the receipt of hazardous waste at a qualified hazardous waste disposal facility," equal to $2.13 per dry weight ton of hazardous waste received at the facility after September 30, 1983, that will remain at the facility after it is closed.[4/] (CERCLA § 231, adding Sections 4681 and 4682 to the Internal Revenue Code of 1954.) The fund will be used for any of the purposes for which the Hazardous Substance Response Fund would otherwise be used,

---

4/ "Hazardous waste" and "qualified hazardous waste disposal facility" are defined with reference to the Solid Waste Disposal Act.

H-10

and for any costs of response, damages to natural resources, or any other loss resulting from a release of a hazardous substance for which there would otherwise be liability under the Act or any other law. (CERCLA § 111(j).)

Finally, EPA is required to determine whether or not it is feasible to establish an optional system of private insurance for post-closure financial responsibility for hazardous waste disposal facilities, under which any party enrolled in the insurance plan would be exempt from the tax on hazardous waste. (CERCLA § 107(K)(4).)

V. Reporting Requirements

The Act also contains two sets of reporting requirements for notification of the National Response Center and the Environmental Protection Agency under different circumstances. The penalty for failure to comply with either of the reporting requirements is a fine up to $10,000, or imprisonment up to one year, or both. (CERCLA §§ 103(b), (c).)

First, any person in charge of a vessel or facility must, "as soon as he has knowledge of any release (other than a federally permitted release)" of a hazardous substance in specified quantities (see Appendix F), notify the National Response Center. The reporting requirement does not apply, however, when Subtitle C of the Solid Waste Disposal Act requires reporting the release, or specifically exempts it from the reporting requirement; or when there is "a continuous release, stable in quantity and rate" and either notification has already been given for a sufficient period, or notification under the second reporting requirement discussed below has been given. If one of these exceptions applies, notification is still required annually or when there is a significant increase in the quantity of any hazardous substance released. (CERCLA §§ 103(a), (f).)

Second, a report to EPA by June 1981 was required of owners and operators (including former owners or operators) of waste storage, disposal, or treatment facilities for hazardous substances, and those who transport hazardous substances and select such facilities. The party was required to report the existence of the facility, and specify the amount and type of any hazardous substance found there, and also "any known, suspected, or likely releases" from the facility. EPA may require any party required to report to retain records relating to the facility and to any hazardous substances found there. The reporting requirement did not apply where the facility had a permit issued under, or had been accorded interim status under, Subtitle C of the Solid Waste Disposal Act. (CERCLA § 103.)

In addition to these reporting requirements, the statute requires the owner and operator of any vessel or facility from which a hazardous substance has been released to provide notice to "potential injured parties" through

publication in local newspapers serving the affected area.
(CERCLA § 111(g).)

APPENDIX I

SPILL REPORTING REQUIREMENTS

Adapted from course materials for the
Executive Enterprises Environmental Regulations Course,
a presentation by Daniel H. Squire

The following outline summarizes the federal regulations for reporting spills of hazardous substances into
the environment and other potential environmental and health
effects.

A. MAJOR APPLICABLE STATUTES

  1. The Clean Water Act covers spills of oil and hazard-
      ous substances into water.

  2. Superfund covers releases of hazardous substances,
      but not oil, into any environmental medium.

  3. RCRA covers discharges of hazardous wastes, and
      discharges that create hazardous wastes subject to
      RCRA regulation, onto land or into water.

  4. TSCA covers spills of chemical substances or mix-
      tures which have serious adverse effects into any
      environmental medium.

B. CLEAN WATER ACT (SECTION 311)

  1. Basic prohibition: The act prohibits discharge of
      oil or listed hazardous substances into navigable
      waters of the United States in reportable quan-
      tities that may be harmful. (Section 311(b)(3).)

      a. Navigable waters of the United States are
          defined broadly to include, e.g., tributaries
          of navigable waters and intrastate waters
          used in interstate commerce. (40 C.F.R. §
          112.2(k).)

b.   _Oil_ means oil of any kind in any form, including but not limited to petroleum, fuel oil, sludge, and waste oil. (Section 311(a)(1).)

c.   An oil discharge is harmful if it violates water quality standards for the receiving body of water or causes a sheen on (an iridescent appearance) or discoloration of the water or adjoining shoreline. (40 C.F.R. Part 110.)

d.   _Hazardous substances_ include approximately 300 substances that EPA has listed under Section 311 of the Clean Water Act. (40 C.F.R. Part 116.)

e.   EPA has established a harmful quantity for each hazardous substance, ranging from 1 to 5000 pounds, and has adopted a 24-hour reporting period. Only the hazardous substance component of a mixture or solution is measured. (40 C.F.R. Part 117.)

2.   _Exemptions_: There are three exemptions from the basic prohibitions. (Section 311(a)(2).)

a.   Discharges in compliance with effluent limitations established in an NPDES permit.

b.   Discharges identified and made a part of the public record for an NPDES permit, and subject to a condition in the permit (e.g., tank ruptures in response to which the permit requires certain response actions)

c.   Continuous or anticipated intermittent discharges identified in a permit or permit application (e.g., upsets and treatment system failures not subject to permit conditions).

3.   _Spill prevention_: Owners or operators of non-transportation-related facilities that, due to their location, could reasonably be expected to discharge oil in harmful quantities must prepare a Spill Prevention Control and Countermeasure Plan ("SPCC Plan"). (40 C.F.R. Part 112.)

a.   SPCC Plans must specify established procedures and methods (e.g., inspections, security, personnel training), and equipment and physical structures (e.g., containers, dikes, retaining wall, drainage system) to prevent discharges of oil, depending on the type of facility.

b.   A SPCC Plan must be prepared within six months after a facility begins operations.

c.   Civil penalties up to $5,000 for failure to comply with spill prevention rules are assessable by EPA. (40 C.F.R. Part 114.)

d.   The Coast Guard has established analogous requirements to prevent discharges of oil from vessels and transportation-related facilities, but SPCC Plans are not required. (40 C.F.R. Part 155.)

e.   In 1978, EPA proposed regulations requiring owners or operators of facilities handling hazardous substances to prepare SPCC Plans. (43 Fed. Reg. 39276 (Sept. 1, 1978).) Currently, however, these facilities are required only to develop a best management practices program to minimize the potential for the release of hazardous substances. (40 C.F.R. Part 125, Subpart K.)

4.   Notice of discharge: Any person in charge of a vessel or facility shall, as soon as he has knowledge of a discharge of oil or a hazardous substance in a reportable quantity, report it to the federal government. (Section 311(b)(5).)

a.   Notice must be given to the National Response Center (800-424-8802).

b.   Failure to give notice is a criminal offense punishable by a fine of up to $10,000 or imprisonment of up to one year, or both.

c.   Both employees and corporate employers may be subject to criminal penalties for failure to report. Apex Oil Co. v. United States, 530 F.2d 1291 (8th Cir.), cert. denied, 429 U.S. 827 (1976).

5. <u>Cleanup</u>: The federal government may seek to force cleanup or undertake cleanup itself and then seek to recover its costs.

   a. The Government may seek a judicial cleanup order against the owner or operator of a vessel or facility if there is an imminent and substantial threat to health or the environment. (Section 311(e).)

   b. Alternatively, the Government may itself clean up the spill and then seek to recover its actual costs from the owner or operator -- up to established limits ($50 million for facilities, lower limits for vessels), unless the spill was the result of the owner's or operator's willful negligence, in which case the limits do not apply. (Sections 311(c) and (f).)

   c. The owner or operator of a vessel or facility may choose to clean up a discharge to avoid potential liability for government cleanup costs.

6. <u>Civil penalties</u> for a discharge may be assessed against any owner, operator, or person in charge of a vessel or facility:

   a. By the Coast Guard up to $5,000; or

   b. By a court up to $50,000, unless the discharge resulted from willful negligence or willful misconduct, in which case the maximum penalty is $250,000. (Section 311(b)(6).)

C. SUPERFUND

   1. <u>Hazardous substances</u> include, in addition to substances listed under Section 311 of the Clean Water Act, RCRA hazardous wastes, toxics under Section 307 of the Clean Water Act, hazardous air pollutants under Section 112 of the Clean Air Act, and chemicals listed under Section 7 of the TSCA; but do <u>not</u> include petroleum or natural gas. (Section 101(14).)

2. Spills now include any release into the environment, i.e., onto land, into navigable waters, surface water and groundwater, and into the air.
(Section 101(8).)

3. Notice of release: Any person in charge of a
vessel or facility must, as soon as he has
knowledge of a release of a hazardous substance in
a reportable quantity, report it to the National
Response Center. (Section 103(a).)

a. EPA has adopted five reportable quantity levels
of 1, 10, 100, 1000, or 5000 pounds based on
the potential for harm from the release of a
hazardous substance in a reportable quantity.
(40 C.F.R. Part 302.)

b. EPA's implementing rule is published at 50 Fed.
Reg. 13456 (April 4, 1985).

(1) Although EPA explicitly deferred final
decision on this issue, the focus of the
Agency's "enforcement effort" will be for
sudden, accidental, or episodic releases
that create serious risks.

(2) Adopts "24-hour" rule for determining
reportable quantity.

(3) Measures only the hazardous substance
component of mixtures or solutions.

(4) Workplace releases that do not reach the
environment need not be reported.

(5) Rejects multimedia approach that would
establish, for each hazardous substance,
a different reportable quantity for each
environmental medium.

c. Federally permitted releases, i.e., releases
in compliance with a federal permit, need not
be reported.

d. Continuous releases: No report is required
when the release is continuous, and has
already been reported for a sufficient period

or is from a waste facility that has been reported under the Superfund closed waste site reporting requirement. (A report annually, or when there is a significant increase in quantity released, is still required.)

e. Failure to give notice is a criminal offense punishable by a fine of up to $10,000 or imprisonment of up to one year, or both. (Section 103(b).)

4. Newspaper notification: The owner and operator of a facility at which a release occurs must also notify potentially injured parties by publication in local newspapers serving the affected area. (Section 111(g).)

5. Cleanup: The federal government may seek to force liable parties to undertake cleanup, or undertake cleanup itself and then seek to recover its costs.

a. Owners and operators and generators and transporters are subject to the cleanup provisions.

b. In response to an imminent and substantial endangerment to health or the environment, EPA may issue an administrative order or seek a judicial order against owners, operators, generators, and transporters to compel cleanup. (Section 106.)

c. Alternatively, the Government may itself clean up the release and then seek to recover its costs from the owner, operator, generator, or transporter. (Sections 104 and 107.)

d. The owner, operator, generator, or transporter may choose to clean up a release to avoid potential liability for possibly higher governmental cleanup costs.

D. RESOURCE CONSERVATION AND RECOVERY ACT ("RCRA")

1. Facility Owners and Operators

    a. Owners and operators of RCRA facilities must
        prepare a contingency plan for responding to a
        fire, explosion, or release of a RCRA hazard-
        ous waste. (40 C.F.R Part 265, Subpart D;
        Part 264, Subpart D.)

    b. In response to an emergency, owners and opera-
        tors must:

        (1) Assess the hazard and clean up the waste.

        (2) If the release could threaten health or
             the environment outside the facility,
             telephone the National Response Center.

        (3) If any release requires implementing the
             facility's contingency plan, report in
             writing to the EPA Regional Office within
             15 days.

2. Transporters

    a. In response to a release of a RCRA hazardous
        waste during transportation, transporters
        must:

        (1) Take immediate action to protect health
             and the environment.

        (2) Clean up the waste.

        (3) Telephone the National Response Center at
             the earliest practicable moment if, as a
             result of the release, a person is killed
             or receives serious injuries, or property
             damages exceed $50,000;

        (4) Report in writing to the Department of
             Transportation within 15 days of the
             release of any quantity of hazardous
             waste. (40 C.F.R. Part 263, Subpart C.)

b.   These reporting requirements also apply to a broader list of hazardous materials under the Hazardous Materials Transportation Act. (40 C.F.R. Part 171.)

3.   Generators

a.   The RCRA generator standards apply to any person who discharges a hazardous waste, or who, by discharging a material, produces a hazardous waste subject to RCRA regulation. (40 C.F.R. Part 262.)

   (1)   Generators and transporters who do not have an EPA identification number, and who discharge or produce hazardous waste in an emergency situation that requires immediate transportation of the waste, may telephone the EPA Regional Office for a provisional identification number. (45 Fed. Reg. 85022 (Dec. 24, 1980).)

   (2)   If a discharge of hazardous waste occurs during transportation and requires immediate removal, a federal, state or local government official may waive the identification number and manifest requirements for the transportation of the waste off-site. (40 C.F.R. § 263.30(b).)

b.   Generators and transporters (and others) who undertake treatment or storage activities in immediate response to the discharge of a hazardous waste need not obtain a RCRA treatment or storage permit or interim status. (40 C.F.R. §§ 264.1(g)(8), 265.1(c)(11); 48 Fed. Reg. 2508 (Jan. 19, 1983).)

   (1)   This exemption allows immediate treatment (e.g., neutralizing the waste) and storage (e.g., containing the waste) activities.

   (2)   Although the exemption is especially useful to generators and transporters without RCRA permits, it also covers owners and operators of treatment and

storage facilities whose permits do not cover these facilities.

    c.   After a generator's immediate response to a hazardous waste discharge, a generator may accumulate hazardous waste on-site for 90 days without a permit or interim status. (40 C.F.R. § 262.34.)

    d.   The EPA Regional Office or state may issue orally or in writing a temporary emergency permit to allow treatment, storage, or disposal of a hazardous waste. (40 C.F.R. § 270.61.)

4.   <u>Cleanup</u>

    a.   In response to an imminent and substantial endangerment to health or the environment, EPA may issue an administrative order or seek a judicial order to compel cleanup. (Section 7003.)

    b.   After providing EPA, the state and responsible parties 90 days notice, private citizens may seek a judicial order to compel responsible parties to take cleanup action if EPA or the state is not cleaning up or pursuing responsible parties. (Section 7002.)

    c.   EPA also may issue an administrative order or seek judicial relief to compel corrective action at an interim status facility. (Section 3008.)

5.   <u>Penalties</u>: Civil penalties of up to $25,000 per day for failure to comply with any provision of RCRA. (Section 3008.)

E.   TOXIC SUBSTANCES CONTROL ACT ("TSCA")

1.   General Recordkeeping and Reporting. (Section 8(a).)

    a.   Requires manufacturer to fill out two-page form ("Manufacturers' Report -- Preliminary Assessment Information") for each site that manufactures listed chemicals. (40 C.F.R. Part 712.)

b. Information required includes:

    (1) Location of manufacturing sites;

    (2) Quantity manufactured;

    (3) Worker exposure estimates;

    (4) Customer uses; and

    (5) Trade names.

c. Report for original 250 chemicals required to be submitted by November 19, 1982 (40 C.F.R. § 712.30(e)); 51 additional chemicals added to list with a reporting date of August 17, 1983 (40 C.F.R. § 712.30(f)); 5 additional chemicals with a reporting date of September 20, 1983 (40 C.F.R. § 712.30(h)); 4 chemicals with a reporting date of March 13, 1984 (48 Fed. Reg. 55685 (Dec. 14, 1983)); 5 chemicals with a reporting date of August 27, 1984 (49 Fed. Reg. 22284 (May 29, 1984)); 17 chemicals with a reporting date of October 8, 1984 (49 Fed. Reg. 25856 (June 25, 1984)); 1 chemical with a reporting date of October 8, 1984 (49 Fed. Reg. 25859 (June 25, 1984).)

d. Automatic reporting requirements for chemicals designated by the Interagency Testing Committee. (40 C.F.R. § 712.30(c).)

e. Two additional specific reporting requirements in effect now.

    (1) Notice of manufacture or importation required for PBBS or Tris 40 C.F.R. §§ 704.195, 704.205); and for chlorinated terphenyl (40 C.F.R. § 704.85). (49 Fed. Reg. 11181 (March 26,1984).)

    (2) Reporting requirement for asbestos. (40 C.F.R. Part 763.)

        (a) Applicable both to miners and primary processors of asbestos and to secondary processors;

        (b) Information on quantities produced, employee exposure, waste disposal,

and pollution control equipment must
be submitted;

(c) Reports were due on November 29,
1982 for primary producers and processors and on October 29, 1982 for
secondary processors; and

(d) Exemption for small manufacturer who
employed no more than 10 full-time
employees in 1981.

2. Health and Safety Studies. (Section 8(d).)

a. Requires submission of unpublished health and
safety studies on specifically listed chemicals (40 C.F.R. Part 716); 4 additional
chemicals listed at 48 Fed. Reg. 55686 (Dec.
14, 1983); 6 chemicals listed at 49 Fed. Reg.
1697 (Jan. 13, 1984); 5 chemicals listed at 49
Fed. Reg. 22286 (May 29, 1984).

b. Definition -- Health and Safety Study

(1) Any study of any effect of a chemical on
health and environment.

(2) Includes analyzed occupational exposure
data but not simply daily monitoring
records.

(3) Also includes measurements of selected
physical properties such as vapor
pressure, water solubility, etc.

c. What must be submitted?

(1) Copies of any studies in possession, and

(2) Lists of ongoing studies and any known
studies not in your possession.

(3) Need only search records where information would ordinarily be kept and the
records of the employees who advise company of health and environmental effects.

(4) Studies already available to government are exempted, as are R & D studies on new chemicals.

(5) Additional limitations if study was on mixtures.

d. Who must report?

(1) Manufacturers and processors of listed chemicals;

(2) Persons who propose to manufacture or process such chemicals -- i.e., management decision to commit financial resources.

e. Data must be submitted within 60 days after chemical is added to list or within 60 days of proposing to manufacture/process or within 30 days of initiating study.

f. The reporting period terminates three years after a substance or designated mixture is added to the list.

g. Chemicals listed for priority consideration for testing are automatically listed with all health and safety data due within 90 days of publication of a notice in the Federal Register. See, e.g., 47 Fed. Reg. 54624 (Dec. 3, 1982).

3. Records of Significant Adverse Reactions. (Section 8(c).)

a. Requires all manufacturers and some processors (those in SIC categories 28 (Chemicals and Allied Products) or 2911 (Petroleum Refining)) of chemical substances or mixtures to keep records on significant adverse reactions to health or the environment alleged to have been caused by the chemical substances or mixture. (40 C.F.R. § 717; proposed rule clarifying persons subject to the requirement, 49 Fed. Reg. 49865 (Dec. 24, 1984).)

b. Definition -- Significant Adverse Reactions to Health or the Environment

(1) "Reactions that may indicate a substantial impairment of normal activities, or long-lasting or irreversible damage to health or the environment."

(2) Human reactions include: cancer, birth defects, or reproductive disorders; or "impairment of normal activities" experienced by a group of persons or reportedly by one person. Does not include known effects.

(3) Environmental reactions include: changes in composition of animal or plant life, abnormal number of deaths, reproductive effects, behavioral effects, or long-lasting or irreversible contamination of components of the physical environment. Does not apply to spills or other accidents if reported to federal government.

c. Records must be retained for:

(1) 30 years, if allegation arises from any employment-related exposure;

(2) Five years for other allegations.

d. Effective for all allegations received on or after November 21, 1983.

4. Notice of Substantial Risk. (Section 8(e).)

a. Requires immediate notification to EPA of any "information which reasonably supports the conclusion that such substance or mixture presents a substantial risk of injury to health or the environment." Policy statement, 43 Fed. Reg. 11110 (Mar. 16, 1978).

b. Applicability

(1) Applies to all persons engaged in the manufacturing, processing, or distributing in commerce of a chemical substance or mixture.

(2) Applies not only to the company __but also to all officers__ and employees who are capable of appreciating the significance of the information.

(3) A company may relieve its officers and employees of any liability by establishing and implementing procedures for employee submission of all Section 8(e) information and for corporate processing of pertinent information.

c. Time Limits

(1) Information must be submitted not later than __15 working days__ after the information is obtained.

(2) For emergency incidents (i.e., __spills__) a person should report to EPA __by telephone__ as soon as he has knowledge of the incident. A written report must follow within 15 days.

d. Studies or information respecting the following human health and environmental effects must be reported:

(1) Information on cancer, birth defects, mutagenicity, death or serious or prolonged incapacitation;

(2) Widespread and previously unsuspected distribution in environmental media;

(3) Pronounced bioaccumulation;

(4) Ecologically significant changes in species' interrelationships;

(5) Facile transformation or degradation to a chemical having an unacceptable risk as defined above.

e. Emergency Incidents -- Spills: A spill must be reported if the chemical substance or mixture may pose any of the adverse effects listed above and which because of "the pattern, extent, and amount of contamination" __seriously threatens humans with cancer, birth__

I-14

defects, mutation, death, or serious or prolonged incapacitation, or seriously threatens
non-human organisms with large-scale or
ecologically significant population destruction.

f.   Notification is not required if the infor-
     mation has already been obtained by EPA, has
     been published in the scientific literature
     and referenced by one of the leading abstract
     services, or is corroborative of other well-
     established and documented adverse effects, or
     has been contained in a previous notification
     to the agency under some other EPA statute
     (provided it is also labeled as a TSCA 8(e)
     notice).

5.   Penalties: Civil penalties of up to $25,000 per
     day for failure to comply with reporting obliga-
     tions under TSCA, and criminal penalties of up to
     $25,000 per day and/or one year imprisonment.
     (Section 16.)

APPENDIX J

INTERIM CERCLA SETTLEMENT POLICY,
<u>50 Fed. Reg. 5034 (Feb. 5, 1985)</u>

ENVIRONMENTAL PROTECTION AGENCY

[SW-FRL 2770-4]

Hazardous Waste Enforcement Policy

AGENCY: Environmental Protection Agency.

ACTION: Request for public comment.

SUMMARY: The Agency is publishing today its interim CERCLA settlement policy in order to solicit public comment on it. The policy governs private party cleanup and contribution proposals under the Comprehensive Environmental Response, Compensation and Liability Act of 1980 ("CERCLA" or "Superfund"). The Agency is also publishing as an attachment a more detailed discussion of issues raised by this policy.

DATE: Comments must be provided on or before April 8, 1985.

FOR FURTHER INFORMATION CONTACT: Debbie Wood, U.S. Environmental Protection Agency, Office of Waste Programs Enforcement, WH-527, 401 M St. SW., Washington D.C. 20460, (202) 382-4829.

SUPPLEMENTARY INFORMATION: This interim policy describes the approach the Environmental Protection Agency is now taking in evaluating private party settlement proposals for cleanup of hazardous waste sites or contribution to funding of response action under the Comprehensive Environmental Response, Compensation, and Liability Act (" CERCLA" or "Superfund"). It reflects our recent reevaluation of Agency settlement policies. The policy is also generally applicable to imminent hazard enforcement actions under section 7003 of RCRA.

The Agency's hazardous waste settlement policies have resulted in numerous comprehensive private party cleanups, and in stronger settlements with private parties. Some potentially responsible parties (PRPs), however, have argued that Agency settlement policies have fostered litigation, and discouraged voluntary private party cleanup actions. They have suggested a number of changes, such as expanded releases from liability for PRPs and routine provision to PRPs of protection against possible contribution actions by non-settling parties. These suggestions have been made with the expectation that such changes would substantially encourage voluntary response.

The Agency's interim policy on CERCLA case settlement has therefore been amended to:

—Include additional incentives for private party cleanup;

—Articulate policy decisions previously made on a case by case basis in evaluating particular settlement offers;

—Address additional policy concerns, including releases from liability and contribution protection; and,

—Include a statement of the general principles governing EPA's CERCLA enforcement program.

This policy sets forth the general principles governing private party settlement under CERCLA, and specific procedures for Regions and Headquarters to use in assessing private party settlement proposals. It addresses negotiations concerning conduct of or contribution to the remedy determined by the Agency as a result of the remedial investigations and feasibility studies. The following topics are covered:

1. General principles for EPA review of private-party cleanup proposals;
2. Management guidelines for negotiation;
3. Factors governing release of information to potentially responsible parties;
4. Criteria for assessing settlement offers;
5. Partial cleanup proposals;
6. Contribution among responsible parties;
7. Releases and covenants not to sue;
8. Targets for litigation;
9. Timing for negotiations;
10. Management and review of settlement negotiations.

The policy does not explicitly address PRP participation in the Agency's selection of remedies for private party cleanups. That topic was addressed in a memorandum from Lee Thomas and Courtney Price, entitled "Participation of Potentially Responsible Parties in Development of Remedial Investigations and Feasibility Studies under CERCLA" (March 20, 1984).

The policies and procedures set forth in the interim policy are guidance to Agency and other government employees. The policy sets forth enforcement priorities and procedures, and internal procedures which are not appropriate or necessary subjects for rulemaking. Thus, the policy does not constitute rulemaking by the Agency, and may not be relied on to create a substantive or procedural right or benefit enforceable by any other person. The government may, therefore, take action that is at variance with policies and procedures contained in this document.

The Agency is publishing and soliciting comment on this interim policy for a number of reasons. The Agency

recognizes that the public is very concerned with hazardous waste enforcement. We believe that this policy will substantially benefit the public by encouraging responsible parties to undertake appropriate and long term remedies through settlements. We also believe that the policy will yield better results if the public and potentially responsible parties understand the policy and our reasons for adopting it.

This policy was originally drafted in December, 1983, has been the subject of extensive review and evaluation by the Agency and the Department of Justice. It is therefore being published as interim policy. We will reevaluate this policy in light of our working experience with implementing it, and the public comments that we receive.

The Agency statement of policy follows. A more detailed discussion of issues for public comment is included in the Appendix.

Dated: January 25, 1985.

Jack W. McGraw,
Acting Assistant Administrator, Office of Solid Waste and Emergency Response.

Dated: January 28, 1985.

Courtney M. Price,
Assistant Administrator, Office of Enforcement and Compliance Monitoring.

Memorandum

December 5, 1984.

Subject: Interim CERCLA Settlement Policy

From: Lee M. Thomas, Assistant Administrator Office of Solid Waste and Emergency Response, Courtney M. Price, Assistant Administrator Office of Enforcement and Compliance Monitoring F. Henry Habicht, II, Assistant Attorney General Land and Natural Resources Division, Department of Justice

To: Regional Administrators, Regions I-X

This memorandum sets forth the general principles governing private party settlements under CERCLA, and specific procedures for the Regions and Headquarters to use in assessing private party settlement proposals. It addresses the following topics:

1. general principles for EPA review of private-party cleanup proposals;
2. management guidelines for negotiation;
3. factors governing release of information to potentially responsible parties;
4. criteria for evaluating settlement offers;
5. partial cleanup proposals;
6. contribution among responsible parties;

7. release and convenants not to sue;
8. targets for litigation;
9. timing for negotiations;
10. management and review of settlement negotiations.

Applicability

This memorandum incorporates the draft, Hazardous Waste Case Settlement Policy, published in draft in December of 1983. It is applicable not only to multiple party cases but to all civil hazardous waste enforcement cases under Superfund. It is generally applicable to imminent hazard enforcement actions under section 7003 of RCRA.

This policy establishes criteria for evaluating private party settlement proposals to conduct or contribute to the funding of response actions, including removal and remedial actions. It also addresses settlement proposals to contribute to funding after a response action has been completed. It does not address private-party proposals to conduct remedial investigations and feasibility studies. These proposals are to be evaluated under criteria established in the policy guidance from Lee M. Thomas, Assistant Administrator, Office of Solid Waste and Emergency Response, and Courtney Price, Assistant Administrator, Office of Enforcement and Compliance Monitoring entitled "Participation of Potentially Responsible Parties in Development of Remedial Investigations and Feasibility Studies under CERCLA". (March 20, 1984)

I. General Principles

The Government's goal in implementing CERCLA is to achieve effective and expedited cleanup at as many uncontrolled hazardous waste facilities as possible. To achieve this goal, the Agency is committed to a strong and vigorous enforcement program. The Agency has made major advances in securing cleanup at some of the nation's worst hazardous waste sites because of its demonstrated willingness to use the Fund and to pursue administrative and judicial enforcement actions. In addition, the Agency has obtained key decisions, on such issues as joint and several liability, which have further advanced its enforcement efforts.

The Agency recognizes, however, that Fund-financed cleanups, administrative acton and litigation will not be sufficient to accomplish CERCLA's goals, and that voluntary cleanups are essential to a successful program for cleanup of the nation's hazardous waste sites. The

Agency is therefore re-evaluating its settlement policy, in light of three years experience with negotiation and litigation of hazardous waste cases, to remove or minimize if possible the impediments to voluntary cleanup.

As a result of this reassessment, the Agency has identified the following general principles that govern its Superfund enforcement program:

• The goal of the Agency in negotiating private party cleanup and in settlement of hazardous waste cases has been and will continue to be to obtain complete cleanup by the responsible parties, or collect 100% of the costs of the cleanup action.

• Negotiated private party actions are essential to an effective program for cleanup of the nation's hazardous waste sites. An effective program depends on a balanced approach relying on a mix of Fund-financed cleanup, voluntary agreements reached through negotiations, and litigation. Fund-financed cleanup and litigation under CERCLA will not in themselves be sufficient to assure the success of this cleanup effort. In addition, expeditious cleanup reached through negotiated settlements is preferable to protracted litigation.

• A strong enforcement program is essential to encourage voluntary action by PRPs. Section 106 actions are particularly valuable mechanisms for compelling cleanups. The effectiveness of negotiation is integrally related to the effectiveness of enforcement and Fund-financed cleanup. The demonstrated willingness of the Agency to use the Fund to clean up sites and to take enforcement action is our most important tool for achieving negotiated settlements.

• The liability of potentially responsible parties is strict, joint and several, unless they can clearly demonstrate that the harm at the site is divisible. The recognition on the part of responsible parties that they may be jointly and severally liable is a valuable impetus for these parties to reach the agreements that are necessary for successful negotiations. Without such an impetus, negotiations run a risk of delay because of disagreements over the particulars of each responsible party's contribution to the problems at the site.

• The Agency recognizes that the factual strengths and weaknesses of a particular case are relevant in evaluating settlement proposals. The Agency also recognizes that courts may consider differences among defendants in allocating payments among parties held jointly and severally liable under CERCLA. While these are primarily the concerns of PRPs, the Agency will also

consider a PRP's contribution to problems at the site, including contribution of waste, in assessing proposals for settlement and in identifying targets for litigation.

• Section 106 of CERCLA provides courts with jurisdiction to grant such relief as the public interest and the equities of the case may require. In assessing proposals for settlement and identifying targets for litigation, the Agency will consider aggravating and mitigating factors and appropriate equitable factors.

• In many circumstances, cleanups can be started more quickly when private parties do the work themselves, rather than provide money to the Fund. It is therefore, preferable for private parties to conduct cleanups themselves, rather than simply provide funds for the States or Federal Government to conduct the cleanup.

• The Agency will create a climate that is receptive to private party cleanup proposals. To facilitate negotiations, the Agency will make certain information available to private parties. PRPs will normally have an opportunity to be involved in the studies used to determine the appropriate extent of remedy. The Agency will consider settlement proposals for cleanup of less than 100% of cleanup activities or cleanup costs. Finally, upon settling with cooperative parties, the government will vigorously seek all remaining relief, inlcuding costs, penalties and treble damages where appropriate, from parties whose recalcitrance made a complete settlement impossible.

• The Agency anticipates that both the Fund and private resources may be used at the same site in some circumstances. When the Agency settles for less than 100% of cleanup costs, it can use the Fund to assure that site cleanup will proceed expeditiously, and then use to recover these costs from non-settling responsible parties. Where the Federal government accepts less than 100% of cleanup costs and no financially viable responsible parties remain, Superfund monies may be used to make up the difference.

• The Agency recognizes the value of some measure of finality in determinations of liability and in settlements generally. PRPs frequently want some certainty in return for assuming the costs of cleanup, and we recognize that this will be a valuable incentive for private party cleanup. PRPs frequently seek a final determination of liability through contribution protection, releases or covenants not to sue. The Agency will consider releases from liability in appropriate situations, and will also consider contribution protection in limited circumstances. The Agency will also take aggressive enforcement action against those parties whose recalcitrance prevents settlements. In bringing cost recovery actions, the Agency will also attempt to raise any remaining claims under CERCLA section 106, to the extent practicable.

The remainder of this memorandum sets forth specific policies for implementing these general principles.

Section II sets forth the management guidelines for negotiating with less than all responsible parties for partial settlements. This section reflects the Agency's willingness to be flexible by considering offers for cleanup of less than 100% of cleanup activities or costs.

Section III sets forth guidelines on the release of information. The Agency recognizes that adequate information facilities more successful negotiations. Thus, the Agency will combine a vigorous program for obtaining the data and information necessary to facilitate settlements with a program for releasing information to facilitate communications among responsible parties.

Sections IV and V to discuss the criteria for evaluating partial settlements. As noted above, in certain circumstances the Agency will entertain settlement offers from PRPs which extend only to part of the site or part of the costs of cleanup at a site. Section IV of this memo sets forth criteria to be used in evaluating such offers. These criteria apply to all cases. Section V sets forth the Agency's policy concerning offers to perform or pay for discrete phases of an approved cleanup.

Sections VI and VII relate to contribution protection and releases from liability. Where appropriate, the Agency may consider contribution protection and limited releases from liability to help provide some finality to settlements.

Section VIII sets forth criteria for selecting enforcement cases and identifying targets for litigation. As discussed above, effective enforcemnt depends on careful case selection and the careful selection of targets for litigation. The Agency will apply criteria for selection of cases to focus sufficient resources on cases that provide the broadest possible enforcemnt impact. In addition, targets for litigation will be identified in light of the willingness of parties to perform voluntary cleanup, as well as conventional litigation management concerns.

Section IX sets forth the requirements governing the timing of negotiations and section X the provision for Headquarters review. These sections address the need

to provide the Regions with increased flexibilty in negotiations and to change Headquarters review in order to expedite site cleanup.

II. Management Guidelines for Negotiation

As a guideline, the Agency will negotiate only if the initial offer from PRPs constitutes a substantial proportion of the costs of cleanup at the site, or a substantial portion of the needed remedial action. Entering into discussion for less than a substantial proportion of cleanup costs or remedial action needed at the site, would not be an effective use of government resources. No specific numerical threshold for initiating negotiations has been established.

In deciding whether to start negotiations, the Regions should weight the potential resource demands for conducting negotiations against the likelihood of getting 100% of costs or a complete remedy.

Where the Region proposes to negotiate for a partial settlement involving less than the total costs of a cleanup, or a complete remedy, the Region should prepare as part of its Case Negotiations Strategy a dreaft evaluation of the case using the settlement criteria identified in section IV. The draft should discuss how each of the factors in section IV applies to the site in question, and explain why negotiations for less than all of the cleanup costs, or a partial remedy, are appropriate. A copy of the draft should be forwarded to Headquarters. The Headquarters review will be used to identify major issues of national significance or issues that may involve significant legal precedents.

In certain other categories of cases, it may be appropriate for the Regions to enter into negotiations with PRPs, even though the offers from PRPs do not represent a substantial portion of the costs of cleanup. These categories of cases include:

- administrative settlements of cost recovery actions where total cleanup costs were less than $200,000;
- claims in bankruptcy;
- administrative settlements with de minimis contributors of wastes.

Actions subject to this exceptions are administrative settlements of cost recovery cases where all the work at the site has been completed and all costs have been incurred. The figure of $200,000 refers to all of the costs of cleanup. The Agency is preparing more detailed guidance on the appropriate form of such settlement agreements, and the types of conditions that must be included.

Negotiation of claims in bankruptcy may involve both present owners, where the United States may have an administrative costs claim, and other parties such as past owners or generators, where the United States may be an unsecured potential creditor. The Regions should avoid becoming involved in bankruptcy proceedings if there is little likelihood of recovery, and should recognize the risks involved in negotiating without creditor status. It may be appropriate to request DOJ filing of a proof of claim. Further guidance is provided in the Memorandum from Courtney Price entitled "Information Regarding CERCLA Enforcement Against Bankrupt Parties," dated May 24, 1984.

In negotiating with de minimis parties, the Regions should limit their efforts to low volume, low toxicity disposers who would not normally make a significant contribution to the costs of cleanup in any case.

In considering settlement offer from de minimis contributors, the Region should normally focus on achieving cash settlements. Regions should generally not enter into negotiations for full administrative or judicial settlements with releases, contribution protection, or other protective clauses. Substantial resources should not be invested in negotiations with de minimis contributors, in light of the limited costs that may be recovered, the time needed to prepare the necessary legal documents, the need for Headquarters review, potential res judicata effects, and other effects that de minimis settlements may have on the nature of the case remaining to the Government.

Partial settlements may also be considered in situations where the unwillingness of a relatively small group of parties to settle prevents the development of a proposal for a substantial portion of costs or the remedy. Proposals for settlement in these circumstances should be assessed under the criteria set forth in section IV.

Earlier versions of this policy included a threshold for negotiations, which provided that negotiations should not be commenced unless an offer was made to settle for at least 80% of the costs of cleanup, or of the remedial action. This threshold has been eliminated from the final version of this policy. It must be emphasized that elimination of this threshold does not mean that the Agency is therefore more willing to accept offers for partial settlement. The objective of the Agency is still to obtain complete cleanup by PRPs, or 100% of the costs of cleanup.

III. Release of Information

The Agency will release information concerning the site to PRPs to facilitate discussions for settlement among PRPs. This information will include:

—Identity of notice letter recipients.
—Volume and nature of wastes to the extent identified as sent to the site;
—Ranking by volume of material sent to the site, if available.

In determining the type of information to be released, the Region should consider the possible impacts on any potential litigation. The Regions should take steps to assure protection of confidential and deliverative materials. The Agency will generally not release actual evidentiary material. The Region should state on each released summary that it is preliminary, that it was furnished in the course of compromise negotiations (Fed. Rules of Evidence 408), and that it is not binding on the Federal Government.

This information release should be preceded by and combined with a vigorous program for collecting information from responsible parties. It remains standard practice for the Agency to use the information gathering authorities of RCRA and CERCLA with respect to all PRPs at a site. This information release should generally be conditioned on a reciprocal release of information by PRPs. The information request need not be simultaneous, but EPA should receive the information within a reasonable time.

IV. Settlement Criteria

The objective of negotiations is to collect 100% of cleanup costs or complete cleanup from responsible parties. The Agency recognizes that, in narrowly limited circumstances, exceptions to this goal may be appropriate, and has established criteria for determining where such exceptions are allowed. Although the Agency will consider offers of less than 100% in accordance with this policy, it will do so in light of the Agency's position, reinforced by recent court decisions, that PRP liability is strict, joint and several unless it can be shown by the PRPs that injury at a site is clearly divisible.

Based on a full evulation of the facts and a comprehensive analysis of all of the listed criteria, the Agency may consider accepting offers of less than 100 percent. Rapid and effective settlement depends on a thorough evaluation, and an aggressive information collection program is necessary to prepare effective evaluations. Proposals for less than total settlement should be assessed using the criteria identified below

1 Volume of Wastes Contributed to Site by Each PRP

Information concerning the volume of wastes contributed to the site by PRPs should be collected, if available, and evaluated in each case. The volume of wastes is not the only criterion to be considered, nor may it be the most important. A small quantity of waste may cost proportionally more to contain or remove than a larger quantity of a different waste. However, the volume of waste may contribute significantly and directly to the distribution of contamination on the surface and subsurface (including groundwater), and to the complexity of removal of the contamination. In addition, if the properties of all wastes at the site are relatively equal, the volume of wastes contributed by the PRPs provides a convenient, easily applied criterion for measuring whether a PRP's settlement offer may be reasonable.

This does not mean, however, that PRPs will be required to pay only their proportionate share based on volume of contribution of wastes to the site. At many sites, there will be wastes for which PRPs cannot be identified. If identified, PRPs may be unable to provide funds for cleanup. Private party funding for cleanup of those wastes would, therefore, not be available if volumetric contribution were the only criteria.

Therefore, to achieve the the Agency's goal of obtaining 100 percent of cleanup or the cost of cleanup, it will be necessary in many cases to require a settlement contribution greater than the percentage of wastes contributed by each PRP to the site. These costs can be obtained through the application of the theory of joint and several liability where the harm is indivisible, and through application of these criteria in evaluating settlement proposals.

2. Nature of the Wastes Contributed

The human, animal and environmental toxicity of the hazardous substances contributed by the PRPs, its mobility, persistence and other properties are important factors to consider. As noted above, a small amount of wastes, or a highly mobile waste, may cost more to clean up, dispose, or treat than less toxic or relatively immobile wastes. In addition, any disproportionate adverse effects on the environment by the presence of wastes contributed by those PRPs should be considered.

If a waste contributed by one or more of the parties offering a settlement disproportionately increases the costs of cleanup at the site, it may be appropriate for parties contributing such waste to bear a larger percentage of cleanup costs than would be the case by using solely a volumetric basis.

3. Strength of Evidence Tracing the Wastes at the Site to the Settling Parties

The quality and quantity of the Government's evidence connecting PRPs to the wastes at the site obviously affects the settlement value of the Government's case. The Government must show, by a preponderance of the evidence, that the PRP's are connected with the wastes in one or more of the ways provided in Section 107 of CERCLA. Therefore, if the Government's evidence against a particular PRP is weak, we should weigh that weakness in evaluating a settlement offer from that PRP.

On the other hand, where indivisible harm is shown to exist, under the theory of joint and several liability the Government is in a position to collect 100% of the cost of cleanup from all parties who have contributed to a site. Therefore, where the quality and quantity of the Government's evidence appears to be strong for establishing the PRP's liability, the Government should rely on the strength of its evidence and not decrease the settlement value of its case. Discharging such PRPs from liability in a partial settlement without obtaining a substantial contribution may leave the Government with non-settling parties whose involvement at the site may be more tenuous.

In any evaluation of a settlement offer, the Agency should weigh the amount of information exchange that has occurred before the settlement offer. The more the Government knows about the evidence it has to connect the settling parties to the site, the better this evaluation will be. The information collection provisions of RCRA and/or CERCLA should be used to develop evidence prior to preparation of the evaluation.

4. Ability of the Settling Parties To Pay

Ability to pay is not a defense to an action by the Government. Nevertheless, the evaluation of a settlement proposal should discuss the financial condition of that party, and the practical results of pursuing a party for more than the Government can hope to actually recover. In cost recovery actions it will be difficult to negotiate a settlement for more than a party's assets. The Region should also consider allowing the party to reimburse the Fund in reasonable installments over a period of time, if the party is unable to pay in a lump sum, and installment payments would benefit the Government. A structured settlement providing for payments over time should be at a payment level that takes into account the party's cash flow. An excessive amount could force a party into bankruptcy, which will of course make collection very difficult. See the memorandum dated August 26, 1983, entitled "Cost Recovery Actions under Section 107 of CERCLA" for additional guidance on this subject.

5. Litigative Risks in Proceeding to Trial

Litigative risks which might be encountered at trial and which should weigh in consideration of any settlement offer include traditional factors such as:

a. *Admissibility of the Government's evidence*

If necessary Government evidence is unlikely to be admitted in a trial because of procedural or substantive problems in the acquisition or creation of the evidence, this infirmity should be considered as reducing the Government's chance of success and, therefore, reducing the amount the Government should expect to receive in a settlement.

b. *Adequacy of the Government's evidence*

Certain aspects of this point have already been discussed above. However, it deserves mention again because the Government's case depends on substantial quantities of sampling, analytical and other technical data and expert testimony. If the evidence in support of the Government's case is incomplete or based upon controversial science, or if the Government's evidence is otherwise unlikely to withstand the scrutiny of a trial, the amount that the Government might expect to receive in a settlement will be reduced.

c. *Availability of defenses*

In the unlikely event that one or more of the settling parties appears to have a defense to the Government's action under section 107(b) of CERCLA, the Government should expect to receive less in a settlement from that PRP. Availability of one or more defenses to one PRP which are not common to all PRPs in the case should not, however, lower the expectation of what an entire offering group should pay.

6. Public Interest Considerations

The purpose of site cleanup is to protect public health and the environment. Therefore, in analyzing a settlement proposal the timing of the cleanup and the ability of the Government to clean up the site should be considered. For example, if the State cannot fund its portion of a Fund-financed cleanup, a private-party cleanup proposal may be given more favorable consideration than one received in a case where the State can fund its portion of cleanup costs, if necessary.

Public interest considerations also include the availability of Federal funds for necessary cleanup, and whether privately financed action can begin more quickly than Federally-financed activity. Public interest concerns may be used to justify a settlement of less than 100% only when there is a demonstrated need for a quick remedy to protect public health or the environment.

7. Precedential Value

In some cases, the factual situation may be conducive to establishing a favorable precedent for future Government actions. For example, strong case law can be developed in cases of first impression. In addition, settlements in such cases tend to become precedents in themselves, and are examined extensively by PRPs in other cases. Settlement of such cases should always be on terms most favorable to the Government. Where PRPs will not settle on such terms, and the quality and quantity of evidence is strong, it may be in the overall interest of the Government to try the case.

8. Value of Obtaining a Present Sum Certain

If money can be obtained now and turned over to the Fund, where it can earn interest until the time it is spent to clean up a site, the net present value of obtaining the sum offered in settlement now can be computed against the possibility of obtaining a larger sum in the future. This calculation may show that the net present value of the sum offered in settlement is, in reality, higher than the amount the Government can expect to obtain at trial. EPA has developed an economic model to assess these and other related economic factors. More information on this model can be obtained from the Director, Office of Waste Programs Envorcement.

9. Inequities and Aggravating Factors

All analyses of settlement proposals should flag for the decision makers any apparent inequities to the settling parties inherent in the Government's case, and apparent inequities to others if the settlement proposal is accepted, and any aggravating factors. However, it must be understood that the statute operates on the underlying principle of strict liability, and that equitable matters are not defenses.

10. Nature of the Case that Remains After Settlement

All settlement evaluations should address the nature of the case that remains if the settlement is accepted. For example, if there are no financially viable parties left to proceed against for the balance of the cleanup after the settlement, the settlement offer should constitute everything the Government expects to obtain at that site. The questions are: What does the Government gain by settling this portion of the case? Does the settlement or its terms harm the remaining portion of the case? Will the Government have to expend the same amount of resources to try the remaining portion of the case? If so, why should the settlement offer be accepted?

This analysis is extremely important and should come at the conclusion of the evaluation.

V. Partial Cleanups

On occasion, PRPs may offer to perform or pay for one phase of a site cleanup (such as a surface removal action) but not commit to any other phase of the cleanup (such as ground water treatment). In some circumstances, it may be appropriate to enter into settlements for such partial cleanups, rather than to resolve all issues in one settlement. For example, in some cases it is necessary to conduct initial phases of site cleanup in order to gather sufficient data to evaluate the need for and type of work to be done on subsequent phases. In such cases, offers from PRPs to conduct or pay for less than all phases of site cleanup should be evaluated in the same manner and by the same criteria as set forth above. Settlements performed at the site. This provision does not cover preparation of an RI/FS, which is covered by a separate guidance document: Lee Thomas and Courtney Price's "Participation of Potentially Responsible Parties in RI/FS Development" (March 20, 1984).

VI. Contribution Protection

Contribution among responsible parties is based on the principle that a jointly and severally liable party who has paid all or a portion of a judgment or settlement may be entitled to reimbursement from other jointly or severally liable parties. When the Agency reaches a partial settlement with some parties, it will frequently pursue an enforcement action against non-settling responsible parties to recover the remaining costs of cleanup. If such an action is undertaken, there is a possibility that those non-settlors would in turn sue settling parties. If this action by nonsettling parties is successful, then the settling parties would end up paying a larger share of cleanup costs than was determined in the Agency's settlement. This is obviously a disincentive to settlement.

Contribution protection in a consent decree can prevent this outcome. In a contribution protection clause, the United States would agree to reduce its judgment against the non-settling parties, to the extent necessary to extinguish the settling party's libility to the nonsettling third party.

The Agency recognizes the value of contribution protection in limited situations in order to provide some measure of finality to settlements. Fundamentally, we believe that settling parties are protected from contribution actions as a matter of law, based on the Uniform Contribution Among Tortfeasors Act. That Act provides that, where settlements are entered into in "good faith", the settlors are discharged from "all liability for contribution to any other joint tortfeasors." To the extent that this law is adopted as the Federal rule of decision, there will be no need for specific clauses in consent agreements to provide contribution protection.

There has not yet been any ruling on the issue. Thus, the Agency may still be asked to provide contribution protection in the form of offsets and reductions in judgment. In determining whether explicit contribution protection clauses are appropriate, the Region should consider the following factors:

• Explicit contribution protection clauses are generally not appropriate unless liability can be clearly allocated, so that the risk of reapportionment by a judge in any future action would be minimal.

• Inclusion should depend on case-by-case consideration of the law which is likely to be applied.

• The Agency will be more willing to consider contribution protection in settlements that provide substantially all the costs of cleanup.

If a proposed settlement includes a contribution protection clause, the Region should prepare a detailed justification indicating why this clause is essential to attaining an adequate settlement. The justification should include an assessment of the prospects of litigation regarding the clause. Any proposed settlement that contains a contribution protection clause with a potential ambiguity will be returned for further negotiation.

Any subsequent claims by settling parties against non-settlors must be subordinated to Agency claims against

these non-settling parties. In no event will the Agency agree to defend on behalf of a settlor, or to provide direct indemnification. The Government will not enter into any form of contribution protection agreement that could requrie the Government to pay money to anyone.

If litigation is commenced by non-settlors against settlors, and the Agency became involved in such litigation, the Government would argue to the court that in adjusting equities among responsible parties, positive consideration should be given to those who came forward voluntarily and were a part of a group of settling PRPs.

VII. Releases from Liability

Potentially responsible parties who offer to wholly or partially clean up a site or pay the costs of cleanup normally wish to negotiate a release from liability or a covenant not to sue as a part of the consideration for that cleanup or payment. Such releases are appropriate in some circumstances. The need for finality in settlements must be balanced against the need to insure that PRPs remain responsible for recurring endangerments and unknown conditions.

The Agency recognizes the current state of scientific uncertainty concerning the impacts of hazardous substances, our ability to detect them, and the effectiveness of remedies at hazardous waste sites. It is possible that remedial measures will prove inadequate and lead to imminent and substantial endangerments, because of unknown conditions or because of failures in design, construction or effectiveness of the remedy.

Although the Agency approves all remedial actions for sites on the National Priorities List, releases from liability will not automatically be granted merely because the Agency has approved the remedy. The willingness of the Agency to give expansive releases from liability is directly related to the confidence that Agency has that the remedy will ultimately prove effective and reliable. In general, the Regions will have the flexibility to negotiate releases that are relatively expansive or relatively stringent, depending on the degree of confidence that the Agency has in the remedy.

Releases or covenants must also include certain reopeners which preserve the right of the Government to seek additional cleanup action and recover additional costs from responsible parties in a number of circumstances. They are also subject to a variety of other limitations. These

reopener clauses and limitations are described below.

In addition, the the Agency can address future problems at a site by enforcement of the decree or order, rather than by action under a particular reopener clause. Settlements will normally specify a particular type of remedial action to be undertaken. That remedial action will normally be selected to achieve a certain specified level of protection of public health and the environment. When settlements are incorporated into consent decrees or orders, the decrees or orders should wherever possible include performance standards that set out these specified levels of protection. Thus, the Agency will retain its ability to assure cleanup by taking action to enforce these decrees or orders when remedies fail to meet the specified standards.

It is not possible to specify a precise hierarchy of preferred remedies. The degree of confidence in a particular remedy must be determined on an individual basis, taking site-specific conditions into account. In general, however, the more effective and reliable the remedy, the more likely it is that the Agency can negotiate a more expansive release. For example, if a consent decree or order commits a private party to meeting and/or continuing to attain health based performance standards, there can be great certainty on the part of the Agency that an adequate level of public health protection will be met and maintained, as long as the terms of the agreement are met. In this type of case, it may be appropriate to negotiate a more expansive release than, for example, cases involving remedies that are solely technology-based.

Expansive releases may be more appropriate where the private party remedy is a demonstrated effective alternative to land disposal, such as incineration. Such releases are possible whether the hazardous material is transported offsite for treatment, or the treatment takes place on site. In either instance, the use of treatment can result in greater certainty that future problems will not occur.

Other remedies may be less appropriate for expansive releases, particularly if the consent order or agreement does not include performance standards. It may be appropriate in such circumstances to negotiate releases that become effective several years after completion of the remedial action, so that the effectiveness and reliability of the technology can be clearly demonstrated. The Agency anticipates that responsible parties may be able to achieve a greater degree of certainty in settlements when the state of scientific understanding concerning these technical issues has advanced.

Regardless of the relative expansiveness or stringency of the release in other respects, at a minimum settlement documents must include reopeners allowing the Government to modify terms and conditions of the agreement for the following types of circumstances:

• Where previously unknown or undetected conditions that arise or are discovered at the site after the time of the agreement may present an imminent and substantial endangerment to public health, welfare of the environment;

• Where the Agency receives additional information, which was not available at the time of the agreement, concerning the scientific determinations on which the settlement was premised (for example, health effects associated with levels of exposure, toxicity of hazardous substances, and the appropriateness of the remedial technologies for conditions at the site) and this additional information indicates that site conditions may present an imminent and substantial endangerment to the public health or welfare or the environment.

In addition, release clauses must not preclude the Government from recovering costs incurred in responding to the type of imminent and substantial endangerments identified above.

In extraordinary circumstances, it may be clear after application of the settlement criteria set out in section IV that it is in the public interest to agree to a more limited or more expansive release not subject to the conditions outlined above. Concurrence of the Assistant Administrators for OSWER and OECM (and the Assistant Attorney General when the release is given on behalf of the United States) must be obtained before the Government's negotiating team is authorized to negotiate regarding such a release or covenant.

The extent of releases should be the same, whether the private parties conduct the cleanup themselves or pay for Federal Government cleanup. When responsible parties pay for Federal Government cleanup, the release will ordinarily not become effective until cleanup is completed and the actual costs of the cleanup are ascertained. Responsible parties will thereby bear the risk of uncertainties arising during execution of the cleanup. In limited circumstances, the release may become effective upon payment for Federal Government cleanup, if the payment includes a carefully calculated premium or other financial instrument that adequately insures the Federal Government against these uncertainties. Finally, the Agency may be more willing to settle for less than the total costs of cleanup when it is not precluded by a release clause from eventually recovering any additional costs that might ultimately be incurred at a site.

Release clauses are also subject to the following limitations:

• A release or covenant may be given only to the PRP providing the consideration for the release.

• The release or covenant must not cover any claims other than those involved in the case.

• The release must not address any criminal matter.

• Releases for partial cleanups that do not extend to the entire site must be limited to the work actually completed.

• Federal claims for natural resource damages should not be released without the approval of Federal trustees.

• Responsible parties must release any related claims against the United States, including the Hazardous Substances Response Fund.

• Where the cleanup is to be performed by the PRPs, the release or covenant should normally become effective only upon the completion of the cleanup (or phase of cleanup) in a manner satisfactory to EPA.

• Release clauses should be drafted as covenants not to sue, rather than releases from liability, where this form may be necessary to protect the legal rights of the Federal Government.

A release or covenant not to sue terminates or seriously impairs the Government's rights of action against PRPs. Therefore, the document should be carefully worded so that the intent of the parties and extent of the matters covered by the release or covenant are clearly stated. Any propsed settlement containing a release with a possible ambiguity will be returned for further negotiation.

VIII. Targets for Litigation

The Regions should identify particular cases for referral in light of the following factors:

—Substantial environmental problems exist;
—The Agency's case has legal merit;
—The amount of money or cleanup involved is significant;
—Good legal precedent is possible (cases should be rejected where the potential for adverse precedent is substantial);
—The evidence is strong, well developed, or capable of development;
—Statute of limitations problems exist;
—Responsible parties are financially viable.

The goal of the Agency is to bring enforcement action wherever needed to assure private party cleanup or to recover costs. The following types of cases are the highest priorities for referrals:

—107 actions in which all costs have been incurred;
—Combined 106/107 actions in which a significant phase has been completed, additional injunctive relief is needed and identified, and the Fund will not be used;
—106 actions which will not be the subject of Fund-financed cleanup.

Referrals for injunctive relief may also be appropriate in cases when it is possible that Fund-financed cleanup will be undertaken. Such referrals may be needed where there are potential statute of limitation concerns, or where the site has been identified as enforcement-lead, and prospects for successful litigation are good.

Regional offices should periodically reevaluate current targets for referral to determine if they meet the guidelines identified above.

As indicated before, under the theory of joint and several liability the Government is not required to bring enforcement action against all of the potentially responsible parties involved at a site. The primary concern of the Government in identifying targets for litigation is to bring a meritorious case against responsible parties who have the ability to undertake or pay for response action. The Government will determine the targets of litigation in order to reach the largest manageable number of parties, based on toxicity and volume, and financial viability. Owners and operators will generally be the target of litigation, unless bankrupt or otherwise judgment proof. In appropriate cases, the Government will consider prosecuting claims in bankruptcy. The Government may also select targets for litigation for limited purposes, such as site access.

Parties who are targeted for litigation are of course not precluded from involving parties who have not been targeted in developing settlement offers for consideration by the Government.

In determining the appropriate targets for litigation, the Government will consider the willingness of parties to settle, as demonstrated in the negotiation stage. In identifying a manageable number of parties for litigation, the Agency will consider the recalcitrance or willingness to settle of the parties who were involved in the negotiations. The Agency will also consider other aggravating and mitigating factors concerning responsible party actions in identifying targets for litigation.

In addition, it may be appropriate, when the Agency is conducting phased cleanup and has reached a settlement for one phase, to first sue only non-settling companies for the next phase, assuming that such financially viable parties are available. This approach would not preclude suit against settling parties, but non-settlors would be sued initially.

The Agency recognizes that Federal agencies may be responsible for cleanup costs at hazardous waste sites. Accordingly, Federal facilities will be issued notice letters and administrative orders where appropriate. Instead of litigation, the Agency will use the procedures established by Executive Orders 12088 and 12146 and all applicable Memoranda of Understanding to resolve issues concerning such agency's liability. The Agency will take all steps necessary to encourage successful negotiations.

IX. Timing of Negotiations

Under our revised policy on responsible party participation in RI/FS, PRPs have increased opportunities for involvement in the development of the remedial investigations and feasibility studies which the Agency uses to identify the appropriate remedy. In light of the fact that PRPs will have received notice letters and the information identified in section III of this policy, prelitigation negotiations can be conducted in an expeditious fashion.

The Negotiations Decision Document (NDD), which follows completion of the RI/FS, makes the preliminary identification of the appropriate remedy for the site. Prelitigation negotiations between the Government and the PRPs should normally not extend for more than 60 days after approval of the NDD. If significant progress is not made within a reasonable amount of time, the Agency will not hesitate to abandon negotiations and proceed immediately with administrative action or litigation. It should be noted that these steps do not preclude further negotiations.

Extensions can be considered in complex cases where there is no threat of seriously delaying cleanup action. Any extension of this period must be predicated on having a good faith offer from the PRPs which, if successfully negotiated, will save the Government substantial time and resources in attaining the cleanup objectives.

X. Management and Review of Settlement Negotiations

All settlement documents must receive concurrence from OWPE and OECM-Waste, and be approved by the Assistant Administrator of OECM in accordance with delegations. The management guideline discussed in Section II allows the Regions to commence negotiations if responsible parties make an initial offer for a substantial proportion of the cleanup costs. Before commencing negotiations for partial settlements, the Regions should prepare a preliminary draft evaluation of the case using the settlement criteria in section IV of this policy. A copy of this evaluation shoud be forwarded to Headquarters.

A final detailed evaluation of settlements is required when the Regions request Headquarters approval of these settlements. This written evaluation should be submitted to OECM-Waste and OWPE by the legal and technical personnel on the case. These will normally be the Regional attorney and technical representative.

The evaluation memorandum should indicate whether the settlement is for 100% of the work or cleanup costs. If this figure is less than 100%, the memorandum should include a discussion of the advantages and disadvantages of the proposed settlement as measured by the criteria in section IV. The Agency expects full evaluations of each of the criteria specified in the policy and will return inadequate evaluations.

The Regions are authorized to conclude settlements in certain types of hazardous waste cases on their own, without prior review by Headquarters or DOJ. Cases selected for this treatment would normally have lower priority for litigation. Categories of cases not subject to Headquarters review include negotiation for cost recovery cases under $200,000 and negotiation of claims filed in bankruptcy. In cost recovery cases, the Regions should pay particular attention to weighing the resources necessary to conduct negotiations and litigation against the amounts that may be recovered, and the prospects for recovery.

Authority to appear and try cases before the Bankruptcy Court would not be delegated to the Regions, but would be retained by the Department of Justice. The Department will file cases where an acceptable negotiated settlement cannot be reached. Copies of settlement documents for such agreements should be provided ot OWPE and OECM.

Specific details concerning these authorizations will be addressed in delegations that will be forwarded to the Regions under separate cover. Headquarters is conducting an evaluation of the effectiveness of existing delegations, and is assessing the possibility of additional delegations.

Note on Purpose and Uses of this Memorandum

The policies and procedures set forth here, and internal Government procedures adopted to implement these policies, are intended as guidance to Agency and other Government employees. They do not constitute rulemaking by the Agency, and may not be relied on to create a substantive or procedural right or benefit enforceable by any other person. The Government may take action that is at variance with the policies and procedures in this memorandum.

If you have any questions or comments on this policy, or problems that need to be addressed in further guidance to implement this policy, please contact Gene A. Lucero, Director of the Office of Waste Programs Enforcement (FTS 382-4814), or Richard Mays, Senior Enforcement Counsel (FTS 382-4137).

Appendix—Discussion of Issues Raised by Interim CERCLA Settlement Policy

This appendix discusses in greater detail certain issues raised by the interim policy and identifies specific issues for public comment. It focuses on issues of broad public concern, rather than issues related primarily to internal Agency management. The section headings of this attachment generally parallel the specific sections of the enforcement policy.

I. General Principles

The discussion of general principles sets out the overall philosophy governing the Superfund enforcement program. To achieve the greatest possible number of timely and effective cleanup actions, the Agency must strike a balance between two opposite approaches. One approach emphasizes quick resort to the Fund and enforcement authorities, and the other features more incentives for private party cleanup.

We have attempted to combine features of both these approaches into a vigorous enforcement program that will encourage private party cleanups. These approaches, and their limitations, are described in greater detail below.

Under one general approach, the Agency would quickly resort to either enforcement action such as litigation and administrative orders, or Federal government cleanup under the Fund. Releases from liability and explicit contribution protection clauses would be strictly limited under this approach, and the time for negotiations prior to enforcement or Fund-financed cleanup action would be short. The limitation of this general approach is that EPA may not always be able to move to clean up enough sites, because of restrictions on the use of the Fund and the time and resources needed to compel cleanup through enforcement. Furthermore, many private parties believe that, as a general matter, they can conduct cleanup activities more quickly and at less cost than the Federal government, and have clamed that this approach may discourage private party initiatives.

Under the other general approach, the Agency would provide additional incentives to encourage PRP cleanup. For example, settlements would allow more expansive releases from liability, contribution protection would be provided, and EPA would take as much time as needed to resolve issues through negotiations before it resorted to enforcement action or Fund-financed cleanup. It is possible that the Agency would reach more negotiated settlements under this approach. One limitation of this approach is that the Agency would assume financial risks if it becomes clear in light of changed circumstances or improved knowledge of site problems that additional cleanup action is needed; expansive releases from liability would preclude the Agency from pursuing responsible parties for additional cleanup costs.

Also, protracted negotiations would delay cleanup of sites. Further, private party cleanups may not increase without an attendant aggressive enforcement program (unilateral administrative orders, imminent hazard enforcement actions under CERCLA section 106, and cost-recovery actions under section 107) because private parties may lack an incentive to reach negotiated settlements.

We have attempted to strike a balance between the two directions, recognizing that no approach may be completely adequate to satisfy all of these concerns. While the Agency remains committed to a strong and vigorous enforcement program, it recognizes that negotiated private party cleanups are essential to a successful cleanup program. The Agency will minimize impediments to voluntary cleanup, and take aggressive enforcement action against those parties whose recalcitrance prevents

settlements or makes complete settlement impossible.

The Agency solicits comments on whether any additional factors or principles should be considered by the Agency in formulating a settlement policy.

II. Management Guidelines for Negotiation

The previous settlement policy included a resource management guideline for use after the Agency has evaluated the case using the settlement criteria and determined that the prospects for successfully pursuing the case were good. The guideline stated that the Agency would generally negotiate only if the initial offer from PRPs was for 80 percent of the remedy or costs of cleanup. This 80 percent threshold was established so that the Regional offices would spend their time and resources negotiating cases where settlement on acceptable terms seems more likely. EPA considered retaining that guideline in this interim policy.

The threshold was not intended to be an absolute barrier to offers for less than 80 percent, and the earliest drafts of this interim policy indicated that offers for less than that amount might be considered. However, some PRPs may have perceived the guideline as an absolute barrier, and been reluctant to approach the Agency with valid settlement offers because those offers were not for 80 percent of the remedy or costs of the cleanup. Minor volumetric contributors of wastes to the site would generally be unwilling to offer 80 percent. It is also possible that a few recalcitrant parties who refused to join a group settlement offer could prevent the others from coming up with an 80 percent offer.

The Agency considered a variety of approaches for providing potentially responsible parties with a greater opportunity and incentive for becoming involved in negotiations. They include:
• Eliminating the threshold;
• Eliminating the threshold for certain categories of PRPs or cases;
• Lowering the threshold;
• Allowing deviation from the threshold when the Region has prepared an evaluation of the case, and Headquarters has reviewed this evaluation; and
• Allowing negotiations with individual parties, as long as the Region ultimately recovers a certain percentage of the costs of cleanup.

The approach in the interim policy combines elements of a number of these options. It eliminates the 80 percent threshold. Instead, the interim policy states that the Agency will negotiate

only if the initial offer from PRPs constitutes a substantial proportion of the remedy or cleanup costs. Regions are asked to weigh the potential resource demands for conducting negotiations against the likelihood of getting 100 percent of costs or a complete remedy. Thus, while an offer of 80 percent is not required to initiate negotiations, there will be cases where offers of 80 percent will de deemed inadequate. Offers to negotiate for a partial settlement or cleanup should be evaluated by Regions using the criteria set forth in section IV of the policy. A copy of these draft evaluations are to be forwarded to Headquarters for review.

The policy announced today also recognizes that in certain limited categories of cases, it may be appropriate for Regions to enter into negotiations even though offers do not represent a substantial portion of costs. These categories include administrative settlements of cost recovery actions where total cleanup costs were less than $200,000, claims in bankruptcy, and administrative settlements with *de minimis* contributors of wastes. The term *"de minimis"* does not include parties who deposited any significant amount or type of waste at a site.

The approach of deleting the resource management guideline should provide a greater incentive for individual or small groups of PRPs to negotiate settlements. It should also give the Regions and the litigation team more flexibility in negotiating and settling with low volume PRPs. In addition, the 80 percent figure will not serve as a point of departure for negotiations, limiting the initial offers to that stated threshold percentage. PRPs should find it easier to develop proposals for settlement, and the ability of recalcitrants to obstruct a settlement will be reduced. However, since the objective of the Agency is still to obtain complete cleanup by PRPs, or 100 percent of the costs of cleanup, there will be cases where offers of 80 percent will be deemed inadequate. If a partial settlement offer is accepted, the Agency is committed to vigorous pursuit on non-settlors.

This approach, however, may increase the likelihood that Regional resources will be consumed by fragmented multiple negotiations with a wide variety of parties. The more intensive and time-consuming negotiations that may be necessary might ultimately limit the number of settlements that can be reached. It also places a higher burden on the Regions and Headquarters to assess the adequacy of settlement proposals in light of the settlement criteria, and to determine that sufficient parties are left to provide the remaining cleanup costs.

The Agency solicits comment on whether substantial settlements will be possible without a threshold and whether eliminating the threshold will encourage a greater number of settlements for either a substantial portion of the costs of cleanup or of the cleanup itself. The Agency also solicits comment on how the term *"de minimis contributor"* should be defined.

III. Release of Information

The Agency will release information concerning the site to facilitate discussions of settlement among PRPs. This information will include:
—Identity of notice letter recipients;
—Volume and nature of wastes identified as delivered to the site;
—Any ranking by volume of material sent to the site.

Release of some of this material to PRPs is discretionary under the Freedom of Information Act (FOIA).

Under the policy announced today, information released to PRPs will generally be conditioned on a reciprocal release of information by PRPs. The Agency solicits comment on whether information exempt from disclosure under FOIA should be made available to PRPs on a discretionary basis.

IV. Settlement Criteria

As discussed above, there will no longer be any specific threshold for considering settlement offers from PRPs. Rather, settlement offers will be evaluated using the criteria in this section. Evaluations under these criteria should result in a full evaluation of the offer and will promote consistency among Regional offices. These criteria will apply in evaluation offers from PRPs (1) to clean up the site, (2) to pay for clean up of the site, and (3) in cost recovery actions. These criteria include:
• Volume of waste contributed by each PRP;
• Nature of waste contributed;
• Strength of evidence tracing waste to settling parties;
• Ability of settling parties to pay;
• Litigative risks in proceeding to trial;
• Public interest considerations;
• Precedential value;
• Value of obtaining a present sum certain;
• Inequities and aggravating factors;
• Nature of case that remains after settlement.

Many of these criteria are typical for assessing offers to settle any type of litigation. Although the Agency will consider offers of less than 100 percent

in accordance with this policy, it will do so in light of the Agency's position that PRP liability is strict, joint and several unless it can be shown by PRPs that injury at a site is clearly divisible. EPA solicits comment on the need, if any, for additional criteria.

V. Partial Cleanups

Under the interim policy, EPA will now, on occasion, consider PRP offers to perform or pay for one phase of a site cleanup. The interim policy discusses the circumstances in which it may be appropriate to enter into settlements for such partial cleanups. ESA solicits comments on these arrangements.

VI. Contribution Protection

Contribution among responsible parties is based on the principle that, where liability is joint and several, a party who has paid more than his proportional share of a judgment or settlement is entitled to reimbursement from other liable parties. When the Agency reaches a partial settlement with some parties, it will frequently pursue an enforcement action against non-settling responsible parties to recover the remaining costs of cleanup. If such as action is undertaken, there is a possibility that those non-settlors would in turn sue settling parties, arguing that the settlors are liable to them for contribution. If this action by non-settling parties is successful, settling parties could end up paying a larger share of cleanup costs than was determined in the Agency's settlement.

A contribution protection clause in a consent decree is one method to prevent this outcome. While maintaining the right to go against non-settlors for all remaining relief, the United States could agree to reduce its judgment against the non-settling parties, to the extent necessary to extinguish the settling party's liability to the non-settling third party. This suggested approach is one of several contribution protection options available to the government. Parties negotiating settlement have frequently sought such protection.

The position taken by the government in litigation involving contribution is that the courts should adopt a Federal rule of decision that follows section 4 of the Uniform Contribution Among Tortfeasors Act. Section 4 provides that, where settlements are entered into in "good faith," the settlors are discharged from "all liability for contribution to any other tortfeasors." Under this interpretation, there is no need to provide contribution protection to PRPs who reach good faith settlements with the government. (We do not support adopting section 1 of the Uniform Act as

a Federal rule of decision. Section 1 would preclude settlors from seeking contribution from non-settlors unless the settlors financed or performed a 100 percent cleanup at a site.)

However, since the right of contribution under CERCLA is not yet a settled question, the Agency can take two approaches in response to requests from PRPs for contribution protection:
• argue that under its legal interpretation, explicit contribution protection clauses are unnecessary;
• provide explicit contribution protection clauses in consent decrees on a case-by-case basis, based on the Agency's ability to clearly apportion liability, the percentage of the cleanup represented by the settlement, and a case-specific consideration of the law which is likely to be applied.

Explicit contribution protection clauses may serve as an incentive for private party settlement, because PRPs may be more confident with a settlement which includes an explicit contribution protection clause as part of an agreement. It is consistent with our position on joint and several liability and our support for a uniform Federal rule of decision in this area. However, explicit contribution protection clauses have several limitations. For example, the Agency may become vulnerable for part of the cleanup costs that would otherwise be borne by responsible parties. In addition, the drafting problems involved with such clauses are complex. Finally, such clauses may embroil the Federal government in complex litigation rather than resulting in final settlements.

In the interim policy published today, the Agency has authorized a very limited use of contribution protection clauses. The Agency is soliciting public comment on whether the interim policy provides for contribution protection in the proper circumstances.

VII. Releases From Liability

Potentially responsible parties have frequently sought total releases from past and future liability as a condition of settlement. The Agency has generally been reluctant to grant such total releases because they impair the Agency's ability to assure cleanup in light of changed conditions or new information concerning a site.

We recognize the current state of scientific uncertainty concerning the impacts of hazardous substances, our ability to detect them, and the effectiveness of remedies at hazardous waste sites. It would be inappropriate for the Agency to assume the responsibility for cleanup if previously unknown or undetected conditions arise or are discovered after settlement, or if new information indicates there may be an imminent and substantial endangerment to public health or welfare or the environment.

Three broad approaches for reconciling the concerns of the Agency and of PRPs are to:

• authorize releases for remedial actions taken pursuant to EPA-approved RI/FS and design;

• authorize total releases for remedial actions taken pursuant to EPA-approved RI/FS and design, but include a reopener clause allowing the Agency to seek additional cleanup action or cleanup costs for unknown conditions that indicate possible imminent and substantial endangerments;

• allow very limited releases with reopener clauses that not only cover imminent and substantial endangerments, but require private parties to respond to all other releases or threats of release from the site.

The guidelines in this policy take the second approach. We recognize that an expansive release policy would be an incentive for private party cleanup, but its value as an incentive must be weighed against the scientific uncertainties surrounding the nature of exposure to hazardous substances, their degree of toxicity, and the effectiveness of remedies.

Generally, the expansiveness of a release will depend on the degree of confidence that the Agency has in a remedy. It may be appropriate to negotiate a more expansive release where responsible parties consent to meeting and continuing to attain health based performance standards. In addition, the Agency is considering allowing more expansive releases where the private party remedy is a demonstrated effective alternative to land disposal, such as incineration.

Under the second approach, designed for remedial actions, PRPs will be required to assume risks of imminent and substantial endangerments attributable to problems not known by the Agency at the time the remedy was selected. In return, EPA will be responsible for responding to future releases of contaminants that do not rise to the level of an imminent and substantial endangerment (assuming that, if PRPs conduct the remedial action, the approved remedy is maintained as required).

Releases will be of a similar scope, whether activities will be conducted by EPA or by private parties. Any release policy that allowed more extensive releases when the Agency conducted the cleanup actions than when private parties conducted the actions would discourage private party cleanup, or, at a minimum, encourage private parties to pay for government cleanups rather than conduct the remedial action themselves. Private party conduct of the remedial action is preferable because it is likely to occur sooner than Agency cleanup, and the use of private money frees the government to use the Fund for other sites with no identified PRPs.

The Agency is also considering whether a more expansive release may be allowed where the PRPs hire an approved contractor to perform the cleanup, and the PRPs' performance is secured by a satisfactory premium payment or surety bond in an amount well in excess of the estimated cost of the work. The term "premium payment" refers to risk apportionment device under which the risk of an ineffective remedy would be mitigated by a cash payment in excess of cleanup costs, or another financial assurance mechanism.

The Agency solicits comments on the interim release policy, including the circumstances under which releases should be granted, reopener conditions that should be included, and when releases should become effective. The Agency also solicits comment on the premium payment or surety bond concept.

VIII. Targets for Litigation

The Agency is not legally required to bring action against all potentially responsible parties at a site. The interim policy provides that the Agency will continue to identify targets for litigation on the basis of factors such as financial viability, strength of the case, and our ability to manage litigation. This policy also provides an additional incentive for voluntary cleanup by targeting recalcitrants for litigation.

The presence of a Federal agency as a potentially responsible party at a hazardous waste site sometimes delays negotiations because the position of the Federal PRP may not be clear to government negotiators or other PRPs. The interim policy provides that Federal facilities are to be treated like other PRPs in most respects except being joined as a party in litigation. The reference to administrative orders is intended to direct the Regions to make more aggressive use of administrative orders in dealing with Federal facilities. Instead of litigation, we will use the procedures established by Executive Orders 12088 and 12146 and appropriate Memoranda of Understanding to resolve issues remaining with these facilities after negotiation ends. EPA will encourage Federal facilities to participate in these negotiations.

[FR Doc. 85-2859 Filed 2-4-85; 8:45 am]

BILLING CODE 6560-50-M

APPENDIX K

DEFINITION OF SOLID WASTE

This schematic description is based on RCRA's revised
definition of solid waste.

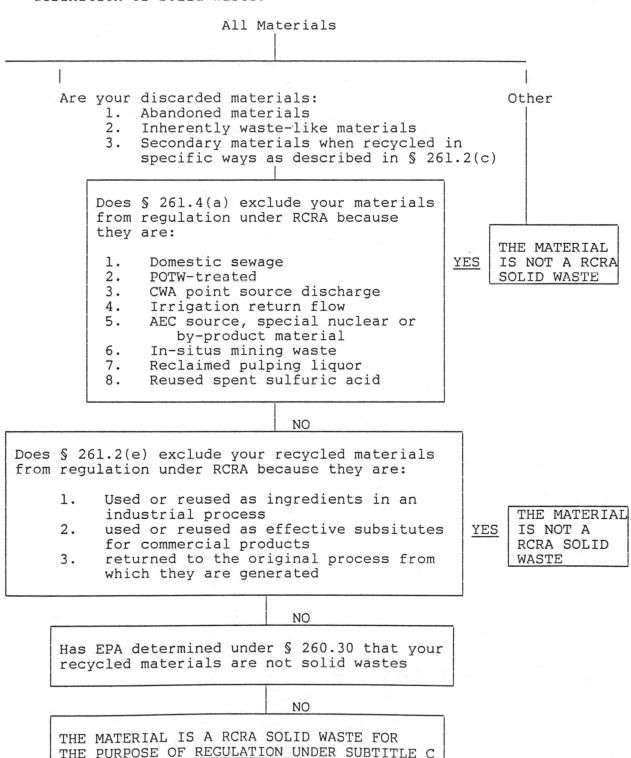

All Materials

Are your discarded materials:
    1. Abandoned materials
    2. Inherently waste-like materials
    3. Secondary materials when recycled in
       specific ways as described in § 261.2(c)

Other

Does § 261.4(a) exclude your materials
from regulation under RCRA because
they are:

    1.   Domestic sewage
    2.   POTW-treated
    3.   CWA point source discharge
    4.   Irrigation return flow
    5.   AEC source, special nuclear or
          by-product material
    6.   In-situs mining waste
    7.   Reclaimed pulping liquor
    8.   Reused spent sulfuric acid

YES → THE MATERIAL IS NOT A RCRA SOLID WASTE

NO

Does § 261.2(e) exclude your recycled materials
from regulation under RCRA because they are:

    1.   Used or reused as ingredients in an
        industrial process
    2.   used or reused as effective subsitutes
        for commercial products
    3.   returned to the original process from
        which they are generated

YES → THE MATERIAL IS NOT A RCRA SOLID WASTE

NO

Has EPA determined under § 260.30 that your
recycled materials are not solid wastes

NO

THE MATERIAL IS A RCRA SOLID WASTE FOR
THE PURPOSE OF REGULATION UNDER SUBTITLE C

K-1

APPENDIX L

DEFINITION OF HAZARDOUS WASTE

This schematic description of RCRA's definition of hazardous
waste is based on 40 C.F.R. § 260.22, Appendix I.

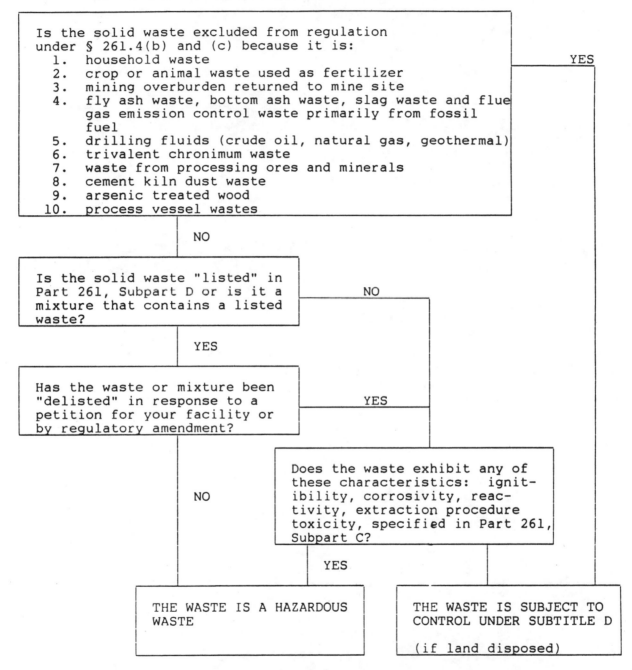

Is the solid waste excluded from regulation
under § 261.4(b) and (c) because it is:
1. household waste
2. crop or animal waste used as fertilizer
3. mining overburden returned to mine site
4. fly ash waste, bottom ash waste, slag waste and flue
    gas emission control waste primarily from fossil
    fuel
5. drilling fluids (crude oil, natural gas, geothermal)
6. trivalent chronimum waste
7. waste from processing ores and minerals
8. cement kiln dust waste
9. arsenic treated wood
10. process vessel wastes

YES

NO

Is the solid waste "listed" in
Part 261, Subpart D or is it a
mixture that contains a listed
waste?

NO

YES

Has the waste or mixture been
"delisted" in response to a
petition for your facility or
by regulatory amendment?

YES

NO

Does the waste exhibit any of
these characteristics: ignit-
ibility, corrosivity, reactivity, extraction procedure
toxicity, specified in Part 261,
Subpart C?

YES

THE WASTE IS A HAZARDOUS
WASTE

THE WASTE IS SUBJECT TO
CONTROL UNDER SUBTITLE D

(if land disposed)

L-1

APPENDIX M

SCHEMATIC OUTLINE OF RCRA

The following outline briefly summarizes the major responsibilities of hazardous waste generators, transporters, and treatment, storage, and disposal facilities.

RCRA HAZARDOUS WASTE GENERATOR REQUIREMENTS
(40 C.F.R. Part 262)

1. Identification

   Identify hazardous waste (by list, testing or experience) and assign waste identification number.

2. Notification

   File separate 3010 notices with EPA for all hazardous waste generation, treatment, storage or disposal facilities (including Class I and IV underground injection wells). Receive identification number.

3. Manifest System

   Implement manifest system and follow rules for tracing and reporting shipments.

4. Packing

   Follow packaging, labelling, marking and placarding requirements under DOT regulations at 49 C.F.R. Parts 172, 173, 178 and 179.

5. TSDF

   Must transport only to RCRA-authorized TSDF.

6. Biennial Report

    Prepare biennial report of transporters and iden-
    tified wastes on EPA Form.

7. Exception Reports

    Whenever generator does not receive signed copy of
    manifest from designated TSDF within 45 days, send
    Exception Report to EPA region including:

        copy of manifest;

        letter describing efforts to locate waste
        and results.

8. Storage

    During storage for less than 90 days, generator must
    comply with storage requirements, including con-
    tingency plan, prevention plan, and staff training
    (40 C.F.R. Part 265, Subparts C, D, J and 265.16).

9. Permit

    If generator retains hazardous waste onsite for
    more than 90 days, generator is subject to require-
    ments for TSDFs including permit.

RCRA HAZARDOUS WASTE TRANSPORTER REQUIREMENTS
(40 C.F.R. Part 263)

1. ## Notification

   File notice with EPA of hazardous waste activity and receive identification number.

2. ## Manifest System

   Apply manifest system:

   > sign, date, return one copy to generator;

   > assure that manifest accompanies waste;

   > obtain date and signature of accepting transporter or TSDF;

   > retain one copy;

   > observe special rules for bulk shipments by rail or water; shipments outside U.S.

3. ## Delivery to TSDF

   Deliver only to RCRA-authorized TSDF.

4. ## Record Retention

   Transporter must retain copies of manifest:

   > signed by generator, himself, and accepting transporter or TSDF;

   > for three years from initial transporter's acceptance (period subject to extension during unresolved enforcement).

5. ## Discharge

   Give notice to National Response Center (800-424-8802 or 202-426-2675).

   Take appropriate immediate action to protect health and environment.

   Report in writing to Department of Transportation.

RCRA HAZARDOUS WASTE REQUIREMENTS FOR TREATMENT, STORAGE, AND DISPOSAL FACILITIES ("TSDFs") (40 C.F.R. Parts 264-265)

1. ## Notification

    File separate 3010 notices with EPA for all hazardous waste treatment, storage and disposal activity (including Class I and IV underground injection wells and waste stored onsite for more than 90 days) and receive identification number.

2. ## Interim Status

    TSDFs.

    Hazardous waste disposal onsite.

    Storage onsite for more than 90 days.

    Transportation and storage of hazardous sludges, listed wastes, or mixtures containing listed wastes intended for reuse.

    Interim Status is achieved by:

    notification (above);

    filing "Part A" of RCRA permit application.

3. ## Interim Status Facility Standards

    General: waste analysis plan, security, inspection plan, personnel training, handling requirements (Subpart B).

    Preparedness and prevention.

    Contingency planning and emergency procedures (Subparts C and D).

Records and Reports: manifest system, operating logs, biennial and other reports (Subpart E).

Groundwater monitoring in effect 18 months after May 19, 1980 (Subpart F).

Closure and post-closure plans (Subpart G).

Financial requirements (Subpart H).

Containers, tanks, surface impoundments, piles (Subparts I, J, K, and L).

Treatment: land treatment, landfills, incinerators, thermal treatment, chemical, physical and biological treatment (Subparts M, N, O, P, and Q).

Underground injection (Subpart R).

4. Permit

For facilities with interim status:

File Part B of RCRA permit application, when so directed by EPA;

Meet final facility standards.

For facilities that do not qualify for interim status:

Apply for permit to EPA or approved state;

Facilities that do not qualify for interim status must cease operations and send waste inventory to RCRA-authorized facility. Operations may resume only after permit is granted.

APPENDIX N

SCHEMATIC OUTLINE OF CERCLA

The following outline briefly summarizes the major provisions of the Superfund statute.

A. COVERAGE: HAZARDOUS SUBSTANCES

    1.   Hazardous substances include:

        Substances listed or designated as hazardous under Sections 307 and 311 of the Clean Water Act, Section 112 of the Clean Air Act, Section 3001 of the Solid Waste Disposal Act (RCRA), or Section 7 of the Toxic Substances Control Act;

        Additional substances designated as hazardous by EPA under the authority of Superfund Section 101.

    2.   Exclusions from regulation as hazardous substances:

        Oil

        Natural and synthetic gas

B. REQUIREMENTS

    1.   Who Is Liable?

        Current owners and operators of facilities that release hazardous substances.

        Persons who owned or operated such facilities at the time the hazardous substance was disposed.

        Persons who arranged for treatment or disposal, or who arranged with a transporter for transportation for treatment or disposal of hazardous substances at such facilities.

        Persons who transported hazardous substances to such facilities.

2. Exemption: Federally permitted releases, or releases from a facility in compliance with a permit issued under:

RCRA

Clean Water Act

Ocean Dumping Act

Underground Injection Control Act

Clean Air Act

Atomic Energy Act of 1954

3. Extent of liability

Costs of removal action -- temporary clean-up activity, including removal of hazardous substances, monitoring, limiting access to the site, or evacuating the area.

Costs of remedial action -- permanent clean-up activity, including dredging, excavation, onsite treatment, incineration, and repair or replacement of leaking containers.

Participation in emergency abatement action if there is an imminent and substantial endangerment to the public health or welfare.

C. SUPERFUND OBLIGATIONS

1. For Generators

Liability for costs of removal or remedial action.

Duty to report spill or release of a reportable quantity of a hazardous substance to the National Response Center (800-424-8802).

2. For Transporters

Liability for costs of removal or remedial action.

Duty to report spill or release of a reportable quantity of a hazardous substance to the National Response Center (800-424-8802).

Duty to report spills to Department of Transportation under the Hazardous Materials Transportation Act.

3.   For TSDFs

Liability for costs of removal or remedial action.

Duty to report spill or release of a reportable quantity of a hazardous substance to the National Response Center (800-424-8802).

APPENDIX O

MAJOR DEADLINES IMPOSED BY THE 1984 RCRA AMENDMENTS

TABLE 1

Schedule for EPA Rulemaking Under
Hazardous and Solid Waste Amendments of 1984

Deadline	Requirement
As promptly as practicable	Amend standards requiring corrective action for hazardous waste treatment, storage, and disposal ("TSD") facilities to require action beyond facility boundaries. (Sec. 207, amending RCRA § 3004(v).)
March 1, 1985	Final permitting standards for underground tanks that cannot be entered for inspection. (Sec. 207, amending RCRA Sec. 3004(w).)
May 8, 1985	List wastes containing chlorinated dioxins or chlorinated dibenzofurans. (Sec 222(a), amending RCRA § 3001(e)(1).)
November 8, 1985	List wastes containing halogenated dioxins and halogenated dibenzofurans. (Sec. 222(a), amending RCRA § 3001(e)(1).)
November 8, 1985	Implement regulations for biennial inspections of TSD facilities. (Sec. 231, amending RCRA § 3007(e).)

TABLE 1 (cont'd)

Deadline	Requirement
November 8, 1985	Propose whether to list or identify as hazardous waste used automobile and truck crankcase oil. (Sec. 241(a), amending RCRA § 3014(b).)
November 8, 1985	Promulgate regulations on export of hazardous waste. (Sec. 245, amending RCRA § 3017(b).)
November 8, 1985	Prescribe form of notice to state/local agencies about underground storage tanks. (Sec. 601, amending RCRA § 9002(b)(2).)
February 8, 1986	Promulgate regulations to minimize disposal of containerized liquid waste in landfills and to minimize presence of free liquids in containerized hazardous waste. (Sec. 201, amending RCRA § 3004(c)(2).)
February 8 1986	Determine whether to list as hazardous certain specified wastes. (Sec. 222(a), amending RCRA § 3001(e)(2).)
February 8, 1986	Promulgate regulations requiring producers, users, distributors, and marketers of fuels derived from or containing hazardous waste or used oil to maintain certain records. (Sec. 204(b)(1), amending RCRA § 3004(b).)

TABLE 1 (cont'd)

<u>Deadline</u>	<u>Requirement</u>
March 31, 1986	Promulgate standards for generation, transportation, and disposal of hazardous wastes from small quantity generators of between 100 and 1000 kilograms per month. (Sec. 221(a), amending RCRA § 3001(d).)
May 8, 1986	Publish guidance criteria for location of TSD facilities identifying areas of vulnerable hydrogeology. (Sec. 202, amending RCRA § 3004(o)(7).)
November 8, 1986	Promulgate regulations establishing standards applicable to producers, users, distributors, transporters and marketers of fuels derived from or containing hazardous waste or used oil. (Sec. 204(b), amending RCRA §§ 3004(q)(1) and 3003(c).)
November 8, 1986	Promulgate regulations identifying additional characteristics of hazardous waste. (Sec. 222(a), amending RCRA § 3001(h).)
November 8, 1986	Determine whether to list used automobile and truck crankcase oil as hazardous waste. (Sec. 241(b), amending RCRA § 3014(b).)
November 8, 1986	Promulgate standards for generation and transportation of recycled used oil. (Sec. 241(a), amending RCRA § 3014(c)(2).)

TABLE 1 (cont'd)

Deadline	Requirement
November 8, 1986	Establish schedule for reviewing eligibility for land disposal of all listed hazardous wastes. (Sec. 201, amending RCRA § 3004(g).)
November 8, 1986	Revise permit regulations to require all new land disposal facilities to meet new minimum technological requirements. (Sec. 202, amending RCRA § 3004(o)(5)(A).)
March 8, 1987	Revise EP toxicity characteristics. (Sec. 222(a), amending RCRA § 3001(g).)
May 8, 1987	Promulgate standards for leak detection systems for all new TSD facilities. (Sec. 202(a), amending RCRA § 3004(o)(4)(A).)
May 8, 1987	Regulations for release detection, prevention and correction at underground storage tanks containing petroleum products must become effective. (Sec. 601, amending RCRA § 9003(f)(1).)
May 8, 1987	Regulations governing financial responsibility of underground storage tank owners must become effective. (Sec. 601, amending RCRA § 9003(f)(1).)
May 8, 1987	Promulgate regulations for monitoring and control of air emissions at TSD facilities. (Sec. 201, amending RCRA § 3004(n).)

TABLE 1 (cont'd)

Deadline	Requirement
August 8, 1987	Revise regulations on hazardous waste in domestic sewage. (Sec. 246, amending RCRA § 3018(b).)
November 8, 1987	Regulations for release detection prevention and correction at new underground storage tanks not containing petroleum products must become effective. (Sec. 601, amending RCRA § 9003(f)(2).)
March 31, 1988	Revise criteria for Subtitle D facilities that may receive hazardous waste from households or small quantity generators. (Sec. 302(a)(1), amending RCRA § 4010(c).)
August 8, 1988	Review 1/3 of listed hazardous wastes to determine whether land disposal should be banned and promulgate land disposal regulations. (Sec. 201, amending RCRA § 3004(g)(4)(A).)
November 8, 1988	Regulations for release detection, prevention and correction at existing underground storage tanks (other than those containing petroleum) must become effective. (Sec. 601, amending RCRA § 9003(f)(3).)

TABLE 1 (cont'd)

Deadline	Requirement
June 8, 1989	Review 2/3 of listed hazardous wastes to determine whether land disposal should be banned and promulgate land disposal regulations. (Sec. 201, amending RCRA § 3004(g)(4)(B).)
May 8, 1990	Promulgate regulations prohibiting land disposal of all listed and identified hazardous wastes, unless a particular method of land disposal of a particular waste is protective of human health and the environment. (Sec. 201, amending RCRA § 3004(g)(4)(c).)

TABLE 2

Schedule For Compliance With New
RCRA Requirements */

Deadline	Requirement
November 8, 1984	**/Prohibition on disposal of hazardous wastes in certain geologic formations. (Sec. 201, amending RCRA § 3004(b).)
November 8, 1984	Hazardous waste from small quantity generators may be disposed of only at RCRA- or state-permitted facilities, until EPA issues standards. (Sec. 221(a), amending RCRA § 3001(d)(5).)
November 8, 1984	Most new or expanded landfills and surface impoundments must have double liners, leachate control systems and groundwater monitoring.
November 8, 1984	All newly permitted incinerators must attain minimum destruction and efficiency standards of regulations of June 24, 1982.
November 8, 1984	All newly permitted incinerators must attain minimum destruction and efficiency standards per regulations of June 24, 1982.

---

*/ Excludes effective dates of new regulations to be developed by EPA. See Table 1.

**/ Takes effect until such time as EPA determines that this method of disposal is protective of human health and the environment.

TABLE 2 (cont'd)

<u>Deadline</u>	<u>Requirement</u>
November 8, 1984	Exporters of hazardous waste must file annual reports by March 1 of each year. (Sec. 245, amending RCRA § 3017(g).)
February 6, 1985	Invoice or bill of sale for fuel containing or derived from hazardous waste or used oil must bear prescribed warning label. (Sec. 204(b)(1), amending RCRA § 3004(r).)
May 7, 1985	New underground storage tanks must meet certain standards. (Sec. 601, amending RCRA § 9003(g).)
May 8, 1985	Prohibition on disposal of bulk or noncontainerized liquid hazardous waste in landfills. (Sec. 201, amending RCRA § 3004(c).)
May 8, 1985	Expansions to interim status facilities must meet same minimum technological requirements as new facilities. (Sec. 243, amending RCRA § 3015.)
May 8, 1985	Prohibition on underground injection of hazardous wastes within 1/4 mile of underground drinking water source. (Sec. 405(a), amending RCRA § 7010(a).)
August 4, 1985	Small quantity generators must use shortened version of Uniform Hazardous Waste Manifest. (Sec. 221(a), amending RCRA § 3001(d)(3).)

TABLE 2 (cont'd)

Deadline	Requirement
August 8, 1985	Permit applications for landfills and surface impoundments must provide information on public exposure to hazardous wastes. (Sec. 247(a), amending RCRA § 3019(a).)
September 1, 1985	Generators must certify that they are minimizing the quantity and toxicity of their hazardous waste. (Sec. 224(a), amending RCRA § 3002(b).)
September 1, 1985	All RCRA permits will require annual reporting on efforts to minimize waste. (Sec. 224(b), amending RCRA § 3002(h).)
November 8, 1986	Prohibition on placement of nonhazardous liquids in landfills (with certain exceptions). (Sec. 201, amending RCRA § 3004(c).)
November 8, 1986	Interim status of land disposal facilities terminates unless specified conditions are met. (Sec. 213(a), amending RCRA § 3005(e)(2).)
November 8, 1986	Exporters of hazardous wastes must notify EPA before each shipment. (Sec. 245, amending RCRA § 3017(c).)
February 8, 1986	Producers, users, distributors, and marketers of fuel derived from or containing hazardous waste or used oil must notify EPA or State agency. (Sec. 204(a)(1), amending RCRA § 3010.)

TABLE 2 (cont'd)

<u>Deadline</u>	<u>Requirement</u>
March 31, 1986	Small quantity generators must comply with additional manifest requirements and dispose of wastes only at RCRA facilities, until EPA issues any other standards. (Sec. 221(a), amending RCRA § 3001(d)(5).)
May 8, 1986	Owners/operators of underground storage tanks must notify state/local agency. (Sec. 601, amending RCRA § 9002(a).)
May 8, 1986	Owners/operators of underground storage tanks that went out of operation after 1973 must notify state/local agency. (Sec. 601, amending RCRA § 9002(b).)
November 8, 1986	<u>*</u>/Prohibition on land disposal (except underground injection) of wastes containing dioxins or certain solvents. (Sec. 201, amending RCRA § 3004(e).)
November 8, 1986	Owners/operators of interim status incinerators must file Part B application or lose interim status five years after enactment. (Sec. 213(c), amending RCRA § 3005(c)(2)(C).)

_____

<u>*</u>/ Takes effect unless EPA determines that this method of land disposal is protective of human health and the environment.

O-10

TABLE 2 (cont'd)

Deadline	Requirement
November 8, 1986	Owners/operators of interim status surface impoundments must apply for applicable exemption from minimum technological requirements or forfeit eligibility for exemption. (Sec. 215, amending RCRA § 3005(j)(5).)
July 8, 1987	*/Prohibition on land disposal (except underground injection) of "California list" wastes. (Sec. 201, amending RCRA § 3004(d).)
August 8, 1988	*/Prohibition on underground injection of "California list" wastes, dioxins, and certain solvents. (Sec. 201, amending RCRA § 3004(f).)
August 8, 1988	*/Prohibition on land disposal of 1/3 of listed hazardous wastes (to be determined by EPA), except at facilities meeting specified standards. (Sec. 201, amending RCRA § 3004(g)(6)(B).)
November 8, 1988	Owners/operators of all interim status facilities (other than land disposal facilities and incinerators) must file Part B application or lose interim status eight years after enactment. (Sec. 213(c), amending RCRA § 3005(C)(2)(c).

_____

*/ Takes effect unless EPA determines that this method of land disposal is protective of human health and environment.

TABLE 2 (cont'd)

Deadline   Requirement

June 8, 1989   */Prohibition on land dispo-
                                sal of 2/3 of listed
                                hazardous wastes (to be
                                determined by EPA), except
                                at facilities meeting spec-
                                ified standards. (Sec.
                                201, amending RCRA
                                § 3004(g)(6)(B).)

May 8, 1990   */Prohibition on land dispo-
                                sal of all listed and
                                identified hazardous
                                wastes. (Sec. 201, amend-
                                ing RCRA § 3004(g)(6)(C).)

_____

*/ Takes effect unless EPA determines that this method of
    land disposal is protective of human health and environ-
    ment.

TABLE 3

Schedule for EPA Studies, Reports,
and Other Implementation Activities

Deadline	Requirement
As promptly as practicable	Report on dioxin emissions from resource recovery facilities burning municipal solid waste. (Sec. 102, amending RCRA § 1006(b)(2).)
Not specified	Study of certain wastewater treatment impoundments. (Sec. 215, amending RCRA § 3005(j)(7)(A).)
November 8, 1984	Begin inspecting all State-operated TSD facilities annually. (Sec. 230, amending RCRA § 3007(d).)
April 1, 1985	Report on study of hazardous waste from small quantity generators. (Sec. 221(c).)
May 8, 1985	Submit inventory of all hazardous waste injection wells. (Sec. 701.)
May 8, 1985	Report on potential for private inspection program for TSDs. (Sec. 231, amending RCRA § 3007(e)(2).)
November 8, 1985	Begin to inspect all privately-owned TSD facilities biennially, and all federal TSD facilities annually. (Secs. 229, 231, amending RCRA §§ 3007(c), 3007(e).)
November 8, 1985	Complete study of underground petroleum storage tanks. (Sec. 601, amending RCRA § 9009(a).)

TABLE 3 (cont'd)

Deadline	Requirement
February 8, 1986	Report on hazardous waste mixed with domestic sewage. (Sec. 246(a), amending RCRA § 3018(a).)
October 1, 1986	Report on feasibility of establishing standards for reduction of quantity and toxicity of hazardous waste. (Sec. 224(c), amending RCRA § 8002(r).)
October 1, 1986	Report on methods to extend useful life of sanitary land-fills and reuse of landfill areas. (Sec. 702, amending RCRA § 8002(3).)
April 1, 1987	Report on study of manifesting system for small quantity generators. (Sec. 221(d).)
April 1, 1987	Report on feasibility of licensing hazardous waste transporters to assume reporting and recordkeeping responsibilities of small generators. (Sec. 221(e).)
April 1, 1987	Report on study of hazard-ous waste from educational institutions. (Sec. 221(f).)
May 8, 1987	Complete activities to educate small quantity generators. (Sec. 221(b).)
November 8, 1987	Complete study of all underground storage tanks. (Sec. 601, amending RCRA § 9009(b).)

TABLE 3 (cont'd)

Deadline	Requirement
November 8, 1987	Study farm and heating oil tanks. (Sec. 601, amending RCRA § 9009(d).)
November 8, 1987	Report on wastewater lagoons at publicly owned treatment works. (Sec. 246, amending RCRA § 3018(c).)
November 8, 1987	Report on study of Subtitle D criteria. (Sec. 302(a)(1), amending RCRA §§ 4010(a), 4010(b).)
November 8, 1987	Evaluate whether states have implemented revised Subtitle D criteria. (Sec. 302(c), amending RCRA § 4005(c)(1)(C).)
November 8, 1988	Review all land disposal permit applications submitted before enactment. (Sec. 213(c), amending RCRA § 3005(c)(2)(A)(i).)
November 8, 1989	Review all incinerator permit applications submitted before enactment. (Sec. 213(c), amending RCRA § 3005(c)(2)(A)(ii).)
November 8, 1992	Review all other permit applications submitted before enactment. (Sec. 213(c), amending RCRA § 3005(c)(2)(A)(iii).)

APPENDIX P

ABOUT THE AUTHORS

SUE M. BRIGGUM is associated with the law firm of Wald, Harkrader & Ross in Washington, D.C. Her principal areas of responsibility are environmental and administrative law and litigation, particularly in the areas of RCRA, Superfund, TSCA, and general hazardous waste handling and liability obligations. She has lectured extensively on environmental and administrative law issues, including RCRA obligations, industry response to environmental inspections, and the new underground storage tank program. Ms. Briggum received her B.A., summa cum laude, from the University of Pittsburgh and her J.D. from Harvard Law School. She received an M.A. and a Ph.D. in British Literature from the University of Wisconsin at Madison, where she taught literature and writing and co-authored three books.

GREER S. GOLDMAN is a partner in the law firm of Wald, Harkrader & Ross in Washington, D.C. Her principal areas of practice are environmental and administrative law and district court and appellate litigation. Prior to entering private practice, Ms. Goldman was a staff attorney in the Appellate Section of the Civil Division of the U.S. Department of Justice and an attorney-advisor with the U.S. Department of Housing and Urban Development. She received her B.A., magna cum laude, from Cornell University and her J.D. from Harvard Law School. She is co-author of the Environmental Audit Handbook: Basic Principles of Environmental Compliance Auditing, Second Edition (Executive Enterprises Press, 1983) and "Racing to the Courthouse, An 'Unseemly' Way to Challenge Agency Orders," The National Law Journal, March 3, 1980. Ms. Goldman is a member of the Natural Resources Law Section and the Section on Administrative Law of the American Bar Association. She served as vice-chairperson of the American Bar Association Committee on Revision of the Administrative Procedure Act, Section of Administrative Law, 1974-1975. Ms. Goldman lectures frequently on environmental law.

DANIEL H. SQUIRE is associated with the law firm of Wald, Harkrader & Ross in Washington, D.C. His principal areas of responsibility are environmental law, particularly environmental liability, and general litigation. Mr. Squire has lectured extensively on Superfund liability, RCRA obligations, and responding to hazardous spills. He also has

written several articles on the subject of environmental
liability, including "How Superfund Affects the RCRA
Financial Responsibility and Liability Insurance
Requirements," 3 Environmental Analyst 10 (September 1982),
and "How to Respond to 'Notice Letters' As a Potential
Superfund Defendant," The National Law Journal, February 8,
1982. He received his B.A., summa cum laude, from Yale
College and his J.D., magna cum laude, from Harvard Law
School.

DAVID B. WEINBERG is a partner in the firm of Porter, Wright,
Morris & Arthur in Washington, D.C. His principal areas of
responsibility are environmental and general administrative
law matters. In 1979 and 1980, Mr. Weinberg served as
Senior Assistant to the Director of the White House Office
of Presidential Personnel, with responsibility for liaison
with the Department of Energy and implementation planning
for the Synthetic Fuels Corporation and Energy Mobilization
Board. He received his B.A. degree from Yale University,
his J.D. degree, cum laude, from the University of
Pennsylvania, and an LL.M. from Georgetown University.
Mr. Weinberg is a frequent lecturer on environmental law, is
co-author of the Environmental Audit Handbook: Basic
Principles of Environmental Compliance Auditing, Second
Edition (Executive Enterprises Press, 1983), and has
authored a number of articles in the environmental, admin-
istrative law, and antitrust fields.

TABLE OF RULES AND REGULATIONS

REGULATIONS

40 C.F.R. Part 264: Standards for Owners
and Operators of Hazardous Waste
Treatment, Storage, and Disposal
Facilities

PREAMBLES, POLICY STATEMENTS, AND PROPOSED RULES

TABLE OF CASES

INDEX

Closure trust fund, 190-92

Commercial chemical products, 31, 32, 39

Common law liabilities, 249-58

Common law, preemption of, 249-50

Compliance monitoring, 183-84

Compliance order(s), 118, 232-33

Consolidation of permit proceedings, 158-59

Container(s), 10, 21, 52, 54, 136-37, 146, 199, 209

Contaminents, 67

Corrective action, 184-87, 225, 233-34

Corrosivity, 45, 70

Cover, 143, 146, 204

Criminal penalties, 236-39

- D -

Delisted wastes, 43-44

Department of Transportation, 20, 85, 89, 108

Detection monitoring, 180-83

Dike(s), 138, 139, 201

Discarded commercial chemical products, 31, 39

- E -

Emergency permits, 165

Emergency repairs, 203

Emergency response procedures, 127, 173-74

Empty containers, 52